The Modern Anthropology of India

The Modern Anthropology of India is an accessible textbook providing a critical overview of the ethnographic work done in India since 1947. It assesses the history of research in each region and serves as a practical and comprehensive guide to the main themes dealt with by ethnographers. It highlights key analytical concepts and paradigms that came to be of relevance in particular regions in the recent history of research in India, and which possibly gained a pan-Indian or even trans-Indian significance.

Structured according to the states of the Indian union, contributors raise several key questions, including:

- What themes were ethnographers interested in?
- What are the significant ethnographic contributions?
- How are peoples, communities and cultural areas represented?
- How has the ethnographic research in the area developed?

Filling a significant gap in the literature, the book is an invaluable resource to students and researchers in the field of Indian anthropology/ethnography, regional anthropology and postcolonial studies. It is also of interest to students of South Asian studies in general as it provides an extensive and critical overview of regionally based ethnographic activity undertaken in India.

Peter Berger teaches Anthropology and Indian Religions at the University of Groningen, the Netherlands. His ethnographic research in highland Orissa focuses on religion, food, ritual, social structure and cultural change.

Frank Heidemann is Professor for Social and Cultural Anthropology at the University of Munich, Germany. His research interests include society and religion in Tamil Nadu and Sri Lanka.

The Modern Anthropology of India

Ethnography, themes and theory

Edited by
Peter Berger and Frank Heidemann

Routledge
Taylor & Francis Group

LONDON AND NEW YORK

First published 2013
by Routledge
2 Park Square, Milton Park, Abingdon, Oxon OX14 4RN

Simultaneously published in the USA and Canada
by Routledge
711 Third Avenue, New York, NY 10017

Routledge is an imprint of the Taylor & Francis Group, an informa business

© 2013 Peter Berger and Frank Heidemann

The right of the editor to be identified as the author of the editorial material, and of the
authors for their individual chapters, has been asserted in accordance with sections 77
and 78 of the Copyright, Designs and Patents Act 1988.

British Library Cataloguing in Publication Data
A catalogue record for this book is available from the British Library

Library of Congress Cataloging in Publication Data
The modern anthropology of India : ethnography, themes and theory / edited by Peter
Berger and Frank Heidemann.
p. cm.
Includes bibliographical references and index.
1. Ethnology--India--History. 2. Ethnology--India--Methodology. 3. Ethnology--India--
Philosophy. I. Berger, Peter. II. Heidemann, Frank.
GN17.3.I4M64 2013
305.800954--dc23
2012042154

ISBN: 978-0-415-58723-5 (hbk)
ISBN: 978-0-415-58724-2 (pbk)
ISBN: 978-0-203-52322-3 (ebk)

Typeset in Times New Roman
by Saxon Graphics Ltd, Derby

MIX
Paper from
responsible sources
FSC
www.fsc.org   FSC® C013056

Printed and bound in Great Britain by
TJ International Ltd, Padstow, Cornwall

For our children

Lena (1988), Kathrin (1990), Teresa (1990)

Lina (2003), Malte (2009), Levi (2012)

Contents

Contributors

Gabriele Alex is Professor of Social and Cultural Anthropology at Tübingen University. Her current research interest is medical pluralism in South India. Her last book is *Medizinische Diversität im Postkolonialen Indien. Dynamik und Perzeption von Gesundheitsangeboten in Tamil Nadu* (2010).

Helene Basu is Professor of Anthropology at Westfaelische Wilhelms-Universitaet Muenster. She has published extensively on the African diaspora (Sidi) in Gujarat (ed., *Journeys and Dwellings: Indian Ocean Themes in South Asia*, 2008). Her recent research concerns psychiatry at the interface of religion and politics ('Contested Practices of Control: Psychiatric and Religious Mental Health Care in India', *Curare,* 2009).

Peter Berger teaches Anthropology and Indian Religions at the University of Groningen, the Netherlands. His ethnographic research in highland Orissa focuses on religion, food, ritual, social structure and cultural change. He is the author of *Füttern, Speisen und Verschlingen* (2007) and co-editor of *Fieldwork: Social Realities in Anthropological Perspective* (2009) and *The Anthropology of Values* (2010).

Marine Carrin is Director of Research with the CNRS at the Centre d'Anthropologie Sociale, Toulouse-Le Mirail. She has worked among the Santals for many years and is the author of *La Fleur et l'Os: Symbolisme et rituel chez les Santal* (EHESS, 1986), *Enfants de la Déesse: Prêtrise et dévotion féminine au Bengal* (CNRS éditions et MSH, 1997) and, with H. Tambs-Lyche, *A Peripheral Encounter: Santals, Missionaries and their Changing Worlds 1867–1900* (Manohar, 2008).

Anthony Carter is Emeritus Professor of Anthropology at the University of Rochester. He was Editor of the Lewis Henry Morgan Lectures and Chair of the Committee on Demography and Anthropology of the International Union for the Scientific Study of Population. In addition to work on Maharashtra, his publications include 'Agency and Fertility: For an Ethnography of Practice' and 'Cultural Models and Reproductive Behavior'.

Manuela Ciotti is Assistant Professor in Global Studies at Aarhus University and a 'Framing the Global' Fellow (2011–14) at Indiana University Bloomington. She has written several essays on Dalits and is the author of *Retro-Modern India: Forging the Low-caste Self* (Routledge, 2010), *Political Agency and Gender in India* (Routledge, forthcoming) and *Femininities and Masculinities in Indian Politics* (Berghahn, forthcoming).

Amit Desai is Lecturer in Anthropology at Brunel University. He has conducted fieldwork in rural Maharashtra and in urban Tamil Nadu and his interests include devotional Hinduism, religious transformation and materiality. He has published in the *Journal of the Royal Anthropological Institute* and is co-editor with Evan Killick of *The Ways of Friendship: Anthropological Perspectives* (Berghahn, 2010).

Henrike Donner is Senior Lecturer in anthropology at Oxford Brookes University. Her research interests include gender and kinship, urban politics and class. She is the author of *Domestic Goddesses: Maternity, Globalization and Middle-class Identity in Contemporary India* (Ashgate 2008) and has edited (with G. De Neve) *The Meaning of the Local: Politics of Place in Urban India,* (Routledge 2006) and *Being Middle-class in India: A Way of Life*, (Routledge 2011).

Christopher A. Gregory holds positions at the Australian National University and the University of Manchester. He first began fieldwork in Bastar District, central India, in 1982 and has made many short return trips over the years, the last being in 2006. He is the author of *Gifts and Commodities* (1982), *Savage Money* (1997) and, with Harihar Vaishnav, *Lachmi Jagar: Gurumai Sukdai's Story of the Bastar Rice Goddess* (2003).

Frank Heidemann is Professor of Anthropology at the University of Munich. His first fieldwork was in Sri Lanka but most of his empirical research was conducted in Tamil Nadu, especially in the Nilgiri Hills, focusing on religion and politics. His interests include visual anthropology and, more recently, he has worked on the Andaman Islands. Among others, he is author of *Akka Bakka* (Berlin, 2006) on the Badaga peasant community.

Carolyn Brown Heinz is Professor of Anthropology at California State University, Chico. Her research interests include construction of identity and community among the Maithil Brahmans, and the internationalization of Mithila art. She is the author of *Asian Cultural Traditions* (Waveland Press, 1999) and numerous ethnographic articles on Bihar.

Aya Ikegame is a Social Anthropologist who studied at both Kyoto and Edinburgh universities. She currently works as a research associate for the ERC-funded project 'Oecumene: Citizenship after Orientalism' at the Open University, UK. She has published several articles on kingship and guruship in Karnataka. Her monograph, *Princely India Re-imagined,* was published by Routledge in 2012.

P. Pratap Kumar is a Professor Emeritus at the University of KwaZulu Natal, South Africa and is currently a visiting faculty member at the Hobart and William Smith Colleges, Geneva, NY. USA. Among others, he is the author of *The Goddess Lakshmi in South Indian Vaishnavism* (1997) and *Hindus in South Africa: Their Traditions and Beliefs* (2000).

Ramdas Lamb, PhD, was a *sadhu* (renunciant) in the Ramananda Sampraday in northern India from 1969 to 1978. Since 1991, he has been teaching at the University of Hawai'i, where his primary areas of research include Hindu monastic traditions, low caste religions, and devotional movements in central and northern India.

Heike Moser is Associate Professor (Akademische Rätin) of Indology at Tübingen University. Further she is the Scientific Coordinator of its Institute of Asian and Oriental

Studies. She focuses on the performing arts of India (especially Kerala's Sanskrit theatre, Kutiyattam) and the culture and language of Kerala. Her main publications are *Nannyar-Kuttu* (Harrassowitz, 2008) and *Between Fame and Shame* (Harrassowitz, 2011).

Tina Otten is currently a researcher at the University of London, School of Oriental and African Studies (SOAS). She takes part in a comparative project about rural change and anthropological knowledge in post-colonial India where she restudies the work of F.G. Bailey in Odisha. Her recent publications include *Healing through Rituals. Illness concepts of Rona in Highland Orissa* (2006, in German) and *Dialogues with Gods. Possession in Middle Indian Rituals* (forthcoming, co-editor).

Georg Pfeffer is a retired Professor of Ethnology at Freie Universität Berlin. Since 1959 he has intermittently spent some seven years in Punjab and written his doctoral thesis on the urban Sweepers of the province, though in the last decades his main work has been concerned with tribal middle India.

William S. ('Bo') Sax (PhD, Chicago 1987) is Chair of Ethnology at the South Asia Institute at Heidelberg. His research in the Western Himalayas focuses on popular religion, ritual, performance and healing. Among his recent books are *Dancing the Self: Personhood and Performance in the Pandav Lila of Garhwal* (2002) and *God of Justice: Ritual Healing and Social Justice in the Central Himalayas* (2008).

Uwe Skoda is Associate Professor of South Asian Studies at Aarhus University, Denmark. He currently focuses on kingship and politics in central-eastern India. His recent publications include *Trysts with Democracy: Political Practice in South Asia* (Anthem Press, 2011) and *State, Power, and Violence* (Harrassowitz, 2010) (both as co-editor).

Martin Sökefeld is Professor of Social Anthropology at the Ludwig-Maximilians-University Munich. He works on Gilgit-Baltistan, Azad Kashmir and the (Azad) Kashmiri diaspora in the UK. In addition he has also worked on Turkish immigrants in Germany. Selected publications include 'Kashmiris in Britain: A Political Project or a Social Reality?' (with Marta Bolognani, in Bolognani and Lyon (eds.), *Pakistan and its Diaspora: Multidisciplinary Approaches*, Palgrave Macmillan, 2011) and *Struggling for Recognition: The Alevi Movement in Germany and in Transnational Space* (Berghahn, 2008).

Tanka B. Subba is the Vice-Chancellor of Sikkim University, Gangtok. His current research interest is in Nepali diasporic communities across the world. His most recent books are *North-East India: A Handbook of Anthropology* (ed., 2012) and *Nature, Environment and Society* (ed. with Nicolas Laine, 2012).

Maxine Weisgrau (PhD in anthropology, Columbia University) has conducted fieldwork in Rajasthan since the late 1980s, studying non-governmental organizations and development programmes in rural communities. She is the author of *Interpreting Development: Local Histories, Local Strategies* (University Press of America, 1997), co-author with Abraham Rosman and Paula Rubel of the ninth edition of *The Tapestry of Culture: An Introduction to Cultural Anthropology* (Altamira Press 2009), and co-editor of *Raj Rhapsodies:Tourism, Heritage and the Seduction of History* (Ashgate, 2007). She is affiliated with The New School

University Graduate Program in International Affairs, and Columbia University School of International and Public Affairs.

Jelle J. P. Wouters is a PhD candidate at the Department of Anthropology, North-Eastern Hill University in Shillong, India. He completed his MPhil in Social Anthropology at the Institute of Social and Cultural Anthropology, University of Oxford. At present, he is carrying out research on hill communities in India's North-East, where he is interested in state and non-state approaches to issues of land, development and indigeneity.

Paul Younger is Professor Emeritus at McMaster University in Hamilton, Ontario. His current research interest is in the Hindu communities formed in diasporic locations. His most recent book is *New Homelands: Hindu Communities in Mauritius, Guyana, Trinidad, South Africa, Fiji and East Africa* (2010).

Preface

The idea of this book emerged many years ago when we were involved in research projects in India and began to teach the anthropology of India. We found it difficult to gain an overview of the ethnographic work conducted in India in general, and in certain regions in particular, and could not offer such an introduction to our students. After discussing the corpus of relevant literature with our colleagues, the textbooks available and introductions to South Asia, we realized the lack of a comprehensive volume dealing with the contemporary ethnographic literature of India in relation to on-going theoretical debates of social and cultural dimensions. Given the obvious need for such a volume, we expected a work like this would appear soon but when this did not occur we decided to do it ourselves.

Several people have contributed considerably to the development of this book. Dorothea Schaefter from Routledge was enthusiastic about the plan when Peter first suggested the project to her in Manchester in 2008 and supported it throughout. We would also like to thank Jillian Morrison from Routledge. The anonymous reviewers (at least three of the four) of the original proposal provided very useful criticisms and suggestions that partly shaped the structure of the chapters in important ways. We want to thank all of our contributors, who willingly and constructively considered our quite specific ideas about the structure of the chapters and showed immense commitment to the project. We are also grateful to Roland Hardenberg who offered his comments on the introduction. Richard Wolf provided valuable support at various stages of the project. Thanks are also due to Birgit Riegler who helped to edit the manuscript in the final stages of the editorial process.

Further reading:

At the end of each chapter, significant literature for further reading is marked in the individual bibliographies with an asterisk.

1 Introduction

The many Indias: the whole and its parts

Peter Berger and Frank Heidemann

Most reviews about the modern anthropology of India focus on grand theories and their interpretation of symbolic and social systems, colonialism and globalization and other titanic topics. This book questions the primacy of the whole of India in relationship to its parts. In anthropology, as in other social and cultural sciences, the discourse about India assumes common features or qualities, and the interpretations of local societies subsequently appear in the light of this whole. We agree that the history of the subcontinent, of postcolonial India and of the processes of cultural identification, is more than the sum of its parts. At the same time, localities, regions and Union states exist in their own right and are more than variants of the whole. In our view, the complex and dialectical relationships of the whole and its parts are often overlooked. In Indian philosophy and in common local discourses an organic metaphor suggests that the parts receive their function and value in relationship to the whole. Most famously, the idea of society as a whole was formulated in the famous Purusha myth in the Rig Veda, where the *varna* originated in the body parts of the cosmic man. The contemporary political sovereignty of India supports the view of dependent parts and underestimates the contributions of the regions towards the greater entity. As anthropologists working in particular settings in India we claim that the idea of common cultural orientations, a shared value system or a collective history, has overshadowed the internal complexities of India's regions.

Key figures in social and cultural anthropology – as in the neighbouring disciplines of Indology and history – have developed ideas about India that gave rise to popular notions of India's unity or wholeness. These notions of wholeness could be extracted from classical texts from the second millennia BCE onwards or from the concrete residue of colonial institutions. 'India is One' is a famous statement from Dumont and Pocock's manifesto on the anthropology of India, this unity supposedly being found at the level of ideas (Dumont and Pocock 1957). Dumont argued that the persisting and ubiquitous idea of purity indicates a shared value system. Bernard Cohn, on the other hand, claimed in his historical writings that British colonialism and administration transformed India as a whole. The British administration created a kind of unity in the nineteenth century through its attempt to analyse and order the subcontinent's cultural complexity. It turned a fluid social organization into a rigid caste system. Most anthropological writings – Burghart's plea against single system approaches and for a sociology of *Indias* being an exception (1983: 282) – followed one or another idea of a whole and contextualized their own field of investigation within a greater framework. The theories of wholeness enabled and encouraged social scientists to interpret their own data within the context of grand theories and of what Redfield and Singer dubbed the Great Tradition of India.

The tendency to consider the encompassing unit as the determining factor has a long history. The name 'India' derives from a pre-colonial Western perspective, namely the idea that the people east of the River Indus have something in common, even the naming of the religious plurality used a singular – Hinduism (see Michaels 1998: 27ff.). Later, most of the landmass south of the Himalayas came under single colonial rule. The British brought their administration, science, law and education to the subcontinent. This system of order and knowledge created models to which the local societies in the hinterlands responded in various ways. One way was to envision the colonial apparatus as a means for creating unity in India. After Independence, Nehru wrote about the 'dream of unity', which has 'occupied the mind of India since the dawn of civilization' (Nehru, quoted in Vora und Feldhaus 2006: 9). His slogan 'unity in diversity' was translated into many Indian languages and became known and shared by millions of citizens.

The 'oneness' of India could be viewed as academically or politically constructed and as opposed to social realities. However, today – as a matter of fact – the people of India are subjects of a centralized administration and even though state institutions are not evenly distributed across the country, the populace face similar problems and seek ways to deal with them. They face corruption and participate in political elections; they are exposed to public rhetoric, including culturally specific forms of protest, hunger strikes and suicides. They admire cinestars and avidly consume Bollywood movies. These films are more than merely about drama, dance and song; they propagate nationalist ideas, family values and messages against the rigidity of caste. Even in remote places people know that cricket is a national sport. They need not share a nationalist view but they have an idea about 'being Indian', at least in relation to Pakistan, with whom India fought wars and competes in cricket world championships. The problematic and often violent relationship between Hindus and Muslims is known to almost all people in India, no matter whether they speak for religious harmony and coexistence or seek the supremacy of their own religion. Many other societal fields could be added. There can be no doubt about a shared knowledge and a common orientation in today's India.

However, alongside this pan-Indian knowledge and orientation, there are other layers of consciousness and horizons of identification. For most Indian citizens a regional affiliation seems to have greater relevance for day-to-day interactions. Their hopes and fears are related to their localities. For most daily affairs, the region, the district or the Union state is the whole and they belong to one of its parts. They can identify the district headquarters and their state capitals. They may view the chief ministers as heroic or demonic figures. In addition to the other languages and dialects they may speak, they relate to the official language of the state and not necessarily to Hindi, a language unknown to hundreds of millions of citizens. In our view, then, the Indian Union in its present form, size and complexity can hardly serve as a starting point for an anthropological interpretation. Cultural understanding must primarily be based in a regional context, and only secondarily refer to greater entities. Therefore, the point of departure of this volume is not the whole of India but its parts. We agree with Leavitt's (1992) argument against 'cultural holism' and with Rothermund and Kulke (1985), who stress the importance of regional cultures. Similarly, Vora and Feldhaus consider both 'region and nation [as] (…) realities in the contemporary period' (Vora and Feldhaus 2006: 10).

The first working title of this volume was 'The many Indias' because it was our aim to highlight the regional diversity and the range of themes and analytical concepts developed in particular settings. Each chapter captures the ethnography of a region and focuses on one theme. By combining locality with themes and theory we intend to offer a systematic approach to anthropological writings to interested readers and to those working on Indian society. It is certainly not our intention to claim that all attempts to generalize about India are futile, nor are we arguing that there is nothing to be gained from a Dumontian approach that stresses unity at the level of values. However, we do argue that the focus on the pan-Indian or South Asian level has eclipsed the significance of the regions, and our emphasis in this volume attempts to counter this tendency.

The Union's states as appropriate parts

A crucial point for the organization of this book concerns the question of the appropriate units that constitute the whole. The regions that constitute the Indian state are cultural complexes in their own right: Kashmir with a strong Islamic influence; Northeast India, including many 'tribal' cultures speaking Tibeto-Burmese languages; the Gangetic plain with an old Sanskrit tradition; the remote hill ranges of central India; and the Dravidian South. In India we find numerous regions named on the basis of being little kingdoms or small empires, on linguistic or ethnic criteria, on geographical or ecological factors. A region – irrespective of its defining criteria – is always a mental and ideological construction. It can be defined from the idea of a centre or of assumed boundaries or through a combination of both. In addition, it can be constructed from an internal view or from an external perspective. As editors we deliberately decided not to create a new spatial order by which to organize the chapters of this book. Considering various possibilities, we decided to take the states of the Indian Union, as they existed in 2011, as our point of departure. As we indicated above, they constitute more than administrative units, influencing social realities as well as various aspects of daily life. On the practical side, they offer a clear orientation to the readers.

The states of the Indian Union came into being in the first decade after Independence and were formed on the basis of linguistic, cultural, political and historical criteria. The Indian Constituent Assembly 1947–1949 shaped a constitution along these lines and formed the first states within the territory of its nation. The Rajput states were integrated into the united state of greater Rajasthan, thirty princely states and adjoining territories became Himachal Pradesh. In 1953 Andhra was formed and in 1956 the States Reorganization Act, the Bihar and West Bengal (Transfer of Territories) Act and the Constitution (Seventh Amendment) Act came into force and gave birth to fourteen linguistic states and six Union Territories. A year later, the territory of Nagaland was shaped, followed by the separation of the bilingual state of Bombay into Gujarat and Marathi-speaking Maharashtra. In 1966 the state of Punjab was divided into Hindi-dominated Haryana and a Sikh-dominated Punjab. Goa was occupied by Indian troops in 1961 and became the smallest Indian state in 1987, comprising about 0.1 per cent of the Indian population. Primarily in the 1970s in Northeast India, further comparatively small states were formed according to what were considered ethnic boundaries. The most recent creation of Indian states took place in November 2000, when Chhattisgarh was separated from Madhya Pradesh, Uttaranchal from Uttar Pradesh, and Jharkhand was formed from the southern parts of Bihar. The intentions behind the new organization of the Indian landmass are manifold, but the creation of new administrative and political units always seem to include – in addition to presumed higher efficiency – a certain division of powers and a smoother governing of the country (see Boland-Crewe and Lea 2002). In short, the creation of states reflects to various degrees – and in various combinations – cultural, historical and linguistic criteria. In many parts of the country, states have constituted a social reality for more than half a century.

Taking the states as our point of departure does not mean to suggest any kind of homogeneity within their boundaries. Often the opposite is true. Considering the internal complexity of the states, several chapters are co-authored by scholars with a particular regional expertise. In three cases – first Northeast India, second Uttarakhand and Himachal

Pradesh and third Punjab and Haryana – a single chapter covers more than one state. We attempted to cover all of the major states but omitted Union Territories, which come under central administration and are either small or far from the Indian mainland. With regard to the outer boundaries of the territory of this work, we decided – also for pragmatic reasons – to limit our discussion of the Indian Union, even though we are aware of cultural continuities. West and East Punjab, territories belonging today to Pakistan and India respectively, have much more in common than regions in the extreme north have with those in the south of India. Similar continuities exist across other Indian borders.

By way of introducing the anthropology within states, we 'relocate' the theoretical debates about pan-Indian themes such as Sanskritization, Westernization, substantialization and discussions about untouchability, resistance, caste-tribe relationships and so on to their places of origin. Each author was asked to deliver a critical overview of the ethnographic work done in a certain state and to identify theoretical or analytical concepts developed in this specific ethnographic field. Obviously, these concepts are objects of transformation when applied in other regions. The 'oneness' of India, then, in addition to being a relational product of the encounter between India and 'the West', appears to also be rooted in its parts.

Modern anthropology – developments after 1947

What then counts as a 'modern' anthropology of India? Anthropology and the idea of a modern, secular and democratic India have strong roots in the second half of the nineteenth century. At least three spheres influenced each other over a period of around one hundred years. Firstly, colonial attempts to control British India by accumulating historical and ethnographic knowledge, introduced – among other institutions – the decennial census (since 1881) and a huge series of district gazetteers describing local 'customs'. Later, collections of 'Castes and Tribes' in various parts of India were published. Secondly, anthropological societies and ethnographic journals were founded and material culture was displayed in museums. This opened the way for anthropology to enter universities. Ethnographers who were in the colonial service, such as John Henry Hutton (1885–1968) and Christoph von Fürer-Haimendorf (1909–1995), became university lecturers in England in 1936 and 1949 respectively. Thirdly, the movement for an independent India commenced towards the end of the nineteenth century, and the Indian National Congress was founded in 1885. The struggle for independence was a reaction to the increasing introduction of mechanisms of colonial control, in which anthropology was decisively involved. However, each sphere had its own complexity. By no means can the roots and the early practice of anthropology be reduced to a colonial tool. Verrier Elwin, the most prominent anthropologist before Independence, turned against the British presence in India, abandoned his missionary task and became an advocate for tribal India. Indian anthropologists such as L. K. A. Iyer (1861–1937) and S. C. Roy (1871–1942) were under strong British influence but their work cannot be reduced to a colonial task. Before Independence the anthropological approach in (and to) India was descriptive and encyclopaedic, and most anthropological writing created an image of an exotic cultural other. In the last decades before Independence, academic anthropology developed its own dynamics and attained a certain degree of emancipation from its administrative roots.

After political independence in 1947 the modern anthropology of India was developed as a distinct discipline within academia in India and within global anthropological discourse and methodology. Trained anthropologists conducted fieldwork in all Indian states and Union Territories. They stayed in remote or urban areas and enquired into religion, economy, politics, social systems and other aspects of culture. Many of these projects resulted in thick descriptions, rich in detail and firmly rooted in the particular locality. Debates in Indian-based journals were interwoven with the international debates in anthropology; they contributed to the discussion on social and symbolic systems, on ideas and values, and on resistance and postcoloniality. Engagement with complex social situations through fieldwork fuelled debates on pan-Indian themes such as 'untouchability', caste, little kingdoms and nationalism. The major themes were shared by the international academic community, but the anthropology of the subcontinent developed its own distinct form.

Unlike the anthropology of the Americas, Africa and Oceania, the anthropology of India refers to old precolonial texts and to a dense colonial account. The anthropology of India was informed by Indology, archaeology and history and discussed cultural continuity and change over long periods of time. Ethnography was combined with the study of Sanskrit texts. North American and European scholars developed structuralist and ethnosociological approaches and claimed the unity of India based on ancient traditions. Postcolonial schools argued that the administrative system – created under colonialism and still in place today – to a large extent created the society of India. Some authors claim that the creation of caste categories for the purpose of census enumeration, the listing of communities for administrative purposes, including positive discrimination, and the emergence of vote banks for elections made India what it is today. All of these approaches created models of Indian society that influenced ethnographic investigations in the regions. The modern anthropology of India was influenced by changing paradigms that made – and questioned – statements about India as a whole.[1] Ethnographic research, however, was conducted within the context of Indian states, examining distinct regions and particular localities.

A further theme in the modern anthropology of India is linked to colonial publications produced in British India. To date, ethnographic compilations first released more than a hundred years ago continue to be reprinted and remain available on the shelves of bookstores. These texts are still influential, feeding public and administrative thought with regard to ethnic minorities, caste hierarchies and ideas of cultural essentialism. Colonial sources also influence academic writings. Many publications by the Anthropological Survey of India are compilations of a descriptive style that did not undergo a major change after Independence. As a governmental institution, the Anthropological Survey of India serves administrative needs, informs decision-makers on ethnic and religious minorities, and prepares statistics, maps and handbooks. Similarly, several Tribal Research Centres – and also, to some extent, anthropology departments at state universities – are asked to deliver advice and information on the hinterland or on minorities in urban areas. Professional anthropologists in state and university positions often write reports for international or Indian NGOs. It is not exceptional for such texts to quote colonial publications referring to an ethnographic presence.

However, there is a distinct discourse on colonial writings, or more generally, on the colonial past, which is explicitly reflective. The debates in the journal *Contributions to Indian Sociology* and the Subaltern Studies series are the result of longstanding academic interactions between scholars from Europe, North America, Asia and Australia. Their views on holism and values, on colonialism and resistance, on the interplay of administrative and academic anthropology, and on native and non-native anthropologists as well as many other fields, have had an impact on the more general debates in academia. This critical approach is a constitutive part of the modern anthropology of India and developed mainly in university departments in India and abroad.

'Tribes' in the anthropology of India

One of the consequences of the regional view concerns the issue of tribes. The use of the word 'tribe' in India has its own history and its own connotations. Originally the term was used in African contexts and was transferred to British India. In many parts of the world – but certainly not everywhere – 'tribe' became a derogatory term and was abandoned due to its lack of political correctness. In India, however, 'tribe' is an administrative category distinguished from 'caste', granting privileges and protection, combined with state paternalism. The term is not free of negative connotations, but it is also used with a lot of pride by many who consider themselves members of this category. Other terms that are used as synonyms are *adivasi*, or in the Dravidian south *adi dravidas*, meaning 'original people' or 'original Dravidians'. In this book, the term 'tribe' will also be used in line with its wide used in academic and public writing; however, the precise use and meaning of 'tribe' will differ in various chapters. Furthermore, the use of this term does not mean to suggest a clear distinction between 'tribe' and 'caste' in all cases. According to an old joke in anthropology, castes turn into tribes at an altitude of around 1,200 metres above sea level!

While ethnography before Independence mainly focused on Indian tribal societies, from 1947 onwards, caste and Hinduism became the dominant themes of anthropological research. The theoretical perspectives that were formulated with reference to Indian culture and society also took little notice of highland societies, which have quite distinct sociocultural features. Louis Dumont famously dismissed tribal people as those 'who have lost contact' (Dumont and Pocock 1970: 3, orig. 1957) with Hindu civilization and did not bother to deal with it any further. Even while dealing on a large scale with 'South Asian Thought', McKim Marriott's work on the ethnosociology of India was concerned with Sanskritic Hinduism and placed a strong emphasis on textual traditions. For scholars of postcolonial studies, 'tribes' are as much a colonial invention as 'castes' and they do not deal with tribal societies except as colonial subjects. The Subaltern Studies Group did contribute research on tribal communities as one example of 'peasant rebellion'. However, as postcolonial studies, these were not empirical contributions based on ethnographic fieldwork. Those few, who were concerned with tribal societies in connection with general theoretical and comparative issues, are rarely acknowledged in pan-Indian discussions.

In contrast to the theoretical neglect of tribes in pan-Indian debates, ethnographic work in many states has been concerned with tribal issues, obviously reflecting a crucial concern in the different regional settings. The contributions to this volume by Alex and Heidemann (Tamil Nadu), Carrin (Jharkhand), Gregory (Chhattisgarh), Kumar (Andhra Pradesh), Lamb (Madhya Pradesh), Subba and Wouters (Northeast India), Otten and Skoda (Orissa/Odisha) and Weisgrau (Rajasthan) partly or mainly deal with the ethnography of tribal communities or *adivasis*, the chapters on Orissa (Odisha) and Rajasthan also discussing more general aspects of the anthropology of Indian tribes. The critical assessment of the anthropological work reveals various issues. Firstly, it is evident that the status of tribes or *adivasis* remains contentious. A possible reason for this is the entanglement of various levels that influence the perception and representation of such communities: local and nationalist politics and reservation, the heritage of colonial classification that found its way into bureaucratic practices after Independence, academic notions of what tribes are – which are in themselves heterogeneous – and global human rights discourses. Depending on the perspective, tribes are a sociological, political or administrative category, and are indistinguishable or completely different from Hindu society and religion. Secondly, the contributions to this volume show that tribal communities are embedded in very specific contexts that need to be taken into account when researching and discussing *adivasi*. Tribes 'as such' do not exist anywhere in India. Carrin demonstrates that being a Santal means having a very particular colonial history and a specific position in the intricate relationship between and discourses of statehood and citizenship. The situation of the Bhil of Rajasthan or the Sora of Orissa (Odisha) is no less specific. Moreover, it is impossible to speak about 'the Santal' or 'the Bhil' in any simple way when such communities comprise millions of people and are heterogeneous in themselves. Yet, this regional embeddedness is not limited to tribal communities. Thus, we think, thirdly, that regional differences should not make generalization and comparison impossible. On the contrary, the fact that tribal issues are apparently relevant in many parts of the country would call for more ethnographic, comparative and analytical efforts than has hitherto been the case. Theories of Hinduization or Santalization, that is, the question of the transformation of communities, have been out of fashion for a while. However, in our view, related questions have not been solved and the relationships between different communities – 'Hindu', 'tribal' and others – deserve more attention.

Key themes of the chapters

While all of the chapters in the volume critically assess the ethnographic work done in the state concerned, each one also selected a particular focus. Whereas all of the chapters discuss the work done in a particular region, some contributions specifically investigate the theme of 'region' itself. Anthony Carter and Amit Desai (Chapter 11) deal with the different ways Maharashtra is conceived and propagated 'as a project' and constructed as a region through nationalist school education, pilgrimage or the exclusionist politics of the Shiv Sena. Christopher Gregory's portrait of Chhattisgarh (Chapter 4) outlines different dimensions of Chhattisgarh 'at the crossroads'. This state is characterized by transitions and encounters, for example in terms of language, kinship or agriculture.

Questions of identity are of crucial importance on many levels of Indian society, for a state as a whole – as in the case of Maharashtra just mentioned – as well as for the many different communities, variously defined, that constitute it. Tribal identities have been constructed by various agents, not least colonial officers and anthropologists, over many decades in Rajasthan (Chapter 15) and Northeast India (Chapter 12). Maxine Weisgrau analyses the various ways identity categories have been put to use in Rajasthan, while Tanka Subba and Jelle Wouters specifically problematize and question the impact of colonial rule on identity formation. Marine Carrin disentangles the complex processes that are involved in the development of new forms of citizenship in Jharkhand (Chapter 7). How does the assertion of an *adivasi* identity relate to the new roles and challenges of a civil society in the making?

Although it could be argued that all of the chapters in the book are about politics in some way – for example, the politics of a region or identity politics discussed above – several chapters deal with relationships of dominance, power and rule in a more specific way. Tina Otten and Uwe Skoda, for instance, discuss relationships between rulers and ruled in Orissa (Odisha) (Chapter 13). They focus especially on 'little kings' and how this segmented political structure related to the tribal social structures of the highlands. Like tribal communities, another marginal social category of Indian society discussed in several chapters of this volume (especially Chapters 5, 16 and 18) are the 'untouchables' or Dalits. Manuela Ciotti argues that the ethnography concerning Dalit groups of Uttar Pradesh (Chapter 18) was not only moulded by questions of purity and ritual status, as in Tamil Nadu, but was particularly concerned with symbolic and political struggles – not only about religion but also about political economy. The economic aspect of social relationships and concomitant relationships of domination is also the focus of P. Pratap Kumar's critical summary of the ethnography of Andhra Pradesh (Chapter 2). He not only describes classical ethnographies of so-called *jajmani* relationships but also economic relations between castes and tribes and across different religious groups. Although social realities of castes and tribes are pertinent in most parts of the country, they are now usually complemented and dissected by distinctions relating to class as well. Accordingly, Henrike Donner (Chapter 19) analyses the formation of a 'Bengali identity' by an elite section of the population, which is to a significant extent the consequence of the colonial legacy with respect to education and agrarian transformations. Finally, power relationships are implicated in the ubiquitous discourse and the influential policies of 'development'. Ramdas Lamb (Chapter 10) critically investigates the relationship between anthropology, especially 'indigenous' applied anthropology, and development.

Several chapters deal with a special form of politics and power relations, namely, violent conflicts. Despite the fact that such contexts are difficult to study ethnographically, anthropologists are increasingly focusing attention on the modes, processes and consequences of violence. The tense and often violent relationship between Pakistan and India undoubtedly has the greatest recognition worldwide, and nowhere is this relationship more delicate or more directly felt than in the Jammu and Kashmir regions, as Martin Sökefeld (Chapter 6) describes. He argues that, caught between an ongoing battle between insurgents and Indian armed forces, the population of Jammu and Kashmir, being diverse in almost all other respects, is mainly unified in its experience of violence. In the case of Bihar, violent conflicts are located on a lower societal level and have different contexts and histories, but are no less endemic and continuous. Carolyn Brown Heinz (Chapter 3) outlines the complex situation in Bihar, where struggles between landowners and the landless masses involve violence-prone agents on all sides, be they Hindu nationalists, Dalits, Naxalites or members of state institutions. Of course, India is not only a place of violence and communalism. In the midst of the violent context mentioned, Hindu–Muslim relationships in Bihar turn out to be friendly and peaceful. That diversity or pluralism need not turn into dispute and conflict is shown by the case of Kerala. In their contribution on this state (Chapter 9), Heike Moser and Paul Younger describe the 'Kerala model', which is based on a commitment to tolerance.

Classic themes such as kinship, status (purity) and religion play a significant role in each state discussed in this book although the foci of the contributions often lie elsewhere. In the chapter on Punjab and Haryana (Chapter 14), Georg Pfeffer provides evidence of the enduring importance of kinship and marriage in modern Indian society and summarizes the ethnographic contributions in this field. The ethnography of Tamil Nadu has contributed significantly to the study of Dalit communities in India. As Gabriele Alex and Frank Heidemann (Chapter 16) show, the emphasis in such studies was less on political struggles, as occurred in Uttar Pradesh, and more on the question of whether or not Dalit communities share the ideology that assigns them a low status. Tamil Nadu – like Orissa (Odisha) and Chhattisgarh – presents quite distinct social configurations when the plains are compared to the highlands. In his discussion of the communities on the Nilgiri plateau, Alex and Heidemann argue that purity in Dumont's sense is relevant in structuring relationships, but hierarchy is also avoided in many contexts. They develop Needham's notion of 'dual sovereignty' to make sense of this situation. As is well known, religion permeates many aspects of Indian society and not only influences political and economic relationships but also the domain of illness and healing. In his contribution on Uttarakhand and Himachal Pradesh (Chapter 17), William S. Sax shows that although under-researched, processes involved in illness and ritual healing are also of crucial relevance in this region, as they are connected to ideas of social justice and family cohesion.

All of the chapters in this volume assess the ethnographies in the respective states in relation to discussions of analytical concepts and theoretical questions. Two chapters, however, specifically focus on particular scholars and the development of their ideas. In her contribution on Karnataka (Chapter 8), Aya Ikegame scrutinizes the fate of the immensely influential concepts of 'dominant caste' and 'Sanskritization' introduced by M. N. Srinivas. The theoretical perspective developed by Srinivas's successor at Oxford – Louis Dumont – is at the centre of Helene Basu's contribution on Gujarat (Chapter 5). What is the value of a theory of hierarchy that is based on ritual purity, or how does it need to be developed when dealing with the ethnography of merchants, Charan bards or Sunni Muslims? The figures of Srinivas and Dumont aptly point to the question of whether there is a difference between a 'sociology of India' and 'Indian sociology'. The former expression figures in the titles of the numerous programmatic articles in the journal founded by Pocock and Dumont (For a Sociology of India), while the latter is part of the title of the journal itself (*Contributions to Indian Sociology*).

Anthropology of India and Indian anthropology

Writing on the modern anthropology of India we must reflect critically on the distinction between the 'anthropology of India', as the international discourse on Indian society and culture, and 'Indian anthropology', as the academic practice of anthropologists working in Indian research institutions and universities. Right from the outset it must be clear that this distinction refers to institutionalized research and not to individuals, since the place of birth or the passport does not determine academic practice.

Generally, in the history of anthropology, intellectual and scientific progress is connected with the transgression of boundaries, be they disciplinary or national, and India is no exception. Anthropological research on Indian societies and cultures has been, and continues to be, informed by various sources. Notwithstanding the different opinions about the relationship between academic anthropology and colonialism it cannot be ignored that both developed in the same places and at the same time. The quality and intensity of mutual influence, however, can be disputed. One aspect of this close association is the dominance exerted by British social anthropology on research in its most important colony, that is, India. As Vidyarthi puts it, 'Indian anthropology (…) had been born and brought up under the dominant influence of British anthropology' (1977: 70f.). Significantly, after Independence in 1947 other academic traditions became important.

One notable influence was American cultural anthropology, which up to the present day shapes scholarship to a great extent. Another influence was the French tradition, particularly in the person of Louis Dumont, who came to fully appreciate the anthropology of Evans-Pritchard while teaching at Oxford. As mentioned above, together with his British colleague David Pocock he founded the most important academic journal on the anthropology of India, the *Contributions to Indian Sociology*, in 1957. Ten years later T. N. Madan, a Delhi-based anthropologist educated in Canberra at the Australian National University, became the editor of this journal and remained responsible for the publication for the next quarter of a century (Madan 2008). The journal and the background of its editors reveal the transnational entanglement of modern anthropology in India and its emancipation from the former colonial centre.

Is there an Indian anthropology? Some scholars argue that anthropology is a Western discipline that developed alongside specific historical processes and a particular configuration of values (cf. Dumont 1986: chapter 8). If such a view were accepted, could there be a non-Western anthropology? In an important volume that focuses on the biographies of twelve anthropologists, Patricia Uberoi, Nandini Sundar and Satish Deshpande (2007) have recently shown that, indeed, Indian anthropology developed its own distinctive and critical style due to local influences and factors. As such, they question earlier criticisms, made by Indian anthropologists, that practitioners of the discipline in India were largely imitative of and dependent on Western scholarship (Béteille 2003: 39; see also Madan 2008: 22). We agree with the editors of that volume (Uberoi *et al.* 2007: 18) 'that "the West" versus "the rest" is not a very productive way of interpreting the history of anthropological practice in South Asia'. The example of Madan itself shows how academic traditions are intertwined with individual biographies. Verrier Elwin is another example, from the other direction, so to say. During his lifelong engagement in and with India, the missionary turned self-trained anthropologist became increasingly alienated from British academia and became an Indian citizen after Independence.

However, there are aspects of Indian anthropology or, rather, anthropologists working in Indian institutions, that make a difference (cf. Uberoi *et al.* 2007: 33–46; Béteille 2003: 57). The most important and consequential feature, it appears to us, is the fact that Indian anthropologists are much more morally and politically involved in the problems of and challenges in their country than are their colleagues from outside. For example, many, if not most, local anthropologists deal with tribal populations in the framework of development. Research is not merely an academic endeavour but is policy- and problem-oriented, dealing with questions of ecology, health and education, among other themes. For them something more is at stake than merely the academy (see Lamb, Chapter 10). The conditions of academic existence are different in comparison with Western anthropologists doing research in India, who can afford a more distanced perspective. This has significant consequences for the kind of research that is conducted. Other distinctive features mentioned by Indian colleagues are the heritage of Sanskrit learning, the administrative classification of anthropology alongside biology, and the widespread lack of interest in doing research outside India. Vidyarthi (1977: 76f.) also mentions an 'Indianness' of anthropology, which he relates to the particular cultural milieu, values and the specific historical experience.

In sum, in this volume we are concerned with the anthropology of India, no matter from where the scholars originate. Anthropology, anthropology of India and Indian anthropology constitute three overlapping fields. At the same time we recognize them as different academic strands and contexts. Individual scholars have been influenced by and engage with all three. They have tested and modified theories developed outside the country in their regionally-based research and developed hypothesis and concepts that gained pan-Indian relevance and at times also influenced the discipline as a whole.

We would like to conclude with a note of caution. Representing Indian cultures in one volume invites critique of various kinds. In addition to the issue of essentialism, the accusation of Orientalism also hangs in the air. Many voices have stressed the dangerous and misleading dichotomy of West and East, or West and the Rest. There is no doubt that the precolonial European view of the 'Hindus', the inhabitants of the Indus valley and beyond, and consequently the related category of 'Hinduism', were misnomers and subsumed an enormous complexity under one term. Without doubt, these external views also influenced history and the self-perception of those categorized as 'Hindus'. However, the editors and at least some of the authors share the view that Europe did not invent India. In South Asia, bound by the Himalayas in the north and by the Indian Ocean on the coasts of peninsular India in the south, cultural orientations emerged over centuries. The question of the whole is captured succinctly by Amitav Ghosh (2002: 250) in the phrase: 'It is impossible to be imperfectly Indian'.

Notes

1   For a critical evaluation of the theoretical developments of the anthropology of India, see P. Berger (2012) 'Theory and Ethnography in the Modern Anthropology of India', *HAU Journal of Ethnographic Theory*, 2 (2): 325–57.

References

Béteille, A. (2003) 'Sociology and Social Anthropology', in Das, Veena (ed.) *The Oxford India Companion to Sociology and Anthropology*. New Delhi: Oxford University Press, pp. 37–61.

Bowland-Crewe, Tara and Lea, David (2002) *The Territory and the States of India*. London and New York: Europa Publications.

Burghart, Richard (1983) 'For a Sociology of Indias: an intracultural approach to the study of 'Hindu Society', *Contributions to Indian Sociology*, 17 (2): 275–99.

Dumont, Louis (1986) *Essays on Individualism: Modern Ideology in Anthropological Perspective*. Chicago: University of Chicago Press.

Dumont, Louis and Pocock, David (1970 [1957]) For a Sociology of India. In: *Religion, Politics and History*. Paris and The Hague: Mouton.

Ghosh, Amitav (2002) *The Imam and the Indian: Prose Pieces*. New Delhi: Ravi Dayal.

Leavitt, John (1992) 'Cultural Holism in the Anthropology of South Asia: The Challenge of Regionalism', *Contributions to Indian Sociology,* 26: 3–49.

Madan, T. N. (2008) '4 January 2008 Contributions to Indian Sociology at Fifty', *Contributions to Indian Sociology,* 42 (1): 7–28.

Michaels, Axel (1998) *Der Hinduismus: Geschichte und Gegenwart*. München: C. H. Beck.

Rothermund, Dietmar and Kulke, Hermann (eds) (1985) *Regionale Tradition in Südasien*. Wiesbanden: F. Steiner Verlag.

Uberoi, Patricia; Sundar, Nandini and Deshpande, Satish (2007) *Anthropology in the East: Founders of Indian Sociology and Anthropology*. Calcutta: Seagull Books.

Vidyarthi, Lalita Prasad (1977) 'The Rise of Social Anthropology in India (1774–1972)', In: Kenneth David, *The New Wind: Changing Identities in South Asia*. The Hague and Paris, Mouton.

Vora, Rajendra, and Anne Feldhaus (2006) 'Introduction', In: Rajendra Vora and Anne Feldhaus (eds) *Region, Culture, and Politics in India*. Delhi: Manohar, pp. 7–23.

2 Andhra Pradesh

Economic and social relations

P. Pratap Kumar

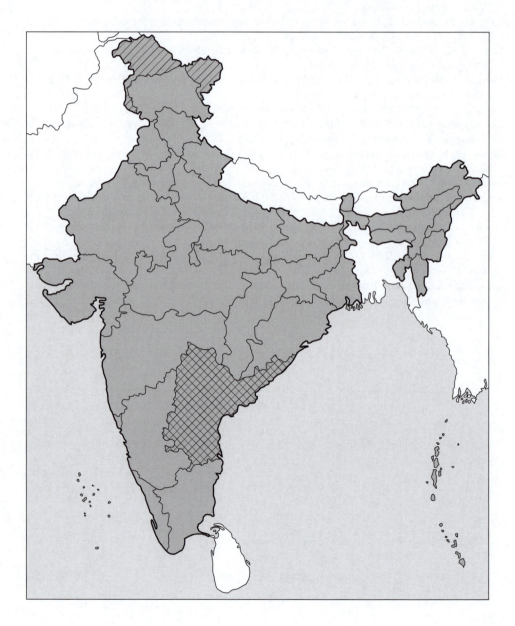

A long time ago, when I used to live in Vijayawada, I had an interesting encounter at the local temple (Kanaka Durga Temple on the bank of the Krishna river). I used to see a Madiga drummer daily performing his occupation as an official drummer during the temple rituals. I asked the priest if his presence at the temple was indeed not considered polluting! The priest remarked as a matter of fact:

> Their caste is obligated to perform this duty for the temple in return for a share of the grains donated to the temple by the devotees. Similarly a washerman washing our clothes can come through the kitchen entrance to collect the clothes and no pollution is warranted. It is purely an arrangement sanctioned by caste rules.

The view of caste as an economic system, as narrated by the priest above, is often overlooked in discussion of the Indian social system. This chapter will focus on the economic relations based on exchange within castes, between castes or castes and tribes, and between religious groups in the State of Andhra Pradesh.

Introduction to the region

The State of Andhra Pradesh was carved out of what was known during the British raj as the Madras Presidency. Although the debate about creating the state boundaries along linguistic lines predates independent India, it is only after Independence that the Telugu people led by Potti Sriramulu, who did not survive to see the formation of the State of Andhra Pradesh, demanded a separate state for Telugus. Under great pressure, the then Prime Minister, Jawaharlal Nehru, conceded the formation of Andhra Pradesh separating the eleven Telugu-speaking districts of the Madras State comprising Coastal Andhra and Rayalaseema regions. It was on October 1, 1953 that the State of Andhra Pradesh came into being under the first Chief Minister, Tanguturu Prakasam Pantulu (well known as Andhra Kesari, the lion of Andhra). On November 1, 1956, the Telanga region of the then Hyderabad State was merged with Andhra Pradesh. The non-Telugu-speaking regions of the former Hyderabad State were merged with Maharashtra and Karnataka. However, the boundaries of the state did not remain uncontested. The Telangana separatist movement began in 1969 and peeked in the mid-1970s. Although it is largely contained, the rumblings continue to the present time with three lobbies—one for a separate Telangana State, one for the creation of a New Andhra State, and another for a combined Andhra Pradesh State.

Today the total population of Andhra Pradesh is 84.6 million with a literacy rate of 67.6 percent (Census 2011). The state is bordered by Tamil Nadu to the south, Karnataka to the west, Maharashtra to the north-west, and Orissa on the north-east. Two major rivers flow through it—Godavari and Krishna. These two river basins are economically most prosperous compared to the rest of the state as the two regions are considered the rice granaries of Andhra. Agriculture remains one of the main economic activities of the state, though in recent years other trades and industries have grown exponentially. It is common knowledge in Andhra that the historically landed castes, mainly the Reddis and Kammas, occupy the seats of economic power in the state.

The various tribal communities that are present in Andhra are as follows—Bodo, Gadaba, Kammara, Kondh, Koya and Lambadas, Malis, Nayaks, Thoti, Yenadis, Yerukulas, and Valmikis. Like the Gadaba, Kond and Koya, the Chenchus are found in both Andhra and Orissa. Among the various caste groups the following are important to note from a demographic point of view—different sub-groups of Brahmins, Komati, Reddy, Kamma, Velama, Kapu, Nayudu, Relli, Mala, Madiga, Yeraka, and Yanadi.

The early history of Andhra Pradesh was reconstructed during the colonial period using dynastic kingdoms as the basis. This certainly obfuscated the social, cultural, and economic details of that early period, even up to the sixteenth and the seventeenth centuries. While the actual historical and social origins of many of these dynasties remain in obscurity, such dynastic histories left the impression that these dynastic rulers were from a homogenous social group identified in Brahmanical ideology as Kshatriyas (ruling varna), which must be understood as a broad social category rather than an endogamous structure as in the jati or caste system. In other words, the historical reconstruction of Andhra Pradesh seems to have assumed that there was some homogeneity of social groups in terms of their ranking system, both within caste communities as well as tribal communities. Such reconstructions also assumed that there was a homogenous region called Andhra. In this regard, Talbot's (2001) study of pre-colonial Andhra is informative in that she rejects both the segmentary state approach as well as king-centered approach used elsewhere in South Indian studies to explain the vast diversity in Andhra. Until the reconstruction of the current State of Andhra Pradesh in the aftermath of Independence (that is the reorganization of Indian states according to languages in the 1950s), the exact boundaries of the linguistic region known as Andhra blurred between the present Maharashtra, Karnataka, and Tamil Nadu States. While the Kakatiya kings might have come from the region of Maharashtra, the Vijayanagara kings might have been Telugus ruled from the present Karnataka region.

Within these fluid boundaries, it is highly problematic to separate groups as castes and tribes in Andhra on the one hand, but also within the various caste groups the boundaries are not always static. Deploying Brahmanical notions of caste to analyze Indian society in general, and Andhra in particular, has certainly caused greater injustice in ascertaining a clearer view of the social and cultural aspects of the Andhra region. As Harrison (1956) suggests, some landed caste groups such as Kammas tended to claim their ancestry being a noble warrior class:

> Kamma lore nurtures the image of a once-proud warrior clan reduced by Reddi chicanery to its present peasant status. Reddi duplicity, recounted by Kamma historian K. Bhavaiah Choudary, was first apparent in 1323AD at the downfall of Andhra's Kakatiya dynasty. Reciting voluminous records to prove that Kammas dominated the Kakatiya court, Choudary suggests that the Reddis, also influential militarists (sic) at the time, struck a deal at Kamma expense with the Moslem conquerors of the Kakatiya regime. The Kammas lost their noble rank and were forced into farming.

(382)

Such instances point to the fact that caste identity has always been in flux in Andhra region and was constructed and reconstructed often for political and economic reasons, as the very same Kamma community today has attempted to claim Backward Class (Other Backward Class/OBC) status.

The present Andhra region is the result of a long history of political hegemonies that oscillated between wet-land controlled powers and dry-land (interior) controlled powers during which many peripheral communities assumed new identities. This flux of society caught between the feudatory lords of the wet-lands on the coast and the predatory lords of the dry up-lands is captured well in the work of Cynthia Talbot (2001) on the Kakatiya period of Andhra. The work of both Talbot (2001) and Susan Bayly (1989) confirms that neither religion nor society of the pre-colonial period of Andhra is to be viewed through the static lenses of the Brahmanical intellectuals.

Research themes in the ethnography of Andhra Pradesh

In line with the national scene, much of the ethnography in Andhra focused on two broadly divided fields—caste studies and tribal studies. In India anthropologists were more concerned with the study of tribes, while sociologists investigated caste. However, scholars from abroad did not make this kind of distinction and both castes and tribes were studied by anthropologists. There were two consequences of this. First, the boundaries of the disciplines became blurred, and second, ritual, kinship, and symbolic forms got more attention at the expense of development studies and socio-economic relations (see Sundar *et al.* 2000: 1999). A similar tendency became visible in Andhra.

Initial studies dealt with broad areas of customs and practices and gradually more detailed studies on kinship, family, marriage, religious beliefs, moral codes, economic and agricultural aspects, inter-caste and inter-tribe relations, as well as caste-tribe relations preoccupied ethnographers. Although in terms of national scenario L. P. Vidyarthi (1976) proffered a three-phase development of anthropological studies—namely, a formative phase (1774–1919) with encyclopedic accounts, a constructive period (1920–1947) with descriptive monographs, and an analytical period (1948–1976) with critical comparative studies—such strict adherence to national developments in Andhra is difficult to assess. However, ethnography in Andhra, particularly in presenting the tribal communities generally was clouded by prehistoric archeology in as much as tribal societies were conceived in terms of stone-age people (e.g. Yenadi, Chenchu). Recent ethnographic studies on Andhra have focused on Marxist-oriented studies on agricultural labor (Kuo-Chun 1957; Jodhka 1997; Prasad and Rao 1997) and the anti-liquor movement (Ilaiah 1992) among other themes. Other studies include performance of caste (Charsley 2004), caste ranking (Hiebert 1969), and role of temples in the integration of tribal societies into the caste society (Durga and Reddy 1992). Topics that have received attention in recent years in the region of Andhra include cultural anthropological studies, ecological studies, the status of women, medical anthropology (e.g. cell disease, inbreeding in population groups, nutrition), and habitation patterns (see Busi and Ravi 2006).

Economic social relations in Andhra Pradesh: a caveat

It is against this background of blurring disciplinary boundaries on the one hand and the dynamic social milieu of Andhra on the other that we begin our exploration of economic relations in this region. I shall argue that the overall picture of society in Andhra can be better explored through economic social relations. This broad theme will enable us to understand the dominance of some castes, and their complex relations with the peripheral communities. The notion of dominant caste is understood largely as to how landholdings were transferred within clan boundaries and not outside.[1] Enmeshed in these contexts are the politics of caste, class, religion, and identity.

While attention to the landed castes such as Kammas and Reddis (the latter not to be confused with the tribal Konda Reddi mentioned below) was given by more recent studies, the earlier studies in anthropology focused on what are traditionally considered untouchable castes and the tribal communities. Whether it is in the case of landed castes or the case of the so-called untouchable castes, the issue seems to be that in each group of castes the notion of superiority of identity seems relative.[2] While the Kammas and Reddis constantly contested each other's status in society, on another level the Madigas and the Malas of the untouchable caste groups contested each other's status within that group. In general, untouchability is often associated with higher versus lower caste relations within the caste society. Many variables of it exist that should enable us to avoid gross and simplistic generalizations. An important case in point is the Lambadas in Andhra, who practice a level of untouchability in relation to their inferior fellow members of Zangats. But this untouchability could be removed by the payment of a price at a ritual (see Rattord 1984).

Contestations of castes in an attempt to position themselves higher than the other often defies the classical Dumontian polarization of castes as pure and impure in view of the competing variables. Most importantly, Dumont's subordination of politics to ideology is problematized. Pointing out that the label of "Untouchable" is a recent construction in the twentieth century notwithstanding the fact that the practice of untouchability existed before and informed caste relations, Simon Charsley (2004) argues that it is the very notion of untouchability that enabled the Madiga group to claim a more respectable status through mythological narratives. He points out that in the Jamba Purana, Adi Purana, and Shakti Purana, as well as through the Basava Purana, the Madigas are able to link their leather-working profession directly with Jambava, the mythological progenitor of the Madigas. Enacting this myth during festivals, the Madigas confront their Brahman counterparts to claim a superior status in the caste hierarchy. Charsley points out that:

> [i]t challenges notions of purity and pollution in terms of which the owners of the purana as traditional leatherworkers, associating these ideas particularly with Brahmans, know themselves to be devalued. Its claim, however, is deeper and more radical. What does not appear is any assertion of primeval kinship with Brahmans, so common a theme in previous discussion of 'Untouchable myths,' nor with the gods. It is precedence rather than coevality which is claimed, calling on cosmogonic traditions emphasizing the female Shakti and making secondary and junior the great male gods of contemporary Hinduism.
>
> (Charsley 2004: 284)

In an earlier study, Paul Hiebert (1969) stresses the role that cooked food and water played in the maintenance of social hierarchy in Andhra. Castes competing for higher status would refuse to accept cooked food from each other—e.g. Smarta Brahmins versus Ayyavaru Brahmins and Chakali (Washermen) versus Mangali (Barbers) (Hiebert 1969: 442). In the case study conducted in Konduru in Andhra Pradesh, Hiebert notes the complexity of caste hierarchy. Using McKim Marriott's technique[3] of ranking by consensus as part of an elaborate structure in a village, Hiebert selects informants from the village and asks them to rank castes. He discovers that the informants ranked castes based on who exchanged food with whom. The results showed, contrary to the homogenous ways of understanding castes through classical Brahmanical classification, a much more nuanced classification that shows individual castes determining how they exchanged food and water. Aside from the complex manner in which the classification appears, more significantly the experiment revealed the different levels of villagers' awareness of each other's social status.[4] The "varna Hindu castes," as Hiebert refers to caste-Hindus, differentiated between different groups of Brahmans whereas the Harijan groups treated them as the same; the high caste groups separated high and low Shudras whereas the low Shudras and Harijans could not; the high caste groups lumped the Mala weavers and Madiga leather-workers into one group, while the Malas and Madigas distinguished themselves sharply (Hiebert 1969: 445–46). However, from the standpoint of oppression against the Mala and Madiga communities by the higher caste groups, there is no distinction between the two—"the atrocities and indignities against the scheduled castes do not distinguish between malas and madigas" (Sankaran 1998: 210). Complementary to the above view, Sankaran describes the competition and tension between the two groups in the context of the government job market.

Exchange and social relations: caste based

Agrarian social relations based on land gifts

Although in recent times, as Surinder Jodhka points out, much anthropological work has covered urban and modern concerns, scholarly interest in agrarian social structure has diminished in recent years. Commenting on Wendy Olson's important work on agrarian social relations in Andhra, Jodhka observes that:

> [t]he study of agrarian social structure and change that had been among the most popular concerns among scholars working on India suddenly seems to have gone out of fashion. Interestingly, this has happened without any significant change in the structure of the Indian economy.
>
> (Jodhka 1997: 1016)

Olson (1996) also makes a similar point and notes that the agrarian markets function as social institutions within which groups establish social relations based on exchange. This tradition refers to a rather long history. Talbot (1991: 336) points to the fact that the practice of exchange, though identified recently by economists in India, dates back to the medieval practice in Andhra of making donations of lands and livestock to temples and deities by the various dynastic rulers (e.g. Kakatiyas, Chalukyas, and the Vijayanagara kings) and later on by various caste groups. In fact, the formation of social groups as castes in Andhra is rooted in this practice of donations based on exchange, which was considered to still be evolving until at least the thirteenth century.

In this exchange, donations and caste titles as well as religious practices are closely linked, e.g. the cases of Reddis, Nayakas, Rajus, Boyas, Settis, and others. In the context of donations in exchange for titles in the medieval period, caste groups reveal an interesting phenomenon of division into right-handed and left-handed based on whether or not they are based on agricultural exchange or non-agricultural donations. This symbolic distinction of right-handed and left-handed refers to the way their women wear their upper garment—whether over the right shoulder or the left—and is not to be confused in the Tantra sense of the usage in Hinduism. The right-handed groups (e.g. *Reddis*) are associated with land and agriculture and had territorial clans and lineages whereas the left-handed groups (*Settis* and *Brahmins*) do not have land-based clans and lineages as they traveled and moved around. As such, from the point of view of religious practice, the landed groups worshipped in local village temples whereas the non-landed groups worshipped at pilgrimage centers and sacred places. The broad category of *Rajus* could have been a minor lord or minister and in some cases a Brahmin occupying such a position as known today under the name of *Niyogis* (conducting secular occupations) as opposed to *Vaidiki Brahmins*. Similarly the *Boyas* may have become associated with tribal communities in recent centuries, but in the thirteenth century they were identified with the occupation of herding cattle like the *Gollas* (Talbot 1991: 321) However, Durga and Reddy (1992: 157–58) suggest that they (*Boyas*) remained independent in the interior Rayalasima region as hunting tribes, and were brought by the medieval kings initially to safeguard the frontier regions. Later they were turned into herders in the southern coastal regions where they cooperated closely with the agricultural groups and became integrated into the caste society. Gift-giving provided the network between caste groups in the medieval period and seems to have continued into the present time.[5] In earlier times, gifts were made to the temple in the name of an overlord by the local lords. But in recent times when such gifts are made, the merit is transferred to parents or significant members of the community (Talbot 1991: 333).

The phenomenon of gifting lands during the period of the dynastic rulers of Andhra gave rise to what was later described as the zamindari system, which entrenched feudal lords functioning under the political control of larger monarchs or kings. Its replacement by the ryotwari system[6] in the nineteenth century gave rise to the power of a new peasantry. The rise of the Kamma community is largely due to this phenomenon in the nineteenth century. What is significant is the proximity between the newly emerging class of capitalists and the peasant caste groups, particularly the Kammas in the coastal regions (Upadhya 1988a). It is for this reason that Upadhya points out:

> In India the term 'business community' refers to castes and religious groups whose traditional occupation is trade. The business-men described here belong to several castes, the traditional occupation of which is cultivation. The members of this new 'business community' are united by their common class and regional origin; that is, they come from the class of landed cultivators of coastal Andhra.
>
> (Upadhya 1988b: 1438)

Economic social relations based on the jajmani system

The theoretical concept that conjured up social relations based on exchange has been covered under the indigenous concept of the jajmani system. Although based on the North Indian social background, it soon came to be applied to the whole of India, including South India. According to Mayer (1993), Wiser (1969) was the first scholar who is credited with describing this system in his classic work in 1936.[7] Much scholarship exists regarding this system, dealing with its origins and modern application, its usefulness for comparative analysis, as well as providing a serious critique (Gould 1958; Beidelman 1959; Good 1982; Miller 1986; Kölver 1988; Mayer 1993; Raheja 1988; Fuller 1989). For our purpose, Janet Benson's (1976) work on Mallannapalle is most useful as it provides some perspective of its application for the region under consideration. Benson's essay provides a useful comparison between the North Indian and South Indian contexts of the jajmani system, while at the same time taking an intensive look at the situation in Andhra. One important point that she makes is that the jajmani system is much more nuanced than is commonly supposed. The common view is that it is a general village system structured around certain castes providing certain services in lieu of either kind or cash payments.[8] She argues that viewing the system purely as high caste versus low caste (Beidelman 1959) or purely through ritual relations (Pocock 1962) is to lose sight of the complexity of the system.[9] For example, while Brahmans and other castes might provide ritual services, they do not live in the village of the jajman or patron, as in the case of Mallannapalle, and therefore are not integral to the village structure, though they have hereditary rights to the services they provide and they can sell those rights to others in the event of no rightful successor. As such, not all local service castes may participate in the jajmani system (e.g. goldsmiths, tailors, weavers) (Benson 1976: 242). The key is whether service providers are permanent or paid on a piecework basis and whether they are paid cash or grain or both. There seems no uniform way in which all service castes participate in the system—some are temporary, paid in kind, paid in cash, not paid or provide in exchange for something nominal (Benson 1976: 243).

Furthermore, the relationships between service providers and receivers, or clients and patrons, can be interrupted through internal rivalry between dominant castes (Benson 1976: 247–48). To bring more complexity into the social relations of caste groups in Andhra, Venkatesu divides the castes that are currently listed as Backward (OBC) into two groups— those who produce commodities, e.g. carpenters (Vadrangi), goldsmiths (Kamsali), and potters (Kummari) *inter alia*, and those who provide services, e.g. washermen (Chakali), diggers (Uppara), and stone-cutters (Vaddera) *inter alia* (Venkatesu 2004: 3687). During the colonial period, many of the castes from both groups became agricultural laborers and began to play a vital role in the agriculture-based rural economy. In the aftermath of Independence, the government of Andhra Pradesh introduced cooperatives to protect the traditional occupations in order to prevent them from becoming dependent on agricultural labor and migrant labor. However, the high caste communities, by virtue of their financial ability to invest in modern technology-driven industries, have weakened the ability of traditional occupation-based cooperatives to be sustainable in the modern economy. Due to privatization, lack of government support, and emerging modern industries, these castes are back in the labor market driven by the higher caste controls (Venkatesu 2004: 3688–89).

In another study conducted by Prasad and Rao (1997) a further subdivision of castes is introduced which brings greater subtlety to the traditional occupation-based caste groupings and their hierarchies. In Ranapuram village in the Anantapur district of Andhra Pradesh, Prasad and Rao divided the castes into four groups: 1) agricultural caste—Kammas; 2) agricultural labor castes—Boya, Kuruva (shepherds), Nese (weavers), Vadde (stone-cutters), Edega (toddy tappers), Balija, Dudekula (mattress makers); 3) service castes—Chakali (washermen), Mangali (barbers), Kummari (potters), Bommalata (puppeteers), Bhatrajulu (bards); and 4) scheduled castes—Madiga (both Hindu and Christian). Although the authors' main purpose is to highlight the adaptation strategies to the environment, they reveal interesting caste-/land-based exchange dynamics. For example, aloe plants used for boundary marking were never considered private property. However, in recent years the rope-making castes, which derived their income from the aloe, have had to seek the permission of the landowner on whose boundary the aloes are harvested: "rope makers who use the plant's pulp have to seek permission from the owner and in return have an obligation to give a length of rope to the owner" (Prasad and Rao 1997: 230). This co-existence of barter system with a modern monetized rural economy has certainly made social relations based on exchange in the context of agricultural labor system more complex. It is in this context that Prasad and Rao (1997) make the distinction between attached or bonded laborers and casual or seasonal laborers. In the traditional cultural system of client-patron relationships, the bonded or attached laborers have a buffer during times of drought and other economic hardships, which the casual laborers do not. Similarly, the service-providing castes, such as Mangali or Chakali (Tskali), would provide regular service to the patron for a fixed payment in kind or cash throughout the year (Prasad and Rao 1997: 231). Under conditions of severe economic hardships, the traditional exchange-based caste relations often provide a buffer to those who are under financial strain. This often works within a Jati framework—financially secure members of the Jati provide for their Jati members—or within a kin/lineage framework— when resources become scarcer then such a buffer is restricted to kin members (Prasad and Rao 1997: 232).

The intrinsic relationship between caste and capitalism on the one hand, and communism on the other is evident in Andhra. Concerning the latter relationship, Harrison (1956) points out the reasons why Kammas are strong in the Communist Party in Andhra whereas Reddis are strong in the Congress Party. Among other reasons related to their mutual economic strongholds—the Kammas in the coastal delta regions and the Reddis in the Rayalaseema region—the most important reason that Harrison cites is that while Kammas rejected the Brahman-dominated leadership of the Congress Party, the Reddis quietly accepted the Brahman leadership. This compelled the Kammas to seek their political aspirations in the Communist Party (Harrison 1956: 384). The relationship between caste and capitalism is grounded in what is known as feudal capitalism or agrarian capitalism, which links certain castes in intrinsic ways in which "formal cash payment is not wages in return for definite labor time but payment in return for unspecified services and labor time" (Mohan 1995: 124). It must also be noted that this relationship between caste and capitalism is something that became intrinsic to politics. In other words, in Indian politics in general and in the politics of Andhra Pradesh in particular, caste identity became the most significant means of advancing individual group's economic self-interests. However, it must be underlined that such proximity between caste and politics is rooted in the formation of state in the colonial period. As Sheth points out:

> [t]he colonial state assumed a dual role: of a super brahmin who located and relocated disputed statuses of castes in the traditional hierarchy and of a just and modern ruler who wished to 'recognize' rights and aspirations of his weak and poor subjects. This helped the state to protect its colonial political economy from incursions of the emerging nationalist movement. Among other things, it also induced people to organize and represent their interests in politics in terms of caste identities and participate in the economy on the terms and through mechanisms set by the colonial regime.
>
> (Sheth 1999: 2503)

One of the lasting impacts of colonialism on caste relations is evident in the new realignment of castes, which were previously organized hierarchically into horizontally aligned social groups. As rituals that upheld the hierarchical relations gradually collapsed due to growing urbanization and new economic opportunities, previously landed caste groups in Andhra began to compete to enter middle-class society. Urbanization effectively and fundamentally changed the caste rules and caste hierarchies to the extent that it relaxed the acceptance of cooked food from lower order castes and inter-dining across caste boundaries. This practice may not have been a conscious process on the part of the various caste groups, but seems inevitable in the face of emerging urban society. Additionally, even endogamous relations are now extended beyond the original ritual boundaries. As Sheth argues,

> [t]he castes which occupied a similar ritual status in the traditional hierarchy, but were divided among themselves into sub-castes and sub-sub-castes by rules of endogamy, are now reaching out increasingly into larger endogamous circles, in some cases their boundaries co-terminate with those of the respective varna in a region to which they supposedly belong.
>
> (Sheth 1999: 2505)

In a study on the Yelnadu Reddis of Andhra, who relocated to Tamil Nadu and Karnataka through gradual urban migration, Montgomery (1977) points out that such an urbanization phenomenon affected even the leadership and authority of the caste. In other words, political power shifted from the traditional village elders to urban leaders in the case of Yelnadu Reddi politics (Montgomery 1997: 185). Srinivas attributed this political shift in caste relations to the establishment of "Pax Britannica which set the castes free from the territorial limitations inherent in the pre-British political system. British rule freed the jinn from the bottle" (1957: 530). This is in line with studies that have indicated the complex role of caste-based politics in modern India, as internal conflicts within a caste can pit their own members against each other in the context of larger group interests or perpetuate old conflicts in the new form, as in the case of Reddis and Kammas in Andhra (Gusfield 1965: 134).

Exchange and social relations: tribe based

I have mentioned above a list of the most commonly found tribal communities in Andhra Pradesh. The term "tribe" in the Indian census reports was used to cover both the groups that domesticated animals and lived a fairly settled life with agricultural activities, as well as those who engaged in a hunting and gathering lifestyle and lived in flux. In terms of economic relations, as well as with reference to general socio-cultural patterns, the distinction is, however, important. Therefore, the term "tribe" will refer to non-peasant cultivators only and does not include hunter-gatherers. Some of the communities that attracted wider academic interest from anthropologists are Yanadi and Chenchus (who are hunter-gatherers), while Konda Reddis have been known to engage in agricultural activities and raising domesticated animals (Allchin 1966). While most of the earlier studies on the tribal communities in Andhra dealt with the ancient roots of these communities, von Fürer-Haimendorf (1943, 1945) comprehensively dealt with the life of the Chenchus and the [Konda] Reddis in the Hyderabad region. He paid attention to their religio-social life as well as their economic activities. However, his particular reference to the economic life of these groups is useful from our point of view. Of the two groups, the Konda Reddis seem to have become more closely related to lowland caste society to the extent that they have engaged in trade relations with the Mala community and become, in many areas, involved in plough cultivation. While mobility strategies such as residential mobility and logistical mobility are important for the survival of the hunter-gatherer communities such as Chenchus (Kelly 1983), in order for them to be effective in their adaptation to the new economic demands, they need to become, what Helms calls, a "purchase society." While "peasant societies" are integral to the political institutions of the state, the "purchase societies" in contrast are linked to the wider society by commercial activities that include wage labor contracts and exchange of natural resources or agricultural produce (Helms 1969: 329). Drawing on the work of Fox (1969), Helm suggests that the hunting and gathering tribal people such as Chenchu, Vedda, and Yanadi[10] in Andhra operate as "occupationally specialized productive units similar to caste groups such as Carpenters, Shepherds, or Leather Workers" (Helm 1969: 339). Items such as honey, wax, rope, baskets, and so on are exchanged for items that the highlanders need from their neighbors on the plains. Von Fürer-Haimendorf has noted this occupational specialization in the case of Konda Reddis who make wooden drums, dug-out canoes, and wooden pounding troughs that other local communities need (von Fürer-Haimendorf 1948: 88). Such economic collaboration or symbiosis is also noted by Sinha (1958).

Although they are considered to be outside the larger Hindu peasant society, Sinha (1958: 505) notes that the tribal communities from both agricultural and hunting and gathering backgrounds are in touch with the organized market system, particularly the Hindu artisan castes, namely the blacksmiths, basket makers, potters, and weavers. He notes that this interaction often extended into "other aspects of social life, such as ceremonial friendship, participation in common festivals, and so on" (Sinha 1958: 505). He makes an interesting distinction between "social field" and "ideological field" and identifies the tribal communities that are part of the Hindu social field, even though they might not share the ideology of the Brahmanical Hinduism. In this sense, the tribal communities in central and southern India are "in a process of transformation which brings them closer to peasant Hindu communities—there is not a single tribe in this belt that is completely un-affected by Hinduism" (Sinha 1958: 505). This view has also been vouchsafed by von Fürer-Haimendorf in his study, for he notes that the Chenchus "have had occasional contacts with pilgrims flocking to a famous Hindu shrine in the heart of their country, and they must have known of the agricultural civilizations in the adjoining plains" (von Fürer-Haimendorf 1948: 88).

The Konda Reddis of the hills seemed to have maintained closer proximity with the plains people because of their ability to raise crops and breed animals as well as gathering food from wild plants (von Fürer-Haimendorf 1948: 88). In his more comprehensive work on the Reddis on the Bison Hill in the Hyderabad region, von Fürer-Haimendorf refers to the Konda Reddis as being the "representative of perhaps the oldest agricultural civilization of the Deccan" on the basis that the Konda Reddis used the "digging-stick cultivation" method (von Fürer-Haimendorf 1945: 337). As such, they are placed in between the hunting and gathering Chenchus, according to von Fürer-Haimendorf "survivals of most ancient India" (1943: 4), and the "more advanced hoe-cultivators, such as Marias, Bondos, Gadabas and Mundas" (von Fürer-Haimendorf 1945: 335). The Bondo and Gadaba tribes of Orissa are even more attuned to the cultivation of crops (von Fürer-Haimendorf 1948: 89). He further points out that the process of what he calls "Dravidianization" gradually resulted among the Raj Gonds, for instance, the adoption of the feudal systems of the peasant communities.

However, what is also important to note is the intrinsic relationship between myth, ritual, and the tools used in cultivation. For instance, Gond mythology details how Gonds first acquired iron tools. Both Gonds and Koyas give ritual importance to the iron tools that they use for their economic activities (von Fürer-Haimendorf 1948: 89). The use of tools for subsistence strategies has also undergone modification in the face of the tribal interaction with the plains people and the gradual acculturation of their cultural practices. For instance, Murty points out that the Dabba Yerukulas and Boyas do not use bows and arrows anymore due to their "acculturation into the village economy as marginal enclaves" (Murty 1985: 196) although they continue to "depend on hunting and foraging for their subsistence and exchange" (Murty 1985: 192). Murty also notes that the introduction of the village system, through the intrusion of village dwellers, e.g. in the case of Kunderu valley (in Kurnool district), resulted in the disruption of the ecological balance of the region and transformed the hunter-gatherers into various specialized professionals to supply meat and other products to the village economy. In other words, the hunter-gatherers gradually began to domesticate sheep, goats, and pigs for the purposes of supplying them to the village system, in contrast with their earlier practice of hunting these animals in the wild (Murty 1985: 201).

Notwithstanding this social interaction based on exchange of products and services, the tribal communities are generally treated separately by the larger Hindu populations in Andhra. As is evident by now, this relationship is always dependent on what different groups bring to each other in an exchange. Nevertheless, it is also important to note that the caste communities generally controlled and dominated this relationship. For instance, in the case of Lambadas[11] in the Hyderabad region, they were mostly used by the mainstream caste society for protection against marauders. In return they were given land to settle on the periphery of the village at the invitation of the village landlords. However, the acquisition of land by the Lambadas from the village landlords generated internal class differentiation among them. The Naiks and the Kharbaris, the sub-castes among them, generally benefitted more than the Lambada tribal community as a whole (Rattord 1984: 49). What is interesting is that while the Lambadas are expected to provide free labor to the caste landlords, such as Reddis, Kammas, and Velamas, they do not provide free labor to their own landlords, namely to the Naiks and Kharbaris (Rattord 1984: 51).

One of the limitations in the study of the castes and tribes in Andhra Pradesh is that while a good deal of it is focused on inter-caste relations, and caste and tribal relations in the context of larger exchange of products and services, not much focus was given to internal hierarchical relations. Rattord's study is unique in this regard in that she brings out the internal stratification and strategies for upward mobility within the Lambada tribe and the associated smaller groups who are considered less equal tribes, such as the Zangads. Although from the outside caste landlord's point of view, all Lambadas are untouchable, there is an internal hierarchy among them in which some groups, such as Zangads, are considered untouchable by other Lambadas and hence carry double untouchable status. However, through a ritual called *dawat*, Zangads can climb up the social ladder within the Lambada tribe by paying a prescribed amount during the ritual to the Naiks or Kharbaris in return for which they are given official certification of their new status. By this process, the Zangads will no longer be called by that name, and any Lambada who violates the rule will be fined (Rattord 1984: 51–54).

Exchange relations across religious boundaries

There is a sizable population of Muslims in Andhra, especially in the Telangana region, whose internal social ranking is of some importance. It is important to include some comments on these relations in this chapter in order to provide not only a comparative perspective, but also some nuance in the exchange relations of different groups. Comparisons by anthropologists have been made between Muslim communities in Tamil Nadu and Andhra Pradesh. Mines (1975) conducted a brief study on Muslims in Tamil Nadu. Benson (1983), using Mines's material on Tamil Nadu , draws a comparison between the two communities and distinguishes the Muslim community in Andhra by the following criteria: first, the use of Urdu among Andhra Muslims, unlike the Tamil Muslims who speak Tamil; second, the distinction based on social ranking among Muslims in Andhra, unlike their counterparts in Tamil Nadu. The Andhra Muslims are divided into seven groups—Sayyid, Sheikh, Mughul, Pathan, Katikawallu, Laddaf (also known as Dudekula), and Fakir. Whereas the first four are associated with either foreign or North Indian origins, the latter three are converts from former lower castes among Hindus. Marriage alliances between the former four and the latter three are not common. Just as the untouchable castes are segregated hierarchically among Hindus, the last three castes among Muslims are also treated lower than the first four (Benson 1983: 46–47).

One of the questions that Benson pursues is how Hindus and Muslims regard each other. She points out that Hindus in the village system place Muslims, regardless of their internal caste differentiation, on a par with the agricultural castes and above the untouchables and other lower castes, such as barbers and washermen. Furthermore, economic status is the common basis in the case of the status of women in both Hindu and Muslim communities in the villages. While working-class Hindu women interact with their male counterparts freely, the wealthy Hindu women observe Purdah like their Muslim counterparts. Likewise, the working-class Muslim women cannot afford to maintain seclusion based on religious grounds due to economic reasons (Benson 1983: 48). Although in the villages, Muslims do maintain their ethnic identity, there is a close exchange and mutual participation between Hindus and

Muslims at the popular festivals, and in some instances, for example in the Mallannapalle area, Muslim ritual practices are influenced by Hinduism (Benson 1983: 49). However, notwithstanding the many similarities, Muslims generally emphasize the differences, such as the religious significance of festivals, language, dress, and so on (Benson 1983: 50). Focusing on mainly the Dudekula Muslims, Saheb (2003) makes the point that, unlike their Hindu counterparts, the Muslim castes are ranked not on the basis of ideology of purity, but on occupational and cultural differences. For the same reason, the Dudekula women do not wear Purdah as they are generally involved in outdoor jobs. While they do not accept food from the two lower caste groups in Andhra, namely Mala and Madiga (cf. Nicholson 1926; Singh 1969), they offer their services, along with other service castes, as agricultural laborers to Reddi farmers (Saheb 2003: 4910–11).

Conclusion: Placing economic relations in Andhra in a broader context

In concluding this essay, let me both sum up as well as place the discussion in the larger context of anthropological studies on India. In the above, we looked at economic relations based on exchange among castes, between castes and tribes, and across religious boundaries in the region of Andhra Pradesh. As is evident both in the case of relations within caste society as well as across hierarchies, relations have always been contested by some within those groups. Therefore, Dumontian notions of pure and impure (Dumont 1980) cannot be applied to social relations within Andhra in some reified sense. As contestations are often political and economic in nature, they cannot entirely be circumscribed through ritual. Strangely, as much as ritual can function as a mechanism to discriminate against the lower order social groups, as in the case of the Brahmanical ritual, it can also be used to obtain higher status, as in the case of Lambadas who are able to do so by making payment during a ritual. Elsewhere, I have made some comment (see Penumala 2010: 413) in the way of problematizing the ideological pre-eminence of the Brahman proffered by Lawrence Babb (1975) and Brian K. Smith (1994). In view of the pervasiveness of caste mobility throughout India, the notion of untouchability in academic analysis needs to be understood in terms of its complexity and variables in real practice, instead of engaging in generalizations. For the higher order social groups no distinctions are visible among the various untouchable castes. The Madigas, for instance, historically used their very "untouchableness" to claim superior status through the invention of myth; untouchability is not merely higher caste versus lower caste through ritual participation, but is practiced between two untouchable castes, e.g. the Mala and Madiga groups and between Lambadas and their inferior counterparts, namely the Zangads. The context of Andhra shows that exchange relations based on the jajmani system are far more complex than is generally considered.

As Benson (1976) pointed out in her analysis of Mallannapalle village, the jajmani system is neither to be circumscribed as a higher versus lower caste relationship nor as a ritually regulated system, but rather we need to recognize the diverse ways in which the service castes relate to each other. As such, exchange relations between castes are not merely hierarchical but horizontal, going beyond ritual boundaries of endogamous groups to incorporate cognate exogamous groups. It is often economic considerations that are at the center of these exchanges. Similarly, the exchange relations between caste groups and tribal communities are based on mutual economic cooperation, albeit the caste society generally retained dominance. It is also economic considerations that are at the basis of placing Muslim caste groups on a par with the agricultural castes rather than with the untouchable castes, notwithstanding the association of some of them with impure services such as leather work. It may be fair to say then that economic considerations among sub-castes, between castes and tribes, and between caste groups and their Muslim counterparts, appear to be of greater significance in the overall picture of the economic and social relations within Andhra. Explaining inter-caste and across-caste relations on the one hand and caste and tribe relations on the other, through circumscribing these relations through the religious ideology of the Brahmins, is too limiting in that it does not take into account the many variables, such as the fact that the Brahmin is on the periphery in most villages as he is an itinerant member and not located in the villages. Therefore, the social relations of castes and their tribal counterparts in various regions of Andhra are structured on the basis of various economic exchanges, and the status of being lower and higher is not necessarily expressed in purity and pollution terms *vis-à-vis* ritual, but rather on the basis of services and products that they can exchange. Privileging the ritual sphere to explain social relations of castes and tribes, as done by Dumont (1980) and many other later anthropologists (Pfaffenberger 1980), is to ignore the economic concerns of society and the many changes that society has undergone in recent years. Social relations in Andhra need to be explained from the standpoint of the great diversity that exists both within groups as well as across groups, but primarily driven by economic concerns.

Notes

1 Raheja, in the case of North India, drawing from Stokes's study, identifies at least two ways in which proprietary rights to land were transferred—first in the Zamindari system in which the proprietary rights were transferred easily; second through the Bhaichara or Pattidari system in which individual families held land titles, the transfer of such rights was restricted to within the clan system (see Raheja 1988: 7). In Andhra Pradesh, land rights were usually sold within the dominant caste families to prevent local political opposition from other groups. It is more likely for another Kamma landlord to sell his land rights to another Kamma landlord than to another Reddi, let alone to a lower caste person.
2 This situation is not peculiar to Andhra, but more general in the South Indian context. For instance, in the case of Vellalars in Tamil Nadu, many lower castes have tended to claim that status, e.g. Nalavars and Pallars (see Pfaffenberger 1980: 205). It is for this reason, Pfaffenberger argues, that the dominant castes continually manipulate ritual "to distinguish themselves from Untouchables, attaching to low-caste persons a stigma of low rank that goes deeper than impurity and that discredits the claims that Untouchables make to a higher rank" (1980: 206).
3 In his 1960 brief study (75 pages) of five regions—Kerala, Coromandel, Upper Ganges, Middle Indus, and Bengal Delta—Marriott introduced a new method of elaborating caste ranking on the basis of the consensus among the villagers to rank the corporate entities within the system (see Marriott 1960).
4 Sheth (1999: 2503) points out that it is precisely due to the contested perceptions of each other's social status that the colonial census enumerators often relied on "their 'reading' of the scriptures as well as local knowledge and practice. But when a name and/or a rank given to a caste were in dispute – and this happened frequently – the census officer's 'anthropological' judgment, albeit tempered by representations received from leaders of concerned caste, prevailed. Thus, despite the diversity of the debate, at the end of the day, the criterion of 'social precedence of one caste over the other', i.e., the scriptural principle of ritual status hierarchy, was explicitly and officially recognized."
5 Mauss (1977) argued that ritual provided the basis for social relations in traditional societies, which he called a "system of total prestation." Many subsequent scholars, including Dumont, pursued their arguments in line with this view, which privileged ritual in explaining social relations.
6 The ryotwari system is distinguished from the zamindari system of large-scale landlords during the British raj. In this (ryotwari) system the farmer is bestowed with the ownership of land.
7 No matter how in modern social scientific terms one defines the jajmani system, the most fundamental use of it is found in the ancient Vedic ritual context where a Yajamana invokes both gods and humans for his personal benefit. Three groups of priests—the Adhvaryu priests concerned with the

material components of the ritual, the Hotri priests concerned with the deities, and the Yajamana priests who are concerned with the prosperity of the Yajamana—all come together for the benefit of the Yajamana (see Wheelock 1985; Fuller calls attention to the original notion of yajamana in the jajmani system: see Fuller 1989: 39).

8   Fuller contrasts the jajmani system with that of the Baluta system, which comes from the Maharashtra region. In the Baluta system, "officials and servants are not clients of patron households, but are attached to the village as a whole or to a division of it, and the remuneration which they receive at harvest time from the cultivators is made on behalf of the entire village or division (except for the often excluded Untouchables)" (Fuller 1989: 38). Fuller also calls into question whether jajmani can be properly described as a "system".

9   From the North Indian perspective, Raheja's study of the relationship between Gujar landholders and Gaur Brahmins in Pahansu village in Uttar Pradesh is very insightful in this context (see Raheja 1988).

10 For a more comprehensive cultural study of Yanadi tribe of Sriharikota island in Andhra, see N. Sudhakar Rao (2002). He provides a comprehensive list of earlier works on Yanadi studies (Rao 2002: 2).

11 Lambadas were initially listed as "Denotified Tribes" and only recently included in the list of Scheduled Tribes in Andhra. They are originally from the North-western region and earned their living by transporting goods on bullock carts. They are said to have supplied the Moghuls with food grains when they (Moghuls) invaded the Deccan (see Rattord 1984: 47).

References

Allchin, Bridget (1966) *The Stone-tipped Arrow: Late Stone-Age Hunters of the Tropical World*. London: Phoenix House.

Babb, Lawrence (1975) *Divine Hierarchy: Popular Hinduism in Central India*. New York: Columbia University Press.

Bayly, S. (1989) *Saints, Goddesses and Kings: Muslims and Christians in South Indian Society 1700–1900*. Cambridge: Cambridge University Press.

Beidelmann, T. O. (1959) *A Comparative Analysis of the Jajmani System*. Locust Valley, NY: J. J. Augustin Inc. for the Association for Asian Studies.

*Benson, Janet (1976) 'A South Indian Jajmani System,' *Ethnology*, 15 (3) (July 1976): 239–50.

Benson, Janet E. (1983) 'Politics and Muslim Ethnicity in South India,' in *Journal of Anthropological Research*, 39 (1) (Spring 1983): 42–59.

Busi, Bhaskar Rao and K. Ravi (eds) (2006) *Anthropological Studies in Andhra Pradesh*. New Delhi: Anthropological Survey of India.

Census (2011) www.censusindia.gov.in/ (accessed January 4, 2013).

Charsley, Simon (2004) 'Interpreting Untouchability: The Performance of Caste in Andhra Pradesh, South India,' *Asian Folklore Studies*, 63 (2): 267–90.

Dumont, Louis (1980) *Homo Hierarchicus: The Caste System and its Implications*, (tr. Mark Sainsbury, Louis Dumont and Basia Gulati). Chicago: University of Chicago Press.

Durga, P. S. Kanaka and Y. A. Sudhakar Reddy (1992) 'Kings, Temples and Legitimation of Autochthonous Communities. A Case Study of a South Indian Temple,' *Journal of the Economic and Social History of the Orient*, 35 (2): 145–66.

Fox, Richard G. (1969) '"Professional primitives"; hunters and gatherers of nuclear South Asia,' *Man in India*, 49: 139–60.

Fuller, C. J. (1989) 'Misconceiving the grain heap: a critique of the concept of the Indian Jajmani system,' in J. Parry and M. Bloch (eds), *Money and the Morality of Exchange*. Cambridge: Cambridge University Press.

*Fürer-Haimendorf, Christoph von (1943) *The Chenchus, Jungle Folk of the Deccan*. London: Macmillan & Co.

*——(1945) *The Reddis of the Bison Hills: A Study in Acculturation*. London: Macmillan & Co.

——(1948) 'Culture Strata in the Deccan,' *Man*, 48 (August 1948): 87–90.

Good, Anthony (1982) 'The Actor and the Act: Categories of Prestation in South India,' *Man*, New Series, 17 (1) (March 1982): 23–41.

*Gould, Harold A. (1958) 'The Hindu Jajmani System: A Case of Economic Particularism,' *Southwestern Journal of Anthropology*, 14 (4) (Winter, 1958): 428–37.

Gusfield, Joseph R. (1965) 'Political Community and Group Interests in Modern India,' *Pacific Affairs*, 38 (2) (Summer 1965): 123–41.

*Harrison, Selig S. (1956) 'Caste and the Andhra Communists,' *The American Political Science Review*, 50 (2) (June 1956): 378–404.

*Helms, Mary W. (1969) 'The Purchase Society: Adaptation to Economic Frontiers,' *Anthropological Quarterly*, 42 (4) (October 1969): 325–42.

Hiebert, Paul G. (1969) 'Caste and Personal Rank in an Indian Village: An Extension in Techniques,' *American Anthropologist*, New Series, 71 (3) (June 1969): 434–53.

Ilaiah, Kancha (1992) 'Andhra Pradesh's Anti-Liquor Movement,' *Economic and Political Weekly*, 27 (45) (November 7, 1992): 2406–08.

Jodhka, Surinder S. (1997) 'Understanding Exchange Relations in Indian Agriculture,' *Economic and Political Weekly*, 32 (19) (May 10–16, 1997): 1016–17.

Kelly, Robert L. (1983) 'Hunter-Gatherer Mobility Strategies,' *Journal of Anthropological Research*, 39 (3) (Autumn 1983): 277–306.

Kölver, Bernhard (1988) 'On the Origins of the Jajmānī System,' *Journal of the Economic and Social History of the Orient*, 31 (3): 265–85.

Kuo-Chun, Chao (1957) 'Agricultural Laborers in India,' *Far Eastern Survey*, 26 (2) (February 1957): 24–31.

Marriott, McKim (1960) *Caste Ranking and Community Structure in Five Regions of India and Pakistan*, Deccan College Monograph Series no. 23. Poona: Deccan College.

Mauss, M. (1977) *The Gift: Forms and Functions of Exchange in Archaic Societies*. New York: W. W. Norton.

Mayer, Peter (1993) 'Inventing Village Tradition: The Late 19th Century Origins of the North Indian "Jajmani System",' *Modern Asian Studies*, 27 (2) (May 1993): 357–95.

Miller, Daniel (1986) 'Exchange and Alienation in the "Jajmani" System,' *Journal of Anthropological Research*, 42 (4) (Winter 1986): 535–56.

Mines, M. (1975) 'Islamisation and Muslim Ethnicity in South India,' *Man*, 10: 404–17.

Mohan, K. Narendra (1995) 'Caste and Politics in Andhra Pradesh,' *Economic and Political Weekly*, 30 (2) (January 14, 1995): 124.

Montgomery, Edward (1977) 'Human Ecology and the Population Concept: The Yelnadu Reddi Population in India,' *American Ethnologist*, 4 (1) Human Ecology (February 1977): pp. 175–89.

Murty, M. L. K. (1985) 'Ethnoarchaeology of the Kurnool Cave Areas, South India,' *World Archaeology*, 17 (2), Ethnoarchaeology (October 1985): 192–205.

Nicholson, Sydney (1926) 'Social Organization of the Malas-An Outcaste Indian People,' *Journal of the Royal Anthropological Institute of Great Britain and Ireland*, 56 (1926): 91–103.

*Olson, Wendy (1996) *Rural Indian Social Relations: A Study of Southern Andhra Pradesh*. Delhi: Oxford University Press.

Penumala, Pratap Kumar (2010) 'Sociology of Hinduism,' in Bryan S. Turner (ed.), *The New Blackwell Companion to the Sociology of Religion*. Oxford: Blackwell Publishing Ltd.

Pfaffenberger, Bryan (1980) 'Social Communication in Dravidian Ritual,' *Journal of Anthropological Research*, 36 (2) (Summer 1980): 196–219.

Pocock, D. F. (1962) 'Notes on Jajmani Relationships,' *Contributions to Indian Sociology*, VI (December 1962): 7995.

Prasad, N. Purendra and P. Venkata Rao (1997) 'Adaptations of Peasants in a Stress Environment,' *Economic and Political Weekly*, 32 (5) (February 1–7, 1997): 228–34.

Raheja, Gloria Goodwin (1988) *The Poison in the Gift: Ritual, Prestation, and the Dominant Caste in a North Indian Village*. Chicago: Chicago University Press.

Rao, N. Sudhakar (2002) *Ethnography of a Nomadic Tribe*. New Delhi: Concept Publishing Company.

*Rattord, B. Shyamala Devi (1984) 'Class and Caste Differences among the Lambadas in Andhra Pradesh,' *Social Scientist*, 12 (7) (July 1984): 47–56.

*Saheb, S. A. A. (2003) 'Dudekula Muslims of Andhra Pradesh: An Ethnographic Profile,' *Economic and Political Weekly*, 38 (46) (November 15–21 2003): 4908–12.

*Sankaran, S. R. (1998) 'Development of Scheduled Castes in Andhra Pradesh: Emerging Issues,' *Economic and Political Weekly*, 33 (5) (January 31–February 6, 1998): 208–11.

Sheth, D. L. (1999) 'Secularization of Caste and Making of New Middle Class,' *Economic and Political Weekly*, 34 (34/35) (August 21–September 3, 1999): 2502–10.

Singh, T. R. (1969) *The Madiga*. Lucknow: Ethnographic and Folk Culture Society.

Sinha, Surajit (1958) 'Tribal Cultures of Peninsular India as a Dimension of Little Tradition in the Study of Indian Civilization: A Preliminary Statement,' *Journal of American Folklore*, 71 (281), (Traditional India: Structure and Change) (July–September 1958): 504–18.

Smith, Brian K. (1994) *Classifying the Universe: The Ancient Indian Varna System and the Origins of Caste*. New York: Oxford University Press.

Srinivas, M. N. (1957) 'Caste in Modern India,' *Journal of Asian Studies*, 16 (4) (August 1957): 529–48.

Sundar, Nandini; Satish Deshpande and Patricia Uberoi (2000) 'Indian Anthropology and Sociology: Towards a History,' *Economic and Political Weekly*, 35 (24) (June 10–16, 2000): 1998–2002.

Talbot, Cynthia (1991) 'Temples, Donors, and Gifts: Patterns of Patronage in Thirteenth-Century South India,' *Journal of Asian Studies*, 50 (2) (May 1991): 308–40.

——(2001) *Precolonial India in Practice: Society, Religion and Identity in Medieval Andhra*. New York: Oxford University Press.

*Upadhya, Carol Boyack (1988a) 'The Farmer-Capitalists of Coastal Andhra Pradesh,' *Economic and Political Weekly*, 23 (27) (July 9, 1988): 1376–82.

——(1988b) 'The Farmer-Capitalists of Coastal Andhra Pradesh,' *Economic and Political Weekly*, 23 (28) (July 2, 1988): 1433–42.

Venkatesu, E. (2004) 'Occupational Cooperatives: All but Defunct,' *Economic and Political Weekly*, 39 (33) (August 14–20, 2004): 3687–89.

Vidyarthi, L. P. (1976) *Rise of Anthropology in India*. Delhi: Concept Publishing Company.

Wheelock, Wade T. (1985) 'Patterns of Mantra Use in a Vedic Ritual,' *Numen*, 32, Fasc. 2 (December 1985): 169–93.

Wiser, W. H. (1969 [1936]) *The Hindu Jajmani System*. Lucknow: Lucknow Publishing House.

3 Bihar

Caste, class, and violence

Carolyn Brown Heinz

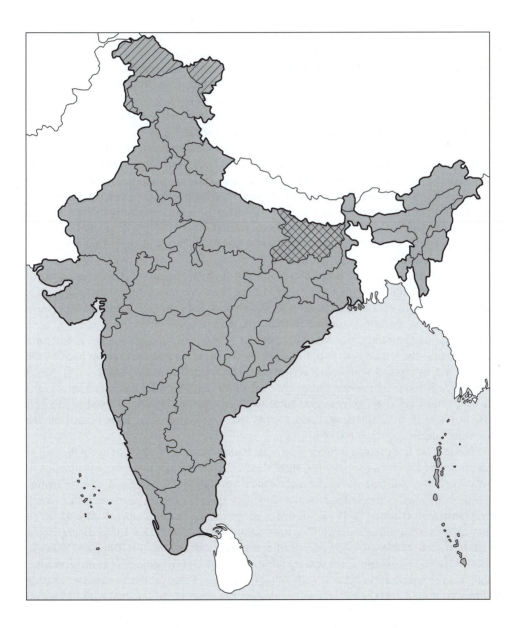

Sanitizing politics

As a young anthropologist hoping to do fieldwork in Bihar in 1979, I waited through a long application period while one by one all the applications for Fulbrights and Indo-US Subcommission Fellows were processed—except mine. I was the sole anthropologist that year, and the hang-up turned out to be some passages in Gerald Berreman's *Hindus of the Himalayas* (1972). Buried deep in the book were references to high caste men taking sexual advantage of low caste women. Although Berreman's book was published in 1972, and had nothing to do with me or my research site, someone in the UP state legislature had just discovered it, and outrage ensued. Why were foreigners coming here and writing these things about us? My visa was put on hold. At the last minute someone was prevailed upon to sign off on it, and I was on the plane a week later. But it was an early lesson learned.

I had with me current newspapers filled with gruesome photos and headlines. The caption of one photo read: "Bodies of Parasbigha carnage victims, roasted alive on Thursday in an armed raid by hired men." The photos did not spare the details of their burned and distorted bodies jumbled inside the clay half-walls from which the thatched roof had burned off. At Patna station, six young men, their hands bound in front of them, a single rope linking them one to another by the neck, were being herded by police across the platform. Were these some of the resisting Dalits, or members of the armed militia?

This was my initiation to Bihar. I knew that although I would pay attention to these troubles during my stay, clipping news stories and documenting any events that happened to emerge in my vicinity, I would not actively inquire about them and I would never write about them. I had come to work with the Maithil Brahmans, and I had been trained to preserve the security and reputation of the people whose culture I was there to study. I was fully indoctrinated in the "sanitizing politics" form of ethnographic research (Ortner 1995: 176). I would engage in "watchful waiting" (Scheper-Hughes 1995: 414), ears alert, eyes wide open, but not overtly investigate these matters.

As I settled into the modest home of a prominent Brahman family in Darbhanga, north of the Ganges in the cultural region known as Mithila, there was much to note but not pursue. Some of it had to do with a black trade in the jewels and other portable wealth of Darbhanga Raj, which was in process of dissolution following zamindari abolition. I was in Bihar at an important turning point in the post-colonial history of the region, at the demise of one form of dominance—the feudal system put in place by the Mughals and then rationalized by the British—and its replacement with a restructured, vigorous, contentious new set of power games made possible by the new patronage democracy, with the state having taken over the role of the old zamindars, an emergent local landlord class, resistance by landless laborers consisting mostly of Dalit castes, and a party politics where elites manipulated all the competing interests for their own ends.

This was a far from serene turning point. The Parasbigha massacre was among the first in a succession of atrocities over the next three decades, culminating in the present situation in which "predatory politicians, 'cockeyed' Mandal revolutionaries, frenzied caste warriors, red-hot Maoists and ethnophobic Hindu nationalists are locked in a vicious no holds barred power struggle" (Kumar 2008: 2). Rajputs, Bhumihars, Yadavas, and Kurmi have all organized private armies (Louis 2002; Kumar 2008; Hauser 2004; Das 1986; Bhatia 1997), which have been responsible for dozens of massacres, most of them in Bhojpur, Nalanda, Jahanabad, and Gaya districts. These were responses to the mobilization of peasant resistance, which has a long history in Bihar (Pinch 1996; Chaudhry 1988), yet the movement has been co-opted by middle and big cultivators, leaving out the poorest, the laborers with little or no land who are now the main partisans of the Naxalite, or Maoist, resistance (Peoples' Union for Democratic Rights 1992; Kunnath 2004, 2006, 2009; Das 2008; Subramanian 2010). This was not the "*jajmani* system" I had studied at the university.

In the anthropology of India during the first post-Independence decades, many writings exoticized the caste system and wrote respectfully, even admiringly, of the distributive economy of the village, the *jajmani* system in which *jatis* with occupational specializations are tied to a dominant landowning caste, the *jajman* (Wiser 1936). While there were critiques of the functionalist model of *jajmani* relations from Marxist scholars, on the whole the dynamics of these settings were treated with the studied relativism of mid-century academic liberalism. These local communities, with their dominant castes, rising backward castes, and exploited scheduled castes, were all subalterns. Dealing with any of the emerging crises produced by relations of inequality, dominance, submission, resistance, and violence in independent India risked various sanctions, from alienating local powers to getting research visas denied to disapproval from peers back home.

Yet anthropology has had little to say about this latest and more violent incarnation of the "*jajmani* system," at least in Bihar. This may be explained in part by the fact that few anthropologists have worked in Bihar, and fewer still have addressed either the violence or the sociocultural factors that have produced it. Rather, much of the anthropology that has emerged in recent years has focused on art (Heinz 1996, 2006; Jain 1997; Szanton and Bakshi 2007), music (Henry 1998), ritual (Henry 2003), and folklore (Narayan 2001). We might expect that foreigners would rarely be welcome to conduct critical research, but Indian anthropologists who have attempted to work in areas of chronic violence have also found this work difficult and dangerous. One anthropologist who has attempted to study the social organization of violence in rural Bihar, Anand Chakravarti (2001a), was bullied by the dominant caste when he attempted to ask questions about unfree labor in an area of Purnea district where fourteen Santhal share-croppers were murdered in 1971. More recently, Kunnath (2004) risked fieldwork in the heart of the "flaming fields" of agrarian violence in Jahanabad district near the sites of the Parasbigha and Pipra massacres, where private armies of landholders have been responsible for dozens more massacres over thirty years and Dalit Naxalites now run a parallel government. His life was in constant danger. Yet we have nothing like Sudhir Kakar's psychoanalytic study of participants in Hindu–Muslim violence in Hyderabad (1996) or E. Valentine Daniel's "anthropography" of violence in Sri Lanka (1996) that systematically focuses on the culture of violence itself.

We could profitably raise more questions about the lack of anthropological inquiry into the forms of domination and human suffering in the places where we work. In American universities since the 1990s, human subjects committees squelch such investigations by, in effect, siding with local oppressors by requiring full disclosure of all possible risks, along with signed consent forms, from anyone the anthropologist talks to. But perhaps a more relevant line of inquiry is to ask what our discipline might contribute to such studies. For other disciplines have not been reticent to investigate Bihar's violence and dysfunction, and the media, from populist local vernacular papers to elite publications like the *Times of India* and the *Economic and Political Weekly,* have made discourse about Bihar's violence, casteism, and the corruption of public culture, a "zone of cultural debate conducted through the mass media, other mechanical modes of reproduction, and the visible practices of institutions such as the state. It is 'the site and stake' of struggles for cultural meaning" (Gupta 1995: 385). We should pay close attention to this public culture, its themes, tropes, and rhetoric. Stories written by local observers reported in the vernacular papers are often emotional and sympathetic to the Dalits who are victims of the crimes. They name powerful landowners in a rhetoric of outrage. The Dalit victims are portrayed for elite readers as real persons suffering horrifying offenses, though without significant agency, even when the massacre is retaliation for targeted murders of hated local strongmen.

A brief profile of Bihar

Bihar within its most recent borders consists of the rich alluvial lands north and south of the Ganges, since the region formerly known as "southern Bihar," the Chotanagpur Plateau, was hived off in 2000 to form the new state of Jharkhand. This leaves the region formerly known as "central Bihar" as the new south Bihar, which renders nomenclature from pre-2000 publications somewhat confusing. Numerous tributaries draining southward from the Himalayas make much of north Bihar a soggy plain, especially in the Kosi area, with its frequent shifts leaving older beds behind as empty or marshy remnants. South Bihar is watered by drainage from the Chotanagpur Plateau in numerous small rivers and streams that create parallel north-south undulations, which do not readily retain moisture without the system of man-made irrigation channels and tanks that make cultivation possible. By contrast, flat north Bihar more readily absorbs the moisture from rainfall. Besides the Kosi River, two other tributaries have major importance, the southward-flowing Gandak and the northward-flowing Son, each of which joins the Ganges near the capital, Patna, the Son somewhat further to the west.

This river system has allowed for three distinct cultural regions and language groups to emerge over Bihar's 3,000-plus year history. Patna was formerly Pataliputra, the capital of the Mauryan empire (323–185BC). The surrounding region was known as Magadh, and the dialect of Bihari spoken there today is known as Magahi. This was the heartland of early Buddhism, a fact still apparent from the Buddhist complexes at Bodh Gaya, which remain centers of worldwide pilgrimage, the ruins of the ancient monastery/university at Nalanda, and various other historic sites. Magadh was thus a heterogeneous region from early on, with the Vedic religion of the Brahmans losing ground to later Buddhist kingdoms, and even later to some of the earliest incursions of Muslim conquerors from the west. The second major region consists of the districts to the west of the Son and Gandak where the predominant dialect is Bhojpuri.[1] This region looks westward as much as eastward in its cultural affinities, especially to Banaras, the center of the Bhojpuri cultural region that includes eastern UP and western Bihar (Freitag 1989: 1), even though Gottschalk's informants in Kaimur district considered themselves "fully and proudly Biharis" (Gottschalk 2000: 58). The third major region is Mithila, consisting of the sixteen districts of north Bihar where Maithili is spoken. Mithila is a culturally conservative region lying between the Gandak and the Kosi, which persisted as a center of Vedic continuity by making distinct adaptations to Buddhist, Muslim, and later British dominance when other parts of Bihar became more heterogeneous. There Buddhism did not displace Brahmanism, and when Muslim conquerors defeated a Hindu raja in 1313, local power was vested in Brahman families by the new Muslim overlords. In British times, Darbhanga Raj was the largest *zamindari* estate of Bihar, and one of the largest and richest in India, ruled by a family of Maithil Brahmans who promoted Brahman influence throughout the region.

Bihar has the reputation of being the most caste-conscious state of India, whose politicians openly appeal to caste interests in their struggles for control of state power, where politics is rarely about governing policies and mostly about contending for communal interests. The four dominant high caste groups (the "Forward castes")—Brahman, Bhumihar, Rajput, Kayastha—together constitute about 12 percent of the population. These are the old elite, from whose numbers came the major *zamindars* and local landowning castes. The so-called "Backward castes," consisting of about half the population of Bihar, were further classified soon after Independence into the Upper Backwards and the Lower Backwards (Blair 1980).[2] The Upper Backwards—Bania, Yadav, Kurmi, and Koiri—constitute about 19 percent of the population, and now include most of the rising "Kulak" class of successful peasants who have acquired land, adopted improved agricultural technology, and become a powerful force in Bihar politics. This is true, above all, of the Yadavas. The Lower Backwards are Shudra castes such as Barhi, Dhanuk, Kahar, Kumhar, Lohar, Mallah, Teli, etc., about 32 percent of the population. The largest components of the Scheduled Castes (14 percent) are the Dusadh, Chamar, and Musahar, the Dalit groups who are in many parts of the state locked in struggles for land and living wages with the rich peasants and landlords of the Forward and Upper Backward castes.

Bihar is also India's poorest state, whose 90 million people live on a per capita income of $160 a year, half the national average. Male literacy is 60.32 percent, female 33.57 percent, according to the 2001 Census of India. (In 1951 the figures were 22.68 and 4.22 percent respectively.) Recently, female literacy has been increasing faster than male literacy. Among the Scheduled castes, literacy is far lower: 40.2 percent (male) and 15.6 percent (female). Only 3.6 percent of Scheduled Caste persons have graduated from university.

Caste and class

The public culture that has emerged around the events described earlier has cast Bihar as the most dysfunctional, backward, violent, and "casteist" state of India. Bihar is at the far end of the spectrum from the energy and economic growth and modernism of Bangalore, Bollywood, and even Delhi. Bihar is the old India that everyone wants to leave behind. But Bihar persists, a troubled place with intractable problems, India's Third World that can't or won't catch up.

Public discourse about Bihar invariably holds "casteism" responsible for much of the state's troubles. Scholars seem to hold their noses when referring to caste, while hardly bothering to study it either. Perhaps this follows the census practice of ignoring caste, as if to pay attention will reify and empower it. The study of caste has also come to be identified as a colonial project: "As this Other, opposed to the British Self, India was that swamp of caste taboos and customs where people, soaked in religion, were entangled in unchanging traditions" (Prakash 1990: 142), a formulation that makes caste itself taboo for scholars. Rather, class is the preferred social formation. Marxian scholars, especially, bring a strong ideological commitment to class analysis that is both intellectual and partisan, the "Left anti-caste strategy" (Devika 2010: 806). Yet there has been little effort on the part of Marxists to theorize caste, even though caste continues to structure social life throughout Bihar.

The persistence of caste consciousness is attributed to the failure of modern institutions to take hold: there is a lack of economic growth and social development to provide incentives to shed caste controls and build cross-caste friendships and partnerships; politicians exploit caste anxieties about changing power valences and reinforce caste solidarity as voting blocs; with a dysfunctional state apparatus, castes provide some security against the encroaching interests of other groups. These points are real enough, yet they resemble explanations for the persistence of religion solely by its functions in intergroup conflict. Castes are also social and cultural systems that provide connectedness and meaning much as religion does. It may seem odd, years after anthropologists turned their attention away from caste (as if all had already been said), to suggest it is time to take another look. We should ask how particular local *jatis* construct their bonds of community such that they appear given, natural, and immutable, the only constant in a world of change. Earlier anthropology provided social-structural explanations, pointing to features of social organization like patrilineal kinship, endogamy, hypergamy, patrilocal residence, and commensality rules, while transactional rules governed inter-caste relations in the village, reinforcing boundaries and enforcing relations of dominance (glossed as hierarchy). More recently, scholars have used other strategies to account for identity formation in groups, such as the use of narratives, performance, and cultural memory to articulate a common past and thus present solidarity. These discourses of identity become crucial features of the cultural content of each *jati*, while a parallel discourse of the other—other castes—provide narratives of difference and justifications for dominance and resistance.

The continuing power of local castes, and their central role in the continuing violence, is documented in study after study in Bihar by scholars from every discipline (Bhatia 1997; Chaudhry 1988; Das 1986; Hauser 2004; Kumar 2008; Louis 2002) and in almost all political writing. Three important anthropological studies should be noted.

The events that occurred in February of 1980 as I was arriving by train are typical of the kind of conflict seen over the subsequent three decades in south Bihar. In the summer of 1981, Nageshwar Prasad spent three months in the villages of Parasbigha, Dohia, and Pipra in order to write *Rural Violence in India: A Case Study of Parasbigha and Pipra Violence in Bihar* (1985), the source of what follows.

Parasbigha and Dohia were neighboring villages five kilometers south of Patna. Most villages in this area are dominated by Bhumihar. With the abolition of the *zamindari* system in 1950, a struggle began for the lands of the former Tekari Raj, and the tenants, mostly Yadavas (cowherds) and Gareris (shepherds), became less submissive than before. A series of clashes reached a climax in 1979 when a faction of Dalit groups, plus two Yadavas, beheaded a notorious Bhumihar strongman. Six months later, after careful planning that even included building a dirt road into Parasbigha, on the night of February 6, 1980, a gang of 150 men arrived in the village, bolted the house of the man they took to be the Naxalite leader, and burned it down with its occupants inside. Eleven members of the family died, as did one Yadava. Two days later, Yadavas led the retaliation, attacking nearby Dohia village, where the main Bhumihar families lived. Most of the men had disappeared after the attack of two days earlier, but the attackers raped two girls, killed an old woman, and looted property.

A similar massacre took place two and a half weeks later in Pipra, a village ten kilometers further south in what is now Jahanabad district. Here, Kurmis were the landowners, a Lower Backward or "rising Kulak" caste. Prior to Independence, the whole village had been owned by a large Muslim *zamindar* who lived in Patna, and twelve Muslim families had rights to portions of the village land. Almost all the agricultural work was done for these local Muslim landholders by bound servants known as *kamias* or by sharecroppers (*bataidars*) from Dalit castes. There was a great deal of security of tenure and even a certain prestige for the *kamias* who ran things for the landowners, at least in Dalit communal memory, which has a certain nostalgia for those days. But at Partition, Kurmi from a nearby village approached the Dalits with a plan to burn the Muslim houses. Instead, they helped their masters escape, some in disguise under cover of night. When things later calmed down, the Muslim owners returned to sell the land to Kurmi buyers. The resentful Dalits were suddenly *kamias* to the Kurmi, who now felt entitled to all the respect once enjoyed by the Muslim *zamindars*.

Over the course of the 1970s, the Dalits became sympathetic to the Naxalite movement, which was most active across the Son River in Bhojpur. Numerous clashes between them and the Kurmis left a trail of rancor, rape, and murder on both sides. Because of historic competition between the middle-caste Yadavas and Kurmis, Yadavas were sometimes involved on the Naxalite side with Dalits. Kurmis began to cut off their Dalit *kamias* as agriculture was increasingly disrupted; a drought worsened things in 1978–1979, and by the end of the decade the Dalits were in a desperate condition. In December 1979 an important Kurmi landowner was murdered, reportedly by Naxalites who were said to be organizing the Dalits in the region. Kurmis decided to strike harshly in order to stop the growing Naxalite movement. On February 25, 1980, 200 heavily armed men set fire to twenty-seven Dalit houses in Pipra, killing five young women, three adults, and six children under ten.

These events demonstrate significant features of caste violence in south Bihar. Dominant caste power comes from traditional Forward castes (such as the Bhumihar) or from Backward castes enabled to move into the role of the former dominant castes (such as Yadava and Kurmi). Each process provokes resentment and resistance among the former landless castes, whose situations have not just stayed the same but actually worsened since British times.

A second case study is offered by Prakash Louis, who describes the failure of Panchayat Tehta of Jehanabad (2002: 84–88), which in 1960 was widely cited as one of two model local societies. There was a school, a center for women's welfare, and a library with 1,100 books. The *panchayat* had made important infrastructural improvements; pulses were being exported as far as Madras and Kerala. The success of this *panchayat* was attributed to the absence of castes like Bhumihars, Kayasths, Brahmans, Rajputs, and Kurmi; neither were there any ex-*zamindars* among village leaders. An educated and hard-working Muslim was the unanimously elected *mukhiya*. Yet by 1999, all had evaporated. The women's organization, the library, and all the common tube wells were defunct. Population increase had driven up land prices, benefitting Kahars and Koiris who had sold to Yadavas, the main buyers, who then set themselves up as the new dominant caste. Louis concludes:

> Caste continued to determine social status as well as destine access to resources, including literacy and education. The dominant castes appropriated the outcome of developmental measures. Whether it is the construction of canals, roadways or railways, the dominant caste arrogated all the fruits. ... There has been a constant interplay between caste and class, at times initiating alignments and at other times leading to antagonism.
>
> (Louis 2002: 88)

For every effort to reform land use in favor of the actual cultivator of the soil, local dominant castes manage to restructure agrarian relations in such a way that the lot of the cultivators is worsened rather than improved.

The third case study, which I describe in some detail, is by Anand Chakravarti, who traced agrarian evolution in one local place, this time in north Bihar, in a series of papers and one monograph (1986, 2001a, 2001b). This study is extremely useful in providing a social history of dominance and violence in one region, showing the evolution of a "*jajmani* system" from the time of the dominance of the large *zamindars* in British India, in this case Darbhanga Raj. Chakravarti then traces the strategies by which the local magnates—read 'dominant caste'— attempted to adapt to changing times and technologies while maintaining their grip on social life.

The village of Aghanbigha (a pseudonym) in Purnea District was established "about two centuries ago" by one Ishwar, the ancestor of the present dominant caste of Bhumihars. Many north Bihar villages similarly report founding ancestors "two centuries ago," which should not be attributed to folklore or the collapsing of history into a single prevalent trope. In fact, in the late eighteenth century, the Darbhanga rajas were desperately trying to keep land grants which they had received from the Mughals but which were at risk under the new British regime. Documents between Madhava Singh of Darbhanga Raj and the Board of Revenue frequently make mention of "inviting people to settle in the Sircar [*sarkar*]" (J. S. Jha 1966) in order to fulfill their obligation to enhance settlement and cultivation and meet their revenue obligations. Aghanpur was part of a revenue unit of Darbhanga Raj, and it is very likely that Ishwar settled there at that time much as high-caste men with grants of land or villages were doing all over the region.

The village Ishwar founded in the late eighteenth century now has forty-five Bhumihar households. He immediately set about assembling a full complement of serving castes to establish a classic *jajmani* system. The Bhumihar landholders were technically "tenure holders" under Darbhanga Raj, a prestigious position as local lords or petty *zamindars* responsible for sending village land revenues up the hierarchy, although they themselves did not work the land. The actual tillers of the soil were *raiyats* (cultivators) of various lower castes who enjoyed semi-permanent use of the land. In an effort to improve security of tenure, the Bihar Tenancy Act of 1885 provided that if a *raiyat* could establish that he had cultivated particular fields for twelve years, he could claim permanent rights as an "occupancy *raiyat*." He might then outsource smaller tracks to "under-*raiyats*." Thus there was a complex hierarchy of rights to land.

Aghanbigha was in a marshy, jungly region that suffered from the inconstant Kosi River, with its frequent floods and deposits of sand. When in 1893 the Kosi did a radical westward course change, Santhals, a scheduled tribe population from the Santhal Parganas, were brought in as simple sharecroppers (*bataidars*) to reclaim the land. *Bataidars* typically worked land for half the produce, but with less security than *raiyats*. When Santhals tried to claim occupancy rights to land under the 1885 Bihar Tenancy Act, Bhumihar landowners refused to provide the receipts necessary to prove continuous cultivation, and began replacing them with Yadavas who were considered to be more pliant in accepting their place in the caste hierarchy. Bhumihars also began calling themselves *kisans,* farmers, rather than "tenure holders." The result was less prestige as petty *zamindars* but tighter control of the local economy. Many of them had enormous holdings—as much as 800 acres despite a legal ceiling of fifteen acres—that could not possibly be cultivated without control of a large labor force. Because the *bataidar* sharecropping system carried too much risk of permanent claims against the land, the owners attempted throughout the early part of the twentieth century to replace sharecroppers with wage laborers. The Yadava *bataidars*, like the Santhals before them, were unwilling to give up hope for greater security of land rights, and from the 1930s on there was a great deal of agitation, much of it led early on by the Bihar Provincial Kisan Sabha (BPKS) led by Swami Sahananda, himself a Bhumihar.

In the 1960s, agriculture began to be restructured along capitalist lines. When several Bhumihar *maliks* acquired tractors in the 1960s, the scale of cultivation increased dramatically. Twenty-five acres which took sixty days to plow with oxen could be completed in twenty hours with a tractor; the tractor could accomplish sixty times the work of a plow team in just one day (Chakravarti 2001a: 95), and oxen and plow disappeared as a form of means of production owned by many poorer *kisans*.

The results of the post-Independence transformations of agriculture and land legislation were much larger tracks of land owned by fewer landholders, almost all of them Bhumihar who now called themselves *kisans*; loss of traditional means of production as ox teams were replaced by tractors; and labor demand reduced to need for a large supply of daily labor (*mazdur*) paid the lowest possible wages. These new calculations and solutions have seriously worsened conditions for the underclass, almost all of them members of lower Backward or Dalit castes.

Chakravarti's theoretical interest in these developments is to evaluate the relative significance of caste versus class in understanding the changes that took place over two centuries. This question needs to be seen in context. India's Leftist intelligentsia tends to deny that caste is relevant (except to denounce 'casteists' who use it for nefarious political purposes) and embrace class analysis; or rather to attempt to dissolve caste in class. As an anthropologist, Chakravarti wasn't so sure, and attempted to clarify the relationship between caste and class at the local level, using classic field methods to empirically define Aghanbigha's classes.

To summarize his findings: the *malik* class (i.e. the dominant caste of Bhumihars) monopolizes social, economic, and coercive power by virtue of their high caste rank, their control of 78.5 percent of the land, their pivotal role in the everyday workings of the agrarian economy, and the oppressive conditions they are able to impose on their large labor force. Another smaller group of upper and upper-middle castes, which Chakravarti labels *grihasts*, model themselves after the *maliks* but lack their social power. That is, they are 'cultivators' whose land is worked entirely by hired labor but they are not members of the dominant caste. *Tenant-cultivators* are those who hire labor in addition to their own household labor, but do not have to hire themselves out to larger landowners. These are mostly middle-caste Yadav and Kurmi, with four households of Dalits (Dhobi and Dusadh). *Petty cultivators* are those who have less than five acres of land, owned or leased, but not enough for subsistence and so must sell their labor to make ends meet. Finally, the *landless laborers*, desperately poor, live entirely on the sale of their labor. These last two categories represent 75 percent of the total village households.

This close examination of a single north Bihar village revealed a process of increasing disempowerment and impoverishment of Bihar's cultivators from British times through Independence wrought by liberal legislation that was systematically undermined by local landowning castes with the collusion of the Bihar government. As recently as February 2010 the Chief Minister Nitish Kumar, speaking to an audience consisting mostly of Bhumihars, assured them that no "Bataidari Bill" exists, and anyone who says it does is "sow[ing] seeds of hatred and discontent" by threatening landowners with loss of their land (Ahmad 2010). The event was, ironically, a celebration of the birthday of Swami Sahajanand Saraswati, the founder of the Bihar Provincial Kisan Sabha and the champion of "kisans" in the original sense of the term.

Chakravarti concludes that "caste continues to be the fundamental basis of social inequality in contemporary Bihar. ... The circumstances of birth into a low-ranking caste tend to determine their social and material conditions" (Chakravarti 2001b: 1459). Chakravarti's work is the most detailed and complete ethnographic account of agrarian life in twentieth-century Bihar we have, and in my opinion should be more widely read by anthropologists. It would be good to have similar historical-ethnographic studies from south Bihar, especially in the districts of greatest social unrest.

"Smouldering Dalit fires"

At least one anthropologist has dared go to the most contentious and violent part of Bihar to write about the Maoist movement in great detail and at first hand. George Kunnath (2004: 6) went to Jahanabad District to study power relations in the agrarian struggle in Dumari village not far from Pipra and Parasbigha. He negotiated with the local police not to be tortured if arrested; he also needed enough support from them to gain access to public records. He describes his methodology as "engaged analysis," which included helping to mobilize demonstrations, traveling with the landless to protests in distant cities, and living in a "gray zone" of fear and evasion.

This part of Bihar was subject to conquest by warrior chieftains who subjected the independent cultivators to slavery conditions and did not produce the typical "*jajmani* system" of peasant stratification familiar across north India. As we have already seen, the Kurmi, an Upper Backward caste, have taken the position of dominant caste in much of Jehanabad district as owners of most of the land. The 118 Kurmi households of Dumari own 95 percent of the land, while none of the 134 Dalit households owned any land when the Maoist movement began in the 1980s. Many were in debt bondage to the Kurmi, which worked in the same way as in Aghanbigha: small loans that could never be paid back kept them tied to *maliks* year after year. Their daily wage as laborers consisted of less than one kilo of *kesari,* a coarse grain of low nutritional value. In the absence of Brahmans and with only two households of Bhumihars and Rajputs, the Kurmis claimed all the forms of deference and service prescribed by the purity/pollution framework, which Dalits have been unwilling to give to an upstart caste.

Organized resistance by Dalits began in 1981 against a Kurmi brick kiln owner. Dalits requested a rise in wages from Rs. 10 to Rs. 25 for every 1,000 bricks they made (Kunnath 2009: 315). The landlord refused, and in the struggle that followed between armed Maoists and armed Kurmi, the landlord was killed and his head hung on a tree at the village entrance. Months later, a second landlord was killed as part of a policy of "selective annihilation" of the most oppressive landlords. In response, landlords organized the Bhumi Sena in 1982, which operated in Patna, Jehananbad, Nalanda, and Nawada districts. Between 1982 and 1985 they killed 65 Dalits and drove hundreds of Dalit families out of the area. The organization that led the Dalit resistance was the Mazdur Kisan Sangram Samiti (MKSS), a front organization of the CPI(ML) Party Unity, known locally as the Sangathan (collective). This armed resistance movement, with a mix of labor boycotts, burning of standing crops and stored harvests, and killing of Bhumi Sena leaders, finally ended in a truce in 1984. In a mango grove outside the village, the Kurmi landlords agreed to cease support for the Bhumi Sena, accepted fines of Rs. 1,368,000 and surrendered nine rifles (Kunnath 2009: 316).

This triumph for the Dalits and the Sangathan changed the power dynamics in Dumari. Old forms of caste discrimination and sexual abuse of Dalit women ended. Wages improved to three kilos of paddy or wheat, the ponds were open to fishing by everyone, and village committees with major Dalit representation handled local grievances. The arming of local Dalits, or the establishment of armed squads that would protect them in their demands for improved conditions, matched and check-mated the martial traditions of the landlords and their *lathi*-wielding muscle men that always underpinned their dominance.

Then a strange thing happened. The Kurmis joined the Sangathan. The MKSS was facing a choice between local armed struggle on behalf of the most impoverished class and "mass mobilization" that would make them competitive in state-level politics. Choosing to play in the bigger field, MKSS began allying with the middle peasants, such as Kurmi and Yadav, who joined the party in order to re-establish their dominance. Kunnath writes about the current disenchantment of the Dalits against the Sangathan, which no longer struggles for wage increases, or an end to bonded labor, has neglected education, and takes large "commissions" for development projects. The party that briefly mobilized the Dalits *en masse* later betrayed them as it sought to enhance its power through strategic alliance with the landowning middle castes.

Kunnath's work, which is exceptional for the length of time he spent immersed in the Dalit community (over a year), is so rigorously class focused that even the biographical portrait of one Naxalite leader, Rajubhai (Kunnath 2006), does not reveal his caste identity. He is Dalit. The son of a bound laborer, he attended midnight meetings in the paddy fields when the Sangathan was being organized, and became commander of an armed squad. He taught himself to read to gain access to Marxist literature. He became an "organic intellectual" (Gramsci 1971), one who challenges the hegemony of the ruling class by formulating analysis of the Dalits' situation, pursuing grassroots empowerment, and raising specific radical possibilities, such as capturing land and redistributing it to the landless. Rajubhai is compared to the nineteenth-century working-class autodidacts in the classic analysis of working-class formation by E. P. Thompson (1963). But the nineteenth-century English Christian bourgeoisie was not the late twentieth-century Hindu caste system, and with no place for caste in the analysis, there is no way to account for puzzling "contradictions" in Rajubhai's behavior. "Traditional religious beliefs persisted" forming "a parallel discourse that shadowed the materialist consciousness of Naxalism" (Kunnath 2006: 16). A sick child is taken to a village exorcist. Rajubhai refuses to explain himself when the anthropologist asks if he really believes in exorcism. On a trip to Calcutta for a political demonstration, everyone heads for the Kalighat Temple. His father's body has to be cremated on the banks of the Ganges. The replacement of traditional cultural values and practices by total class consciousness is incomplete.

One is reminded of a point made by Prakash Louis:

> Had the ivory-tower theorists of Naxalite struggle cared to feel the pulse of common people in central Bihar, and listened to them, they would not have failed to see the major role caste affinity played in spreading the Naxalite ideology in the first phase of the struggle and continues to play even today.
>
> (Louis 2002: 270)

I would like to know more about how caste and class identities interconnect in Dalit communities.

Caste and culture

There are many ways to think about caste in Bihar. Most commonly, we speak of the caste *system*, a form of dominance mystified by an ideology of ritual purity and pollution. It is certainly that, but also much else. It is a form of *identity* in which, because of the near-universality of intra-caste marriage, almost everyone has one and only one *jati*. The folk theory of *jati* holds that there are "kinds" of human groups as fixed as animal species, with traits built into the "blood" and "substance" that are unchanging and heritable. Anthropologists should question this assumption, not by dismissing caste as a research topic, but by investigating how given castes have constructed such assumptions in the past and now think about such matters in light of the obvious changes wrought by history and politics within people's lifetimes.

For example, Maithil Brahmans have elaborated a theory of identity over a period of six centuries that constructs a firewall around the caste while allowing for complex, cross-generational strategies for raising the *innate* quality (also referred to as *jati*) of kinship lines (U. N. Jha 1980; Heinz 1983, 1988). This system was slowly elaborated in the centuries following the initiation of written genealogies (*panjis*) in the fourteenth century as a defense against the non-Hindu political order established by the Afghans. Brahman genealogists theorized that every boy is a composite of thirty-six lines of descent (females "carrying" the blood of patrilineages to mix with their husband's seed), and that these ancestral lines might be of varying quality, thus affecting the status of each generation of offspring as calculated by the genealogists. Marriage-making involved a complicated calculus, as powerful and/or high-status families sought elevating marital ties. It also became a form of *jati*-wide discipline that the maharajas of Darbhanga could manipulate in controlling the entire caste of Maithil Brahmans, along with endowments of land that created local level *zamindars* under Darbhanga Raj.

Of course, people do not have only one identity, as Gottschalk (2000) shows in his elegant study of identity in Arampur, to which I shall return. But caste identity is uniquely rich and content-filled. Two important studies have taken as their topic the epic narratives of Dalit groups, the Tulsi Bir tale of the Bhuinya (Prakash 1990) and the Chuharmal tale of the Dusadhs (Narayan 2001).

Bhuinya cultural traditions are the starting point in Gyan Prakash's social history of labor servitude (1990). Their rich oral traditions include sung epics that extol their caste history as descent from an apical ancestor, the hero Tulsi Bir, which are typically performed at the climax of marriage ceremonies that affirm the two parties' common descent and identity as Bhuinya. These epic tales are "a form of historical consciousness deployed dynamically to construct the Bhuinya identity" (Prakash 1990: 44). From these stories we come to see how Bhuinya construct the social world and their own relationship to other powerful groups. Most variants of the Tulsi Bir story contain a central narrative involving an independent hero who is petitioned by a Bhumihar to mend a broken embankment. With the blessings of the gods, he sets forth to do so. He is given grants to villages by Brahma and Vishnu to do this work, so that thousands of Bhuinyas, plus Rajputs, Bhumihars, and Dusadhs hope for work from him. But Tulsi Bir is tricked into eating the placenta of a cow, which permanently pollutes him and by implication all his descendants. Nevertheless, his success in mending the breach has made agriculture possible. Although this narrative is similar to the many myths of Dalit groups accounting for their early high status and later subordination, there is something else going on here.

> By patterning their birs [heroes] as warriors the Bhuinyas point to the construction of kamia-malik relations in terms of power. By representing it not as a labor relationship but as ties of dependence between warriors of different ranks, they point to the centrality of power constructed as physical prowess, control over material resources, ritual status, and military command.
>
> (Prakash 1990: 53)

Prakash, a historian who uses anthropological methods together with historical methods, traces the origin of these legends to Islamic conquests after the thirteenth century, evidence of a "protracted diffusion of Islamic culture and of people from the north into areas hitherto dominated by non-Hindu lineages or tribal chiefs" (Prakash 1990: 63). These accounts came from late nineteenth- and early twentieth-century ethnographic reports, supplemented by interviews Prakash conducted with Bhuinya informants in the 1980s. It would be good to know the status of such traditions since the Naxalite struggles in more recent times.

More attention should be paid, as Prakash (1990) has done, to the ways in which Dalit castes use their cultural traditions dynamically both among themselves and in relations with other castes. A rich source of materials belongs to the Dusadhs, who have a wide distribution in Bihar and a reputation that suggests multiple strategies of resistance to the dominant order, not least their reputations as "thieves," along with the more normative role of watchmen. An annual fair in the month of Chaitya at the Chuharmal temple complex east of Patna draws hundreds of thousands of participants, and the epic tale of Chuharmal and Reshma is probably the most popular *nautanki* (dance drama) in Bihar. Badri Narayan (2001, 2003) attempts to show how this story serves to construct Dusadh identity and strike at upper-caste claims to moral superiority. The key point of conflict in the many versions of the Chuharmal story is the seduction of the Dusadh hero by Reshma, a Bhumihar (in south Bihar) or a Brahman (in north Bihar) girl. Their love ends badly for both of them, with Chuharmal nobly "taking *jal samadhi*" (ritual suicide by drowning). The fate of real-life cross-caste love matches between high-caste girls and low-caste boys is usually even worse than in the story, but even the performance of this plaintive tale, particularly popular in the Bhojpur area, has resulted in dozens of violent interruptions by angry Bhumihars. Narayan argues that the Chuharmal tale is a collective memory that should be seen not as the unitive property of a single caste, but as part of a contested and fragmented whole that includes the high castes who object to it (Narayan 2003: 9). This argument, perhaps not fully developed in Narayan's work, nevertheless suggests ways in which cultural texts may "belong" to certain communities, contributing to communal consciousness and identity as social capital in Bourdieu's sense, while other groups attempt to control and limit social capital along with other aspects of a subaltern group's identity. These struggles take place within a power structure where class is only one factor among many.

Cultural texts like the Chuharmal story, together with their contextual uses, even in very politicized settings, could be a productive starting point for cultural anthropologists interested in revisiting caste-as-culture, and the contestatory potential of cultural forms.

Hindu and Muslim identities

Individual Biharis do not have solely a caste identity, as the very term Bihari suggests, but numerous other ones as well. Some identities appear as given as one's own body and blood (gender and *jati*). Others are assumed, as one chooses to join organizations (CPI(M-L) or BJP), while still others are associated with residence and the soil (the village, the *mohalla*). Some identities seem more "imagined" than others (Bihari, Indian). And then there is religion. Hindu and Muslim identities were the starting point in Peter Gottschalk's research in Bhabhua district, the most southwestern district of Bihar in the Bhojpuri-speaking region. Published in 2000, his work comes at the end of a decade of communal tensions following the destruction of the Babri mosque. In Arampur, he found Hindus and Muslims living together peacefully and was curious to know why. Like Narayan and Prakash, Gottschalk uses collective memories as a means of exploring group identities.

The coming of Muslim rulers is the starting point of many group memories in Bihar. For two dominant castes in Bhabhua district, one Hindu, the other Muslim, their connectedness is remembered through a story of shared descent from two brothers who came to the region with the Delhi sultan. They defeated a local raja and were given all the land as a reward. One brother remained a Hindu and named his village Naugrah ("new house"), while the other brother converted to Islam and founded a neighboring village. The descendants of these two brothers consider themselves relatives and share Hindu and Muslim celebrations. The same event is remembered differently by Chamars. The name of the village for them means "nine houses," referring to the nine households they had in the village before the Khans came and took their land.

A more powerful cultural memory for residents of Arampur and its nexus of eleven surrounding villages is the story of the raja, the sultan, and a dead Brahman, Shastri Brahm, whose shrine is a famous place of pilgrimage in Arampur. Both Hindus and Muslims tell this story, though with separate twists on it, and both respect the power of the ghost in the shrine. There are also powerful Sufi tombs which, like Shastri Brahm, have authority to heal. In unpacking the complex strands of the stories told him by Hindu and Muslim informants, Gottschalk demonstrates the ways in which individuals assert their membership in that community while simultaneously respecting the other. Gottschalk credits these interwoven narratives and multi-stranded identities for the mutual respect between these religious communities that has kept Hindu–Muslim relations peaceful in Bhabhua district despite all the communal violence that has marred the last few decades elsewhere.

Gottschalk's own narrative style, telling *his* stories with vivid details of the tea stalls and verandahs where Arampur residents related their local knowledge, is an excellent model for how anthropology might be done in Bihar's many perplexing regions, including the narratives of conflict in the Burning Fields of south Bihar.

Cultural production in Mithila

In north Bihar there has been greater cultural continuity and less turbulence than south of the Ganges, for reasons not entirely clear. The people are poorer, agriculture less developed. The Mithila region—the central tracks lying between the Gandak and Kosi rivers—have long been dominated by the Maithil Brahmans. This dominance began at the time of the Muslim invasions in the fourteenth century, when a few Brahman families benefitted from the conquests much as Bhumihars and Rajputs did in the south. By the fifteenth century, there was a Brahman court under a dynasty known as the Oinivaras, who supported Brahman scholarship, poetry, literature, and music, making Maithili the only Bihari language to have a written literature before the twentieth century (Thakur 1956). The Mughals brought another family to power, the Khandavalas, who became the Darbhanga rajas. This long history of patronage by Maithil Brahman elites has made Mithila a center of cultural richness (Mishra 1979), if also of Brahmanic conservatism.

Until recently, it was the achievements of male intellectuals that were celebrated in Mithila. Nyaya and Mimamsa schools of philosophy originated there. The poet Vidyapati, a star of the Oinivara court, is celebrated throughout India, and his verses are the basis of much of the folk music in Mithila to this day. In recent years, however, it has been the cultural productions of Mithila women that have attracted the attention of scholars, from music to painting. Maithil women's distinctive musical tradition may be slowly dying out under competition from Bollywood (Henry 1998), but the *jayamala* rite in weddings seems to be spreading, also influenced by the film industry (Henry 2003). Above all, the ritual wall paintings once produced privately for marriages by Maithil Brahman and Kayastha women have become something of an international phenomenon. If there is a Bihar product that has entered the global economy (broadly defined), it is Mithila Art. This has been a radical cultural shift in which ritual art that performed agentive action on bride and groom has been transformed into art for its own sake in a new system of circulation, monetization, and international prestige systems (Heinz 2006). There has also been a small industry of scholarly support for this effort, from the applied anthropology of Erika Moser, Ray Owens, and more recently David Szanton in the "painting villages" around Jitwarpur in Madhubani district to the ethnographic writings of others (Heinz 1996, 2006; Jain 1997; Szanton and Bakshi 2007). The energy of this recent burst of cultural innovation may be contributing to improved relations between elite and Dalit castes, as Dusadh painters have joined the effort with innovative contributions such as replicating the look of village walls with a first wash of cowdung on the paper art. When one thinks of the effort by elite castes to suppress performance of Chuharmal and Tulsi Bir by Dalits in south Bihar, the embracing of Mithila Art by all caste communities in the north seems a very hopeful sign for the future.

Conclusion

There may be numerous reasons for the paucity of anthropological research in Bihar. We are a small discipline and India is a large country. Bihar is a difficult place to work, but that should not deter anthropologists, who have long romanticized the difficulty of fieldwork. The danger of working in areas of chronic violence is another matter, as is the difficulty of gaining access to such regions from authorities that do not want observers around or another thing to worry about. It can also be difficult to gain trust from embattled groups, whether they are attempting to maintain hegemony or resist it. Yet these are not unusual challenges for anthropologists to face.

A serious difficulty, it seems to me, is the challenge to the moral obligation many anthropologists feel to represent a local lifeway in positive and even romantic tones in our ethnographies. Our thick descriptions are meant to be deeply humanistic and sympathetic accounts, rather than political exposés, and we tend to avoid elites. Yet the rural elite cannot be separated from their relations with subalterns. We cannot study, say, the Bhumihars and brush aside their harsh efforts to restructure local economies and insure a secure supply of labor. How do we write about the dominating strategies, the self-justifications, the interaction patterns with Bhuinya and other subaltern groups? Can the Bhuinya be represented without thickly describing the cultural symbols by which they encode and deploy their resistance as well as their accommodations with elites? The topic of caste is avoided because the topic was so absorbing to colonial scholars, because caste consciousness is backward, because casteism is an essential principle of political struggle in Bihar. And yet caste values, like religious ones, give these political and economic struggles their form and their depth of meaning. Good ethnography should be able to treat this topic without succumbing to outmoded theorizing about the "unchanging" nature of the caste system. It *has* changed; what are its dimensions now? We need to know.

Notes

1   In using this nomenclature, I am adopting the controversial classification of George Grierson, who invented the term "Bihari"—a language no one claimed to speak—to identify the close relationship of the three main dialects, Magahi, Bhojpuri, and Maithili, that he found in this eastern India region. Advocates of Maithili and Bhojpuri argue for the status of each of these as full and distinct languages, as evidenced by written literature of several hundred years' depth.
2   Castes have not been enumerated in the Indian census since 1931, but here I follow Harry Blair's shrewd and still classic 1980 estimates of the numbers of Forwards, Backwards, and Scheduled Castes. These numbers, however, included the population now removed to Jharkhand, which skews all the percentages, and especially the more numerous Scheduled Tribes.

References

Ahmad, F. (2010) 'Where is Bataidari Bill? Asks Nitish,' *The Times of India,* 21 February. Available at: www.timesofindia.indiatimes.com (accessed July 16, 2010).
Berreman, G. (1972) *Hindus of the Himalayas: Ethnography and Change.* New Delhi: Oxford University Press.
Bhatia, B. (1997) 'Massacre on the Banks of the Sone,' *Economic and Political Weekly*, 32: 3242–45.

Blair, H. W. (1980) 'Rising Kulaks and Backward Classes in Bihar: Social Change in the Late 1970s,' *Economic and Political Weekly*, 15: 64–74.

Chakravarti, A. (1986) 'The Unfinished Struggles of Santhal Bataidars in Purnea District, 1938–1942,' *Economic and Political Weekly*, 21: 1947–65, 1987–89.

——(2001a) *Social Power and Everyday Class Relations: Agrarian Transformation in North Bihar*. New Delhi: Sage Press.

——(2001b) 'Caste and Agrarian Class: A View from Bihar,' *Economic and Political Weekly*, 36: 1449–62.

Chaudhry, P. K. (1988) 'Agrarian Unrest in Bihar: A Case Study of Patna District 1960–1984,' *Economic and Political Weekly*, 23: 51–56.

Daniel, E. V. (1996) *Charred Lullabies*. Princeton: Princeton University Press.

Das, A. N. (1986) 'Landowners' Armies take over "Law and Order",' *Economic and Political Weekly*, 21: 17–18.

——(2008) 'Swami and Friends: Sahajanand Saraswati and Those who Refuse to Let the Past of Bihar's Peasant Movements Become History', in W. R. Pinch (ed.), *Speaking of Peasants: Essays on Indian History and Politics in Honor of Walter Hauser*. Delhi: Manohar.

Devika, J. (2010) 'Egalitarian Developmentalism, Communist Mobilization, and the Question of Caste in Kerala State, India,' *Journal of Asian Studies*, 69: 799–820.

Freitag, S. (1989) *Culture and Power in Banaras: Community, Performance, and Environment, 1800–1980*. Berkeley: University of California Press.

*Gottschalk, P. (2000) *Beyond Hindu and Muslim: Multiple Identity in Narratives from Village India*. New York: Oxford.

Gramsci, A. (1971) *Selections from the Prison Notebooks of Antonio Gramsci*. Q. Hoare and G. N. Smith (eds and trans.). New York: International Publishers.

Gupta, A. (1995) 'Blurred Boundaries: The Discourse of Corruption, the Culture of Politics, and the Imagined State,' *American Ethnologist*, 22: 375–402.

*Hauser, W. (2004) 'From Peasant Soldiering to Peasant Activism: Reflections on the Transition of a Martial Tradition in the Flaming Fields of Bihar,' *Journal of the Economic and Social History of the Orient*, 47: 401–34.

Heinz, C. B. (1983) 'The Gift of a Girl: Hierarchical Exchange in North Bihar,' *Ethnology*, 22: 43–62.

——(1988) 'Raja and Rank in North Bihar,' *Modern Asian Studies*, 22: 757–82.

——(1996) 'Contested Meanings: Tantra and the Poetics of Mithila Art,' *American Ethnologist*, 23: 717–37.

——(2006) 'Documenting the Image in Mithila Art,' *Visual Anthropology Review*, 22: 5–33.

Henry, E. O. (1998) 'Maithil Women's Song: Distinctive and Endangered Species,' *Ethnomusicology*, 42: 415–40.

——(2003) 'The Jayamala Rite in Eastern North India: Outsiders and Insiders' Misunderstandings,' *Journal of Anthropological Research*, 59: 511–30.

Jain, J. (1997) *Tradition and Expression in Mithila Painting*. New Delhi: Mapin.

Jha, J. S. (1966) 'History of Darbhanga Raj,' *Journal of the Bihar Research Society*, 48: 1–4, 14–104.

Jha, U. N. (1980) *Genealogies and Genealogists of Mithila*. Varanasi: Kishor Vidya Niketan.

Kakar, S. (1996) *The Colors of Violence: Cultural Identities, Religion, and Conflict*. Chicago: University of Chicago Press.

*Kumar, A. (2008) *Community Warriors: State, Peasants, and Caste Armies in Bihar*. London: Anthem.

*Kunnath, G. J. (2004) 'Under the Shadow of Guns. Negotiating the Flaming Fields of Caste/Class War in Bihar, India,' *Anthropology Matters Journal*, 6: 1–12.

——(2006) 'Becoming a Naxalite in Bihar,' *The Journal of Peasant Studies*, 33: 89–123.

——(2009) 'Smouldering Dalit fires in Bihar, India,' *Dialectical Anthropology*, 33: 309–25.

Louis, P. (2002) *People Power: The Naxalite Movement in Central Bihar*. Delhi: Wordsmith.

Mishra, V. (1979) *Cultural Heritage of Mithila*. Allahabad: Mithila Prakasana.

Narayan, B. (2001) *Documenting Dissent: Contesting Fables, Contested Memories, and Dalit Political Discourse*. Simla: Indian Institute of Advanced Studies.

——(2003) 'Honour, Violence and Conflicting Narratives: A Study Of Myth And Reality,' *New Zealand Journal of Anthropological Studies*, 5: 5–23.

Ortner, S. B. (1995) 'Resistance and the Problem of Ethnographic Refusal,' *Comparative Studies in Society and History*, 37: 173–93.

Peoples' Union for Democratic Rights (1992) *Bitter Harvest: The Roots of Massacres in Central Bihar*. Delhi: P.U.D.

Pinch, W. R. (1996) *Peasants and Monks in British India*. London: Oxford University Press.

Prasad, N. (1985) *Rural Violence in India: A Case Study of Parasbigha and Pipra Violence in Bihar*. Varanasi: Vohra.

*Prakash, G. (1990) *Bonded Histories: Genealogies of Labor Servitude in Colonial India*. London: Cambridge University Press.

Scheper-Hughes, N. (1995) 'The Primacy of the Ethical: Propositions for a Militant Anthropology,' *Current Anthropology*, 36: 409–40.

Subramanian, K. S. (2010) 'State Response to Maoist Violence in India: A Critical Assessment,' *Economic and Political Weekly*, 45: 23–26.

Szanton, D. and Bakshi, M. (2007) *Mithila Painting, The Evolution of an Art Form*. San Francisco: Ethnic Arts Foundation.

Thakur, U. (1956) *History of Mithila*. Darbhanga: Mithila Institute.

Thompson, E. P. (1963) *The Making of the English Working Class*. London: Victor Gollancz.

Wiser, W. H. (1936) *The Hindu Jajmani System*. New Delhi: Munshiram Mansharlal.

4 Chhattisgarh

At the crossroads

Christopher A. Gregory

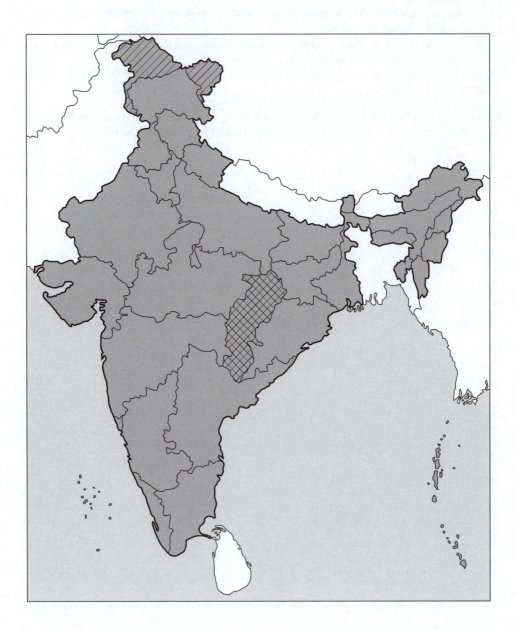

The crossroads

Jagdalpur, the former capital of the Princely State of Bastar, is popularly known as the 'city of crossroads.' This image, says a recent political commentator, best represents the political disconnect between the state and the people in the Bastar region today (Mahaprashasta 2010). The idea of the crossroads also best represents the deep history of economy and culture in Chhattisgarh as a whole. The uniqueness of Chhattisgarh as a region in India is defined by its position at the crossroads of a north/south division of India into Indo-Aryan and Dravidian-speaking linguistic regions and an east/west division into wet-rice and dry-grain producing farming regions. These oppositions, in turn, have been modified by the deep and shallow history of Chhattisgarh. The arrows on the maps drawn by archaeologists (Bellwood 2005) of the movements of Dravidian, Indo-Aryan, and Munda speakers into India meet in Chhattisgarh; the sons and daughters of the Chhattisgarh soil speak dialects born of this clash. Meanwhile, the agrarian frontier has moved slowly westward as rice has asserted its dominance over millet and with it, in the mythical allegories of the oral epics of farmers, the dominance of Lakshmi (as goddess of rice) over her elder sister Alakshmi (as goddess of millet) as the main co-wife of Narayan. Rice's victory was complete on the lower, well-watered Raipur plain, but is a never-ending conflict on the higher, marginal farmlands of the Bastar plateau. The history of Chhattisgarh is a long one of migration into the area, but one that has intensified over the past 75 years as DDT has transformed the region from an endemic malarial area to an epidemic one, and as high-yielding varieties of rice have ushered in the green revolution. The arrival of steel, and the human sacrifices this new god demands (Parry 2008b), has pushed the region in new directions: a relatively peaceful melting pot of people from different castes, classes, and regions here (Parry 2008a), a red revolution there as forests are cleared and the mountains raided for their mineral treasures. The new state of Chhattisgarh is at a new crossroad. The old debate between 'tribe' and 'caste,' previously restricted in the main to academic journals, is now fought out at all levels in the political arena as politicians, Naxalites, Hindu nationalists, unions, and villagers try to define the key terms in a new debate about Chhattisgarhi identity: *adivasi* (original-dweller), *vanvasi* (forest-dweller), *dharati putr* (son of the soil)? This has wrought changes that contemporary ethnographers strive to document. The following account locates these studies in their geographical and historical context.

The Raipur plain and the Bastar plateau

The state of Chhattisgarh was formed on November 1, 2000 when the sixteen easternmost states of Madhya Pradesh gained statehood; it has an area of 135,194 square kilometers and, in 2001, had a population of 20,834,000. This rectangular-shaped state, which measures roughly 700 kilometers north-south and 200 kilometers east-west, is on the westernmost boundary of monsoon Asia, a fact that has shaped the economy and culture of the region. The state is divided into two distinct physiographic regions: the Raipur plain to the north, which contains about 90 percent of the state's population, and the Bastar plateau to the south.

The Raipur plain is drained by the Mahanadi river system into the Bay of Bengal. The plain averages 250 meters and the surrounding hills to the north and east rise to between 700 and 1,000 meters. It is popularly known as the 'rice bowl of India' but it is also the site of much heavy industry including the Bhilai Steel Plant, the BALCO Aluminium Plant, and the National Thermal Power Corporation, whose plants at Korba and Bilaspur supply electricity to a number of Indian states. Chhattisgarhi is the *lingua franca* and the state's capital, Raipur, is located in the centre of the state on the plain.

The Bastar plateau is a distinctive ecological zone that begins abruptly at Keshal ghat, some 170 kilometers south of Raipur. It is bounded on the west and south by the Godavari River and in the east by the deforested hills of Orissa. The undulating plateau, with its hilly ranges to the west and south, is rich in forest and mineral resources. Rain-fed rice cultivation provides the staple, but the unreliable rains require that this be supplemented by millet, a dry-area grain whose importance rises as one moves westward across the plateau out of the monsoon zone toward Maharashtra. Jagdalpur, the capital of the former Princely State of Bastar, is situated on the banks of the Indravati River. This drains to the west into the Godavari and bisects the region into the plateau proper in north Bastar and lower lands of south Bastar that fall gradually to sea level. Halbi was the *lingua franca* of the region and, along with Bhatri and other local Indo-Aryan languages, remains the mother tongue of approximately half of the indigenous people of the plateau. Gondi and other Dravidian languages are also spoken by the other half of the population. Hindi is the language of administration and commerce for the state as a whole.

The stark ecological contrast between the Raipur plain and the Bastar plateau, along with its equally obvious socio-economic correlates, has provided the basis for the popular image of the Bastar plateau as a remote, 'backward', tribal homeland, far removed from the modern, industrialized Raipur plain where caste Hindus predominate. The pioneering ethnographic work of Elwin in the 1930s and 1940s did much to promote this image; indeed, a prominent anthropologist of Elwin's generation described Bastar as an "unblemished tribal haven" (von Fürer-Haimendorf 1982: 201). Whatever merits this image may have had in the past, post-war ethnographers have struggled to present a more historically-informed description of Chhattisgarh that reflects the complexity of the present situation, one where Hindu nationalists, Maoist insurgents, and migrant merchants have created religious division, social conflict, and new class cleavages. Comparative theorists for their part have a theoretical interest in Chhattisgarh ethnography because the state straddles the 'frontier zone' between the cultures of the Indo-Aryan north and those of the Dravidian south. This has enabled them to gain new insights into the values that give the region its cultural and historical specificity.

Elwin's legacy

Any account of ethnographic work in Chhattisgarh must, perforce, begin with the pioneering work of Elwin. Fieldwork was a way of life for him rather than a mere academic pursuit. A Christian missionary, turned Gandhian, turned Indian civil servant, he married into a tribal community and became the self-appointed scribe and advocate of tribal people in general. He spent over two decades conducting research on the tribal cultures of central India, an area that included the hill areas of the Raipur plain, the central Bastar plateau, and its eastern rim land in the Orissan mountains. He then moved onto the north-east frontier where he continued to research and write. His output was prodigious and he left behind an encyclopaedic documentation of tribal India the like of which has few parallels in the history of anthropology. His studies of central India, for example, included six substantial ethnographies (Elwin 1939, 1942, 1947, 1950a, 1950b, 1955), five collections of the oral traditions (Hivale and Elwin 1935; Elwin 1944, 1946, 1949, 1954), as well as three other books (Elwin 1943, 1951, 1958) and numerous articles. His life and work has attracted the attention of two biographers (Misra 1971; Guha 1999) but, because he was not a theorist, his writings have had little impact on mainstream academic thought. For the student of Chhattisgarh culture, however, his work remains an invaluable encyclopaedic reference on tribal culture even though his somewhat romantic portrayal of the tribal has provided contemporary ethnographers with many an antithesis to structure their own work (Gell 1992; Vitebsky 1993). Perhaps the most important, and ongoing, general question his work begs is that of the notion of 'tribe' and its relationship to caste.

Tribes and caste in Chhattisgarh

The notion of 'tribe' is a master concept in anthropology; indeed, there was a time when the study of 'tribes,' the semantic successor of 'primitives,' defined the scope and limits of anthropology. While use of the concept in Africa and Oceania was, and to some extent still is, relatively unproblematic the same cannot be said for India where the word 'tribe' has always excited very strong emotion. This is because the descriptive content of the term immediately invites comparison with 'caste,' a contrast that has hotly disputed prescriptive implications. For example, Elwin's use of the word 'tribal' in his first book, *The Baiga* (1939), drew strong criticism from the Indian anthropologist Ghurye (1943), who argued that they were 'backward Hindus' rather than '*adivasis*' (literally 'aborigines'). Elwin, the tribal advocate, was well aware of the prescriptive implications of the term and did not shy away from drawing out the policy implications of his work. He witnessed firsthand the internal colonial conquest of the indigenous people and advocated policies of protection; his opponents caricatured these as tantamount to the establishment of an anthropological zoo (Guha 1999: chapter 8).

Subsequent work by anthropologists concentrated initially on the descriptive adequacy of the tribe-caste distinction. Bailey (1961), for example, developed the idea of the tribe-caste continuum, an idea that has attracted much debate. For the people of Chhattisgarh the problem of the descriptive adequacy of the term is not a matter of academic debate; it is a question of cultural identity that has far-reaching political and economic consequences. This is because the term 'tribe' acquired a legal status in the Indian constitution: people so classified are deemed to be underprivileged and entitled to receive government funds and benefits. With the formation of the new state of Chhattisgarh this question has acquired a new salience because the notions of 'Chhattisgarhi identity' and 'tribal identity' are intimately related. The following exchange between a journalist and Chhattisgarh's first Chief Minister, Ajit Jogi, illustrates this.

> Q. *There is a controversy over your tribal identity, which is being used by the Opposition and also some members of your own party to demand your resignation.*
>
> A. This is an absolutely false campaign. I very much come from a tribal family. Jogi is not my surname, it is a title relating to Jogisar, the place from which my ancestors hail. My great-grandfather fled the village after he had eloped with a Rajput girl of the same village. My ancestors later settled in another village called Gorella and converted to Christianity. But the conversion does not alter my tribal identity. It is obvious that the controversy has been generated with political motives. I cannot be bothered with such pettiness.
>
> (Chaudhuri 2001: 18, 24)

Disputations about tribal identity are the stuff of endless discussion everywhere in modern Chhattisgarh, be it in state parliament in Raipur or in the remotest village on the Bastar plateau. The word *adivasi* is the term used by non-English speakers and increasingly by English speakers. But this term is unacceptable to the Hindu nationalists for whom India is fundamentally Hindu; they prefer *vanvasi*, forest dweller (Froerer 2007: 33). Terms such as 'tribe,' 'adivasi,' and the like are, therefore, heavily loaded in India and this fact poses special problems of ethnographic description and analysis. One way out of the problem is to avoid the term altogether and to ask what values, if any, define Chhattisgarh—and central India more generally—as a distinctive cultural region of India.

Chhattisgarh as a cultural region

The question of the unity and diversity of Indian culture is much debated but the ethnographic evidence reveals significant cleavages between the Indo-Aryan north and the Dravidian south, especially in the realm of kinship, gender relations, life-cycle rituals, and annual rituals, as Fuller's (1992) synthesis of the ethnographic literature on 'popular' Hinduism illustrates. Even Dumont (1966), for whom 'India is One,' acknowledges this diversity. However, a significant omission from the bibliography of both writers is any reference to the work of Elwin and, as such, any serious attempt to grapple with the cultural specificities of central India. As Pfeffer (1997: 5) has noted, Dumont simply ignores the 'tribal' issue in the sociology of India; his large oeuvre contains just one cryptic comment to people who have 'lost contact' with the wider society.

In this respect Trautmann's (1981) classic work on Dravidian kinship is exceptional: for him ethnographic data on the 'frontier zone' between the Indo-Aryan north and the Dravidian south was the key to unlocking the problem of Dravidian kinship in India. As he put it, "the future of the inquiry into the nature, and necessarily also the history, of the Dravidian kinship system lies in Central India" (1981: 236). He hypothesized the existence of a third kinship system in Central India, but lamented that he was unable to develop the argument further because of the poor quality of the extant ethnography. He considered Elwin's data on the kinship system of the Baiga, noting that the terminology "was predominately Indo-Aryan in its vocabulary, but Dravidian in semantic structure" (1981: 137). Of more interest to him was Grigson's (1938) ethnography of the Maria Gonds of the Bastar plateau because the kinship system here was "thoroughly Dravidian" in structure. "We shall have to rethink the Dravidian terminology in the light of the intriguing case of the Maria Gond," he argued (Trautmann 1981: 200), calling for more data on other Gondi speakers and the speakers of other central Dravidian languages (1981: 207).

Trautmann's insights into central Indian kinship were simultaneously developed by Pfeffer (1982, 1983) and elaborated in subsequent publications based on extensive fieldwork in Orissa (Pfeffer 1996, 1997, 2004). He noted the importance of the notion of seniority and alternate generations as general features of central Indian kinship; but a consideration of his analysis of the specific variations found in the Orissan highlands is beyond the scope of this chapter, important though they are for a general understanding of Indian kinship.

Parkin's (1992) *The Munda of Central India* is an exhaustive survey of the extant data on the Munda speakers of central India; it established beyond any doubt the existence of a distinctive form of central Indian kinship. The distinguishing features of this Munda kinship system, as he called it, are alternate generation equivalence and the division of kin within a generation into named marriageable and non-marriageable categories. He also went further than Trautmann by noting the social and religious correlates of the Munda kinship system. For example, reincarnation beliefs in central India, he noted, are intimately related to "the conceptual unity of alternate generations" (1992: 203).

The Munda system, like the Tamil and other southern systems, permits cross-cousin marriage, but a peculiarity of the Munda system is that marriage with the cross-grandparent is a logical possibility. Elwin (1939: 141) and Grigson (1938: 245) both noted this logical possibility and reported actual cases of its occurrence. A peculiarity of the Tamil case, by contrast, is the possibility of an elder sister's daughter's marriage, a form of marriage that is taboo in central India. These different marriage types are the effects of two quite distinct forms of generational merging: alternate generation equations in central India, adjacent generation merging in the south.

The Trautmann-Parkin theory has the advantage of getting us beyond the language of tribe and caste, but in doing so raises new problems because linguistic categories like 'Munda' and 'Dravidian' are inadequate descriptors of the socio-cultural reality to which they refer. Parkin, to his credit, was well aware of this problem.

> The present work is essentially an account of Munda social organization. This does not mean that it attempts to argue in favour of any sort of linguistic determinism—quite the contrary, for it is clear that the Munda share many if not most of their values with neighbouring low-status groups who speak Indic or Dravidian languages instead.
>
> (Parkin 1992: ix)

Parkin (1992: 16) also noted another problem of significance for his analysis: "the outmoded or indifferent quality of much of the published [ethnographic] work." This point is well taken because, at the time his book was written, relatively little ethnographic work had been done in Chhattisgarh since Elwin's time, especially on Indo-Aryan speakers both on the Raipur plain and on the Bastar plateau. Recent decades have seen a revival of ethnographic interest in the area but much more work needs to be done, not only in the area of anthropology but also in archaeology and history. Cultural geography must be historically informed as Trautmann's method of analysis demonstrates. His distinction between the cultural consequences of 'deep' and 'shallow' historical relations of contiguity gives us a new way of approaching the cultural specificities of a region in a descriptively adequate way; however the language of historical linguistics is manifestly inadequate for the Chhattisgarh case as Parkin notes: the term 'Munda' avoids some of the problems of the term 'tribe' but only by introducing new ones.

Recent research on the Bastar plateau

If an indigenous person can be defined as a migrant whose ancestors have lived in the same region for more than five generations, then the indigenous population of Bastar can be said to be made of roughly equal numbers of Indo-Aryan and Dravidian speakers, with Halbi and Gondi being the major languages of the respective groups. This definition of an indigene, which is advanced here for the sake of exposition, is not accepted by the Hindi-speaking administrators and other outsiders who visit Bastar. For them Gondi language is the marker of the 'true' tribal; Halbi speakers are low-caste Hindus. We can be certain that these classifications, which have been accepted uncritically by many academics, were not based on any anthropological evidence because, prior to the recent work of Gregory (Gregory 1988, 1997, 2004; Gregory and Vaishnav 2003) and Prevot (2005) and the linguistic studies of Woods (1973, 1980; Woods and Bowman 1978), no one had ever made a serious study of the Halbi-speakers of Bastar. Meanwhile, a number of studies have been made of Dravidian speakers, including Simeran Gell (1992), Alfred Gell (1980, 1982, 1986, 1997), Savyasaachi (1992, 1993), Popoff (1980) and Thusu (1965). In addition, Huber (1984) and Sundar (2007) have written anthropological histories of the district, informed in both cases by fieldwork in Dravidian-speaking areas.

The work of these scholars and others enables us to move beyond the image of Bastar as an 'unblemished tribal haven' and to see the place as the historical product of a range of cross-cutting forces that inform the present diversity found in the region. From Orissa in the east has come rice farming; this has been a process of agrarian transition that has been going on at glacial pace for millennia. Rice, the undisputed king of the grasses in terms of yield, ousted millet, an inferior grain that can be grown on drought-prone hilly country; this happened as rice farmers slowly moved westward to exploit the rice-growing potential of the monsoon rains. They appropriated the lower-lying fertile ground, cleared the forests, and levelled the land to create bounded fields to catch the rains. This forced the millet farmers westward into the forests and upwards into the hills where they could continue to practice swidden cultivation, a process that continues to this day (Savyasaachi 1993). This agrarian extensification was accompanied by an intensification process as millet farmers acquired rice-farming skills and began to grow rice on their lower-lying farmlands and millet on their higher lands.

The process of agrarian transition has left its mark in every village of Bastar, an ecological reflection of the fact that the Bastar plateau describes part of the westernmost boundary of monsoon Asia. Millet and rice are grown in almost every village but as one moves west across the undulating plateau the proportion of land devoted to millet slowly rises and becomes the sole crop in the Abujmarh hills on the Maharashtra border (Agarwal 1967: chapter 6). Within each village the intensification process sees rice move slowly upward to the higher farm lands as millet is forced to conquer the steeper slopes of newly expropriated forest land (Gregory 1997: chapter 3; Gell 1992: chapter 2).

The status of rice as the premier crop of Bastar is enshrined in its rich cycle of agrarian rituals where rice is worshipped as the goddess Maha Lakhi, as Lakshmi, one of the three great goddesses of the Hindu pantheon, is called in Halbi. This association of Lakhi with rice is perceived of as an identity rather than an equation: rice is Lakhi, Lakhi is rice, as every Bastarian will tell you. This identity is celebrated in its most elaborate form during the singing of the Lachmi Jagar epic, literally 'the wake for Lakshmi,' an annual harvest ritual held in the cold season from November to January. The ritual takes a fortnight to perform and involves the singing and ritual enactment of an oral epic of some 31,000 lines long. This is sung by women (*gurumai*) and it tells of the birth and marriage of Lakshmi. The culmination of the event is the ritual harvest of a sheaf of rice, representing Lakshmi, and its symbolic marriage to a coconut, representing Narayan. This, the story tells us, is his second marriage; his first was to Akisrani, 'the 21 queens,' representing the various millets. They get very jealous of Lakshmi and cause her many problems. She runs away, famine ensures, and they beg her to come back (Gregory and Vaishnav 2003).

This tale is an obvious allegory of the deep history of agricultural transition in Bastar for it highlights the antagonistic relationship between the rice, the newcomer, and millet, the existing resident who must now make way for the newcomer. Rice has won this cultural war on the Bastar plain (and the Raipur plain) but not in the Abujmarh hills where a millet culture prevails, threatened though it is on its lower reaches by immigrant rice farmers, their new gods, and their new rituals (Savyasaachi 1993).

Religion and ritual in Bastar is defined by the annual agrarian cycle on the one hand and the life-cycle of people on the other. In both cases the rituals are local variations on a general Hindu theme. In the wet season, for example, the Halbi-speaking *gurumai* sing another epic called *dhankul*, which is also ritually enacted by participants. This ritual, which often lasts for two to three months, tells the story of Mahadev (= Shiva) and Parbati. Gondi speakers participate in this ritual but also sing their own songs about Mahadev whom they called Lingo. As Elwin (1947: 174) noted, the religion of the Gondi speakers "is undoubtedly a religion of the Hindu family with special affinities to its Shaivite interpretation." He adds the contradictory rider "yet at the same time it is but little 'Hinduized'." It is not clear what he means by this but it does pose the question of the specificity of Bastar Hinduism. One important sense in which Bastar religion has not been 'Hinduized' is the fact that the Bastar caste system has neither top nor tail, neither indigenous Brahmins nor sweepers. As such, the caste system has an egalitarian twist, an ideology that still prevails in villages today despite the migration of many high-caste Hindus from different parts of India into the area. This ideology also prevails within castes between wife-givers and wife-receivers, but not within the patriarchal family. This ideology permeates the Lachmi Jagar epic, too, where castes are equal and defined by occupation, not ranked by degrees of pollution. The only violence sung about in this long epic is wife-bashing, a fact that, alas, is a feature of Bastar households (as it is of households everywhere in the world).

A sharp contrast is evident in the male and female approaches to religion and ritual in Bastar: female ritual practitioners tend to be concerned with the all-India goddesses of the Hindu pantheon, male ritual practitioners with highly localized spirits of the recently dead who have become deities; women (*gurumai*) sing epic myths about the goddesses, men do not tell myths but become the medium (*siraha*) through which the local spirits speak and act; female ritual is based around the domestic hearth, male ritual happens on those special market days (*dev bazaar*) when the clan gods come out to 'play.'

Little work has been done on male religion save for Alfred Gell's prize-winning essay (Gell 1980), which describes male spirit possession rituals he observed in Manjapur village, an essay that offers a speculative interpretation of possession as analogous to autism. A detailed ethnographic account of the *dev bazaar* ritual was conducted by Prevot (2005), a French ethno-musicologist who worked with a Halbi-speaking musician-caste in Barkai village. His French PhD thesis is yet to be translated and published.

Oral epics are sung everywhere in India but Bastar is unique in that it is the only place, it seems from the extant evidence, where women are the principal singers (Blackburn *et al.* 1989). However, it is possible that this is an artefact of bias in reporting. The Bastar women's oral tradition has passed by largely unnoticed, even by Elwin who makes only one passing reference to it (Elwin 1947: 188). This seems to have been due to his methodology. "My custom," he reports (Elwin 1954: x), "was to translate the stories on the spot, as they were narrated or interpreted to me." "The narrators," he adds, "were in the main elderly men, the headmen, priests and shamans of the village." Some of the stories he collected from these men and reproduced are obviously potted fragments from the epics sung by women. For example, a brief twenty-line myth about the origin of rice that Elwin (1954: 163–4) reproduces takes up 5,200 lines of the Lachmi Jagar epic. Even the long prose version of a myth about Lakshmi that Woods (1980) recorded and transcribed as the basis of her unpublished thesis, is a fragment of a Sanskritized version of the Lachmi Jagar epic sung in villages near the district capital of Jagdalpur that Vaishnav has recorded, transcribed, and which he and Gregory are in the process of translating. Their method has been to record actual sung performances rather than to ask people to relate their myths in summary prose form.

This women's oral epic tradition is not limited to the Bastar plateau (Gregory 2004). While its limits are yet to be determined, recent research by Gregory and Vaishnav in Bastar and surrounding regions, and ongoing work by Otten (2009, in press) in the Koraput District of Orissa, has revealed that it spreads as far south as Dhamtari on the Raipur plain and over the Eastern Ghats of Orissa. Variations on the Lakshmi rice epic can be found all the way down to coastal Orissa. However the myth takes some classic Lévi-Straussian double-twists as it wends its way down to the seaside: an allegorical tale sung by women in the Bastar plateau about rice and wife-beating husbands becomes a didactic literary treatise written in Oriya by men about theological consequences of the bad behaviour of wives (Sahu 1965).

The oral epics women sing also vary in a way that reflects the natural and cultural history of the particular micro-region of the Bastar plateau in question. For example, millet and rice have a complementary rather than antagonistic relationship in the Koraput hills on the eastern rim of the Bastar plateau. Here rice grows in the shallow river beds and millet on the banks of the river valleys (Rousseleau 2008; Berger 2007). The rice farmers of Koraput extract high yields using highly skilled transplantation techniques, a marked contrast to the relatively inefficient farmers on the Bastar plateau who broadcast-sow their rice and rely on rain-fed irrigation. Yields of around 0.5 tonnes per hectare or less are achieved, making the Bastar plateau quite literally the most marginal rice farming area in monsoon Asia but one of the richest in terms of mythical and ritual elaboration.

To the west of the Bastar plateau the millet culture in the dry lands of western India prevails. Very little is known about this part of central India from an ethnographic perspective. Savyasaachi's (1992) restudy of Grigson's (1938) work remains an unpublished PhD. Further to the east in Maharashtra little has been done since the sociological surveys of Singh (1944) and Thusu (1980). There is no evidence that Maharashtra's millet culture has influenced Bastar but some evidence of cultural influence in the other direction is that Halbi is spoken in those districts of Maharashtra that border onto the Bastar plateau. What we can be sure of, though, is that the contemporary society and culture of the Bastar plateau has been greatly influenced from Andhra Pradesh in the south and the Raipur plain in the north. If the agrarian history of Bastar has been shaped by rice farmers to the east, its political history has been shaped by rulers and revolutionaries from the south and its modern commercial history by merchants and migrants from the north.

Sundar's (2007) anthropological history of Bastar covers the period from mythical times to the present day, with a primary focus on the period since 1854. The Kakatiyas, the royal family who ruled Bastar until 1947, claim to have come from Warangal in Andhra Pradesh in 1323, when they allegedly supplanted the Naga kings whose ruined Shiva temples can still be found at their capital in Barsur. The inscriptions in these ruins, Sundar (2007: 47–8) notes, indicate the presence of high Hinduism, a fact that contradicts the popular image of Bastar as 'primitive,' 'tribal,' and 'isolated' (see also Cooper 1997; Postel and Cooper 1999: chapter 2). The Kakatiyas, after much moving around, eventually established their capital at Jagdalpur, the present-day administrative capital. They also established Danteswari as the tutelary goddess of Bastar, whom they regard as a form of Durga. She is still worshipped annually, both in the capital and villages, during the Dussehra ritual during the first half of the lunar month of Asvina (September–October).

The spectacular fifteen-day long ritual in Jagdalpur has received more scholarly attention than any other ritual in Bastar and its interpretation has been much debated (Crooke 1915; Gell 1997; Mallebrein 1994; Sundar 2001). Sundar's (2001, 2007: chapter 2) scholarly historical account shows how it is critical for understanding the Bastar polity, both its transformations over time and for the different stories the sovereigns and subalterns tell about this. An example of the latter comes from the myths the Ghadwa people of Kondagaon tell about the king and his goddess (Baghel 1982). They say that the king did not come from Warangal but emerged from a home-grown pumpkin. Danteswari, they assert, is not Durga but a local goddess who was born with teeth (*dant*) on the banks of the Sabri river in Konta, from whence her name. Thus *dant* plus Sabri gives *dantsabri*, which becomes Danteswari. Furthermore, they argue, twisting the standard Brahmanic myth upside down, that whereas Durga won the battle with the buffalo demon, Danteswari lost it. These myths informed the sculptures the Ghadwa traditionally cast for use in temples. Today their art is part of the global 'tribal art' market and Bastar bronzes, renowned all around the world, have attracted the attention of scholars interested in material culture (Hacker 2000, 2004; Postel and Cooper 1999). Leaders of the community, such as Jaidev Baghel who relates these myths in Halbi, are locked in a battle with the government over their official classification as non-tribal (Gregory 1995–96). "The government promotes our work as 'Tribal Art'," notes Baghel, "but classifies us as low caste Hindus; if our art is Tribal then we are Tribals" (Gregory, fieldnotes).

While the political history of the sovereigns and subalterns of Bastar has been a verbal battle involving the use of myths and sculptures as weapons, the recent political history of Maoist insurgency in Bastar is of a radically different order involving guns and violence, looting and burning. Sundar (2007: chapter 10) chronicles the origins of the Maoists from Andhra Pradesh in the 1980s and subsequent formation of the so-called people's movement against the Maoists called Salwa Judum. This government-sponsored program has had devastating consequences for the people of Dantewada District in South Bastar. Some 150,000 people have been displaced, approximately one-third of whom were officially living in camps as of February 2006; some 500 to 1,000 people have been killed and over 3,000 houses burnt (Sundar 2007: 287). Maoist activity has now spread all the way up the eastern side of the Bastar plateau but not as yet on the scale seen in Dantewada, where the intensity of counter-insurgency activity is correlated with mining activity and plans for further industrialisation.

The modern commercial history of Bastar can be traced from the north via the national highway that links Raipur with Jagdalpur. This road has long been the main trunk route to the Bastar plateau and the recent construction of a bridge over the Godavari River in the south, together with a planned upgrade of the road that will establish good road links with Hyderabad, will obviously influence future commercial developments. There is still no road link across the Godavari River in the west to Maharashtra but a track (now a pot-holed bitumen road) has long existed on the eastern route to the coast via the deforested mountains of Orissa. The absence of trees along this eastern route—a sign of the long history of agrarian transformation from monsoon east—stands in stark contrast to the forests that line the roads in every other direction.

The livelihood of Bastar farmers is intimately tied up with the forests, a theme explored by all ethnographers of the region. However, the forests are also intimately tied up with the Indian state and commercially-minded outsiders interested only in its value as a commodity. The large-scale commercial exploitation of the forests in the name of 'development' has never harmonized with its small-scale exploitation by farmers who have long used the forests to hunt animals and harvest its fruits, and cleared it to establish rice farms as their numbers grew (Gregory 1997: chapter 3). The farmers have often been victims of the development projects but not always so, as Anderson and Huber's monograph, *The Hour of the Fox: Tropical Forests, the World Bank and Indigenous People in Central India* (1988) illustrates. This book reveals how the views of the indigenous people, who have a long history of resistance to the commercial exploitations of their forests, were probably decisive in terminating a major World Bank forest project.

Meanwhile, rich Marwari merchants from Rajasthan, poor landless laborers from the Raipur plateau, along with migrants from almost every other state in India, migrated to Bastar to capitalize on the commercial opportunities the economic development on the plateau presented. The merchants exploited the opportunities presented by the traditional periodic marketing system and enabled it to flourish to the mutual advantage of all. Villagers take their cash crops and minor forest products to the local markets where they sell them in order to buy the clothes, jewellery, and groceries they desire. The markets also provide landless people with a source of income from petty trading, a commercial opportunity that has attracted many landless people and marginal farmers. Gregory's monograph, *Savage Money:*

The Anthropology and Politics of Commodity Exchange (1997), describes this dynamic showing how the all-Indian kinship networks of the Marwaris enables them to monopolize the lucrative trade in high status, high valued commodities such as jewellery and cloth, leaving the trade in low valued commodities, such as glass bangles and trinkets, to the locals. The trade in these commodities, too, is kin-based but, unlike the Marwari situation, the Bastar lineages do not supply a source of trading credit, the lifeblood of a successful merchant.

Recent work by Gregory (2009, 2010) has concentrated on the kinship and life-cycle rituals of the Halbi speakers, a theme developed by Simeran Gell (1992) in her study of the mixed-sex dormitory of the Gondi-speaking Muria. Gell's monograph corrects the romantic vision of the *ghotul* "as a dreamland of adolescent sexual bliss" (Gell 1992: 21) by locating it in its social context. This book is a classic village ethnography in the best sense of the term and one of the few village studies available. She provides a micro-analysis of the relationship between the forest, swidden millet farming, and wet-rice cultivation at the village level; an account of the clan structure, land tenure, kinship system, and village politics; and a detailed descriptive account and intepretation of the *ghotul*. The village in which she worked, like many in Bastar, contained approximately roughly equal numbers of Gondi and Halbi speakers. Centuries of contiguous residence has created a convergent culture, especially in the domain of kinship and marriage and in the performance of rituals of an annual and life-cycle kind. However, the various cultures of Bastar define themselves in opposition to others by adopting distinctive cultural traits.

Language is one way they do this. Hindi has replaced Halbi as the *lingua franca* in Bastar today but it remains the mother tongue of many communities, Murias, Gandas, Kalars, Maraars, Gadwa, Lohar, Panka etc., some of whom (Gadwa, Lohar, Panka) have their own private dialects they call *bhaasadi* or *phaarasii* (Vaishnav, pers. comm.). A variety of other Indo-Aryan languages are also found in Bastar such as Bhattri, Bastari, Chhattisgarhi, Marathi, and Oriya, with the latter three, of course, being the language of people whose ancestors migrated to Bastar many generations ago. Woods' study of sentence patterns in Halbi (Woods 1973) is the only serious linguistic study of a Bastar language. A socio-linguistic analysis of language in Bastar as a marker of local identity is yet to be done.

The other way communities within Bastar differentiate themselves is through variations in the performance of rituals. Gell's interpretation of why the mixed-sex *ghotul* is found among the Muria and not other groups develops this argument. What is at stake is a relatively small, but highly significant, variation in the order of life-cycle rituals. Pre-puberty weddings were the norm among many Halbi-speaking groups such as the Maraars. These weddings were celebrated with full pomp and ceremony. The young married girls would stay at home with their parents until they reached puberty, when they would, after a second minor wedding ceremony, move in with their husbands. The Gonds, by contrast, only had one post-puberty wedding but, at the time Maraar girls were getting married, the Gond girls would enter the *ghotul*. As Gell was told by her informants: "The Maraars get married when they are little. We don't. We go to the *ghotul* instead" (Gell 1992: 245). With the present-day demise of pre-puberty weddings among the Maraars and the demise of the *ghotul*, this cultural difference is becoming a thing of the past.

Today the indigenous people of Bastar—defined for the sake of the argument of this paper as those whose ancestors have lived on the plateau for more than five generations—see themselves in opposition to new migrants from all over India who have taken up residence in the major urban areas and peri-urban villages. These migrants include the richest of the rich and the poorest of the poor. Many of the latter have married into the local communities and adopted their culture; indigenous farmers, for their part, are joining the ranks of the economically disadvantaged as their landholdings become ever smaller through population growth. The forest lands that they traditionally cleared, now the property of the state, are no longer available for them to expand onto; those who are forced, by economic necessity, to expropriate forest land find themselves strangers on their own traditional lands, their livelihoods dependent on the whim of corrupt forest guards (Gregory 1997). Others move to urban areas, surviving on daily labor and petty trading, where they continue to celebrate their weddings at great cost to the parents of the bride and groom, and where the performance of rituals such as Lachmi Jagar continues to thrive.

Recent research in the Raipur plain

The Raipur plain, also known as the Chhattisgarh plain, is the most populous region of the modern state of Chhattisgarh as well as being the political and economic heartland today. It has always been thus. Its fertile, flat, and well watered soils shaped its deep agrarian history of rice cultivation and commerce; Nehru's decision to establish a steel plant in Bhilai has shaped its recent industrial history. This has accelerated the rate of migration of people from other parts of India into the area creating a complex multicultural society, but one where tribal identity, religious identity, and regional identity are asserted and contested. Early post-war work continued the tradition of focussing on the *adivasis* in the surrounding hills (Fuchs 1960), but recent ethnographic research has focused on contemporary issues and has begun to fill the large gap in our understanding of the plain.

   The Raipur plain is an exemplar of one of the five basic types agronomists use when analysing the rice cultures of monsoon Asia; the other four basic types include intermontane basins, deltas, volcanic foothills, and tidal swamps. Rice farming in these different terrains requires specialist labor and distinct forms of social organisation. For example, ethnographers in Java, Bali, and insular Southeast Asia have carried out extensive studies of how the control of the abundant water supplies in the volcanic foothills of these countries has shaped culture; so, too, have ethnographers working in the intermontane basin areas of northern Burma, Thailand, Vietnam, China, and Japan, where rice rituals were important affairs of the state (and still are in Japan and Thailand). However, ethnographic studies of the relatively unstable rain-fed tank irrigation of the plains, of which the Raipur plain is the classic example along with southern Southeast Asia, are almost non-existent. In this respect, *The Aghira: A Peasant Caste on a Tribal Frontier* (Skoda 2005) fills an important gap in the literature, even though the location of the fieldwork was the Orissan village of Mundaloi, rather than the modern state of Chhattisgarh. However, we must not let the location of modern state boundaries constrain our thinking about the cultural ecology of region. The pre-colonial state of Chhattisgarh, from which the modern district and the modern state derived its name, included territory such as Mundaloi village that is now part of Orissa; it also included parts of Maharashtra.

   The pre-colonial state of Chhattisgarh, literally 36 forts, consisted of two kingdoms (*raj*) of the Haihaibansi dynasty (Wills 1919). One king, an elder brother, was based in Ratunpur in the north and controlled eighteen forts (*atharahgarh*); another king, his younger brother, controlled the other eighteen forts from Raipur in the south. Each fort contained 84 villages (*chaurasi*) under the control of a chief (*diwan* or *thakur*), and seven *talugs* composed of twelve villages (*barhons*) under a minor chief (*gaontia*, literally village headman). The numerical basis of this kingdom is clearly based on Hindu numerology rather than empirical fact, but these terms for office holders, and some of their functions, remain today. For example, the *gaontia*, as Earth Mother priest, still plays a central role in village affairs on the

Bastar plateau and no ritual can be performed without his presence. In the Raipur plain, where agrarian social structure was more class-based, the *gaontia* was a landlord. This at least was the case in the village Skoda studied. However, unlike the situation for intermontane rice-growing areas of monsoon Asia, there is no evidence that rice rituals were ever affairs of the pre-colonial state in Raipur plain, something that may be related to the relatively low status of farming in the Hindu caste system.

Skoda's ethnography consists of a detailed description and analysis of the life-cycle, the annual cycle, and the accompanying rituals. It is clear from this study of religion and social organisation that it is a variation on the general theme for central India defined by Trautmann and Parkin. What distinguishes this area from Bastar is the extent of Brahmanical influence. For example, rice rituals, as in the Bastar case, are based on the identification of rice with the goddess Lakshmi: rice *is* Lakshmi, Lakshmi *is* rice, and the aim of the annual rituals is to invite her into your kitchen because when she is a resident good fortune ensues. However, whereas the Bastar rituals are informed by oral epics sung by low-status women, the rituals Skoda describes are informed by Orissan texts written by Brahman men. East-central India has the richest source of vernacular oral and textual tradition concerning Lakshmi in India, and the fact that one of the major varieties of rice, *indica*, probably has its origins in Orissa may have something to do with this. Both the textual and oral sources associate rice, an aquatic plant with the highest yield of any grass ever cultivated by *homo sapiens*, with good fortune, and its 'opposite,' low-yielding millet, with misfortune. This is hardly surprising given that the yield ratio of rice is around ten times that of a dry grain like millet or wheat (Tanaka 2002). This rich vernacular tradition of Lakshmi worship in Chhattisgarh and Orissa remains largely unknown; thus the claim by the author of a recent book on Lakshmi (Chaturvedi 1996) that there is no legendary text (*purana*) devoted to Lakshmi needs correction in the light of this extensive textual and oral evidence from Chhattisgarh and Orissa.

It is a comment on the richness of the oral traditions of Chhattisgarh that Elwin's vast writings on the subject barely scratch the proverbial surface. For example, he does not document the extensive women's oral epic tradition that extends over north Bastar, the Koraput hills of Orissa (Gregory 2004) and the southern Raipur plain. Flueckiger's multi-sited ethnographic research on women's folklore in the latter region has added to our knowledge of the latter (Flueckiger 1983, 1987, 1991a, 1991b, 1996; Flueckiger and Sears 1991). The position of women in the rice cultures of eastern India, she notes, differs from that in the wheat-growing areas of the west. This is because rice is a labor-intensive crop requiring the participation of women in the transplanting, weeding, and harvesting stages; wheat, by contrast, requires less labor. Women, who spend months working closely together in rows in the fields, pass the time singing and/or listening to elders singing fantastic tales about deities and ordinary people. They also participate in many rituals involving rice. One of these is the parrot dance, a harvest dance genre performed by female land laborers, "a performance that transforms harvested paddy into ritual wealth, the goddess Lakshmi herself" (Flueckiger 1996: 24). Another tradition is that of the *bhojali* ritual where women plant wheat seedling in a basket, worship the sprouts for the duration of a ritual that takes nine days, and then, on the final day, immerse the baskets in water and use the sprout to create ritual friendship with other women.

Men also create ritual friendship in the Raipur plain (Jay 1973) and it seems to be a phenomenon widespread throughout Chhattisgarh and central India more generally (Skoda 2005: 164). A multitude of different types of ritual friendship are found in Chhattisgarh that cross-cut gender, caste, religion, and communities. Some ritual friendships, as Skoda (2005:

chapter 3.4) notes, create relations of ideological *identity* between friends, and raise fundamental questions about notions of *equality* and *hierarchy* that have dominated anthropological debates about the sociology of India.

The general question of 'popular' religion in the Raipur plain was addressed in Babb's oft-quoted study, *The Divine Hierarchy: Popular Hinduism in Central India* (Babb 1975), a triple-sited ethnography based in the capital city of Raipur, a small village some 48 kilometers to the north of Raipur, and a major temple and pilgrimage site. This book, while it contains an informative chapter detailing the ethnographic specificities of the region, is mainly concerned to provide a systematic account of popular Hinduism by focusing on the generalities. A picture of Chhattisgarhi Hinduism emerges but one deliberately severed from its social structure. Babb is concerned to understand popular Hinduism as a "cultural domain which displays a pattern and consistency of its own" (1975: xvii). This was the only account of Chhattisgarhi religion until the work of Lamb (2002) and Dube (1998) on 'Untouchable' religion and Froerer's *Religious Division and Social Conflict: The Emergence of Hindu Nationalism in Rural India* (Froerer 2007), a detailed village-based ethnography that complements Babb's study by anchoring contemporary religious practice firmly in its social and historical context.

Froerer's study raises the question of Christianity among the Aboriginal (*adivasi*) population, something that all previous studies have ignored. Her concern is to understand the reason for violence against Christians by means of a 'grass roots' study of the spread of Hindu nationalism, the Rashtriya Swayamsevak Sangh (RSS), throughout the area. Her fieldwork was based in a village near Korba in the northern area of the Raipur plain but it is not a village study in the classic sense; it is a study *from* a village rather than *of* a village, a strategy that enables her to address general questions about religious division and social conflict from a particular standpoint.

The village she studied consisted of some 43 households, which can be divided either by official status, religion, language, migration history, or economic status, and all of which tell a different story. Official status divides by ST (scheduled tribe), SC (scheduled caste, i.e. 'Untouchable'), OBC (other backward classes); religion by Hindu or Christian; language by Indo-Aryan speaker (Chetriboli or Chhattisgarhi) or Dravidian (Kurukh); migration history by the number of generations one's family has been resident in the village; and economic status by measures of wealth such as landholdings, off-farm income, etc. Another division is by subjective linguistic divisions used by different groups. On this score she makes the important observation that the RSS prefer the term *vanvasi* (forest-dweller) to *adivasi* (tribal) because the latter word implies that the tribal people are the original inhabitants of India, a threat to the RSS claims that they, as Aryans, were the original inhabitants of India. Another term Froerer uses is "sons of the soil," a theoretical concept she borrows from Weiner (Weiner 1978).

The conflicting objective and subjective classifications of people at the household level in a village immediately raises the general question of the adequacy of the tribe/caste opposition that has informed so much debate in the past. Froerer's use of the 'sons of the soil' notion has the advantage that it raises the empirical question of the migration history of various groups of people, one that if pushed to the limits gives various answers according to whether we are talking about years, generations, or millennia; in other words, it has the potential to problematize any notion of 'original inhabitant' because the deep history of people anywhere is one of continual mobility and migration. In this respect Froerer's use of the notion of 'sons of the soil' resonates with the pragmatic definition given above of Bastar indigenes as migrants whose families have been living in Bastar for more than five generations.

For the Ratiya Kanwar people of Mohanpur village, history begins nine to ten generations ago when their ancestors first settled in the village; they divide others into those who have been in the village for seven generations and those who have been in the village for just one generation. In this particular case it so happens that the latter group are all Christians from the Dravidian-speaking Oraon community who were granted land to settle on and who have become relatively wealthy over the past two decades through their own hard work and from off-farm income; their relative wealth is such that they lend money to others in the village taking land as security. Froerer's close analysis of local approaches to sickness and healing, local corruption, land tenure, and liquor reveals how the RSS have worked with members of the Ratiya Kanwar 'sons of the soil' to exploit the divisions within the village and to spread their influence within the area.

Froerer's study of 'modern' Chhattisgarhi religious life complements Skoda's more 'traditional' ethnography; considered together they tell us much about contemporary rural life on the Raipur plain. Rice economies and the religious beliefs associated with them involve repetitive cycles that reproduce themselves year after year, decade after decade, and century after century, but never in exactly the same way because the reproduction of tradition is always subject to the historical contingencies of the moment.

Parry's recent work on the Bhilai Steel Plant (BSP) poses the question of a radically different kind of modernity, one that creates a radically new concept of 'tradition' for those people involved. Steel making is governed by the unpredictable short-term history of the commercial trade cycle rather than the relatively predictable annual cycle of rice production, governed as it is by the cycles of the sun and moon. The study of a steel plant poses special problems for the ethnographer, too. Parry, one of India's foremost ethnographers and well known for his earlier work in the Himalayas and in Benares, found that he had to develop new methods of a biographical and historical kind because there were no 'rules' and 'customs' of the classic type to be found.

The BSP began production in 1959. When Parry began his fieldwork in 1993 it had 55,000 employees and covered an area of seventeen square kilometers. It is now one of the largest steel plants in Asia even though the number of employees had fallen to 39,000 by 2003. The plant has had a profound effect on the economy of Chhattisgarh as a whole and the Durg District in particular. Parry's work has focused on the lives of the workers, their values, and their social relationships. While the situation he describes is extremely complex, one theme that has echoes with Froerer's work is the notion of 'sons of the soil,' which here has an indigenous expression, *dharati putr* (Parry and Struempell 2008: 51). Migrants from all over India have moved to Bhilai to take advantage of the new economic opportunities offered, but the *dharati putr* bitterly complain about the disproportionate share of BSP jobs these people have taken. Parry was surprised to find little nostalgia for old village ways among these 'sons of the soil,' noting the disdain those raised in the town had for village labor (Parry 2008b: 237). New values such as these are found throughout monsoon Asia where industrialisation has led to a relative decline in the economic importance of agriculture as a percentage of GNP. In other words, the 'great transformation' experienced by the wheat cultures of Europe in the nineteenth century are now affecting all the rice cultures of monsoon Asia notwithstanding the political resistance of the agrarian lobby in many parts of Asia (Ohnuki-Tierney 1993; Bray 1986, 1998).

Parry's writings on BSP consist of a series of essays on various topics rather than a monograph. Almost half of the essays deal with specific industrial topics such as unions, labor relations, and social relations between migrants and other workers (Parry 1999, 2003, 2008a), some with more general comparative issues dealing with corruption and violence

(Parry 2000; Parry and Struempell 2008), and others on more classic anthropological themes such as kinship and marriage (Parry 2001, 2004, 2005) and religious beliefs about industrial development (Parry 2008b). These essays defy simple summary suffice to say that they are rhetorically designed to present an ethnographically-informed challenge to accepted ideas about Indian society and culture.

Take his essay on 'Ankalu's Errant Wife: Sex, Marriage and Industry in Contemporary Chhattisgarh' (2001) for example. This challenges accepted ideas about endogamy and marital instability in India through the presentation of rich ethnographic data analysed in its broader comparative context. Parry argues that "certain pockets of the country sustain divorce rates quite comparable to contemporary California" (2001: 786), the Chhattisgarh region as a whole being one of these. He quotes statistics from Gell's work on the Gondi-speakers of Bastar to the effect that more than 50 percent of first marriages ended in divorce. These are bolstered with statistics of his own but, more tellingly, with fine-grained case studies dealing with the emotions excited and moral dilemmas posed by affairs, divorce, remarriage, and intermarriage between castes. These stories also tell of the influence of employment at BSP on marriage patterns; they show, for example, that marriages among the 'labor aristocracy' tend to be more stable.

Of more general and contemporary interest is a joint paper with Struempell (Parry and Struempell 2008) that examines the problem of ethnic and communal violence through a telling comparative analysis of Bhilai's steel plant in Chhattisgarh with the Rourkela steel plant in Orissa where Struempell conducted research, telling because, in spite of the many commonalities, the Rourkela plant has been racked with ethnic conflict whereas ethnic relations in Bhilai have been relatively benign. Their detailed ethnographic analysis of the reasons for this contrast enables them to challenge received ideas in the political science literature on postcolonial nationalism.

Which way?

If Chhattisgarh is at the crossroads again then which way will it go? If history is any guide then the region will take the paths it has always taken and go off in all directions simultaneously, with all this implies for the becoming of the economy, society, culture, and peoples of the region.

References

Agarwal, P. C. (1967) *Human Geography of Bastar District*. Allahabad: Garga Brothers.

Anderson, R. S. and Huber, W. (1988) *The Hour of the Fox*. Seattle: University of Washington Press.

Babb, L. A. (1975) *The Divine Hierarchy: Popular Hinduism in Central India*. New York: Columbia University Press.

Baghel, J. (1982) Of 'Devis' and 'Devas' (as told to Roshan Kalapesi). In Kagal, C. (ed.) *Shilpakar: The Craftsman*. Bombay: Crafts Council of Western India.

Bailey, F. G. (1961) "Tribe and Caste in India," *Contributions to Indian Sociology*, 5(1): 7–19.

Bellwood, P. (2005) *First Farmers: The Origins of Agricultural Societies*. London: Blackwell.

Berger, P. (2007) *Füttern, Speisen und Verschlingen: Ritual und Gesellschaft im Hochland von Orissa* (Feeding, Eating and Devouring: Ritual and Society in Highland Orissa). Berlin: Lit.

Blackburn, S. H., Claus, P. J., Flueckiger, J. B. and Wadley, S. S. (eds) (1989) *Oral Epics in India*. Berkeley: University of California Press.

Bray, F. (1986) *The Rice Economies: Technology and Development in Asian Societies*. Oxford: Basil Blackwell.

——(1998) 'A Stable Landscape? Social and Cultural Sustainability in Asian Rice Systems', in Dowling, N. G., Greenfield, S. M. and Fischer, K. S. (eds) *Sustainability of Rice in the Global Food System*. Manila: IRRI.

Chaturvedi, B. K. (1996) *Lakshmi*. Delhi: Books For All.

Chaudhuri, K. (2001) 'Special Feature Chhattisgarh: Interview with Chief Minister Ajit Jogi,' *Frontline*, 18.

Cooper, Z. (1997) *Prehistory of the Chitrakot Falls*. Pune: Ravish Publishers.

Crooke, W. (1915) 'The Dasahra: Autumn Festival of Hindus,' *Folklore*, 26, 28–59.

Dube, S. (1998) *Untouchable Pasts: Religion, Identity, and Power Among a Central Indian Community, 1780–1950*. Albany, NY: SUNY Press.

Dumont, L. (1966) 'Marriage in India, The Present State of the Question: III. North India in Relation to South India,' *Contributions to Indian Sociology*, 9: 90–114.

Elwin, V. (1939) *The Baiga*. London: John Murray.

——(1942) *The Agaria*. Calcutta: Humphrey Milford.

——(1943) *The Aboriginals*. Oxford: Oxford University Press.

——(1944 [1980]) *Folk-Tales of Mahakoshal*. New York: Arno Press.

——(1946) *Folk-Songs of Chhattisgarh*. Oxford: Oxford University Press.

——(1947) *The Muria and their Ghotul*. Oxford: Oxford University Press.

——(1949) *Myths of Middle India*. Oxford: Oxford University Press.

——(1950a) *Bondo Highlander*. Bombay: Oxford University Press.

——(1950b) *Maria Murder and Suicide*. Bombay: Oxford University Press.

——(1951) *The Tribal Art of Middle India: A Personal Record*. London: Oxford University Press.

——(1954) *Tribal Myths of Orissa*. Oxford: Oxford University Press.

——(1955) *The Religion of an Indian Tribe*. Oxford: Oxford University Press.

——(1958) *Leaves from the Jungle: Life in a Gond Village*. London: Oxford University Press.

Flueckiger, J. B. (1983) 'Bhojali: Song, Goddess, Friend: A Chhattisgarhi Women's Oral Tradition,' *Asian Folklore Studies*, 42: 27–43.

——(1987) 'Land of Wealth, Land of Famine: The Sua Nac (Parrot Dance) of Central India,' *Journal of American Folklore*, 100: 3–38.

——(1991a) 'Genre and Community: the Folklore System of Chhattisgarh' in Appadurai, A., Korom, F. J. and Mills, M. A. (eds) *Gender, Genre, and Power in South Asian Expressive Traditions*. Philadelphia: University of Pennsylvania Press.

——(1991b) 'Literacy and the Changing Concept of Text: Women's Ramayana Mandali in Central India' in *Boundaries of the Text: Epic Performances in South and Southeast Asia*, Michigan Papers on South and Southeast Asia, no. 35. Ann Arbor: Center for South and Southeast Asian Studies, University of Michigan.

——(1996) *Gender and Genre in the Folklore of Middle India*. Ithaca: Cornell University Press.

Flueckiger, J. B. and Sears, L. J. (1991) *Boundaries of the Text: Epic Performances in South and Southeast Asia*. Ann Arbor: Center for South and Southeast Asian Studies, University of Michigan.

Fuchs, S. (1960) *The Gond and Bhumia of Eastern Mandla*. Bombay: Asia Publishing House.

Fuller, C. J. (1992) *The Camphor Flame: Popular Hinduism and Society in India*. Princeton: Princeton University Press.

*Froerer, P. (2007) *Religious Division and Social Conflict: The Emergence of Hindu Nationalism in Rural India*. New Delhi: Social Science Press.

Gell, A. (1980) 'The Gods at Play: Vertigo and Possession in Muria Religion,' *Man*, 15: 219–248.

——(1982) 'The Market Wheel: Symbolic Aspects of an Indian Tribal Market,' *Man*, 17: 470–91.

*——(1986) 'Newcomers to the World of Goods: Consumption Among the Muria Gonds', in Appadurai, A. (ed.) *The Social Life of Things*. Cambridge: Cambridge University Press.

——(1997) 'Exalting the King and Obstructing the State: A Political Interpretation of Royal Ritual in Bastar District, Central India,' *Journal of the Royal Anthropological Institute*, 3: 433–50.

Gell, S. M. S. (1992) *The Ghotul in Muria Society*. Reading: Harwood Academic Publishers.

Ghurye, G. S. (1943) *The Aborigines — So Called — and their Future*. Poona: Gokhale Institute of Politics and Economics.

Gregory, C. A. (1988) 'Village Money Lending, the World Bank and Landlessness in Central India,' *Journal of Contemporary Asia*, 18: 47–58.

——(1995–96) 'Vision of the Aboriginal Artisan,' *Artonview*, 4: 24–27.

*——(1997) *Savage Money*. London: Harwood.

*——(2004) 'The Oral Epics of the Women of the Dandakaranya Plateau: A Preliminary Mapping,' *Journal of Social Sciences*, 8: 93–104.

——(2009) 'Brotherhood and Otherhood in Bastar: On the Social Specificity of "Dual Organisation" in Aboriginal India,' in Pfeffer, G. and Behera, D. K. (eds), *Structure and Exchange in Tribal India and Beyond*. New Delhi: Concept Publishing.

——(2010) 'Siblingship as a Value' in Berger, P., Hardenberg, R., Kattner, E. and Prager, M. (eds) *The Anthropology of Values: Essays in Honour of Georg Pfeffer*. Delhi: Dorling Kindersley (India) Pvt. Ltd.

Gregory, C. A. and Vaishnav, H. (2003) *Lachmi Jagar: Gurumai Sukdai's Story of the Bastar Rice Goddess*. Kondagaon: Kaksad Publications.

Grigson, W. V. (1938) *The Maria Gonds of Bastar*. Oxford: Oxford University Press.

*Guha, R. (1999) *Savaging the Civilized: Verrier Elwin, His Tribals, and India*. Delhi: Oxford University Press.

Hacker, K. F. (2000) 'Traveling Objects: Brass Images, Artisans, and Audiences,' *Res*, 37: 147–65.

——(2004) 'Retooling Tradition: Image Making as Practice in Bastar District, Chhattisgarh,' in Dursum, B. A. (ed.) *Change and Continuity: Folk and Tribal Art of India*. Miami: Lowe Art Museum.

Hivale, S. and Elwin, V. (1935) *Songs of the Forest: The Folk Poetry of the Gonds*. London: George Allen and Unwin.

Huber, W. A. (1984) 'From Millennia to the Millennium: An Anthropological History of Bastar State,' Department of Anthropology and Sociology. British Columbia: University of British Columbia.

Jay, E. J. (1973) 'Bridging the Gap between Castes: Ceremonial Friendship in Chhatisgarh,' *Contributions to Indian Sociology*, 7: 144–58.

Lamb, R. (2002) *Rapt in the Name: The Ramnamis, Ramnam, and Untouchable Religion in Central India*. Albany, NY: SUNY Press.

Mahaprashasta, A. A. (2010) 'In the War Zone,' *Frontline*, 27 (9). Available at: http://www.flonnet.com/fl2709/stories/20100507270901000.htm

Mallebrein, C. (1994) 'Dantesvari, the Family Goddess (Kulsvmi) of the Rajas of Bastar, and the Dasahara-Festival of Jagdalpur,' in Michaels, A., Vogelsanger, C. and Wilke, A. (eds) *Wild Goddesses in India and Nepal*. Bern: Peter Lang.

Misra, B. (1971) 'Verrier Elwin's Field Methods and Fieldwork in India: An Appraisal,' *Asian Folklore Studies*, 30: 97–132.

Ohnuki-Tierney, E. (1993) *Rice as Self: Japanese Identities Through Time*. Princeton: Princeton University Press.

Otten, T. (2009) 'King, Tribal Society and Fertility in Koraput: Different Aspects of the Ritual Bali Jatra,' in Pfeffer, G. and Behera, D. K. (eds) *Tribal Studies 8: Structure and Exchange in Tribal India and Beyond. Contemporary Society*. New Delhi: Concept Publishing.

——(in press) 'Bali Jatra: An Oral Epic and a Ritual for Well-being,' in Kulke, H., Mohatny, N. and Pathy, D. (eds) *Imaging Orissa*. New Delhi: Manohar.

*Parkin, R. (1992) *The Munda of Central India: An Account of their Social Organization*. Delhi: Oxford University Press.

Parry, J. (1999) 'Two Cheers for Reservation: The Satnamis and the Steel Plant,' in Guha, R. and Parry, J. (eds), *Institutions and Inequalities: Essays in Honour of André Béteille*. Oxford: Oxford University Press.

——(2000) '"The Crisis of Corruption" and "The Idea of India": A Worm's Eye View,' in Pardo, I. (ed.), *The Morals of Legitimacy*. Oxford: Beghahn.

——(2001) 'Ankalu's Errant Wife: Sex, Marriage and Industry in Contemporary Chhattisgarh,' *Modern Asia Studies*, 35: 783–820.

——(2003) 'Nehru's Dream and the Village "Waiting Room": Long Distance Labour Migrants to a Central Indian Steel Town,' *Contributions to Indian Sociology*, 37: 217–49.

——(2004) 'The Marital history of "A Thumb Impression Man",' in Arnold, D. and Blackburn, S. (eds) *Telling Lives in India: Biography, Autobiography and Life History*. Oxford: Permanent Black.

——(2005) 'Changing childhoods in industrial Chhattisgarh,' in Chopra, R. and Jeffrey, P. (eds), *Educational Regimes in Contemporary India*. London: Sage Publications.

——(2008a) 'Cosmopolitan Values in a Central Indian Steel Town,' in Werbner, P. (ed.) *Anthropology and the New Cosmopolitanism*. Oxford: Berg.

——(2008b) 'The Sacrifices of Modernity in a Soviet-built Steel Town in Central India,' in Pina-Cabral, J. and Pine, F. (eds), *On the Margins of Religion*. Oxford: Berghahn.

*Parry, J. and Struempell, C. (2008) 'On the Desecration of Nehru's "Temples": Bhilai and Rourkela Compared,' *Economic and Political Weekly*, 10 May, 47–57.

Pfeffer, G. (1982) *Status and Affinity in Middle India*. Wiesbaden: Franz Steiner.

——(1983) 'Generation and Marriage in Middle India: The Evolutionary Potential of Restricted Exchange,' *Contributions to Indian Sociology*, 17: 87–121.

——(1996) 'The Young and the Junior Set in Tribal Middle India: On the Category of Age,' in Pfeffer, G. and Behera, D. K. (eds), *Contemporary Society: Childhood and Complex Order*. New Delhi: Manak Publications.

——(1997) 'The Scheduled Tribes of Middle India as a Unit: Problems of Internal and External Comparison,' in Pfeffer, G. and Behera, D. K. (eds), *Contemporary Society: Tribal Studies*. New Delhi: Concept Publishing.

——(2004) 'Order in Tribal Middle Indian "Kinship",' *Anthropos*, 99: 381–409.

Popoff, T. (1980) 'The Muriya and Tallur Mutte: A Study of the Concept of the Earth Among the Muriya Gonds of Bastar District, India.' Unpublished PhD thesis, University of Sussex.

Postel, M. and Cooper, Z. (1999) *Bastar Folk Art: Shrines, Figurines, and Memorials*. Mumbai: Project for Indian Cultural Studies, Publication VIII.

Prevot, N. (2005) 'Jouer avec les dieux. Chronique ethnomusicologique d'un rituel annuel de village au Bastar, Chhattisgarh, Inde centrale.' Paris: Université de Paris X – Nanterre.

Rousseleau, R. (2008) *Les créatures de Yama: Ethnohistoire d'une tribu de l'Inde (Orissa)*. Bologna: CLUEB.

Sahu, I. (1965) *Mahalakshmi Puran*. Cuttack: Sarda Press.

Savyasaachi (1992) *A Sociology of Agriculture*. Unpublished PhD thesis, University of Delhi.

——(1993) 'An Alternative System of Knowledge: Fields and Forest in Abujhmarh,' in Banuri, T. and Marglin, F. A. (eds), *Who Will Save the Forests? Knowledge, Power and Environmental Destruction*. London: Zed.

Singh, I. (1944) *The Gondwana and the Gonds*. Lucknow: Universal Publishers.

Skoda, U. (2005) *The Aghira: A Peasant Caste on a Tribal Frontier*. New Delhi: Manohar.

Sundar, N. (2001) 'Debating Dussehra and Reinterpreting Rebellion in Bastar District, Central India,' *Journal of the Royal Anthropological Institute*, 7: 19–35.

*——(2007) *Subalterns and Sovereigns: An Anthropological History of Bastar (1854–2006)*, Second Edition. Delhi: Oxford University Press.

Tanaka, K. (2002) 'Crop-Raising Techniques in Asian Rice Culture: Resemblances to Root and Tuber Crop Cultivation,' in Yoshida, S. and Matthews, P. J. (eds), *Vegeculture in Eastern Asia and Oceania*. Osaka: National Museum of Ethnology.

Thusu, K. N. (1965) *The Dhurwa of Bastar*. Calcutta: Anthropological Survey of India.

——(1980) *Gond Kingdom of Chanda with Particular Reference to its Political Structure*. Calcutta: Anthropological Survey of India.

Trautmann, T. R. (1981) *Dravidian Kinship*. Cambridge: Cambridge University Press.

Vitebsky, P. (1993) *Dialogues with the Dead: The Discussion of Mortality Among the Sora of Eastern India*. Cambridge: Cambridge University Press.

Von Fürer-Haimendorf, C. (1982) *Tribes of India: The Struggle for Survival.* Berkeley: University of California Press.

Weiner, M. (1978) *Sons of the Soil: Migration and Ethnic Conflict in India.* Princeton: Princeton University Press.

Wills, C. U. (1919) 'The Territorial System of the Rajput Kingdoms of Mediaeval Chhattisgarh,' *Journal of the Asiatic Society of Bengal*, 15: 197–262.

Woods, F. (1973) 'Sentence Patterns in Halbi,' in Trail, R. L. (ed.), *Patterns in Clause, Sentence, and Discourse in Selected Language of India and Nepal. Part I, Sentence and Discourse.* Norman, USA: Summer Institute of Linguistics of the University of Oklahoma.

Woods, F. M. (1980) *The Interrelationship of Cultural Information, Linguistic Structure, and Symbolic Representations in a Halbi Myth.* Arlington: University of Texas at Arlington.

Woods, F. and Bowman, H. (1978) *Stratificational Analysis*, Research Papers of the Texas SIL at Dallas. Dallas: Summer Institute of Linguistics.

5 Gujarat

Transformations of hierarchy

Helene Basu

For a few days in November 2009, the small town of Unjha in North Gujarat could pride itself on being a Hindu sacred centre boasting at least half a million devotees, allegedly all from one caste. The station where farmers normally take their cumin and cotton crops was humming with people arriving in special trains from Ahmadabad to attend the 'Silver Jubilee' of the temple of their caste goddess, the *kuldevi* Umiya Mataji of the Kadva Patidar. For weeks, lists of large donations from well-known industrialist houses and wealthy farmers were publicly circulated. The temple buildings had been refurbished, and the compound enlarged and equipped with 24 air-conditioned rooms for the temple guesthouse. Large tents were put up around the temple to shelter the masses of Patidars coming from elsewhere in Gujarat and India, as well as from faraway places such as the US, the UK, Tanzania and Uganda, to feast the goddess. Even the guesthouses attached to a Muslim pilgrimage centre in the neighbouring village were asked to keep most of their rooms available for Umiya Mataji's devotees. Gujarat's chief minister, Narendra Modi, gave a moving speech about his devotion to the *kuldevi* of his *njati* (caste) when opening the *havan* (vegetarian sacrifice) performed by twenty-one Brahmans. During the days of the festival, the temple trust had thought of a spectacular way to show devotion to Umiya Mataji by offering helicopter flights to those who wished to have *darshan* (divine sight) from above and were willing to pay 25,000 R.s for it. The local press covered the event extensively, praising the economic achievements and unrelenting devotion of Patidars as utterly beneficial for Gujarat in particular and India in general.

Celebrations of castes revelling in an almost Durkheimian fashion is a common practice that enjoys widespread popularity in Gujarat, but the Patidar feast for Umiya Mataji was exceptional in scale. The Patidar success story unfolded in a region where trade has played an important role for at least two millennia. Today, Gujarat is one of the most highly urbanized and industrialized states of the Indian Union, with a large diasporic population residing outside the state. The rise of Gujarat to the forefront of Indian modernity is epitomized by the ascent of the Patidars from a peasant caste in the nineteenth century to a regionally dominant and globally dispersed business community in the twentieth and twenty-first centuries.

Economic success in a globalized market economy, state power, migration and diasporic consciousness, regional pride, religious devotion and nationalist sentiments are obviously not incompatible with a social institution once held by scholars to signify the core of India's difference from modern Europe. For Louis Dumont in particular, one of the salient features of the caste system consisted in its undervaluation of the political sphere and economic competition compared to the religious domain of values. Politics and economics, he argued, are central values and spheres of action in modern societies, whereas in the non-modern Indian society these are encompassed by superior religious values through the holistic order of the caste hierarchy (Dumont 1980a). As the contemporary debate on caste is still so heavily influenced by Dumont – or rather by critiques of his theoretical model (e.g. Gupta 2004) – I shall include a critical reading of some of his propositions in relation to ethnographic findings specific to Gujarat. Dumont's theory of caste hierarchy has been criticized in relation to a range of issues, beginning with McKim Marriott's objection to Dumont's dualist approach (Marriott 1976), but few of his critics have considered theoretical problems related to trade and the merchant castes. These, as will be seen below, figure importantly in social anthropological research conducted in Gujarat. Not many ethnographers engage directly with the implications of their findings for the theory of hierarchy proposed by Dumont, but even a cursory glance at the historical and ethnographic literature pertaining to Gujarat raises doubts as to whether there ever was such a well-knit, coherent society consistently structured by the single ideological principle of purity and pollution as Dumont imagined. Still, in Gujarat we are faced with multiple social and religious formations expressing different types of hierarchical values, which are simultaneously acclaimed, contested or become transformed by being juxtaposed with other forms of ranking and social stratification. It is therefore apt to ask if the theory of hierarchy can still offer useful explanations of contemporary social processes and religious conflicts.

This chapter is concerned with the history of anthropological research on caste and hierarchy in different religious settings in Gujarat after independence. Even before British colonialism established its supremacy over the region, societies in Gujarat were thoroughly pluralized in terms of rural and urban settings, agriculture and trade, as well as religion (both within the fold of Hindu traditions, as well as with regard to Islam). The word commonly used by Hindus and Jains for 'caste' is *njati*, 'a known person', i.e. a kinsman (see also Cort 2004: 78). It is used in the sense of *jati*, 'kind' or 'birth'. Muslims more often employ the term *jamat*, a term referring to kinship units that may also be extended to denote a sect or a guild. Similarly, in Hindu contexts *njati* and *sampradaya* ('sect') may sometimes overlap with the term for a merchant guild (*mahajan*).

Gujarat: a brief overview

As trade has played such a prominent role in the history of Gujarat, the region is dotted with both small and big towns. Formerly a major textile-producing region, the state has turned into a diversified industrial site producing chemicals, fertilizers, pharmaceuticals, cement, and more recently oil off the coast near Jamnagar. In the nineteenth century, the expansion of the British colonial empire and the ending of slavery within the Indian Ocean region incited movements of large groups of Indians to Africa, Fiji and Trinidad, partly as indentured labourers (Basu 2008a). But even before, movements across the Indian Ocean had been common and Gujaratis had already formed small trading communities in East Africa by the sixteenth century (Pearson 1998). Conversely, Arabs, Africans and others from elsewhere in the Western Indian Ocean region came to settle in Gujarat. In the nineteenth and twentieth centuries, Patidars and members of other Gujarati castes migrated to Bombay, South Africa, East Africa and elsewhere in the world; later, especially since the 1970s, a growing number of people migrated from Gujarat to Great Britain, the US and Canada.

As a state, in 1960 Gujarat was separated from Maharashtra and the larger Bombay state. It borders on Sindh in contemporary Pakistan in the west, Rajasthan in the north and Madhya Pradesh and Maharashtra in the east and south. Conceding to the demands of the 'Mahagujarat movement' for a separate state on linguistic grounds, the Gujarati language spoken from Bombay to Kacchch provided the justification for including the peninsulas of Kacchch and Saurashtra in the west within the folds of the new state, while Bombay became part of Maharashtra. The state of Gujarat was created out of a region which, a hundred years ago, consisted of a mosaic of semi-independent Rajput little kingdoms, dispersed territories under the dominion of the ruling Gaekwads of the Baroda princely state and British colonial districts. Rajputs in Saurashtra and Kacchch remained in power much longer than in central and southern Gujarat where Muslim governors had ruled since the fifteenth century. Saurashtra and Kacchch are sometimes said to share more cultural traits with Rajasthan than with mainland Gujarat. Moreover, the alluvial plains in mainland Gujarat are conducive to variegated agricultural production and contrast with the large semi-arid areas characteristic of Saurashtra and Kacchch, where pastoralism is often the primary source of livelihood. Finally, along the coastline of Gujarat, littoral societies emerged characterized by highly mixed populations engaged in fishing, overseas trade and maritime industries (Basu 2008a; Simpson and Kresse 2007). This was particularly true for the peninsula of Kacchch, which, until the 1960s, was more easily accessible from the sea than from the land. Historically, Gujarat has evolved as a region of thresholds, with littoral societies overlapping with agrarian systems based on agriculture, as well as with merchant societies rooted in trade.

Gujarat is home to a multitude of religions. The majority of Gujaratis are Hindus (89.53 per cent), followed by 8.53 per cent Muslims, 1.37 per cent Jains, 0.03 per cent Zoroastrians (Parsi), 0.39 per cent Christians, 0.02 per cent Buddhists, 0.07 per cent Sikhs and 1.96 per cent 'other religions' (Singh 2003: 17). In addition, Scheduled Tribes (Adivasis) constitute 14.22 per cent of the total population of the state (Singh 2003: 8). Caste and religion figure importantly in postcolonial Gujarati politics. In the 1950s and 1960s, industrial development and modernization were the main goals, and Indian politics was governed by ideals of progress and social change. In Gujarat, land reforms under the slogan 'land to the tiller' aimed at breaking the power of 'feudal' landlords, and social practices of 'untouchability' were declared illegal. In those days, the Patidar caste was already at the forefront of movements of social mobility. Until the mid-1970s politics in Gujarat was dominated by the Congress Party and by Gujarati high castes (Baniyas, Patidars, Brahmans). This changed when Congress-I led by Indira Gandhi developed a new electoral alliance between Kshatriyas, Harijans, Adivasis and Muslims called KHAM (Nandy *et al.* 1995: 102ff.). In the 1980s, the political success of KHAM led to an eruption of violence between high and low castes in Gujarat, sparked by anti-reservation campaigns. When the BJP became increasingly popular in the late 1980s, what had started as conflicts between castes over material and symbolic capital was gradually transformed into religious antagonism between Hindus and Muslims articulated in the idiom of nationalism. With the infamous campaigns for the demolition of the Babri Masjid in Ayodhya, the Hindutva movement gained unprecedented success and Gujarat turned into a major stronghold of the movement. Since 1995 Gujarat has been ruled by the BJP. In 2002, by far the worst outbreak of violence against Muslims rocked Gujarat. Muslims were accused of having set a train bogey on fire in which 56 Hindus returning from campaigning to have a Rama temple built in Ayodhya died. In the ensuing violence, more than 1,000 Muslims lost their lives, women were raped and set on fire in front of their families, and hundreds of thousands of Muslims lost their homes. In spite of the widespread criticism of the ways in which the Gujarat government handled the violence, which continued for weeks, the BJP remained in power.

Economic considerations, the dynamics of change and history figure importantly in many ethnographies that deal either directly or indirectly with caste in Gujarat. Broadly speaking, the ethnographies produced since the 1950s reflect the major political and economic transformations engendering modern Gujarat from the perspectives and experiences of its people. Here, I shall confine myself to anthropological studies dealing with caste in Hindu, Jain and Muslim contexts. Compared to the former two, ethnographic studies of Muslims are still rare. The modest interest anthropologists have shown in Muslim social and religious life might be seen as a reflection of the successful production of the image of Gujarat as the 'sacred earth' of Hinduism purified by the value of non-violence (*ahimsa*) and as the birthplace of Gandhiji, the 'father of the nation'. There is, however, nothing natural or given about present-day Gujarat, as Simpson has recently demonstrated (Simpson 2011; Simpson and Kapadia 2010). Rather, the 'making of modern Gujarat' as a unified state of the Indian Union through texts produced by Hindu intellectuals has been very much a project of high-caste male Hindu writers in which the voices of Muslims – and women – were rarely heard. What kind of 'Gujarati society' emerges from the ethnographic studies conducted by social anthropologists? I shall explore this question by looking in greater detail at the ethnographies produced by anthropologists on caste and hierarchy during the last 50 to 60 years.

Tradition and modernity: two approaches to changing caste

In the 1950s and 1960s, sociological theories of modernization flourished, and Indian policies were governed by ideals of progress, industrial development and social change. In response to these theories, two quite different monographs appeared in the early 1970s based on fieldwork in the 1950s and 1960s. Both were concerned with transitions from tradition to modernity focused on the changing nature of caste in Gujarat. The first was by Jan Breman, who adopted a Marxist approach in dealing with the relationships between the landowning and landless castes. The second was David Pocock's study of a Patidar village, which reflects his early involvement with Louis Dumont in the project 'For a Sociology of India' (Breman 1974; Pocock 1972, 1973).

Breman conducted his first ethnographic study in 1962–63 in two villages, one irrigated, the other non-irrigated, in southern Gujarat. As part of a Dutch anthropological project (van der Veen 1972), Breman worked closely with I. P. Desai (Desai 1964a, 1964b; Breman 1985, 1997). For decades to come, much historical and social-science research in Gujarat proceeded along the lines pursued by Breman, in which economic and political development were placed centre stage (Breman 1985). Breman came to wield great influence in the overlapping fields of the social sciences, Indian sociology and anthropology and subaltern history in regard to Gujarat (Breman 1997; Hardiman 1987, 1996; Shah *et al.* 2002). In his view, caste served the internal distinctions of a peasant society and roughly corresponded to classes involved in processes of agrarian production. In both villages, landowners belonged to a Brahman subcaste, the Anavils, whose members did not perform any priestly services but dominated agricultural production. The labourers, who owned no or very little land, mostly came from a 'tribal' community known as Dublas. Breman's main question concerned the relationships between landowners and agricultural labourers and the changes whereby traditional forms of patronage were eliminated in the transition from a 'closed village economy of a peasant society' to a capitalist economy (Breman 1974: 36). In the traditional economy, Breman argued, agrarian labour relationships were cast in the form of permanent service relationships between patrons and clients known in South Gujarat by the term *halipratha* (ibid.). A *hali* was a farm servant in the permanent employ of a landlord (*dhaniamo*) (Breman 1974: 36ff.). The system of *halipratha* implied bondage and was compared to slavery by some colonial writers. At the beginning of the relationship stood a loan that the agricultural labourer had incurred for arranging his marriage. As his debt increased in the course of time, making it impossible for him to repay it during his lifetime, his son inherited it and continued to serve the same master. For his own marriage the son again needed a loan from the master, meaning that the cycle started all over again. Not all servants labouring in the fields of landlords, however, were bonded. Breman noted a blurred distinction between *bhandela hali* (bonded labourers) and *chuta hali* (free labourers).

This system of bonded labour was shaped by the norms that governed patronage as part of the division of labour between castes (*jajmani*). Not only did agricultural labourers often belong to servant castes associated with a specific profession (e.g. leatherworking), but agricultural labour itself was 'thought to be defiling' (Breman 1974: 14). High castes derived prestige from the fact that they did not perform manual labour themselves. The traditional relationship between patrons (*jajman*) and clients (*kamin*) entailed mutual rights and moral obligations which, for the patron, consisted in providing food, clothes and general aid to the *kamin*, who in turn was both obliged as well as entitled to perform services for the patron. In the 1960s agriculture was modernized and landowners had turned to growing cash crops of fruit. Wage labour replaced the old patron–client relationship.

At the time when Breman conducted his research, 'Village Studies' were the paradigm of the day, engaging social anthropologists from north to south India (Marriott 1955; Srinivas 1955). While Breman was critical of this approach because of the apparent neglect of processes of agrarian production, David Pocock found other reasons not to follow this line of inquiry (Breman 1974: xiii; Pocock 1972). Instead of focusing on relations between castes, Pocock concentrated on the internal dynamics of a single caste. He had spent eighteen months between 1953 and 1956 doing fieldwork in a village in Charottar, which later became Kheda District in central Gujarat. In this village, as in the district as a whole, the Patidar were the dominant landholding caste. The 'dominance' they exercised in Kheda District differed in important respects from how anthropologists had described the 'dominant caste' elsewhere (Srinivas 1952). Significantly, Patidars hardly patronized ritual service castes. A 'real' dominant caste in a hierarchical set-up would have depended on the services performed by ritual specialists and other servants to maintain their superior status. But for Patidars it sufficed to know that Brahmans were superior, 'Untouchables' inferior (Pocock 1972: 27).

Although Pocock considered economic developments important for the changes he observed in regard to the Patidar caste, his point of departure for determining the traditional system was the caste hierarchy. Like Dumont, he regarded the tripartite scheme of caste (separation, division of labour/interdependence, graded status/relative ranking) proposed by Célestin Bouglé to be a major theoretical foundation for comprehending the caste hierarchy (or rather, the *varna* hierarchy, Bouglé 1958). Caste was to be understood as a holistic system constituted by ranked categories differentially related by the opposition of pure and impure (Dumont and Pocock 1957). In contrast to Dumont, however, Pocock argued for a restriction of the term *jajmani* to ritual service relationships that assisted the higher castes in maintaining their purity and that he saw as distinct from 'secular' service relationships related to economic production (Pocock 1962). The fact that Patidars did not act as patrons (*jajmans*) demanding ritual services was thus an important indicator denoting transformations of traditional caste realities. According to Pocock, these were best captured by studying 'the view which the people themselves have of their castes' (Pocock 1957a: 22).

According to Pocock, the Patidar view of caste was deeply influenced by processes of upward social mobility. These began in the nineteenth century when the Patidars emerged from Kanbi cultivators as a superior and upwardly mobile section of the caste. Originally, *pati* was a title tied to a particular system of taxation. Those who held this title profited specifically from the changes introduced by the colonial government and prospered in unprecedented ways. At first, 'Patidar' became the name of a prestigious section superior to other Kanbis. Over time, all Kanbi came to call themselves Patidar. They are also known by the surname 'Patel', formerly the title of the village headman. In addition to cultivation, Patidar Patels entered the domain of urban commerce, trade and enterprise, and by the mid-twentieth century farmers growing cash crops such as tobacco and cotton had become most successful in the development of commercial agriculture in Gujarat. Patidars also have a significant history of migration. At the end of the nineteenth century, they migrated to East Africa and Fiji. By the time of Pocock's fieldwork, young Patidar men were studying at universities in the United States and England (Pocock 1957a: 20). In the US today, the name 'Patel' has become almost synonymous with owners of motel chains;[1] in the UK the figure of 50 Patel millionaires living in the country was disclosed by the BBC in its special programme, *Meet the Patels*.[2]

'Patidar society is intensely hierarchical and competitive', Pocock told his readers on the first page of *Kanbi and Patidar* (Pocock 1972: 1). The book contains an ethnographic description of kinship and marriage. Marriage practices provided the arena in which economic differences were converted into competition for prestige and rank within the Patidar caste. As in the past, when the upper strata of Patidars had differentiated themselves from the lower levels by contracting hypergamous marriages, the practice of women marrying upwards still channelled competition for higher standing between the households of different patrilineages. Wealth was an important criterion for determining superior status within the endogamous Patidar caste. However, wealth alone did not suffice for connoting social superiority: not only was the Patidar caste internally stratified economically, but social and ritual practices also varied greatly. Social distinctions were vested in 'customary practices' (Pocock 1972: 52). The claim to higher standing was usually accompanied by Patidars abandoning practices that were considered low from the perspective of Brahmanical norms, especially widow remarriage, the consumption of meat and alcohol, and payments of bride wealth instead of dowry. While hypergamy provided Patidars with an important strategy with which to raise their rank, Pocock also discovered another tendency, which to some extent counterbalanced hypergamy, namely marriages contracted in particular villages grouped into closed marriage circles (*ekadas*). According to Pocock, Patidars adopted this practice in the 1940s. Within an *ekada*, villages exchanged an equal numbers of girls. Such marriage circles rejected hierarchical ranking by professing nominal equality at the top level of the Patidar caste, which was concerned to demarcate and guard its members' superior social standing against competitors from below (cf. also Patel 1961).

Breman and Pocock were both sensitive to the historical context in which they conducted ethnographic research in post-independence Gujarat. They differed most obviously in what was to be taken as 'tradition' and what represented the changing present of caste. Breman proceeded from the concept of a closed peasant economy opened up by the forces of the market; Pocock took his lead from an ideal-typical hierarchical system of caste deprived of its integrative social functions. He referred to the modern trend he observed in changing the view of the caste system as involving 'difference' towards discussing it in terms of 'identity' (Gupta 2004). Drawing on Bouglé, Pocock argued that, under modern conditions, one of the three structural features characterizing the caste system, namely 'separation', had gained greater weight over the remaining two (interdependence and hierarchical gradation). In 1957 Pocock published an article that showed that his perspective on the Patidar caste in Gujarat was as much influenced by his earlier research experiences in East Africa as by studying Bouglé and other classics on caste (such as Hocart, 1968, or Dumézil; for other discussions of the influence of fieldwork in East Africa on Pocock's view of India, see Simpson and Kresse 2009; also Pocock 1957b: 289). In the African context, Pocock dealt with a shift from 'caste as a system' to 'individual castes', which he had observed in East Africa. 'Gujarati Hindus' came from a range of different castes, such as the Bhattia, Lohana and Baniyas, all large merchant castes, as well as from the Patidar caste. But since there were neither Brahmans performing priestly services for them, nor 'Untouchables', Pocock concluded that Gujarati castes in East Africa did not relate to each other in terms of hierarchy. Rather, members of different castes perceived each other as different, and therefore, perhaps, as 'impure'. 'Castes exist and are like each other in being different', Pocock wrote, the similarity consisting in 'being Indian' (1957b: 298). The notion of hierarchy implied the inclusion of pure and impure status (for Dumont: encompassment), whereas in East Africa no such complementary relationships between castes existed. For Pocock, the future of caste was not its disappearance (as modernization theories suggested and as Indian politicians believed), but a transformation from hierarchical interdependence to separation, with an emphasis upon difference and competition (Pocock 1957a, 1957b).

Unlocking complementarity

In his second book, *Mind, Body, and Wealth* (1973), Pocock explored this process further in a Patidar village in central Gujarat, this time in the domain of religious beliefs and practices. Just as the system of ritual exchanges of services (*jajmani*) was marked by the opposition of pure and impure, the local Hindu pantheon consisted of higher and lower deities distinguished by the offerings they received. Higher deities, mostly male, received pure, vegetarian offerings, whereas the lower deities, usually female, were given animal sacrifices that were considered relatively impure. During his fieldwork, Pocock observed that Patidars were giving up the practice of offering blood sacrifices. Since it was mainly goddesses who were worshipped with animal sacrifices, he concluded that they must have been abandoned as well. Although the goddess remains important, as the feast of Umiya Mataji recently staged by Patidars proves, Pocock was right in his assessment that a de-centred Hinduism with its 'all-pervading relativism' (1973: 93), rendering those who are superior gods in one context inferior in another, was slowly turning into an 'authoritarian, unambiguous centre in matters of belief' (ibid.). As evidence for this process, Pocock pointed to the changing religious practices of Patidars. The worship of Shiva and *shakti*, the feminine power activating the universe, in which blood sacrifices to the goddess complemented the vegetarian sacrifices offered to her consort, was gradually replaced by devotion to the modern faith offered by the Swaminarayan 'sect' (*sampradaya*) centred upon the god Krishna (Williams 1984).

The Vaishnava movement of the Swaminarayan *sampradaya* arose in the nineteenth century in Gujarat. Initially, it drew most of its followers from Hindu merchant castes. Swaminarayan theology was specifically directed against the worship of goddesses and thus against the ritual pattern of Rajput kingship and power practised in Saurashtra and Kacchch. The rise of the Swaminarayan *sampradaya* was closely connected to the expansion of colonial sovereignty in the region and to pre-existing political differences between mainland Gujarat and the peninsulas of Saurashtra and Kacchch, to which I shall return below. By the 1950s, economically successful Patidars had increasingly joined the Swaminarayan *sampradaya*. Claims to higher social status were bolstered by 'reforming' (*sudharavun*) religious practices. The worship of goddesses, depending on animal sacrifices and low-caste priests, was no longer compatible with Patidar claims to high-caste status. As Pocock pointed out, by rejecting meat offerings in favour of exclusively vegetarian offerings, the 'old', complementary pattern of the pantheon constituted by relatively pure and impure deities was dislocated.

Today, the largest Swaminarayan temple is in London. Patidars and the Swaminarayan *sampradaya* are perhaps the most frequently studied diasporic caste and Hindu movement originating in Gujarat (e.g. Barot 1972, 1987, 2002; Dwyer 1994; Tambs-Lyche 1980).

Distinctions

As mentioned before, Gujarat state is not a natural, homogenous cultural region. Although similar caste names are found across mainland Gujarat, Saurashtra and Kacchch (Shah 1982), local configurations of hierarchy and power evolved from diverse historical constellations. These manifest themselves in a series of distinctions. The first is the distinction between the peninsulas and the mainland in terms of political history. On the mainland, Rajputs, who are representatives of the Kshatriya *varna* category, had lost their traditional status as kings since the fifteenth century. Although in many areas Rajputs still dominated in villages as landholders, on the state level a succession of Sultans, Mughal governors, Mahratta kings and British colonial administrators came to rule. Saurashtra and Kacchch, on the other hand, were ruled until 1948 by a host of Rajput little kings. The largest Rajput kingdoms were those of Kacchch and Nawanagar (Jamnagar) ruled by the Jadeja lineage in the west, and Bhavnagar ruled by the Gohils in the southeast. Though since the nineteenth century Rajput polities had been subjected to Mahratta and British colonial suzerainty executed from the mainland, Rajputs in Saurashtra and Kacchch still retained considerable power and prestige. The second distinction concerns what historians have referred to as 'dual systems of power' on the peninsulas (Spodek 1974: 448). In these kingdoms, political and economic power was divided between Rajputs and merchant elites. While the power base of the Rajput rulers was rural, resting on their control of land and agrarian production, merchants dominated in urban areas and wielded economic power drawn from commercial activities. Although merchants were nominally the subjects of a Rajput king, they enjoyed considerable autonomy. Their profession as traders made them mobile, so that merchants could always counter political pressures with the threat to leave the kingdom and settle elsewhere.

These broad divisions, characteristic of the region, are also reflected in anthropological research on caste in Gujarat. Given that the classical *varna* scheme is taken to provide the reference model for any local configuration of the caste hierarchy, ethnographers encountered a somewhat divergent version in Gujarat. This seemed to further confirm the unlocking of the hierarchical complementarity of the values of purity and pollution in processes of social change. In the early phase of post-independence anthropology, castes attempting to rise in status were thought either to be striving to emulate the norms and standards of conduct of the highest caste, the Brahmans, or those of the former rulers and the West. Srinivas distinguished these processes as 'Sanscritization' and 'Westernization' (Srinivas 1966). For Patidars, however, Pocock noted that it was not Brahmanical norms and practices but those associated with the Baniyas that provided the most highly valued model of lifestyle to which they aspired. A. M. Shah and Shroff made a similar observation, even claiming that the *varna* categories were used in contemporary Gujarat differently from what the textual model suggested (Shah and Shroff 1959). Here, Baniyas, who are Vaishyas according to the *varna* scheme, were accorded a higher status than Rajputs or the Kshatriya *varna* as a whole.

Unlike the treatment of trade and traders reported from elsewhere in India, in Gujarat Baniyas were not 'socially ostracised' (Tambs-Lyche 1997: 225ff.; cf. also Hardiman 1996). Baniyas profess a specific ethos related to their calling as traders. Trading (*vepar*) is a highly valued calling associated with autonomy, contrasted with service likened to 'slavery' (Tambs-Lyche: ibid.). Baniya values emphasize vegetarianism and place great weight on purity, *ahimsa* (non-violence) and asceticism. Following Max Weber, Baniya religiosity has often been compared to Protestantism.

Shah and Shroff attributed changes in the evaluation of traditional status categories to the effects of colonial policies (1959: 62–63). In a study of the history of Rajputs in Kheda District (where Pocock had worked on the Patidars), Shah traced the decline of Rajput status to changing patterns of landholding (Shah 1978). The village was in an area that had come under the sovereignty of Muslim rulers as early as the fifteenth century. The dominant Rajput landowners in this village identified with the Rathod lineage, which encompassed branches of both Hindu and Molesalam (Muslim) Rajputs. The Rathods controlled most of the land jointly, were served by Brahman priests and patronized a range of lower service castes. They also shared specific social and ritual practices, such as employing genealogists to record births, marriages, deaths and other important events in the life of a lineage. When the area came under direct colonial administration, new revenue settlements were introduced in 1860 which brought an end to the joint ownership of land (*wanta*). Since Rajputs thus lost the primary symbol of Kshatriya power, namely land, Shah argued that they also lost the prestige and status associated with it (Shah 1978: 355). Their place in the hierarchy was taken by the Baniyas, who followed more 'sanscritized' practices than the Rajputs, who still consumed meat and offered blood sacrifices to the goddess. Moreover, the Baniyas also excelled in acquiring Western education and wealth. According to Shah and Shroff, the Baniyas' rise in the *varna* hierarchy was confirmed by other castes (such as the Patidars), who now considered commerce and business, the traditional vocation of Baniyas, the most desirable professions, ones to which they now aspired as well.

The proposition that a 'business model' has replaced the traditional 'kingly model' of prestige and conduct in Gujarat rests on the assumption that hierarchy is constituted by power and wealth alone. From a Dumontian perspective, however, such an understanding of hierarchy reflects Western values and categories, whereas Indian notions suggest a different construction of hierarchy, a hierarchy of values. Hierarchy in this sense means that values are segmented, related as superior and inferior, and encompassing. The encompassing quality of this type of hierarchy becomes manifest in the relative relationship between the higher and the lower, which mutually define each other. This kind of logic underlies, according to Dumont, the ranking of the *varna* categories, in so far as their further differentiation into numerous local and regional *jatis* can be encountered in the present. The Kshatriya *varna* (and the Rajput caste) embody the domain of political power and economics, which, in Dumont's interpretation of the Indian hierarchy, is a domain relatively inferior to the superior moral, spiritual and cosmological domains represented by the Brahman priesthood. But the relationship between king and priest is not fixed. In the realm of religion, epitomized spatially by the temple, the priest is superior, whereas in everyday life the priest is dependent upon the king and his gifts.

If we translate this model into empirical realities in Gujarat, it does not fit if one expects to find there the same social categories associated with the same values of purity and pollution as everywhere else in India. In Gujarat, Baniyas came to represent Brahmanical notions of purity. Purity defines practices of vegetarianism, non-violence (*ahimsa*) and forms of (Vaishnava) devotion. This emphasis on purity, on the other hand, does not mean that we are back to the original Dumontian hierarchy structured by complementary relationships between pure and impure categories. Pure status, Shah and others argued, no longer depends on patronising relatively impure servants engaged in removing impurities from the corporeal existence of higher castes, thereby helping them to maintain their purity and superiority. The encompassing dynamic, that is so crucial in Dumont's concept of hierarchy, has disappeared, at least in the contexts considered so far. In the same way in which wealth alone did not lead to a rise in caste status, the reform of practices alone was not sufficient to convince others of one's higher status. If such claims were to be accepted, the reform of practices must be accompanied by education, economic success and the accumulation of wealth. Thus, in modern Gujarat, status is now defined as 'purity + wealth + education'. In terms of hierarchy this would mean that, for those at the bottom, the unlocking of complementarity implied a shift from encompassment to exclusion. Low status, poverty and impurity became parameters of social difference and, ultimately, discrimination and exclusion.

The ethnographies discussed so far have said little about low-status social categories, i.e. castes such as the Dhed, Vankar, Bhangi and others who permanently carry the stigma of being impure and polluting. Since the 1960s, similar processes of upward social mobility as described for Patidars had been observed for at least some sections of those who were formerly described as 'Untouchables' (Parmar 1987). I. P. Desai observed in his survey that untouchability continued to be practised in domestic and religious contexts, although it had lost its influence in the public sphere (Desai 1976). Concerning the concepts of pollution and

Dalit castes in Gujarat, however, Shalini Randeria (1992, 2010) has provided significant further insights that partly confirm and partly contradict Moffatt's (1979) arguments of a consensus among 'Untouchables' that supports the high-caste ideology (see Chapter 16 on Tamil Nadu in this volume). Her ethnography shows that pollution and untouchability are not constructed in a unified discourse but rather involve a plurality of representations (Randeria 1989: 172) and concludes that 'the hierarchical order is based on an exercise of power rather than on value consensus' (ibid.: 189).

Rajput kingship and the absent Brahman

Anthropologists doing research on caste in post-independence mainland Gujarat have focused mostly on the contrast between modern changes and a more or less abstract 'tradition' (closed peasant society, hierarchy). Seen from this perspective, A. M. Shah's historical account of the declining esteem accorded to Rajputs in mainland Gujarat was somewhat exceptional (Shah 1978). What these theoretically diverse works had in common was the explanatory force they attributed to how political and economic constellations were altering social realities pertaining to caste in general and the dominant caste in particular. Often, moreover, transformations observed in mainland Gujarat were contrasted with the more 'traditional' societies of Saurashtra and Kacchch, where Rajputs retained political dominance, prestige and status for much longer. Until the 1990s, however, few anthropological studies dealt with caste on the peninsulas (but cf. Trivedi 1954, 1986). The first comprehensive account of the caste system in Saurashtra and the role of the Rajput kings was published by Harald Tambs-Lyche in 1997 (Tambs-Lyche 1997). My own study of caste, relationships of patronage between bardic castes (Charans) and Rajputs in Kacchch appeared almost a decade later (Basu 2004b). By taking history and people's own ideas about the past into account, these studies uncover 'traditional systems' of caste and kingship, which again depart in significant respects from the Dumontian model of hierarchy and the place of kingship accorded in it (Dumont 1980b).

In the 1980s, Indian kingship became a major concern of anthropologists working in South Asia (Fuller and Spencer 1990; Galey 1989). Dumont proposed the ideological separation of status from power (or religion from politics) as exemplified in the relationship between Brahmans and Kshatriyas (Dumont 1980b). The Brahmans' superiority derives from the value of purity (vegetarianism), the Kshatriyas' relative inferiority from the martial values of heroism, violent action (war), strength and the consumption of meat and alcohol, which render them relatively impure in relation to the Brahman. As a corollary, spiritual values encompass 'secular' (political) ones, which do not represent values by and in themselves. This position was seriously challenged by ethnosociologically-oriented approaches followed by anthropologists, Indologists and historians studying Indian kingship in relation to caste in various regions of the subcontinent or in texts (e.g. Dirks 1987; Inden 1982; Quigley 1993; Raheja 1988a). I cannot enter into this debate in detail here, but the main point of contention concerns the place of power and the role of the king. Most of Dumont's critics have emphasized the centrality of the king and his pivotal role as sacrifier or giver of gifts (*dan*) and thus identified power rather than purity as the main factor for the ranking of castes in a local hierarchy (Dirks 1987). The opposition of purity and pollution, moreover, was disqualified by some of these authors as the principle values of hierarchy and replaced by the dichotomy between auspiciousness and inauspiciousness (Raheja 1988b). Thus, according to Raheja, for those wielding political power, Brahmans were not considered higher because of their inherent purity but were rather treated like any other ritual servants (e.g. like washermen) in being expected to remove inauspicious influences from their masters in exchange relationships (Raheja 1988a: 504).

Turning to Saurashtra and Kacchch, neither ethnosociological nor structuralist approaches offer a single comprehensive perspective to account for the social constellations characterising this region. Apart from the fact that it would be hard to deny the almost passionate concern with the value of purity demonstrated by high-caste Hindus in Gujarat, both approaches share two major flaws: first, neither the concept of hierarchy nor the ethnosociological concepts of power and ritual exchange allow for a recognition of the social and religious pluralism that characterizes these peninsular societies; and secondly, such studies do not pay attention to trade and the role of merchants in systems of caste and kingship (for a detailed critique of this point, cf. Cort 2004). One is therefore not surprised to find very little reference to either school in Tambs-Lyche's ethnohistorical study of the emergence of Rajput states and the caste system in Saurashtra.

A major challenge to Dumont's theory of hierarchy is the notable absence of Brahmans in rituals of kingship (Tambs-Lyche 1997: 271). According to Tambs-Lyche, the absence of Brahmans from royal Rajput rituals of kingship was compensated by Charan bards and genealogists, who mediated the kings' relationship with the state deity in rather unusual ways. Tambs-Lyche worked as an 'anthropologist among historians', to paraphrase Cohn's famous dictum, in exploring the historical emergence of Rajput states. For him, power constitutes the 'central dimension in the construction of the state', though it cannot be divorced from religious concepts (Tambs-Lyche 1997: 9). He stresses that Rajput conceptions of power are entrenched in notions of divine female power or *shakti*. Unlike in other Hindu kingdoms, where a male god, usually Vishnu, installed a king as the protector over people and lands, in this case it is the goddess, or rather *shakti*, who assumed supreme moral authority and the power to 'make kings'. Tambs-Lyche takes this as evidence that the Charans had taken the place of the Brahman priests – or were competing with them – in legitimating the rule of a Rajput king (1997: 268). From the perspective of the Charan bards, Brahman priests were 'corrupted'. Without giving further evidence of the ritual pattern of kingship, Rajput power in Saurashtra was legitimized not from above but by the people from below.

However, this kind of people's orientation as the foundation of medieval Rajput kingship is not supported by the ritual pattern of Rajput kingship. As my ethnographic findings from Kacchch demonstrate (Basu 2010a), in this medieval state, which had been ruled by Jadeja Rajputs since the fifteenth century, it was also a goddess who 'made' the king and who is still worshipped today as the state deity or *deshdevi* (Basu 2004b). As in Saurashtra, Charan bards and genealogists served their Rajput patrons by singing their praises and recording the histories of their lineages, while the goddess was often born in a Charan house (Basu 2004a). But Charans did not replace Brahman priests in the rituals of the goddess, and it is only partly true that the latter were absent from the public celebrations of the goddess during the Navratri rituals performed annually by the king. During the nine days of the festival, the king worshipped *shakti*, the goddess, in her various manifestations. Of crucial importance here were the *kuldevi* protecting the king's lineage and the *deshdevi* protecting his kingdom. Lineage and state goddesses were distinct, as were the locations of their temples. At the temple of the *kuldevi*, Brahman priests served the king. At the temple of the *deshdevi*, by contrast, ascetics belonging to the tantric monastic order of the Kapdia mediated the royal sacrifices offered by the king to the state goddess. In this setting, then, tantric ascetics had assumed priestly functions. The ascetic-priest did not carry out the act of killing the sacrificial animal himself. This was done by a Rajput, while a Charan woman collected the blood from the dying animal and drank it, thereby becoming transformed into an embodiment of the goddess Kali.

During the annual festival of Navratri, the hierarchical order of power was enacted during the royal sacrifice entailing complex ritual exchanges between the king, ascetics of the Kapdia and Kanphata order and the representatives of the various castes settled in his dominion (Basu 2004b: 125ff.). Even though Rajputs no longer wield political power, the model of the sacrificial order of the kingdom is still remembered in bardic poetry, in the books kept by genealogists and through rituals performed in the present (Basu 2004a). Charan bards legitimized the Rajputs' capacities to rule by praising their heroic actions. The relationship is expressed in categories of kinship and gender: the Charan caste is 'sister' to the superior 'brother' caste of Rajputs (Basu 2004b: 122ff.; Tambs-Lyche 1997: 174ff.). In this context, however, the values of purity and pollution played no role. The tantric path of Hinduism practised by Rajputs and the king emphasized the overcoming of dualism (on the Aghoris, see Parry 1994). Relationships between the king and client castes such as the Charan and other pastoralist or servant castes were embedded in encompassing values of loyalty and self-sacrifice. Thus, when a new king was installed on the throne (*gadi*), a Meghval, who would be considered impure from a Brahmanical perspective, blessed the king by placing a *tilak* on the king's forefront with his blood (on the Meghval see Skoda 2002). Here, one is faced with a ritual reversal that seems relatively played down in India because of the concentration on hierarchy.

While the tantric orientation of Hinduism practised by Rajputs and the king was shared by the Charans and other servant castes, the merchants in the kingdom followed distinct paths of religion (Vaishnava, Jain, Muslim). Nevertheless, they attended the royal rituals along with Brahmans. Moreover, in the history of the kingdom of Kacchch, the temple of the state goddess Ashapura was built and rebuilt with donations from merchants, whose diverse religious institutions were in turn patronized and protected by the kings.

Further ethnographic research on rituals of kingship in the society of the peninsulas therefore shows that the apparent absence of the Brahmans should not be confused with an absence of hierarchical values: they were simply relocated. As Burghart had argued against Dumont, according to Hindu notions power is not secular, nor can the Hindu social system be reduced to a single hierarchal formula (Burghart 1978). Instead, on the basis of his work in Nepal, Burghart proposed three distinct models of hierarchy which differ according to the social aspect they focus upon. Priestly, royal and ascetic hierarchies place different categories at the top in each case. These categories may combine locally in different configurations or remain separate. In the regions of Saurashtra and Kacchch, values of renunciation are of paramount importance, being expressed in multiple religious contexts ranging from Jains to specific castes such as the Charan (Basu 2000). The devaluation of Brahman priests noted by Tambs-Lyche must therefore be seen in the light of the values of renunciation. In this case, they rest on the opposition between the sexual reproduction of householders and the renunciation of sexuality by ascetics. In the kingdom of Kacchch, the values of renunciation provided a shared conceptual space beyond purity and pollution. In relation to the king, tantric ascetics, not Brahman priests, represented the superior spiritual domain – although they consumed the sacrificial meat. In this, the tantric orientation of Rajput kingship comes to the fore. Ascetics mediated the king's relationship to the state goddess and controlled the process in which his powers to rule were regenerated.

Multiple hierarchical models, moreover, are not confined to Brahmans, kings and ascetics. In Kacchch people easily switch between several and diverse hierarchical schemes depending upon the context. Charans, for example, perceive themselves as different from the '*varna* castes' (Brahmans, Rajputs, Baniyas) because the first reference for Charan status is the hierarchy of *maldhari*, pastoralists. This hierarchy ranks social categories according to the relative purity of the animals they are supposed to keep. The Ahirs come first because of their traditional profession as herdsmen of the cow, the purest beast, the Charan who raise water buffaloes second, and nomadic Rabari or camel-breeders third; the fourth category, interestingly, encompasses Hindu Bharvads and, significantly, Muslim Jat who both keep sheep and goats. A fifth category, the Meghvals, who process the animal skins and wool they receive from the other pastoralists, are by profession weavers and leatherworkers. Meghvals are considered 'impure' in relation to the other four 'pure' pastoralist castes. Although this hierarchical scheme formally resembles the *varnas*, for the people it is the different content that matters. When we now turn to the merchant estate, we find not only plural notions of hierarchy internal to Hinduism, but also the different hierarchical values of the religious communities of Hindus, Jain and Muslims.

The merchant's difference

Tambs-Lyche proceeded from the observation that Saurashtra is a pluralistic society reflected in the dual systems of Rajput kingship and the merchant estate, as well as in the diverse and coexisting traditions or 'paths' (*marg*) of Hinduism. The merchant estate, however, includes not only Hindu and Jain Baniyas but also Muslim merchants, especially Shia Khojas and Daudi Bohras. While there is a large ethnographic literature dealing with Jain religiosity (e.g. Banks 1992, 1994; Cort 1999; Luithle-Hardenberg 2010; Flügel 2005), comparatively little anthropological research has been conducted on the Shia Ismaili communities of the Khoja and the Daudi Bohra in Gujarat (Blank 2001; Engineer 1989; Misra 1964; Mallison 2001). Beyond their differences of religion and faith, these groups share specific structural features, especially a strongly sectarian social and religious organisation in which the boundaries between caste, sect and religious community tend to collapse. This creates a strong sense of being different. Castes-cum-sects emphasize being different from other castes in their respective religious communities that also engage in business. Baniyas consider themselves superior to Hindu Gujarati Lohanas and Bhattiyas, whereas Daudi Bohras deny sharing 'Muslimhood' with Sunni Bohras and the other Sunni Muslim *jamats* (castes) in Gujarat.

The Sunni Muslim hierarchy

In the last sections of this chapter, I shall now turn to ethnographic research on Sunni Muslims in Gujarat. This will take us to the littoral dimension of the Gujarat region and add other models of hierarchy and caste to those already discussed. Sunni Muslims do not form a homogenous religious community but are divided into numerous endogamous *jamats* related by descent and affinity. They have settled in towns and villages all over Gujarat. Many of them trace their origin to a region beyond Gujarat, typically one situated along an old trading route, either across the Indian Ocean or along one of the long-distance land trade routes leading to the coast of Gujarat. They include Arabs, Makranis (from the Makran coast in Persia), Turks, Bucharians, Africans (Sidi) and those who remember their conversion in the fifteenth or sixteenth century (often from the Lohana caste) by a Sufi saint.

For Dumont, Muslims lived in a society distinct from Hindus because, in terms of values, Islam was a distinctly egalitarian religion. At the same time he admitted that Muslim society in India was influenced by the surrounding Hindu environment (Dumont 1980a: 211). Later on, anthropological research on Muslims in India was promoted by Imtiaz Ahmad who published several collections of articles on caste, kinship, ritual practices and the modernity of Indian Muslims, which included a few articles on Muslims in Gujarat (Ahmad 1976a,

1976b, 1978, 1981; Lambat 1976; Masselos 1978; Pfleiderer 1981; Wright 1976). These amply demonstrated that Muslims were 'stratified' in ranked groupings related by kinship and marriage referred to as *jamat*. The question of values, however, was rarely addressed.

Hierarchical values come to the fore when one looks at the ritual practices of Gujarati Muslims related to the veneration of *pirs* (Sufi saints) and *dargahs* (Muslim shrines), often referred to nowadays as 'old' or 'traditional' Indian Islam. Saints and shrines are arranged hierarchically and overlap with the status ranking of local Sunni Muslim *jamats*. In Gujarat Muslims do share notions of purity and impurity, but they concern the individual and do not generally attach to groups. Descent from the family of the Prophet, closeness or distance to the sacred centre of Islam and purity of blood are all highly valued. They are epitomized in the category of '*aql*, social reason, which is a significant element constitutive of the Muslim person and of social categories. In relation to the individual person, '*aql* is contrasted with *nafs*, the lower component of the human person consisting of sexual desires and selfish emotions in need of control and refinement through '*aql*. '*Aql* is contrasted with non-reason, or rather, with an ambiguous conception of 'holy madness' (*majnun*) known all over the Islamic world (Dols 1992).

Descent, pure blood, closeness to the sacred centre of Islam and '*aql* constitute important principles in evaluating status among Muslims. The Sayyids are followed by those deemed of honourable descent, such as Mughal or Afghan *jamats* supposedly related to former rulers. Foreign descent – in North India categorized as *ashraf* (nobility) – distinguishes higher from lower ('converted') Sunni Muslims. The majority of less prestigious Muslims belong to a range of service castes. A middle rank is accorded to the Sunni merchant *jamat* of the Memon and to the Sunni Bohra *jamat*, who engage in both trade and agriculture (Lambat 1976).

The Muslim hierarchy in Gujarat diverges from Sunni Muslim settings described elsewhere on the subcontinent. Whereas in the Punjab, for example, the bottom of the hierarchy has been identified as consisting of converted untouchable castes (Werbner 1990), in Gujarat it is represented by Sidis, i.e. former slaves from Africa. During my fieldwork in the 1980s among the Sidi *jamat* in Gujarat, they stressed 'holy madness' or 'non-reason' as part of their self-image ('we Sidis are mad') (Basu 1995). Sidis embodying 'holy madness' are contrasted with the Sayyids, who embody '*aql* and exemplary moral personhood.

The category of 'holy madness', moreover, was historically associated with the notion of the slave. Historically, the Muslim system of stratification distinguished between free and unfree, aristocratic and enslaved social categories. Slavery was prevalent in the littoral societies of Arabia and East Africa, where the majority of slaves originated from the African hinterlands. Although in Gujarat labour was organized differently, there were slave markets where African slaves were sold to the landed and merchant elites (Basu 2003, 2008b). Former African slaves (both men and women) were absorbed in the society, mainly as domestic servants. At least since the nineteenth century, a distinct Muslim caste of African origin, the Sidi *jamat*, has emerged in Gujarat. Sidis are specialists of a distinct cult dedicated to African saints closely associated with performances of possession and the healing of demonic illnesses (Basu 2008c).

According to Dumont, the Hindu caste society absorbed outsiders on only two levels: as rulers or as untouchable castes. The difference lies in the degree of permanent impurity attributed to the foreigner. With regard to the Sidi this is a tricky issue because, as in the case of untouchable castes discussed by Randeria (1992, 2010), representations and relationships are multiple and varied. At Rajput courts in Kacchch and Saurashtra in the past, for example, Sidis were even sometimes employed as cooks. But Hindu peasant castes in contemporary Gujarat will not accept food and water from Sidis and will serve them, if the situation ever arises, on separate plates reserved normally for members of untouchable castes. However, the Sidis' situational pollution is not related to their African origins, nor to a specific occupation, but to their status as Muslims. Just as untouchable castes are not perceived as internally differentiated by non-untouchable castes, Muslims, too, are represented en bloc by (some) Hindus as impure because of their consumption of meat.

It is not, however, the Hindu hierarchy and the categories of purity and impurity that provide the frame of reference for representations and self-representations of the Sidi *jamat*. Rather, it is the Sunni Muslim *ummah* or worldwide community of believers with the Sayyid at its apex. Significantly, although Sidis are not treated as 'impure' and 'untouchable' by other Muslims, the relationships between Muslim *jamats* of different status are modelled upon those features of hierarchical interdependence which Dumont proposed as fundamental. As I have demonstrated in my work on the Sidis, the hierarchy of Sufi saints and Islam practised at shrines provides the main frame of reference for Sidi status and their self-representations (Basu 1993, 1995). Like Sayyids, Sidis have inherited and embody charisma in the form not of the powers of *'aql*, but of the powers of non-*'aql*, of 'holy madness', as becomes manifest in Sidis embodying saints in performances of possession.

Patron–client relationships and status competition

As we have seen, patron–client relationships figure importantly in the organisation of agricultural productive labour, in the organisation of a Rajput kingdom and in the production of a regional Sunni Muslim hierarchy. Patron–client (or master-servant) relationships structured interactions between castes in the past and continue to do so in the present, often merging 'secular' and 'ritual' forms of labour and service. In this last section, I shall deal with patron–client relationships in the littoral society of Gujarat and the organization of seafaring through patron–client relationships between merchants and seafarers (cf. Simpson 2006).

Edward Simpson conducted fieldwork in the second half of the 1990s in the shipbuilding yard controlled by the Bhadala *jamat* in Mandvi, an old Indian Ocean port town in Kacchch. Mercantile and maritime activities in Kacchch rested on a division of labour between merchants (*vepar*) and sailors (*khalaasi*) or labourers (*mahjur*) organized along the lines of patron–client relationships: 'Merchants traded from their offices in ports; merchants employed – either directly or on contract basis – a captain and a crew, on whose loyalty they relied; and sailors conveyed goods and occasionally merchants between ports' (Simpson 2006: 31). These class divisions cut across religious differences, as both merchants and sailors belonged to both Hindu and Muslim castes.

Simpson describes how the patronage of shipbuilding and seafaring in this town had shifted from Hindu merchants and sailors to Muslims in postcolonial Gujarat. In this process, formerly modest seamen of the Bhadala caste emerged in the present as wealthy ship-owners and merchants. In the past, Bhatiya merchants had been the patrons of sailors, who came almost exclusively from the Kharva caste. From among Muslim merchants, Khoja had been the patrons of sailors from a range of different Muslim *jamats*. Both gave up ship-building, Khoja merchants in the late 1940s, Bhatiyas in response to the 'oil boom' in the 1970s (see also Simpson 2008). Their position was taken by Bhadalas from among the ranks of former sailors, who became prosperous merchants making fortunes in the 1970s by trading between the free port of Dubai and India (Simpson 2006: 52).

The separation of power from status, Simpson argues, is relevant and very much operational among Muslims in Mandvi, too – by this he means the relationship between economic wealth and social status. The Bhadalas' transformation from a low Muslim caste of seafarers and labourers to powerful merchants, shipbuilders and employers was not accompanied by a corresponding change of status and prestige. Rather, in the hierarchical context dominated by Sayyid values of closeness to the sacred centre, charismatic leadership and learning, the Bhadalas' status remained subordinate. Like Hindu castes, Bhadalas turned to a competitive strategy of status-seeking by stressing the need for 'reform' and investing their new wealth in religious symbols and practices. In the case of Bhadala, this entails a pronounced rejection of the traditional Muslim hierarchy with the Sayyid at the top, which subordinates them. Bhadala ship-owners are especially anti-Sayyid *pirs* and denounce religious discourses of saintly mediation and flows of *baraka* embedded in practices of shrine Islam as corrupt and archaic superstitions (ibid.: 87). 'True' Muslims, by contrast, follow the exemplary life of the Prophet, the *sunnah*, pray in the mosque and need no intermediaries such as Sayyid *pirs* to communicate with god.

This, however, is only half of the story. In his analysis, Simpson shows how the Bhadala are able to enforce their values upon their clients through the labour process in the shipyards they own. In these, a hierarchy emerges which differs from the one dominated by Sayyids, a hierarchy of class (Bhadala capitalists and labourers) in which 'demands and orders [are] given downwards, silence [is] proffered upwards' (ibid.: 85).

In the process of apprenticeship, 'old' hierarchical values are deliberately destroyed. When apprentices enter the shipyard they come with an understanding of themselves, of their bodies and persons, embedded in conceptions of hierarchy suggesting the place of each as ontologically given. In the shipyards, however, this understanding of 'bodies, hierarchy and respect' is challenged, often in violent ways (ibid.). For example, a son of a Sayyid, accustomed to deferential and respectful behaviour towards him by others, is initially subjected as an apprentice in the shipyard to humiliating, disrespectful and sometimes cruel behaviour from the master until he learns the physical and social ways of the shipyard and acts accordingly. Simultaneously and through these practices, the ideas of a reformed Islam are spread. Simpson shows how a religious idiom has interpenetrated the language of building ships (2006: 66ff.). The 'pure' religious ideals and practices of the reformers invoke the mosque and the Quran. Bhadala masters urge their workers to attend religious gatherings and follow the *sunnah*. In such meetings, Sayyid *pirs* 'were often portrayed as "magic men" (although many of the speakers were Sayyid)' (Simpson 2006: 71), and music and drumming on religious occasions were condemned.

Beyond hierarchy

Anthropologists dealing with caste in multiple religious settings in Gujarat have brought to the fore entangled dynamics of changing economic conditions, status competition and transformations in the interactions of different value systems. Arguably, in recent decades these dynamics have turned into religious nationalism. Notwithstanding the great diversity of Islamic traditions and Muslim communities, the ideology of the Hindutva movement constructs them as a monolithic block threatening the Hindu majority. The unfolding of the Hindutva movement in Gujarat in recent decades testifies to the close relationship between processes of cultural modernity, with the central role of the state and nationalism as a major modern ideology (Chatterjee 1995; Veer 1994). At this point, however, I can only summarize the most recent research, which focuses increasingly on the political side. The bulk of the literature on religious politics and violence against Muslims in the state of Gujarat has been produced by non-anthropologists (e.g. Sondhi and Mukarji 2002). Notable exceptions are the studies conducted by Parvis Ghassem-Fachandi (2008), Farhana Ibrahim (2009) and also Simpson. While Simpson's book contains a detailed ethnographic description of the mutual representations of Hindus and Muslims in the town of Mandvi (Simpson 2006), Ghassem-Fachandi has shown how vegetarianism remains crucial to the dissociation of Hindus from Muslims. According to him, the value of vegetarianism has turned 'hyperbolic' and invades the most personal and emotional dimensions of Hindu selves (Ghassem-Fachandi 2009). Having experienced the Muslim pogrom in Ahmadabad in 2002 during his fieldwork, Ghassem-Fachandi presents a subtle analysis of how the effects of violence transformed the social geography of this city (Ghassem-Fachandi 2008). Farhana Ibrahim conducted an 'ethnography of the state' by examining the effects of the political construction of the border between Kacchch and Sindh (India and Pakistan) upon pastoralist Jats in the northern part of the peninsula (Ibrahim 2009).

Conclusion: transformations of hierarchy

Anthropologists have come a long way from the abstract ('static') construction of hierarchy against which Pocock contrasted his findings of a competitive Patidar caste engaged in upward social mobility. Instead of a single model of hierarchy integrating a range of castes according to their status defined by relative purity, coexisting rural and urban systems of power are recognized as having emerged, advancing diverse Hindu and Muslim religious traditions. Hinduism itself has historically emerged as internally plural (cf. Malinar 2010). In this region, Hinduism's plural nature is reflected in the Vaishnava orientation of the merchants and some other castes, and the Tantra (and Shaiva) orientations of Rajputs, Charans and other allied castes. Although Vaishnava 'merchant values' do generally correspond to Brahmanic notions of purity – and one could therefore conclude that the relative impurity of the Rajput pattern of tantric Hinduism would ultimately prove Dumont's claim of a single, pan-Indian hierarchical model right – ethnographic evidence does not support such a conclusion. The heterogeneity of urban, rural and littoral social formations and the pronounced element of competition expressed by the tendency of merchant communities to separate themselves socially from other castes worked against a unified single social hierarchy. As Tambs-Lyche demonstrated, the relationship between merchants and rulers was shaped by rivalry and competition even before the nineteenth century. This kind of competition also fed into popular imaginations of mainland Gujarat as progressive and 'forward' against archaic and backward Saurashtra and Kacchch.

Moreover, the notion of purity itself was not uniform, as Cort has shown for Jain Baniyas. And while the Muslim social order is not based on the opposition of pure and impure social categories, in its Sufi version it still displays the formal features of a hierarchical logic by relativizing sacred bodies. The higher (Sayyid) encompasses the lower (Sidi), and both are contrasted with 'non-sacred' Muslim bodies. Taken together, ethnographic studies of Hindu and Muslim social formations manifest shifting methodological approaches from predominantly cognitive concerns with hierarchical categories to performances embodying, and corporal practices inscribing, diverse values of hierarchy. They demonstrate an ongoing interplay of multiple hierarchies and representations invoking different social and cosmological values and oppositions.

A significant aspect emerging from most ethnographic studies discussed in this chapter pertains to master-servant or patron–client relationships. Because of their central importance in both religious and labour organisations, they perhaps constitute a site where transformations of values become most immediately manifest. The Patidars' route to dominance did not entail emulation of the high-caste patronage of ritual servants, while the Anavils' turn to capitalist farming was accompanied by stripping the relationship of patrons and farm labourers of its moral content. Rajputs have lost the material base for acting as givers of gifts (*dan*), while Charan bards have turned to praising religious leaders and world-renouncing Gurus. The Sayyid *pirs*' authority is challenged by Islamic reformers, and their clients are torn between conflicting loyalties and the demands of employers who are themselves engaged in processes of status rising and upward social mobility.

Hierarchical values are neither immutable nor irrelevant. Gujaratis continuously redefine and contest caste and hierarchical values in a competitive pluralistic social environment. In postcolonial Gujarat, the merchant culture and its values of purity *and* economic wealth have prevailed over plural notions of hierarchy (Tambs-Lyche 1982). The Vaishnava and Jain values of vegetarianism and non-violence (*ahimsa*) had been contained and relativized in the past by the power of Rajput states in Saurashtra and Kacchch, as well as by Muslim states in mainland Gujarat. When this religious pattern of Rajput kingship (non-vegetarianism, regenerative violence and *shakti*) was no longer supported by political power, the values of purity were left to reign supreme, stripped of their former encompassing nature. In this way, first in mainland Gujarat and later in Saurashtra and Kacchch, configurations of values (purity and impurity) became fragmented. In the 1990s, older members of the royal Jadeja house remembered that the heir to the throne had continued to perform the royal buffalo sacrifice (even after he was no longer the ruler of a state) until the late 1960s, when influential Baniyas had urged him to give up this 'low' ritual practice. In 1974, the Gujarat government issued an act valid in all districts which prohibited animal sacrifice. Since then, goddesses as well as many formerly meat-eating castes, including Charans, turned vegetarian. Baniya religious values have risen in the scale alongside the devaluation of other traditions, first of the religious pattern of former Rajput rulers, and secondly of Muslims being turned into an essentialized 'Other'.

Finally, to conclude this chapter it must be noted that there are an increasing number of studies dealing with Gujarati migrants in the US and the UK (Simpson 2011). Although it is common knowledge that both the Hindutva movement and Islamic reform movements in Gujarat receive much impetus from Gujaratis living abroad, there are as yet no serious studies examining the influence of transnational experiences on the transformation of values in Gujarat or in the diasporas.

Acknowledgements

I wish to thank the editors for their careful editing work. My gratitude also goes to Robert Parkin for taking the pain of language corrections as well as providing valuable comments on theoretical points.

Notes

1 See, e.g., 'America's Patel Motels', at http://news.bbc.co.uk/2/hi/south_asia/3177054.stm (accessed 18 September 2010).
2 http://www.bbc.co.uk/programmes/b00kvryj (accessed 18 September 2010).

References

Ahmad, Imtiaz (1976a) 'Caste and Kinship in a Muslim Village of Eastern Uttar Pradesh', in I. Ahmad (ed.), *Family, Kinship, and Marriage Among Muslims in India*. Delhi: Manohar, pp. 319–45.

——(ed.) (1976b) *Family, Kinship and Marriage Among Muslims in India*. Delhi: Manohar.

——(ed.) (1978) *Caste and Social Stratification Among Muslims in India*. Delhi: Manohar.

——(1981) *Ritual and Religion Among Muslims in India*. Delhi: Manohar.

*Banks, Marcus (1992) *Organizing Jainism in India and England*. Oxford: Clarendon Press.

——(1994) 'Jain Ways of Being', in R. Ballard (ed.) *Desh Pardesh: The South Asian Presence in Britain*. London: Hurst & Company.

Barot, Rohit (1972) 'Swaminarayan Sect as a Community', *New Community*, 2: 34–37.

——(1987) 'Caste and Sect in the Swaminarayan Movement', in R. Burghart (ed.) *Hinduism in Great Britain: The Perpetuation of Religion in an Alien Cultural Milieu*. London: Tavistock Publications.

——(2002) 'Religion, Migration and Wealth Creation in the Swaminarayan Movement', in D. F. Bryceson and U. Vuorela (eds), *Transnational Family: New European Frontiers and Global Networks*. Oxford: Berg, pp. 197–213.

Basu, Helene (1993) 'The Sidi and the Cult of Bava Gor in Gujarat', *Journal of the Indian Anthropological Society*, 28: 289–300.

——(1995) *Habshi-Sklaven, Sidi-Fakire: Muslimische Heiligenverehrung im westlichen Indien*. Berlin: Das Arabische Buch.

——(2000) 'Local Concepts of Women Ascetics: Living Goddesses of the Charan', *Journal of Social Sciences*, 4: 313–21.

——(2003) 'Slave, Soldier, Trader, Fakir: Fragments of African Histories in Gujarat', in S. D. S. Jayasurya and R. Pankhurst (eds) *The African Diaspora in the Indian Ocean*. Asmara: Africa World Press, pp. 223–50.

*——(2004a) 'Practices of Praise and Social Constructions of Identity: Charan Bards of Kacch', *Archives de Sciences Sociales des Religions*, 130: 81–106.

——(2004b) *Von Barden und Königen: Ethnologische Studien zum Gedächtnis und zur Göttin in Kacch*. Berlin: Peter Lang Verlag.

——(ed.) 2008a. *Journeys and Dwellings: Indian Ocean Themes in South Asia*. Hyderabad: Orient Longman.

——(2008b) 'Music and the Formation of Sidi Identity in Western India', *History Workshop Journal*, 65: 161–78.

——(2008c) 'A Gendered Indian Ocean Site: Mai Mishra, African Spirit Possession and Sidi Women in Gujarat', in H. Basu (ed.) *Journeys and Dwellings: Indian Ocean Themes in South Asia*. Hyderabad: Orient Longman, pp. 227–55.

——(2010a) 'Navratri Celebrations in Kacchch in the 1990s', in P. Berger, R. Hardenberg, E. Kattner and M. Prager (eds), *The Anthropology of Values: Essays in Honour of Georg Pfeffer*. Delhi: Pearson.

Blank, Jonah (2001) *Mullahs on the Mainframe*. Chicago: University of Chicago Press.

Bouglé, C. (1958) 'The Essence and Reality of the Caste System', *Contributions to Indian Sociology*, II: 7–30.

Breman, Jan (1974) *Patronage and Exploitation: Changing Agrarian Relations in South Gujarat India*. Berkeley: University of California Press.

*——(1985) *Of peasants, Migrants and Paupers: Rural Labour Circulation and Capitalist Production in West India*. Oxford: Clarendon Press.

——(1997) 'Labour Nomads in South Gujarat: Wage Hunters and Gatherers', in G. Shah (ed.), *Social Transformation in India: Essays in Honour of I. P. Desai*. Jaipur: Rawat Publications, pp. 532–80.

Burghart, Richard (1978) 'Hierarchical models of the Hindu social system', *Man*, 13: 519–36.

Chatterjee, Partha (1995) 'History and Nationalization of Hinduism', in V. Dalmia and H. V. Stietencron (eds), *Presenting Hinduism: The Construction of Religious Traditions and National Identity*. New Delhi: Sage.

Cort, John E. (1999) *Open Boundaries: Jain Communities and Cultures in Indian History*. Delhi: Sri Satguru Publications.

*——(2004) 'Jains, Caste and Hierarchy in North Gujarat', *Contributions to Indian Sociology, (N. S.)* 38: 73–112.

Desai, I. P. (1964a) *The Patterns of Migration and Occupation in a South Gujarat Village*. Poona: Deccan College Postgraduate and Research Institute.

——(1964b) *Some Aspects of Family in Mahuva*. London: Asia Publishing House.

*——(1976) *Untouchability in Rural Gujarat*. Bombay: Popular Prakashan.

Dirks, Nicholas B. (1987) *The Hollow Crown: Ethnohistory of an Indian Kingdom*. Cambridge: Cambridge University Press.

Dols, Michael (1992) *Majnun: The Madman in Medieval Islamic Society*. Oxford: Clarendon Press.

Dumont, Louis (1980a) *Homo Hierarchicus: The Caste System and its Implications*. Chicago: University of Chicago Press.

——(1980b) *Homo Hierarchicus: The Caste System and its Implications,* Appendix C: The Conception of Kingship in Ancient India. Chicago: University of Chicago Press.

Dumont, Louis and Pocock, David (1957) 'For a Sociology of India', *Contributions to Indian Sociology,* 1: 23–41.

*Dwyer, Rachel (1994) 'Caste, Religion, and Sect in Gujarat: Followers of Vallabhacharya and Swaminarayan', in R. Ballard (ed.), *Desh pardesh: The South Asian experience in Britain*. London: Hurst & Company, pp. 165–90.

Engineer, Asghar Ali (1989) *The Muslim Communities of Gujarat: An Exploratory Study of Bohras, Khojas and Memons*. Delhi: Ajanta Publications.

*Flügel, Peter (2005) 'Beyond the Hindu Frontier: Jaina-Vasinava Syncretism in the Gujarati Diaspora', *International Journal of Tantric Studies*, 7: 1–43.

Fuller, C. J. and Spencer, J. (1990) 'South Asian Anthropology in the 1980s', *South Asia Research,* 10: 85–105.

Galey, Jean-Claude (1989) 'Reconsidering Kingship in India: An Ethnological Perspective', *History and Anthropology*, 4: 123–87.

*Ghassem-Fachandi, Parvis (2008) 'Bridge over the Sabarmati: An Urban Journey into Violence and Back', *Journeys: The International Journey of Travel and Travel Writing,* 9: 68–94.

——(2009) 'The Hyperbolic Vegetarian. Notes on a Fragile Subject in Gujarat', in J. Bornemann and A. Hammoudi (eds), *Being There: The Fieldwork Encounter and the Making of Truth*. Los Angeles: University of California Press, pp. 77–112.

Gupta, Dipankar (ed.) (2004) *Caste in Question: Identity or Hierarchy?*. New Delhi: Sage.

Hardiman, David (1987) *The Coming of the Devi: Adivasi Assertion in Western India*. Delhi: Oxford University Press.

*——(1996) *Feeding the Baniya: Peasants and Usurers in Western India,* Chapter 4: The Baniya's Life and Faith. Delhi: Oxford University Press.

Hocart, A. M. (1968) *Caste: A Comparative Study*. New York: Russell & Russell.

Ibrahim, Farhana (2009) *Settlers, Saints and Sovereigns*. London: Routledge.

Inden, Ronald (1982) 'Hierarchies of Kings in Early Medieval India', in T. N. Madan (ed.), *Way of Life: King, Householder, Renouncer*. Paris: Editions de la Maison de l'Homme.

Lambat, Ismail A. (1976) 'Marriage among the Sunni Surati Vohras of South Gujarat', in I. Ahmad (ed.), *Family, Kinship and Marriage Among Muslims in India*. Delhi: Manohar, pp. 49–82.

Luithle-Hardenberg, Andrea (2010) 'The Pilgrimage to Shatrunjaya: Refining Shvetambara Identity', in P. Berger, R. Hardenberg, E. Kattner and M. Prager (eds), *The Anthropology of Values: Essays in Honour of Georg Pfeffer*, Delhi: Pearson, pp. 317–30.

Malinar, Angelika (2010) 'Religiöser Pluralismus in Indien'. Zürich: Inaugural Lecture, 4 October 2010.

*Mallison, Francoise (2001) 'Resistant Ginans and the Quest for an Ismaili and Islamic Identity among the Khojas', in V. Dalmia, A. Malinar and M. Christof (eds), *Charisma and Canon: Essays on the Religious History of the Indian Subcontinent*. New Delhi: Oxford University Press, pp. 360–75.

Marriott, McKim (1955) *Village India: Studies in the Little Community*. Chicago: University of Chicago Press.

——(1976) 'Interpreting Indian Society: A Monistic Alternative to Dumont's Dualism', *Journal of Asian Studies,* 36: 189–95.

Masselos, J. C. (1978) 'The Khojas of Bombay: The Defining of Formal Membership Criteria during the Nineteenth Century', in I. Ahmad (ed.), *Caste and Social Stratification among Muslims in India.* Delhi: Manohar, pp. 97–116.

Misra, Satish C. (1964) *Muslim Communities in Gujarat*. Bombay: Asia Publishing House.

Moffatt, M. (1979) *An Untouchable Community in South India: Structure and Consensus*. Princeton: Princeton University Press.

Nandy, Ashis; Trivedi, Shikha; Mayaram, Shail and Yagnik, Achyut (1995) *Creating a Nationality: The Ramianmabhumi Movement and Fear of the Self.* Delhi: Oxford University Press.

Parmar, Y. A. (1987) *The Mahyavanshi: The Success Story of a Scheduled Caste*. Delhi: Mittal Publications.

Parry, Jonathan (1994) *Death in Benares*. Cambridge: Cambridge University Press.

Patel, H. G. (1961) *Status and Prestige by Marriage among the Lewa Patidras of Five Villages in Mehsana District*. Baroda: University of Baroda (MA thesis).

Pearson, M. N. (1998) 'Indians in East Africa: The Early Modern Period', in R. Mukherjee and L. Subramaniam (eds), *Politics and Trade in the Indian Ocean World*. Delhi: Oxford University Press, pp. 227–49.

Pfleiderer, B. (1981) 'Mira Datar: The Psychiatry of a Muslim Shrine', in I. Ahmad (ed.), *Ritual and Religion among Muslims in India.* Delhi: Manohar, pp. 195–234.

Pocock, D. (1957a) 'Inclusion and Exclusion: A Process in the Caste System of Gujarat', *South Western Journal of Anthropology,* 13: 19–31.

——(1957b) 'Difference in East Africa: A Study of Caste and Religion in Modern Indian Society', *Southwestern Journal of Anthropology,* 13: 289-300.

——(1962) 'Notes on Jajmani Relationships', *Contributions to Indian Sociology*, 6: 78–95.

——(1972) *Kanbi and Patidar*. Oxford: Clarendon Press.

*——(1973) *Mind Body and Wealth: A Study of Belief and Practice in an Indian Village*. Oxford: Basil Blackwell.

Quigley, Declan (1993) *The Interpretation of Caste*. Oxford: Clarendon Press.

Raheja, Gloria Goodwin (1988a) 'India: Caste, Kingship and Dominance Reconsidered', *Annual Review of Anthropology,* 17: 497–522.

——(1988b) *The Poison in the Gift: Ritual, Prestations, and the Dominant Caste in a North Indian Village*. Chicago: University of Chicago Press.

Randeria, Shalini (1989) 'Carrion and Corpses. Conflict in Categorizing Untouchability in Gujarat', *Sozialanthropologische Arbeitspapiere, FU Berlin* 21.

——(1992) *The Politics of Representation and Exchange Among Untouchable Castes in Western India (Gujarat)*. Berlin: Freie Universität Berlin (dissertation).

*——(2010) '"We are in the World in Order to Exchange": Mortuary Exchange and Memorialization Feasts among Dalits in Gujarat (Western India)', in A. Bigger, R. Krajnic, A. Mertens, M. Schüpbach and H. W. Wessler (eds), *Release From Life – Release in Life*. Bern: Peter Lang, pp. 177–96.

Shah, A. M. (1978) 'Lineage Structure and Change in a Gujarat Village', in M. N. Srinivas, S. Seshaiah and V. S. Parthasarathy (eds), *Dimensions of Social Change in India*. Bombay: Allied Publishers Private Limited, pp. 339–67.

*——(1982) 'Division and Hierarchy: An Overview of Caste in Gujarat', *Contributions to Indian Sociology, (N. S.)* 16: 1–33.

——Shroff, R. G. (1959) 'The Vahivanca Barots of Gujarat: A Caste of Genealogers and Mythographers', in M. Singer (ed.), *Traditional India Structure and Change*. Philadelphia: American Folklore Society, pp. 40–70.

Shah, Ghanshyam; Rutten, Mario and Streefkerk, Mario (eds) (2002) *Development and Deprivation in Gujarat: In Honour of Jan Breman*. New Delhi: Sage.

Simpson, Edward (2006) *Muslim Society and the Western Indian Ocean: The Seafarers of Kacchch*. New York: Routledge.

——(2008) 'Sailors That Do not Sail: Hinduism, Anthropology and Parochialism in the Indian Ocean', in H. Basu (ed.) *Journeys and Dwellings: Indian Ocean Themes in South Asia*. Hyderabad: Orient Longman, pp. 90–124.

——(2011) 'Two Historians, a Research Society and a Freedom Fighter: On the Life of the Sociological Ideas in the Mesocephalic Province of Gujarat' in E. Simpson (ed.), *Society and History of Gujarat Since 1800: A Select Bibliography of the English and European Language Sources*. New Delhi: Orient Blackswan, pp. XIII–XXXVI.

Simpson, Edward and Kapadia, Aparna (eds) (2010) *The Idea of Gujarat: History, Ethnography and Text*: Hyderabad: Orient Blackswan.

Simpson, Edward and Kresse, Kai (eds) (2007) *Struggling with History: Islam and Cosmopolitanism in the Western Indian Ocean*. London: Hurst & Company.

Simpson, E. and Kresse, K. (2009) 'Mombasa-Mandvi: Exploring the Social Dimension of a Trans-oceanic Axis', Connecting Histories across the Indian Ocean, Goa, 19–21 November 2009.

Singh, K. S. (ed.) (2003) *The People of India: Gujarat*, Vol. XXII. Mumbai: Anthropological Survey of India. Popular Prakashan PVT.LMD.

Skoda, Uw (2002). *Forever Yours: Mobility and Equilibrum in Indian Marriage*. New Delhi: Mosaic Books.

Sondhi, M. L. and Mukarji, A. (eds) (2002) *The Black Book of Gujarat*. Delhi: Manak.

Spodek, H. (1974) 'Rulers, Merchants and Other Groups in the City-States of Saurashtra, India, around 1800', *Comparative Studies in Society and History,* 16: 448–70.

Srinivas, M. N. (1952) *Religion and Society among the Coorgs of South India*. Oxford: Clarendon Press.

——(ed.) (1955) *India's Villages*. Calcutta: West Bengal Government Press.

—— (1966) *Social Change in Modern India*. New Delhi: Orient Longman.

Tambs-Lyche, Harald (1980) *London Patidars: Case Study in Urban Ethnicity*. London: Routledge & Kegan Paul.

——(1982) 'The Merchantization of Saurashtra', *Journal of Social Science* (Dhaka), 16: 39–50.

——(1997) *Power, Profit and Poetry: Traditional Society in Kathiawar, Western India*. Delhi: Manohar.

Trivedi, Harshad R. (1954) 'Some Aspects of Kinship Terminology among the Mers of Saurashtra', *Journal of the Maharaja Sayajirao University of Baroda,* 3: 157–68.

——(1986) *The Mers of Saurashtra Revisited and Studied in the Light of Socio-cultural Change and Cross-cousin Marriage*. New Delhi: Concept.

Veen, Klass van der (1972) *I Give Thee My Daughter: A Study of Marriage and Hierarchy Among the Anavil Brahmans of South Gujarat*. Assen: Van Gorcum.

Veer, Peter van der (1994) *Religious Nationalism: Hindus and Muslims in India*. Berkeley: University of California Press.

Werbner, Pnina (1990) *The Migration Process: Capital, Gifts and Offerings Among British Pakistanis*. Oxford: Berg.

Williams, Raymond B. (1984) *A New Face of Hinduism: The Swaminarayan Religion*. Cambridge: Cambridge University Press.

Wright, Theodore (1976) 'Muslim Kinship and Modernization: The Tyabji Clan of Bombay', in I. Ahmad (ed.), *Family, Kinship and Marriage Among Muslims in India*, Delhi: Manohar.

6 Jammu and Kashmir

Dispute and diversity

Martin Sökefeld

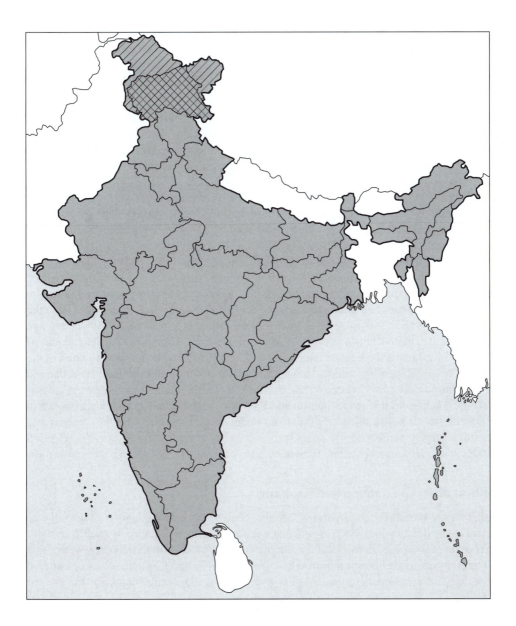

> The spectre of death and state violence haunts Kashmiri civil society each day. Violence is anticipated, experienced, and intimate to lives. (…) Violence permeates daily life, regulates bodies and conditions behavior.
>
> (International People's Tribunal on Human Rights and Justice in Kashmir 2010)

This quotation from a press note of a human rights organization in Kashmir, issued in June 2010, goes on to refer to extra-judicial killings of Kashmiris by Indian armed forces. The note is just one example to contradict the claims that, after the insurgency or the 1990s, 'normalcy has returned to Kashmir'. Particularly in the Kashmir Valley, the expectation and experience of violence is still part of everyday life and while other parts of Jammu and Kashmir State are less directly exposed to violence they are still subject to the predicament of the Kashmir dispute.

Jammu and Kashmir: shared historical and political predicament of a culturally fragmented region

Jammu and Kashmir is perhaps the most controversial region portrayed in this collection. It is an area to which any conception of a 'region' based on cultural, linguistic or even geographical homogeneity can be applied with great difficulties only. As a consequence of the Kashmir dispute it is even not unambiguously clear which geographical tracts are parts of the region. Indian maps generally show the historical State of Jammu and Kashmir as it existed before the partition of the subcontinent in 1947. This region that is politically claimed by India includes large areas which, as a consequence of territorial conflict, are currently controlled by Pakistan and China. This chapter focuses on those areas which are under the present administration of India. Towards the end of the chapter, however, I will have a brief look at Jammu and Kashmir beyond the Line of Control.

Jammu and Kashmir is more characterized by difference than by unity as a region. Roughly, the area currently administered by India is made up of three parts. Jammu in the south consists of plains and hills, including the Pir Panjal range, which separates it from the Kashmir Valley. 'The Valley', as it is often simply called, is a large basin with an average altitude of 2,000 metres between the Pir Panjal and the Great Himalaya. The largest part of Jammu and Kashmir is the high mountain area of Ladakh, situated in the east and north of the Kashmir Valley. Regarding culture, language, religion, ethnicity and similar factors, Jammu and Kashmir is extremely diverse. Abraham (2003), however, argues that a region is created by political action. In this sense, Jammu and Kashmir is established as a region exclusively through the area's political history. Pointedly it can be said that the 'unity' of Jammu and Kashmir is largely produced by its shared predicament of being a disputed area. Therefore an introduction to Jammu and Kashmir would be utterly incomplete without a historical outline.

Political history of Jammu and Kashmir

Kashmiris are proud of '5,000 years of history' (Puri 1997) and Kashmir is famous for its ancient historiography laid down in Kalhana's Rajatarangani, written in the twelfth century, which spans the time from mythical ages to the author's present. In this chapter, however, I will limit myself to the history of the modern State of Jammu and Kashmir, which constituted the region under consideration as a region and which is highly significant for the present dispute.

The State of Jammu and Kashmir is a product of colonial history. It was created out of the remnants of the Ranjit Singh's Sikh Empire in 1846 when, in order to cover what they considered war indemnities, the British sold 'all the hilly or mountainous country with its dependencies situated to the eastward of the River Indus and the westward of the River Ravi including Chamba and excluding Lahul' to Gulab Singh, the Raja of Jammu.[1] Thereby Gulab Singh became Maharaja of Jammu and Kashmir, the largest of British India's 562 princely states. Jammu and Kashmir State consisted of the three provinces of Jammu, Kashmir, and Ladakh and Baltistan. Beside the provinces there was the Jagir of Poonch and the Gilgit Agency. Gulab Singh's Hindu Dogra dynasty ruled the state until 1947. The British considered Jammu and Kashmir as a region of utmost strategic importance because the state bordered on Russian Central Asia. In spite of indirect rule, the British therefore repeatedly intermingled with the government of the state and severely curbed the powers of Maharaja Pratap Singh, Gulab Singh's grandson, by instituting a state council in 1889. British worries about Russian interventions were also the reason for installing a British agent in Gilgit.

The rule of the Maharajas was notorious for the exploitation of its subjects. All agricultural land belonged to the Dogras. Peasants suffered from high taxation and forced labour (begar). In conjunction with untimely rains, the system of revenue which extracted all surpluses from the villages caused a famine in 1877–78 in which large parts of the Valley's population died (Lawrence 2002: 213ff.). While the Maharaja was Hindu, about three-quarters of the population were Muslims who were completely excluded from the administration of the state. Originally, the administration was almost monopolized by Kashmiri Hindus (Kashmiri Pandits), a rather small minority in the Valley. Yet after the establishment of the State Council and further changes in the administration, which included switching from Persian to Urdu as the administrative language, the Pandits who lacked the knowledge of 'modern' administrative procedures were increasingly replaced by Punjabis (Zutshi 1986: 176ff.). The ensuing unrest among the formerly privileged Pandits had significant consequences for the further history of Kashmir because it led to increasingly restrictive formulations of state subject status intended to favour the employment of subjects of the State in public service. Initially, the regulation had many loopholes for non-Kashmiris (ibid.: 184), resulting in the Kashmir for Kashmiris movement by the Pandits, until a more exclusive State Subjects Regulation was issued by Maharaja Hari Singh in 1927. This regulation limited not only public service but also the acquisition of land to state subjects (Rai 2004: 249f.). Still today, the State Subjects Regulation and the connected privileges are an important issue in political struggles about Kashmir.

However, the State Subjects Regulation of 1927 did not help to soften the de facto exclusion of Muslims from education and service. In the 1920s, a handful of Muslims pursued higher education outside of the state, enrolling at Punjab University or Aligarh College. They became the nucleus for a new Muslim leadership in the state. At the same time, Muslim movements outside of the state took increasing interest in what they considered the discrimination of Kashmiri Muslims. The turning point for Muslim political mobilisation in Kashmir was 1931, when, following an alleged desecration of the Quran in Srinagar, events escalated. On 13 July 1931, a Muslim crowd and the police clashed in the city, and general rioting followed. These events are frequently considered as the beginning of anti-Dogra agitation and the freedom struggle in Jammu and Kashmir, yet they can also be seen as the beginning of communalist politics in the state (Zutshi 2004: 211ff). In any case, a new Muslim elite emerged after the events, which included Sheikh Abdullah, the later Prime Minister[2] of Jammu and Kashmir, and this demanded, and to some extent achieved, significant political reforms. Under the leadership of Sheikh Abdullah, Muslims organized politically in the Jammu and Kashmir Muslim Conference, which was renamed in 1939 as the Jammu and

Kashmir National Conference, intending to decommunalize politics and to include Kashmiri Pandits, too. From the 1930s, politics in Kashmir oscillated between mobilization drawing on religious communities and the emphasis of a pan-Kashmiri, plural yet non-communalist identity framed in the concept of Kashmiriyat (see Madan 2006 and Puri 1995).

Limited space in this short introduction does not allow going into the depths of the turbulent developments of the 1940s.[3] With Independence coming closer, the Muslim League and Congress Party took an increasing interest in the affairs of Jammu and Kashmir. Partition of the subcontinent resulted in the first war between India and Pakistan. The war ended on 1 January 1949 with a ceasefire that was mediated by the United Nation's Security Council. Resolutions of the Security Council envisaged a referendum about the future affiliation of Jammu and Kashmir to either Pakistan or India as a final solution of the dispute. However, neither of the states involved was ready to fulfill the preconditions for the plebiscite, which included the demilitarization of Jammu and Kashmir. The continuing result of the dispute is the de facto, though not de jure, division of the state into two Pakistani- (Azad Kashmir and Gilgit-Baltistan) and one Indian-administered section.[4]

Later, in 1956, China also entered the game by occupying a considerable section of Indian-administered Jammu and Kashmir, Aksai Chin (Schofield 1996: 178). In 1963 China acquired a smaller part of Gilgit-Baltistan in the course of a border settlement with Pakistan (Schofield 2000: 101). Kashmiris were marginalized in the politics of Jammu and Kashmir as significant decisions concerning the state were made in the capitals of India and Pakistan.

The Maharaja's terms of accession with India[5] initially secured a special status for the state, laid down in Article 370 of the Indian constitution. Subsequently, however, this special status was increasingly eroded by Delhi (Bose 2003: 68ff.) and today only the continuing application of the State Subjects Regulation remains. Within the Indian Union, Jammu and Kashmir holds an ambivalent position as being both at the margins of India and at the centre of its identity. Being the only Muslim majority state of the Union, Jammu and Kashmir is considered to be a litmus test for Indian secularism. Yet many Kashmiris, not only Muslims, felt increasingly neglected and alienated by India (Ganguly 1997). After the obvious rigging of the 1987 state elections, mass protest grew and was turned, under the leadership of the Jammu and Kashmir Liberation Front (JKLF) and with considerable support by Pakistan, into armed struggle against India. As the JKLF favoured independence of Jammu and Kashmir instead of accession with Pakistan, Pakistan quickly shifted its support to a number of Islamist groups that turned the Kashmiri nationalist struggle into a jihad (Sikand 2001). The 1990s were a decade of extreme violence, especially in the Kashmir Valley.[6] Thousands of people were killed by either militants or Indian military and paramilitary forces. Most of the Kashmiri Pandits left the Valley, settling in Jammu or in Delhi (Evans 2002). Abduction, extra-legal execution and rape became part of the 'game' of insurgency and counter-insurgency.[7] After the late 1990s, Pakistan largely withdrew support from the militants and Islamist violence became less frequent. The JKLF had already renounced armed struggle in the mid-1990s. Still, at least 500,000 Indian troops continue to be stationed in the state. Although Indian observers assumed that Kashmir was on the verge of returning to 'normalcy', discontent and protest has by no means subsided, as a new mass movement emerging in the summer of 2008 showed (Sökefeld, 2012).

The Kashmir Valley is the centre of insurgency. Consequentially, a considerable polarisation between the Valley on the one hand and Jammu as well as Ladakh on the other ensued. In Jammu, militant Hindu nationalists who demand the abolition of the last remnants of the state's special status gained considerable foothold. A political movement of Buddhists in Ladakh struggled for dissociation from the state and, after conflicts with local Muslims, achieved a semi-autonomous status as an Autonomous Hill Development Council. A considerable momentum of political fragmentation notwithstanding, Kashmiri nationalists from all parts of Jammu and Kashmir invoke Kashmiriyat as a culture of diversity and tolerance that provides the fundament of a Kashmiri nation comprising all different communities and spanning all parts of the state, including those under Pakistani and Chinese administration. This is an extension of earlier notions of Kashmiriyat, which were centred on the Valley and Koshur- (Kashmiri) speaking people.

Ethnography of Jammu and Kashmir

For centuries, the valley of Kashmir has fascinated outsiders – South Asian invaders like the Moghuls, and European travellers, explorers and administrators alike. Many reports by European observers are available, starting with François Bernier who visited the Valley in the seventeenth century. A number of reports and gazetteers that contain much useful ethnographic detail have been written by European authors, some of whom were in the service of the Maharaja, during colonial times.[8] Alexander Evans (2008) speaks of Kashmiri exceptionalism as a mode of representation that marks Kashmir – more than Kashmiris – in various ways as unique and that continues from colonial times to the present. In the postcolony this has been most prominently expressed in a great number of Hindi films that portray Kashmir as India's 'territory of desire' (Kabir 2009). While writings in history and politics on Jammu and Kashmir abound, there is a striking scarcity of ethnography. For the last two decades this can be explained by the very unfavourable conditions for fieldwork that have prevailed, given the high incidence of violence by militants and security forces as well as strict control of access by the government. One explanation for earlier ethnographic neglect could be that the dominant theme of the ethnography of India, (Hindu) caste and social stratification, was almost irrelevant for the most prominent part of Jammu and Kashmir, the Valley, because the limited number of Hindus was concentrated in a few caste groups only. All of them were Brahmans and hierarchy is of comparatively little significance among them. The ethnography of Jammu and Kashmir largely falls into three categories: firstly, studies of Kashmiri Pandits (Kashmiri Hindu Brahmans), and more recently also of Pandit migrants and refugees in Delhi; secondly, studies of nomadic Bakkarwals, mobile herdsmen that move between Jammu and the mountains north and east of the Kashmir Valley; and lastly, studies of Buddhists and Muslims in Ladakh. Further, a few articles by anthropologists that deal with the Kashmir dispute have appeared more recently, but this work, although most significant for present situation of the state, is still quite limited.

The ethnography of Kashmiri Pandits

The first and for a number of decades only anthropological monograph on Kashmir was T. N. Madan's study *Family and Kinship: A Study of the Pandits in Rural Kashmir*, originally published in 1965 (Madan 2002). Based on his PhD thesis at the Australian National University, the book is a descriptive ethnography written from a structural-functionalist perspective. Madan, who is a Kashmiri Pandit born in Srinagar himself, studied the Pandits' kinship and social organization in two adjoining villages in South Kashmir, close to the town of Anantnag. In a separate article, he explains that he chose to study 'his own people' as a consequence of intense uneasiness in a fieldwork situation with total (personal and cultural) strangers (Madan 1995: 114ff). At the time of fieldwork, 90,000 Pandits lived in Kashmir, about 5 per cent of the population. The Pandits are mainly divided into two endogamous sub-groups based on occupation: the gor or bhasha took priestly duties, and the karkun, the larger group enjoying higher status and generally a better economic position, followed secular occupations. Both sub-castes are divided into exogamous gotras. Only 20 per cent of the inhabitants of the larger village studied by Madan were Pandits, all of them karkun. There were, however, some gor families in the adjoining smaller village. Madan describes in great detail the composition and developmental cycle of the Pandits' households as well as family relations and marriage patterns, before turning to the household economy. The household (chulah) is the basic structural and functional unit of the Pandit community in terms of social relations, production (including landownership) and consumption. Several households may share a house. Most of the Pandits in the villages live on the produce of their land and government salaries, while some are shopkeepers and servants or labourers. Individual households are part of larger family clusters and patrilineages.

Only in the conclusion of his book does Madan refer to Pandit-Muslim relations in the village. He writes that Pandits are more dependent on Muslims than vice versa because they rely on a number of services which are offered only by Muslims. Still, Pandits and Muslims live largely separately. They neither inter-dine nor intermarry. In a later article (Madan 1984) he focuses also on the Muslims in the main village of his fieldwork. They are divided into three larger categories: zamindars or peasants, nangar or traditional service groups, and herdsmen (Gujjar and Bakkarwal). Each category is made up of a number of sub-categories. The Pandits regard the Muslims as ritually impure and avoid physical contact. They accept only uncooked food from them and do not offer them any services, though Muslim zamindars may be regarded as less impure than members of the service groups (ibid.: 43ff.). In turn, Muslims regard food cooked by Pandits as haram (prohibited by Islam). Both groups largely disregard the internal differentiations of the respective other. Although both Pandits and Muslims emphasize the importance of zat ('jati'), Madan argues that both categories should not be conceived of as being part of a single 'caste system' but that a dual social organization prevails within an overarching framework of being Kashmiri (ibid.: 61).

Since the time of Madan's fieldwork, the situation of the Kashmiri Pandits has changed dramatically. Instead of 5 per cent, they now make up less than 2 per cent of the Valley's population. After the beginning of the insurgency, in early 1990, most of the Pandit families left Kashmir for Jammu, Delhi or other places in India. It is still disputed whether the Pandits' exodus was caused by actual intimidation by the (Muslim) militants or whether they were encouraged to leave by the Indian governor Jagmohan, a 'hardliner' who was deputed to Kashmir by the government in Delhi in order to counter the insurgency. Alexander Evans concludes that the Pandits left out of fear, even if not explicitly threatened by the insurgents, and that the administration did nothing to keep them in the Valley (Evans 2002). Since then the ethnography of the Kashmiri Pandits has had to be turned into the ethnography of exile.[9]

In the late 1990s, Haley Duschinski did fieldwork among Kashmiri Pandits in Delhi. Her unpublished PhD thesis (Duschinski 2004) revolves around the public spaces in the Indian capital in which the Pandit community emerges as a distinct political actor and develops imaginations of community, homeland and nation.[10] She particularly follows the stories told by the Pandits, which are shaped by the interaction between community organizations and state agencies. Through these stories, the Kashmir Valley becomes visible as an '"inconstant homeland": a shifting and unstable place where one might encounter the unexpected and the strange' (Duschinski 2004: 9).

A central actor for Kashmiris in Delhi is the Kashmiri Samiti, a non-profit organization that has helped to manage the large number of displaced Kashmiris in the city, and that through its monthly journal *Koshur Samachar* authors a community discourse of forced exodus and the right to return to the homeland. The journal also disseminated the concept of Panun Kashmir, i.e. the idea of a separate territory for Kashmiri Pandits within the Valley. It portrays the Pandits in a discourse intertwined with Hindu nationalist notions as a unitary community that shares collective subjecthood and nationhood in the allegiance to the homeland of the Valley. Yet this political discourse of a stable belonging to the Valley contrasts with the antinomies of the uncertain and provisional conditions of living and working in the capital's neighbourhoods and markets where identities are contested and have to be redefined and renegotiated, and where city development schemes threaten a second displacement. The political discourse of the Pandits' right to return to the Valley does not correspond to their fragmented stories of violence, loss and uncertainty in which the possibility of simple 'return' appears highly improbable, although some stories seem to open spaces beyond the simple dichotomization of Hindus (Pandits) versus Kashmiri Muslims. Duschinski reports a scene where Pandits and Muslim activists who happen to meet in order to petition their separate agendas in front of the UNHCR office in Delhi start to debate and exchange arguments. While they start accusing one another for the miseries of their respective communities, the argument is concluded in the assertion that both sides have suffered and that 'the government has abandoned us all' (ibid.: 211).

Mobile herdsmen: the ethnography of Bakkarwals

Bakkarwals (literally 'goat people') are Muslim pastoralists who move annually with their flocks of goat and sheep between the hills and plains of Jammu in the winter and the summer pastures in the high mountains of Kashmir. Bakkarwals have been studied ethnographically by Aparna Rao and Michael Casimir. While Casimir focuses largely on the cultural ecology of Bakkarwals like nutrition and the sustainability of pastoral strategies (Casimir 1991, 2003), the work of Rao is related to ethnic identity formation, kinship, gender, life-cycle and concepts of the person, to mention just the major topics. As an 'ethnic group' the Bakkarwals have emerged only since the beginning of the twentieth century from a conglomerate of other groups of pastoralists and peasants, including Gujjars[11] and Awans, who migrated to Jammu and Kashmir from the Kunhar and Allai valleys in what is today the North West Frontier Province of Pakistan. Ethnogenesis was a complex process that took place in a colonial context of power relations and unequal access to resources (Rao 2001). The Bakkarwals' patterns of mobility were strongly affected by the Kashmir dispute because their traditional summer pastures in Gilgit and Baltistan became largely inaccessible after 1947 (Rao 1988). Migration between summer and winter terrains has become difficult in recent decades because of the lack of accessible pasture and fodder en route. Rao states that increased herds, a consequence of higher meat prices, which require the stricter safeguarding of pasture have led to the increasing territoriality of the Bakkarwals' pastoral practices (Rao 1992, cf. Rao 2003). While winter pastures are located below 1,000 metres, summer pastures are situated in the alpine belt up to or even above 4,000 metres. Rich families possess several thousand animals while one hundred animals are considered the minimum to support a family (Casimir and Rao 1985). Bakkarwals are subdivided into a number of kinship groups; they live and move in small groups of several families, all of which generally belong to the same zat (patrilineal clan). The origin of Bakkarwal groups from either Kunhar (Kunhari) or Allai (Alaiwal) is socially significant even to date (Rao 2001).

Rao frames her book-length ethnography of the Bakkarwal (Rao 1998) within the debate about individual and person in South Asia, which revolves around the question of the extent to which human beings in South Asian cultures can be regarded as individuals endowed with agency or whether individual and agency are totally alien concepts in subcontinental cultural worlds. The idea that the individual is not a significant category of the sociology of India was originally proposed, from different theoretical backgrounds, by Louis Dumont (1965, 1970), McKim Marriott (1976, 1989) and McKim Marriot and Ronald Inden (1977), yet it has also been opposed (McHugh 1989, Mines 1994, Sökefeld 1999a). Departing from Clifford Geertz's (1993: 5) conceptualization of the human being as 'an animal suspended in webs of significance he himself has spun', Rao endeavours to identify the 'webspinners' among the Bakkarwals, 'to enquire into their genesis, to discuss their growth, their life and death' (Rao 1998: 3). She is quick, however, to point out that not all individuals among the Bakkarwal are recognized by others as such 'spiders', endowed with agency, which 'spin the web'. The book is based to a great extent on the analysis of local concepts of procreation, socialization, gender and the life-cycle. Linked to norms and values they are expressed and symbolized in rites that transform the 'individual individual' (shakas) into a 'social/communal individual' (banda) and enable the reproduction of the community. Connected to others in camps and kinship groups, Bakkarwal households strive to find a balance between independence and cooperation (ibid.: 243). In this context, agency and well-being are closely related: the ability to take the right decisions enables well-being, and well-being in turn is seen as evidence of superior knowledge, prudence and legitimate authority (ibid.: 245 ff). According to Rao, individualism and holism are two sides of the same coin among Bakkarwals; agency needs to be conceived of as being grounded in social context.

The ethnography of Ladakh

Of all the regions of Jammu and Kashmir, Ladakh, the high mountain area beyond the Valley, has attracted by far the largest ethnographic attention. Ladakh lies mostly above 3,000 metres and has very little precipitation. It is a sparsely populated high mountain desert in which agriculture is restricted to irrigation oases.

While Ladakh is often popularly – and also academically – perceived as a Buddhist region,[12] about half of the population is in fact Muslim. Martijn van Beek and Fernanda Pirie (2008) observe that the scholarship of Ladakhi culture and society occupies an ambiguous disciplinary position between Tibetan and South Asian studies. Politically, however, the South Asian context is dominant and includes the uneasy and contested relationship of Ladakh with Jammu and Kashmir.

Both Muslims and Buddhists in Ladakh are subdivided into different religious communities. Among Muslims, for instance, there are Sunnis, Shias and Nurbakhshis. The Nurbakhshis are a small Muslim community related to a Sufi order that was brought to Kashmir in the late fifteenth century by Shams ud-Din Iraqi. Nurbakhshis survived only in Ladakh and Baltistan and merged elsewhere into the mainstream Twelver Shia (Rieck 1995). In 1979 Ladakh was divided into two districts, Leh and Kargil. Leh is dominated by Buddhists and Kargil has a majority of (Shia) Muslims. For many years Ladakh has seen various political movements that sought to distance Ladakh from Jammu and Kashmir by demanding the recognition of Ladakhi language and identity and political autonomy for the region. Sometimes, these movements operated along religious lines, pitting Buddhists against Muslims. Accordingly, relationships between Buddhists and Muslims are a major topic of the ethnography of Ladakh. In 1995, the area was finally granted autonomous status within Jammu and Kashmir as Ladakh Autonomous Hill Development Council. Ethnographies have focused on different valleys and regions of Ladakh, including the Nubra and Shyok Valleys (Srinivas 1998), Kargil (parts of Aggarwal 2004), Suru (Grist 1999), Zanskar (Gutschow 2004) and Leh (van Beek 1996).

Martijn van Beek's unfortunately still unpublished PhD dissertation is a political ethnography of the developments that led to the establishment of Ladakh's new status as Autonomous Hill Development Council (van Beek 1996).[13] He traces the 'grammars of identification and representation' of Ladakh in the political and bureaucratic sphere; elaborating a concept of 'identity fetishism' that refers to the hegemonic imagining of discreet and unambiguous 'groupness' which operates in both political and academic practice. Focusing on the 'social boycott' that was imposed from 1989 to 1992 by the Ladakh Buddhist Association on Muslim Ladakhis in the course of the demand for Union Territory Status, van Beek seeks an answer as to why the agitation followed communal lines. The boycott defined Sunni Muslims especially as 'outsiders' and sought to prevent inter-dining, intermarriage and social interaction in general of Buddhists with Muslims in Ladakh. Van Beek analyses three distinct but interlinked processes of 'constructing' Ladakh: the bureaucratic demarcation and representation of Ladakh and Ladakhis, the classification of Ladakh's population in the Census of India, and the academic construction of Ladakh as being 'Buddhist'. He then looks at how local actors articulate their politics of difference within this framework, claiming unity and homogeneity while suppressing internal difference and heterogeneity. In this context, a (self-)representation of Ladakhis as poor and backward but innocent and patriotic evolves against a depiction of a Kashmir government that is inherently communal and anti-Ladakhi. Van Beek shows that although communal ideas were already present in Ladakh since the 1930s, mobilisation along communal lines in the 'social boycott' agitation of 1989 was by no means 'natural' but required careful organization. He points out that the 'solution' for the demands for autonomy, the institution of the Ladakh Autonomous Hill Development Council, did not overcome the fragmentation engendered by the politics of difference but rather institutionalized it by dividing Ladakh into separate constituencies, reserving seats for particular 'minorities' and by, in fact, multiplying the opportunities for communal articulation and mobilization.

Other ethnographies that address political conflict in and about Ladakh include Ravina Aggarwal's *Beyond Lines of Control* (Aggarwal 2004) and Fernanda Pirie's *Peace and Conflict in Ladakh* (Pirie 2007). Drawing mainly on fieldwork in a village close to the Line of Control, Aggarwal analyses diverse kinds of cultural and political performances in Ladakh, including Independence Day celebrations, village rituals and archery shows. She observes how the separation of religious communities increasingly invaded different areas of life and shows how rituals have become sites to contest and negotiate status and power. Pirie's (2007) book is about how order is maintained in a society that changes quickly under pervasive outside influences. Combining rural and urban ethnography, she analyses concepts of social order and practices of conflict resolution in a context of intersecting power relations. Smriti Srinivas's ethnography (Srinivas 1998) is set in two villages in the Nubra region, a rather peripheral part of Ladakh that is separated from the Indus Valley by the Ladakh range. Both villages have a Buddhist majority and Muslim minority population. Srinivas focuses on households and social integration within and across the villages and shows that households are drawn into what she calls 'political patrilinies' (ibid.: 106ff.), i.e. regional organizations of Buddhists and Muslims. The Ladakhi Buddhist Association, especially, with its local representation had a growing influence on social organization and relationships within the villages.

The ethnography of Ladakh is too voluminous and diverse to be adequately surveyed in the limited space available here.[14] As just one significant example of ethnography beyond the dominant political framework that has been stressed so far, Kim Gutschow's monograph on Buddhist nuns in Zanskar deserves to be mentioned (Gutschow 2004). The book gives a unique insight into relations of gender and inequality within the Ladakhi Buddhist context. Drawing on a concept of the economy of merit, Gutschow analyses the rather miserable living conditions of the nuns: donations confer moral/religious merit on the donor, but the measure of merit acquired by a donor depends on the moral position of the recipient. Thus, donations tend to be concentrated on those monks and monasteries that are regarded as most prestigious. As women, including nuns, are regarded as less prestigious than men, nunneries receive very few donations. Nuns are therefore required to work for their own subsistence and have much less time for religious teaching and practice, which in turn limits their ability to acquire merit and donations. The economy of merit thus sustains gender and general social inequality. Recently, however, Buddhist feminism has questioned this inequality and certain changes appear to be forthcoming.

The ethnography of violence in Kashmir

Since 1989, Jammu and Kashmir – not only the Kashmir Valley – has been the site of violent insurgency and counterinsurgency. The militantly voiced demand for 'freedom' (azadi) on part of the insurgents has been countered by the Indian state and its forces with strict repression and violence, torture, disappearance and extrajudicial executions (Human Rights Watch 2006). The conflict has disrupted normal life to the extreme and after more than twenty years, normalcy has not returned. In particular, the Valley continues to be highly militarized. If anything, the conflict has increased polarization between the Indian state and the Kashmiri population. In spite of all attempts by the state to silence and repress discontent, grievances and protests are easily taken to the streets, especially in the cities. Thus, daily life is not only frequently interrupted by actual instances of violence but also by demonstrations, strikes and curfews.

Most of the ethnographies referred to in this chapter have noted the pervasive and disrupting consequences of the Kashmir dispute – that is, the conflict between India and Pakistan as well as the militant insurgency in Jammu and Kashmir and its repression by Indian forces – for culture and society in the state. The seasonal migration of the Bakkarwal was strongly affected by the closure of the 'ceasefire line', the later Line of Control, and also by the more recent militancy. Madan deplores the forced migration of the Pandits from the Kashmir Valley and Duschinski analyses the consequences of this migration in the Kashmiri community in Delhi. The disputed and unstable condition of Jammu and Kashmir is a very significant context for political movements in Ladakh, too. Aggarwal (2004: 51) notes that during the Kargil war of 1999 Kargili refugees in Leh were dubbed 'Pakistani agents'. Even Gutschow, in her ethnography of Ladakhi Buddhist nuns, points out that 'the militant struggle for political autonomy in Jammu and Kashmir has brought religious identities to center stage' (2004: 254f).

Yet such references notwithstanding, the violence of the Kashmir dispute itself, rather than its consequences, has only rarely been made an object of anthropological study. Addressing Kashmir together with the insurgency in the Punjab, Cynthia Mahmood (2000) enquires into the dynamics of terror. She points out that counterinsurgent violence does not only aim at 'technically' quelling the rebellion but at humiliating the subjected population. Sexual violence is a frequently employed strategy and similarly the purpose of torture is not restricted to the elicitation of information but intends the destruction of the victims' selves and self-respect. Mahmood concludes that both acts of 'terrorism' and of 'counterterrorism' are more expressive than instrumental. She notes that 'acts of state terror like torture and the bombing of religious places are more than simple military tactics, that responses to them resonate with meanings far beyond the strategic, and state responses to insurgent violence again cannot be really understood as pragmatic politics. To understand them as forms of performance or ritual, while risking trivialization of the bloodshed involved, is an important antidote to the hyperrational war discourse that merely skims the surface of the violent area' (Mahmood 2000: 82).

Duschinski also points to the 'real social suffering' that militarization produced for the local population (Duschinski 2009: 693). In Kashmir, security governance legitimizes the suspension of legal, political and cultural rights. Special acts allow the state forces to arrest people without warrant and even to kill people if that is deemed necessary for the maintenance of 'public order'. The pervasive presence of Indian forces 'produces a collective experience of being under siege, subjected to a military occupation of home and homeland' (ibid.: 705). People are living in a constant situation of threat and insecurity, effected by the 'security forces' that may stop, search and arrest persons at any time, without judicial control or challenge. Drawing on encounters with human rights activists in Kashmir, Duschinski notes that 'the realities of war leave Kashmiris with no real choices. Simply being Kashmiri – living under conditions of permanent captivity, existing in a state of social abandonment, struggling day after day to breathe – is itself framed as an act of resistance, presented as evidence or proof of terror. In this war against the people, Kashmiris by virtue of their existence are transformed into terrorists, enemies of the state' (ibid.: 712).

In another article Duschinski focuses on 'fake encounters' in Kashmir (Duschinski 2010). A fake encounter is an extrajudicial killing of civilians by the state forces legitimized by the claim that the victim was a terrorist or an infiltrator from Pakistan who was killed in a military 'encounter'. Over the years it has become clear that many of the 'terrorists' who were killed by Indian troops in Kashmir were in fact 'ordinary people'. Duschinski analyses the situation in Kashmir with reference to Giorgio Agamben's notion of 'states of exception' (Agamben 2005) in which the sovereign power of the state operates to the extent of stripping the state's subjects of their rights and reducing them to 'bare life'. The sovereign becomes absolute, beyond accountability, and the distinction of the legal and the illegal is blurred. In the resulting regime of impunity, the violence of the state is not a secret affair; it is 'part and parcel of the way in which sovereignty is practiced' (Duschinski 2010: 119). Still, in Jammu and Kashmir the sovereignty of the state has not yet become absolute but is challenged by media and sometimes even by the judiciary. Duschinski refers to cases in which it was revealed that persons who had been killed in fake encounters were in fact not militants. Media disclosed that the police and army kill their victims in order to claim awards and promotions. It is significant that in the Indian mainstream media these cases are not reported as elements of the state's policy and strategy but as the actions of some individual aberrant criminal officers. For Kashmiris, however, it is clear that 'state agents who kill civilians in order to receive bounties and stars are acting, not outside of the law, but rather inside of its interstices and folds, within a system that effectively legitimizes violence and terror against and among Kashmiris in the name of the national effort to protect public safety and public order' (ibid.: 125).

Jammu and Kashmir beyond the Line of Control

In spite of strict control and surveillance, the Line of Control between Indian- and Pakistani-dominated parts of Kashmir is porous. While India points to the infiltration of militants from the Pakistani side, many Kashmiris took shelter in refugee camps in Azad Jammu and Kashmir (AJK) because of the insecure situation in Indian-administered Jammu and Kashmir.

Cabeiri deBergh Robinson who did ethnographic research with refugees from the Indian side, mainly in Muzaffarabad District (Robinson 2005), comes to the conclusion that both phenomena, hijrat (flight, migration) and jihad (struggle) are closely interlinked – although not in the straightforward way in which it is often assumed that refugee camps are simply training grounds of 'Islamic fundamentalists'. On the basis of life-history interviews with muhajirs (refugees) and mujahids (warriors) – or muhajirs turned mujahids – Robinson spells out the ambiguities of her interlocutors' subjectivity in local, national and transnational contexts. She argues that the shift towards jihad is an outcome of 'sustained but failed attempts to engage the "international community" through an appeals [sic] for protection in the language of universal human rights. In Kashmir, the conception of jihad as a continuum of moral engagement with the production and maintenance of just society is marked by an emphasis on social evaluations founded in the moral structure of the refugee family. Militant and jihadist organizations have taken up the organization of jihad as a project of protecting human rights rather than territorial sovereignty' (ibid.: 455).

India claims the whole of Jammu and Kashmir as its 'integral part', including those areas that are currently under the control of other states. Similarly, Pakistan argues that, being Muslim majority territory, the whole of the erstwhile state awaits accession with Pakistan. Kashmiri nationalists who struggle for the independence of Jammu and Kashmir from both India and Pakistan emphasize that current political division and cultural diversity notwithstanding, Kashmir is basically a nation that needs to be territorially united. My look beyond the Line of Control, which nationalists refer to as the 'line of division', is not meant as acceptance of the legitimacy of any of these claims but rather as recognition that under the current conditions any portrait of the 'region' that is restricted to only one side of the Line of Control remains incomplete.[15]

Pakistani-administered Jammu and Kashmir is divided into two politically and ethnographically very different parts. On the one hand there is AJK, a narrow tract of hilly territory to the west of Jammu and the Kashmir Valley, and on the other hand there is Gilgit-Baltistan, a vast and sparsely populated high mountain area. While AJK is formally a separate state that has entrusted only some competences like currency and defence to Pakistan, Gilgit-Baltistan is directly ruled by the government of Pakistan.[16] Due to its ambiguous status and the propinquity of the Line of Control access to AJK is highly restricted. Until now, DeBergh Robinsons's dissertation is the only ethnographic work situated there. Gilgit-Baltistan, in contrast, is much more accessible – it is the ethnographically best-known part of Jammu and Kashmir beside Ladakh. However, the categorization of Gilgit-Baltistan as part of Jammu and Kashmir is rejected by a significant local political perspective which emphasizes that in 1947 the people of the area fought successfully for freedom from Kashmir (Sökefeld 1997b, 1999b, 2005). According to this perspective, Gilgit-Baltistan is not part of Jammu and Kashmir but only part of the Kashmir dispute.

There is a significant body of colonial ethnography of the region.[17] Since the 1950s, a strong German anthropological research focus developed on the area that was established within a specific cultural-historical framework by Karl Jettmar (1960a, 1960b, 1980) but has subsequently completely changed its scope and theoretical perspective. Politics in the broadest sense, including ethnicity, sectarianism and general political history, are at the centre of ethnographic attention to the area.[18] More recently, ethnographies of Gilgit town focused on women, kinship and space (Gratz 2006) and on the medical situation of women in the context of sectarian conflict (Varley 2010).

Conclusion

At the outset of this chapter I emphasized that Jammu and Kashmir does not fit easily with a concept of 'region'. The great cultural diversity within and across more readily identifiable 'sub-regions' like Jammu, the Kashmir Valley, Ladakh or Gilgit-Baltistan is mirrored by multifaceted ethnographic topics and interests. Historically, the 'unity' of the 'region' was established by the colonial creation of Jammu and Kashmir State under Maharaja Gulab Singh with the help of the British and had been prefigured already by the Dogra's conquest of Ladakh. Today, culturally definable sub-regions are divided by the Line of Control, which separates southern AJK from Jammu, northern AJK from the Kashmir Valley and Baltistan from Ladakh. Given the pervasiveness of disputes within Jammu and Kashmir, it is not surprising that much ethnography of the area is characterized by a political focus. It can be concluded that the 'region' is ultimately held together by its disputes and that the Line of Control not only divides Jammu and Kashmir but also holds it together in a shared condition.

Notes

1 The transfer of Kashmir was part of the Treaty of Amritsar. For the full text of the treaty, see Anand 2004: 342f. Under the treaty, Gulab Singh had to pay 7.5 million rupees for Kashmir.
2 As a token of Jammu and Kashmir's special status within the Indian Union, the head of the state's government was called Prime Minister and not Chief Minister as in the rest of the Indian states. Similarly, there was a President of Jammu and Kashmir and not a Governor. In the course of Jammu and Kashmir's further integration in the Indian Union, these special offices were abolished in 1965 (Bose 2003: 81f).
3 One of the best accounts of the events in the 1940s is still Bazaz 1954.
4 On the war between India and Pakistan and the involvement of the Security Council see Das Gupta 1968, Dasgupta 2002 and Korbel 1966.
5 For the sake of completeness it needs to be added that the accession of late October 1947 is not undisputed. Many Kashmiri activists deny that the Maharaja possessed the competence of signing an instrument of accession as the political movement of 1947 had effectively dethroned Hari Singh. Further, some historians dispute on the basis of a meticulous analysis of sources and events that Hari Singh indeed signed the instrument of accession on 26 October, as is claimed by India. See, for instance, Lamb 1997, chapter 6, and Schofield 1996, 148ff.
6 For a chronicle of events, see Joshi 1999.
7 See Human Rights Watch 2006.
8 Among the most prominent instances of this literature are Hügel 2000 [1845], Drew 1980 [1875], Lawrence 2002 [1895] and Knight 1991 [1905].
9 Pandits had emigrated from Kashmir long before the twentieth century. See Sender 1988 for an account of Pandit settlements in different parts of northern India.
10 Parts of the dissertation have been published in separate articles, see Duschinski 2007 and 2008.
11 Some of the publications refer also to Gujjars in Kashmir. See Rao 1999 and Casimir and Rao 2008.
12 For the construction of Ladakh as 'essentially Buddhist' see van Beek 1996: 141ff.
13 See also van Beek 2000a, 2000b, 2003; van Beek and Bertelsen 1997.
14 The collections edited by van Beek, Bertelsen and Pedersen (1999) and van Beek and Pirie (2008) give a good impression of the broad diversity of Ladakh studies.
15 Because there is no ethnography of the territories under Chinese rule this section must be limited to the parts of Kashmir that are controlled by Pakistan.
16 As a separate state, AJK is, however, not recognized by any other state and the ultimate control of AJK affairs is executed by Pakistan. See Asif 2006; Hussain 2005; and Rose 1992 on the political status of AJK.
17 See, for instance, Leitner 1985 [1889] and Biddulph 1971 [1880]. D. L. R. Lorimer's material has been published by Müller-Stellrecht (1979, 1980). Both Biddulph and Lorimer served as British Political Agents in Gilgit.
18 Examples are Frembgen 1985, Stellrecht 1998, Sökefeld 1997a, 1998, Lentz 2000.

References

Abraham, Itty (2003) 'State, Place, Identity: Two Stories in the Making of Region', in Sivaramakrishnan, K. and Agrawal, A. (eds), *Regional Modernities: The Cultural Politics of Development in India*. Stanford: Stanford University Press, pp. 404–25.

Agamben, Giorgio (2005) *State of Exception*. Chicago: University of Chicago Press.

*Aggarwal, Ravina (2004) *Beyond Lines of Control: Performance and Politics on the Disputed Borders of Ladakh, India*. Durham: Duke University Press.

Anand, A. S. (2004) *The Constitution of Jammu and Kashmir: Its Development and Contents*. Delhi: Universal Law Publishing.

Asif, Bushra (2006) 'How Independent is Azad Jammu and Kashmir?' in Sidhu, Waheguru Pal Singh, Asif, Bushra and Samii, Cyrus (eds), *Kashmir: New Voices, New Approaches*. London: Lynne Rienner, pp. 33–48.

Bazaz, Prem Nath (1954) *The History of Struggle for Freedom in Kashmir*. New Delhi: Kashmir Publishing Company.

Biddulph, John (1971 [1880]) *Tribes of the Hindoo Koosh*. Graz: Akademische Druck- und Verlagsanstalt.

*Bose, Sumantra (2003) *Kashmir: Roots of Conflict, Paths to Peace*. Cambridge, MA: Harvard University Press.

Casimir, Michael J. (1991) *Flocks and Food: A Biocultural Approach to the Study of Pastoral Foodways*. Köln: Böhlau.

——(2003) 'Pastoral Nomadism in a West Himalayan Valley: Sustainability and Herd Management', in Rao, Aparna and Casimir, Michael J. (eds), *Nomadism in South Asia*. Delhi: Oxford University Press, pp. 81–103.

Casimir, Michael J. and Rao, Aparna (1985) 'Vertical Control in the Western Himalaya: Some Notes on the Pastoral Ecology of the Nomadic Bakrwal of Jammu and Kashmir', *Mountain Research and Development*, 5: 221–32.

——(2008) 'A Black Dog's Gaze: Some Insights into the Mortuary Rites and Conceptual Transformations among the Gujar and Bakkarwal of the Kashmir Valley', in Rao, Aparna (ed.), *The Valley of Kashmir: The Making and Unmaking of a Composite Culture?*. Delhi: Manohar, pp. 401–87.

Das Gupta, Jyoti Bhusan (1968) *Jammu and Kashmir*. The Hague: Martinus Nijhoff.

Dasgupta, C. (2002) *War and Diplomacy in Kashmir, 1947–1948*. New Delhi: Sage.

Drew, Frederic (1980 [1875]) *The Jammoo and Kashmir Territories: A Geographical Account*. Karachi: Indus Publications.

Dumont, Louis (1965) 'The Functional Equivalent of the Individual in Caste Society', *Contributions to Indian Sociology*, 8: 85–99.

——(1970) 'The Individual as an Impediment to Sociological Comparison and Indian Sociology', in Dumont, Louis, *Religion, Politics and History in India: Collected Papers on Indian Sociology*. The Hague: Mouton, pp. 133–50.

Duschinski, Haley (2004) 'Inconstant Homelands: Violence, Storytelling, and Community Politics among Kashmiri Hindu Migrants in New Delhi, India'. Department of Anthropology, Harvard University (unpublished PhD thesis).

——(2007) '"India Displacing Indians for the Sake of India": Kashmiri Hindu Migrant Vendors and the Secular State', *Political and Legal Anthropology Review*, 30: 90–108.

——(2008) '"Survival is Now Our Politics": Kashmiri Hindu Community Identity and the Politics of Homeland', *International Journal of Hindu Studies*, 12: 41–64.

——(2009) 'Destiny Effects: Militarization, State Power, and Punitive Containment in Kashmir Valley', *Anthropological Quarterly*, 82: 691–718.

*——(2010) 'Reproducing Regimes of Impunity: Fake Encounters and the Informalization of Everyday Violence in Kashmir Valley', *Cultural Studies*, 24: 101–32.

Evans, Alexander (2002) 'A Departure from History: Kashmiri Pandits, 1990–2001', *Contemporary South Asia*, 11: 19–37.

——(2008) 'Kashmiri Exceptionalism', in Rao, Aparna (ed.), *The Valley of Kashmir: The Making and Unmaking of a Composite Culture?*. New Delhi: Manohar.

Frembgen, Jürgen (1985) *Zentrale Gewalt in Nager (Karakorum): Politische Organisationsformen, ideologische Begründungen des Königtums und Veränderungen in der Moderne*. Stuttgart: Steiner.

Ganguly, Sumit (1997) *The Crisis in Kashmir: Portends of War, Hopes of Peace*. Cambridge: Cambridge University Press.

Geertz, Clifford (1993) *The Interpretation of Cultures*. London: Fontana Press.

Gratz, Katrin (2006) *Verwandtschaft, Geschlecht und Raum: Aspekte weiblicher Lebenswelt in Gilgit/ Nordpakistan*. Köln: Köppe.

Grist, Nicola (1999) 'Twin Peaks: The Two Shiite Factions of the Suru Valley', in Van Beek, Martijn; Bertelsen, Kristoffer Brix and Pederson, Poul (eds), *Ladakh: Culture, History, and Development between Himalaya and Karakoram*. Aarhus: Aarhus University Press, pp. 131–52.

Gutschow, Kim (2004) *Being a Buddhist Nun: The Struggle for Enlightenment in the Himalayas*. Cambridge, MA: Harvard University Press.

Hügel, Baron Charles (2000 [1845]) *Travels in Kashmir and the Panjab, Containing a Particular Account of the Government and Character of the Sikhs*. Delhi: Low Price Publications.

Human Rights Watch (2006) *"Everyone Lives in Fear:" Patterns of Impunity in Jammu and Kashmir*. New York: Human Rights Watch. Available at: http://www.hrw.org/en/reports/2006/09/11/everyone-lives-fear (accessed 15 October 2009).

Hussain, Rifaat (2005) 'Pakistan's Relations with Azad Kashmir and the Impact on Indo-Pakistani Relations', in Dossani, Rafiq and Rowen, Henry S. (eds), *Prospects for Peace in South Asia*. Delhi: Orient Longman, pp. 109–37.

International People's Tribunal on Human Rights and Justice in Kashmir (2010) *Fake Encounters and State Terror in Kashmir*. Press Release. Available at: http://www.kashmirprocess.org/reports/ machil/pressrelease.html (accessed 11 June 2010).

Jettmar, Karl (1960a) 'The Cultural History of Northwest Pakistan', *Yearbook of the American Philosophical Society*, 492–99.

——(1960b) 'Soziale und wirtschaftliche Dynamik bei asiatischen Gebirgsbauern (Nord-West Pakistan)', *Sociologus*, 10: 120–38.

——(1980) *Bolor and Dardistan*. Islamabad: Lok Virsa.

Joshi, Manoj (1999) *The Lost Rebellion: Kashmir in the Nineties*. New Delhi: Penguin.

*Kabir, Ananya Jahanara (2009) *Territory of Desire: Representing the Valley of Kashmir*. Minneapolis: University of Minnesota Press.

Knight, E. F. (1991 [1905]) *Where Three Empires Meet: A Narrative of Recent Travel in Kashmir, Western Tibet, Gilgit, and the Adjoining Territories*. Lahore: Sang-e-Meel.

Korbel, Josef (1954) *Danger in Kashmir*. Princeton: Princeton University Press.

Lamb, Alastair (1997) *Incomplete Partition: The Genesis of the Kashmir Dispute 1947–1948*. Karachi: Oxford University Press.

Lawrence, Sir Walter R. (2002 [1895]) *The Valley of Kashmir*. Srinagar: Gulshan.

Leitner, G. W. (1985 [1889]) 'Dardistan in 1866, 1886 and 1893', *The Hunza and Nagyr Handbook*. Karachi: Indus.

Lentz, Sabine (2000) *Rechtspluralismus in den Northern Areas/Pakistan*. Köln: Köppe.

McHugh, Ernestine (1989) 'Concepts of the Person Among the Gurungs of Nepal', *American Ethnologist*, 16: 75–86.

Madan, T. N. (1984) 'Religious Ideology and Social Structure: The Muslims and Hindus of Kashmir', in Ahmad, Imtiaz (ed.), *Ritual and Religion Among Muslims in India*. Delhi: Manohar, pp. 21–63.

——(1995) 'On Living Intimately with Strangers', in *Pathways: Approaches to the Study of Society in India*. Delhi: Oxford University Press.

*——(2002 [1965]) *Family and Kinship: A Study of the Pandits of Rural Kashmir*. Delhi: Oxford University Press.

——(2006) 'Kashmir, Kashmiris, Kashmiriyat', in *Images of the World: Essays on Religion, Secularism, and Culture*. Delhi: Oxford University Press, pp. 175–206.

Mahmood, Cynthia Keppley (2000) 'Trials by Fire: Dynamics of Terror in Punjab and Kashmir', in Sluka, Jeffrey A. (ed.), *Death Squad: The Anthropology of State Terror*. Philadelphia: University of Pennsylvania Press, pp. 70–90.

Marriott, McKim (1976) 'Hindu Transactions: Diversity Without Dualism', in Kapferer, Bruce (ed.), *Transaction and Meaning*. Philadelphia: Institute for the Study of Human Issues, pp. 109–42.

——(1989) 'Constructing an Indian Ethnosociology', *Contributions to Indian Sociology* (ns), 23: 1–39.

Marriott, McKim and Inden, Ronald B. (1977) 'Toward an Ethnosociology of South Asian Caste Systems', in David, Kenneth A. (ed.), *The New Wind: Changing Identities in South Asia*. The Hague: Mouton, pp. 227–38.

Mines, Mattison (1994) *Public Faces, Private Voices: Community and Individuality in South India*. Berkeley: University of California Press.

Müller-Stellrecht, Irmtraud (1979) *Hunza*. Graz: Akademische Druck- und Verlagsanstalt.

——(1980) *Gilgit*. Chitral und Yasin, Graz: Akademische Druck- und Verlagsanstalt.

Pirie, Fernanda (2007) *Peace and Conflict in Ladakh: The Construction of a Fragile Web of Order*. Leiden: Brill.

Puri, Balraj (1995) 'Kashmiriyat: The Vitality of Kashmiri Identity', *Contemporary South Asia*, 4: 55–63.

——(ed.) (1997) *5000 Years of Kashmir*. Delhi: Ajanta Publications.

Rai, Mridu (2004) *Hindu Rulers, Muslim Subjects: Islam, Rights, and the History of Kashmir*. London: Hurst.

Rao, Aparna (1988) *Entstehung und Entwicklung ethnischer Identität bei einer islamischen Minderheit in Südasien*. Berlin: Verlag Das Arabische Buch.

——(1992) 'The Constraints of Nature or Culture? Pastoral Resources and Territorial Behaviour in the Western Himalayas', in Casimir, Michael J. and Rao, Aparna (eds), *Mobility and Territoriality: Social and Spatial Boundaries among Foragers, Fishers, Pastoralists and Peripatetics*. New York: Berg, pp. 91–134.

*——(1998) *Autonomy: Life Cycle, Gender and Status among Himalayan Pastoralists*. Oxford: Berghahn.

——(1999) 'The Many Sources of Identity: An Example of Changing Affiliations in Rural Jammu and Kashmir', *Ethnic and Racial Studies*, 22: 56–91.

——(2001) 'Levels and Boundaries in Native Models: Social Groupings among the Bakkarwal of the Western Himalayas', in Madan, T. N. (ed.), *Muslim Communities of South Asia*. Delhi: Manohar, pp. 269–306.

——(2003) 'Access to Pasture: Concepts, Constraints, and Practice in the Kashmir Himalayas', in Rao, Aparna and Casimir, Michael J. (eds), *Nomadism in South Asia*. Delhi: Oxford University Press, pp. 174–212.

Rieck, Andreas (1995) 'The Nurbakhshis of Baltistan. Crisis and Revival of a Five Centuries Old Community', *Die Welt des Islams*, 35: 159–88.

Robinson, Cabeiri deBergh (2005) *Refugees, Political Subjectivity, and the Morality of Violence: From Hijrat to Jihad in Azad Kashmir*. Cornell University (unpublished PhD thesis).

Rose, Leo E. (1992) 'The Politics of Azad Kashmir', in Thomas, Raju G. C. (ed.), *Perspectives on Kashmir: The Roots of Conflict in South Asia*. Boulder: Westview Press, pp. 235–53.

Schofield, Victoria (1996) *Kashmir in the Crossfire*. London: I. B. Tauris.

——(2000) *Kashmir in Crossfire: India, Pakistan, and the Unfinished War*. London: I. B. Tauris.

Sender, Henny (1988) *The Kashmiri Pandits: A Study of Cultural Choice in North India*. Delhi: Oxford University Press.

Sikand, Yoginder (2001) 'Changing Course of Kashmir Struggle: From National Liberation to Islamist Jihad?', *Economic and Political Weekly*, 36 (3): 218–27.

Sökefeld, Martin (1997a) *Ein Labyrinth von Identitäten in Nordpakistan: Zwischen Landbesitz, Religion und Kaschmir-Konflikt*. Köln: Köppe.

——(1997b) 'Jang Azadi: A major theme in Northern Areas' History', in Stellrecht, Irmtraud (ed.) *The Past in the Present: Horizons of Remembering in the Pakistan Himalaya*. Köln: Köppe, pp. 61–82.

——(1998) '"The People who Really Belong to Gilgit": Theoretical and Ethnographic Perspectives on Identity and Conflict', in Stellrecht, Irmtraud and Bohle, Hans-Georg (eds), *Transformation of Social and Economic Relationships in Northern Pakistan*. Köln: Köppe, pp. 95–224.

——(1999a) 'Debating Self, Identity, and Culture in Anthropology', *Current Anthropology*, 40: 417–47.

——(1999b) 'Balawaristan and Other ImagiNations: A Nationalist Discourse in the Northern Areas of Pakistan', in van Beek, Martijn; Bertelsen, Kristoffer Brix and Pedersen, Poul (eds), *Ladakh: Culture, History, and Development between Himalaya and Karakoram*. Aarhus: Aarhus University Press, pp. 350–68.

——(2005) 'From Colonialism to Postcolonial Colonialism: Changing Modes of Domination in the Northern Areas of Pakistan', *Journal of Asian Studies*, 64: 939–74.

——(2012) 'Secularism and the Kashmir Dispute', in Bubandt, Nils and van Beek, Martijn (eds), *Varieties of Secularism: Anthropological Explorations of Religion, Politics, and the Spiritual in Asia*. London: Routledge, pp. 101–119.

Srinivas, Smriti (1998) *The Mouths of People, the Voice of God: Buddhists and Muslims in a Frontier Community of Ladakh*. Delhi: Oxford University Press.

Stellrecht, Irmtraud (1998) 'Trade and Politics: The High Mountain Region of Pakistan in the 19th and 20th Century', in Stellrecht, Irmtraud and Bohle, Hans-Georg (eds), *Transformation of Social and Economic Relationships in Northern Pakistan*. Köln: Köppe, pp. 5–92.

van Beek, Martijn (1996) 'Identity Fetishism and the Art of Representation: The Long Struggle for Regional Autonomy in Ladakh'. Cornell University (unpublished PhD thesis).

*——(2000a) 'Beyond Identity Fetishism: "Communal" Conflict in Ladakh and the Limits of Autonomy', *Cultural Anthropology*, 15: 525–69.

——(2000b) 'Dissimulations: Representing Ladakhi "Identity"', in Driessen, Henk and Otto, Ton (eds), *Perplexities of Identification: Anthropological Studies in Cultural Differentiation and the Use of Resources*. Aarhus: Aarhus University Press, pp. 164–88.

——(2003) 'The Art of Representation: Domesticating Ladakhi Identity', in Dollfus, Pascale and Lecomte-Tilouine, Marie (eds), *Ethnic Revival and Religious Turmoil: Identities and Representations in the Himalayas*. Delhi: Oxford University Press, pp. 283–301.

van Beek, Martijn and Bertelsen, Kristoffer Brix (1997) 'No Present Without Past: The 1989 Agitation in Ladakh', in Dodin, Thierry and Räther, Heinz (eds), *Recent Research on Ladakh 7: Proceedings of the Seventh Colloquium of the International Association for Ladakh Studies*. Ulm: Universität Ulm, pp. 43–65.

van Beek, Martijn; Bertelsen, Kristoffer Brix and Pederson, Poul (eds) (1999) *Ladakh: Culture, History, and Development between Himalaya and Karakoram*. Aarhus: Aarhus University Press.

van Beek, Martijn and Pirie, Fernanda (eds) (2008) *Modern Ladakh: Anthropological Perspectives on Continuity and Change*. Leiden: Brill.

Varley, Emma (2010) 'Targeted Doctors, Missing Patients: Obstetric Health Services and Sectarian Conflict in Northern Pakistan', *Social Science and Medicine*, 70: 61–70.

Zutshi, U. K. (1986) *Emergence of Political Awakening in Kashmir*. Delhi: Manohar.

*Zutshi, Chitralekha (2004) *Languages of Belonging: Islam, Regional Identity, and the Making of Kashmir*. New York: Oxford University Press.

7 Jharkhand

Alternative citizenship in an "Adivasi state"

Marine Carrin

In 2007, at the issue of a seminar I gave in Ranchi on "Education and youth agency in Jharkhand", I addressed the audience with a final question: "Don't you think that after fifty years of struggle, you might propose an alternative model of citizenship to the rest of India?" I had in mind that in Jharkhand, many people were against caste feelings and atrocities committed against Dalits and Adivasis (from the Hindi word *adi*, "beginning" and *vasi*, "resident", an equivalent of the word "aboriginal"). Then, somebody answered: "Yes, in principle, but you know we have also lost any hope of having a civil society." This declaration was followed by a deep silence and then the discussion became private.

It seems true that the disenchantment with the state is a major reason for the interest in civil society. Gupta (1999) argues that in India, over the past five decades, the state has been unable to deliver a better life to most of its citizens in spite of its repeated promises, since technological advance has been monopolized by an elite. The majority of Indians, and certainly tribal people or Adivasis, have been in that situation, having witnessed only the negative consequences of technology, since they have been victims of industrial pollution, such as uranium waste.

This does not explain why civil society was no longer possible in Jharkhand. In fact, the day following my lecture, a friend took me for a visit to a neighboring government coal-field where, in the early morning, hundreds of people were busy filling up their baskets with coal before disappearing on their bicycles. My companion added sadly, "Don't you see that they steal from the state because they have no fuel? But that explains why there is no more civil society here." I tried to convince my interlocutor that his remark was proving that somebody was still connecting the state with some kind of moral community.

I will first provide a brief general introduction to the region before reviewing general ethnographic works on Jharkhand. We shall see how the ethnographic discussion evolves into a debate on citizenship and identity. I will then present the historical background of the region and the Mundari political and social structures followed by the emergence of the modern state of Jharkhand, a recently created state of Central India. I will then talk about how Adivasis have been reordering the world since colonial times and we shall see how they have reinvented their traditions. We shall see how the present society produces the debate on civil society and citizenship to which I referred in my introductory anecdote. I shall explore how the legacy of the Jharkhand movement has influenced the construction of civil society in the region.

General introduction

Most of Jharkhand (from *jhar*, "grove" and *khand*, "country") lies on the Chota Nagpur plateau, which is the source of the Koel, Damodar, Brahmani, Kharkai and Subarnarekha rivers, whose upper watersheds lie within Jharkhand. Much of the state is still covered by forest. The state has vast mineral resources accounting for 37 percent of the total mineral wealth of India (George 2009: 157). In 1950, the Scheduled Tribes represented 60 percent of the population of Jharkhand, but they form only 23 percent of the population today (Prakash 2001). The state of Jharkhand was founded in 2000 from the southern districts of Bihar, including the Chota Nagpur plateau and the Santal Parganas. Though a 'tribal' state, with the Munda, Santal, Ho and Oraon as the largest tribal populations, it has a Hindu majority, due to immigration from the plains. Muslim, Christian, Sikh, and Jain minorities are included in a religious landscape structured by the opposition between tribal religion and Hinduism. Tribals are often called Adivasis and they refer to themselves by that term. Adivasis claim to be the first settlers on the land. But this term, coined in the 1930s by the leaders of the Munda tribe in Bihar, also reflects the awareness of the exploitation suffered by the tribals in colonial times when these groups became conscious of the exploitation they suffered from Hindu castes. Jharkhand, as imagined—in Anderson's sense (1983)—by its Adivasi population, includes the non-Adivasis as *dikus*, "foreigners", though this appellation concerns both *marang diku*, the high castes and *hurin diku*, the artisan castes who often live in multi-ethnic villages with the Santal.

Mining has been at the heart of the development debate since officials and middle-class spokesmen assessed that the surest way to development was to intensify mining. Mining in Jharkhand starting in 1774; Adivasi labor in the coal fields has a long history (George 2009), but the situation of the workers has greatly deteriorated both in terms of stability of employment and conditions of safety. Similarly, forest laws in Jharkhand have been an instrument of oppression. The Forest Act of 2006 at least acknowledges some of the everyday violence that forest laws impose on Adivasi existence. The urbanization of the region has been organized around industrial towns, such as Dhanbad and Jamshedpur, but Ranchi became the capital of the state in 2000. Failure to supply potable water in the slum areas of the major towns raises critical questions. In brief, Jharkhand has huge economic potential but many problems. While mining and industrialization have been promoted, their environmental cost has been disastrous. There is no political space that allows representatives of the people to dialog with government and mining companies.

The term Jharkhand is also used to designate the tribal party that was founded in 1950 by Jaipal Singh, an Oxford-educated Munda leader. Jaipal Singh's inability to create a solid front was criticized by the educated Adivasi who were often Christian. For fifty years, the Jharkhand movement has supported the creation of the state, while splitting into several parties. Far from reproducing the values of the dominant castes, the Adivasis defend an alternative cultural model rooted in egalitarian values. The foundation of the Jharkhand state should allow Adivasis to negotiate new identities and new forms of citizenship inspired by their cultural inheritance.

Ethnographical work in and on the region

Ethnographic work done before Independence provides valuable information on the social organization and worldview of the Mundari groups. An Indian lawyer, S. C. Roy (1912, 1925, 1928, 1937), published important monographs exploring the social and religious structures of the Mundari groups and of the Dravidian-speaking Oraon. Furthermore, the sustained presence of the Belgian Jesuits in the region resulted in the production of an impressive corpus of ethnographic data, ranging from linguistics and religion to folklore and folk medicine (Hoffman and van Emelen 1990). Bodding (1925–29; 1932–36), a Norwegian Lutheran missionary, published extensively on Santal language, religion, and folk medicine. After Independence, Vidyarthi (1972) tried to define the situation of the tribes in relation to the mainstream caste society, stressing the appraisal of tribal leadership. Mahapatra (1972) and Sinha (1972) were concerned with solidarity movements among Adivasis. McDougall (1977) argues that such tribal movements are produced by various types of agrarian transformation. Singh (1972) also focuses on agrarian issues. The history of tribal labor has been analyzed by Rothermund and Wadhwa (1978) while Simeon (1995) wrote about the union movement. More recently, Corbridge (1988) has analyzed the tribal economy, taking into account the impact of land alienation, mining, and casual labor.

Other literature, equally important in assessing the profile of Jharkhand as an Adivasi state, concerns work on colonial transformations, ethnicity, and religious movements (Singh

1983; Sen 1984; Sarkar 2002; Samaddar 1998). Dasgupta (1999) and Banerjee (1999) show how the Oraon and the Santal tried to reconstruct their worldview through opposing the discipline imposed by colonialism on Adivasi societies. Devalle (1992) stresses the importance of class consciousness rather than ethnicity for understanding Adivasi resistance by reconstructing the history of forcible harvesting from 1968 to 1980. Singh (1983) analyzes the emergence of charismatic figures such as Birsa Munda, the leader of the Munda rebellion. Munda and Mullick (2003) have developed the concept of internal colonization, explaining how industrialization of the region has led to further exploitation of the Adivasis. Carrin (Carrin-Bouez 1986; Carrin 1997, 2002; Carrin and Tambs-Lyche 2008a, 2008b) has worked on ethnicity, language, and religious movements from the beginning of the colonial period. Carrin and Tambs-Lyche (2008a) analyze the encounter between Santals and working-class missionaries in the nineteenth century. Areeparampil (1988), Corbridge *et al.* (2004) stress the emergence of indigenous knowledge based on environmental issues. Claims related to the exploitation of the forest are not isolated incidents, as noted by Damodaran (2005) and Kelkar and Nathan (1991). Ghosh (2006) relates the consequences of the implementation of a hydraulic project to the transnational imaginary of the idea of indigenous people.

One may wonder if the identity of Jharkhand is still an Adivasi identity. It seems clear that the Adivasis are increasingly aware of their exploitation and try to assert their rights as citizens, promoting the idea that they are competent to manage their own resources (Corbridge 2002; Corbridge *et al.* 2005). This last trend has been discussed in a book edited by Sundar (2009) in which the authors examine rights, laws, and policies on land, forest, water, and mining. They question how people use notions related to customary laws to formulate political claims and to distance themselves from the state, seeking alternative forms of citizenship. The work of Shah (2006, 2007, 2010) is crucial to understand the functioning of politics in Jharkhand and, more specifically, how the actual strengthening of the customary offices of leadership could voice peoples' demands for self-government.

Disenchantment with the state has taken different manifestations (Kothari 1998), such as the demand for the strengthening of intermediate institutions, like councils, which would realize the promise of constitutional democracies (Béteille 1996). Interactions between the state and society emerge from different sources (such as politicians and media), producing a multiplicity of discourses, expressed through different images of the state (Nugent 1997; Trouillot 2001; Das and Poole 2004; Krohn-Hansen and Nustad 2005).

The resurgence of the term "civil society" in an intellectual circle in Ranchi made me question if the term was not interpreted as a return to a traditional moral ordering of communities in the region. My long-term experience with the Santals made me wonder how the Adivasis in Jharkhand today could experience the idea of a civil society. Was this idea rooted in community ties, and if so, to what extent was it linked to the renewal of Adivasi institutions of self-governance? Was the constitutional definition of citizenship, as Sundar (2009: 191) puts it, suspended "between the liberal and the communitarian notions?" Sundar argues that on the one hand, protective measures concerning Adivasis are undertaken by the state—such as the scheduling of areas and communities—while on the other hand, some laws like the Land Acquisition Act, the Indian Penal Code, and the Forest Act of 1927, though presented as neutral, tend to disadvantage the Adivasis.

The Adivasi stage their assertions of identity around the question of access to land and other material and symbolical resources, arguing that such access is manipulated by the dominant communities. The dominated resist, wanting to create a kind of jurisprudence able to target the opaque bureaucracy and the intricate strategies of the different illegal enterprises ("mafias"), which operate at different levels of clandestine production, such as exploiting mines that are legally closed. Among these resources, indigenous knowledge is particularly important since Adivasi communities articulate their discourse as "custom."

The historical background

In the early eighteenth century, Chotanagpur was a region composed of many chiefdoms that were mostly under the influence of Bengal. The independent kingdom of Chotanagpur came under the East India Company and soon the region started feeling the increased tax burden, as from 1780 the tribal heads had to pay a fixed sum to the Company. Tribal revolts broke out in Chotanagpur from the late eighteenth century until the end of the nineteenth. From 1806, rights to land previously held by tribals were given to landlords (zamindars), though such practices had existed since the eighteenth century. The later revolts, which broke out in the second half of the nineteenth century, corresponded to the development of colonial administration, which brought a large number of Hindu middlemen to the tribal areas.

The system of land taxation was increasingly perceived as a foreign system that violated indigenous practice. The tribal population protested against the hierarchical system of colonial administration represented by police officers, by the jagirdars (landowners), and by moneylenders who charged exorbitant interest, despoiling the tribals of their land since the latter were unable to repay their debts. The introduction of money completed the destruction of the traditional economy, forcing the local communities to turn to moneylenders who sought by all means to deprive them of their lands. The protest movements of the different Adivasi communities thus had a common motive: the struggle against the alienation of their land. Amendments were made to the Chotanagpur Tenancy Act and to the Santal Parganas Settlement Regulation in 1903 and 1908 respectively, to prohibit transfer of land to outsiders. Despite these regulations, alienation of land continued in the twentieth century.

Two opposed ideological currents pervaded the religious movements: some were strongly anti-Hindu, like the Santal rebellion of 1855, while others were inspired by Hindu reform, such as the Kherwar movement among the Santals, or the Tana Bhagat movement among the Oraon who rejected shakti cults and adopted vegetarian offerings. Religious movements generally developed in two phases: the first phase implied driving away the old "impure" deities, held responsible for the rampant epidemics conceptualized as witchcraft, while the second phase aimed at consolidating a new faith inspired by Hinduism, Vaishnavism, and sometimes Buddhism or Islam into a new doctrine (see Verardo 2003; Dasgupta 1999; Areeparampil 1993).

Among the Ho, in the 1930s, the resurgence of witchcraft ended in the founding of a religious movement which included Vaishnavite and Buddhist elements, and Muslim influence, propagated through local Sufi shrines that attracted a large number of Adivasi devotees, seeking healing. The reform movements tried to refute a group image that reflected the rejection of the dominant society, while the tribal rebellions rather tried to reactivate a glorious past.

The Scandinavian Lutheran missionaries, who settled in the Santal Parganas in 1867, undertook linguistic work and also contributed to land and legal reforms (Carrin and Tambs-Lyche 2008a). Missionary education expanded considerably from 1905 to 1920. The Christian ideal of justice conformed to the egalitarian values which the Adivasis felt they had lost in the nineteenth century, values guaranteed by the authority of the village chiefs. The Munda and Oraon leaders of the 1930s strove to render all Adivasis equal, regardless of their position in tribal society where chiefs and priests were of higher status. Christian influence was important in transforming rebellion into legal political opposition.

The Mundari political and social structures

Chotanagpur is the place of origin of the Munda tribes, i.e. those communities who speak languages belonging to the Austro-Asiatic Mundari family. However, other communities such as the Oraon who speak a Dravidian tongue, share the general socio-cultural pattern of the tribal communities of the region. Mundari-speaking groups can be defined by their language, their ecological adaptation, and by their social and political organisation[1] (see Parkin 1992). In most of these groups we find a kinship system of exogamous clans. In the Munda khuntkatti villages, the land was collectively owned by the lineage (khunt). All the male descendants of the village were known as khuntkattidars (holders of lineage lands) while other lineages who had settled later were called rayats and had to pay rent to the former. The pahan or priest was usually the senior member of the khuntkatti lineage while the Munda or headman was his junior. Among the Munda, the Ho, and to a certain extent the Santal, the founder clans own the land while others only have usufruct. Such ownership allowed Munda chiefs, during the last two centuries, to grant land to Brahmans and Hindu soldiers, thus contributing to the immigration of Hindu landlords and to state formation (Roy 1912: 109–10). This did not happen among the Ho, whose land remained in control of the village assembly (panch). Among the Ho, the clans are more numerous, and divided into sub-clans who live in separate hamlets of the village (see Bouez 1985). Each Ho clan represented in the village has its own megalithic graveyard (sasan), and those who share a common ossuary are seen as agnates and should not marry (Koichi 1969: 99). Among all Mundari tribes, myths relate how the migrations of the ancestors produced segmentation into sub-clans, which gradually become exogamous,[2] co-operative units, exchanging labour and sharing the bride-price. Among the Munda the sub-clan has both ritual and economic significance, while among Santals only the ritual is common to the group. Most Santal clans have a mythical territory and occupational specialization, perhaps inspired by the neighbouring caste society, though except in the contexts of birth and death they do not recognize the notion of purity, which is so central to Hindus. Ho and Munda sub-clans are ranked, while Santal sub-clans are more equal in practice (see Koichi 1969; Carrin-Bouez 1986; Roy 1937; Harimohan 1990). Among Hill Kharia the Dudh and Dhelki clans are ranked. Dhelki eat beef, while Dudh, meaning "milk," is a reference to ceremonial purity (Parkin 1992: 32). Dudh do not eat beef and are considered purer by the Hindu castes. The Birhor, a hunting and gathering community, are organized in semi-nomadic bands, but have twelve clans like the Santal (Roy 1925: 43–50; Adhikari 1984). Some groups (Birhor, Juang, Santal, Kharia, Asur) affirm the descent of the clan from the totem, which is no longer worshipped but which still validates the position of clans as dominant in a village, locating memory in a shared landscape where animals and plants dialog with men. Each village is a ritual unit, whose members share the sacrificial food during agricultural rituals and avoid intermarriage.

The tribes have often, to an extent, adopted Hindu elements in their traditional cults, especially when the group is numerically weak, such as the Mal Paharia who had to call in Brahmans to celebrate their rituals. Santal, Munda, and Ho share to some extent a symbolic system that values the forest, represented in the village by the sacred grove. Similarly, according to myth, the Munda and the Ho originate from an ancestor pair, while the Santal descend from an incestuous union of seven brothers and seven sisters, ancestors of the first seven clans.

Patrilineal ideology gives men access to land and to the most prestigious goods, such as the heads of the sacrificial animals or the hunted game. Taboos relate to key production activities such as roofing and plowing, and refer to ritual order to maintain women in a subaltern position in the family (Kelkar and Nathan 1991: 62). Women's activity is defined as gathering forest produce and tubers, which they sell in the market along with rice-beer manufactured at home. Here, women develop initiatives that allow them to plan their economic activities, through block development projects or NGOs.

Adivasi women are freer than women in the Hindu castes, since they can divorce, remarry, and dispose of their own money (Carrin 2006). But this superior position is now partly eroded through social change and Hinduization, as when the dowry system is introduced in Santal marriages instead of the traditional bride-price (gonon) or when girls are prevented from schooling. In short, traditional inequalities involving property rights and political participation are based on the ranking of clans and on gender (Rao 2005; Carrin 2006).

During the colonial period, the chiefs collected the land taxes, and acceded to a prestigious position, beyond the power they traditionally held. The settled Munda groups share a similar organization with a council of five elders, a headman, and a priest taking care of agricultural rituals.

The council does not correspond to the modern panchayat. The Santal assembly meets before the manjhi than, a shrine dedicated to the spirits of past chiefs. In some parts of Chotanagpur there is a division of the village between the priest's (junior) and the headman's (senior) clan. The Munda, the Santal, and the Ho have an elaborate system of traditional rights that was to some extent acknowledged by British authorities and is still considered important, especially when land is at stake (Archer[3] 1984).

Reordering the world: from colonial writing to revealed script

During the colonial period, the Mundari groups gained a more global view of history and the Christian elites started to use legal channels in their resistance to exploitation. As collaborators of the missionaries the Santals became narrators in their own right, and they felt the urge to reorder their world after the rebellion of 1855. The ethnic movements of the Adivasis present a symbolic dimension, where the assertion of values proper to their society is essential. Centering on the idea of a lost kingdom, these assertions affirm the separate identity of the population concerned.

Santal and Ho traditional structures of authority have been partly reinvented through the influence of religious movements—such as the Sarna Dhorom ("Return to the Sacred Grove")—which originated in the 1970s among the Santal in Mayurbhanj. One of the architects of the Sarna Dhorom was Ragunath Murmu, an intellectual who in 1941 perfected an alphabet for the Santal language that was popularized and taught in the schools from then on. R. Murmu denounced the class interests which split the Santals and criticized the urban elite, who showed no interest in maintaining the links with the mass of landless peasants.

The "Return to the Sacred Grove" is known under different names in the different communities, but the phenomenon is always linked to séances of public possession where religious brotherhoods celebrate their own rituals. Even so, this quest expresses the pan-tribal dimension of the Jharkhand movement, whose leaders organize "conferences" to imagine the hard core of a common tribal religion. They have redefined the meaning of the sacred grove, the emblem of the ancestors, symbolized by a grove of sal trees (Shorea Robusta) sheltering the stones that represent the tribal deities. Intertribal commissions of village priests have decreed the equivalence of certain religious festivals as celebrated by different tribes. In the 1970s, these assemblies aimed to defend the cult of the Sarna from borrowing Hindu elements (Carrin 2002: 233–63).

The village chiefs have revived the village political system, insisting on the importance of the council of intertribal hunts, which traditionally allowed everyone, irrespective of ethnic origin, to appeal to the "judgment of the burnt forest" (Carrin-Bouez 1986: 87). More recently, the construction of custom, such as cults inspired by ecological movements, have become part of the subtle process of reinvention of tradition.

The political identity of the state of Jharkhand

Despite the egalitarian ideology of the tribes, class relations developed with urbanization. In the urban context, the Munda elite consider themselves more advanced while the Santal elite stress their education. The Oraon who have been depending economically on the Munda in the villages, claim to be the best Christians and assert transnational solidarities by converting to globalized churches such as the Pentacostalists (see also Ghosh 2006). The Jharkhand movement has become famous for its ethno-nationalist grassroots character. Without entering into detail of the different phases of the movement,[4] we may note that the project of a separate state was launched in the 1970s. In the 1980s the central government opposed the idea of a separate Jharkhand state, but became more open to the idea ten years later. Finally, in 1998 the Bharatiya Janata Party (BJP) decided to include the proposal of a separate state, the Vananchal, in its election manifesto, aiming to replace the Jharkhand project. The Jharkhandi-BJP alliances led to a compromise, implying the creation of a state limited to the districts of South Bihar including the plateau of Chota Nagpur and the Santal Parganas. More importantly, the project of a separate state no longer corresponded to the demands of the low castes and the Adivasis but was the result of a political bargain among political elites (Corbridge 2002). The dominant castes remained influential within the BJP. Certainly, the Hindu nationalists in general did not care about the exploitation of lower castes and Adivasis, nor about protecting the cultural unity of Mundari groups. In March 2005, neither the ruling National Democratic Alliance (NDA), led by the BJP, nor the United Progressive Alliance (UPA, led by the Congress Party) won a clear majority. Shibu Soren, the Santal leader of the Jharkhand Mukti Morcha ("Jharkhand Freedom League," a party which has grown from the left wing of the Jharkhand movement), was invited by the Congress Governor to form the state government. The NDA mobilized the media and the courts against the Governor's action, Soren resigned and Marandi (BJP) became chief minister (Sundar 2009: 189). Let us also mention the Jharkhand Vikhas Party, advocating the idea of an Adivasi religion founded by the intellectual Ram Dayal Munda. The extreme left includes the Maoist Coordination Comity (MCC) and the People's War Group (PWG), which are seen as engaged in terrorist activities.

Thus the struggles over citizenship in Jharkhand are rooted in different images of democracy: on the one hand a liberal democracy where people choose between different parties through elections—"the constitutional path" —and, on the other hand, a popular self-government where local and ethnic communities assert their own affiliations in a political process leaving room for autonomy (Sundar 2009: 191). The latter path, based on a non-party grassroots organization, of course implies resistance to the state. The Adivasi communities have raised the banner of custom and indigeneity to project themselves as citizens, while the Hindu high castes have fought for politics inscribed in a religious idiom, pervaded by fundamentalist ideas.

The political discourse that was developed by the Jharkhand Party involved a difficult compromise between the idea that indigenous people had rights over the land and that they also represented indigenous knowledge and wisdom, which implied their ability to deal with non-tribal populations. These ideas have contributed to creating the political space of

Jharkhand where Adivasi populations have been emotionally invested in asserting their identity, but other factors related to the exploitation of natural resources (forests, mines) have brought dispossession and exploitation.

The political systems of parha and chiefs are considered as paradigms of self-governance. The Munda, the Santal, and the Ho are promoting their traditional structures of authority to avoid direct confrontation with the state administration, perceived as oppressive and corrupted. The Santal launch grassroots initiatives and cultural strategies, trying to conciliate the traditional forms of self-government with political participation.

As Sundar argues (2009: 194), this search for relative autonomy has only been possible since Jharkhand laws concerning tenure rights have been related to the pre-colonial system of leadership. This search for an alternative citizenship through a revival of traditional leadership does not exclude people from addressing the government as in other parts of India. Jharkhand, then, offers a labyrinth of ideologies built on laws, reinvention of "traditional" institutions, religious movements, and political forces such as the MCC (Maoist Communist Center) which have taken to armed resistance, but are also infiltrating the state apparatus and the market economy (see Shah 2010).

An ethnographic example of grassroots initiatives

The people of the village I call Jobradaga here (Hazaribagh District) and the neighboring sixty-five villages are mostly inhabited by Santals. The description is based on my recent fieldwork in the village. Most of the locals have been deprived of their lands and are currently trying to regain some of them. Formerly, the Santal here worked as casual laborers for the Hindu Mahtos (small landowners), who used to harass Santal women, leading to conflicts. Nowadays, the Santals try to avoid working for the Mahtos, who treat them as untouchables, and the communities keep apart. Because of this defiance, the Santals often hold the Mahtos responsible when they fail to find niches in the local market. Since most Santals have insufficient land, men prefer to work casually in illegal mines, carrying coal on their bicycles to sell it to illegal networks, whose heads are generally high caste people. The latter, who are the traditional landlords, are seen as associating themselves with the state in order to monopolize contracts. These villages have benefitted from the work of an NGO founded by a Christian nun who built a residential school for the children. She died recently, but during the last twenty years, the villagers have been involved in irrigation works and other initiatives such as trying to cultivate mushrooms, organize fisheries, or rear a new breed of pig.

The villagers felt they could control technical knowledge, but social knowledge was more problematic. The Santals are known for their egalitarian ethos, though contests over property reflect and shape relationships between people. In Jobradaga, it is the headman (manjhi) who controls the distribution of ration cards and BPL (Beyond Poverty Line) cards and supervises any collective undertaking. He has gained a considerable influence in the neighboring villages by obtaining sarkari (government) resources, as well as NGO grants, to implement projects such as improving irrigation. His main success was to help the NGO to found the school, since teachers were not coming to this remote area. The villagers decided to have Adivasi teachers but school fees were too high for most parents, and to solve the problem the villagers appealed to the NGO. These decisions were made through the Kulhi durup (literally, "Sitting in the street"), the meeting where people discuss local politics.

Reinvention of traditional authority

The old system of self-governance implies trust in the traditional chiefs. This is not easy, since in the past some chiefs have been criticized for usurping the rights of their subjects and monopolizing lands. There are cases where villagers complain against their manjhi to the Council of the Burnt Forest, chaired by the parganait—a territorial chief presiding over twelve villages—who embodies the customs of the ancestors. I have met parganaits who were politicians in the modern sense of the term, and exercized considerable power. Some parganaits were enthroned like kings, received a mark of investiture (tika) on the forehead, and wore royal insignia. In the 1980s I knew territorial chiefs who were MLA or even MP, using both their political position and their ritual status to reinforce their authority.

In Hazaribagh, few parganaits try to influence their fellow villagers to return to self-government, though people do not thrust the development promoted by the state, since they feel it privileges outside investors. Yet, my informants stress that no panchayat elections had been held, and that there were now "other ways to power," alluding to Maoist activities. Briefly, the Santal in Hazaribagh have not yet turned to other forms of citizenship, unlike the Munda and the Ho whose chiefs have tried to initiate a return to self-government.

Is indigenous knowledge seen as a resource for developing grassroot initiatives or other forms of participation in civil society? The Munda, the Santal, and the Ho are putting forward their traditional structures of authority, considered as paradigms of self-governance, to avoid confrontation with the state administration, perceived as oppressive and corrupted.

Shah (2007) argues that the Munda dissociate themselves from the state, perceived as foreign and dangerous. Thus the Bero parha, which regroups twenty-one villages and represents a sacred and political entity, is presided by a chief "who protects his parha as his sphere of influence where he has (…) to maintain harmony, settling intra-village and inter-village conflicts over land as well as forbidden amorous relationships" (ibid.: 132). In the years preceding 1967, one Oraon leader revived the parha by launching a festival (mela) dedicated to local deities, to gain electoral support as a Congress MLA. Later, his opponent in the next elections, a representative of the Jharkhand Mukti Morcha (JMM), held a separate mela to launch his campaign (ibid.: 132). In 2000, when the state of Jharkhand was formed, the JMM MLA tried to destroy the traditional system of parha raja by using democratic elections to establish himself as a second raja. He was careful to dissociate the idea of democracy from the state, claiming that an elected raja was authentic Munda custom.

This kind of conflict may involve religious oppositions (Christian and Sarna Dhorom) as well as political differences. Each MLA and parha chief seems to accuse the other of being unable to protect the parha from the state, illegal enterprises, and corruption. Sundar (2009: 208) gives another example from the Koel Kero region, where Adivasis were to be displaced by a big dam (see also Baviskar 1995, and Carrin and Tambs-Lyche 2008b). When the project was stopped, villagers developed initiatives such as managing their forest through collective patrolling, starting a school and establishing a hospital. This parha had taken steps to introduce reforms, such as reducing marriage expenditure. Sundar argues that villages use both customary institutions and "the constitutional path," declaring themselves as gram sabha, "village assembly," by sending formal letters to the Chief Minister or Governor in order to get development funds channeled through the gram sabha. Clearly different groups of citizens struggle to get acknowledged so as to manage their own affairs. But, as informants told me, the government wants the parha to work only to resolve disputes on the model of a caste association. Sundar (2009: 209) stresses the danger of framing alternative citizenship through the parha. Is the prestige of customary chiefs becoming crucial in Jharkhand, or are politicians simply claiming to be emblematic of tradition? We should keep in mind that when traditional chiefs are MLA they are de facto government representatives and can distribute development contracts. Sundar (2009: 209–10) stresses that the history of the parha "has been closely tied with state formation and sacred power." Shah (2007) notes that the parha rajas have high caste supporters. To what extent, then, do non-Adivasis in the parha subscribe to this idea of an idealized polity embedded in the sacred realm? Perhaps this idea fits their own strategy as members of dominant castes.

Strengthening the parha may contribute to idealizing charismatic figures and silencing other actors, such as women. Thus, Sundar (2009:199–204) argues in favor of "the constitutional path"—communities should address the relevant channels for their rights to be acknowledged, since "citizenship is organized as a set of juridical or quasi-legal practices. Among these laws, the Panchayats Extension to Scheduled Areas Act (PESA)[5] of 2001, which should empower communities, does not work properly, since democratic village assemblies have been replaced by "a government functionary who convenes a village assembly" (Sundar 2009: 203). Sundar quotes cases where communities have difficulties in addressing the High Court to have their land rights restored. As Shah (2006: 303–05) notes, however, the legalist view is fragilized in Jharkhand, where votes and ideologies may become commodities. How, then, should we interpret the Adivasi choice to keep apart from the state, as well as from Maoists who racket them, a trend I observed in Hazaribagh and on the Orissa border? Certainly, villagers feel defiant towards the state, associated with the repressive interventions of police and forest department officers (see Corbridge *et al.* 2004: 92). They feel that high caste people use their connections with mining companies and government officials to prevent them from having their rights acknowledged, especially when they want their lands restored, as Corbridge (1988) underlines.

Conclusion

Traditional knowledge has helped the Mundari groups to imagine themselves as a moral community, a samaj, able to generate religious leaders, as well as writers. The Adivasi cultural renewal is explicit and asserted in religious and literary movements, but it conceals class conflicts since actors speak in the name of custom (colon) and silence others, in particular women and minority groups. During discussions with Santal writers in recent years, I felt they were convinced of their mission to voice silent distress, which pervades everyday relations and concerns internal segments of Adivasi communities: kinship, neighborhood, and labor relations. Young Adivasi who fail to find a job with their diploma, look for social models to find a "track to follow." Some work with NGOs, write articles on the problems of rural life, or engage in artistic pursuits, while others convert to Christianity (Carrin, in press). Others, and not just the young, make films documenting conflict over natural resources, employment, land, and the struggle for education. Thus, youth are ready to struggle over the possible idea of citizenship voiced in artistic, religious, or even environmental idioms.

The creation of Jharkhand has raised new questions concerning the future of Adivasis. How has the acknowledgement of indigenous forms of knowledge by the state helped Adivasi communities to conciliate their "tribal identity" with their identity as citizens? Tribal identity has become a tool of protest, and ethnic symbols such as bow and arrow are now associated with political campaigns launched by the Jharkhand parties. Subtle signs of resistance appear when Adivasis organize demonstrations in the Ranchi streets, or when they stage conflicts in village theaters while knowing that the message is not understood by the Hindu castes.

Resistance also implies "to play tribal" as when children are asked to perform dances before officials, and caricature their "tribal culture." This everyday resistance is directed against the hegemonic values of high castes who show contempt towards Adivasis, seen as "jungly." Other forms of resistance articulate political claims and the idea that Adivasis should be part of decision-making regarding the exploitation of natural resources.

While some Adivasi resist the state and claim a return to self-governance as the only way to recapture citizenship, others feel they should follow "the constitutional path." The recent history of struggles against mining companies shows how some evicted communities challenge the state through the High Court when they fail to gain compensation (George 2009: 171–72). Are Adivasis ready to negotiate new identities and new forms of citizenship so as to reconcile custom and democracy? Does Jharkhand, where the extreme left opposes the extreme right, allow its citizens to disentangle themselves from ethnic identities and essentialist assumptions? This seems difficult since the political class itself is ethnically conscious, which favors the big communities to the detriment of the small ones. The inequalities that put urban elites in opposition to the rural poor reinforce Adivasi withdrawal to remote areas, a trend which also existed in the past. In other words, are Adivasis condemned to become semi-clandestine forest citizens?

A strong sense of justice and the problems of the legal paths inspired the rebellions of the past, and the struggles of the Jharkhand movement. Today, the priorities of the state and of the Adivasi communities are diverging, since for the latter, land remains a key element of their social identity. Given the incapacity of different legislative measures to protect Adivasi rights, Adivasis have few options for survival. One option is exemplified by the Santal of Hazaribagh who work out collective decisions through consensus, and keep apart from the state, looking to NGOs to sponsor their projects. Still, they take advantage of government welfare measures such as ration cards. Another option is associated with the emergence of literacy among the Santal, provided writers become influential enough to voice and empower Adivasi interests in the way that Dalit literature has become a political force in these last decades.

Notes

1 Important social categories are often blurred by scholars who want to avoid "essentialist views" and analyze "tribal leadership" as a general pattern without taking into account ethnic differences.
2 While some authors state that clans are mainly important for marriage regulations (Ryuji 1972), Bouez (1985) stresses that among the Munda only clan members have full ancestral rights to land. While the Santal have twelve clans, the Munda and Ho have about a hundred.
3 W. Archer who was in the Indian Civil Service in Bihar in the forties has worked on Santal law and "custom."
4 From 1949 to 1963, the Jharkhand movement was strengthened and became a party, which was joined by caste people.
5 The provisions of the PESA declare the rights of the Adivasi communities regarding acquisition of lands, management of water and mining leases regarding minerals, allowing the local communities (*panchayats, gram sabha*) to control local plans and resources (Sundar 2009: 218).

References

Adhikari, Ashim Kumar (1984) *Society and World View of the Birhor*. Calcutta: Anthropological Survey of India.

Anderson, B. (1983) *Imagined Communities: Reflections on the Origins and Spread of Nationalism*. London: Verso.

Archer, W. G. (1984) *Tribal Law and Justice: A Report on the Santal*. Delhi: Concept.

Areeparampil, M. (1988) 'Forests and Tribals: Victims of Exploitation.' Chaibasa: Tribal Research and Training Centre (TRTC).

——(1993) 'Socio-Cultural and Religious Movements among the Ho Tribals of Singhbhum District in Bihar, India,' in M. Miri (ed.), *Continuity and Change in Tribal Society*. Shimla: Indian Institute of Advanced Study.

Banerjee, Prathama (1999) 'Historic Acts? Santal Rebellion and the Temporality of Practice,' *Studies in History*, 15: 209–46.

Baviskar, Amita (1995) *In the Belly of the River: Tribal Conflicts over the Narmada Valley*. Delhi: Oxford University Press.

Béteille, A. (1996) 'Civil Society and its Institutions,' First Fullbright Memorial Lecture delivered in Calcutta, 12–13 March.

Bodding, P. O. (1925–29) *Santal Folk-tales*, vol. 1, 1925; vol. 2, 1927; vol. 3, 1929. Oslo: H. Aschehoug and Co.

——(1932–36) *A Santal Dictionary* (five vols). Oslo: Det Norske Videnskaps Akademi.

Bouez, S. (1985) *Réciprocité et Hiérarchie: L'Alliance chez les Ho et les Santal de l'Inde*. Paris: Société d'Ethnographie.

Carrin-Bouez, M. (1986) *La Fleur et l'Os: symbolisme et rituel chez les Santal*, Cahiers de l'Homme. Paris: EHESS.

Carrin, M. (1997) *Enfants de la Déesse: Dévotion et prêtrise féminine au Bengale*. Paris: Editions du CNRS et MSH.

*——(2002) 'Le retour du bosquet sacré. Réinvention d'une culture Adivasi,' in M. Carrin and C. Jaffrelot (eds), *Tribus et basses castes: résistance et autonomie dans la société Indienne*. Paris: EHESS, pp. 233–64

——(2006) 'Women, Adivasis, Subalterns: Perspectives on the Empowerment of Santal Women,' in Kamal K. Misra and J.Huber Lowry (eds), *Recent Studies on Indian Women: Empirical Work of Social Scientists*. Jaipur: Rawat Publications, pp. 281–301.

——(in press) 'The Santal as an intellectual,' in M. Carrin, P. Kanungo and G. Toffin (eds), *The Politics of Ethnicity in India, Nepal and China*. Delhi: Primus.

Carrin, M. and Tambs-Lyche, H. (2008a) *An Encounter of Peripheries: Santals, Missionaries and their Changing Worlds, 1867–1900*. Delhi: Manohar.

——(eds) (2008b) *People of the Jangal: Reformulating Identities and Adaptations in Crisis*. Delhi: Manohar.

*Corbridge, S. (1988) 'The Ideology of Tribal Economy and Society: Politics in the Jharkhand 1950–1980,' *Modern Asian Studies*, 22: 16–42.

——(2002) 'The Continuing Struggle for India's Jharkhand: Democracy, Decentralisation and the Politics of Names and Numbers,' *Commonwealth and Comparative Politics*, 40 (3): 55–71.

*Corbridge, S., Jewitt, S. and Kumar, S. (2004) *Jharkhand: Environment, Development, Ethnicity*. Delhi: Oxford University Press.

Corbridge, S., Williams, G., Srivastava, M. K. and Véron, R. (2005) *Seeing the State: Governance and Governmentality in India*. Cambridge: Cambridge University Press.

Damodaran, Vinita (2005) 'Indigenous Forests: Rights, Discourses and Resistance in Chotanagpur, 1860–2002,' in G. Cederlof and K. Sivaramakrishnan (eds) (2006) *Ecological Nationalisms: Nature, Livelihoods and Identities in South Asia*, pp. 115–50.

Das, Veena and Poole, Deborah (eds) (2004) *Anthropology in the Margins of the State*. Santa Fe and Oxford: School of American Research.

Dasgupta, Sangeeta (1999) 'Reordering the World: the Tana Bhagat Movement 1914–1919', *Studies in History*, 15: 1–41.

Devalle, Susana B. C. (1992) *Discourses of Ethnicity: Culture and Protest in Jharkhand*. Delhi: Sage.

*George, Ajitha Susan (2009) 'The Paradox of Mining and Development,' in N. Sundar (ed.) (2009) *Legal Grounds: Natural Resources, Identity, and the Law in Jharkhand*. Delhi: Oxford Univeristy Press, pp. 158–88.

Ghosh, Abhik (2006) *The World of the Oraon: Their Symbols in Time and Space*. Delhi: Manohar.

Ghosh, Kaushik (2006) 'Between Global Flows and Local Dams: Indigenousness, Locality, and the Transnational Sphere in Jharkhand, India,' *Cultural Anthropology*, 21 (4): 501–34.

*Gupta, Dipankar (1999) 'Civil Society or the State: What Happened to Citizenship', in Ramachandra Guha and Jonathan Parry (eds), *Institutions and Inequalities: Essays in Honour of André Béteille*. Delhi: Oxford University Press, pp. 234–54.

Harimohan, (1990) 'Leadership and Development: A Study of the Role of Tribal Leaders in Self-governing Institutions in Bihar,' in S. P. Sinha (ed.), *Tribal Leadership in Bihar*, pp. 7–70.

Hoffman, J. and van Emelen, A. (1990) *Encyclopaedia Mundarica*, vols. 1–13 (1st edition 1930). Delhi: Gian.

*Kelkar, Govind and Nathan, Dev (1991) *Gender and Tribe: Women, Land and Forests in Jharkhand*. New Delhi: Kali for Women.

Koichi, Sugiyama (1969) *A Study of the Mundas: Village Life in India*. Tokyo: Tokai University Press.

Kothari, Rajni (1998) *State Against Democracy: In Search of Humane Governance*. Delhi: Ajanta Publications.

Krohn-Hansen, C. and Nustad, K. G. (2005) *State Formation: Anthropological Perspectives*. London: Pluto Press.

McDougall, J. (1977) 'Agrarian Reform versus Religious Revitalization: Collective Resistance to Peasantization among the Mundas, Oraons and Santals, 1858–95,' *Contributions to Indian Sociology*, n.s., 11 (2): 295–327.

Mahapatra, L. K. (1972) 'Social Movements Among Tribes in India,' in K. Suresh Singh (ed.), *The Tribal Situation in India*, pp. 399–409.

Munda, Ram Dayal and Bosu Mullick, S. (2003) *The Jharkhand Movement: Indigenous People's Struggle for Autonomy in India*, IWGIA Document No. 108. Copenhagen: IWGIA.

Nugent, D. (1997) *Modernity at the Edge of Empire: State, Individual, and Nation in the Northern Peruvian Andes, 1885–1935*. Stanford: Stanford University Press.

Parkin, R. (1992) *The Munda of Central India: An Account of their Social Organization*. Delhi: Oxford University Press.

*Prakash, A. (2001) *Jharkhand: Politics of Development and Identity*. Delhi: Orient Longman.

Rao, Nitya (2005) 'Kinship Matters: Women's Land Claims in the Santal Parganas Jharkhand,' *Journal of the Royal Anthropological Institute*, 11: 725–45.

Rothermund, D. and Wadhwa, D. C. (1978) *Zamindars, Mines and Peasants*. New Delhi: Manohar.

Roy, S. C. (1912) *The Mundas and their Country*. Calcutta: City Book Society.

——(1925) *The Birhors*. Ranchi: Man in India.

——(1928) *Oraon Religion and Customs*, K. M. Banerjee (ed.), Calcutta: Industry Press.

——(1937) *The Kharias*, vols I–II. Ranchi: Man In India.

Ryuji, Yamada (1972) *Cultural Formation of the Mundas* (1st edition 1967). Tokyo: Tokai University Press.

Samaddar, Ranabir (1998) *Memory, Identity, Power: Politics in the Jungle Mahals 1890–1950*. London: Sangam Books.

Sarkar, Tanika (2002) 'Missionaries, Converts and the State in Colonial India,' *Studies in History*, 18: 121–33.

Sen, Suchibrata (1984) *The Santals of the Jungle Mahals: An Agrarian History, 1793–1861*. Calcutta: Ratna Prakashan.

Shah, A. (2006) 'Markets of Protection: The Maoist Communist Centre and the State in Jharkhand, India,' *Critique of Anthropology*, 26: 297–314.

——(2007) 'Keeping the State Away: Democracy, Politics, and the State in India's Jharkhand,' *Journal of the Royal Anthropological Institute*, 13 (1) March: 128–45.

——(2010) *In the Shadows of the State: Indigenous Politics, Environmentalism, and Insurgency in Jharkhand, India*. Durham: Duke University Press.

Simeon, Dilip (1995) *The Politics of Labour under Late Colonialism: Workers, Unions and the State in Chotanagpur 1928–1939*. Delhi: Manohar.

Singh, K. Suresh (1972) 'Agrarian Issues in Chotanagpur,' in K. S. Singh (ed.), *The Tribal Situation in India*, Indian Institute of Advanced Studies. Delhi: Shimla and Motilal Banarsidass, pp. 374–87.

——(1983) *Birsa Munda and his Movement 1874–1901: A Study of a Millenarium Movement in Chotanagpur*. Calcutta: Calcutta University Press.

Sinha, Surajit (1972) 'Tribal Solidarity Movements in India: A Review,' in K. Suresh Singh (ed.), *The Tribal Situation in India*. Delhi: Shimla and Motilal Banarsidass, pp. 438–53.

Sundar, N. (2009) (ed.) *Legal Grounds: Natural Resources, Identity, and the Law in Jharkhand*. Delhi: Oxford University Press.

*Trouillot, M. R. (2001) 'The Anthropology of the State in the Age of Globalization,' *Current Anthropology*, 42 (1): 125–38.

Verardo, Barbara (2003) 'Rebels and Devotees of Jharkhand: Social, Religious and Political Transformations among the Adivasis of Northern India,' PhD thesis, Department of Anthropology, London School of Economics.

Vidyarthi, L. P. (1972) 'An Appraisal of the Leadership Pattern among the Tribes of Bihar,' in K. Suresh Singh (ed.), *The Tribal Situation in India*. Delhi: Shimla and Motilal Banarsidass, pp. 438–53.

8 Karnataka

Caste, dominance and social change in
the 'Indian village'

Aya Ikegame

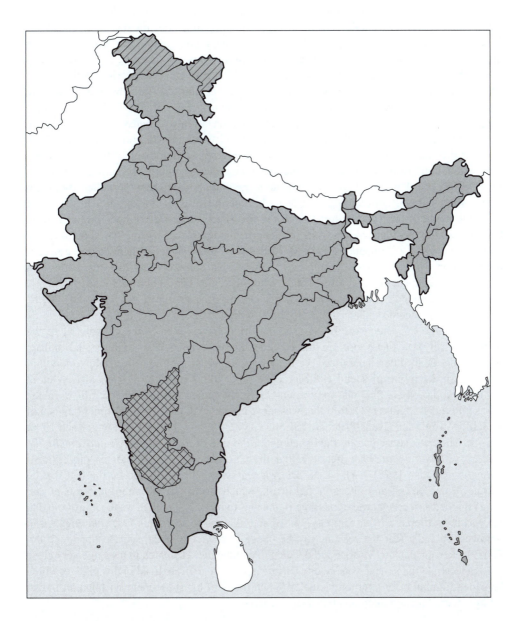

In 2006, Karnataka became the first southern state to be ruled by the Hindu nationalist party, Bharatiya Janata Party (BJP). The success of the BJP in Karnataka arose because the party secured considerable support from the Lingayat community (followers of Veerashaivism), the dominant caste in northern Karnataka. Many journalists and scholars believed that the BJP utilized Hindu monasteries (*mathas*) as their vote banks. However, the other major political parties in the state, such as the Indian National Congress and Janata Dal (Secular) have similar interests in monasteries. The inclination of the Lingayat community to favour the BJP may appear rather puzzling at first sight, since the Lingayat philosophy, developed by Basavanna, a twelfth-century religious reformer, is considered to be strongly opposed to caste hierarchy and Brahminical values. Since the BJP is commonly considered to be a party of high castes and supporters of orthodox Brahminical values in north India, this alliance in the south requires some explanation. From the very beginning of the twentieth century, Lingayats have been making tremendous efforts to 'up-lift' their community, particularly through modern education, in order to compete with Brahmins who monopolized high government offices both in the princely state of Mysore and in British-ruled territories. After having secured an improvement in their social and economic capital, they felt the need to acquire concomitant cultural capital as well. In this sense, one may ask if this new alliance between Lingayats and the BJP could be regarded as a political form of 'Sanskritization' through which the Lingayats manifest themselves as a community that upholds Hindu spiritual values.

Several of the terms used in the introductory paragraph – 'dominant caste', 'vote bank', 'Sanskritization' – were invented or popularized by an Indian sociologist/social anthropologist, M. N. Srinivas (1916–99). It would not be an exaggeration to call him the father of modern Indian socio-cultural anthropology, since he brought about a significant shift in the social scientific methods practised in India from the so-called 'historical method' propagated by G. S. Ghurye in pre-Independent India to modern ethnographical writing based on long and intensive fieldwork (Deshpande 2007). M. N. Srinivas' sociology also changed the subject of investigation from 'preliterate communities' (i.e. tribal communities) towards a focus on social relationships amongst castes, tribes, peasants, cults, etc., within a bounded concrete space, 'a space which is a macrocosm of our culture': the village (Patel 1998: 50). M. N. Srinivas thus pioneered village studies in India in the 1950s.

As his name suggests, Mysore Narashimha Srinivas was born in the capital city of the former princely state of Mysore. He studied under the supervision of G. S. Ghurye in Bombay, but it was at Oxford that he realized the increasing importance of intensive fieldwork within the modern discipline of social anthropology. As a DPhil student, he spent two years at Oxford and turned his PhD dissertation on Coorg, submitted to the University of Bombay, into a DPhil dissertation at Oxford that was more in tune with the structural-functionalism of Radcliffe-Brown and Evans-Pritchard (Srinivas 1973: 139–44; Fuller 1999: 5–7; Shah 1996: 203–6). The book subsequently published under the title of *Religion and Society among the Coorgs of South India* (hereafter, I call it the Coorg book) established his professional reputation (Madan 1978: 2–4). M. N. Srinivas was, however, frustrated by the fact that he had never carried out any intensive fieldwork, which British social anthropologists at that time regarded as a crucial rite of passage if one was to be truly qualified as an anthropologist. He was then offered a lectureship at Oxford and allowed to spend his first year engaged in fieldwork in India (for the reason why he chose to return to India, see Deshpande 2000: 106–9). He went back to Mysore and decided to conduct field research in a village very close to his ancestral village near Mysore city (Srinivas 1976: 4–10). He lived in this village, which he called Rampura, for ten months in 1948, and many of his subsequent writings on Indian villages were founded upon this fieldwork experience.

In this chapter, we will revisit two of the most influential and important theoretical concepts of M. N. Srinivas: Sanskritization and the dominant caste. Academics have argued fiercely over the validity of these concepts. At the same time, they were widely used and have almost become a part of the daily language of social and especially caste analysis in South Asia. It is important therefore to re-examine and re-problematize these unique contributions from Karnataka state to the social anthropology of South Asia, not only in their own terms, but also in relation to their continuing importance and validity within the state itself. Beginning with M. N. Srinivas, we will then move on to discuss lesser known ethnographers within Karnataka who have substantiated or otherwise contradicted his ideas, and conclude by proposing some alternative ways in which we might explore the dynamics of caste and social change within South India.

Karnataka: A brief profile

Karnataka (formally known as Mysore) is a southern Indian state with a population of nearly fifty-three million. Culturally and geographically, the state, most of which is situated on the Deccan plateau, can be divided into four regions. Firstly, there is the southern region, which was the territory of the princely state of Mysore during colonial times. This region, especially the areas around Mysore, the former capital of Mysore state, and Bangalore, the current state capital, have well-irrigated, rich agricultural lands that produce commodity crops such as rice and sugar cane. Secondly, there is the northern region, most of which formerly came under the Bombay Presidency, which is dry and poorer, and often suffers from severe droughts. Thirdly, there is the coastal region facing the Arabian Sea, which was under the Madras Presidency before Independence. Fourthly, there is Malenadu ('hill or rain land' in Kannada), which covers the western and eastern slopes of the Western Ghats. Kodagu (or Coorg in an anglicized spelling), which was once an independent kingdom with a distinct language and culture, is a part of Malenadu. The official language of the state is Kannada, but each region has different languages and dialects. Tulu is spoken in the coastal region, Kodagu or Kodava in Coorg (now Kodagu district), and Marathi is used either in its pure form or a form mixed with Kannada in the northern region. There are also many migrant communities who settled in Karnataka several centuries ago. Many of them maintain their mother tongue amongst themselves. Languages such as Tamil, Telugu, Malayalam, Konkani and Urdu are thus very much alive, not as the language of a particular locality but as the language of discrete communities.

Sanskritization

The notion of Sanskritization is undoubtedly one of the most widely used and problematic sociological terms (for a more detailed genealogy of this concept, see Charsley 1998). M. N. Srinivas may not have been the first person to use this term, but certainly he was the one who popularized the term and defended it vigorously (S. K. Chatterjee wrote about Sanskritization in 1950, but M. N. Srinivas claimed that he used this term for the first time in 1947 in his DPhil thesis). Sanskritization generally refers to a process by which a lower caste or tribal group adopts certain customs, forms of rituals, beliefs, ideologies and the lifestyle of a higher, and especially a twice-born (Brahmin, Kshatriya and Viasha) caste (Srinivas 1996: 88). This phenomenon had been already recognized in the early twentieth century when certain caste groups claimed a higher caste rank in the census reports and had begun employing symbols of the twice-born on themselves, such as the wearing of sacred thread (Srinivas 1966: 16). M. N. Srinivas used the term 'Sanskritization' for the first time in his Coorg book in 1952:

> The caste system is far from a rigid system in which the position of each component caste is fixed for all time. Movement has always been possible, and especially so in the middle regions of the hierarchy. A low caste was able, in a generation or two, to rise to a higher position in the hierarchy by adopting vegetarianism and teetotalism, and by Sanskritizing its ritual and pantheon. In short, it took over, as far as possible, the customs, rites, and beliefs of the Brahmins, and the adoption of the Brahminic way of life by a low caste seems to have been frequent, though theoretically forbidden. This process has been called 'Sanskritization' in this book, in preference to 'Brahminization,' as certain Vedic rites are confined to the Brahmins and the two other 'twice-born' castes.
>
> (Srinivas 1952: 30)

It was rather peculiar that M. N. Srinivas developed the idea of Sanskritization from studying Coorgs (Kodavas or Kodagis), who proudly maintain their rather warrior-like culture, openly consume meat (they even eat pork, but not beef) and alcohol, and enjoy hunting. The only group amongst the Coorgs who demonstrated their strong tendency to Brahminize or Sanskritize their customs was the Amma Coorgs (*amma kodagas*), who formed no more than 2 per cent of the entire Coorg population. Amma Coorgs were vegetarians and teetotallers, wore the sacred thread and offered only vegetarian food to their ancestors (ibid.: 34). They claimed that they were descendants of the union between a Coorg man and a Brahman girl and had been observing their Brahmin mother's customs, hence their name (mother = *amma*).

While there certainly has been a general tendency to claim higher status than their own position in the caste hierarchy by adopting a new lifestyle, we could also observe that there is more than one model that lower castes could follow. Indeed, M. N. Srinivas himself wrote in the same book that increasing numbers of non-Kodagi speakers (Wynad Chettis, Kannada Okkaligas, Tulu Gaudas and others) aspired to be Coorgs by taking up Kodagi language and imitating the dress, customs and manners of the Coorgs, who are non-vegetarians and non-teetotallers (ibid.: 9). Their action seems to be quite opposite to what the Amma Coorgs were aspiring to do. M. N. Srinivas did not, though, make any distinction between the two seemingly opposing tendencies. Instead, he kept the concept of Sanskritization more inclusive by not calling it 'Brahminization'. However, we remain puzzled and wonder which particular actions can be called 'Sanskritic' practice and which actions non-Sanskritic.

There was an ambiguity in the term Sanskritization from its very conception. It was not clear whether the term had to be used exclusively for describing the adoption of Brahminical practices (typically vegetarianism and teetotalism) or could include the more general tendency to imitate whatever upper castes do (in this case, certain practices could be mutually inconsistent). The concept itself was, however, underlined by other anthropological concepts of the era, such as the great and little traditions introduced by Robert Redfield, or Milton Singer's distinction between textual and contextual (Staal 1963: 263; Carroll 1977: 359). In the Coorg book, M. N. Srinivas carefully described the process of incorporation of non-Hindu communities and cults into the Hindu social order and way of life (Madan 1978: 3) as well as the notions of purity and pollution. This view, of marginal communities observing certain elements of 'high' culture, was very much in tune with the sociological trend at that time. Sankritization therefore corresponds with a movement from a little tradition to a greater one.

After carefully tracing never-ending efforts by M. N. Srinivas at redefining the term, historian Lucy Carroll has questioned whether Sanskritization is:

really anything other than that phenomenon common to all societies where to a greater or lesser degree the plebeians follow the social and cultural lead of the elite, emulating the latter to the extent that their own financial resources and the presence or absence of social sanctions supporting elitist prerogatives permit.

(Carroll 1977: 359)

She further argued that the definition given to the term by M. N. Srinivas was so broad and flexible that it could include all possible social change occurring in India (ibid.: 360). She has also pointed out that the result of using culturally-specific terminology might be to inhibit cross-cultural comparison and might further imply that the phenomena could be applied only and uniquely to cases within India (ibid.: 368). This is an extremely significant remark, which characterizes both M. N. Srinivas' ambition to present a case study in Karnataka as a pan-Indian issue, and his life-long academic enterprise to make sociology 'Indian' (see also Deshpande 2007).

Another significant criticism came from an Indologist, J. F. Staal. He has questioned to what extent the term 'Sanskritization' related to Sanskrit as a language or to Vedic or Sanskritic culture in general (Staal 1963). He rightly pointed out that there was a general tendency amongst anthropologists to label certain practices and beliefs as non-Sanskritic religion or popular Hinduism and to contrast them with Sanskritic tradition, which ranges from the worshipping of Sanskritic deities and engaging the service of Brahmans, to classical ideals and beliefs expressed in the philosophical schools (especially the Vedanta), the Bhagavat Gita and the *bhakti* movement (ibid.: 261–2). He then argued that even the act of possession, which has been regarded by anthropologists as a non-Sanskritic practice par excellence, could be found in classical texts such as the Rigveda (ibid.: 267). We could find that gods and priests trembled when they drank the *soma*, and it is well known that animal sacrifice (including that of cows) was very common, if not the core of the Vedic rituals, and that their gods were very fond of the meat of sacrificed animals (see also Jha 2002). Indeed, many cultural and religious practices described in Vedic literature ironically shared more similarity to what modern anthropologists identify as elements of non-Sanskritic, or the little, tradition. The admonition of Staal was therefore significant in suggesting that there was a clear lack of historical consciousness amongst anthropologists, who were too eager to generalize cultural and religious phenomena. The obvious question would be how certain practices such as vegetarianism and teetotalism came to be regarded as elements of higher culture, and at what point high castes began to adopt such practices. The elements of Sanskritic culture might have been much newer than M. N. Srinivas and other anthropologists had assumed.

Sociologist Sujata Patel has argued that M. N. Srinivas determined the way in which Indian sociology treated the caste system thereafter. For him, the best, and the correct, way to identify various groups in India was 'in terms of empirically perceivable markers that define (the) boundaries of such groups' (Patel 1998: 57). These markers were occupation, endogamy and purity-pollution. For M. N. Srinivas, what characterized the caste system was thus primarily *jati* not *varna*. According to Patel, the fact that M. N. Srinivas rejected a more hierarchical aspect of the caste system (*varna*) because he thought that the *varna* hierarchy was empirically non-verifiable made Indian sociology 'at best an unsophisticated one' (ibid.). This also reflects M. N. Srinivas' positioning as a western-educated, liberal but politically neutral intellectual, which makes a sharp contrast with the political engagement of the subaltern study group (see also Khare 1996: 66).

Dominance in rural Karnataka

It was approximately thirty years after he had conducted his first and last intensive fieldwork in a village called Rampura that M. N. Srinivas published a monograph, titled *The Remembered Village*, in 1976. He began the book with the shocking episode of a fire at Stanford, where he was about to write this much-awaited monograph. The fire destroyed most of his fieldnotes, which he had collected in 1948 and processed over several years, and the reader is immediately dragged into this half tragic, half comical journey of his 'remembering' of the ethnography and the notes that have been destroyed. This style of writing, in which the narrator himself (M. N. Srinivas) is always present in the story, continues throughout the book and contributed greatly to the very engaging and emotional nature of his ethnography.

The story is mainly structured around a young, urban Brahmin man, who goes to a village near to his ancestral village in South India. On his arrival, he appears almost like the hero from the Bollywood film *Swades* (2004), played by Shahrukh Khan, a NASA engineer who could only visit a village with a huge camping car equipped with the latest domestic gadgets and conveniences. In 1947, M. N. Srinivas appeared in Rampura with a cook of his own, and twenty-six pieces (!) of luggage. He was, of course, ridiculed by the villagers whose entire possessions would be much less than that. Again, this was a clever trick by which a definite cultural distance was introduced between him and the villagers at the same time as a sense of equality was somehow maintained (by being laughed at). This cultural distance that M. N. Srinivas often emphasized between himself and the people he worked with was not just an honest self-description of an awkward urban intellectual but was ideologically crucial to legitimize himself as a professional social scientist who could maintain objective distance (Khare 1996: 63; Patel 1998: 45). The fact that Rampura was not so far from Mysore city, and the language that the villagers spoke was the same language he spoke (although not the language of his house), does not affect this cultural distance. In fact, he even said that caste-wise the segregation of the residential areas of Mysore city was so strict that if he entered the Kuruba (shepherd caste) street just behind the Brahmin street where he lived, he could discover a variety of costumes and rituals totally different from his own (Srinivas 1998: 204–5). In the international academic context, the distance was therefore necessary to place him in a similar position to that of Malinowski in the Trobriand Islands (which makes M. N. Srinivas less of a 'native' anthropologist).

Meanwhile, in the Indian context, his position as a member of the western-educated urban high-caste elite made it possible for him to speak to his fellow elites about what was going on in the village. Village India was after all the true India, and Rampura was represented not so much as a village in southern Karnataka with its own distinct culture, but as 'the microcosm of social life in India steeped in tradition(s)' (Patel 1998: 54). In this sense, Rampura has become the quintessential Indian village in the same way as Malgudi, a creation of R. K. Narayan, another intellectual from Mysore and M. N. Srinivas' close friend, has been regarded as the quintessential Indian small town. M. N. Srinivas wrote extensively in the popular media and spoke on many occasions to non-academic audiences. His role in the era immediately after Independence was to give his audience a sense of their responsibility to know their own nation (i.e. Village India) and simultaneously to satisfy them with nostalgic depictions of the village, which Indian urban elites had left a few generations ago. The nostalgic nature of M. N. Srinivas' village was also enhanced by the fact that he did not pay much attention to the progress of the time and particularly the fundamental changes that the introduction of universal suffrage was slowly bringing about. Many have suggested that this makes Rampura static, and we do not know whether we are reading about the village of 1948 or of his imagination of it in the early 1970s (Patel 1998: 60; Mayer 1978: 42–3). This criticism may also be applied to the tendency of village studies in the 1950s and 1960s in general.

The concept of dominant caste has been developed through the writings of M. N. Srinivas, based on his Rampura experience, from the early 1950s onwards. He wrote in 1955:

> caste may be said to be 'dominant' when it preponderates numerically over the other castes, and when it also wields preponderant economic and political power. A large and powerful caste group can more easily be dominant if its position in the local caste hierarchy is not too low.
>
> (Srinivas 1955: 18)

The definition he gave here was again rather vague, as was his definition of Sanskritization, although he claimed that the 'vagueness' was deliberate and that he intended to develop this idea later (Srinivas 1987: 4). Is numerical strength sufficient to be politically powerful? Or can economic eminence compensate for numbers? While his original idea about the dominant caste contained several possibly contradictory qualifications, the popular usage of the term has been fixed to designate simply a numerically large caste group; hence the dominant castes in Karnataka were Lingayats in the north and Okkaligas in the south. Especially in the era of electoral politics, numerical strength was immediately translated into the number of votes a group could cast. The image of dominant caste described by M. N.Srinivas was, however, not so much concerned with collective dominance, but with personal power and dominance in the village. The elders of the dominant Okkaliga caste (he simply called them 'Peasants') administer the village council, where not only their own castes but others, including Muslims, seek justice in order to settle their disputes (Srinivas 1955, 1959: 9–10). Of course, being an Okkaliga does not automatically assure this difficult office. A member of the village council has to be a man of quality and respect. M. N. Srinivas later added modern factors to the criteria of dominance: western education, jobs in the state administration, and urban sources of income (Srinivas 1959: 2, 1966: 10–11).

Whenever M. N. Srinivas discussed concrete examples of dominance, although he often brought up cases of individual dominance and superiority, he nonetheless considered numerical strength to be what matters. Louis Dumont has criticized this numerical criterion of the dominant caste introduced by M. N. Srinivas and has instead claimed that the ownership of land, or the possession of superior rights over land, is the sole source of dominance. He further insisted that a caste powerful in terms of land does not have to be numerous, for such a caste can easily attract clientele (Dumont 1980: 161–2). In response to this, M. N. Srinivas has again defended the importance of numbers saying that 'strength of number does provide some protection against the worst forms of oppression and abuse, particularly amongst non-Untouchable castes. In other words, strength of numbers can be translated into social rank' (Srinivas 1987: 5).

S. C. Dube, on the other hand, has questioned the validity of dominance of a caste over the other castes by drawing on his ethnographic data from four villages in Madhya Pradesh (Dube 1968). He has shown that with certain castes, although they fulfil most of the criteria of the dominant caste (number, land possession, economic and political power, ritual status, and western education and occupation), the important and powerful individuals were often hostile to each other and did not contribute towards the unity of their caste. Powerful individuals who belonged to a particular caste exercised their power through abuse, beatings, economic and sexual exploitation, holding representative positions in the village and inter-village councils, and control of votes and settlement of intra-caste and inter-caste disputes, but nonetheless power was not diffused throughout the caste as a whole, and the gap between the rich and poor was significantly wide. He therefore claimed that 'caste is not the power-wielding unit; multi-caste power alliances are' (ibid.: 80). M. N. Srinivas responded to this criticism by pointing out that 'both "dominant individuals" and the "dominant faction" hail from the dominant caste except in areas where there are two rival castes each striving to establish its dominance' (Srinivas 1987: 12). He also claimed that the unity of caste is neither static nor constant, but dynamic and contextual (ibid.).

Rather typically, M. N. Srinivas made his definition wider and looser in order to accommodate irregularities and exceptions. As a consequence, the term 'dominant caste' has become vague but remains a useful descriptive tool. There is no doubt that the numerically dominant castes in Karnataka, the Lingayats in the north and the Okkaligas in the south, have continued to enjoy political power in the state. With a few exceptions, the chief ministers of the state have been from one of these two castes during the past several decades. It seems that they are now following the Brahmins and moving from rural areas to cities, from agriculture to more modern occupations. It is said that communities classified as Other Backward Classes (OBCs) are buying land from former landlords and acquiring power. Whether this new phenomenon will create new dominance in rural Karnataka will require another sociological enquiry.

Veerashaivism in Karnataka: modernising religion or Sanskritizing agent?

After the publication of the Coorg book, M. N. Srinivas elaborated and refined the notion of Sanskritization (1956a, 1956b, 1996 [1967]). To show the complexity of Sanskritization, he drew upon two examples from Karnataka. One was the Lingayats (followers of Veerashaivism) and the other was the Vishwakarma. He called the Lingayats 'a powerful force for the Sanskritisation of the custom and rites of many low castes of Karnataka' and noted that Lingayats in Mysore claimed equal status to that of the Brahmins, and that the more orthodox Lingayats refused to take food cooked or handled by Brahmins (1956b: 482). The Vishwakarma, whose traditional occupations were goldsmiths, ironsmiths, silversmiths, bronzesmiths and stone masons (for a detailed ethnography, see Brouwer 1995), call themselves Vishwakarma Brahmins, wear the sacred thread and have Sanskritized their rituals (Srinivas 1956b: 482).

Although the Lingayats in rural Karnataka seem to have managed to claim high caste status, if not one higher than Brahmin, the Vishwakarma appear to have failed to do the same. According to M. N. Srinivas, they were considered to belong to the left-hand division of the castes. No caste belonging to the right-hand division, including Holeyas (Untouchables), would eat food touched by them and Vishwakarma (left-hand caste) wedding and other processions were not allowed to pass through streets where the right-hand castes lived (ibid.: 482). This division between right- and left-hand castes can be found elsewhere in India. Generally, the left-hand castes follow the Brahminical model of respectability, and the right-hand castes tend to adopt the kingly model of interaction (Brouwer 1995: 25–6; Mines 1982), although which caste belongs to which hand varies from region to region. The reason why certain castes seem to have succeeded in raising their status through Sanskritization while some have failed despite the adoption of Sanskritic customs was not explained at all by M. N. Srinivas.

The tradition of Veerashaivism or Lingayatism has made the religio-political cultures of Karnataka distinctive from other parts of South India. The Lingayats are also one of the two most numerically and therefore politically powerful dominant castes, alongside the Okkaligas. Veerashaivisim has developed since the twelfth century as a popular reformist movement. The saint-politician Basavanna, who lived in northern Karnataka in the twelfth century, was responsible for turning a sectarian philosophy into a mass movement that attracted many lower castes as well as Hindu elites. Although he was Brahmin himself, Basavanna denied the ritual authority of Brahmin priests in temples who claimed a monopoly on the role of mediating between people and the Supreme Being. Instead, Lingayats perform *puja* on their own hand (*hasta puja*), which enables them to communicate directly with Siva. They do not recognize the concept of purity and pollution, which many scholars regard as a core concept of caste hierarchy in India (Dumont 1980), as much as other Hindu high castes do. The personal lingam that they wear on their body purifies any pollution that may occur (see the study on puberty by Parvathamma 1972: 23–43). Rather than relying solely upon the Brahminical authority of Vedas and Agama texts (sets of scriptures evolved from the Upanishad), they place more importance on *vacanas*, short poems in colloquial Kannada written by Basavanna and other mystic-saints (*sharanas*). *Vacanas* convey ethical codes, doctrine, values, devotion and philosophy in simple everyday language. Although their original ideology was clearly opposed to the caste hierarchy based on ritual status, over the centuries the Lingayats themselves have developed caste-like endogamous divisions and a sort of hierarchy within their community.

Since the philosophy of Basavanna was very strongly against the caste system and Brahmin authority, the way in which M. N. Srinivas and others treated Lingayats as agents of Sanskritization or followers of a mere branch of the mainstream Brahminical tradition has troubled many other social scientists, especially Lingayat scholars. K. Ishwaran, himself a Lingayat, claimed that Lingayats were not mere agents of Sanskritic tradition, but rather propagators of a 'populistic tradition' that upholds pluralistic non-elitist ideology (Ishwaran 1983: 13, see also 1977: 2–12). Instead of the dichotomous model of great and little traditions, Ishwaran proposed a more dynamic model in which both *marga* and *desi* traditions communicate with one another. According to him, the *marga* signifies an elitist, minority cultural pattern, while the *desi* typifies a localized, popular cultural pattern. Ishwaran claimed that the Lingayat tradition is partly a selective blending of the *marga* and the *desi*, and partly a selective conflict of the two (1983: 5). By tracing the historical development of their philosophy, ideals and institutions, he further argued that the Lingayat 'populistic' community exemplified an indigenous and internal pattern of modernization in contrast to the modernization imposed by the west. In this modernization, the local populistic community was flexible enough to absorb new ideas such as nation-centred institutions, modern political structures and modern economy, and provided a 'grassroot' basis for the modern political system (ibid.: 133–47). It seems that Ishwaran attributed the success of the Lingayat community in achieving political and economical dominance in the state to their non-elitist ideology, but he failed to explain how Lingayats maintained a dominant position over other communities despite their 'non-elitist' ideology.

C. Parvathamma, another prominent scholar from Mysore and perhaps the first female Dalit sociologist, has provided another interesting interpretation of Lingayat ideology in relation to Sanskritization. Although she has dismissed M. N. Srinivas' *The Remembered Village* as 'a Brahminical odyssey' (Parvathamma 1978), she nonetheless considered that Sanskritization could still be retained as a useful concept (1972: 15). Referring to the rather confusing identification of Lingayats as Sanskritizing agents by M. N. Srinivas despite the fact that

Lingayats have a clear anti-Brahminical tendency, especially their ritual independency from Brahmins, she argued that once a certain community has gained dominance in rural society, their ideological orientation does not matter so much in persuading other lower castes to imitate their patterns of life (ibid.: 18–20). Rather than thinking in terms of behaviour (such as teetotalism and vegetarianism), she suggested that we should pay more attention to the economic, political and ritual interdependence of castes to understand the 'structure in action' (ibid.: 20).

The recent study of the Lingayat community by V. M. Boratti tells us that the idea that Lingayat philosophy has been more humanistic and anti-Brahminical itself has to be historicized (Boratti 2010). The detailed work of Boratti demonstrates how some Lingayat intellectuals endeavoured to re-fashion Lingayat ideals as more modern and 'secular' by rejecting the mythical, supernatural and fanatical legends. They instead promoted *vacanas* as humanistic moral messages that resist against caste discrimination and religious superstition, and propagate work ethics and the equality of women. The promotion and subsequent institutionalization of *vacanas* captured the imagination of the urban middle classes and has helped to form a modern Lingayat identity. Boratti's work also shows that this process of making the Lingayat identity modern did not necessarily go smoothly. In fact, the promotion of *vacanas* and the portrayal of Basavanna as 'a champion of [the] downtrodden and an anti-varna crusader' did not appeal to the conservative Lingayat elites whose aspiration was to gain equal status with Brahmins (ibid.: 183). This tension between two conflicting self-images, modernising religion or Sanskritizing agents, seems to continue to exist even today.

The morality of dominance in rural Karnataka

The village remained the main site of ethnography in Karnataka throughout the 1960s, 1970s and 1980s and up until the 1990s (Epstein 1962, 1973; Ishwaran 1968; Beals 1974; Charsley and Karant 1998; Vasavi 1999). Pioneered by M. N. Srinivas, many followed in his steps by conducting intensive fieldwork and participant observation, but brought different perspectives. The three volumes of ethnography on a majority Lingayat village called Shivapur in northern Karnataka by K. Ishwaran (1966, 1968, 1977) focused on the economy of the village by analysing the complex network of social relations. Ishwaran endeavoured to find out not only how the economic system functioned but also the spirit of the system itself. In the first volume, he explained in detail the transactional economic system called *aya*. The *aya* system that Ishwaran described involves a series of economic transactions in kind between *ayadakulas* (the family giving *aya* – mostly landed farmers), and the *ayagara* (the recipient of *aya* – service castes) and does not operate in a profit-maximising or exploitative way, but centres around the values of honour, pride and prestige (1966: 36–49). He claims that the *aya* system works because all participants want to perform their duty (*dharma*).

One cannot help thinking that Ishwaran was rather romanticizing this system, or simply acting as an apologist for a caste system that many scholars consider rather exploitative, especially when he says things like:

> Since the occupations are graded into a hierarchy of their own, with purity and pollution rules affecting relations with other occupations, and since the occupations are born into via the institution of caste, the question of higher and lower in a simple form does not arise. You are just where you are, and there is no external standard by which you can feel the sense of 'lower' and 'higher'.
>
> (Ishwaran 1966: 38)

Nevertheless, he brought up an interesting example in which a carpenter voted against a Lingayat farmer during the Panchayat elections. When the farmer (an *ayadakula*) tried to intimidate him, the carpenter (an *ayagara*) refused to collect the *aya* from his *ayadakula* (ibid.: 44). It might be a matter of perspective whether one calls this an act of moral superiority on the part of a recipient, or a form of passive resistance, but it could have been developed into a more nuanced form of dominance in village society. Studies on gift-giving in Karnataka did not move to more elaborate theories such as ones concerning the negative components (inauspiciousness, sin, etc.) in gift-giving that developed elsewhere (Raheja 1988; Parry 1980). Gift-giving remained positive and moral in Karnataka.

Alan Beals added ecology as an important dimension to village studies in Karnataka (1974) (see also Gurumurthy 1982). He tried to understand a complex set of relationships within a particular natural environment, which is also constantly being changed by natural forces, modern technology and state intervention. In his study of three villages within different environmental settings, he tried to establish a clear link between ecological necessities and religio-cultural practices. While describing charitable works by temples and monasteries (*mathas*), and mass feedings during religious festivals, he notes that:

> the functions of religious institutions and rituals in South India is not so much to regulate the eco-system directly as to provide a flexible set of options that can compensate for problems arising in the operation of regional ecological and social systems.
>
> (Beals 1974: 159)

He claimed that a large population could survive even at a time of local famine by referring to an incident in 1952 when the areas east of Namhalli (one of his three villages) were affected by drought. Starving people from those areas passed through the Namhalli region and were given small amounts of grain (ibid.: 158).

A. R. Vasavi has further developed the ecological analysis of Beals and others into a much more nuanced ethnography (1999). She not only described the more complex natures of inter-caste relationships in rural Karnataka, but also successfully incorporated historical sources into ethnographical descriptions, which scholars of previous generations failed to do. Madhavi, the village where she conducted her fieldwork in the late 1980s, was situated in a drought-prone area of Bijapur district in northern Karnataka. Contrary to the romantic image of *aya* transactions described by Ishwaran, Vasavi found that *aya* and *dana* (another form of gift-giving) were only made during harvests, which are not periods of resource stress. The harvest season is a period of high employment, and even the poor of the village are able to sustain themselves (ibid.: 77). She further claims that '[t]he inability of these transactions to cater to either the ecologically induced risks of production or to address the established socially-based discrepancies of resource allocation necessitates the underscoring of the characteristics of these transactions' (ibid.: 81). As Vasavi argued, the 'moral economy' has to be examined in the context of power, dominance and cultural norms.

If *aya* transaction is considered to be incumbent on the landowners' families (Vasavi 1999: 81), the receiving of *aya* must also evoke a sense of loyalty amongst recipients. Regarding the strategies of lower castes, especially Dalits, in the complex interdependency of village life, many scholars of Karnataka have produced detailed ethnographies of oppressed classes (see especially Charsley and Karant 1998). G. K. Karant gives us details of subtle but determined everyday protests amongst Dalits (Karant 1998: 102–4). As a part of the terms of contract, landowners serve meals during the day for the agricultural labourers who are mostly lower castes and Dalits. However, the quality of food and the way the food and water is served often makes them feel humiliated. In order to avoid this humiliation, they demand to be paid separately for their food rather than having meals provided (ibid.: 103). The morality of dominance therefore must be considered in the context of complex cultural norms and changing social and economic conditions.

Beyond the village: the city and middle classes

After the economic liberalisation in the 1990s, anthropologists and sociologists began to move their site of ethnography from the village to the city, and from rural agrarian society to urban industrial and post-industrial society. In step with the national trend, Bangalore changed its image and functions from a haven of pensioners and a sleepy garden city to India's Silicon Valley, one of the largest information technology (IT) hubs in India. Bangalore thus became one of the cities that attracted scholarly enquiries. Outstanding works such as Smriti Srinivas' *Landscapes of Urban Memory* (2001), James Heitzman's *Network City* (2004) and Janaki Nair's *The Promise of the Metropolis* (2005) provide detailed historical and ethnographical accounts of how Bangalore has changed its nature from a typical colonial double-city (the 'Indian' old city and the British military cantonment) to a high-tech city. They show how the use of certain public spaces has nurtured and limited the growing sense of civil society, and point to the way in which migrant professionals have developed new religiosity in new suburban residential areas, where people with different languages, religions and castes share spaces of everyday life. The rapid growth of IT and other service industries since the 1990s has attracted new high-tech labourers to the city. The collection of ethnographical essays on IT workers, *In an Outpost of the Global Economy* (Upadhya and Vasavi, 2008), is a much-awaited study that helps us to understand what kind of influence the work culture of the globalizing workforce has upon workers in the high-tech industry and how a competitive and controlling work ethic is producing new psychological imperatives concerning stress relief, self-improvement and success.

While M. N. Srinivas' *The Remembered Village* was primarily a description by an urbanized Brahmin scholar of a village which most of the Brahmins had already left, the Brahmins themselves have never become an object of ethnographical investigation. Their role has always been to describe, not to be described. In this relationship, they remain a neutral agent, free from the world of greed and conflict. In a recent study of Brahmin caste associations in Karnataka, Ramesh Bairy broke with this convention and revealed how Brahmins endeavoured to construct a modern and secular Brahmin identity at the same time as making full use of their kin and *jati* networks to maximize their material gains (Bairy 2010). At last, Brahmins have come under the sociological gaze in Karnataka.

Conclusion

The fact that Karnataka has produced probably the most influential Indian sociologist since Independence, who successfully refashioned the discipline of Indian sociology, ironically did not make Karnataka an attractive region for sociologists and anthropologists to explore. This was perhaps because the findings and attractive narratives drawn from the state of Karnataka by M. N. Srinivas were projected in his writing as voices and theories representing India as a whole. Karnataka itself therefore remained relatively understudied: an apparently normative and unchanging place with very little that was new to attract the engaged scholar. The reality, of course, is quite different, and the 'timelessness' of M. N. Srinivas' work on Karnataka could be said to have done the region a disservice. This chapter has endeavoured to critically engage with the theories of M. N. Srinivas by bringing his theories and implications back to specific situations within Karnataka and by introducing less well-known ethnographical works concerning the rapidly changing social, political and caste structure of the region. Undoubtedly, caste and dominance remain as the most crucial aspects of people's life in Karnataka. Electoral politics in the state is said to be more caste-divided than the other states, and dominant landlord castes (Lingayats and Okkaligas) are still major political players in the state. However, M. N. Srinivas' emphasis on the role of dominant castes has diverted attention from the still more important influence of 'big men' within Karnataka politics and society. In reality, the dominant castes are represented and controlled, both within the village and the state as a whole, by a handful of powerful families, often with a single charismatic leader. This is a feature Karnataka shares in common with neighbouring Tamil Nadu and Andhra Pradesh (see, for example, Price 1989, 2005; Mines and Gourishankar 1990). It has its roots in the highly centralized rule of Mysore state in pre-colonial times and the development of a powerful economy of 'honours', which consolidated ritual, social and political leadership in the hands of the Mysore king and a number of powerful gurus whose wealth and influence progressively increased in the colonial period (Ikegame 2012). The central role of gurus within Karnataka society derives from its anti-Brahminical Veerashiva and other traditions. These were established in pre-modern times but grew spectacularly in prominence in the early twentieth century and still more since Independence, with the rise of OBCs as a political category and the provision of targeted patronage by successive state governments (Ikegame 2010).

As elsewhere in India, the village has ceased to be the sole location of ethnographic study, and many scholars have shifted their focus from the village towards newly emerging sites and issues. In part, this reflects social developments within Karnataka society itself: as cities have grown, dominant castes have followed Brahmin elites and have relocated from villages and established themselves within the economy of Karnataka's spectacularly flourishing urban centres. This, however, has left a lacuna in the social anthropology of the region, since the impact of urbanisation on the village has been entirely neglected. The village of M. N. Srinivas' time has clearly changed dramatically, but there is little ethnography to chart this development. The time, therefore, is now ripe for another visit to Rampura.

References

Bairy, R. T. S. (2010) *Being Brahmin, Being Modern: Exploring the Lives of Caste Today*. New Delhi: Routledge.

Beals, A. R. (1974) *Village Life in South India: Cultural Design and Environmental Variation*. Chicago: Aldine Publishing Company.

Boratti, V. M. (2010) 'The "Discovery" of Vachanas: Notes on Fakirappa Gurubasappa Halakatti's secular interpretation of the texts and Lingayath community in colonial Karnataka', *South Asia: Journal of South Asian Studies*, 33 (2): 177–209.

Brouwer, Jan (1995) *The Makers of the World: Caste, Craft and Mind of South Indian Artisans*. Delhi, Oxford: Oxford University Press.

*Carroll, L. (1977) '"Sanskritization," "Westernization," and "Social Mobility"': A Reappraisal of the Relevance of Anthropological Concepts to the Social Historian of Modern India', *Journal of Anthropological Research*, 33 (4): 355P–71.

Charsley, S. (1998) 'Sanskritization: The career of an anthropological theory', *Contributions to Indian Sociology*, 32 (2): 527–49.

Charsley, S. and Karant, G. K. (eds) (1998) *Challenging Untouchability: Dalit Initiative and Experience from Karnataka*. New Delhi: Sage.

Deshpande, S. (2000) 'M. N. Srinivas on sociology and social change in India: extracts from an interview', *Contributions to Indian Sociology*, 34 (1): 105–17.

*——(2007) 'Fashioning a Postcolonial Discipline: M.N. Srinivas and Indian Sociology', in Uberoi, P. Sundar, N. and Deshpande, S. (eds), *Anthropology in the East: Founders of Indian Sociology and Anthropology*. Ranikhet: Permanent Black.

Dube, S. C. (1968) 'Caste Dominance and Factionalism', *Contributions to Indian Sociology*, 2: 58–81.

Dumont, L. (1980) *Homo Hierarchicus: The Caste System and its Implications*. Chicago: University of Chicago Press (original French edition, 1966).

Epstein, T. S. (1962) *Economic Development and Social Change in South India*. Manchester: Manchester University Press.

——(1973) *South India – Yesterday, Today and Tomorrow: Mysore Villages Revisited*. London: Macmillan.

Fuller, C. J. (1999) 'An interview with M. N. Srinivas', *Anthropology Today*, 15 (5): 3–9.

Gurumurthy, K. G. (1982) *Indian Peasantry: Anthropological Essays on Peasantry*. Delhi: B.R. Publishing Corporation.

Heitzman, J. (2004) *Network City: Planning the Information Society in Bangalore*. New York: Oxford University Press.

Ikegame, A. (2010) 'Why do backward castes need their own gurus? The social and political significance of new caste-based monasteries in Karnataka', *Contemporary South Asia*, 18 (1): 57–70.

——(2012) *The Princely India Re-Imagined: A Historical Anthropology of Princely Mysore from 1799 to the Present*. London: Routledge.

Ishwaran, K. (1966) *Tradition and Economy in Village India*. London: Routledge & Kegan Paul.

——(1968) *Shivapur: A South Indian Village*. London: Routledge & Kegan Paul.

——(1977) *A Populistic Community and Modernization in India*. Leiden: E. J. Brill.

——(1983) *Religion and Society among the Lingayats of South India*. Leiden: E. J. Brill.

Jha, D. N. (2002) *The Myth of the Holy Cow*. London: Verso.

Karant, G. K. (1998) 'Escaping Domination: Rajapura's Untouchables', in Charsley, S. and Karant, G. K. (eds), *Challenging Untouchability*. New Delhi: Sage.

Khare, R. S. (1996) 'Social Description and Social Change: From Function to Critical Cultural Significance', in Shah, A. M., Baviskar, B. S. and Ramaswamy, E. A. (eds), *Social Structure and Change, Vol. 1: Theory and Method – Evaluation of the Work of M. N. Srinivas*. New Delhi: Sage.

Madan, T. N. (1978) 'M.N. Srinivas's earlier work and "The remembered village": an introduction', *Contributions to Indian Sociology*, 12 (1): 1–14.

Mayer, C. (1978) 'The remembered village: from memory alone?', *Contributions to Indian Sociology*, 12 (1): 39–47.

Mines, M. (1982) 'Models of caste and the left-hand division in South India', *American Ethnologist*, 9 (3): 467–84.

Mines, M. and Gourishankar, V. (1990) 'Leadership and Individuality in South Asia: The Case of the South Indian Big-man', *Journal of Asian Studies*, 49 (4): 761–86.

Nair, J. (2005) *The Promise of the Metropolis: Bangalore's Twentieth Century*. New Delhi: Oxford University Press.

Parry, J. (1980) 'Ghosts, Greed and Sin: The Occupational Identity of the Benares Funeral Priests', *Man* (NS) 15: 88–111.

Parvathamma, C. (1972) *Sociological Essays on Veerasaivism*. Bombay: Popular Prakashan.

——(1978) 'The remembered village: a Brahminical odyssey', *Contributions to Indian Sociology*, 12 (1): 91–96.

Patel, S. (1998) 'The nostalgia for the village: MN Srinivas and the making of Indian social anthropology', *South Asia*, 21 (1): 49–61.

Price, P. (1989) 'Kingly Models in Indian Political Behavior: Culture as a Medium of History', *Asian Survey*, 29 (6): 559–72.

——(2005) 'Ideological Integration in Post-colonial (south) India: Aspects of a Political Language', in Bates, C. and Basu, S. (eds), *Rethinking Indian Political Institutions*. London: Anthem Press.

Raheja, G. (1988) *The Poison in the Gift: Ritual, Presentation and the Dominant Caste in a North Indian Village*. Chicago: University of Chicago Press.

Shah, A. M. (1996) 'The Man and His Work', in Shah, A. M., Baviskar, B. S. and Ramaswamy, E. A. (eds), *Social Structure and Change, Vol. 1: Theory and Method – Evaluation of the Work of M .N. Srinivas*. New Delhi: Sage.

Srinivas, M. N. (1952) *Religion and Society among the Coorgs in South India*. Oxford: Oxford University Press.

——(1955) 'The Social System of a Mysore Village', in M. Marriott (ed.), *Village India*. Chicago: University of Chicago Press.

——(1956a) 'Sanskritization and westernization', in Aiyappan, A. and Bala Ratnam, L. K. (eds), *Society in India*. Madras: Social Science Association.

——(1956b) 'A Note on Sanskritization and Westernization', *The Far Eastern Quarterly*, 15 (4): 481–96.

——(1959) 'The Dominant Caste in Rampura', *American Anthropologist*, 61 (1): 1–16.

——(1966) *Social Change in Modern India*. Berkeley, LA, London: University of California Press.

——(1973) 'Itineraries of an Indian Social Anthropologist', *International Social Science Journal*, 25 (1–2): 129–48.

*——(1976) *The Remembered Village*. Berkeley: University of California Press.

*——(1987) *The Dominant Caste and Other Essays*. Delhi: Oxford University Press.

——(1996) 'The Cohesive Role of Sanskritization', in *Village, Caste, Gender and Method*. Oxford: Oxford University Press. Originally published in Mason, P. (ed.) (1967) *Unity and Diversity, India and Ceylon*. London: Oxford University Press, pp. 67–82.

——(1998) *Village, Caste, Gender and Method*. New Delhi: Oxford University Press.

Srinivas, S. (2001) *Landscapes of Urban Memory*. Minneapolis, MN: University of Minnesota Press.

Staal, J. F. (1963) 'Sanskrit and Sanskritization', *Journal of Asian Studies*, 22 (3): 261–75.

Upadhya, C. and Vasavi, A. R. (eds) (2008) *In an Outpost of the Global Economy: Work and Workers in India's IT Industry*. New Delhi: Routledge.

*Vasavi, A. R. (1999) *Harbingers of Rain: Land and Life in South India*. New Delhi: Oxford University Press.

9 Kerala

Plurality and consensus

Heike Moser and Paul Younger

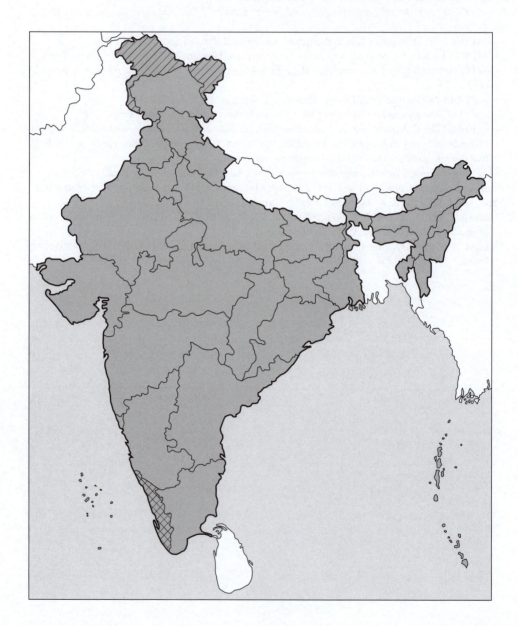

God's own comrade

> It matters little to the ordinary Keralite if the Marxist he voted for was a closet believer. What galls him is the subterfuge.
>
> (*India Today*, February 26, 2007)

Because of its distinctive social makeup, Kerala is a favorite place for ethnographic study. As ethnographic research of Kerala began, a surprising number of Kerala's own researchers joined in the study of their neighbors. As early as 1926, the Brahman scholar L. K. Ananta Krishna Ayyar wrote *Anthropology of the Syrian Christians*. A few years later A. Aiyappan was writing about Nayadis, Nayars, Izhavas, and Paniyas, and K. Saradamoni and A. Ayrookuzhiel have continued that trend with more recent studies of Pulayas and other low castes. Outside ethnographers, on the other hand, focused immediately on what appeared to them to be the exotic dimensions of Kerala's society, such as the widespread matriliny, the presence of an ancient Christian church, and the early success of the Communist-inspired "model" society.

History and ethnography are difficult to disentangle in the case of Kerala. Most communities have legendary accounts of how they came to be part of Kerala society, and while both historians and ethnographers express skepticism about those legends, they tend to tell the story of that community as if there is some truth in the legendary perspective. As they then go on to describe the reform stories of the nineteenth century, the political stories of the middle of the twentieth, or the recent stories of working abroad and globalization, the interaction of the different communities can be traced in more detail and statistical and observational evidence takes over from the older stories. In order to preserve a sense of how these different historical eras give rise to different scholarly styles, after a brief historical overview we will divide our study into four major parts. Thus Section II will describe the approaches that have been made to understanding the traditional communities and will introduce the ethnography about those communities; Section III will deal with the reforms of the nineteenth and early twentieth centuries; Section IV with the era of political unification and the accomplishments of the "model" society; and Section V will concern itself with the current social scene.

I Kerala: a brief historical overview

Kerala is one of the smaller states of the Indian Union (38,863 square kilometers) with about 31.8 million inhabitants (Census 2008), and yet its official language of Malayalam is divided into many dialects and sociolects in accord with the social divisions of the society. The etymology of the name "Keralam" is not clear: some derive it from "kera" (coconut tree) and "alam" (land)—from the view of a philologist quite problematic—while others take it to mean "cera-alam," "the land of the Ceras." The state is distinctive partly because of its semi-isolated geography as a coastal strip in the deep Southwest, cut off from the rest of India by the Western Ghat mountain range. In mythology it is said that it was Parasurama who created Kerala by throwing his axe into the sea in order to create the coastal region.

Thanks to its historical contacts with West Asia, Europe, Sri Lanka, Southeast Asia, and Northern India through its coastal ports, a variety of different communities settled in Kerala and chose to maintain their distinctive culture, religion, and social forms, even as they agreed to live in a pluralist, and in many ways harmonious, society.

Kerala was ruled for many centuries by Cera-kings (first century BCE–CE twelfth century). In this period Jewish, Christian, and Muslim merchants settled down and enjoyed religious freedom. According to the Census of 2001, Kerala's main religious groups are divided into 56.2 percent Hindus, 24.7 percent Muslims, 19.0 percent Christians, and 1.1 percent "Others." The Later Cera Kingdom, the Kulashekara dynasty, came to an end largely because of invasions by the Pandya and Cola dynasties to the east. After this, Nayar chieftains became powerful and the country was divided into small principalities in the absence of a strong central power. After 1498, when Vasco da Gama arrived in Kappad (Kozhikode), Europeans started to control much of the lucrative spice trade characteristic of the region and to interfere with the religious life of the area. The initial Portuguese role in this regard was followed by a briefer contact with the Dutch East India Company in the eighteenth century. Hyder Ali (ruler of Mysore) and his son Tipu Sultan invaded the northern half of the region in the late eighteenth century, but were soon driven out by the British, who took over the rule of Malabar or the northern area of the state in 1792. After India gained independence, the state of Kerala was formed on November 1, 1956 by merging the Malabar district and the former local kingdoms of Travancore and Cochin. The first elections of the Kerala Assembly in 1957 became famous because they resulted in the election of one of the first democratically elected Communist governments in the world. The state is recognized today around the world for its high life expectancy, low fertility rate, low infant and maternal mortality rates, "natural" sex ratio, and high literacy. At the same time the economy of Kerala now suffers from a lack of local employment opportunities and is heavily dependent on remittances from its large expatriate community.

II The traditional communities of Kerala

The first communities

One of the odd things about Kerala ethnography is that so little is known about the early communities. Publications like those of Iyer (1909) or Thurston (1909) are of only little help. Aiyappan has struggled to address this silence and has studied both the archaeological evidence of burial sites (1982) and communities such as the Muduga, Nayadis, Kurichiyas (Aiyappan and Mahadevan 1990), and Paniya (Aiyappan 1992) that claim legendary links with the distant past. In an amazing article in 1999, Uchiyamada picks up this story of tribal communities and burial sites and shows how the Kurava community today clings to land it thinks of as traditionally its own. What the Kuravas do is watch from nearby as the spirits of their ancestors haunt those who they say have taken their land from them. In his account, Uchiyamada argues that the Pulayas, who constitute the major class of agricultural labor, follow some of the same practices concerning their *badha* or ancestral spirits. One example of the evidence of this that he cites comes from an article by Kathleen Gough (1959) where she describes the necessity Nayar landlords feel to allow their Pulaya workers to bring sorcerers to pacify the ancestral spirits that still claim to have a prior right to what is now ostensibly Nayar agricultural land.

The religious life of these early communities seems to have been largely preserved in the Teyyam practices of today described by Ayrookuzhiel (1983) in the village of Chirakkal in North Malabar, a practice that has now been studied further in new theses by Freeman (1991), Ashley (1993), and Uchiyamada (1995). Both the deities and unhappy ancestral spirits of these communities are thought to abide in groves or *kavu* from where they come out to take form in Teyyam dancers from time to time. By expressing themselves in traditional songs or *tottams* these spirits are sometimes linked up with the deities of Tiyyas (Ezhavas) and Nayars, or even make references to Brahman, Mappila (the moslems of Kerala), or Christian spirits. Teyyam practices are not only a good example of how a cult of one group can be woven into the religious life of the whole society, but also can serve as a ritual performing art that serves the whole society as both "theater" and "ritual" (Ashley and Holloman 1982).

Tamil literary records would seem to indicate that Kerala had a fascinating forest culture at one time. The Tamil grammarian, Tolkappiyan, describes the Kurinchi or mountain people of the Western Ghats and their deities and romantic customs. Revealing more sophistication as the forest culture met the coastal, the author of the slightly later *Cilapattikaram* describes his heroine, Kannaki, fleeing into the Kerala mountains after setting fire to the city of Madurai, and then explains how she was hailed by the local women and eventually buried and worshipped in the annual festival in the coastal city of Muziris (Kodungalur) (Induchudan 1969; Obeyesekere 1984).

The Mukkuvar or fishermen caste who now live along the coast seem to have some links with the early inland communities, but they also have ties with other coastal fishing communities in Tamil Nadu and Sri Lanka. Records of their earlier history are difficult to reconstruct because they developed their own distinctive cultural enclave when many of them became Roman Catholic after the Portuguese arrived in the early sixteenth century (Houtart and Nayak 1988; Bayly 1989).

The Christian presence

Today Christians constitute almost 20 percent of the population of Kerala, but prior to the unification of the state in 1956 they seem to have been about half the population in the southern half of the state, the area in which they traditionally carried out trade. There is much evidence that the Kerala coast was trading with western Asia and even Rome well before the beginning of the Christian era, and there are still both synagogues and churches that claim ancient origins in places such as Parur, just beside the island port of Muziris (Bayly 1989; Visvanathan 1993). The Christian legends hold that the apostle Thomas himself landed in Muziris in 52 CE and that he preached to Brahmans there and established seven churches in the area. A separate tradition that is passed on in the small Canaanite community is that their ancestor, Thomas of Cana, arrived in the fourth century with a large company and insisted they remain endogamous, which they claim they have largely done (Visvanathan 1993). The Jewish and Christian communities early on served as the trading community of Kerala and established links between trade in pepper and spices and the coastal trade. In both Quilon and Muziris copperplate grants of rulers in 849 and 1225 CE respectively specify that land and servants are to be given to the Christians, along with ceremonial privileges and responsibilities over trade and the official scales (Kuriakose 1982). While the rulers honored this semi-autonomous community in this way, by the time of the latter copperplate they were beginning to do much the same by designating large tracts of land to the Brahmans and Nayars as well. During much of Kerala's history these three elite communities apparently all had military units, intermarried to some extent, and contributed money and ceremonial support to each others' temples and churches (Visvanathan 1993).

Fuller (1976b) has argued that the Syrian Christians should be considered a "caste" in that they maintain the ideology behind the strictly hierarchical social arrangements of Kerala. They insist on the same touch and distance pollution rules of the other high castes over against the Ezhavas and the "slave" castes, and even among themselves they maintain a strict hierarchical arrangement that is most evident at the time of marriage when very large payments of *stridanam* or dowry are expected from brides whose families want to marry them into a family of higher status (Visvanathan 1993; Chacko 2003; Philips 2004).

While Fuller uses the static all-Indian category of "caste" to describe the position of the Syrian Christians in Kerala society, Bayly (1984), Visvanathan (1993), and Dempsey (1998) describe the Christians as a powerful community that played a central role as events in society developed. In describing the initiatives of Martanda Varma (1729–48) in establishing the Travancore state, Bayly demonstrates how he relied heavily on the elite Christian military units as he reduced the role of the Nayars in local administration and insisted that they swear to support him in the ceremony he initiated in the Sri Padmanabha temple. When he then went on to employ exclusively Desastha Brahmans from Tamil Nadu in his civil service, the Namboodri Brahmans, too, lost the privileged link with royalty that they had once enjoyed. Visvanathan describes in detail the marriage arrangements and worship traditions that make the Syrian Christian community internally strong, but then describes how difficult the issues of spiritual lineage have been, as first the Portuguese in the sixteenth century questioned the legitimacy of the Syrian liturgy they use, and then the British Church Missionary Society did the same thing in the nineteenth century. Dempsey (1998, 2000, 2005) describes the way the Christian and Hindu communities recognize each other's spiritual traditions and speak of Mary as the older sister, and Bhagavati as the younger whose procession cannot start until a Christian family from the Manarkat church takes its role as the first to pull on the ropes of the processional cart (Younger 2002: 118–24).

The Namboodiri elite

Although the Brahmans of Kerala now represent hardly one percent of the population, they are scattered in settlements throughout the state where they were once given title to the agricultural land (*janmi*). They established landholding temples, introduced Sanskrit vocabulary into the basically Dravidian Malayalam language, and taught the people the rules of caste. In a valiant effort to link legend with history, Kesavan Veluthat (1978) followed the clues of his teachers at Calicut University, E. K. Pillai and M. G. S. Nararayanan, and identified almost every one of the 32 legendary "settlements" of Brahmans with an existing temple community. Many of these settlements were given to Brahmans by members of the Cera dynasty when it briefly revived near Muziris between the ninth and thirteenth centuries, but weaker rulers had certainly started the practice earlier and Brahman landholdings continued to accumulate in the centuries that followed.

Scholars working on the matrilineal castes in the 1950s began to take note of the way matriliny allowed high-status Nayar women to have hypergamous relationships with Brahman men, so in 1962 Joan Mencher (Mencher and Goldberg 1967) studied the Namboodiri system of marriage to figure out what implications that arrangement had for Brahman families. She found that Namboodiris insisted not only on patriliny but on primogeniture, so that only the eldest son would marry and keep strict control of the family land as it was passed from generation to generation. Although younger Brahman men bore children with Nayar women, this arrangement did not lead to extended ties between the communities, and the Namboodiri house or *illam* remained a distant, monastery-like place where the unmarried youth were busy with religious and domestic duties.

Being quite resistant to modernization until the early twentieth century, the Namboodiris kept old traditions alive that have vanished in other parts of India (for a glimpse into the modernization of a Namboodiri family, see Parpola 2000). One example is the "altar of fire," *Agnicayana*, which is considered to be the greatest Vedic ritual and one of the oldest rituals of humanity. In 1975 Frits Staal documented the full twelve-day performance of such a ritual (Staal 1983). Based on his observation of this ritual, he later went on to develop his well-known theory on the "meaninglessness of ritual" and the similarity of ritual and grammar (Staal 1989). Another example of Namboodiri culture is Kutiyattam, India's sole surviving traditional Sanskrit theater, which is indigenous to Kerala (Raja 1964; Richmond 1990). Until the 1950s Kutiyattam was exclusively staged in prosperous Brahmanized temples as a ritual theater, patronized by the Namboodiris and performed by high-caste actors and actresses. In the twentieth century, when temples began to lose their rich landholdings, Kutiyattam had to leave the protective environment of the temple playhouse and present itself on secular stages to audiences who were not educated in the traditional arts. This makes Kutiyattam a perfect example of the re-invention and innovation of tradition as it conserves an art form by opening itself to a wider audience in a newly public space (Byrski 1967; Moser 2011).

The Nayars

Between 1947 and 1949 E. Kathleen Gough, on a student scholarship from Cambridge, conducted fieldwork in Nayar *taravads* of three villages of what she called "Central Kerala" (Southern Malabar). During the 1950s she published five articles on her findings and in 1961 wrote two-thirds of the classic study called *Matrilineal Kinship* (edited with David Schneider). Her analysis is a brilliant example of the structural-functionalist anthropology associated with Britain in her day, and everyone since has begun from her explanations of matriliny or *marumukatayam* as descent through the female line. This line is established by the ceremony of tying the *tali* for a group of small girls that prepares them for fertility, and by the subsequent creation of *sambandhams* or sexual relationships with one or more men of higher status. The mother legitimizes the child by identifying the father, who in turn gives it a small gift, but then she raises it in her own house or *taravad* along with her sisters' children and the management of her eldest brother or *karanavan*. The debates that raged about matriliny, marriage ceremonies, hypergamy, and polyandry after these definitive studies were complex.

Because the style of structural-functional argument Gough used made "Nayars" appear to be an abstract entity following a clear logic, Aiyappan (1965, 1982) had to remind readers that Ezhavas, like himself, followed a similar system of marriage and that he had written extensively about the polyandry part of the practice in the 1930s. Mencher (1962) had to try to figure out why the system was changing so fast, and Fuller (1976a) had to point out that there were very different styles of *taravad* in different regions and different social classes. Moore joined the debate late (1985, 1988) to point out that from the point of view of symbolic anthropology the *taravad* might better be described as a house-and-land arrangement (she did not mention the Syrian Christian use of the word "*taravad*" and its many similarly complex arrangements for managing and passing on land; a pattern to be discussed in detail by Visvanathan in 1993), and the genealogical dimension as a mother and child linked together by a "shared-biological substance" tie. For her the *tali*-tying becomes a *mangalam* or auspiciousness ritual, to be followed later by a first menstruation ritual, and later still by the cloth-gift or *purdavakada (sambandham)* as one of many hypergamous gift-giving rituals that link groups in Indian society together.

The Ezhavas (Tiyyas)

By far the largest single community in Kerala is that of the Ezhavas (1.8 million or almost 40 percent of the total in the 1931 census). Their legends link them with the island of Sri Lanka

(Ezham) and with the introduction to Kerala of the coconut palm and the production of the intoxicating drink *toddy*. Aiyappan (1944, 1965, 1982), himself of Ezhava heritage, acknowledges the two parts of the legendary history, even as he argues that there could not have been such a large migration, and that Ezhava identity is loosely constructed and should be understood in all-Indian "caste" terms.

We will see below how centrally Ezhavas became involved in the reforms of the nineteenth and twentieth centuries, the politics of the mid-twentieth century and the social changes involved in the current employment in the Gulf countries, but definitive accounts of their various roles in pre-modern Kerala are almost non-existent. Velayudhan (1991, 1998) traces their version of the matrilineal system, and they are mentioned as servants assigned to the Syrian Christians in the inscription of 849 CE. They also figure in accounts of traditional temple rituals (Osella and Osella 2003), sometimes participate as a group of *veliccapatu* or sorcerers that Nayars control (Tarabout 1986; Younger 2002: 41–50), and, at other times, as temple owners at whose temple the lower caste Teyyam dancers perform (Younger 2002: 125–32). Because their primary work in coconut groves left them free of the "slave" status imposed on the Pulaya and others in rice cultivation, both women and men seem to have been free to do agricultural work, own their own agricultural land, engage in commercial enterprises of various kinds, and find themselves in a great variety of religious roles.

The Muslims

Arab traders seem to have replaced Christians along the coast at some point, and by the ninth century most coastal cities had mosques built, some of which are still standing. Miller (1992) and Bayly (1989) have tried to explain when and how the extensive pattern of marriage between Muslim men and local women (many of whom had traditionally followed a matrilineal form of descent) began and how the agricultural community known as the Mappila was formed in the Malabar area.

This community was jolted out of its traditional role by the way Muslim invaders from Karnataka briefly entered the area in the eighteenth century before being driven out by the British in 1792. The pattern of change initiated at this time continued during the Mappilas' bitter conflict with the Brahman and Nayar landowners or *janmi* when those two groups tried to use the British courts to regain their rights in the late nineteenth and early twentieth centuries, the era of post-Independence politics, and also in the current era of employment in the Gulf countries (Osella and Osella 2008a, 2008b). In understanding the different struggles the Mappila community went through, it is important to remember that for a thousand years before these changes the Mappilas had little contact with the Muslim world in the north of India and were very much a local community that shared some of the matrilineal traditions of the Nayars and Ezhavas and the ritual traditions of the Teyyam.

Traditional pluralism

Each of the communities making up traditional Kerala society seemed keen to perpetuate its own identity by maintaining legendary accounts of its outsider origins and by keeping to the complex rules on separation, whether they were defined by a pollution ideology or by the traditional patterns of economic activity. What is even more interesting than these rules on separation, however, are the patterns of ritual engagement that make the different communities intimately aware of one another's marriage arrangements, politics, and especially religion. The hypergamous marriage arrangements between Nayars and Namboodris are the most famous example of contact, but Christian and Muslim links with other communities through both religion and marriage worked more slowly and also integrated both those communities into specific niches in society. Political ties were never as dominant as they were in nearby Tamilnadu and other places, but they did give economic advantages to Christians, Namboodris, and Nayars at various times, and so there was not much resistance when after Independence political forces took away some of those privileges in order to serve the good of the whole society. Most important of all, however, seems to be the way religious ritual governed inter-community relations. In addition to the examples already given, where two communities were linked in a ritual festival (like in Teyyam or Kutiyattam), there were also general features of religious behavior that linked communities, and not necessarily in the lower-emulating-upper pattern described as "Sanskritization" in other parts of India. Hospital (1984) described the social impact of the Onam festival in which all communities share and link all of Kerala society with the demon king Mahabali who was sent into the underworld only to return to his people once a year. Tarabout (1993) described how often competition between communities is established by ritual rivalry at festival time and by the legendary boat races that allow one community to challenge another without resorting to violence. He also (Tarabout 1999a, 2000) described the way in which the ubiquitous use of witchcraft makes it possible for the apparently losing community to continue the struggle as it waits upon the supernatural for new opportunities. Freeman (1999a) even argues that the permeability of the person that one sees in Teyyam possession is still part of the religious logic of the Brahmans' *tantric* image worship.

III The reform movements of nineteenth- and early twentieth-century Kerala

Political and educational reform

New opportunities for social change rather suddenly became available at the beginning of the nineteenth century when the British colonial regime found a way to reach into the Kerala hinterland. Susan Bayly (1984) is anxious that we remember that the local political reform of Martanda Varma (ruler of Travancore) began in the middle of the eighteenth century. He was, however, only able to resist the later invasions of Hyder Ali (ruler of Mysore) and his son Tipu Sultan from the north because the British came to his rescue, so it was the establishment of British rule in Malabar in 1792 that defines the beginning of the new era. The royal states of Cochin and Travancore continued on in the center and south of the Malayali-speaking area, but they, too, were influenced by the British Resident appointed to assist them, and by the Tamil-speaking Brahman civil servants who kept close touch with the colonial office in Madras.

The first British Residents, Macauley and Munro, were eager reformers, and, as E. T. Mathew (1999) describes, they assisted the London Mission Society and the Church Mission Society in setting up some of the first schools, and encouraged the Travancore Rani (or Queen), who declared in 1817 that the state would "defray the cost of the education of its people" (cited in Census of India 1941, vol. XXV, part 1, p. 155 as the primary reason for the high literacy rate). Schools established in Alleppy in 1816 and Kottayam in 1817 encouraged the education of girls and the lower castes, and the combination of state schools and mission schools was soon followed by those started by other communities and by private parties.

Almost as important as the educational reforms of the time was the introduction of a colonial judicial system that was soon sorting out land disputes in all three jurisdictions. It was the judicial system that began to examine the central role of the Nayar *taravad* and the

Namboodiri entitlement (*janmi*) in matters of land use that pushed along the reforms initiated with the opening of schools.

The Nayar entanglements

In some ways the community that responded most dramatically to the opportunities that opened up in the field of education and land reform was that of the Nayars. Because the eldest brother in the matrilineal house or *taravad* was considered the sole manager, younger males and females had always had some time for education, and they now eagerly moved from the village teachers to the new schools being established. Political opportunities were, however, oddly in decline because the royal families continued to rely on Tamil Brahmans as their senior civil servants, and the zealous Resident Munro had insisted that judicial powers be taken from the local Nayar officials and given to trained judges, who were initially often of Syrian Christian background (Jeffrey 1976a).

In the process of being exposed to new ideas through education and to new economic opportunities, both the cultural and the economic viability of the larger matrilineal *taravad* houses was being called into question. The missionaries lost no opportunity to criticize the matrilineal system as immoral, but the real challenge came from the clumsiness of the *taravad* management and the fact that it left no opportunity for the community to take advantage of the new business atmosphere and the salaried income many members were now receiving. The real crunch came from the colonial courts' interpretation of the rule that a *taravad* could only be divided if there was unanimous consent. Fuller (1976a), Jeffrey (1976a) and Arunima (2003) all describe how, in effect, the courts were handing a monopoly of land management to the *karanavan* (the senior maternal uncle in a matrilineal family), and how both the women and the younger brothers of the household began to rebel against that monopoly. As the controversy spread from land management to the whole of the matrilineal system, voices within the Nayar community led the revolt and began to echo the Victorian morality they were now reading about. Kodoth (2001) and Arunima (2003) provide detailed historical accounts of this period and of the arguments involved in the writing of the Madras Marriage Commission Law of 1891. Those two scholars explicitly contrast their historical style with the ahistorical character of the earlier anthropological accounts of Gough, Fuller, and Moore that looked for explanations of the "unnatural" character of matriliny either in the hypergamy forced on the Nayars by the Namboodiris or in the absence from the home of men who were serving in local militias. For Kodoth and Arunima the weakness that brought the matrilineal system down was primarily in the area of land management. The disintegration of the matrilineal system and the status of Nayar women today is discussed in Renjini (2000).

While the inheritance provisions of matriliny and the *taravad* were only changed by legislation in 1933 and 1976, the forces in favor of change within the community were clearly in the ascendency by 1890 when the educated youth turned their attention in the *Malayali Memorial Agitation* to seeking a better representation for local people in the Travancore civil service (Jeffrey 1976a). The decision of Martanda Varma to use primarily Tamil Brahmans in his civil service had from the beginning been a severe blow to the traditional roles of both the local Nayar officials and the Namboodiris, but the newly educated Nayars were able to take up the cause in their own way when in the *Memorial* they argued that it was a matter of enlightened democratic practice to employ the educated youth of the locality rather than an alien elite from Tamilnadu. The fact that the logic of that demand would later lead to changes in land tenancy rights and even radical political realignment was not yet clear, but with that petition the Nayar youth of Kerala took over the intellectual leadership of society and began the push for more changes in the years ahead.

The Christian advantages

The schools built in the early years of the nineteenth century were open to all communities, but the male and female Christian youth felt most at home in them and soon their literacy, and subsequent employment, rates were well ahead of the average. Almost more important was the fact that their traditional role as traders blended in with the development of a new commercial economy, and they were soon recognized by all as the wealthy in society (Jeffrey 1976a; Visvanathan 1993; Osella and Osella 2000a). With their new level of wealth they were also in a position to take advantage of the Namboodiris and Nayars, who were finding it necessary to divest themselves of their difficult-to-manage land wealth. Finally, their understanding of the new economy made it possible for them to see the opportunities available in upland agriculture, first in Central Travancore and later on in North Malabar (Freeman 1999b).

As Visvanathan notes, however, it was not a happy time for the Syrian Christians internally. The Portuguese had earlier on questioned the traditional theological connections they maintained with minor bishops of west Asia, and only after a bitter struggle did half of them push aside the Portuguese effort to link them with Rome. Munro, one of the early Residents, was a zealous reform-minded Protestant Christian, and he once again dismissed the west Asian links and described the poor education of the local priests. When the Anglican Church leadership tried to assist the Syrian churches through education and social reform, a significant group among them supported the push towards an educated clergy (Thomas 1977) and they developed into the Mar Thoma Church. By 1889, however, the courts held that the conservative faction, which in the meantime had again come into favor with the west Asian bishops, was entitled to most of the traditional church property. The Mar Thoma group pushed on in spite of this ruling and took an active role in the *Malayali Memorial* of 1890 and in the development of hill tracts in the early part of the twentieth century.

The Ezhava reforms

The community that was at the center of the social changes that characterized the nineteenth and twentieth centuries was the large amorphous group in the middle ranges of Kerala society known as the Ezhavas. Fortunately, we know a lot about how this group became an "imagined community" (Anderson 1983) during this period because a number of their leaders became newspaper editors and publishers. The renowned anthropologist, A. Aiyappan, was born in their midst and wrote about them, many studied their great reformer Narayana Guru, and the Osellas (2000a) conducted detailed fieldwork on them as recently as the 1990s.

In spite of the demeaning pollution rules it was subjected to, the community had always maintained its distance from the slave-like arrangements of others in the agricultural sector, and when plantation agriculture opened up the hilly sections of Kerala and provided other opportunities to work in labor gangs in Malaysia and Sri Lanka the Ezhavas were prepared to go. Soon these first initiatives developed into a major coir manufacturing industry in Alleppy and other coastal cities, and the Ezhavas rushed there for work and schooling. By 1931 male literacy among them was 43 percent, and above the Kerala average, and many were attending English-medium schools in order to maximize their opportunities (Jeffrey 1976b).

While the Ezhavas of Central Kerala were taking advantage of their new opportunities in the integrated society, the related community of Nadars (Shanars) in the southern corner of

Travancore lived more or less alone and were deeply influenced by the newly arrived missionaries (Hardgrave 1969; Gladstone 1984). When the Resident Munro insisted that the new female converts among them should be allowed to cover their breasts, most Nadar as well as Ezhava women began to do so and a bitter controversy arose with the upper castes who considered this a first step in tearing away the caste barrier. Unlike the situation that developed in the Nayar community, where matriliny could not easily be changed because it was in many ways the cultural support of the *taravad* landholding system, Ezhavas moved away from matriliny more quickly and began to use a variety of different marriage systems as the social environment around them changed (Aiyappan 1944, 1965).

By the end of the nineteenth century there was enough wealth in the Ezhava community that they were, like the Mar Thoma Syrian Christians, buying up land, and a few of the best educated in the community were prepared to take a new initiative. The founding of the famous SNDP Yogam in 1903 ("Sri Narayana Dharma Paripalana Yogam," a charitable society working for the spiritual and educational uplift of the Ezhava community) brought together the three brilliant voices of Dr. Palpu, a medical doctor who had gone to Madras for his education and to Mysore for work because Ezhavas were still barred from those roles in Kerala; Narayana Guru, the saintly figure who had been, for some time, tearing down traditional Ezhava temples, dedicating new ones, and calling for the end of all caste practice; and Kumaran Asan, the brilliant poet trained in Sanskrit. Having committed themselves to reform through this efficiently run organization, Ezhavas took center stage in Kerala's social change over the decades to come. In the 1920s and 1930s the newspaper editor, C. V. Kunjuraman, raised the question as to whether a mass conversion into the Mar Thoma Church, into which many were already moving through conversion or marriage, was a good idea, but when the Temple Entry Proclamation was finally issued in 1936, and Ezhavas were free to think of themselves as proper Hindus, that idea was dropped (Jeffrey 1976b; Houtart and Lemercinier 1978). By that point T. K. Madhavan was the energetic secretary of the SNDP, and the Ezhava movement focused less on religion and evolved into the beginning of a mass movement of the lower classes, which in a couple of years would lead to the birth of the Communist Party of Kerala (Namboodripad 1966).

IV Political unification and the recognition of the Kerala "model"

Civic culture

During the middle decades of the twentieth century Kerala suddenly developed a remarkable sense of civic culture. This was a very local development, because while it was the period of the India-wide national struggle in which Gandhi's leadership was prominent, Kerala was not at the heart of that struggle and found itself dealing with a host of local issues. Jeffrey (1976a, 1978) and Isaac (1986) provide detailed accounts of the variety of different issues addressed, demonstrate why the Indian National Congress never got its leadership role in Kerala right, and explain why its left-wing leaders moved to become the Congress Socialist Party in 1934 and then the Communist Party of Kerala in 1940. It is Manali Desai (2001, 2002) who later on described the way in which the formation of the Communist Party developed around the issues brought forward in the developing civic culture, and how a perfect synergy between the Party and the civic culture developed before 1957 and largely continues. However, it was the leader of the first Communist ministry, E. M. S. Namboodripad, who in 1966 stepped back from his party duties temporarily to provide his account of Kerala's civic culture, which shows us how close culture and politics had become in that era.

In Namboodripad's view it is the misinterpretation of both the Moplah (Mappila) Rebellion of 1921 in Malabar and the Vaikom temple entry agitation in Travancore in 1924–25 that was the undoing of the Congress and the signal to the masses that their movements would prove successful only when they were in a position to interpret them themselves. In Malabar the land tenure issue had been festering for generations by the 1920s because the British interpreted the traditional *janmi* system as a matter of simple ownership and allowed the absentee Brahman and Nayar landlords back into control after they had been chased out of the area by the invasions of Hyder Ali and his son Tipu Sultan. The Mappila peasant tenants rebelled over and over about the way the courts interpreted their rights, and in 1921 were hopeful only because the Congress offered to lead their cause. At the first whiff of violence, Gandhi ordered the agitation closed down, but the restless peasants were still outraged and a mass movement had been formed. The Vaikom issue was similar only in that the massive demonstrations were being led by the increasingly confident Ezhava leader T. K. Madhavan, who had the support of the nearby Ezhava coir factory workers. Again, it was Gandhi who suggested the demands be watered down, and the aroused public was deeply disappointed.

When the youthful leaders of the mass action movements were put in jail together, they began to read Marxist literature for the first time. By 1934 they felt they should not only try to control the Congress apparatus democratically, as they had been doing, but that they should also join the Congress Socialist Party in order to give a clearer ideological edge to the various mass movement activities they found themselves engaged in. After the mass agitation for responsible government to replace princely rule in Travancore in 1938, which was largely led by the Ezhava coir workers, they decided they needed an even clearer ideological lead and became the Communist Party of Kerala in January 1940. Once the Second World War started and the Germans attacked the Soviet Union, the newly formed Party had to make an awkward shift from opposing the British war effort to supporting it, but it was still able to concentrate on local issues affecting the lower classes as food shortages and issues around land rights became acute. When the war ended and the central local issue became the ending of princely rule and the uniting of all Malayali-speaking people in one nation, the political energy was in full flood and the pluralist society was speaking with one voice (Namboodripad 1966).

Governing from the Left

When the first Communist ministry came to power between 1957 and 1959, outsiders asked whether it would be tolerated by the Center or the governing party in New Delhi, and how it would deal with the apparatus of government. People within the civic culture of Kerala were curious as to how it would continue to lead the masses that had come to expect so much. The initial decisions to provide a basic framework for land tenancy legislation and to protect families against eviction from their huts proved popular, but the effort to bring the management of the schools within government purview proved more controversial and enticed the church authorities and some in the Nayar leadership to declare how nervous they were about the rapidly developing civic culture. While the Center dismissed the first government and called for new elections, the political consensus remained. With different party coalitions in each of the subsequent elections (the United Democratic Front, UDF, often continued with the policies of the Left Democratic Front or LDF), the government continued to lead the development of a welfare state providing health, education, rationing, and equality of opportunity in accord with the local consensus (Lieten 1982, 2002; Menon 1994).

The "model"

In the 1980s the United Nations decided to create a Human Development Index in order to give a qualitative measure to its push for development. Alas, the world discovered Kerala and the remarkable way in which it had achieved indices of human development that were comparable to those in the developed world, in spite of its relatively low per capita income levels. In 1986–87 Franke and Chasin went to a village where data were available from Joan Mencher's earlier research, and in their writing of 1992–93 declared that Kerala was a "model" of human development all could aspire to follow. They set out the indices in a simple chart as follows (adjusted in a later paper published in 1996 to the 1995 figures used by both the government of Kerala and the World Bank) in Table 9.1.

A host of studies quickly produced more sophisticated analyses of the numerous indices, and debated the explanations of these interesting figures. Jeffrey (1992, 2005), Gita Sen (1992), and Bhat and Rajan (1990, 1997) tried to argue that these developments in Kerala society go back to momentum developed from earlier patterns of female agency (from matriliny) and initiatives in the field of education. Franke and Chasin (1992), Franke (1993), and Lieten (1982, 2002) were inclined to credit primarily the mass movement that preceded the election of the 1957 government and the government implementation of the equality of opportunity that made house sites, health clinics, ration shops, and schools available to all in the years to follow. Amartya Sen (1994, 1997, 2000) developed from the Kerala story a theory of development that identified the way in which freedom gives agency to the subordinate classes to identify and articulate their needs in such a way that "growth-mediated" development might continue. Desai's (2001, 2002) comparisons with West Bengal highlight the way in which the dispersed settlement pattern and the rural/urban blend of Kerala allowed the earlier caste movements to smoothly evolve into a class consciousness movement and then into a civic culture, as no self-interested landlord class, such as the *jotedhars* of West Bengal, came forward to block those developments. In an even more complicated explanation of Kerala's success, Casinader (1995) compares Kerala with Sri Lanka, which has similarly high indices of human development. He points out that Kerala's strong sense of national or Malayali identity is not torn apart by a linguistic divide in the way Sri Lanka's is, and that Kerala enjoys relatively peaceful ethnicity in spite of its rich pluralism.

Many in Kerala's own scholarly community were not as comfortable about the rosy picture the human development indices seemed to present as the international scholarly community was. In 1995 John Kurien wrote a much quoted article on the fishing community along the Kerala coast, which had initially been totally left out of the welfare state developing right on its doorstep. Isaac and Tharakan's summary (1995) of the huge (1,600 participants) international conference on Kerala held in Tiruvananthapuram in 1994 tried to report in a neutral voice, but was clearly quite skeptical about the sustainability of the model in the face of the declining economic indicators. Part of the issue was the fiscal crisis of the government

Table 9.1

	Kerala	India	Low income countries	United States
Per capita income ($)	180	300	300	24,700
Adult literacy (%)	91	48	51	96
Life expectancy (years)	71	61	56	76
Infant mortality (per 1000)	13	80	89	9
Birth rate (per 1000)	17	29	40	16

that developed as the welfare state took shape (George 1993; Oommen 1999) and grants from the Center for Social Development ceased because the social goals had been achieved. The strongest summary critique of the positive reading that many make of the "Kerala model" came from Joseph Tharamangalam in his article "The Perils of Social Development without Economic Growth: The Development Debacle of Kerala, India" (1999). He reviews the impressive record of social development, but then goes on to argue that the dismal economic picture emerging in the 1990s was a direct result of the positive social story earlier in the century. He sees the fiscal crisis as a direct result of the obligatory welfare payments and subsidies the state has taken on, the decline in agricultural production as a result of the only partly resolved land tenure issues and the new culture of educated leisure, and the absence of industrial initiative as a result of the disappearance of entrepreneurial energy as people learned to wait for the government to act (see also Tharamangalam 2006). Most scholars at the end of the century found Tharamangalam's analysis somewhat too bleak, and felt the model of a peaceful pluralist society was still something to be proud of, even if undertaking migratory work in India or abroad now seemed to pose more interesting challenges than the government-sustained "model" that was so much talked about in an earlier generation.

V The current social scene

A new reading on the social situation

During the period 1989–96 Filippo and Caroline Osella lived quietly in a village of South-Central Kerala they call "Valiyagramam" and focused their attention on the Ezhava community of that village. Although the story they tell is about "social mobility," the Ezhavas they write about are not the dramatic social reformers following Narayana Guru (1855–1928, Hindu saint and social reformer from an Ezhava family) in the beginning of the twentieth century, or the leaders of the mass movement that put the Communist Party in power in the middle of the century. While the story is still about this unusual community at the center of Kerala society, the focus is no longer on the dramatic agency this community is seen to have exerted on historical events earlier in the century, but on the ambiguous role it now accepts within the renewed pluralist field of Valiyagramam society.

The village is full of new houses and shops, many of them the result of remittances brought back from the Gulf and other outside employment, and now has a busy consumer culture with shops, restaurants, and drinking establishments used by all communities in the society. In spite of this, older caste-like patterns seem to continue as people hesitate to eat in one another's home, and enormous amounts of energy are spent on marriage arrangements. Ezhavas often try to emulate the wealthy Christians by paying expensive dowries in order to raise their family's status by linking it with a more traditionally respected family.

The state's political situation is recognized in the village not for the way it once led the mass movement into land reform and the creation of schools, health clinics, and equal opportunity for all, but the way in which community members now need to keep in touch with both the Left Democratic Front and the United Democratic Front through their networks of power brokers. Social changes now allow Ezhavas with money from the Gulf to raise their status by participating in temple festivals traditionally reserved for Nayars (Osella and Osella 2003), and practitioners of the various forms of sorcery now tend to appeal to a wide spectrum of communities as they offer their services to the people of the village.

Migration and its implications

Kerala has long had contact with distant places, and, perhaps more important, recognizes itself as having had those contacts. Because of the high level of female education, nurses from Kerala began going to Europe and North America a half century ago, and recent studies (Goel 2008; Raj 2008; Ternikar 2008) show that they both established themselves there and kept in close touch with relatives in Kerala. Larger numbers of both professionals and laborers also settled in India's large cities during this time, and, once again, they maintained contact with Kerala. By the 1960s significant numbers of nurses and other professionals were finding their way to Saudi Arabia and some of the Gulf states, and they in turn introduced ordinary laborers to the employment opportunities of the Gulf. What was different about this last form of migration is that the Gulf countries decided to bring in all-male groups of laborers on fixed contract and ensure that they left at a specific time and enjoyed none of the rights of ordinary citizens. The numbers of Malayali males gaining employment in the latter way had risen to 1.4 million by 1996, and the remittances being returned to Kerala were $15 billion or one-quarter of the state's Gross Domestic Product. An even newer migration of technical graduates to the Indian computer industry based in Hyderabad and Bangalore promises to keep the mobility of Kerala's population a pattern the society will have to continue to live with for some time.

The impact these patterns of migration are having on Kerala society is just beginning to be studied. The economic impact is, of course, great in that not only are remittances sustaining the state's economy but the construction industry is also transforming the dispersed settlement pattern and creating a new environment of concrete houses and suburban malls. What is most interesting socially is the way in which those returning from outside Kerala relate primarily with their family and the sub-community of which it was traditionally a part, and are less involved in the state-wide political scene than their parents were (Gulati 1993; Osella and Osella 2000b, 2008b). Because the different sub-communities went after these outside employment opportunities as a group of close friends and relatives, the earliest impact was primarily within that community. As a result, the pluralist nature of Kerala society actually began to become more visible again (or, as P. Kurien, 1994, argues, a new ethnicity began to develop). Initially Christians benefitted the most and they were the primary group involved in the migration to Indian cities, Europe, and North America, and in the early migration of trained medical personnel to west Asia. Although they had their own local Kerala church traditions, they shared in a set of religious values that linked them to others in the outside world to some extent. They had already begun seeking wider horizons during the economic and educational reforms in the first half of the twentieth century, and when the opportunity for outside employment arose they acted quickly. The bishops of their different denominations were at first reluctant to take the local Kerala rituals to the far-flung Malayali settlements in New Delhi, Toronto, and Riyadh, but their members insisted, and now each of their denominations have churches in a host of locations across the globe (Raj 2008).

Once west Asia began welcoming less highly skilled laborers, Muslim and Ezhava migrants quickly outnumbered Christians (Gulati 1993). For the Mappila Muslims, who had not participated in a major way in the educational reforms of the first half of the twentieth century, this opportunity allowed them to leapfrog into whatever status wealth could bring and also allowed them to reflect on their Muslim identity, which had until now developed in a semi-isolated way in the local environment of Kerala (Osella and Osella 2008a, 2008b). As Filippo and Caroline Osella's study of Ezhavas (2000a) has shown, the migration to west Asia allowed them to continue the quest for social mobility that had characterized their identity since the time of Narayana Guru early in the century, even though they often found it hard to translate their cash into a comfortable new identity back home (Osella and Osella 2000b). Interestingly, the upper-class Nayars and their former agricultural workers, or Pulayas, both seem to have understood their cultural roots as more Kerala-bound than did the Christians, Muslims, and Ezhavas, and they have shown much less interest in migrating to other places for employment (Gulati 1993; Saradamoni 1980, 1981, 1999).

VI Conclusion

By the beginning of the twenty-first century, Kerala society expressed itself through a set of values that was increasingly hard to sort through. The pluralism of sub-communities that had long characterized the society had been shaken both by the unified set of values that described the distinctive nature of the left-leaning political era and by the wide diversity of the personal experiences migrants discovered when they lived abroad for long periods of time. The new forms of pluralism no longer focus on the ties that once connected most other groups with the Nayars as the primary landowners, but the old sense of inter-group rivalry controlled by a general commitment to tolerance, compromise, and the good of all still seems to be the prevailing consensus. While there may be a new ethnicity, it does not seem to take the communal forms sometimes found in other parts of India. As James Chiriyankandath (1996) has shown, the RSS with its narrow ideology of Hindu nationalism has worked hard to disrupt the local political consensus of Kerala, but it has found little support outside some isolated Nayar and Tamil-speaking Desastha Brahman families. And, in the same vein, the Osellas (2008a, 2008b) show how difficult radical Islam finds it to interest Kerala Muslims in the issues that intrigue other Muslims the world over.

The tension between local cultural traditions and universal values is evident in a new way. Murphy Halliburton's (2004) study of how people in Kerala now seek to deal with mental illness serves as a good example. Once Kerala society was famous for its exorcists and its ability to deal with "spirit possession." The *velicappatu* in most temples and the more specialized exorcist sites, such as the Chottanikkara temple and the Beemapalli mosque, were among the places where spirit possession was regularly dealt with (Caldwell 1999; Freeman 1999a; Tarabout 1999a, 1999b; Uchiyamada 1999). In studying this phenomenon at the turn of the present century, however, Halliburton found that both allopathic and ayurvedic doctors are now getting many of these patients. Even more interesting is the fact that both the doctors and the exorcists at the temples and mosques find that people seldom identify the offending spirit by name, but strive to express their problem in more universalistic terms as a "depression" or a "tension." Halliburton picks up on this shift from local to universal forms of cultural expression, and quoting from A. K. Ramanujan's (1989) widely read article on the way in which all Hindus move back and forth between very local idioms and fairly universal ones, he shows how this ambivalence has become a special concern of twenty-first-century Malayalis.

Malayalis today seem prouder than ever of their exposure to the outside world and of the pluralistic and harmonious society they have been able to create for themselves as a result of that exposure. They hesitantly accept the praise that has been accorded to the Kerala model and appreciate the fact that people in their society are not plagued by hunger or ethnic conflict. In a similar vein, they appreciate the phenomenal power their ancient pilgrimage site in Sabarimala has developed as it brings huge numbers from all over South India to its annual pilgrimage (Daniel 1984; Younger 2002: 17–25; Osella and Osella 2003), and they even seem to enjoy the way the commodification of their Teyyam dance tradition encourages tourism (Tarabout 2005).

The most dramatic example of a local tradition of Kerala transposing itself into a very modern and universal form is that of the fishing-caste girl who has become the global spiritual leader Mata Amritanandamayi. The devotees of her mission, which is scattered around the world, come to experience Mata Amritanandamayi when she hugs them each in turn just as a mother in her home village would. While this very local ritual symbol is the heart of the ritual tradition of this Mission, her followers revere her because they consider her totally modern in requiring of them no particular beliefs and in establishing an organization that now runs hospitals and science colleges and maintains religious centers all over the world (Warrier 2005). Devotees who come to her headquarters in the fishing village where she was born sometimes find the social and material conditions of Kerala offputting, but to those who know Kerala better, the idea of a hugging mother figure with a universal and modern outlook on life is one that seems to have an earlier history.

References

Aiyappan, A. (1944) *Iravas and Culture Change*. Madras: Government Press (Bulletin of the Madras Government Museum 5.1).
——(1965) *Social Revolution in a Kerala Village*. Bombay: Asia Publishing House.
——(1982) *The Personality of Kerala*. Trivandrum: University of Kerala.
——(1992) *The Paniyas: An Ex-slave Tribe of South India*. Calcutta: Institute of Social Research and Applied Anthropology.
Aiyappan, A. and Mahadevan, K. (1990) *Ecology, Economy, Matriliny and Fertility of Kurichyas*. Delhi: B. R. Publishing Company.
Anderson, B. (1983) *Imagined Communities*. London: Verso.
*Arunima, G. (2003) *There Comes Papa – Colonialism and the Transformation of Matriliny in Kerala, Malabar c. 1850–1940*. New Delhi: Orient Longman.
Ashley, W. (1993) 'Recodings: ritual, theater, and political display in Kerala State, South India,' unpublished thesis, New York University.
Ashley, W. and Holloman, R. (1982) 'From ritual to theatre,' *The Drama Review*, 26 (2): 59–72.
Ayrookuzhiel, A. M. A. (1983) *The Sacred in Popular Hinduism: An Empirical Study in Chirakkal, North Malabar*. Madras: Christian Literature Society.
Ayyar, L. K. A. K. (1926) *Anthropology of the Syrian Christians*. Ernakulam: Cochin Government Press.
Bayly, S. (1984) 'Hindu kingship and the origin of community: religion, state and society in Kerala, 1750–1850,' *Modern Asian Studies*, 18 (2): 17–213.
——(1989) *Saints, Goddesses and Kings: Muslims and Christians in South Indian Society, 1700–1900*. Cambridge: Cambridge University Press.
Bhat, P. N. M. and Rajan, S. I. (1990) 'Demographic transition in Kerala revisited,' *Economic and Political Weekly*, 25 (35/36): 1957–80.
——(1997) 'Demographic transition since independence,' in K. C. Zachariah and S. Irudaya Rajan (eds), *Kerala's Demographic Transition: Determinants and Consequences*. New Delhi: Sage, pp. 33–78.
Byrski, M. C. (1967) 'Is Kudiyattam a museum piece?,' *Sangeet Natak Akademi Journal*, 5: 45–54.
Caldwell, S. (1999) *Oh Terrifying Mother: Sexuality, Violence and Worship of the Goddess Kali*. New Delhi: Oxford University Press.
Casinader, R. (1995) 'Making the Kerala Model more intelligible: comparisons with Sri Lankan experience,' *Economic and Political Weekly*, 30 (48): 3085–92.
Chacko, E. (2003) 'Marriage, development and the status of women in Kerala, India,' *Gender and Development*, 11 (2): 52–9.
Chiriyankandath, J. (1996) 'Hindu nationalism and regional political culture in India: a study of Kerala,' *Nationalism and Ethnic Politics*, 2 (1): 44–66.

Daniel, E. V. (1984) *Fluid Signs*. Berkeley: University of California Press.

Dempsey, C. (1998) 'Rivalry, reliance, and resemblance: siblings as metaphor for Hindu-Christian relations in Kerala State,' *Asian Folklore Studies*, 57 (1): 51–70.

——(2000) *Kerala Christian Sainthood: Collisions of Culture and Worldview*. New York: Oxford University Press.

——(2005) 'Nailing heads and splitting hairs: conflict, conversion, and the bloodthirsty Yaksi in South India,' *Journal of the American Academy of Religion*, 73 (1): 111–32.

Desai, M. (2001) 'Party formation, political power, and the capacity for reform: Comparing left parties in Kerala and West Bengal, India,' *Social Forces*, 80 (1): 37–60.

——(2002) 'The relative autonomy of party practices: a counter-factual analysis of left party ascendancy in Kerala, India 1934–1940,' *American Journal of Sociology*, 108 (3): 616–57.

Franke, R. W. (1993) *Life is a Little Better: Redistribution as a Development Strategy in Nadur Village, Kerala*. Boulder: Westview Press.

*Franke, R. W. and Chasin, B. H. (1992) *Kerala: Development Through Radical Reform*. Delhi: Promilla and Co.

Freeman, J. R. (1991) 'Purity and violence: sacred power in the Teyyam worship of Malabar,' unpublished thesis, University of Pennsylvania.

——(1999a) 'Dynamics of the person in the worship and sorcery of Malabar,' in J. Assayag and G. Tarabout (eds), *La Possession en Asie du Sud*. Paris: Purusartha, pp. 149–82.

——(1999b) 'Gods, groves and the culture of nature in Kerala,' *Modern Asian Studies*, 33 (2): 257–302.

*Fuller, C. J. (1976a) *The Nayars Today*. Cambridge: Cambridge University Press.

——(1976b) 'Kerala Christians and the caste system,' *Man (New Series)*, 11 (1): 53–70.

George, K. K. (1993) *Limits to Kerala Model of Development: Analysis of Fiscal Crisis and its Implications*. Thiruvananthapuram: Centre for Development Studies.

Gladstone, J. W. (1984) *Protestant Christianity and the People's Movements in Kerala 1850–1930*. Thiruvananthapuram: Seminary Publications.

Goel, U. (2008) 'The seventieth anniversary of "John Mathew": On "Indian" Christians in Germany,' in K. A. Jacobsen and S. J. Raj (eds), *South Asian Christian Diaspora: Invisible Diaspora in Europe and North America*. Surrey: Ashgate, pp. 57–75.

Gough, K. (1959) 'Cults of the dead among the Nayars,' in M. Singer (ed.), *Traditional India: Structure and Change*. Philadelphia: The American Folklore Society, pp. 240–72.

Gough, K. and Schneider, D. M. (eds) (1961) *Matrilineal Kinship*. Berkeley: University of California Press.

Gulati, L. (1993) *In the Absence of Their Men: The Impact of Male Migration on Women*. New Delhi: Sage Publications.

Halliburton, M. (2004) '"Just some spirits": the erosion of spirit possession and the rise of "tension" in South India,' *Medical Anthropology*, 24 (2): 111–44.

Hardgrave, R. L. (1969) *The Nadars of Tamilnad*. Berkeley: University of California Press.

Hospital, C. (1984) *The Righteous Demon: A Study of Bali*. Vancouver: University of British Columbia Press.

Houtart, F. and Lemercinier, G. (1978) 'Socio-religious movements in Kerala: a reaction to the Capitalist mode of production,' Part I, *Social Scientist*, 6 (11): 3–34; Part II, *Social Scientist*, 6 (12): 25–43.

Houtart, F. and Nayak, N. (1988) *Kerala Fishermen: Culture and Social Organization*. Louvain-la-Neuve: CETRI.

Induchudan, V. T. (1969) *The Secret Chamber: A Historical, Anthropological and Philosophical Study of the Kodungallur Temple*. Trichur: Cochin Devaswom Board.

Isaac, T. M. T. (1986) 'The national movement and the Communist Party in Kerala,' *Social Scientist*, 14 (8/9): 59–80.

Isaac, T. M. T. and Tharakan, P. K. M. (1995) 'Kerala, the emerging perspectives: overview of the International Congress on Kerala Studies,' *Social Scientist*, 23 (1/3): 3–36.

Iyer, L. K. K. (1909) *The Cochin Tribes and Castes*, two vols. London: Government of Cochin.

Jeffrey, R. (1976a) *The Decline of Nayar Dominance: Society and Politics in Travancore, 1897–1908*. Sussex: Sussex University Press.

——(1976b) 'Temple-entry movement in Travancore 1860–1940,' *Social Scientist*, 4 (8): 3–27.

——(1978) 'Matriliny, Marxism and the birth of the Communist Party in Kerala, 1930–1940,' *Journal of Asian Studies*, 38 (1): 79–98.

——(1992) *Politics, women and Well-being: How Kerala Became "A Model"*. New Delhi: Oxford University Press.

——(2005) 'Legacies of matriliny: the place of women and the "Kerala model",' *Pacific Affairs*, 77 (4): 647–64.

Kodoth, P. (2001) 'Courting legitimizing custom? Sexuality, sambandham and marriage refined in late nineteenth century Malabar,' *Modern Asian Studies*, 3 (2): 349–84.

Kuriakose, M. K. (1982) *History of Christianity in India: Source Materials*. Madras: Christian Literature Society.

Kurien, J. (1995) 'The Kerala model: its central tendency and the outliers,' *Social Scientist*, 23 (1) and 3: 70–90.

Kurien, P. (1994) 'Colonialism and ethnogenesis: a study of Kerala, India,' *Theory and Society*, 23 (3): 385–417.

Lieten, G. K. (1982) *The First Communist Ministry in Kerala, 1957–9*. Calcutta: K. P. Bagchi.

——(2002) 'The human development puzzle in Kerala,' *Journal of Contemporary Asia*, 32 (1): 47–68.

Mathew, E. T. (1999) 'Growth of literacy in Kerala: state intervention, missionary initiatives and social movements,' *Economic and Political Weekly*, 34 (39): 2811–20.

Mencher, J. P. (1962) 'Changing familial roles among South Malabar Nayars,' *Southwestern Journal of Anthropology*, 18 (3): 230–45.

Mencher, J. P and Goldberg, H. (1967) 'Kinship and marriage regulations among the Namboodiri Brahmans of Kerala,' *Man (New Series)*, 2 (1): 87–106.

Menon, D. (1994) *Caste, Nationalism and Communism in South India: Malabar 1900–1948*. Cambridge: Cambridge University Press.

Miller, R. E. (1992) *Mappila Muslims of Kerala: A Study in Islamic Trends*. New Delhi: Orient Longman.

Moore, M. A. (1985) 'A new look at the Nayar Taravad,' *Man*, 20 (3): 523–41.

——(1988) 'Symbol and meaning in Nayar marriage ritual,' *American Ethnologist*, 15 (2): 254–73.

Moser, H. (2011) 'How Kutiyattam became kuti-attam: the changing role of women in the Kutiyattam tradition of Kerala,' in H. Brückner, H. de Bruin, and H. Moser (eds), *Between Fame and Shame: Performing Women / Women Performers in India*. Wiesbaden: Harrassowitz, pp. 169–88.

Namboodripad, E. M. S. (1966) *Kerala: Yesterday, Today and Tomorrow*. Calcutta: National Book Agency.

Obeyesekere, G. (1984) *The Cult of the Goddess Pattini*. Chicago: University of Chicago Press.

Oommen, M. A. (ed.) (1999) *Rethinking Development: Kerala's Development Experience*. New Delhi: Concept Publishing Company.

*Osella, F. and Osella, C. (2000a) *Social Mobility in Kerala: Modernity and Identity in Conflict*. London: Pluto Press.

——(2000b) 'Migration, money and masculinity in Kerala,' *Journal of the Royal Anthropological Institute*, 6 (1): 117–33.

——(2003) 'Migration and the commoditisation of ritual: sacrifice, spectacle and contestations in Kerala, India,' *Contributions to Indian Sociology*, 37 (1/2): 109–39.

——(2008a) 'Islamism and social reform in Kerala, South India,' *Modern Asian Studies*, 42 (2/3): 317–46.

——(2008b) '"I am Gulf": the production of cosmopolitanism among the Koyas of Kozhikode, Kerala,' in E. Simpson and K. Kresswe (eds), *Struggling with History: Islam and Cosmopolitanism in the Western Indian Ocean*. New York: Columbia University Press.

Parpola, M. (2000) *Kerala Brahmins in Transition: A Study of Namputiri Family.* Helsinki: Finnish Oriental Society.

Philips, A. (2004) 'Gendering color: identity, femininity and marriage in Kerala,' *Anthropologica*, 46 (2): 253–72.

Raj, S. J. (2008) 'New land, new challenges: the role of religion in the acculturation of Syro-Malabar Catholics in Chicago,' in K. A. Jacobsen and S. J. Raj (eds), *South Asian Christian Diaspora: Invisible Diaspora in Europe and North America.* Surrey: Ashgate, pp. 183–96.

Raja, K. K. (1964) *Kutiyattam: An Introduction.* New Delhi: Sangeet Natak Akademi.

Ramanujan, A. K. (1989) 'Is there an Indian way of thinking? An informal essay,' *Contributions to Indian Sociology*, 23 (1): 41–58.

Renjini, D. (2000) *Nayar Women Today: Disintegration of Matrilineal System and the Status of Nayar Women in Kerala.* New Delhi: Classical Publishing Company.

Richmond, Farley (1990) 'Kutiyattam,' in F. Richmond, D. Swann and P. Zarrilli (eds), *Indian Theatre: Traditions of Performance.* Honolulu: The University of Hawaii Press, pp. 87–117.

Saradamoni, K. (1980) *Emergence of a Slave Caste: Pulayas of Kerala.* New Delhi: Peoples Publishing House.

——(1981) *Divided Poor: Study of a Kerala Village.* Delhi: Ajanta Publications.

——(1999) *Matriliny Transformed: Family, Law and Ideology in Twentieth Century Travancore.* New Delhi, Walnut Creek, London: Sage Publications and Altamira Press.

Sen, A. (1994) 'Freedoms and needs: an argument for the primacy of political rights,' *The New Republic*, 210 (1/2): 31.

——(1997) 'Radical needs and moderate reforms,' in J. Dreze and A. Sen (eds), *Indian Development: Selected Regional Perspectives.* Delhi: Oxford University Press, pp. 1–32.

——(2000) *Development as Freedom.* New Delhi: Oxford University Press.

Sen, G. (1992) 'Social needs and public accountability: the case of Kerala,' in M. Wuts *et al.* (eds), *Development Policy and Public Action.* Oxford: Oxford University Press, pp. 253–77.

Staal, F. (1983) *Agni: The Vedic Ritual of the Fire Altar*, two vols. Berkeley: Asian Humanities Press.

——(1989) *Rules Without Meaning: Ritual, Mantras and the Human Sciences.* New York: Peter Lang.

*Tarabout, G. (1986) *Sacrifier et donner à voir en pays Malabar: Les fêtes du temple au Kerala.* Paris: Publication de l'EFEO.

——(1993) 'Ritual rivalry in Kerala,' in H. Brückner, L. Lutze and A. Malik (eds), *Flags of Fame: Studies in South Indian Folk Culture.* New Delhi: Manohar, pp. 81–108.

——(1999a) '"Psycho-religious therapy" in Kerala, as a form of interaction between local traditions and (perceived) scientific discourses,' in M. Carrin (ed.), *Managing Distress: Possession and Therapeutic Cults in South Asia.* Delhi: Manohar, pp. 133–54.

——(1999b) 'Corps possédés et signatures territoriales au Kérala,' in J. Assayag and G. Tarabout (eds), *La possession en Asie du Sud: Parole, corps, territoire.* Paris: Purusartha, pp. 313–56.

——(2000) '"Passions" in the discourses on witchcraft in Kerala,' *Journal of Indian Philosophy*, 28: 651–64.

——(2005) 'Malabar gods, nation-building and world culture: on perceptions of the local and the global,' in J. Assayag and C. J. Fuller (eds), *Globalizing India.* London: Anthem Press, pp. 185–210.

Ternikar, F. (2008) 'Indian Christians and marriage patterns,' in K. A. Jacobsen and S. J. Raj (eds), *South Asian Christian Diaspora: Invisible Diaspora in Europe and North America.* Surrey: Ashgate, pp. 197–208.

Tharamangalam, J. (1999) 'The perils of social development without economic growth: the development debacle of Kerala, India,' *Bulletin of Concerned Asian Scholars*, 30 (1): 92–112.

*——(ed.) (2006) *Kerala: The Paradoxes of Public Action and Development.* Delhi: Orient Longman.

Thomas, M. M. (1977) *Towards an Evangelical Social Gospel: A New Look at the Reformation of Abraham Malpan.* Madras: Christian Literature Society.

Thurston, E. (1909) *Tribes and Castes of Southern India*, four vols. Madras: Government Press.

Uchiyamada, Y. (1995) 'Sacred land (kavu): ancestral land of "landless agricultural labourers" in Kerala, India,' unpublished thesis, London School of Economics.

——(1999) 'Soil, self, resistance: late-modernity and locative spirit possession in Kerala,' in J. Assayag and G. Tarabout (eds), *La Possession en Asie du Sud*. Paris: Purusartha, pp. 289–312.

Velayudhan, M. (1991) 'Caste, class and political organisation of women in Travancore,' *Social Scientist* 19 (5/6): 61–79.

——(1998) 'Reform, law and gendered identity: marriage among Ezhavas of Kerala,' *Economic and Political Weekly*, 33 (38): 2480–83.

Veluthat, K. (1978) *Brahman Settlements in Kerala: Historical Studies*. Calicut: Sandhya Publications.

Visvanathan, S. (1993) *The Christians of Kerala: History, Belief and Ritual Among the Yakoba*. Chennai: Oxford University Press.

Warrier, M. (2005) *Hindu Selves in a Modern World: Guru Faith in the Mata Amritanandamayi Mission*. London: Routledge Curzon.

Younger, Paul (2002) *Playing Host to Deity: Festival Religion in the South Indian Tradition*. New York: Oxford University Press.

10 Madhya Pradesh

Anthropology and development

Ramdas Lamb

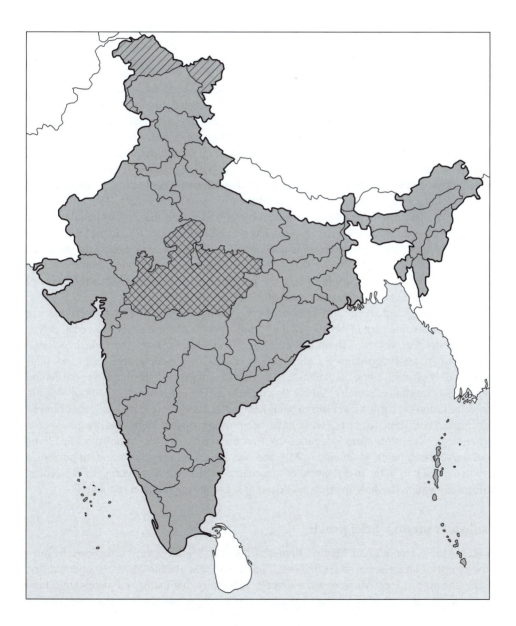

Anthropology is not the study of man but is the science for the service to mankind.[1]

Sitting under the large banyan tree at the edge of the village, a Baiga tribal elder and I were taking advantage of the shade that the Baiga goddess who lives in the tree provided us. As we talked about the various changes that government programs have attempted to bring to his life, his tribe, and his forest over the last several decades, I asked what he thought about these and what he would like, if anything, in the way of assistance. "Water. That's all we need. Without water, there are no crops, there is no life. We will all die. If there is water, we will have everything we need. Please ask the government to just help us get water. We need nothing else from them." His comments and plea reflected both his sense of powerlessness and his frustration in the face of all the government activity occurring in his area that had altered his life in many ways, while doing little or nothing to solve what he saw as the real issues his people are facing.

In Madhya Pradesh (MP), *'vikas'* (the term the government usually translates as 'development') means something very different to most tribal peoples than it does to the government. For the former, it generally means greater access to water and to the forest resources upon which they have long depended for their existence. For the government, it also means access to water and forest resources, but often for the purpose of profiting from their sale to capitalistic interests. Any rights that tribal peoples believe they have tend to be ignored in the process. Anthropology and the kinds of development taking place in central India have been integrally connected since the early twentieth century. The information gained by scholars has helped the government better understand the various peoples of the state and their needs However, their research has also helped it better realize the vast amount of natural resources and profit potential in traditionally tribal homelands. Seeing the problems that this can and has brought about, many anthropologists have sought to use their increasing knowledge of the land and people to help the populace preserve their rights in the face of increasing governmental participation, and often intrusion, in the region.

In order to comprehend post-Independence anthropology in MP, and its role in governmental involvement in the lives of the region's people, these must be viewed in part as a response to the way the discipline developed and was used by the British colonial government in pre-Independence India to gain control over people and their land. This chapter will begin with a brief explanation of some relevant general information about central India, the largest state of which is MP. Following this will be an overview of anthropology in British India and the form it had prior to being indigenized and adapted by local practitioners. The chapter will then focus on what have become the major forms and themes in the anthropology of the state since Independence. Because relatively little is known outside India about the research being conducted in MP, and non-Indian scholars have seldom published on issues specific to it, the major theme of this chapter will be the highlighting of indigenous ethnography within the state in relation to development and applied anthropology.[2]

Madhya Pradesh: a brief profile

Located in the center of India, Madhya Pradesh (literally, 'Middle Land') is bordered by most of the country's larger states and provinces. It has a land area of nearly 120,000 square miles, roughly the size of New Mexico, and a diverse geography that includes a plateau region in the northwest, portions of two mountain ranges, the Vindhyas and the Satpuras, and the only major Indian rivers that flow in a westerly direction and empty into the Arabian Sea. Close to half of the land area is used for agriculture, although only a small percentage of it is irrigated. The remainder depends upon the annual monsoons for water, and this limits both the length of the growing season and the types of crop that can be planted. Just over 30 percent of the state is covered by forests, and it is in these areas that the majority of the state's tribal peoples (*adivasi*) reside.³ The recorded history of the region dates back to the time of the Buddha more than 2,500 years ago. Since that time, the area that now comprises the state has been a part of various kingdoms and politically designated regions. In 1956, it officially became its own state, with Bhopal as its capital. Its present borders have existed since November 2000, when sixteen eastern districts became the new state of Chhattisgarh. The current population of MP is approximately 75 million.

Over the millennia, various dynasties, *adivasi* groups, bands of refugees, wanderers, and other ethnic and cultural groups have immigrated into the state from bordering lands, as well as from places beyond the subcontinent. Due to this, one can find pockets of nearly all the major Indian ethnic and linguistic communities, as well as the religious traditions and movements they brought with them. In addition, the state hosts the largest population of tribal peoples in India with nearly four dozen recognized groups. Numerically dominant among these are the Bhil and the Gond, the latter having more than fifty sub-groups. Counted together these two comprise close to 75 percent of the state's tribal population, which itself accounts for just over 20 percent of the total population of the state.⁴ Hindi and the many indigenous dialects, including those of the various *adivasi* groups, are the most frequently spoken languages in MP and are found throughout the village areas. Among the more common languages that have been brought in from neighboring states are Gujarati, Marathi, Oriya, Punjabi, Sindhi, and Urdu. These introduced languages remain almost exclusive in the urban portions of the state. MP, then, is a mix of indigenous and immigrant, rural and urban, tribal and non-tribal, and the distinctive character of each group has tended to influence to some extent the other cultures and traditions amidst which it exists. With time, there has come to be a richly interwoven fabric of diverse religious and cultural customs and practices, and most have found a way to live together more harmoniously than has been the case in some of the surrounding provinces.

Colonial anthropology

Due to the number of tribal peoples in the state and the interest that British ethnographers took in them, the development and direction of anthropological research in MP has been largely centered around some aspect of *adivasi* life, either directly or indirectly. This focus began rather early in British India with some of the first ethnographic work on tribes in the region occurring in the late eighteenth century under the influence of William Jones and the Asiatic Society of Bengal (Mann 1996: 68).

In 1823, the Royal Asiatic Society of Great Britain and Ireland was founded by Henry Thomas Colebrooke as a British counterpart to the society started by Jones. The newer organization soon began its annual *Journal of the Royal Asiatic Society* (*JRAS*). The publication was initially devoted to ethnographic and historical studies of all of Asia, although research on India tended to dominate in its pages. An increase of writings on central India and the *adivasi* communities there began to appear. Once the British established control over the entire country in the mid-nineteenth century, the colonial administration began an enhanced approach to data collection on nearly every aspect of the lives of the people of the country. The amassing of ethnographic material on customs, beliefs, and habits of the tribes and castes required patience for detail, but little in the way of scholarly insight, insider perspective, or respect for the people being studied. A high percentage of English who wrote about India were employed by the East India Company, the British colonial administration, or various Christian missionary organizations, and these affiliations not only affected the data they chose to collect but how it was interpreted and presented. Most depicted the lifestyles of the people they wrote about as being extremely primitive in comparison to their own European lives and existence, while they considered the prevalent religious beliefs and practices too alien to their own Judeo-Christian viewpoints and cultural conceptions to have any merit. This attitude came to be reflected in their writings. An example can be found in the works of Walter Hamilton, an early ethnographer who was the first to attempt a large-scale collection of data in India. In an 1820 publication, he expresses this negativity and embellishes his writings with the kind of deprecating rhetoric frequently found in European accounts of India during that era. In the quote below, Hamilton expresses his view of Indians' lack of what he considers to be historical information and knowledge. He claims that Hindus' understanding of their past was "either mere traditions preserved among [the] ignorant, or legends mixed with the most monstrous fables, for it may be safely asserted that the Hindoos have nothing deserving of being dignified with the name of history" (Hamilton 1971 [1820]: 649).

There is no shortage of similarly degrading comments about Hindus and their beliefs in the writings of the British at the time. After all, the intended purpose of the observations and investigations of the East India Company, colonial officials, and missionaries was to establish control in India. Empathetic understanding was hardly a consideration. Nevertheless, some of the scholarly writings of the time provide valuable insight today into life in nineteenth-century India. In 1871, the Royal Anthropological Institute of Great Britain and Ireland was formed, and it began publishing *Indian Antiquary* (*IA*) the following year. The aim of this journal was slightly different from *JRAS*, concentrating more on customs, rites, festivals, and other dimensions of religion and culture. Some translations of ancient texts also appeared, as did occasional writings by Indians. The material in both the *JRAS* and *IA* remained European in sensibility and outlook, for even the infrequent indigenous author had been trained by western scholars and usually looked at India through westernized eyes. Consequently, throughout most of the 1800s, nearly all ethnographic work on tribes was approached from a strictly European mindset and perspective. Information not relevant to church, government, or economic control tended to be downplayed or ignored completely. By the end of the century, however, a variety of Indians who had been educated in the British system were beginning to participate and influence the ethnographic work being conducted and the resulting publications brought an indigenous perspective to the work being produced.

The first extensive ethnographic study of central India was conducted in the early twentieth century by Robert Vane Russell, Superintendent of Ethnography for the Central Provinces, and an Assistant Commissioner, Rai Bahadur Hira Lal. Their four-volume publication, *The Tribes and Castes of the Central Provinces of India* (1916), was patterned after Sir Herbert Risley's *Tribes and Castes of Bengal*. Like several former works of the same genre, theirs was meant to benefit colonial officials working in central India. In the 'Preface' to the first volume, Russell acknowledges his indebtedness to previous anthropologists like J. G. Frazer and E. B. Tylor, and one can see the influence of their perspectives in the text.[5] Irrespective of the agenda, the four-volume publication provides a relatively rare look into the world of the tribal communities and lifestyles of the region at that time, and Hira Lal was one of the first Indian anthropologists to be recognized for his work in the region.

Developing an indigenous anthropology

The early twentieth century gave rise to more than a dozen important figures, both Indian and non-Indian, whose ethnographic research, writings, and activism are credited with helping to establish the discipline and its development in MP. For our purposes here, a brief look at the work of several of these individuals will help to shed light on the growth and contemporary form of anthropology in the state. Although only one of them, Verrier Elwin, undertook major portions of his work in what is now MP, all had great influence on the way anthropology has developed and been conducted there.

Sarat Chandra Roy (1871–1942) was one of the first Indian scholars to have a significant effect on the development of anthropology in central India. His willingness to present an indigenous perspective, side with the people he studied, and challenge the way many ethnographies before him had been done have continued to influence the way ethnography has been undertaken in MP. Roy had seen how many of the British researchers and colonial officials looked down upon the subjects of their studies, so from his earliest days as a lawyer and continuing throughout his career as an anthropologist and activist, he sought to develop an approach to anthropology that reflected the reality of life 'on the ground' as he understood it, and also what he considered the unique Indian experience based on the classical understanding of truth. He believed the study of humans should, among other goals, be aimed at understanding their true qualities, and "the eternal spiritual reality behind life and society, the *Sat* [truth] behind the *Asat* [untruth]" (Roy 1937: 243).

Roy earned a degree as a lawyer in 1895, but he started his career working in education in what is now Jharkhand. There, he was exposed to tribal peoples of the area and to the difficulties they faced when dealing with outsiders, especially government officials. His concern led him to set up a legal practice there to help them. In order to better understand the people and their needs, he began an in-depth study that included both their languages and their cultures. Roy's emphasis on 'participant observation' preceded Bronislaw Malinowski's use and labeling of the method. Roy's monograph on the Munda tribe published in 1912 is one of the first writings by anyone to address the topic of *adivasi* with a focus on the indigenous perspective. His close connection with the people is alluded to in the 'Introduction' to his first book, written by E. A. Gait, the Indian Census Commissioner at the time. In it, he calls Roy "the sturdy champion of the Mundas" and writes that he defends the tribals whenever they and their interests come into conflict with outside people and the government (Gait 1912: i). Gait was so impressed with Roy's work that he financed his next research project on the Oraon tribe (Upadhyay and Pandey 1993: 395–96)

In 1921, Roy launched his own journal, *Man in India*, with the goal of creating a forum for a uniquely Indian approach to anthropology. This publication quickly became an important outlet for presenting the work of indigenous anthropologists in the region as well as all over India. Until his death in 1942, Roy worked to help *adivasi* communities have autonomy in their lands and lives. Although his work was not conducted in MP, it has been an important source of inspiration for many of the anthropologists there. His academic lineage has also produced a variety of important scholars working in central India. One of Roy's students, Nirmal Kumar Bose (1901–72), has been called one of the most important figures in the development of a uniquely Indian anthropology. As with Roy, the effect Bose has had on the researchers in the region has had to do with his approach to the craft and commitment to the people he studied.

Bose received a graduate degree in Anthropology from Calcutta University in 1925. After but a few years of working in academia, he left to devote his time to Gandhi's freedom movement, which he had joined nearly a decade before. He was eventually jailed in 1931 for his anti-government activities. In his own unique fashion, he became an ardent devotee and follower of Gandhi's teachings, and even became the latter's private secretary at one point during the last few years of the Mahatma's life. After Independence, he returned to his academic pursuits, bringing Gandhi's spirit of activism with him, as can be seen in his subsequent work and writings. This spirit attracted and inspired many young scholars who eventually helped the government in the Central Provinces in its efforts to understand the vast array of tribes living in its lands. Like Roy, Bose saw anthropology as a way to understand and to serve humanity and also believed it helped reveal a connection with India's roots and culture.

About the same time that Bose left academia to immerse himself in the freedom movement, Verrier Elwin (1902–64) arrived in India as a British Christian missionary with the zeal of his predecessors and a desire to covert pagans. However, within a short time, he too came to be influenced by the work and person of Gandhi, and his life was altered forever. Elwin was moved by Gandhi's vision of India and of the world and wanted to understand it better. He eventually cut most ties with the missionaries and began spending long periods of time at Gandhi's ashram in Gujarat. Some of Elwin's first ethnographic work was actually studying the people at the ashram and their beliefs and practices. He writes with great admiration of Gandhi's frugal living, which he considered not all that different in its simplicity from the *adivasi* whom he would eventually devote his life to studying. Gandhi allowed no caste stratification among his followers, and Elwin saw this, too, as being more like the general social structure of many tribes, which have relatively little hierarchy in comparison to non-tribal society in India.

Elwin eventually settled in a Gond village, immersed himself in learning about life there, and married a girl from the tribe. Essentially unfamiliar with anthropology as a discipline and lacking any formal fieldwork training with which to formulate—or narrow—his approach, he began by simply watching, participating in, and learning from whatever took place. In seeking to understand the people, he had no reason to doubt the validity of tribal thinking or to utilize an academic paradigm to analyze the people or compare them to other groups. Instead, he worked to learn indigenous views and gain their insight about their communities and ways of living. He perceived the uniqueness of each group he studied and sought to present this in his writings. In the process, he rejected Freudian and other universalist concepts as having any applicability to the people and communities he studied.

Because of his anti-colonial stance, Elwin became quite popular with Indian nationalists and even something of a celebrity. This led various non-academia media to take note of his writings as well, which broadened the interest and readership in tribal studies. Over the years, the more Elwin came to understand the people with whom he lived and worked and the problems they faced, the more he sought to educate them and generate assistance for them (Elwin 1964: 105–09) Like Roy before him, he developed his own form of 'action anthropology,' and it added impetus to the anthropologists who followed him in studying the *adivasi* of the region. It would be hard to overemphasize Elwin's influence on the development and direction of ethnography in central India. Because of his extensive fieldwork through years of immersion in the life of the communities he studied and his great respect for the people, Lalita Prasad Vidyarthi sees his presence and work as bringing about an important "turning point in the history of Indian ethnography" (Vidyarthi 1978: 141). Prior to him, virtually all the outsiders who studied tribes had peripheral contact with the people at best, used a few select informants to gather data, and did so with the goal of supporting the colonial government, church, or missionary organization for which they worked. Elwin had no such attachments or loyalties except to his desire to improve the lives of the people he studied.

Post-independence anthropology

By the time of Indian Independence, the direction and form of indigenous anthropology in central India had been essentially established, thanks in large part to the efforts, teachings, and writings of those mentioned above, as well as to the inspiration of Gandhi and the freedom movement, which had garnered great support among the academics and intellectuals in the region. Since such a significant number of anthropologists, sociologists, and other tribal researchers have worked for the government in the field, there has developed among them a keen awareness of the negative impact that so many government programs have had, especially on the tribal peoples of the state. Many of the researchers have consequently adopted an approach that seeks to promote tribal rights and a sense of autonomy amidst the inevitable changes resulting from what the government promotes as 'development.' Referred to variously as 'action anthropology,' 'social anthropology,' or 'applied anthropology' in the region, much of the ethnographic research on peoples and communities has been undertaken with the goal of helping those studied toward maintaining at least some autonomy and control over their own community's direction and future. This inevitably forces many anthropologists there to walk a fine line between furthering the goals of their governmental employers and helping to serve the interests of the people.

There are a variety of higher education institutions in MP where anthropologists and other scholars doing ethnography have trained and worked. In 1946, the first university in what is now MP was established through the monetary donation of a single individual, Dr. Hari Singh Gour, a wealthy attorney and educator from the city of Sagar. Initially called University of Saugar, its name was eventually changed to Doctor Harisingh Gour Vishwavidhyalaya ('University'). In 1954, the teaching of anthropology was added to the curriculum, and the university became an important center for tribal and rural studies for the next half century. In 1957, Professor S. C. Dube became head of the new Anthropology Department there. He was instrumental in turning the focus of the study to the tribal peoples of the state. Dube's initial tribal ethnography on the Kamar was published six years before. In it, he gives credit to his predecessors like D. N. Majumdar, Elwin, and others as sources of inspiration for his approach, but he is also highly critical of the popular four-volume work on central India by Russell and Hira Lal. He points out the flaws in their data collection as well as in the information they present, claiming it was gathered second-hand from undependable sources, and also misunderstood (Dube 2003: xxii–6). In this way, he set the tone of critical scholarship that he expected of his students and his faculty. Today, the university is the only state institution where a doctorate in anthropology can be earned.

In 1964, Pandit Ravishankar Shukla University was founded in the city of Raipur (now the capital of Chhattisgarh), and anthropology was one of its initial offerings. Bhopal University was established in 1970 in the state capital, and in 1988 it was renamed Barkatullah Vishwavidhyalaya ('University'). Two years after its founding, the institution's faculty began producing writings on the various tribes in the state. From its early years, sociology and social anthropology were emphasized in its curriculum. In 1978, the Indian Institute of Forestry Management (IIFM) was begun in Bhopal with its stated goal of promoting education for the development, management, and conservation of forest lands. Since nearly all the state's forest lands are either inhabited or used by various *adivasi* groups, research on them and their lifestyles has been integral to the institute's work.

Caste studies

The last colonial Constitution of India was called the 'Government of India Act of 1935'. It contains a list, or 'Schedule,' of sub-caste groups (*jatis*) relegated by long-held tradition to the bottom of the social hierarchy, those previously referred to in English as 'Untouchable.' The official designation for them became 'Scheduled Castes' (SC), while the more common term, which was popularized by Gandhi, was 'Harijan.' In a similar fashion, the 1950 Constitution of Independent India contains a list of 'Scheduled Tribes' (ST) that was created for the purpose of classifying those groups officially identified as constituting a 'tribe.' The latter document also designates both groups as having a 'marginalized' status and thus deserving of special government assistance. The pattern of ethnographic study by indigenous scholars in the region has been centered around *adivasi*, with the goal of both learning about and helping the various groups and communities. It would seem natural, then, for anthropologists to seek out and undertake the study of other marginalized groups as well, such as SC. However, this has rarely been the case. Since Independence, very few university-related studies have occurred in this regard, and next to none have been published. There seems to be several reasons for this.

When asked about the lack of ethnographic studies of SC in MP, academics at various institutions refer to the Dr. Babasaheb Ambedkar National Institute of Social Sciences, centered in Bhopal. It was established by the state government in 1988 for research into and promotion of the teachings of Dr. Bhimrao Ambedkar, arguably the most popular and influential Untouchable/SC in the twentieth century. Courses at the institute deal with a variety of issues surrounding various minority communities and groups. However, its efforts tend to be more theoretical and apologetic than empirical and academic. There is some ethnographic research conducted under the auspices of the institute, but it is often guided by overt political agendas that limit its objectivity and highly contextualize its usefulness. Because of the influence of the Ambedkar Buddhist socio-political movement among SC in the state, and the presence and work of the institute, academic study of the lowest caste there is essentially left to the institute to undertake. This has functioned to pigeonhole such study to a single place and perspective and remove it from the broader academic landscape. The institute is overt in its interest in the promotion of Ambedkar Buddhism and the SC who have converted to it and who self-identify as 'Dalit.' The research conducted there essentially ignores those SC who have converted to Christianity or Islam, or the vast majority who have chosen to remain Hindu.

Another pivotal factor that limits research on SC communities is the lack of government funding. Unlike the situation with the study of *adivasi*, in which there are ample sources of support for undertaking a wide variety of research projects, those wanting to study SC are limited in the sources and amount of funding available to them. The central government has a variety of programs for the upliftment of SC, but when it comes to funding research on them, there is very little in comparison to what is available for tribal studies. A general feeling among various officials interviewed is that the problems SC face are not because of a lack of understanding of them and the kinds of difficulties they face, but because of the continued prevalence of traditional biases. The officials suggested that what the SC community really needs is better access to education and jobs. *Adivasi* communities, on the other hand, are relatively unknown and therefore funding research projects to understand them is necessary. Of course, one could make a good case that the continuing prejudice against SC is a direct result of ignorance about them and their lives as well, but this seems to matter little at the official level.

The issue of the caste status of researchers must also be considered here when speculating on the shortage of SC ethnographies. When one looks at indigenous scholars who have studied SC all over India, high caste names predominate. Since the early days of indigenous anthropology, those scholars near or at the top of the caste hierarchy have long shown a reticence about doing research requiring close and personal interaction with those at the bottom. This can likely be traced, in part at least, to the effect of social norms and prejudices that restrict such interactions. Instead, the writings on low castes by such scholars has often depended on the study of classical texts, census data, or the field work of others, including non-Indians. Very few include data from questionnaires and formal interviews requiring one on one contact. Such methods obviously do not require much field research work, and many of these studies include none at all. Unfortunately, these impersonal and non-contact approaches have been quite common since the earliest days of indigenous anthropology of India.

A good example of this can be seen in the work of M. N. Srinivas, considered one of the most distinguished and influential Indian social anthropologists in the latter half of the twentieth century. In his *The Remembered Village*, he discusses the religious beliefs and practices of the residents of the village focused upon in a particular ethnographic study he conducted. Although he limited his actual contact to those belonging to the 'touchable' upper castes, he presents his findings as applying to all the members of the village. Then, in the final chapter of the book, he acknowledges the limited sources for his information and understanding but nevertheless claims, "I think it is true of the Harijans [SC] also, though they are likely to regard with skepticism, if not reject, at least some parts of upper caste ideology and world-view" (Srinivas 1980: 319). Srinivas emphasized participant observation and ethnographic method in his writings, but he apparently did not seem to think it was necessary when learning about those at the bottom of the caste system. He has not been alone in his approach. Another example can be seen in Chandra Mouli Jha's article from the mid-1990s about the Chamars (a leather worker sub-caste of SC) of Chotanagpur. In it, he describes them as "[d]ark-complexioned, stocky in structure and with rather unseemly features, the Chamars are easily distinguishable for the other Hindu castes" (quoted in M. Jha 1997: 59). It can be safely assumed from such a stereotyping comment that the author had no close and personal contact with members of the group. Comments and commentaries throughout indigenous works on the subject often leave one with the sense that they are as much guided by preconceptions and prejudices as factual analysis. At the same time, it must be noted that C. M. Jha's piece appears in a volume entitled *Scheduled Castes Today*, edited by Makhan Jha (1997), a renowned anthropologist. Although some of the articles in the book reflect the same prejudices mentioned above, still others are based on seemingly solid ethnographic study and possess a much more objectively-oriented content.

Professor Bhawani Muhkerjee, retired head of the Department of Anthropology and Tribal Development at Guru Ghasidas Vishwavidhyalaya in Bilaspur (CG), also believes that the main reason there has not been a scholarly focus on SC or caste studies in MP and CG over the last several decades has to do with the presence of caste barriers, prejudices, and related issues, as well as political factions that are inevitably encountered when conducting ethnographic studies in non-tribal villages. These function to inhibit open communication, both alone and simultaneous, with members of various caste groups in the same village, especially if low caste and SC are involved. In tribal villages, on the other hand, there tends to be more opportunity for open and honest communication and a greater commonality of thinking on issues about and affecting the entire village. While social factions and tensions do exist in many *adivasi* villages, these are far less the norm than in non-tribal villages so tend to be less a factor in data collection.

Nevertheless, there have been a few well-known ethnographies on caste in the state, such as *Caste and Kinship in Central India* (1960) by British anthropologist Adrian C. Mayer. This is the product of important on-the-ground ethnographic work in the mid-1950s and provides useful insight into the lives of the rural people he studied, but its focus is almost exclusively on the upper castes with whom Mayer resided. He acknowledges this limitation in the 'Preface', where he notes that, due to "village sentiment", his contact with low caste members was "transitory" (Mayer 1960: xiv). Four years later, K .C. Mathur's *Caste and*

Ritual in Malwa Village (1964) appeared. The high-caste Mathur was a professor of Anthropology at the University of Lucknow and focused his study on the higher castes of western MP. In it, he attempts to show that the Hinduism of the villagers in the region accurately reflects the pan-Indian tradition. However, he falls short of contextualizing much of the information he provides, so the reader is unable to discern whether his comments and quotes from the people he interviews are reflective of the entire region or specific to a village or individual. Since that time, research on caste in the state has been limited primarily to articles in various journals and other periodicals, such as Subas Kumar Biswas's 'Potters of Madhya Pradesh and the distribution of handmade pottery industry in India' in the *Bulletin of the Anthropological Survey of India* (1962). Various works continue to appear that make reference to caste issues in the state but only as a small part of a broader geographical study. The consequence is that ethnographic research that focuses on SC in the region is almost non-existent, except the few that have been conducted by foreign scholars.

Among the studies that have been done on both SC and *adivasi* groups by non-Indians, many have been undertaken by Christian missionaries, starting in the nineteenth century. Of those that occurred post-Independence, one of the earliest is *The Children of Hari* (1951), a rather extensive study by the Catholic scholar/missionary Stephen Fuchs. The focus of his research is a Hindu SC community, the Nimar Balahis, in the southwestern region of the state.[6] He followed it with a variety of articles on SC. One of his last works that addresses caste issues in the region is *At the Bottom of Indian Society* (1981). In it, he attempts to give a broad and generalized view of Harijans in the country. Although he acknowledges in the 'Preface' that much of his information is superficial and inadequate, and also that many of his sources were likely inaccurate, he nevertheless defends his broad assumptions about groups he never met, stating "from my general knowledge of the Harijans all over India I am fairly sure that in general the situation of each Harijan caste has been recorded much as it exists today" (Fuchs 1981: vii-viii). However, similar to the situation with the Ambedkarites and the bulk of colonial period ethnographers, the primary goals of these have been driven by ideology rather than conducted with the primary goal of broadening scholarly understanding.

In the case of the missionaries, most research had the end goal of conversion, and many find justification in 'interpreting' the data they have collected to enhance that end. In 2001, several American evangelical groups joined together and started a conversion campaign targeting India. Initially called 'AD2000 & Beyond', it later became 'Joshua Project I' and 'Joshua Project II.' According to its website, the project "is a research initiative seeking to highlight the ethnic people groups of the world with the least followers of Christ. Accurate, regularly updated ethnic people group information is critical for understanding and completing the Great Commission."[7] The data collection efforts of the group is a contemporary Protestant version of what Catholic missionaries began doing in tribal areas in the nineteenth century, with both having the same ultimate goal. In MP, the Joshua Project has targeted several sub-caste groups, including Yadav, Sonar, Gawaria, and Kashmiri Muslims. In each case, its volunteers obtain as much detailed information as they can to assist them in crafting plans for evangelization patterned to each group. Nevertheless, there are some volunteers who have the opportunity and desire to spend longer periods of time in the field, and the resulting knowledge and insight they gain of the people they are studying has been useful to other ethnographers as well.

Tribal studies

As mentioned above, by the early twentieth century the relatively new field of indigenous ethnography in central India had turned its focus toward tribal communities. Because MP has both the largest and the most diverse tribal population in the country it has been a fruitful region for such research, with the bulk of it being conducted under the auspices of various governmental agencies and departments. One of the first government agencies to focus on economic efforts in the tribal lands of central India was the Tribal Research and Welfare Institute at Chhindwara, established in 1954 in what is now southern Madhya Pradesh. Once the state was formed, the institute was shifted to Bhopal, the state capital, and its name was first changed to the Tribal Research and Development Institute, then eventually shortened to the Tribal Research Institute. In 1973, it began publication of what has become an important medium through which much of the ethnographic research has been made available to the public. Over the decades, more than a dozen other institutes, centers, and programs have been started in the country to expand official contact with and understanding of *adivasi* communities.

Anthropologists in government forestry management programs who conduct ethnographic work, such as those at IIFM, undertake some of the most extensive study of tribal forest lands and the people whose lives depend upon them. Because they tend to have access to a greater understanding of the overall planning and interests of the government than do university scholars in departments of Anthropology and Sociology, this affords them a good perception of the longer-term benefits and drawbacks of government designs on the various forested areas. Many of the forest researchers who undertake ethnographic studies have come to appreciate the diversity, complexity, and uniqueness of the various cultural communities and ecological areas. This can be seen in the approach they use in understanding and writing about people and places. Often, one can read cautionary tales and subtle warnings of the long-term damage that can and will happen if outside interests, both government and private, are allowed to exploit the natural and human resources there. In the last two decades, thanks in part to the research of Professor Debashis Debnath, the IIFM has produced a plethora of government reports and writings in various media on the tribes in the region. These have included research on social and religious customs, on the maintenance efforts and non-timber uses of the forests by the tribes that reside in them, and on the need for a better working relationship between the tribal peoples and the state and central governments. Although dealing with tribes in West Bengal, Debnath's *Ecology and Tribal Rituals* is a good example of how ethnographic research can and does play a vital role in governmental understanding and subsequent approach to tribal issues. Articles such as Debnath's 'Role of Non-timber Forest Products in Traditional Economic System and Cultural Practices of a Primitive Tribal Group' (2005) and 'Anthropology of Tribal Religiosity' (2006) show the importance of ethnographic research to the Forestry Department in the state. They also reveal an empathy for tribal peoples that has become typical in the writings of so many government researchers who study *adivasi* groups.

In addition to issues involving government projects in tribal lands, researchers have studied language, customs, religious beliefs and practices, cultural traditions, and social and economic structures. The vast majority of such ethnographic writings appear in academic journals, other periodicals, and governmental reports. The relatively few books that have focused exclusively on the state have either been in the form of monographs of individual tribes or studies that have taken a more comparative approach while looking at aspects of tribal life, such as religious beliefs and practices, art, and music, or agriculture, health, and education. Many detail the extensive field research that has occurred in MP during the last eighty or so years, and especially since Independence. Yet, most are relatively unknown outside the country. Researchers working in the state have found it difficult to disseminate their writings to a broader audience, and there is a dearth of such works among the offerings of international publishers in India as well as the larger Indian publishers. There are several reasons for this, one being that a significant percentage of the work has been written in Hindi, which clearly limits the potential audience. Another is a general lack of international researchers in the region to bring the work to the attention of foreign publishers. As a consequence, the bulk of writings on ethnographic research conducted in the state ends up with various smaller publishing houses, locally and in Delhi, as well as in journals.

Some of the authors whose work on tribal life in the state has appeared in book form are S. K. Tiwari, D. Debnath, B. H. Mehta, B. D. Sharma, T. B. Naik, and P. D. Khera. Tiwari is one of the most prolific of the last several decades. He trained as a zoologist and developed an intense interest in the forests of MP. This led him to his extended study of tribal life in the region. Among the academic positions he held was Head of the Department of Tribal Studies at Rani Durgawati Vishwavidyalaya in Jabalpur (MP). Two of his many volumes that focus on the state are *Baigas of Central India: Habitat and Culture of a Primitive Tribe* (1997), and *Tribal Situation and Development in Central India* (1995). In addition, he authored a two-volume work entitled *Encyclopedia of Indian Tribals* (1994).

Although the bulk of Debnath's writing is found in journals and government reports, some have been published in book form as well. Examples of the latter include 'Role of Non-timber Forest Products in Traditional Economic System and Cultural Practices of a Primitive Tribal Group: The Baiga Case of Mandla district in M.P.' (2005) and 'Anthropology of Tribal Religiosity' (2006). B. H. Mehta's *Gonds of the Central Indian Highlands* (1984), a two-volume study of several villages, provides good insight to the life and culture of the people of the time. It is often cited by researchers in the region as a valuable resource on the tribe and is popular among anthropology students in the state. As a sociologist, Khera studied the Baiga for many years. His 'Baiga and Sal Forests' (1990) is typical of his writing and takes a decidedly pro-tribal approach in addressing the importance of forest resources to the people who reside in them. So impressed was he with the Baiga way of life that he retired, rid himself of his responsibilities in Delhi, and moved to a Baiga village in the eastern part of the state. A variety of other government officers have done the same. T. B. Naik did the bulk of his research while employed in various departments of the MP Government, so much of his writing on tribes is contained in various government documents. Of this ethnographic research that appeared in book form, his *Impact of Education on the Bhils* (1969a) is a good example and addresses the issue of the influence of government schools in *adivasi* villages in both MP and Chhattisgarh. Although the vast majority of B. D. Sharma's writing can be found in government documents, his work in MP continues to be an inspiration to academics and other government officials who work in tribal areas. As an Indian Administrative Service (IAS) officer working for both MP state and central government, he came to have a great respect for the people and a distrust of government development programs, which he saw generally as intrusion into the people's lands. He was consequently pivotal in seeking to adapt policies and programs to better serve the needs and honor the rights of tribal peoples in central and eastern India. He ultimately left government service to become an activist against such programs. Two of his books that show a deep understanding of the people and the situation they face are *Tribal Development* (1976) and *Tribal Affairs in India – The Crucial Transition* (2001).

The Korkus of the Vindhya Hills (1988) by Fuchs is a comprehensive monograph constructed from contact with members of the tribes over several decades. A better contextualizing of the material presented within would make it much more useful. Other texts include Sachchidananda's *Man, Forest and the State in Middle India* (2004), which takes a pro-tribal approach in addressing the practical issues faced by his *adivasi* subjects on the ground when dealing with government designs on their forested lands. V. K. Shrivastava's

The Tribal Scenario in Madhya Pradesh and Chhattisgarh (2003) is another good example of ethnographic writing by an IAS officer whose knowledge of the people and subject matter is the result of spending years of living and working in their midst. His presentation is straightforward and attempts an objective look at the people and the government policies that are affecting their lives. Lastly, S. K. Tiwari's *Madhya Pradesh ki Janjatiyaṅ* (1999) written in conjunction with K. Sharma, and his sole-authored *Madhya Pradesh ki Janjatiya Sanskriti* (1999) are both Hindi language works on tribal culture. The first presents various aspects of tribal life as well as tribal concepts and methods of '*vikas,*' while the latter focuses more directly on social life and customs.

Among the main academic journals that carry ethnographic work conducted in the state are *Man in India, Journal of the Anthropological Survey of India, Indian Anthropologist, Society and Culture, Indian Journal of Regional Science, Bulletin of Tribal Research Institute*, and *Social Welfare*. Articles in both Hindi and English can be found in their pages. Since the 1970s, the Institute of Social Research and Applied Anthropology in West Bengal has been producing a journal entitled *Man in Life*. This has become one of the more popular academic literary vehicles for disseminating knowledge about MP tribes. Ethnographic research on tribes by those working for forestry agencies and institutes appears in publications like *Forest Survey of India, International Forestry Review, The Indian Forester*, etc. In addition, a few periodicals from other disciplines present opportunities for MP anthropologists to publish. These include such diverse titles as the *Indian Journal of Agricultural Economics, Economic and Political Weekly, Journal of Family Welfare*, and *Indian Journal of Human Genetics*. The sole academic research journal originating in the state is *Madhya Bharati*. Produced by Dr. Hari Singh Gour University, it covers many disciplines. However, anthropological work seldom appears in its pages.

In the last two decades, the *International Journal of Rural Studies* (1994), *The Anthropologist* (1999), and *Studies of Tribes and Tribals* (2003) have been added to the list of publications open to MP ethnographers. All three also provide Internet access to their articles, which come from a diverse field of academic disciplines and a broad range of topics. Among the primarily Hindi language publications in the state that include articles drawn from ethnographic work on tribes, and some on castes as well, are *Madhya Pradesh Sandesh, Madhya Pradesh Varshiki, Purvagraha, Vanyajati*, and *Sarvahara*. These all provide field researchers opportunities to make their work available to the regional Hindi-speaking public.

Another medium through which ethnographic research on MP has been published is the Indian census. Starting in the colonial period and continuing through the 1961 Census, it has contained articles on customs, arts, festivals, etc., as well as monographs on the people of the various sub-districts. The authors of many of these articles in the 1961 report include K. S. Bhatnagar, P. K. Dixit, and K. C. Dubey (see 1961 Census of India, Madhya Pradesh, Parts VI–VII). However, in subsequent census reports most ethnographic information has been omitted.

Development gone wrong: an example

Among the more controversial government development projects in the state is the Narmada Valley Development Project. Officially begun in 1987, it is actually a continuation of government plans begun shortly after Independence to build more than 3,000 dams along the Narmada River, nearly 90 percent of which is in MP. The claimed goal of the project is to generate electricity as well as divert water to several drought-prone areas of Gujarat. By garnering international attention and controversy, it has inspired a variety of ethnographic studies to be undertaken and made more broadly available. Once researchers in both states began looking into the project and the people who would be impacted, it became apparent to most that large sections of forest land and countless villages, both tribal and non-tribal, would be destroyed with little likelihood that the affected people would be adequately compensated for their losses. The project has thus created a further source of conflict between many anthropologists and the government agencies that finance their research. Several NGOs were formed to mount a resistance to what they saw as the government takeover and destruction of tribal and village land. These organizations have financed their own ethnographic research in the state to document the lives and cultures of the peoples in order to publicize the destruction that has and will occur. Although the research is undertaken with an obviously stated agenda, it has nevertheless unearthed some valuable data about the people being affected.

According to data collected by NGOs fighting the project, the lands and livelihoods of more than an estimated one million people in Madhya Pradesh alone will be negatively affected by the project, in addition to several hundred thousand in Maharashtra and Gujarat. The primary organization leading the fight is the Narmada Bachao Andolan ('Save the Narmada Movement'). It coordinates most of the anti-government protests against the project and publishes occasional articles that utilize ethnographic research on the Internet website of its correlate organization, Friends of River Narmada (www.narmada.org). In addition, articles that address problems faced by the peoples being displaced have been published in various journals, newsletters, and on other websites. Some of the research has been conducted by established scholars and trained anthropologists from universities in India, as well as by those working either for government organizations or in the private sector. Others conducting research are self-taught, having committed themselves to studying the people and the problems for years, including journalists or volunteers with little or no academic training. Sometimes it is hard to tell fact from agenda-based rhetoric in their accounts. At other times, the information suggests some thoughtful and extensive ethnographic research. Nevertheless, efforts are being made and some good ethnographies have come from the process. In addition, not only has the project inspired a significant interest in the region, but also in the people, and this has led many more to take an interest in anthropology as an academic discipline, including some of the tribal youth. Texts such as Amita Baviskar's *In the Belly of the River: Tribal Conflicts over Development in the Narmada Valley* (2004 [1995]) is the product of much fieldwork and takes a highly critical look at the government's so-called development of the river. The author pulls no punches in her castigation of what she sees as shortsightedness and greed on the part of many of the officials involved.

Conclusion: problems and possibilities

The practice of ethnographic research developed primarily as a method through which colonial powers sought to learn about and more efficiently control their colonized subjects. Once indigenous researchers in India entered the field, they began to replace the older approach by introducing the combined goals of learning, helping, and empowering. Throughout the last century, much of the anthropological research in MP has followed this pattern and has, in the process, provided great insight into the lives and lifestyles of the *adivasi* communities in the state. It has also been used to benefit many of those studied. However, some of the research has also served to facilitate intrusion in the lives of the people by both government and private interests.

With respect to tribal communities and their lands in the state, anthropologists and others who conduct ethnographic research have long been aware of the difficulties that arise when short- and long-term government interests conflict with the interests of the people. In the eyes of the government, tribal lands are under-utilized to the detriment of the tribal people and the country as a whole. The untapped rich natural resources need to be drawn from and made available, while *adivasi* need to increase their participation in agricultural and other forms of economic productivity in the state. In other words, their traditional lifestyles that take a less active approach to agriculture and a less invasive and intrusive approach to forest lands are seen as counter-productive to government interests and plans. In their efforts to have greater access and control, officials often find ethnographic studies to be useful in promoting their goals and agendas. Here, the rhetoric of respect for tribal lands and culture is clearly at cross purposes with governmental interests and thus remains little more than empty verbiage to many. At the same time, however, there are a significant number of government officials who seek to carry out policies using a less intrusive approach and one that brings as much benefit as possible to those affected. Because so many anthropologists in the state also understand the problems, many find innovative ways to make their research efforts more directly beneficial to the subjects of their study. Many realize that there are definite cases in which government programs do good for the poorer *adivasi* and work in conjunction with tribal concepts of development.

There has been some success as ethnographic publications have led to an increased recognition and awareness among the educated classes of the plight and need for social justice for members of tribal and other minority groups. Thanks to the efforts of the researchers, important issues have been highlighted, and various programs, both governmental and non-governmental, have been created to address some of the more glaring problems. In addition, not only are anthropologists' research and writings used by officials, but many serve in an advisory capacity in various government agencies, and are called upon as instructors in workshops from time to time to help incoming government administrators familiarize themselves with tribal issues in the state. Anthropologists such as F. Mollick and B. M. Mukherjee also provide input into the formation of government development projects. In their co-written article, 'Gondwana: Whether Political or Socio-Cultural Reality' (1999), they look at the various Gond forms of resistance against what is seen by many members of the tribe as an attempt by the government to take their land and resources. They also attempt to show the roots and current manifestations of the dissatisfaction in hopes of bringing greater awareness of the problems. In many ways, then, anthropologists in MP stand in a central and pivotal position when it comes to the planning and instrumentation of development policies affecting the lives of the state's *adivasi*. This gives them the opportunity to try to use the knowledge they have gained through their research toward helping create a situation whereby governmental claims of respect and support for tribal peoples do not simply remain rhetoric but move in the direction of reality.

In his brief piece entitled 'Urgent Research in Social Anthropology' (1969b), T. B. Naik mentions nearly two dozen areas or topics that he sees as in need of research in MP. More than four decades later, most are still left unstudied. The state remains a fertile land with much as yet to be uncovered and learned, and also a hot bed of tension between tribal peoples and the government over what '*vikas*' means and what shape it should take. Hopefully, it will not take another four decades before those in power and the outside world take a deeper interest in and a sincere concern for the situation in MP. The people, especially the *adivasi* there, are worthy of respectful treatment as autonomous beings and communities. Any development in the region that occurs should be done in consultation with them, taking into serious consideration their needs, aspirations, and lifestyles rather than treating them as obstacles to the fulfillment of current imprudent political and shortsighted capitalistic interests.

Notes

1 A statement attributed to Professor P. K. Bhowmick by Debashis Debnath, Professor of Anthropology at the Indian Institute of Forestry Management, Bhopal, Madhya Pradesh on August 4, 2010. Debnath was a student of Bhowmick, and in an interview stated that the quote expresses the approach that Bhowmick encouraged all his students to take when doing anthropology.
2 The material for this chapter is drawn from years of traveling in and interacting with villagers, scholars and students in both MP and Chhattisgarh. In addition, I spent the summer of 2010 in central India doing research at various colleges and universities as well as interviewing faculty and students to collect information specifically relevant to the topic at hand.
3 The term '*adivasi*' literally means 'original resident' and is thus somewhat of a misnomer. Various DNA studies conducted over the years suggest that while some tribal groups possess unique genetic characteristics in relationship to the non-tribal peoples of the region, most do not. Instead, the distinction seems largely the result of lifestyle, primary sources of food (forest as opposed to agriculture), and relationship to the broader caste-based society. Nevertheless, both '*adivasi*' and 'tribal' are in common usage by anthropologists, government officials, and other researchers when speaking or writing in English. While some of those thus labeled use the terms for self-identity, most tend to prefer the name of their tribe instead, i.e. Baiga, Gond, etc. However, for purposes of clarity only, both 'tribal' and '*adivasi*' will be used herein.
4 http://censusindia.gov.in/Tables_Published/SCST/dh_st_madhya_pradesh.pdf
5 Several years before Russell's first volume, Frazer published *Totemism and Exogamy*, which includes a chapter on tribals in the Central Provinces.
6 At the time Fuchs did his research and writing, 'Harijan' was arguably the most common general term for members of the lowest of the Indian castes. In more recent years, 'Scheduled Caste' has become the most common, while many of those who no longer identify with Hinduism self-identify as 'Dalit.'
7 'Joshua Project – India' at www.joshuaproject.net/joshua-project.php (accessed January 4, 2011).

References

1961 Census of India, Madhya Pradesh, Parts VI–VII. New Delhi: Office of the Registrar General, India.
Baviskar, A. (2004 [1995]) *In the Belly of the River: Tribal Conflicts Over Development in the Narmada Valley*. New Delhi: Oxford University Press.
Biswas, S. K. (1962) 'Potters of Madhya Pradesh and the Distribution of the Handmade Pottery Industry in India', *Bulletin of the Anthropological Survey of India*, 11(2): 95–110.
*Debnath, D. (2003) *Ecology and Rituals in Tribal Areas*. New Delhi: Sarup & Sons.
——(2005) 'Role of the Non-timber Forest Products in Traditional Economic System and Cultural Practices of a Primitive Tribal Group: The Baiga Case of Mandla District in M.P.,' in Choudhary, S. and Coudhary, S. S. (eds), *Primitive Tribes in Contemporary India*. New Delhi: Mittal Publications.
——(2006) 'Anthropology of Tribal Religiosity,' in Paramanick, S. K. and Manna, S. (eds), *Explorations in Anthropology: P. K. Bhowmick and His Collaborative Works*. Bidisa: The Institute of Social Research and Applied Anthropology.
Dube, S. C. (2003 [1951]) *The Kamar*. New Delhi: Oxford University Press.
*Elwin, V. (1964) *The Tribal World of Verrier Elwin: An Autobiography*. Bombay: Oxford University Press.
Frazer, J. G. (1910) *Totemism and Exogamy*, four vols. London: Macmillan.
Friends of River Narmada (www.narmada.org)
Fuchs, S. (1951) *The Children of Hari: A Study of the Nimar Balahis in the Central Provinces of India*. New York: Frederick A. Praeger.
——(1981) *At the Bottom of Indian Society*. New Delhi: Munshiram Manoharlal Publishers.
——(1988) *The Korkus of the Vindhya Hills*. Delhi: Inter-India Publications.
Gait, E. A. (1912) 'Introduction' in Roy, S. C., *The Mundas and Their Country*. Calcutta: The City Book Society.

'Government of India Act of 1935.' Available at: www.legislation.gov.uk/ukpga/1935/2/pdfs/ukpga_19350002_en.pdf

Hamilton, W. (1971 [1820]) *A Geographical, Statistical and Historical Description of Hindostan and Adjacent Countries,* Vol. I. Delhi: Oriental Publishers.

Jha, M. (1997) *Scheduled Castes Today.* New Delhi: M. D. Publications Pvt. Ltd.

'Joshua Project' (www.joshuaproject.net)

Khera, P. D. (1990) 'The Baiga and Sal Forests,' *The Eastern Anthropologist*, 43(3): 241–50.

Mann, R. S. (1996) *Tribes of India: Ongoing Challenges.* New Delhi: M. D. Publications Pvt. Ltd.

Mathur, K. C. (1964) *Caste and Ritual in Malwa Village.* New York: Asia Publishing House.

Mayer, A. C. (1960) *Caste and Kinship in Central India.* Berkeley: University of California Press.

Mehta, B. H. (1984) *Gonds of the Central Indian Highlands.* New Delhi: Concept Publishing Company.

Mollick, F. and Mukherjee, B. M. (1999) 'Gondwana: Whether Political or Socio-Cultural Reality,' *Anthropologist*, 1(4): 279–282.

Naik, T. B. (1969a) *Impact of Education on the Bhils.* New Delhi: Research Programmes Committee, Planning Commission, Government of India.

——(1969b) 'Urgent Research in Social Anthropology (with Reference to Madhya Pradesh),' in Abbi, B. L. and Saberwal, S. (eds), *Urgent Research in Social Anthropology.* Simla: Indian Institute of Advanced Study.

Risley, H. (1891) *Tribes and Castes of Bengal.* Calcutta: Bengal Secretariat Press.

Russell, R. V. and Hira Lal, R. B. (1916) *The Tribes and Castes of the Central Provinces of India*, four vols. London: MacMillan and Co.

Roy, S. C. (1912) *The Mundas and Their Country.* Calcutta: The City Book Society.

——(1986) 'The Study of Anthropology from the Indian View-Points,' *Man in India*, 66(1): 81–93.

Sachchidananda (2004) *Man, Forest and the State in Middle India.* New Delhi: Serials Publications.

Sharma, B. D. (1976) *Tribal Development: The Concept and the Frame.* New Delhi: Prachin Prakashan.

——(2001) *Tribal Affairs in India – The Crucial Transition.* New Delhi: Sahyog Pustak Kuteer.

Shrivastava, V. K. (2003) *The Tribal Scenario in Madhya Pradesh and Chhattisgarh.* Bhopal: Energy Environment and Development Society.

Srinivas, M. N. (1980) *The Remembered Village.* Berkeley: University of California Press.

Tiwari, S. K. (1994) *Encyclopaedia of Indian Tribals.* Delhi: Rahul Publishing House.

——(1995) *Tribal Situation and Development in Central India.* New Delhi: M. D. Publications Pvt. Ltd.

——(1997) *Baigas of Central India: Habitat and Culture of a Primitive Tribe.* New Delhi: Anmol Publications Pvt. Ltd.

——(1999) *Madhya Pradesh ki Janjatiya Sanskriti.* Bhopal: Hindi Granth Academy.

Tiwari, S. K. and Sharma, K. (1999) *Madhya Pradesh ki Janjatiyaň.* Bhopal: Hindi Granth Academy.

Upadhyay, V. S. and Pandey, G. (1993) *History of Anthropological Thought.* Delhi: Concept Publishing Company.

*Vidyarthi, L. P. (1978) *Rise of Anthropology in India: A Social Science Orientation*, two vols. Delhi: Concept Publishing.

11 Maharashtra

Constructing regional identities

Anthony Carter and Amit Desai

Introduction

Looking towards the border with the neighbouring state of Chhattisgarh, Hira said 'Maharashtra ends where the tarred road ends'. For him, as for many others living in the eastern borderlands of the state, Maharashtra represents a vision of modernity at odds with the image he has of Chhattisgarh. Tarred roads, urban culture, selfish people, even the method of sowing paddy, all offer a contrast to the place across the border. They are the muddle in the middle, neither properly Marathi nor fully Chhattisgarhi, and uncomfortable in both places. Yet, both places exert a pull and are desired for different reasons. State and social power, however, work to denigrate this muddle and engage in projects of purification to clarify and channel senses of belonging.

This chapter is concerned with three recent ethnographies that discuss the ways in which Maharashtra is made an object of desire in various articulations of regionalism. Thus, rather than being studies merely in Maharashtra, they place Maharashtra itself at or near the centre of their analyses. Thomas Hansen's *Wages of Violence* (2001) is a study of exclusionist politics and urban life in late twentieth-century Bombay. Anne Feldhaus's *Connected Places* (2003) examines the ways in which places in Maharashtra are connected to one another by various kinds of pilgrimages and accompanying religious texts. Veronique Bénéï's *Schooling Passions: Nation, History, and Language in Contemporary Western India* (2008) follows the politics of Maharashtrian and Hindu nationalism into the primary schools of Kolhapur, asking how such sentiments are naturalized or made 'banal' in the lives of school-age children.

In the terms of Bernard Cohn's classic paper on the study of regions in India, *Wages of Violence* and *Schooling Passions* are studies of regionalism, i.e. 'calls to action', or the creation of 'symbols, behaviors, and movements which will mark off groups within some geographical boundary ... for political, economic, or cultural ends' (Cohn 1967: 21). If 'connected' is taken as an adjective, as Feldhaus apparently intends, then *Connected Places* should be read as a study of Maharashtra as a cultural and historical region, an area with 'widely shared cultural traits and patterned behavior' and 'in which there are sacred myths and symbols ... regarding the relationship of people to their "past" and the geographical entity' (Cohn 1967: 6–7). However, *Connected Places* can also be read as a study of regionalism. If 'connect' is taken as a verb, then pilgrims can be seen as attempting to create Maharashtra and to claim a place in it for themselves.

The chapter is divided into three parts. In the first part we sketch the ethnographic work done in Maharashtra during the last nearly fifty years. In the second part we outline the ethnographic argument in each of our core works. In the third part we critically examine our authors' arguments in the light of other research in Maharashtra and, where necessary, elsewhere in India or beyond.

Ethnography in and of Maharashtra

Established on 1 September 1960, largely from parts of the State of Bombay and the Central Provinces, Maharashtra is now the second largest state in the Indian Union by population (98 million according to the 2001 census) and third largest by area. It is also one of the wealthiest, if measured by GDP. As one might expect for such a large state, it has a varied geography ranging from the mountainous littoral that forms the northern extent of the Western Ghats (known as the Sahyadri), the central plateau which comprises most of Maharashtra, and the dense deciduous forests in the north and east.

Until recently ethnographic research has been in Maharashtra, but not of Maharashtra. Though the creation of Maharashtra in 1960 as a linguistic state with Bombay as its capital was the outcome of a heated contest, ethnographers generally have taken the state as a given and treated it as context rather than subject.

Since Orenstein's (1965) *Gaon*, a study of a village in southern Pune District, most ethnographic work in Maharashtra has focused on villages and small towns in the countryside. Much of this work is concerned with religion and ritual (Carter 1982; Malhotra 1988; Sontheimer 1988; Feldhaus 1995; Desai 2010). Other topics include agriculture (Schlesinger 1981; Appadurai 1984; Attwood 1992); co-operative societies, especially sugar factories (Baviskar 1980); domestic groups and families (Carter 1984, 1988; Kolenda 1970; Dandekar 1999); gender (Bagwe 1995; Contursi 1996; Kumar 2006); politics (Baviskar 1968; Carter 1974a; Schlesinger 1977); kinship and marriage (Carter 1974b; Bénéï 1996, 1999); personhood (Carter 1982); primary health care centres (Kamat 1995); ritual healing (Skultans 1987a, 1991), and rural-to-urban migration (Dandekar 1986).

Ethnographic research in Maharashtra has been confined geographically and culturally as well. Most studies were carried out in just three districts in Western Maharashtra: Pune, Satara, and Kolhapur. Studies in the coastal Konkan Division or in Nashik, Aurangabad, Amravati, and Nagpur Divisions in the north and east are rare (Rubinoff 1988; Bagwe 1995; Kamat 1995; Burman 2001; Desai 2010), as is ethnographic work on the Maoist (Naxalite) insurgency, which has been active in the eastern districts of the state for over twenty years (though see Desai 2009). Ethnographic researchers have also tended to concentrate on Hindus. Only a handful of ethnographic studies focus on Adivasis (Kumar 2006; Desai 2008, 2010), Dalits (Patwardhan 1973; Fitzgerald 1997; Burra 1996), or Muslims (Burman 2001) in any sustained fashion.

Karve's (1962) and Deleury's (1960) accounts of the pilgrimages to Pandharpur undertaken by the Varkaris, Maharashtra's most prominent surviving medieval devotional cult, are early exceptions to the general pattern. These are studies of Maharashtra rather than in Maharashtra. In their view, Maharashtra is the land of the Varkaris. People from all over Maharashtra join the vast procession travelling from Alandi to Pandharpur; other very large groups journey to Pandharpur by their own independent routes from sites across the state. Feldhaus's *Connected Places* resumes this mode of research, as does Youngblood's (2003) more recent account of Varkari pilgrimage during a period of rising Hindu nationalist sentiment in the state.

As one of the most urban states in the Indian Union, much ethnographic work in Maharashtra over the last twenty years has been carried out in cities or peri-urban areas, with a large proportion of this in the megacity of Mumbai. Some of this work has involved research with new populations and on new topics. Among the new populations are urban slum dwellers – Buddhist Dalits (Contursi 1989, 1993), formerly Harijans or Scheduled Castes; Hindus (Appadurai 2000, 2001; Sen 2004, 2007) and Muslims (Hansen 2000) – as well as Parsis (Luhrmann 1996) and Bombay advertising creatives (Mazzarella 2003). Some of the topics addressed by urban ethnographers – e.g. HIV/AIDS (Kielmann 2002; Kielmann *et al.* 2005; Datye *et al.* 2006) – continue the tradition of working in but not on Maharashtra. However, with the growing prominence of exclusionist politics, ethnographers have increasingly focused on contests about the definition of Maharashtra and claims to belong. It is to these issues that we turn in the remainder of this chapter.

Maharashtra as a region and as a project

In this section, we treat *Connected Places* as an investigation of Maharashtra as a cultural and historical region. According to many participants and some observers, the cultural unity of Maharashtra pre-exists and is the grounds for the nationalist politics analysed by Hansen. In turn, according to Bénéï, important features of primary schooling are shaped by and reproduce the passions of nationalist politics.

Maharashtra as a place

In *Connected Places*, Feldhaus explores the Hindu religious geography of Maharashtra. Is Maharashtra, she asks, more than the physical area in which the majority of the people are Marathi-speakers (on Maharashtra as a linguistic region, see Bennett 1980) or a state in the federal republic of India? Does it also have 'a distinct identity and significance' at least for those who 'live in it and for others who think and care about it'? Is it, in other words, a 'kind of place' or a set of connected places (2003: 5)?

As we noted above, previous studies of Maharashtra as a region focused on the Varkaris and argued that Maharashtra was 'the land whose people go to Pandharpur for pilgrimage' (Karve 1962: 22; Deleury 1960). *Connected Places* differs from this work in several ways. First, Feldhaus uses a much larger palette. She examines the Hindu geography of Maharashtra using texts that Maharashtrians read and write, stories that they tell, and a variety of contemporary pilgrimage festivals. Second, Feldhaus analyses this material using concepts of place, region, and connection. A place is a 'concrete, particular, and differentiated' location 'with a distinct identity and significance' in which one's social relationships take place and about which one cares. '[T]he place par excellence is the domestic residence, the home'. However, the sense of place may be extended to include a village, town, or region. A region is a 'large place' or, alternatively, a collection of connected places that have 'coherence and meaning' and comprise a here 'or indexical' for some person or persons (2003: 5). Places are connected when deities, people, or rivers move from one location to another or when they are linked conceptually. Third, Feldhaus comes to a different conclusion.

Here we pass over Feldhaus's valuable analysis of textual connections between places and focus instead on her observations of contemporary pilgrimages, 'rituals in which people physically move across or around in an area' (2003: 27). Many pilgrims travel to express their personal devotion or 'to fulfill a private *navas*-vow', but Feldhaus is especially concerned with pilgrimage festivals (*jatras*) in which people converge on a temple or river at more or less the same time in organized groups, what she calls 'local community project[s]' (2003: 72–3).

Feldhaus devotes an entire chapter (2003: 45–87) to the very popular Caitra (March–April) festival at the Shingnapur Mahadev Temple, in the Mahadev Mountains in northeast Satara District. This *jatra* combines features that occur widely in pilgrimage festivals in Maharashtra. Many pilgrims bring river water from near their homes to cool the god, and 'recreate the image of Shiva with the Ganges on his head'. The water is carried in *kavads*, decorated poles that can be 'slung over the shoulder with a water vessel … hanging from each end' (2003: 47, 67). The effort involved in carrying a *kavad* of water from one place to another over substantial distances and up the steep hill to the Mahadev Temple expresses 'a kind of fierce, athletic, ascetic devotion (*bhakti*) to Shiva' (2003: 47, 57, 67). Other groups of pilgrims bring the goddess Parvati (Shakti), represented by a decorated pole (*kathi*), from Bhatangali, a village six days' walk northeast of Shingnapur, in Usmanabad Distict, to celebrate her marriage to Mahadev (Shiva) (2003: 67–71).

Prominent among the 'community project[s]' involved in the Shingnapur Mahadev festival are six groups that carry particularly large, heavy, and elaborately decorated *kavads* and have the right (*man*) to be the last to climb Mungi Ghat, a very steep slope on the northwest face of the mountain on which the temple sits, at the climax of the festival at the end of the twelfth (*baras*) day of Caitra. The senior *kavad* is the one carried by successors of Bhutoji Teli, a Shaivite *bhakta* who lived in Sasvad, in Purandar Taluka, Pune District. The other *kavads* come from other villages or groups of villages in Purandar Taluka and Phaltan Taluka in Satara Distict. The *kavads* climb Mungi Ghat in reverse order, the Saswad group last. Another organized group of pilgrims includes the men who carry the pole representing Parvati from Bhatangali (2003: 55–6).

Feldhaus reports that members of these groups of Shingnapur pilgrims see themselves as creating Maharashtra as a region. On the one hand, they imagine themselves as representing the places from which they come. '[M]en from many different households in a village' should accompany the community's *kavad* or pole to Shingnapur. In Belsar, Feldhaus was told, every household is to contribute grain or cash to feed the pilgrims accompanying the village's *kavad*. The amount is determined by a meeting of 'the whole village'. Before leaving for Shingnapur and/or when arriving home, 'each large *kavad* or pole travels in a festive procession throughout what the men describing it generally identify as its "whole" village or town'. People living in the village or town 'greet' the *kavad* or pole 'on their own doorsteps' as it passes by, or come in from outlying homes to 'pay their respects' in a central area. In many places the festival of the local guardian deity is timed to coincide with the return of the *kavad* or pole. Many places celebrate the return of their *kavad* with 'a community meal, usually called *bhandara*, to which "everyone" in the village is invited'. On the other hand, pilgrims who go to Shingnapur, like Irawati Karve (1962) 'on the road' with the Varkaris, feel that they are joined by people from all over Maharashtra and that Maharashtra is the land from which such pilgrims come (2003: 50, 71–87).

However, Feldhaus also observes that the practices that connect places in Maharashtra are not themselves interconnected. For example, Jejuri, a town southeast of Pune on the old highway to Satara, figures in *Connected Places* in multiple ways. It is on the Karha river and connected to other places by the river. It is the site of a famous temple of the god Khandoba, family deity (*kula devat*) to many Maharashtrians. It is the 'starting point and terminus' of the pilgrimage in which the descendents of Nago Mali carry the goddess Janai back to her temple in Navkhan. It is an important early stop on the journey of the *kavads* from Saswad and other places in Purandar Taluka to Shingnapur. And it is a stop on the Varkari pilgrimage from Alandi to Pandharpur. It would be difficult to miss the crowds connected with the Varkaris, but '[p]eople can live in Jejuri without being aware of the Shingnapur festival, without knowing the story of the origin of the Karha river, and even without taking cognizance of the pilgrimage festival of Janai' (2003: 214–25). And this is to speak only of Hindus. As Feldhaus notes, Jains, Sikhs, Christians, Jews, Buddhists and Muslims – one should add Parsis (Luhrmann 1996) – also live in Maharashtra and inhabit connected places of their own (see Burman 2001 on connections between Hindu and Muslim places).

Thus, though Feldhaus accepts that connected places comprise regions, she does not see any of these regions or the sum of them together as equivalent to Maharashtra. The many regions that intersect in the area of modern Maharashtra State do not add up to the whole of Maharashtra, nor is any one of the regions studied in this book coextensive with the one that became the State of Maharashtra in 1960. Maharashtra is a collection of overlapping but otherwise quite separate 'small worlds' (2003: xv, 211–2).

Turbulent politics and unstable names

Thomas Blom Hansen's book, *Wages of Violence* (2001), examines the processes by which an organization called the Shiv Sena (Shivaji's Army) transformed the nature of politics, regionalism and state-making in late twentieth-century Mumbai and Maharashtra. Founded in 1966 by Bal Thackeray, a journalist and satirical cartoonist, the Shiv Sena represents the apogee of regional exclusionist politics in India. Claiming to speak for the interests of the ordinary Marathi *manus* ('Marathi person'), the Shiv Sena has over the years advocated controls on the migration and employment of Indians from other states and appointed itself the protector of Marathi Hindus from the depredations of North and South Indians, Muslims and Mumbai's 'cosmopolitan elite'. Yet Hansen's argument is that the appeal and success of the Shiv Sena cannot be explained solely by its commitment to Marathi nativism. As a plebeian challenge to elite understandings of democracy, law and the state, the movement is centrally concerned with refashioning the meaning and practice of politics itself. By pursuing an agenda of permanent (and often violent) public performance, the Shiv Sena reveals what politics looks like when it is stripped of ideological content. Thus, Hansen suggests that 'region' is not of particular analytical importance in understanding the Shiv Sena phenomenon; rather we need to explore the public performance of region: 'regionalism'.

Regionalism as 'a call to arms' in Maharashtra begins and ends with Shivaji, the famous Maratha ruler of the seventeenth century and the establishment of the Maratha state in the early modern period. By this we do not mean that the possibilities of regionalism are closed, predictable or eternal. Such characterizations are in fact the analytical consequence of the position taken by a number of historians who have seen Shivaji and the Marathas as proto-nationalists. One strand claims them as inspiration for the anti-colonial struggle (e.g. Ranade 1961 [1900]) while another sees the old regional nationalisms of Maharashtra, Bengal and the Tamil country as laying the foundations for a broader Indian nationalism (Bayly 1998).

Hansen argues that, in their emphasis on continuity, the approaches outlined above fail to properly appreciate the radicalism of new narrative frames and the constantly changing ways in which a collective past – the 'regional ethnohistorical imaginary' (2001: 230) – can be reflected upon and claimed (2001: 28, see also Rao 2009: 40–1). This is precisely the sort of challenge he suggests is posed by Shiv Sena politics. Central to these new frames is the indexical act of naming, which, contrary to the intention of the act, contributes to the incompleteness and instability of that which is named. An important practice of naming in Maharashtra is that of the identification of castes. Hansen contends that 'caste groups or religious communities ... are not "out there" as groups *an sich* but only exist as collective identities when they are named in public rituals, organized, and reproduced through performative practices as groups and categories for themselves' (2001: 10). Refracted through the histories of Shivaji and the Maratha state, the production of regionalism intersects with the production of caste identities and caste antagonism in Maharashtra to create changing forms of identification and political contests over 'who belongs'. One key axis of antagonism in western India is between Brahmans and Marathas; another is that between Marathas and Dalits (former Untouchables). The ways in which these castes have come to be named offers insights into the constitution of Maharashtrian regionalism in India today.

Though the period of virtual kingship by Brahmans had come to an end after the Peshwa's final defeat at the hands of the British in 1818, non-Brahmans saw the dominance of Brahmans in the new colonial administration as deeply problematic and inimical to their own claims to higher status. As Hansen (2001) demonstrates, the Maratha response to this was to argue that Brahmans were foreigners to the land of Maharashtra (and indeed to India) and the products of miscegenation. By painting Brahmans as foreigners, Marathas could assert their own indigeneity, and claim a rightful dominance in the nascent anti-colonial nationalist movement in western India (Rao 2009: 96). Hansen argues that the formation of the Maratha caste as a symbol bound together elements such as martiality, the legacy of Shivaji, rural virtues and a regional identity, just as Brahman in this imaginary linked together effeminacy, the legacy of the Peshwas, urban culture and a pan-Indian solidarity (2001: 34).

The debates over who could claim indigeneity were therefore sharply inflected by the processes of caste formation in colonial western India. The success of the Marathas in excluding Marathi Brahmans from the leadership of the regional Congress Party, while at the same time challenging Dalit claims to equal status has led to three of the most powerful political formations in contemporary Maharashtra: the Shiv Sena; the Dalit movement (see Rao 2009); and the Rashtriya Swayamsevak Sangh (RSS) (see Hansen 1999). These have defined not only the contours of regionalism in Maharashtra but also the content and style of postcolonial Indian politics.

The Shiv Sena did not appear at first to challenge the long-established regional imaginary. The extreme adaptability of the movement was shown by the way in which it combined a regionalism associated with the Marathi-speaking middle class with the aspirations of entrepreneurs, together with more subaltern voices belonging to the urban poor (Hansen 2001: 47) and women (Sen 2007). Hansen's key insight in his analysis of the appeal of the Shiv Sena, one which echoes his discussion of on-going and unstable caste formation in Maharashtra, is that political parties do not reflect pre-existing interests or groups but that 'they create and reiterate the precarious boundaries of a group through the act of naming' (Hansen 2001: 98). Just as the very naming of the Maratha, Brahman or Dalit castes creates doubts as to the limits and potentialities of those castes, so Hansen argues, the Shiv Sena's constituency 'is not built on who people are or how they behave but rather on who they wish to become' (2001: 98).

Central to this mode of understanding participation in politics as 'becoming' rather than 'being' in Maharashtra, Hansen suggests, was the articulation and mobilization of a Maharashtrian and later Hindu masculinity, which was refracted through the deeds of Shivaji and his Maratha warriors. This masculinity was plebeian, disdainful of the 'cultured classes', and wedded to forms of violent enactment. However, this plebeian masculinity itself was unstable because of the desire of the men who engaged in it to pursue projects of aspiration and respectability. Hansen explores these tensions through a discussion of the *dada* ('elder brother'), a gangster-like political operator. The ambiguities of the *dada*, which pre-date the rise of the Shiv Sena, suited the emerging leadership of the party: it combined the plebeian emphasis on engagement in the rough and tumble of neighbourhood politics with the desire for respectability of Mumbai's *parvenu* elite brought about through participation in large commercial ventures (2001: 72–4; 109–12). Thus the production of regionalism also intersects with the compulsions of social mobility and class in contemporary Maharashtra.

One might have expected that the ostensible egalitarianism of the Shiv Sena and the value placed on lower-class and lower-caste masculinities would lead to solidarities with the important Dalit movement in Maharashtra. That this has not happened signifies for Hansen the tensions inherent within the Shiv Sena's aspirational plebeianism. He suggests that the violent reaction of many Shiv Sena activists towards the assertion of Dalit consciousness can be explained by the Dalit movement's explicit rejection of any stab at middle-class and elite respectability, thus undermining the Shiv Sena activists' (known as Shiv Sainiks) desire for conventional social mobility.

This failure of a Maharashtrian lower-caste solidarity reveals that for Shiv Sena activists the naming of 'Dalit' makes obvious concerns of 'lack' of proper Marathi- or Hindu-ness that is the lower-caste Maharashtrian condition. The refusal of the leadership to allow the organization to engage in and as 'groups' also reveals, for Hansen, the way in which the Shiv Sena operates to mould popular identities and therefore cannot surrender to the perspective of any one such identity (2001: 97–8).

The Shiv Sena's radicalism and flexibility was also apparent in the way it repeatedly and deliberately flouted the conventions designed to secure the peaceful conduct of politics, such as adhering to the law and respecting opponents. It was instrumental in organizing the Bombay Riots of 1992 and 1993 during which 1,000 Muslims were murdered and an estimated 250,000 became refugees within and outside the city. What was extraordinary was that the party's leadership did not disown the perpetrators but publically rejoiced in having 'taught the Muslims a lesson'. Undoubtedly then, by incorporating rather than repudiating violent acts, the Shiv Sena expanded the notion of the 'legitimately political' in Maharashtra; though, as Hansen recognizes, the Shiv Sena also built on broader processes of the 'banalization' of public commemoration in Maharashtra (Hansen 2001: 230–1).

Making nationalism banal

In *Schooling Passions*, Bénéï is concerned with the production of what, following Billig (1995), she calls 'banal nationalism', nationalism that is 'so integral to people's lives that it goes unnoticed most of the time' (Bénéï 2008: 1–2). How, Bénéï asks, does nationalism in Maharashtra become 'visceral'? How is passionate devotion to versions of Maharashtra and India 'irrefragably' inscribed in the body and made instinctual?

Bénéï is especially concerned with primary schools. In her view, schools and schooling are, in part, '*upstream*' of and prior to episodes of communal violence. Schooling is shaped by debates among 'Hindu nationalist[s] [such as the Shiv Sena] … secularists … minorities, social activists, intellectuals, and scholars' but it also may become the source, for children in school, of 'senses of belonging' and 'exclusivist political projects' (2008: 2, 5, 132; author's emphasis).

In the six Kolhapur primary schools in which Bénéï worked, nationalism was performed in school-wide assemblies (*paripatha*), and 'moral education' (*naitik siksan*) that opened the school day, in skits performed during holiday celebrations, in textbooks, in the routine language of instruction, and in the insistence on proper Marathi pronunciation. We will discuss the first in some detail and the others very briefly.

At the private Varsity Marathi School, the morning assembly and moral education contain a great deal of Hindu material. The students assemble in rows in the playground, one row for each class or grade, standing still with their arms at their sides. At a signal from Mandabai, the Brahmin woman teacher in charge, the school peon pounds out a beat on a large drum. The students give a 'military salute' with their right hands and 'rock to and fro' as the teacher calls out, in Hindi, her voice amplified by a public address system, '"one-two one-two …" (ek-do ek-do …)'. At the command, again in Hindi, 'Attention! Ready to start [the national anthem]: start!', the children sing the national anthem. This is followed by the pledge of allegiance; a school prayer to Saraswati, the goddess of learning, or Ganesh, the remover of obstacles; a patriotic song; various 'song-prayers' (*shloks*); a moral story; news items, and another collective song, usually secular. The song-prayers consist of material that is central to the Hindu history of Maharashtra. For example, the 'City of Alankar, holy land of religious merits', was composed by Shivaji's spiritual guru, the seventeenth-century saint Ramdas, and celebrates the virtues of Alandi (also called Alankar) where Sant Dnyaneshwar, the thirteenth-century translator of the Bhagavad Gita, attained release from the coils of consciousness (*samadhi*). Moral education consists of moral stories and news items read to the assembled students following the song-prayers. The school-wide assembly concludes with 'the vigorous shouting, in military fashion, of slogans such as "Bharat Mata ki Jay" (Victory to Mother India), "Hindustan zindabad" (Long live India), with right fists raised'. All this may be accomplished in as little as 'ten minutes', though in some schools it takes longer (2008: 38–9, 53, 76).

The work in each classroom begins in a similar manner. After worship (*puja*) of Saraswati, the seven-year-old pupils in Mandabai's room at the Varsity Marathi School sang or chanted hymns of praise (*stotras*) to Ganapati and Maruti. And then, 'without pausing' and in less than ten minutes, a song about 'the love of, and for, mothers'; salutes (*namaskars*) to country, parents, teachers and others; the months of the year in Marathi and English; the days of the week; the lunar days of the Hindu calendar; the seasons, in Marathi and English; the astrological mansions of the moon (*nakshastras*); multiplication tables, and 'all the songs and poems thus far learned from the Class 2 standard Marathi-language textbook'. All in 'repetitive tones' and while 'rocking their bodies to and fro' (2008: 49).

Morning assembly is similar at other Marathi-medium schools. However, at the public Urdu Corporation School, serving Muslim pupils, it consists of 'singing the national anthem, reciting the pledge and the *dua*, the Urdu morning prayer, all the rituals being a Muslim equivalent to the Hindu practice in Marathi schools with Hindu *shlok*' (2008: 197).

Nationalism and a Hindu version of Maharashtra similarly figure prominently in government-produced Marathi-language textbooks. The Class 4 textbook, for example, focuses on the exploits of the aforementioned Maratha warrior hero, Shivaji Maharaj. Shivaji's aim is to wrest *Hindavi swaraj* from Muslim invaders. Though the book explains that '[a]nyone who lived in Hindustan, no matter to what community or religion he belonged, was a *Hindavi*', Shivaji's Muslim officers are portrayed as loyal to him despite their religion. Shivaji is small, valiant and cunning. His Muslim opponents are huge, stupid and treacherous. The violence involved in Shivaji's disembowelment, during hand-to-hand combat, of the Bijapuri Muslim general, Azfal Kan, is portrayed in bloody detail. The Muslim contribution to the history of Maharashtra and India is elided (2008: 145–6, 185).

Patriotic themes also dominated in skits performed in annual school shows and municipal Republic Day celebrations. Designed by teachers and performed by students, presumably for audiences of parents, these skits were strikingly warlike and gendered in the months and years immediately following the conflict with Pakistan in Kargil, Kashmir. At the Varsity Marathi School, the kindergarten section of the annual show featured four-year-old boys marching in fatigues, cutting off the heads of imaginary enemies, and following their teacher in shouts of 'Hindustan Jindabad'. At the private All India Marathi School, in January 2000, six kindergarten boys aged three to five mimed infantrymen in Kargil, lying prone and firing their weapons (pieces of wood) at the enemy (2008: 102–3, 119–21).

Regardless of the language or form of Marathi they speak at home, students at Marathi- and English-medium schools are expected to use 'proper' or 'standard' *pramanit* Marathi. Spoken Marathi (*boli basha*) varies widely by region and socio-economic status. *Pramanit* Marathi derives from the work of codification and standardization done in the nineteenth century by British colonial officials and Pune Brahmins. It formed the basis for the vernacular print literature that led to the creation of Maharashtra as an imagined community (see also McDonald 1968). Students are continually urged to pronounce Marathi in the standard fashion and corrected if they lapse. In a metaphorical extension of undergoing a Hindu rite of passage (*samskar*), to be made to speak in this way is to be polished, embellished or purified, to learn how to behave correctly, to become a proper person (2008: 60–1, 71–2, 80–1, 93–4).

The definition of and devotion to Maharashtra and India presupposed by regionalist and nationalist practices becomes 'visceral' or beyond question, Bénéï argues, in several ways. The practices themselves are performative. By singing the national anthem every day, killing India's enemies in battle, and pronouncing Marathi properly, the children create their state and the nation of which it is a part and make it real in their lives (2008: 24, n20). Speaking standard Marathi, conforming to a language ideology, is also 'emblematic of self and community' (2008: 80, quoting Fishman 1989). In Hansen's terms, the reiteration of names is central to becoming rather than merely being Marathi, though it is also inherently unstable. More broadly, Bénéï draws on Walter Benjamin's (1999) concept of 'sensorium', i.e. the combined sensory functions of the body: sight, sound, movement, speaking, and so on. Students may not understand what they are collectively reciting in the morning assembly and moral education until they are in Class 3. In Bénéï's view, however, the students' engagement with nationalism through multiple sensory media causes them to 'phenomenologically ... "feel" the nation within their own bodies' and to do so enduringly. She quotes a story from the Class 3 Marathi textbook as an example both of the lessons given to students and of the effects of those lessons on students. Embedded in a story of the first day of school for children new to the routines is a story of a retired army officer who is walking by carrying a jug of water as school begins. Hearing the call to attention and the national anthem, the old soldier instinctively snaps to attention, dropping the water jug. The textbook enjoins students to emulate the officer during *paripatha*. Bénéï imagines that they will in fact do so, at least unconsciously, for the rest of their lives (2008: 24–6, 78).

Maharashtra as a project

As we noted in the introduction, if 'connected' is read as a verb rather than an adjective, then *Connected Places*, like *Wages of Violence* and *Schooling Passions* can be taken as a study of regionalism. Though most of the pilgrimages and texts with which Feldhaus is concerned apparently are quite old, all of the regionalist projects described in these volumes occur contemporaneously. They also refer to one another. The Patil of one of the Panchakroshi villages involved in the Shingnapur pilgrimage festival had a clipping from a 1994 issue of the Shiv Sena newspaper that spoke of how water is brought to Shingnapur from all the rivers of Maharashtra, 'from the Tungabhadra to the Narmada', carried by villages from 'all corners' of the state (Feldhaus 2003: 71–87). The nationalism performed in Kolhapur primary schools is influenced by the views of Shiv Sena and other right-wing political parties and employs passages from texts composed by famous Varkari poet saints and by Shivaji's guru, Ramdas. Here we draw together our three core ethnographies to examine the symbols through which regions are invoked, the ways in which people are recruited to regionalist projects, and competing voices in the wider conversations of which regionalist projects are a part.

Symbols

In the regionalist projects on which we focus here, the symbols used, the practices in which they occur, and the manner in which they are thought to operate are quite diverse. For the people studied by Feldhaus, Maharashtra is made manifest by means of acts of devotion that connect places: telling stories of the movements of gods, goddesses and rivers from one place to another and going on pilgrimages that recall those sacred movements. The Shiv Sena seeks to create its Maharashtra by naming places such as Mumbai and categories of people such as Marathi *manus* in acts of legislation, speech making and rioting. Teachers in Kolhapur primary schools create Maharashtra by making their pupils enact nationalist discourse: reciting key Varkari and national texts, performing skits, speaking *pramanit* Marathi and so on.

Though versions of Maharashtra are invoked by diverse symbols, all of them have a virtual existence. Like the Tamil village deities and festivals studied by Mines (2005), regional deities and pilgrimage festivals in Maharashtra are metonymic symbols, parts that stand for the whole for someone in some way. Their meanings for different someones – Shaivites and Vaishnavites, Hindus or Muslims, men and women – are not the same. Similarly, acts of naming, whether Shiv Sena legislation or primary school performances, are indexical. They do not refer to or connote entities that exist as things-in-themselves. Rather they point to or invoke phenomenon whose existence is dependent upon the act of naming (Hansen 2001: 1–4).

Recruitment

Regionalist projects and the regions they create take shape only if sufficiently large and powerful 'assemblage[s] … of elements – actors, institutions, knowledges, and so forth' (Greenhalgh 2008: 9 citing Latour 2005; see also Mosse 2005) are recruited to sustain them.

Not infrequently, people align themselves with a regionalist project without sharing the concerns of the project's leaders. Devotees traveling to Pandharpur or Shingnapur may come to see these pilgrimages as manifestations of Maharashtra, but other research suggests that the concerns that set them on the road are the fates of their dead loved ones, their own fertility, the health of their children, and, for the elderly in particular, release from rebirth (*moksha*) (on the concerns of women and their families with the birth and health of children, often leading to vows to deities and journeys to rivers, see Feldhaus 1995: 118–45; also Gold 1988; Skultans 1987a, 1987b, 1991). In his study of Mahanubhav devotion, Desai (2007: 174–8) shows that Adivasis or Chhattisgarhis from the linguistically heterogeneous eastern borderlands of Maharashtra, who feel acutely marginalized by the dominant Marathi regionalism of the state, come to recognize a sacred geography proper to Maharashtra on becoming Mahanubhav devotees and going on pilgrimage (see also Feldhaus 2003).

Atreyee Sen's book, *Shiv Sena Women* (2007), a study of members of the female wing of the Shiv Sena, the Mahila Aghadi, offers another example of how recruitment into the politics of regionalism goes hand in hand with intimate experiences of the region and the pursuit of personal projects. Sen shows how in the first instance these Bombay slum women's Marathi-ness was produced by the change in urban settlement patterns caused by the collapse of the textile industries:

> Within the party the continuing need for support and self-protection merged localized identities into an overarching 'Marathi' identity. During the initial phase of their migration women had developed a security system around the familial and regional divisions of Maharashtra (by living in family or kin enclaves). But within the Sena they felt 'connected'; the feeling of community that was lost through rural-urban and intra-urban migration was replaced by 'Maharashtrianism'.
>
> (Sen 2007: 30)

Indeed, this association with the Shiv Sena and an emphasis on Marathi-ness worked to further distance these urban migrant women from their rural kin (2007: 37). As projects of self-fashioning, older activists tried to suppress their own rural pasts and histories of migration in order to better fit the ideal of the violent, aggressive, fully urban and fully Marathi woman. By doing this, women articulated a regionalism firmly centred in the regional urban experience of de-skilling and marginality.

The ethnohistorical imaginary also came to furnish women's understandings of their place in the production of regionalism. Sen describes the importance for women activists of telling stories about Shivaji. Complementing Bénéï's insights into the emotional nation-making capacities of public ritual in India, Sen shows how, in the performance of plays put on by their children, the Shiv Sena women sought to recover a role in history by suggesting that if they were only given an opportunity they could create a militaristic, Hindu-dominated society in the future. They portrayed Shivaji as combining both the 'strength of a man and the heart of a woman' (ibid.), thus drawing him closer to their own experience as violent yet compassionate people. Sen argues that, for the women, the exploits of Shivaji and the Maratha Empire cannot be understood as a linear progression of episodes that lead inexorably to the present day. Rather, Shivaji exists synchronically with them: 'their narrations of history were performative, ritualistic and flexible and had no relationship with unitary truths. Within the constraints of a masculinist discourse, these tales restored women to history and history to women' (2007: 159, 162).

Sen's account therefore offers a complexly gendered portrait of the tense articulation of regionalism in Maharashtra. Whereas Hansen explains Shiv Sena activists' enactments of masculinity by drawing on Lacanian notions of 'lack' (a psychoanalytical resonance), Sen explores the ways in which members of the Mahila Aghadi make meaning out of the intimate experiences of history and kinship. Sen explores in vivid fashion the sphere of everyday social relations (with, for example, children, spouses, kin, friends, workmates, employers) that Hansen neglects and which also come to constitute the political for these Shiv Sena women.

As we have seen, Bénéï argues that nationalist discourses in primary schools are of interest because, for the children, they are 'upstream' of violent nationalism, recruiting them into exclusionist regional projects. However, the ethnography in support of this claim must be regarded as inconclusive. In her fieldwork, Bénéï apparently was seen by both staff and students as one of the adults in charge. She stands with the staff turning the morning assembly. She has lunch and chats with them in the school office. Asking students in Class 2 at one school about the material included in the morning assembly, each of her questions is repeated to the class and expanded on by the teacher.

> 'After you have sung the national anthem, what do you say?'
>   The teacher repeated, breaking up the words and emphasizing thus: 'You have sung the national anthem, haven't you? "Jana Gana Mana," haven't you? Then after this, what do you actually say?'
>
> (Bénéï 2008: 116)

During a tour of another school, the headmistress introduces Bénéï to each class and then 'tests' the students (2008: 187). Accompanying an official from the municipal education department on a surprise visit to an Urdu-medium school for Muslim children, Bénéï is '[s]uddenly "invited"' to question the children on the syllabus and their knowledge of Marathi. Aware of the hostility to which Muslim children who do not speak Marathi at home may be exposed, an embarrassed Bénéï can only 'mitigate the command' by speaking in Hindi (2008: 175–6, 182–3). Only at the private military academy where she was introduced by a parent, did the students 'not take [her] for an inspector of sorts invested with a mission to spy on them' (2008: 253).

Schooling Passions often shows us the children doing what is required of them by their teachers. We catch a glimpse of the students in one classroom being unruly and of the teacher throwing chalk at the worst offenders. We also see the student Bénéï knows best at the military academy watching 'sullenly and noncommittally' as he and his classmates are ordered to sing the daily prayer (2008: 227). More generally, she attempts to present the perspectives of children in brief interludes of 'experimental' writing, 'collages' of what she knows of specific young people, that separate the descriptive chapters (2008: 31). Nevertheless, the children and their views of their teachers' nationalist projects remain inaccessible (2008: 28–9).

If we are to learn something about how primary-school children – Dalits and Adivasis as well as upper and middle castes, girls as well as boys – understand and respond to nationalist discourse in school we must take a very different approach. We must recognize the agency of children, their capacity to participate in 'the construction and determination of their own social lives, the lives of those around them and of the societies in which they live' (Prout and James 1997: 2). We must also listen to children's voices (Coles 1993: 9, 24).

Only two ethnographic studies in India speak to the effects of nationalist discourse in schools and attend to the agency and voices of children: Das' (1989) work with Punjabi and Sikh children in Delhi slums and Sen's (2007) study of a Mumbai neighbourhood. These studies reach sharply contrasting conclusions. Sen's observations are not inconsistent with Bénéï's argument. The older male children of the Shiv Sena women with whom Sen worked, boys aged ten to fifteen years old, felt that their teachers supported them and provided them with knowledge that 'helped them develop a Hindu militant "gang" identity' (Sen 2007: 141). However, it is clear that in this setting schools are not the sole source of banal nationalism. During the 1992–93 Hindu–Muslim riots, the boys 'were taken out of school and kept in the home with their mothers and television sets. They spent their days indoors, watching broadcasts of the riots and listening to the tales of gore propagated by the women' (2007: 137).

The effects of schooling on the children with whom Das worked appear to be far more limited. The communities in which these children live were devastated in the riots following the assassination of Prime Minister Indira Gandhi. Many members of the children's families were violently murdered. Das finds that the language of schools contrasts sharply with that surrounding children and women in Punjabi homes. Consistent with Bénéï's observations, the former involves a great deal of direct questioning and many imperatives. The latter revolves around 'causing someone to hear something rather than directly 'tell[ing] someone something' (Das 1989: 270). In their play, children marked the alien character of the 'images' they had learned in school 'by tone of voice, rigidity of gesture, and a standardized speech that [Das] ... characterize[s] as "school speech"' (1989: 282–3). More generally, Das argues, the play of the children in the Sikh slums indicated that they comprehended that the world in which they found themselves

> did not go by the stated rules, for the preservation of the self depended on knowing how to avoid adult aggression, how to answer questions of visiting bureaucrats so as to conceal certain truths, and how to avoid sexual aggression of certain known pimps. Just as they created games that mirrored the dark and macabre reality of their lives, so they learned that the underlying rules of the game are quite different from the stated rules.
>
> (Das 1989: 284–5)

Other voices

The regionalist projects examined in our core ethnographies do not occur in isolation and do not reflect a uniform culture; they are part of an intensive and sometimes violent debate in which the identities of Maharashtra and Maharashtrians are produced and distributed. Our authors are well aware that '"[r]egional consciousness" can ... be a matter of contention and opposition' (Feldhaus 2003: 7), that all localities – places that might be connected as well as regions – are deeply unstable, always subject to contestation. Nevertheless, the work on which we focus privileges a small set of Hindu voices: *bhakta* devotees, the Shiv Sena and Hindu nationalists. Other voices, notably those of Dalits, Muslims and secular intellectuals, are largely missing.

Secular intellectuals may share Bénéï's distaste for Hindu nationalist discourse in primary schools (Sen 2007: 144–8), but they also have other concerns about the state of primary education across India (for a survey of recent literature see Kingdon 2007). Schools often are badly equipped and teachers frequently fail to appear for work. There are significant fees attached to 'free' public schools. Drop out rates are high, especially among girls and children from disadvantaged Scheduled Castes and Scheduled Tribes. According to the 2002 Human Development Report of the Government of Maharashtra, 14 per cent of boys and 15 per cent of girls drop out of school before Class 5. Better off parents increasingly send their children to private schools, while girls and SC/ST children remain in government schools. Teachers, many from upper castes, commonly treat Dalit and Adivasi pupils with contempt, ignoring them or singling them out as people unable to learn. Guru (1997: 1879–80) reports that in the late 1990s the Shiv Sena-BJP government of Maharashtra issued an order requiring distinctive blue school uniforms for Dalit students. (Other male students were to wear khaki shorts and white shirts.) This order was withdrawn following protests in the Assembly, but it was followed by another order announcing a plan to create separate schools for Dalit children. Unfortunately, we hear nothing about these issues in *Schooling Passions*.

The absence of Dalit and Muslim voices in our core ethnographies may be due in part to the violence of the debate about regionalism in Maharashtra. As we noted above, both Hansen and Sen found it all but impossible to associate with Muslims in Mumbai while working with Shiv Sena activists. The Kolhapur municipality offered Urdu-medium schools for Muslims, but Muslim pupils in Marathi-medium schools felt compelled to keep a low profile. While taking Bénéï on a tour of her private school, the headmistress questioned the students in Class 2 about 'the plural form', a diagnostic of the difference between *pramanit* and *boli* Marathi. Only one student was willing to venture a response and the headmistress asked him:

> 'What do you speak at home?'
> [*The child instantly began to show signs of nervousness.*]
> Kirari Bai rephrased her question thus: 'What does Mummy speak at home?'
> A shadow darkened the little boy's face as he pleadingly answered: 'Now, now I speak Marathi.'

Realizing that the student probably was a Muslim who spoke Hindi at home, the headmistress 'reassure[d] him] by saying, "You can speak your language at home, there is no problem, nothing will happen," precisely suggest[ing] otherwise, especially in public spaces in this part of Maharashtra' (2008: 188–9). Dalit children are invisible in Bénéï's ethnography.

Fortunately, our understanding of debates about naming, politics and regionalism in Maharashtra has been enriched by Anupama Rao's (2009) recent study of the formation of

Dalit subjectivity in Maharashtra, *The Caste Question*. Histories of region and caste produced different forms of Dalit subjectivity in different parts of India. From the nineteenth century onwards, radical Dalits in Maharashtra, like many non-Brahmans, were contesting Brahman origin stories and claims to indigeneity. But their agenda of social equality conflicted with the unstable formation of the Maratha caste since the latter was based on drawing to it those sections of Marathi society guided by an interest in aspiration rather than egalitarianism.

Following Independence in 1947, Congress came to be associated with Maratha power; this sense only increased after 1960, following the successful campaign for a separate Maharashtra state organized on linguistic lines. It is not surprising then that the key Dalit leader in Maharashtra (and India), Bhimrao Ambedkar, opposed the formation of a linguistic state on the grounds that 'a focus on language would only deepen caste dominance' (Rao 2009: 183, 185–6).

In Maharashtra, 'the deepened significance and symbolisation of region and caste incited new mappings of political violence and new spatialisation strategies' (Rao 2009: 204). We noted above the animosity of the Shiv Sena in Bombay to the political assertiveness of Dalits. Rao's account shows the parallel ways in which the public (often violent) performance of politics came to constitute both Dalit and Shiv Sainik subjectivities. For instance, the Dalit Panthers, a militant Dalit organization, was formed in 1972 and mirrored the activities of the Shiv Sena in many ways, not least in their public meetings which 'served as ecstatic commemorations and public affirmations of a despised and denigrated identity now resignified as political potential' (2009: 189–90). And as Rao reports, there was intense street fighting in Bombay between the Panthers and the Shiv Sena until 1980 (2009: 204).

Thus, the Dalit and anti-Dalit movements together created new arenas of politics in Maharashtra. Whereas Hansen largely ignores the role of Dalit radicalism in the political transformation of Bombay, Rao makes a case for understanding the ways in which Dalit activism was involved in the formation of Marathi (and Indian) political subjectivities, rather than simply being external or reactive to them.

A site of such transformation was the campaign to rename Marathwada University in Aurangabad as Dr Babasaheb Ambedkar Marathwada University. The renaming (or *namantar*) had long been desired by Dalit activists but was opposed by mainly upper-caste elites, who argued that the university ought not to be defined by one caste group. Throughout the anti-renaming campaign, 'the depiction of Ambedkar as a Dalit icon and *namantar* as a casteist demand defined upper-caste resistance' (Rao 2009: 209); violence was committed against Dalits in the region and also came to define the Dalit response to such attacks. Rao shows how the *namantar* controversy was yet another occasion when Dalits were stereotyped as militant malcontents who would sacrifice national interest in the pursuit of public recognition. She discusses a newspaper editorial that reminded readers that Ambedkar's caste, the Mahars, had fought on the side of the British against the Maratha forces in 1818 and as such were colonial collaborators. Regionalism was once again being shaped to exclude Dalits from the Maharashtrian ethnohistorical imaginary and to cast them in the mould of anti-national agitators. And, Ambedkar ceased to be an uncontested Marathi hero (Rao 2009: 215).

Dalits were thus made hostile to the project of Maharashtra and excluded from it; their relative absence from Hansen and Bénéï's ethnographies are uncomfortable reminders of this. But Rao recovers the integral role played by radical Dalits in the formation of Maharashtrian political subjectivity, while at the same time showing how Dalits have come to be defined by violent antagonism. Their relative powerlessness is thrown into sharp relief by comparison with the Shiv Sena whose performances of violence are attributed to assertions of martial Marathi pride.

In the exchange with the Muslim child, the Kolhapur private school headmistress seems to suggest that the language he speaks at home does not threaten the project of Maharashtra: invisible and silent, it cannot possibly contribute to the conversation. But Sen's ethnography tells us otherwise about the saliency of the 'private': in the Bombay slums, the politics of regionalism has become kinship. Rao similarly tells us that there is no space (private or public) in Maharashtra in which a Dalit is not portrayed as violent and threatening. The bind is considerable: unable to play a legitimate part in the politics of regionalism, the politics of regionalism does not grant Dalits or Muslims the luxury of private subjectivities either.

Conclusion

The politics of regionalism in Maharashtra is inseparable from the broader social and cultural implications of the act of naming. Naming is an on-going performative process that attempts to fix that which is being named. Key to naming is desire, which is the expression of the 'becoming' of the object that is named. Of the three ethnographies we have considered, Hansen's study is most explicit about this and furnishes the frame through which he analyses the politics of Mumbai. The consideration of names and the act of naming here is primarily an ethnographic point because it is the rise of exclusionist visions of Marathi regionalism in the twentieth and early twenty-first centuries that has laid bare the ways in which such naming works in India today. Drawing on Judith Butler's discussion of the authority to bestow names (1993: 208–17), Hansen argues that official names (of a city or monument for instance) are performances of the sovereignty of the state. He suggests that the popularity and use of these names becomes 'indexical of the authority of the state ... to make ... the name ... effectively designate and thus authorize, a particular history, myth, reference as more authentic than those it seeks to displace' (Hansen 2006: 204). But it can only be successful if it accurately represents local desires and aspirations. This is why the renaming of Bombay as Mumbai by the Shiv Sena-BJP Maharashtra state government in 1995 has largely stuck (ibid.: 221), and in turn made the state government's vision of 'Mumbai' more authoritative.

That 'Maharashtra' itself is such a name is amply testified to by Bénéï's discussion of schooling in the state, and of Feldhaus' ethnography of pilgrimage. Feldhaus shows how the practices of Hindu devotion offer material that can service an imaginary of the region, a region that was named as a state in 1960. That imaginary is then actively promoted through performative acts of naming by state institutions such as the schools discussed by Bénéï. Importantly, however, we have also drawn out the ways in which such performances are always subject to contestation and slippage, and are thus ultimately unstable. This may be expressed as conflict at the level of the 'local' that we raise in our discussion of Feldhaus, or by the discomfort experienced by the Muslim pupil described by Bénéï, when he was questioned over language use by his teacher.

Understanding public, performative acts of naming as an assertion of sovereignty also illuminates the place of 'Maharashtra' in the context of the Indian state. By authorizing the name, the Indian state engages in a performance of sovereignty that also indexes a particular ethnohistorical imaginary of what 'India' is: an uncontestable place consisting of many named places. Or, rather more simply: 'Unity in Diversity'.

References

Appadurai, A. (1984) 'Wells in western India: irrigation and cooperation in an agricultural society', *Expedition*, 26: 3–14.

——(2000) 'Spectral housing and urban cleansing: notes on millennial Mumbai', *Public Culture,* 12: 627–51.

——(2001) 'Deep democracy: urban governmentality and the horizon of politics', *Environment and Urbanization,* 13: 23–43.

Attwood, D. W. (1992) *Raising Cane: The Political Economy of Sugar in Western India.* Boulder: Westview Press.

Bagwe, A. (1995) *Of Woman Caste: The Experience of Gender in Rural India.* Calcutta: Stree.

Baviskar, B. S. (1968) 'Co-operatives and politics', *Economic and Political Weekly,* 3: 490–5.

——(1980) *The Politics of Development: Sugar Co-operatives in Rural Maharashtra.* Delhi: Oxford University Press.

Bayly, C. A. (1998) *Origins of Nationality in South Asia.* Delhi: Oxford University Press.

Bénéï, V. (1996) *La Dot en Inde: Un fléau social? Socio-anthropology du mariage au Maharashtra.* Paris: Karthala.

——(1999) 'Changing house and social representations: the case of dowry in Pune district', in I. Glushkova and R. Vora (eds), *Home, Family and Kinship in Maharashtra.* New Delhi: Oxford University Press.

——(2008) *Schooling Passions: Nation, History and Language in Contemporary Western India.* Stanford: Stanford University Press.

Benjamin, W. (1999) *The Arcades Project* (Prepared after the Gergman volume edited by Rolf Tiedemann). Cambridge, MA: Belknap Press.

Bennett, C. (1980) 'The morphology of language boundaries: Indo-Aryan and Dravidian in peninsular India', in D. Sopher (ed.), *An Exploration of India.* Ithaca: Cornell University Press.

Billig, M. (1995) *Banal Nationalism.* London: Sage Publications.

Burman, J. (2001) 'Shivaji's myth and Maharashtra's syncretic traditions', *Economic and Political Weekly,* 36: 1226–34.

Burra, N. (1996) 'Buddhism, conversion and identity: a case study of village Mahars', in M. N. Srinivas (ed.), *Caste: Its Twentieth Century Avatar.* New Delhi: Viking.

Butler, J. (1993) *Bodies That Matter: On the Discursive Limits of "Sex".* New York: Routledge.

Carter, A. T. (1974a) *Elite Politics in Rural India: Political Stratification and Political Alliances in Western Maharashtra.* Cambridge: Cambridge University Press.

——(1974b) 'A comparative analysis of systems of kinship and marriage in South Asia', *Proceedings of the Royal Anthropological Institute,* 1973: 29–54.

——(1982) 'Hierarchy and the concept of the person in Western India', in Á. Östör, L. Fruzzetti and S. Barnett (eds), *Concepts of Person.* Cambridge, MA: Harvard University Press.

——(1984) 'Household histories', in R. Netting, R. Wilk and E. Arnould (eds), *Households: Comparative and Historical Studies of the Domestic Group.* Berkeley: University of California Press.

——(1988) 'Household dynamics and land transactions in Western Maharashtra', in D. W. Attwood, M. Israel and N. K. Wagle (eds), *Countryside, City and Society in Maharashtra.* Toronto: University of Toronto, Center for South Asian Studies.

Cohn, Berhard (1967) 'Regions subjective and objective: their relation to the study of modern Indian history and society', in R. Crane (ed.), *Regions and Regionalism in South Asian Studies: An Exploratory Study,* Program in Comparative Studies on South Asia, Monograph No. 5. Durham, NC: Duke University.

Coles, R. (1993) *The Call to Service: A Witness to Idealism.* Boston: Houghton Mifflin.

Contursi, J. (1989) 'Militant Hindus and Buddhist Dalits: hegemony and resistance in an Indian slum', *American Ethnologist,* 16: 441–57.

——(1993) 'Political theology: text and practice in a Dalit Panther community', *Journal of Asian Studies,* 52: 320–39.

——(1996) 'Language and power in images of Indian women', in A. Feldhaus (ed.), *Images of Women in Maharashtrian Literature and Religion.* Albany: State University of New York Press.

Dandekar, H. (1986) *Men to Bombay, Women at Home: Urban Influence on Sugar Village, Deccan Maharashtra, India, 1942–1982*. Ann Arbor: Center for South and Southeast Asian Studies, University of Michigan.

——(1999) 'A house of your own: the value of *ghar* for village women in Maharashtra', in I. Glushkova and R. Vora (eds), *Home, Family and Kinship in Maharashtra*. New Delhi: Oxford University Press.

Das, V. (1989) 'Voices of children', *Daedalus*, 118: 262–94.

Datye, V., Kielmann, K., Sheikh, K., Deshmukh, D., Deshpande, S., Porter, J. and Rangan, S. (2006) 'Private practitioners' communications with patients around HIV testing in Pune, India', *Health Policy and Planning*, 21: 343–52.

Deleury, G. A. (1960) *The Cult of Vithoba*. Poona: Deccan College Postgraduate and Research Institute.

Desai, A. A. (2007) 'Witchcraft, religious transformation, and Hindu nationalism in rural central India', unpublished thesis, University of London.

——(2008) 'Subaltern vegetarianism: witchcraft, embodiment and sociality in Central India', *South Asia: Journal of South Asian Studies*, 31: 96–117.

——(2009) 'Anti- "anti-witchcraft" and the Maoist insurgency in Maharashtra, India', *Dialectical Anthropology*, 33: 423–39.

——(2010) 'Dilemmas of devotion: religious transformation and agency in Hindu India', *Journal of the Royal Anthropological Institute*, 16: 313–29.

Feldhaus, A. (1995) *Water and Womanhood: Religious Meanings of Rivers in Maharashtra*. New York: Oxford University Press.

——(2003) *Connected Places: Region, Pilgrimage, and Geographical Imagination in India*. New York: Palgrave.

Fishman, J. A. (1989) *Language and Ethnicity in Minority Sociolinguistic Perspective*. Clevedon, UK: Multilingual Matters.

Fitzgerald, T. (1997) 'Ambedkar Buddhism in Maharashtra', *Contributions to Indian Sociology*, 31: 225–51.

Gold, A. G. (1988) *Fruitful Journeys: The Ways of Rajasthani Pilgrims*. Berkeley: University of California Press.

Greenhalgh, S. (2008) *Just One Child: Science and Policy in Deng's China*. Berkeley: University of California Press.

Guru, Gopal (1997) 'Understanding Dalit protest in Maharashtra', *Political and Economic Weekly*, 32 (30): 1879–80.

Hansen, T. B. (1999) *The Saffron Wave: Hindu Nationalism and Democracy in Modern India*. Princeton: Princeton University Press.

——(2000) 'Predicaments of secularism: Muslim identities and politics in Mumbai', *Journal of the Royal Anthropological Institute*, 6: 255–72.

——(2001) *Wages of Violence: Naming and Identity in Postcolonial Bombay*. Princeton: Princeton University Press.

——(2006) 'Where names fall short: names as performances in contemporary urban South Africa', in G. vom Bruck and B. Bodenhorn (eds), *The Anthropology of Names and Naming*. Cambridge: Cambridge University Press.

Kamat, V. (1995) 'Reconsidering the popularity of primary health centers in India: a case study from rural Maharashtra', *Social Science and Medicine*, 41: 87–98.

Karve, I. (1962) '"On the road": a Maharashtrian pilgrimage', *Journal of Asian Studies*, 22: 13–29. (Originally published in 1951 as 'Watcal' in *Paripurti*. Poona: Deshmukh and Company.)

Kielmann, K. (2002) 'Theorizing health in the contest of transition: the dynamics of perceived morbidity among women in peri-urban Maharashtra, India', *Medical Anthropology*, 21: 175–205.

Kielmann, K., Deshmukh, D., Despande, S., Daty, V., Porter, J. and Rangan S. (2005) 'Managing uncertainty around HIV/AIDS in an urban setting: private medical providers and their patients in Pune, India', *Social Science and Medicine*, 61: 1540–50.

Kingdon, G. G. (2007) 'The progress of school education in India', *Oxford Review of Economic Policy*, 23:168–95.

Kolenda, P. (1970) 'Family structure in village Lonikand, India: 1819, 1958 and 1967', *Contributions to Indian Sociology*, 4: 50–72.

Kumar, P. (2006) 'Gender and procreative ideologies among the Kolams of Maharashtra', *Contributions to Indian Sociology*, 40: 279–310.

Latour, B. (2005) *Reassembling the Social: An Introduction to Actor-Network-Theory*. Oxford: Oxford University Press.

Luhrmann, T. (1996) *The Good Parsi: The Fate of a Colonial Elite in a Postcolonial Society*. Cambridge: Harvard University Press.

McDonald, E. E. (1968) 'The growth of regional consciousness in Maharastra', *Indian Economic and Social History Review*, 5: 223–43.

Malhotra, K. C. (1988) 'The birth of a god: Ram Mama of the Nandiwalas', in E. Zelliot and M. Berntsen (eds), *The Experience of Hinduism*. Albany: State University of New York Press.

Mazzarella, W. (2003) *Shovelling Smoke: Advertising and Globalisation in Contemporary India*. Durham, NC: Duke University Press.

Mines, D. P. (2005) *Fierce Gods: Inequality, Ritual, and the Politics of Dignity in a South Indian Village*. Bloomington: Indiana University Press.

Mosse, D. (2005) *Cultivating Development: An Ethnography of Aid Policy and Practice*. London: Pluto Press.

Orenstein, H. (1965) *Gaon: Conflict and Cohesion in an Indian Village*. Princeton: Princeton University Press.

Patwardhan, S. (1973) *Change among India's Harijans: Maharashtra; a Case Study*. New Delhi: Orient Longman.

Prout, A. and James, A. (1997) 'A new paradigm for the sociology of childhood? Provenance, promise and problems', in A. James and A. Prout (eds), *Constructing and Reconstructing Childhood: Contemporary Issues in the Sociological Study of Childhood*. London: RoutledgeFalmer.

Ranade, M. G. (1961 [1900]) *The Rise of the Maratha Power*. Bombay: Bombay University Press.

*Rao, A. (2009) *The Caste Question: Dalits and the Politics of Modern India*. Berkeley: University of California Press.

Rubinoff, J. A. (1988) 'Vangad: the context of lineage in Goan corporate villages', in D. W. Attwood, M. Israel and N. K. Wagle (eds), *Countryside, City and Society in Maharashtra*. Toronto: University of Toronto, Center for South Asian Studies.

Schlesinger, L. (1977) 'The emergency in an Indian village', *Asian Survey*, 17: 627–47.

*——(1981) 'Agriculture and community in Maharashtra, India', *Research in Economic Anthropology*, 4: 233–74.

Sen, A. (2004) 'Mumbai slums and the search for "a heart": ethics, ethnography and dilemmas of studying urban violence', *Anthropology Matters*, 6: 1–7.

*——(2007) *Shiv Sena Women: Violence and Communalism in a Bombay Slum*. Bloomington: Indiana University Press.

Skultans, V. (1987a) 'The management of mental illness among Maharashtrian families: a case study of a Mahanubhav healing temple', *Man*, (N.S.) 22: 661–79.

——(1987b) 'Trance and the management of mental illness among Maharashtrian families', *Anthropology Today*, 3: 2–4.

——(1991) 'Women and affliction in Maharashtra: a hydraulic model of health and illness', *Culture, Medicine and Psychiatry*, 15: 321–59.

Sontheimer, G.-D. (1988) 'The religion of Dhangar nomads', in E. Zelliot and M. Berntsen (1982) (eds), *The Experience of Hinduism*. Albany: State University of New York Press.

Youngblood, M. D. (2008) 'Negotiating hierarchy and identity: cultural performance on the meaning of the Demon King Bali in rural Maharashtra', in M. Bhagavan and A. Feldhaus (eds), *Speaking Truth to Power: Religion, Caste, and the Subaltern Question in India*. New Delhi: Oxford University Press.

12 North-East India

Ethnography and politics of identity

Tanka B. Subba and Jelle J. P. Wouters

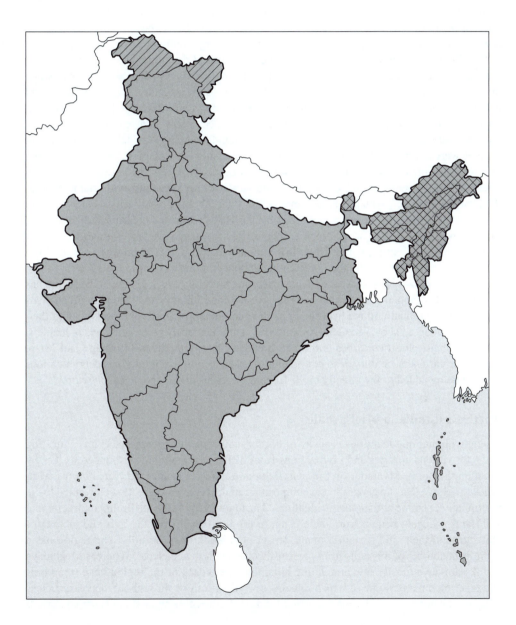

'Do not accept *guwa pan* (areca nut and betel leaf invariably offered by the Khasis of Meghalaya as a sign of hospitality) from a Khasi girl.' This was how one of the authors of this chapter was cautioned by his mother when he was about to leave for Shillong to join North-Eastern Hill University as a Reader in September 1991. When asked why, she said: 'If you do that you will be under her spell throughout your life.' His mother's construction of the Khasis was certainly not based on her first-hand knowledge of the people in question but on the basis of what she had heard from her relatives who came to Meghalaya from the eastern hills of Nepal in the 1890s to work in the forests and on the roads.

The identities of 200-odd communities of the region called North-East India are similarly constructed by people who have gone there from outside, as missionaries, travellers, administrators or as those in search of employment, such as the relatives of one of the authors mentioned above. Of all such constructions of local identities the ones by the colonial administrators were perhaps the most influential for they continue to be questioned even today. The colonial administrator-ethnographers dominated the construction of identities by not only enumerating and classifying the people of this region, but also by publishing numerous articles in reputed journals published from India and the United Kingdom and exhaustive monographs on some important tribes of the region like the Khasi, Garo, Ao, Angami, Sema, Lotha, Karbi, Kachari and Lepcha. As regards the names of these tribes they did not create any but appropriated those that they thought were most widely known. In doing so, they were more often than not influenced by what names the Assamese plains people used for different hill tribes that they notionally controlled. This was so because the British interacted relatively more, for commercial and administrative reasons, with plains peoples than with hill peoples, which was instrumental for their labelling of hill tribes. This certainly does not mean that all names popularized by the British were taken from the Assamese; 'Kutcha Nagas', who are now known as Zeme Nagas, was, for instance, a name given by their neighbour Angamis (Kamei 2004: 13). Similarly 'Lepcha' in Sikkim was a corrupt form of 'Lapche', a name given by their western neighbour Limbus.

When one takes a local perspective, however, one finds that every village in the region has its own identity, and although many people have left their villages and settled in urban areas for better educational and medical facilities they continue to identify themselves with their respective villages. They also identify themselves simultaneously with their *khel*s or hamlets, lineages, clans, phratries, tribes and much broader generic identities like Naga and Mizo. During the past half a century or so new identities based on religion or religious denominations are also being added to the already multi-layered identities of the people of the region.

North-East India: a brief profile

Living with multiple identities is a way of life for the people of this region, as it is a meeting place for various cultures and civilizations from different directions, surrounded as it is by Tibet on the north, Myanmar on the east, Bangladesh on the south, and Nepal on the west. We also believe that the geographical composition of the region has greatly contributed to the multiplicity of ethnic and linguistic identities. The three fertile valleys – Brahmaputra, Imphal and Barak – hugely benefit from the erosion of top fertile soil from the hills and mountains that surround them and sustain a much denser population than the hills. The region has a significant number of migrants from present-day Bangladesh and Nepal. Whereas Meghalaya and Assam have mostly low undulating hills, the other states of the region have steep hills and taller mountains, some of which remain covered with snow throughout the year, such as those on the northern border of Arunachal Pradesh. Some of these mountains are sources of origin stories and myths, as are the small and big rivers cutting the hills and mountains into deep gorges, which are sometimes broad enough to allow a village to be established along the river bank and pursue wet-rice cultivation in the terraces for which some of the tribes like Angami and Apatani are famous. The search for fertile cultivatable lands has led many hill tribes like Hill Miri and Tiwa to migrate to lower altitudes or plains, which has over the years led to different identities for them from those who are left behind in the hills. The highly fertile river islands of the mighty Brahmaputra continue to be one such major destination for land-hungry migrants.

The linguistic diversity of the region, which largely corresponds with its ethnic diversity, is something to be reckoned with. The diversity of languages in this region, constituting about 9 per cent of the total landmass of India, can be guessed from the fact that the region has more than 200 languages. Among the hill tribes of the region the bilinguals constitute more than 75 per cent (Miri 1982), which is phenomenal compared to the national average of bilinguals, which is just 8 per cent. Although most of the languages in the region belong to the Tibeto-Burman sub-family of the Sino-Tibetan family, the languages are highly heterogeneous and are often not mutually intelligible. The region also boasts a large number of Indo-Aryan and Austro-Asiatic language speakers. Although debatable, this diversity may have something to do with the rugged and harsh terrain, which may have constrained intensive interactions between villages and so perhaps long prevented a commonly shared language from coming into existence.

The region consists of eight states today: Meghalaya, Manipur, Mizoram, Arunachal Pradesh, Nagaland, Tripura, Assam and Sikkim. Meghalaya and Tripura are located on the southern border with Bangladesh; Manipur, Mizoram, Nagaland, and part of Arunachal Pradesh occupy the eastern border with Myanmar; Assam connects Bangladesh and the rest of India with all the states of the region except Sikkim; most of Arunachal Pradesh shares the border with the Autonomous Region of Tibet whereas Sikkim, the last state to be part of the region, is surrounded by the Autonomous Region of Tibet on the north, Bhutan on the east, Nepal on the west and Darjeeling District of West Bengal on the south. This state is geographically not contiguous with the remaining seven states but has ecological and cultural similarities with most states of North-East India, which perhaps justifies its inclusion in the region.

Colonial ethnography

The debate between those who accuse earlier anthropologists of collaborating with colonial governments by implicitly reassuring the cultural hegemony of the ruler (Asad 1973; Said 1978) and those who have tried to play down the alleged relationship between anthropology and colonialism like James, who called anthropologists 'reluctant imperialists' (James 1973), seems not to apply in North-East India. Rather in this region the relationship between colonialism and ethnography was fairly straightforward as ethnographers were at the same time colonial administrators whereas academic anthropology in the region, here seen as only a specific aspect of a broader field of ethnographic practices (Pels and Salemink 2002: 7), is largely a post-colonial phenomenon. As Elwin remarked, colonial ethnography in North-East India is not to be confused with anthropological investigations. Those ethnographic accounts referred to by anthropologists today were often written by administrators, missionaries, travellers and explorers rather than by trained anthropologists (Elwin 1959a: xv). Even the two most well-known colonial ethnographers of the area – J. H. Hutton who wrote *The Angami Nagas* (1968 [1921a]) and *The Sema Nagas* (1969 [1921b]) and J. P. Mills, who is the author of *The Lhota Nagas* (1922), *The Ao Nagas* (1973 [1926]) and *The Rengma Nagas* (1937) – did not receive any formal training in anthropology and were recognized as anthropologists only after they left the British Indian Civil Service and returned to Great Britain, a fact Hutton admits in the preface to his work on *The Angami Nagas* in the following words: 'I had little knowledge of anthropology at that time and having been always a poor linguist and with a bad ear for music, I found the highly tonal languages of the Naga Hills difficult to acquire' (Hutton 1921a: xi). If one would nevertheless insist on placing colonial ethnography in an anthropological framework it is certainly to be seen as 'applied anthropology', meant to render the population visible and to find ways to effectuate colonial policies, rather than 'academic anthropology'.

In the remainder of this section we will, besides briefly introducing some other major colonial ethnographies, criticize the post-colonial reading of colonial accounts on castes and tribes in North-East India, which, we argue, is partial and biased in highlighting certain forms of 'negative stereotyping' while also suffering from measuring colonial ethnographic writings with the yardsticks of contemporary anthropological standards. We argue that the debate within post-colonial anthropology about the 'truth' of colonial ethnographic writings on the region becomes largely redundant when one realizes that what is called colonial ethnography today is rather a non-academic ethnographic tradition that emerged from colonial policies and practices (Pels and Salemink 2002: 7).

It is difficult to claim when the first European traveller or missionary visited the present North-East region of India, but formal contact with the colonial rulers was established with the signing of the Treaty of Yandaboo in 1826, which ended the first Anglo-Burmese war and demarcated the north-eastern political boundaries of British India. Colonial ethnography emerged in a context of political contestations, and the often hostile relations between British colonialists and many hill tribes found its reflection in the often mocking and scornful descriptions, which especially characterize early, colonial ethnographic accounts. For instance, Major John Butler (1847, 1855) talks about the 'treacherous neighbours' of Singphos, 'general degeneracy' of the Assamese people and their 'pernicious opiate'. He describes Singphos as 'a rude and treacherous people', Abors (now called Adis) as 'void of delicacy as they are of cleanliness', Nagas as 'a very uncivilized race, with dark complexions, athletic sinewy frames, hideously wild and ugly visages, reckless of human life' (quoted in Elwin 1959a: xvi). These disdainful attitudes towards hill tribes were widespread and as late as 1911 the wife of an officer attached to an Abor expedition said, 'it is such a bore that my husband has to go off on that silly Abor Expedition to fight those stupid aborigines with their queer arboreal habits' (quoted in Elwin 1959a: xvi).

It was perhaps due to the lack of such hostility in Sikkim that all colonial writers have used highly positive and some even bordering on paternalistic words like 'docile', 'amiable', 'cheerful', 'helpful', 'careful', 'faithful' and so on about Lepchas (Po'dar and Subba 1991: 80). In fact, Gorer (1984 [1938]) made a lot of effort to understand why the Lepchas lacked aggressiveness, and Morris (1938), who accompanied Gorer to Lingthem, a Lepcha village in north Sikkim, greatly agreed with Gorer although on many other matters they differed greatly. The ethnographies of Gorer and Morris based on the same village and people are actually depictions of often different aspects of the Lepcha culture and society. The former being trained by Mead and Benedict was more interested in the psychological aspects of the people whereas Morris, with a long military background before coming to ethnology, was more interested in subjects like magic and spells, family life, sex and festivals.

The beginning of the twentieth century marked a significant change in the history of the ethnography of North-East India. After many decades of political turmoil the British succeeded in pacifying and administering certain parts of the hills. In order to implement effective forms of administration the colonial government needed to know more about the people to be administered. Sir Bampfylde Fuller, then Chief Commissioner of Assam, thus proposed that a series of monographs be prepared on important castes and tribes of Assam. Those monographs were to be written by experienced administrators with intimate knowledge of the people concerned and, suggested by the similarities in indexes, in accordance with book structures set by the influential 'teach yourself ethnography guidebook' *Notes and Queries on Anthropology* (1874). The proposal was accepted by the then government of India and resulted in a wide range of monographs like *The Khasis* by Gurdon (1906), *The Mikirs* by Lyall (1908), *The Garos* by Playfair (1909), *The Kacharis* by Endle (1911), *The Naga Tribes of Manipur* by Hodson (1911) and *The Lushei Kuki Clans* by Shakespear (1912). This colonial project indeed suggests that there was no separation between science and government in the task of accumulating ethnographic data (Dirks 2002: 170).

Although most colonial ethnographic accounts, except those on the Lepchas of Sikkim, are more often than not marked by derogatory comments and are often biased, judgemental, ridden with awkward comparisons and stress colonizer's sense of all-round superiority over the colonized, the problem with the use of selected passages is that one tends to make a partial assessment of the authors, which has been a general malaise about the critique of colonial ethnography. Critiques of early colonial anthropology have picked up selected words and sentences, like Elwin (1959a) has done, to prove their point about colonial ethnography, which does not give a complete picture of the ethnography or the ethnographer. Dalton (1872), for example, criticized the absence of any 'proper religion' among hill tribes yet he rarely missed an opportunity to compliment them. For instance, he describes the Chulikata Mismis as having many virtues, praises the 'practical utility' of the Abor dormitory, of Miri women making 'faithful and obedient wives', and of the Apatani men as 'fighting effectively as well as honourably' (cited in Elwin 1959a: xvii). Likewise, one can find belittling remarks about the tribes of Manipur in Johnstone's *Manipur and the Naga Hills* yet he says in the same source about the Europeans themselves:

> unfortunately, our so-called statesmen are carried away by false ideas of humanitarianism, and a desire to pose in every way as the exponents of civilization, that is the last fad that is uppermost, and the experience of ages and the real good of primitive people are often sacrificed to this *Ignis fatuus*.
>
> (Johnstone 1971 [1896]: 115)

> it cannot, I fear, be denied, that as a race we are a little careless of the feelings of others. It is possibly due in a great measure to our insularity: but, whatever be the cause, it is an undesirable quality to possess.
>
> (Johnstone 1971 [1896]: 276)

Such a balance of negative and positive evaluations can also be found in Hutton (1921b: 27) and Mills (1926: 66). Therefore reconstruction of the colonial ethnography based on selected words used by the colonial administrators is perhaps unfortunate, but also inevitable because all reconstructions are in a way selective.

Most of the colonial monographs mentioned above share the following characteristics. First, the evolutionary paradigm is rather dominant in all monographs, which at times exists even between tribes, e.g. Khasis are put on a higher level of civilization than the Mikirs by

Lyall (1908: 151). With evolutionists such as Tylor, Morgan, Spencer and Frazer standing as leading figures in the field of anthropology it was only natural that the colonial monographs reflected the evolutionary interest. Second, they are all written in a uniform style, although minor variations in the naming and sequencing of chapters were obviously permitted. Although the chapter headings are often the same the contents differ quite significantly from one monograph to another, which could be partly due to the ethnographers' personal interest and partly the data they had access to. Third, they are neither aimed at presenting a monolithic image of the tribes nor are they aimed at representing them as 'primitive isolates', which is clear from the manner they drew affinities with other tribes, plains Assamese or Manipuris, and even the Europeans. The affinities in appearances, character, material culture, religious practices, etc. clearly indicate that they did not wish to project any tribe as a 'primitive isolate', as is often alleged by critics (e.g. Misra 1998). Nonetheless, colonial authors made a rather sharp division between hill tribes and Hindus and Muslims with administrators like Johnstone and Endle warning against tribes coming under the influence of the 'miserable, bigoted, caste-observing Mussulman of Bengal' (Johnstone 1971 [1896]: 44) or the 'destructive vortex of Hinduism' (Endle 1911: 53). Fourth, although most monographs show what might be called 'negative stereotyping' of the studied groups in question, a full assessment of the ethnographic archive may show many instances of 'positive stereotyping' too. Fifth, there is clearly a Eurocentric evaluation of the appearances and habits of the tribes described, with progressively lesser degree as the colonial period came to an end. Sixth, most of them highlighted the positive role played by Christian missionaries and remarked that the Christian houses were cleaner and better than the non-Christian ones. Finally, none of the monographs touch upon any politically sensitive subjects like the local opposition to proselytisation, taxation on house or cattle, imposition of new administrative and judicial systems, the survey and acquisition of tribal land, and the resistance to colonial rule. It is difficult to presume that the colonial ethnographers were not aware of all this, but their loyalty to the crown perhaps prevented them from writing on such matters.

Indeed, British colonialists entered the hills of North-East India with dominant theories of culture, utilitarianism and race taught to them in established universities in the United Kingdom. With the advantage of hindsight we may now argue that their dominant views were a product of British hegemony. Yet this reflexivity cannot reasonably be expected from the colonial authors themselves. It may further be remembered that they wrote what they did for their own European audience and colonial administrators; their accounts were never meant to be read in the light of post-colonialism or by the 'natives'.

The post-colonial ethnography

The work of Fürer-Haimendorf may be seen as a bridge between colonial and post-colonial ethnography. He was the first formally trained anthropologist who executed several field trips in the region and with his arrival the previously described distinction between 'applied' and 'academic anthropology' blurred. Although his ambitions were academic he not only closely befriended senior administrators, who apparently facilitated his fieldwork, but his book *The Naked Nagas* (1939) is partly a narration of how he joined the administrator Mills in a punitive expedition to Pangsha village (in present-day Nagaland) in order to punish its inhabitants for captivating slaves and headhunting, a practice that was made illegal by the British colonial government. Fürer-Haimendorf's dependence on the colonial regime became even more marked during the Second World War when, being an Austrian with a German passport, he was first arrested but later, largely due to his high connections in the British colonial administration, curiously offered the post of Special Officer to the North-East Frontier Agency (now Arunachal Pradesh). This enabled him to do fieldwork among Apatanis, which resulted in his *The Apa Tanis and Their Neighbours* (1962). During his career Fürer-Haimendorf published widely on North-East India and his contributions are perhaps better remembered for their ethnographic richness than for their theoretical insights.

Elwin, who arrived in India in 1927, may be considered as the second bridge between the colonial and post-colonial ethnographers. Pandit Nehru, the first prime minister of India and a close friend of Elwin, was instrumental in sending him to this region. He was appointed in 1953 as Consultant for Tribal Areas in North-Eastern Frontier Agency, the former name for Arunachal Pradesh. In 1959 he published *A Philosophy for NEFA* (1959b) wherein he outlined the tribal policy for India, and the book is still considered as the bible for tribal administrators. Although he had no formal degree in anthropology, his long and intimate knowledge of the tribes of Orissa and Madhya Pradesh gave him the identity of an anthropologist that even his most staunch critic, Ghurye, did not contest.

Fürer-Haimendorf and Elwin had a large presence in the region. But we must hasten to add that both of them held high administrative positions in North-East India, and although we could say that they served as 'bridges' between the colonial and post-colonial ethnography they had at the time the aura of colonial administration. Although both of them often sounded paternalistic they rarely ever used derogatory words to describe the tribes they wrote about; they actually had deep concern for the future of the tribes in the region, changing as they were at a pace unprecedented in their history. Between the two, Fürer-Haimendorf has had a more lasting impact on academics and Elwin on tribal policy in India. Fürer-Haimendorf's and Elwin's refreshing contributions notwithstanding one could argue that the post-colonial ethnography of North-East India, here understood in a historical, i.e. post-independence sense, is to a large extent modelled after the colonial monographs discussed in the previous section. This is particularly true of the ethnographic monographs by Roy (1960 [1977]), Sarma Thakur (1985), Sarkar (1987) and Sharma (1988). Although the post-colonial monographs mentioned above do not strongly exhibit any sense of paternalism or 'negative stereotyping', which is rather common in colonial monographs, they frequently lack the rich ethnographic details found in colonial contributions.

Compared to the 'seven sisters' by which the rest of North-East India is referred to, Sikkim became a part of India only in 1975. Until then it was ruled by hereditary, theocratic rulers. Its status vis-à-vis the colonial rule in India was more or less similar to the status of the other two kingdoms in the region, namely Manipur and Tripura, i.e. as a 'protectorate state'. Therefore it is difficult to categorize Siiger's monumental work on the Lepchas of Tingvoong village in north Sikkim published in 1967 or the monographs on the Lepchas of Lingthem village in north Sikkim by Gorer (1984 [1938]) and Morris (1938) as colonial ethnographies. On the other hand, ethnographies on Lepchas by Thakur (1988) and Bhasin (1989) represent what Po'dar and Subba call 'home-grown Orientalism' (1991: 78) in the way they look at the tribal societies of the region. There is clear 'othering' of the tribes in their ethnographies, which is comparable to the othering of non-Western societies in Orientalist discourse. In corollary to Said's *Orientalism* (1978), Po'dar and Subba argue that there is a further division of the Orient where the dominant Hindu society in India extends the received dominant discourse from the West to the study of tribes, which are their objects of enquiry, without challenging it.

We now deal with some edited volumes on the region containing articles on all the branches of anthropology, but we are presenting here only some ethnographically rich chapters. These volumes were prepared by anthropologists with considerable experience in

North-East India, with the primary objective of providing some good reading materials for undergraduate as well as postgraduate students of anthropology in the region. The anthropology students of the region badly needed such books because the monographs on various tribes of the region, written both during colonial and post-colonial times, did not address the curricular requirements of anthropology students. Although the volumes mentioned below do not fully meet the expectation of students in the region, they are of considerable help to them. Some of the issues like social organization, agrarian relations, folklore and shifting cultivation, which are covered below, are old but they have been approached from development perspectives and are linked with the dynamics of identity in the respective societies. Some other issues such as the ethnography of lesser known tribes, gender, indigenous knowledge systems, urbanization and the impact of Christianity have huge relevance to the contemporary politics of identity.

Two senior Indian anthropologists, who have trained generations of ethnographers of the region, are Bhagabati and Misra. Bhagabati's article (2009) deals with the changes taking place in the relations between the hill and plains people in India's North-East over the centuries. Through various ethnographic accounts he shows how the relationship of symbiosis that existed in the past is gradually eroding. The article by Misra (1990) analyses the symbolism of the sharing of betel leaf and areca nut among the Khasis of Meghalaya. Another article Misra wrote, with Rangad (2008), contains over a dozen folk narratives that are woven together by them to construct the Khasi cosmology and worldview.

We now wish to discuss a number of ethnographers from the West. Two anthropologists who came to the region in the 1950s and did excellent fieldwork are Robbins Burling and Chie Nakane. What perhaps separates these two anthropologists from Fürer-Haimendorf and Elwin is the fact that they did not enjoy any power or privilege, as their predecessors did. They lived in the villages, experienced life the way the villagers did, and depended on the villagers' cooperation for the success of their fieldwork. Except for a letter from their home university they had no other authority to show. It is perhaps because of this difference that the arrival of Burling and Nakane personified the start of a new phase in post-colonial ethnography in the region.

Burling did his fieldwork in a village called Rengsanggri in the Garo Hills of Meghalaya from October 1954 to October 1956. He went there 'because of their unique combination of kinship traits, particularly their matrilineal descent and their matrilateral cross-cousin marriage' (1963: 3). The book shows that the distance between cousins entering into such a marriage is not important because cross-cousins can be both real and classificatory. The book also shows the importance of avuncular authority on cross-cousin marriage. The book on the whole is one of the most balanced accounts of life and living of the Garo tribe. The language of the book shows that the author was keen to make it neither a scientific treatise nor a literary fiction. The author shows a lot of empathy for the people but does not romanticize their social and sexual life. Theoretically, the book may be labelled as a functional representation of the Garo society, with both change and conflict depicted as occasional and secondary (for more details, see Subba 2004).

The other anthropologist who came to the region around the same time was Chie Nakane (1967), a Japanese who had spent many years in UK and US universities and was very much a part of the Western world, at least for academic purposes, and who came to Meghalaya to explore the theoretical problems of Khasi and Garo social organization in comparative perspective. Based on her theoretical interest, she focused on the marriage system in relation to the village community among the Garos and on variation in marriage forms related to the structure of descent groups among the Khasis. She conducted her fieldwork from October

1955 to February 1956 with the help of interpreters. She had earlier (1953–55) worked among the tribes of Tripura and Tangkhul Nagas of Manipur, which helped her considerably while doing her fieldwork among the tribes of Meghalaya.

Several decades after Fürer-Haimendorf, ethnographic work among the Apa Tanis has recently been continued by Stuart Blackburn. His research mainly focuses on oral traditions and the analysis of shamanic ritual chants (Blackburn 2008, 2010).

Erik de Maaker's doctoral thesis (2006) is an example of a more recent contribution by an ethnographer from the West. In his work, De Maaker describes and analyses in minute detail the processes of negotiation surrounding death rituals. In particular, he focuses on intricate patterns of gift-exchange and the 'replacement' of deceased spouses by affinal groups. Through these transactions 'houses' can be continued through the generations. His work is not only a rich account of the fast-changing Garo society but his combined usage of ethnography and visual anthropology is an innovative way of conducting and presenting research in the region.

In 2007 the *Journal of South Asian Studies* brought out a special volume on the North-East and its neighbouring areas. In their introduction the editors, de Maaker and Joshi, lament the multiple marginalization of the region and the lack of ethnographic research, although the castes and tribes of the region were the focus of the very first set of major Indian ethnographies (de Maaker and Joshi 2007: 382). This ethnographic void is partly due to the restrictions imposed on foreigners and related difficulties in obtaining visas but also, so they argue, due to the particular geographical location of the region, which is at the margins of three major academic 'area study' regions – South Asia, South-East Asia and East Asia – but in the academic mainstream of none. However, with restrictions being lifted in Assam, Tripura, Manipur and Meghalaya during the mid-1990s a surge of new research has taken place in the area and this edited volume sets out to celebrate that efflorescence. A central tendency in most of the contributions is the idea that the region has experienced, or is still experiencing, changes that are both rapid and radical. Joshi (2007), de Maaker (2007) and Marak (2007) focus on the social and cultural effects of religious and denominational conversions. Aisher (2007) writes about the changing relationship between spirits, humans and forest, an idea which is, of course, not new in India (see Vidyarthi 1963), whereas Longkumer (2007) links changing land patterns due to state interventions to the Heraka millenarian movement among the Zeme Naga in colonial times and explains how this movement has changed Zeme Naga social organization. Using the Garos as her case, Bal argues how processes of identity and ethnicity are not given but attain shape in the course of ever-changing circumstances (Bal 2007). Especially interesting in relation to the politics of identity is Burling's (2007) contribution in which he deconstructs the influential idea, which is also loaded with ethnic sentiments in the region, that tribes have migrated as coherent groups and that these migratory movements explain both their history and present distribution. Rather, Burling claims, the question 'where did so-and-so come from?' is meaningless because the present distribution of ethnic groups is the outcome of adjustments to environmental, political and economic conditions rather than the result of migratory groups at one point of time collectively settling themselves at one place or the other.

We wish now to take up some articles by Ramirez, which have clear linkages to the politics of identity. In one article (2005), Ramirez argues that Arunachalese myths represent 'a true political cosmology, at the same time deeply egocentric – everything is centred on me and my fellows – and eminently egalitarian – no higher authority is able to infringe on individual designs' (2005: 21). In another article (2007) he takes up three Tibeto-Burmese speaking communities, namely Dimasa (formerly Kachari), Karbi (formerly Mikir) and Tiwa (formerly

Lalung), who live in the fringes of the hills and plains of central Assam. He suggests that to understand anything about the mechanisms of identity in this region one has to admit the dissociation between social structures, cultural patterns and cultural practices, thereby confirming the assumption made by Leach in his *Political Systems of Highland Burma* (1954) that the cohesion of societies cannot be established without assuming the dissociation of identity, cultural patterns and practices. In a third article (2011) he follows the direction of his first article and provides more examples to illustrate the diversity of identities in the region. Although he does not abandon the concept of identity, his examples in this article are of identities based on a network of villages cutting across political boundaries. He shows how the study of 'uncertain ethnic identities' helps to understand how ethnic identities themselves may have emerged.

The other ethnographer from the West who has made a substantial contribution to the understanding of the politics of identity in this region is Karlsson from Stockholm University. From his numerous publications we take the following three important ones. In the first article (2005), he traces the rise of awareness about the pre-eminence and efficacy of traditional institutions among the Khasis of Meghalaya but argues that the revival of traditional institutions is a much more complex and significant event than most scholars seem to believe. In the second article (2006) he describes the struggles of people over forests and land in Meghalaya and argues that the 'politics of nature is intrinsically linked to ethnic mobilization and aspirations for increased political autonomy' (2006: 176). In his book titled *Unruly Hills: Nature and Nation in India's Northeast* (2012), Karlsson traces the social consequences of extractive economy, mainly mining and logging, and advocates empowering traditional institutions and traditional ecological knowledge.

Finally, we highlight some of the forthcoming ethnographic works on the region. The first is on rituals of healing in a community called Karow by Berit Fuhrmann, and the second is on Khasi matriliny by Namrata Gaikwad. Third, Nicolas Laine is working on his doctoral thesis on the ethnography of the relationship between elephants and humans among the Tai-Khamti people of Arunachal Pradesh. This people's identity has changed significantly due to the change of economy after the ban on timber felling imposed by the apex court of India in December 1996. In addition, we particularly look forward to two forthcoming publications by Toni Huber, who has been researching the Upper Subansiri region of Arunachal Pradesh for several years now, looking at narratives of origin and migration among the highlands of the far-eastern Himalaya and micro-migrations of the hill peoples of Northern Subansiri, Arunachal Pradesh, and how all that is intricately linked with issues of identity.

Conclusion

The mapping of colonial and post-colonial ethnographies shows a few emerging trends. First, while ethnographers from the West and from caste Hindu societies of India continue to study the tribes of the region as the study of Other cultures, newly emerging tribal scholars are also studying their own respective tribes, which may be described as 'auto-ethnography' or 'self-culture studies', although coming as they do from urban centres of the region and being westernized they may find themselves almost as alien amidst their own people as someone from the West or India's metropolises. There are some indications that such 'self-culture studies' suffer from the following shortcomings. First, the respondents often do not share details once they know the ethnic and educational background of the researchers. They are often told 'You know it better than we do'. As a result their ethnographies are usually very poor in detail. Second, there is no methodological rigour in the selection of the locale or the respondents, for they usually conduct their fieldwork among their own people who they know personally. Such locales may not always be ideal for the subject under investigation, which often forces the researchers to compromise on the quality of data collected. On the positive side, the researchers do not face language problems in communicating with the people and often receive close cooperation. They also do not suffer from the sense of alienation or frustration that a researcher from the West or elsewhere often experiences.

Second, although colonial ethnographers were by no means a homogenous group one could nevertheless argue that they had similar cultural backgrounds and intellectual exposure before they entered India's North-East. In contrast, post-colonial ethnographers are from highly diverse backgrounds. Therefore it is quite natural that the close similarity in organisation of chapters and style of representing tribal life found in colonial ethnography is missing from the post-colonial ethnography, which is indeed characterized by diverse methods of chapter organization, styles of representation and quality of ethnography.

Third, the other important shift we notice is in the conceptualisation of the tribal world itself. For a very long time, the words 'hill tribes' were synonymous with the tribal world, although some hill tribes like Tiwa and Miri had begun to settle in the plains and valleys long before they came into contact with the colonial administration. Consider how Fürer-Haimendorf starts his book on the Apatanis: 'The tangle of wooded hill-ranges which enclose, horse-shoe like, the fertile plains of Assam is the home of tribal populations distinct in language, race and culture from the Hindu and Muslim peasantry of the Brahmaputra valley' (1962: 1). It is not clear how the tribes living in the plains like the Garo, Tiwa, Dimasa, Karbi and Bodo were not a part of the tribal world in the colonial imagination. The post-colonial tribal world of the region clearly includes the plains tribes, although the colonial hangover cannot be ignored when imagining the hills as the original homelands of tribes.

Fourth, whereas it is never clear from most colonial ethnography what methodology of data collection was followed, it is quite evident that they were very meticulous about details and often rechecked the important data they collected. It is also obvious that they wrote their ethnographies on the basis of extensive travel in the areas inhabited by a tribe as well as a careful scrutiny of the published literature on the same. This made it possible for them to provide sufficient comparative data on other neighbouring tribes as well. The methodology of data collection in post-colonial ethnography is always explained to the readers and recent monographs are based on intensive fieldwork of a single village or tribe. They rarely make reference to other neighbouring tribes, not only perhaps because the concerned ethnographers do not undertake extensive travels in the region but also because within contemporary anthropology in-depth investigations of one place are often preferred over more ambitious comparative studies.

The post-colonial ethnographies are often rather poor in detail in comparison with the colonial ones, except perhaps those written by anthropologists from the West, which are not just ethnographically richer but are also couched in theoretical debates, both of which are incidentally amiss in most ethnographies written by Indian anthropologists, be they from caste Hindu or tribal background. In claiming so, we are far from being judgemental; it is there for everyone to see the difference.

Finally, we question the very widely supported theory of Cohn (1996), Inden (1990), Dirks (2001) and recently also followed by Scott (2009) that the colonial administration was responsible for labelling the population through its census operations and thereby changing their identity from fluid to fixed. We admit that the colonial administration was largely responsible for choosing a certain name out of several names available to them and giving currency to the name they chose, but several such names have already been discarded by the people concerned and several others are in the process of being replaced. Thus, we think that subscribing to the views of, most recently, Scott amounts to giving too much agency to colonial rule. We further think that identities have always been fluid and have remained so both during and after colonial rule.

Scott may be correct to some extent in arguing that name-giving processes as an aspect of state-making – in the context of North-East India the expansion of colonial administration and ethnographic mapping into the hills – 'fixed' units that were once fluid or unnamed (2009: 229). Yet one has to make a distinction between fixing a term for official documentation and how such a term is 'lived' by the people it is supposed to apply to. Colonial rule may have changed identities from fluid to fixed, but often merely on paper because people continued to refer to themselves by identities other than the ones given to them by the colonial ethnographers-cum-administrators. As a matter of fact, many of the colonial labels are not only lying in disuse, but are being contested by those who were labelled so, and some of them have successfully replaced the colonial labels such as Abor with Adi, Dafla with Nyishi, Mikir with Karbi, Lalung with Tiwa, Lushai with Mizo and so on. Had identities popularized by the colonial rulers been rigid all this and more would not be possible.

Regarding the fact that most post-colonial anthropologists have studied tribes as if they are autonomous and self-contained units, it is only to be stated that it is in line with colonial administrators-cum-ethnographers who, for reasons of governance, seem to have preferred to think of tribal groups in terms of stable and coherent groups occupying clearly separated and demarcated territories. This continuity is all the more remarkable when one notes that in the adjacent hills of Myanmar, Leach popularized an altogether different model, which is corroborated by Ramirez above, in which he called attention to the intangibility of social boundaries, the symbiotic relations between hills and valley peoples, and the idea that social and political structures of tribal groups are not static and fixed but rather oscillate between forms of feudal hierarchy and republicanism. Despite Leach arguing that literature on Naga tribes has remarkable similarities with that of highland Burma (now Myanmar) (1964 [1954]: 291) his emphasis on flux, blurred boundaries and interdependence between groups has, until recently (see Sadan and Robinne 2007), not really been followed by anthropologists working on North-East India.

In conclusion we argue that in colonial ethnographic literature the issue of identity was not considered as problematic as it is in the ethnographic literature on post-colonial North-East India, which indicates that the independence of India unleashed certain forces – education, infrastructure development, reorganization of states, affirmative action, secessionist movements – which apparently created the need for redefining colonial identities. The articulation of identities is, however, not always well-orchestrated but, as Karlsson argues in all his publications mentioned above, such articulation is increasingly being shaped by indigenous peoples' fight for their rights.

References

Aisher, Alexander (2007) 'Voices of Uncertainty: Spirits, Humans and Forests in Upland Arunachal Pradesh, India', *South Asia: Journal of South Asian Studies*, 30(3): 479–98.

*Asad, T. (1973) *Anthropology and the Colonial Encounter*. New York: Humanity Books.

Bal, Ellen (2007) 'Becoming the Garos of Bangladesh: Policies of Exclusion and the Ethnicisation of a "Tribal' Minority"', *South Asia: Journal of South Asian Studies*, 30(3): 439–55.

Bhagabati, A. C. (2009) 'Transformational Process in Northeast India: The XIV Verrier Elwin Endowment Lectures', *The NEHU Journal*, 7(1): 1–16.

Bhasin, Veena (1989) *Ecology, Culture and Change: Tribals of Sikkim Himalayas*. New Delhi: Inter-India Publications.

*Blackburn, Stuart (2008) *Himalayan Tribal Tales: Oral Tradition and Culture in the Apatani Valley*. Leiden: Brill.

——(2010) *The Sun Rises: A Shaman's Chant, Ritual Exchange and Fertility in the Apatani Valley*. Leiden: Brill.

Burling, Robbins (1963) *Rengsanggri: Family and Kinship in a Garo Village*. Philadelphia: University of Pennsylvania Press.

——(2007) 'Language, Ethnicity and Migration in North-Eastern India', *South Asia: Journal of South Asian Studies*, 30(3): 391–404.

Butler, John (1847) *A Sketch of Assam*. London: Smith, Elder.

——(1855) *Travels and Adventures in the Province of Assam during a Residence of Fourteen Years*. London: Smith, Elder.

*Cohn, B. S. (1996) *Colonialism and Its Forms of Knowledge: The British in India*. Princeton: Princeton University Press.

Dalton, E. T. (1872) *Descriptive Ethnology of Bengal*. Calcutta: Office of the Superintendent of Government Printing.

*de Maaker, Erik (2006) 'Negotiating Life: Garo Death Rituals and the Transformation of Society', unpublished thesis, University of Leiden.

——(2007) 'From the Songsarek Faith to Christianity: Conversion, Religious Identity and Ritual Efficacy', *South Asia: Journal of South Asian Studies*, 30(3): 517–30.

de Maaker, Erik and Joshi, Vibha (eds) (2007) 'Introduction: The Northeast and Beyond: Region and Culture', *South Asia: Journal of South Asian Studies*, 30(3): 381–90.

*Dirks, N. (2001) *Castes of Mind: Colonialism and the Making of Modern India*. Princeton: Princeton University Press.

——(2002) 'The Crimes of Colonialism: Anthropology and the Textualization of India', in P. Pels and O. Salemink (eds), *Colonial Subjects: Essays on the Practical History of Anthropology*. Ann Arbor: University of Michigan Press.

Elwin, Verrier (1959a) *India's North-East Frontier in the Nineteenth Century*. London: Oxford University Press.

——(1959b) *A Philosophy for NEFA*. Shillong: Government Printing.

Endle, S. (1911; 2nd ed. 1975) *The Kacharis*. Delhi: Cosmo Publications.

Fürer-Haimendorf, C. von (1939) *The Naked Nagas*. London: Methuen & Co. Ltd.

——(1962) *The Apa Tanis and Their Neighbours*. London: Routledge and Kegan Paul.

Gorer, Geoffrey (1938; 2nd ed. 1984) *The Lepchas of Sikkim*. Delhi: Cultural Publishing House.

Gurdon, P. R. T. (1906; 2nd ed. 1975) *The Khasis*. Delhi: Cosmo Publications.

Hodson, T. C. (1911) *The Naga Tribes of Manipur*. London: Macmillan & Co. Ltd.

Hutton, J. H. (1921a; 2nd ed. 1968) *The Sema Nagas*. London: Oxford University Press.

——(1921b; 2nd ed. 1969) *The Angami Nagas*. London: Oxford University Press.

Inden, R. (1990) *Imagining India*. Oxford: Blackwell Publishers.

James, W. (1973) 'The Anthropologist as Reluctant Imperialist', in T. Asad (ed.), *Anthropology and the Colonial Encounter*. New York: Humanity Books.

Johnstone, J. (1896; 2nd ed. 1971) *Manipur and the Naga Hills*. Delhi: Vivek Publishing House.

Joshi, Vibha (2007) 'The Birth of Christian Enthusiasm among the Angami of Nagaland', *South Asia: Journal of South Asian Studies*, 30(3): 541–57.

Kamei, Gangmumei (2004) *A History of the Zeliangrong Nagas: From Makhel to Rani Gaidinliu*. New Delhi: Spectrum Publications.

Karlsson, Bengt G. (2005) 'Sovereignty through Indigenous Governance: Revising "Traditional Political Institutions" in Northeast India', *The NEHU Journal*, 3(2): 1–16.

——(2006) 'Indigenous Natures: Forest and Community Dynamics in Meghalaya, North-East India', in Gunnel Cederlof and K. Sivaramakrishnan (eds), *Ecological Nationalism: Nature, Livelihoods, and Identities in South Asia*. Seattle, Washington: University of Washington Press.

*———(2012) *Unruly Hills: Nature and Nation in India's Northeast*. New York: Berghahn.

Leach, E. (1954; 2nd ed. 1964) *The Political Systems of Highland Burma: A Study of Kachin Social Structure*. Cambridge: Harvard University Press.

Longkumer, A. (2007) 'Religious and Economic Reform: The Gaidinliu Movement and the Heraka in the North Cachar Hills', *South Asia: Journal of South Asian Studies*, 30(3): 499–515.

Lyall, C. (1908) *The Mikirs*. Gauhati: United Publishers.

Marak, Caroline (2007) 'The Role of the Mahari in A'Chik Society: Change and Continuity', *South Asia: Journal of South Asian Studies*, 30(3): 531–40.

Mills, J. P. (1922) *The Lhota Nagas*. London: Macmillan & Co. Ltd.

———(1926; 2nd ed. 1973) *The Ao Nagas*. Oxford: Oxford University Press.

———(1937) *The Rengma Nagas*. London: Macmillan & Co. Ltd.

Miri, Mrinal (1982) *Linguistic Situation in Northeast India*. Shillong: North East India Council of Social Science Research.

Misra, P. K. (1990) 'The Mediating Role of Objects in the Functioning of Social Structure: A Case Study of Kwai', in Stephen H. Riggins (ed.), *Beyond Goffman*. New York: Mouton de Grayten.

Misra, P. K. and Rangad, Angela (2008) 'Sacred Grove, Khasi Society and Worldview', *The NEHU Journal*, 6(1&2): 19–54.

Misra, S. (1998) 'The Nature of Colonial Intervention in the Naga Hills, 1840–80', *Economic and Political Weekly*, 33(51): 3273–79.

Morris, John (1938) *Living with Lepchas*. London: William Heinemann Ltd.

Nakane, Chie (1967) G*aro and Khasi: A Comparative Study in Matrilineal Systems*. The Hague: Mouton & Co.

*Pels, P. and Salemink, O. (2002) 'Introduction: Locating the Colonial Subjects of Anthropology', in P. Pels and O. Salemink (eds), *Colonial Subjects: Essays on the Practical History of Anthropology*. Ann Arbor: The University of Michigan Press.

Playfair, A. (1909) *The Garos*. London: David Nutt.

Po'dar, Preym K. and Subba, Tanka B. (1991) 'Demystifying Some Ethnographic Texts on the Himalayas', *Social Scientist*, 19(8–9): 78–84.

*Ramirez, Philippe (2005) 'Enemy Spirits, Allied Spirits: The Political Cosmology of Arunachal Pradesh Societies', *The NEHU Journal*, 3(1): 1–28.

———(2007) 'Politico-ritual variations on the Assamese fringes: Do social systems exist?', in M. Sadan and F. Robinne (eds), *Social Dynamics in the Highlands of Southeast Asia: Reconsidering Political Systems of Highland Burma*. Leiden: Brill.

———(2011) 'Belonging to the Borders: Uncertain Identities in Northeast India', in Joanna Pfaff-Czarnecka and Gerard Toffin (eds), *The Politics of Belonging in the Himalayas: Local Attachments and Boundary Dynamics*. Delhi: Sage.

Roy, Sachin (1960, 2nd ed. 1977) *Aspects of Padam Minyong Culture*. Itanagar: Directorate of Research, Government of Arunachal Pradesh.

*Sadan, M. and Robinne, F. (eds) (2007) *Social Dynamics in the Highlands of Southeast Asia: Reconsidering Political Systems of Highland Burma*. Leiden: Brill.

Said, Edward W. (1978) *Orientalism*. Harmondsworth: Penguin.

Sarkar, Jayanta (1987) *Society, Culture and Ecological Adaptation Among Three Tribes of Arunachal Pradesh*. Calcutta: Anthropological Survey of India.

Sarma Thakur, G. C. (1985) *The Lalungs (Tiwas)*. Guwahati: Tribal Research Institute.

*Scott, James (2009) *The Art of Not Being Governed: An Anarchist History of Upland Southeast Asia*. New Haven and London: Yale University Press.

Shakespear, J. (1912) *The Lushei Kuki Clans*. London: Macmillan & Co. Ltd.

Sharma, R. R. P. (1988) *The Sherdukpens*. Itanagar: Directorate of Research, Government of Arunachal Pradesh.

Siiger, Halfdan (1967) *The Lepchas: Culture and Religion of a Himalayan People. Part I*. Copenhagen: The National Museum of Denmark.

Subba, T. B. (2004) 'Rereading Rengsanggri: A Text on Post-Colonial Northeast India', in P. K. Misra (ed.), *Studies in Indian Anthropology*. Jaipur and New Delhi: Rawat Publications.

Thakur, R. N. (1988) *Himalayan Lepchas*. New Delhi: Archives Publishers.

Vidyarthi, L. P. (1963) *The Maler: A Study in Nature-Man-Spirit Complex of a Hill Tribe in Bihar*. Calcutta: Bookland.

13 Odisha

Rajas and Prajas in a multi-segmented society

Uwe Skoda and Tina Otten

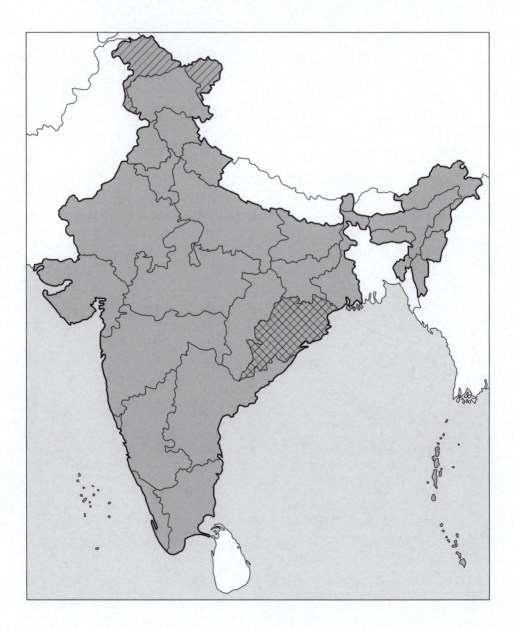

'Your Ancestors have chosen my Ancestors': a Raja in north-western Odisha[1] frequently opened his speeches with this slogan in the election campaign of 2004. It immediately reminded voters – predominantly classified as Scheduled Tribes in this reserved constituency – of the ancient ties between the royal family and the villagers, the bonds between Raja as 'king' in the former princely state and Praja as 'subjects' (the wider semantic scope including 'client', 'dependent', 'ruled', 'tenant' etc., but also denoting a social category in southern Odisha; see also Rousseleau [2008, 2009]). He then usually continued:

> Up until today I have served for 55 years [on the throne] and you call me king, but the day after tomorrow you may call me babu or Sir or sriman [*various honorific titles – the authors*]. That matters little to me; but the love and affection and relations which we have, nobody can cut that.
>
> (Election speech, Kadamba Kesari Chandra Deo, Rajasahib of Bonai, April 2004)

The occasional clapping in the audience appeared to signal affirmation, while the Raja revived memories of the domain, played on sentiments and tried to renew his central role vis-à-vis various communities under changing political equations turning kingdoms into parliamentary constituencies. Fifty years ago Bailey (1960) encountered a similarly complex structural co-existence of frames of reference – 'Tribe, Caste and Nation' among Konds in Odisha and stressed that it 'induced an unusually large degree of "anomie"' and 'created an unusually extensive field of political choice' (1960: 243). More recently, and going beyond Odisha, Price and Ruud (2010) dwelt on the political segmentation that had emerged historically and argued that, even as a modern nation state, 'India can maintain high degrees of segmentation amidst vast expanses of porous central and state bureaucracies' (2010: xxii).

Taking up the question of segmentation and the multitude of domains with reference to Odisha, here we focus on how rulers and ruled are linked. We concentrate particularly on 'little kingdoms' (and their avatars as princely states or *zamindaris*) as hitherto neglected yet crucial domains and sites of interactions, insubordination and historically evolving syncretisms, interfaces between imperial kingdoms and lower 'tribal' chiefs, as well as mediating or acting as a buffer between 'coastal belt' and 'hinterland'. Combining an anthropological with a historical approach, we suggest that Rajas and Prajas have been and are mutually implicated in a multi-segmented Odishan society with co-existing and overlapping realms and patterns of classification including the 'tribal' political system. While older 'frames' such as kingdoms, 'princely states' or clan divisions have often shown remarkable resilience, new orders have evolved transforming kingship and the state and leading to new 'little political systems' in a democratic set-up.

Odisha: a brief profile

Odisha, the province on the Bay of Bengal, has a territory roughly the size of Ireland. About half of its 36 million inhabitants live in the fertile coastal plain or on the banks of the river Mahanadi, flowing eastwards from the Chhattisgarh border into the Bay of Bengal through the centre of the province. The other half lives in the western highlands, that is, the extension of the Chota Nagpur Plateau to the north of the river and to the south the Eastern Ghats (with an average of over 1,000 metres in altitude) that continue in Andhra Pradesh.

Almost 90 per cent of the population lives in villages, with most villages and a few large cities being situated in river valleys (e.g. centres of heavy industry such as Rourkela) and in the intensively cultivated lowlands yielding two to three harvests annually. The largest city and seat of government is the state capital, Bhubaneswar, itself an ancient centre which took over from adjoining Cuttack in 1948. Yet, Cuttack, the political, military and administrative centre during the Mughal period, remained an important commercial centre. Some of India's most famous antique temples in the coastal zone refer to an imperial past. Apart from sacred buildings in the centre of little kingdoms, many temples in the highlands have instead been constructed relatively recently, a recent boom often linked to the rise of Hindu nationalism.

For administrative purposes, more than eight million people are classified as Scheduled Tribes (ST), that is, around 22 per cent of the total population of Odisha (http://censusindia. gov.in/Tables_Published/SCST/dh_st_orissa.pdf, accessed 4 November 2010). They are divided into more than 60 indigenous groups and are under pressure in several parts of the state due to mineral resources found in the hills, rapid industrialization and internal colonization.

Little kings and overlords in Odisha

Little kingdoms, segmented political structures and notions of the state

Throughout India, the 'little kingdoms' have been a regular feature. Cohn (2001a [1959], 2001b [1962]) coined the term while analysing the political system of eighteenth-century Benares. He distinguished several levels within the political system, ranging from the 'local level' as the lowest or most basic administrative stratum, consisting of local revenue collectors, indigenous chiefs and lineages, via the 'regional' and 'secondary' level up to the 'imperial' level (Cohn 2001b [1962]: 485–86). Within these strata one finds smaller and greater kings, as paradigmatically expressed in the distinction between 'Raja' (king) and 'Maharaja' (great king), claiming superiority or having to accept an inferior rank at least temporarily and using very different titles.

This notion of a political system and state was further extended by Stein (1975) when he worked on the medieval state in South India. He argued in favour of a segmentary state rather than a unitary one. It was characteristically multi-centred, with prime centres being mirrored by others. Power, or political sovereignty, was distributed in all centres – and therefore not monopolized – but ritual sovereignty was more concentrated in higher centres. An identical kind of executive authority implied that an overlord 'demanded submission to his claim of superiority, rather than obedience to his orders' (Stein 1975: 77). As Cohn (2001b [1962]: 489) stressed, little kings did have power but needed the superior kings' authority, derived from ritual sovereignty and proven by privileged access to divinities. Being ranked, this access could not automatically be translated into power.

The idea of a 'segmentary state' was further modified by Tambiah (1985), who referred to the concept of the *mandala*, which he understood as a 'galactic polity'

> standing for an arrangement of a center and its surrounding satellites and employed in multiple contexts to describe, for example: the structure of a pantheon of gods; the deployment spatially of a capital region and its provinces; the arrangement socially of a ruler, princes, nobles, and their respective retinues; and the devolution of graduated power on a scale of decreasing autonomies.
>
> (Tambiah 1985: 258)

Thus, Tambiah linked the cosmological topography with the spatial configuration and developed the idea of a political system as a '"center-oriented" space' (ibid.: 259), in which the centre stood for a totality. Yet, boundaries were not permanently fixed but varied according to shifting power scenarios.

Cohn also argued that the king's authority was expressed through the exchange of gifts, superior kings accepting tributes and transferring honours, such as titles, but also by service, that is, little kings serving overlords. This central relevance of gift exchanges was emphasized even more strongly by Dirks, who argued: 'As decentralized as the little kingdom appears, the king was the symbolic head of the system of redistribution, which even as it allotted rights to local power configurations underscored the pre-eminence of the king and the king's rights' (1979: 177). Land – or rather sharing of the king's right to land – played the major role in this subinfeudation. In this way, he questioned the distinction between the religious and political spheres, a crucial element in Stein's model of the segmentary state. In Geertzian style, Dirks rather understood royal gift exchange as constituting inseparable ritual *and* political relations, thus both engineering and performing incorporation into a realm.

Little kingdoms in Odisha

With special reference to Odisha, the above models were applied and developed further by historians and anthropologists alike (Kulke 2001 [1976], 1979; Berkemer 1993; Schnepel 2002; Skoda 2011a). Kulke (2001 [1976]), writing on the Mughal period, identified the four levels of Cohn's model as those of the Mughals (imperial), the Nawab of Bengal and later the Bhonsle Marathas (secondary), the Subahdars in the provincial capital of Cuttack (regional), and the Rajas and local chiefs of the Garhjat states in the hills. However, the Odishan political system appears to offer empirical evidence for more than four levels if one includes tribal chiefs below the kings of the Garhjat states (Schnepel 2002; Skoda 2012).

This multitude of levels is closely tied to the question of where 'little kings' should be located in such a ranked, yet dynamic political system. It is important here to distinguish between the analytical level and the empirical level. As Berkemer (1993: 319) pointed out, a 'little kingdom' should not be understood as a historical entity, but as a relational construct, with a 'little king' being subordinated to the overlord(s) and often simultaneously subjugating others. Irrespective of the levels, scholars do agree that the size of the territory is relatively irrelevant. More importantly, each 'little kingdom' is embedded in a wider network of relationships, in which sovereignty is primarily a question of political alliances (Berkemer 1993: 22ff.).

Ritual sovereignty, Lord Jagannath and the ideology of the Gajapati kingdom

The aspect of authority as related to ritual sovereignty and legitimacy has been taken up by Gell (1997) and Skoda (2012). While Cohn and Stein had suggested that the smaller kings partake in the overlord's ritual sovereignty, Gell's study of *dossehra* rituals in the Bastar kingdom (see Gregory, this volume) rather reveals the king's dependence upon the tribal Gond chiefs. Similarly, Skoda, in view of royal chronicles and ritual practices in Western Orissa, finds evidence that, as an additional element, an authority from below may substantially add to the sovereignty of an overlord. The Raja, in a rather precarious position in the early colonial and pre-colonial periods, also depended on the 'authority of the soil', that is, on the influential tribal Bhuiyan community who considered themselves to be 'masters of the land'.

Combining historical and anthropological perspectives, Schnepel (2002) considers the former kingdom of Jeypore as a distinctive subtype of 'little kingdom': the 'jungle kingdom'

– presumably inspired by the term 'jungle mahals' used for kingdoms further north (see Samaddar 1998). In contrast to Stein, Schnepel (2002: 44) speaks of a segmented structure rather than a segmentary one, thereby avoiding misleading perceptions caused by debates on 'segmentary systems' in anthropology. Like Dirks, Schnepel draws attention to the interrelatedness of politics and ritual as exemplified in *dossehra* rituals. He defines a state as a *'totality of politico-ritual relationships between a great king and the little kings subject to him'* (Schnepel 2002: 83). The presiding deity and king form a nexus – the 'ritual policy' – in the 'jungle kingdom' that resembles and is modelled on the relationship between the Gajapati kings and Lord Jagannath.

The sacred city of Puri, with the temple of Lord Jagannath ('Lord of the World'), is widely considered to be one of the *char dham*, the divine abodes covering the four cardinal points of India. From the thirteenth century onwards, a direct relationship between the cult of Jagannath and kingship in Orissa was established, with political power and religious practices mutually informing and enforcing each other (Kulke (2005 [1978]: 139ff.; also 1979). Under Anangabhima III (ca. 1211–39) the idea of Jagannath as the 'king of the Orissan Empire' (Odisa-rajya-raja) emerged, and henceforward the king ruled as his deputy (*rauta*) and son (*putra*) under Jagannath's overlordship (*samrajya*) (Kulke 2005 [1978]: 139). From the fifteenth century onwards, under Purusottam, a 'pontifical ideology' was established, the king being understood as 'servant-priest' or 'first servitor' (*adya sevaka*) of the god. It was also in this period that one of the most important rituals was introduced: the Raja's 'sweeping' of the Lord's path during the car festival (*ratha yatra*), marking the Raja as servitor of the Lord. In yet another transformation, the so-called '*pratima* ideology' of the nineteenth century, the king (Gajapati) was identified with the god as '*thakur-raja*' (*deva-raja*) and venerated under the honorific title of '*calanti Vishnu*' (walking Vishnu), that is, the king was considered to be an image (*pratima*) of the Lord.

In her anthropological study of the Devadasis, the female temple dancers seen as wives of the god-king and simultaneously as a symbol of kingship, Marglin (1989 [1985]) argued that the king occupies a rather paradoxical position: divine, irrespective of the historical transformations mentioned above, yet inferior to the highest category of Brahmins (*sasan Brahmin*, see Pfeffer 1976) and not fitting into the *varna* categories. Besides his ethnographic work on the ritual renewal of the wooden statues of the Jagannath temple, in which the king is also involved, Hardenberg (1999, 2000, forthcoming) looked more than Marglin specifically at the structure and meaning of the royal rituals in Puri. He illustrates the close entanglement between collective representations of kingship with religious cults in Orissa and the way the kingdom is perceived as a microcosm. Not being content with the mere functionalist argument in terms of providing legitimacy, Hardenberg observes how the royal rituals accommodate a temporary state of affairs, the microcosm, to an absolute order and to the highest cosmological values. The king continues to play a decisive role in this process of creating an ideal microcosm religiously, particularly during the car festival, despite the formal abolition of kingship in the political sphere. This separation of spheres is in turn linked to colonial rule, which reduced the king to the position of the highest temple servant.

Garhjat and Mughalbandi

The Mughal emperors, who conquered Odisha from 1576 onwards, divided the region into two major constituents: the Garhjat and the Mughalbandi. The former, literally 'fortress-born' states (Mubayi 2005: 19), formed clusters in the hilly hinterland (e.g. Sambalpur Garhjats) and around Cuttack (later referred to as the Cuttack States or Tributary Mahals), while the Mughalbandi, literally the 'crown land' (ibid.), in the coastal plains remained under the more direct control of the Mughals. This division continues to influence regional identities, for example, in relation to demands for a separate state of Koshal comprising the western or Odishan districts. Though obliged to pay tribute to the Mughal governor (Subahdar), the Garhjat states, controlled by little kings, were able to maintain some independence even after 1751, when the overlordship passed into the hands of the Marathas. In 1803 the British East India Company occupied Odisha – the strategically important coastal belt as well as the Sambalpur Garhjat tracts – which finally came under British paramountcy in 1818, though control was only tightened in subsequent decades.

The British encounter with the Garhjat chiefs varied. Some were deposed for reasons such as murder or rebellion. British annexations led to relatively discontinuous territories in Odisha. The map of directly ruled 'British India' and of the feudatory states, as the Garhjat states came to be known, resembled a rag rug. Yet, after the uprising in 1857–58 and the policy revision towards the native states, it was this geographical patchwork structure with its dispersed boundaries that was more or less frozen, new treaties (*sanads*) being issued to the 'ruling chiefs' specifying their position vis-à-vis the British, their powers and tribute. Disputes and uncertainties about the status of former kingdoms as states or estates (*zamindaris*) were increasingly resolved from the point of view of the British, who were eager to order society unambiguously.

'Prajas' in the 'hinterlands'

The 'tribal' encounter

The British initially encountered the 'ordinary' western highlanders of Odisha during the so-called Gumsur wars. Stationed in the central Kond Mountains, the Raja of Gumsur was accused of withholding tribute, thus prompting military action. After the Raja's death in 1836 his territory was put under direct British rule (Niggemeyer 1964: 7; Padel 1995). During the campaign the British officers came into contact with the Konds and their rituals. Their reports state that every spring human sacrifices were offered to the earth goddess, that is, young men and women, called *meriah* (Campbell 1986; Niggemeyer 1964: 7; Boal 1982: x). In their own accounts the British were successful in abolishing human sacrifice by having humans replaced with buffalos. Yet, critical historians like Bates (2006) argue that a principal function of the 'Meriah agency', the British administration established in the territories of the Gumsur Raja meant specifically to suppress human sacrifice, was to provide evidence to justify the displacement of indigenous rulers and their advisers, who were forced to give up the practice of human sacrifice. This enabled the British to control the area directly or to install rulers complying with their interests (Bates 2006: 29), while also legitimizing their rule in India. For Bates there is no convincing evidence of the *meriah* sacrifice, and thus he tends to regard the allegations as myths (Bates 2006: 43). However, anthropological field research suggests that these early accounts were not entirely based on colonial fantasies alone. Niggemeyer (1964: 204f.) records how the Kuttia Kondh beg forgiveness from the earth goddess for not supplying human victims. To this date they relate in their prayers how they had to follow the orders of two individually named Scottish officers. While in the 1980s Pfeffer (personal communication) witnessed several on-going buffalo sacrifices among the Dongria Kond, Hardenberg (2005) offers the first detailed description and analysis of this total social fact, which he understands as the fundamental expression of a holistic worldview. The value of Bates' contribution (2006: 44) lies in the way he illuminates how the *meriah* was strategically used by British and local rulers alike, the latter quickly trying to manipulate the British for their own ends, that is, by pointing to certain rulers and their alleged practice of human sacrifice, which was intended to trigger punitive action by the British.

Sahlins' model

Since the Kond and other highlanders are frequently distinguished by the adjective 'tribal', the concept must be mentioned here without rehearsing its contentious history, often with political overtones and repercussions (see Weisgrau, this volume). However, we would like to stress some of Sahlins' (1968) insights, which are relevant in this context, particularly his idea of a tribal system as a 'segmentary system', that is, 'the tribe represents itself as a pyramid of social groups … [t]he smallest units, such as households, are segments of more inclusive units, such as lineages, the lineages in turn segments of larger groups, and so on' (ibid.: 15), while from within a tribe the structure would be perceived as a range of 'concentric circles of kith and kin', with the household occupying the central position. On the periphery one encounters an 'ambiguous zone of transition' (ibid.: 16), in which segments develop affinities and share traits with neighbouring communities.

Sahlins stressed the idea of a tribe as a segmentary system 'not simply because it is built of compounded segments, but also because it is *only* so built: its coherence is not maintained from above by public political institutions (as by a sovereign authority)' (ibid.). Therefore, the whole is often the weakest unit in terms of social cohesion or 'sociability' (ibid.: 16). At the same time, he argues that '*segmentary tribes* proper' may develop into chiefdoms, that is, 'towards integration of the segmentary system at higher levels' as a hierarchical society 'anticipating statehood in its complexities' (ibid.: 20, emphasis in original). In line with such transitions, petty chieftains with hardly any influence – '[o]ne word from him and everyone does as he pleases' (ibid.: 21) – as one pole of the tribal design could be distinguished from chiefs in 'a *system* of chieftainships, a hierarchy of major and minor authorities holding forth over major and minor subdivisions of the tribe: a chain of command linking paramount to middle-range and local-level leaders, and binding the hinterland to the strategic heights' (ibid.: 26, emphasis in original). Thus, a chiefdom is relatively more united and linked by Sahlins to processes of redistribution (in contrast to reciprocity), which is 'chieftainship said in economics' (ibid.: 95).

Tribes in Middle India

The British colonial power gave an altogether different meaning to the term 'tribe', that is, one belonging to the administrative realm and not to be confused with the anthropological notion of 'tribe' or 'tribal society' (Pfeffer 2002, 2004a). The colonial state classified communities like the Kond as 'Scheduled Tribes' (ST), a distinction adopted by the Indian constitution of 1950 to provide special forms of protective discrimination. Pfeffer was probably the first to end the confusion between an analytical category of anthropological theory and an administrative category designed to correct social disabilities. Stressing, like Bailey, the close interaction between communities in the 'hinterland' that had been going on for centuries, Pfeffer preferred to speak of a 'tribal society' consisting in the middle Indian context not only of 'Scheduled Tribes', but also of 'Other Backward Classes' (OBC) and 'Scheduled Castes' (SC) (Pfeffer 2007: 249) otherwise divided by state classifications.

Yet, while Pfeffer by and large agreed with Sahlins' outline of a 'tribe' or 'tribal society', he developed a regional 'middle Indian type' (Pfeffer 1997: 13–14, also 2009) primarily segmented by the principle of seniority. The principle of seniority indicates status differences and hierarchy or unequal rank (senior/junior) of interrelated parts with reference to the common whole, yet seniority does not refer to power differences but to social classification. Found on every level of society (Pfeffer 1982, 1997, 2000), it is shared by most tribal communities in Odisha and beyond. In the 'Chotanagpur complex' of tribes one finds the Delkhi and Dudh Kharia, the Ho and the Munda as well as the Kisan and the Oraon linked in this way. Following the same pattern the 'senior' Bhuiyan live with the 'junior' Juang (McDougal 1963) in the Keonjhar complex, while in the Mayurbhanj complex the Bhumiji are senior to the Santhal (Pfeffer 2003: 71f.).

The binary principle is applied in a general fashion and without exception to all aspects of social life, for example, village ties or political relations with the kings or royal service, first settlement, a status as clients and patrons (Berger 2002, 2007; Otten 2006, 2008) and the kinship system. With regard to the latter, seniority implies the distinction between elder and younger siblings and is often interwoven with the principle of equating alternate generations (McDougal 1963; Parkin 1992; Pfeffer 2004b; Skoda 2005; Otten 2006; Berger 2007). Far from being limited to a tribal society in the 'hinterland', the pervasiveness of this value-idea is mirrored in the genealogies of the royal families of Odisha (Rajaguru 1968/72, vol. 1: 198; Berkemer 1993).

At the same time, in his analysis of the Desia society of Koraput, Berger (2002: 69f.) found a threefold, but relational distinction, which resembled the given categories of 'Other Backward Class', 'Scheduled Tribe' and 'Scheduled Caste', yet was entangled with the principle of seniority. The 'Other Backward Classes' enjoy highest rank and are senior. In the middle is the 'Scheduled Tribe' category, amongst which the Bondo are often regarded as most senior, followed by the Gadaba. The Scheduled Caste category with the Dom is seen as being of lower rank, and in it the Gorua are considered the most junior. However, on the village level, the people of the Scheduled Tribe category as landowners and 'communicators with [the] divine' (see below) are accorded the most senior position, calling themselves 'earth people' (*matia*) in contrast to those who arrived subsequently (Berger 2002: 76f.).

Tribal society in highland Odisha is further characterized by a complementary relationship between patrons and clients, the former usually classified as Scheduled Tribes, or landowners (*roit*) like the Rona, who received land for their services for the royal court, while the latter are considered to be Scheduled Castes by the state administration. The patrons own the land, are cultivators and conduct the important village rituals, while the clients are landless and provide services to the patrons. Pfeffer (1997: 13) opposes the patrons as 'communicators with [the] divine' and the clients as 'communicators with human beings'.

Inter-village organization and state formation

In the tribal society of highland Odisha the village represents the most important social unit. Multi-clan villages might be found occasionally, but more commonly the villages belong to a single territorial clan (Bailey 1960), which is subdivided further into local descent groups (i.e. local lines) whose members assemble on occasions to take public decisions and for innumerable ritual obligations that are due to the divine authorities of the village as a sacred unit. Though individual male elders carry honorific titles indicating the sacred and secular posts of priest and headman respectively, they would often not (be able to) assume decision-making powers.

Villages are often incorporated into larger units, called 'village federations' by Parkin (1992: 74f., 90f.), for example, of twelve villages, a unit known as *mutha* among Konds. The head of a *mutha* was often a person from a society of the plains who migrated to the highlands. Bailey describes (1960: 178) how the British installed administrative divisions in the middle of the nineteenth century. Drawing upon clan territories, the British appointed mutha headmen. For the British these headmen, often Paik or retainers of the Rajas, were an essential part of the political structure in otherwise hardly accessible tribal areas and were allies in suppressing the *meriah,* even though they considered it vital for their welfare. For the Oriya the posts promised some riches, yet they found themselves in an uncomfortable position between the Kond and the British (Bailey 1957: 182ff.).

Similar inter-village organizations are known, such as *bar, pirh, desh* or *pargana* among Bhuiyan or Ho (Mahapatra 1987) or as *patti* or *parha* among Munda and Oraon. They continue to play an important role in a modified way, even in the twenty-first century (Roy 1970 [1912]: 65; Shah 2007). The Munda also installed their own chiefs through this system, that is, the most influential among the headmen of the villages became the *patti* or chief, also called *Manki* or *Parha-Raja* (Shah 2007: 132), while the remaining headmen swore allegiance to them. They presented him with gifts periodically, which with the passage of time became rightful dues, and the position of Manki became gradually hereditary. However, the Manki was a chief among equals, a leader not a ruler. In disputes between villages the Manki with the *patti* or *parha panch* was called upon to adjudicate (Roy 1970 [1912]: 65f.). Roy (ibid: 74) also retells the myth about how the Mankis elected their first king, who originated not from the Munda community but was elected because of his 'superior intelligence' (ibid.: 76), his mother being a Brahmin, his father a snake. This myth of a chosen stranger king mirrors other myths of royal family chronicles (*vamshavali, bansaboli*), which in turn have often been written by royal priests. Most rulers, however, also highlighted their Rajput credentials in their chronicles. In contrast, some British authors such as Dalton (1872) argued that the Rajas were tribal in origin. In a nutshell, either tribal chiefs are believed to have started making claim to Rajput or Kshatriya descent, or it is argued that Aryans or Rajputs settled in or conquered tribal areas.

In contrast to such relatively static descriptions, subsequently more nuanced and dynamic perspective was introduced. Kulke (2001 [1976]: 82ff.), inspired by Srinivas' theory of Sanskritization, highlighted processes of Kshatriyaization (Rajputization) in the 'hinterland' states occurring from above as well as from below. By a process from above Kulke means a sharing of the authority and legitimacy of the Gajapati rulers of Khurda and Puri in the form of rights and privileges granted to the feudatory chiefs while visiting the temple of Lord Jagannath. The latter from below refers to cases of the appropriation of royal symbols and rituals, including the emergence of new institutions such as temples and land donations to Brahmins (*sasan*). These initiatives, for example, to construct temples to worship Lord Jagannath, were often connected with polyvalent claims, such as to fulfil a *rajadharma* expected of a legitimate Hindu Raja, but they were also attempts to symbolize autonomy or even independence vis-à-vis an overlord. Family chronicles composed by royal priests and sometimes written 'on demand' of the colonizers in order to gather knowledge might be seen in this light too and could be considered status symbols.

Hinduization, 'Hindu' Rajas and tutelary deities

The repertoire of insignias of power also included elements from tribal communities that commanded an authority from below, as in the case of the Bhuiya community. Moreover, Rajas of 'little kingdoms' also promoted and accommodated cults of a number of tribal goddesses in Odisha, processes often labelled Hinduization (for Odisha recently, see Mallebrein 2004, 2006). Eschmann (1978, 1994) suggests placing 'tribal' (aniconic signs, e.g. wooden posts) and 'Hindu' (anthropomorphic icons) at opposite ends of a continuum in a similar way in which Bailey (1961) had contrasted 'tribe' and 'caste'. While Eschmann rejects the term Sanskritization because of the inherent text/language-bias, she understands Hinduization primarily as two interlinked developments: either a) tribal gods accepted into the Hindu fold or b) tribal cults may take over, at times temporarily, elements from Hinduism (termed 'tribalisation' by Schnepel 2002). Though she allows for the possibility of a retrogressive development from icon to sign, by and large she sees a decisive development towards Hinduization, with specific Sakta, Vaisnava and Saiva typologies. Her understanding of an emergent regional tradition functioning as a mediating zone between 'Little Tradition' and 'Great Tradition' might have been influenced by McKim Marriott's work on universalization and parochialization (possibly followed by re-universalizations) (Stewart 2002: 267).

Treating these concepts as ideal types, Schnepel is not adverse to the idea of identifying 'possible developmental stages in the process of Hinduization' (2002: 8). In contrast to Eschmann, he highlights the role of 'Hindu little kings who were originally outsiders' (ibid.: 241) and who competed over privileged access to tribal deities in order to legitimize their rule and to ensure stability, as well as the loyalty of their tribal subjects. Such royal patronage included the performance and financing of rituals such as *dossehra* (often identified with Durga Puja) as an important state ritual in most Odishan kingdoms (Hardenberg 2000; Schnepel 2002) or the construction of temples turning tribal goddesses into the tutelary deities (*ishta devis*) of little kings, the court culture being a site of mediation. While Rousseleau (2008, 2009) agrees with Schnepel that kingdoms were major sites of interaction between Rajas and Prajas, he differs from him by highlighting the long-standing mutual exchange between tribal communities and the 'Hindu world'. According to him, the aspect of the Hinduization of a tribal culture or religion has been overemphasized, and institutions or cults labelled somewhat uncritically as 'tribal' may have come under Hindu influence much earlier.

In a critique of the Hinduization theories mentioned above, Hardenberg (2010) warns us that forms, practices or rituals that superficially resemble each other may be tied to very different meanings or value-ideas. While the former may circulate more freely, they still need to be incorporated into one's own community, becoming indigenized and acquiring new meanings in the process. Thus, Hardenberg reminds us that communities may have different and distinct ideologies and that Hinduization as an open-ended, multidimensional process, or rather as a number of related and simultaneously operating processes, involves ideas, concepts and knowledge as much as material objects, and that these may not be transferred together.

While gradual processes of Hinduization and indigenization can be observed in many tribal communities radical changes also occur. A recent example is provided by Vitebsky whose earlier ethnography focused on the Sora's dialogues with their dead via female shamans (Vitebsky 1993). The young generation have completely abandoned this key-aspect of their traditional culture either because they have become evangelical Christians or fundamentalist Hindus (Vitebsky 2008). Such conversions among Sora, but also among Rona under the influence of Mahima Dharma (Guzy 2002), a religious movement emerging from a Hindu fold and actively proselytising in the 'hinterland', exemplify religious fissures that may acquire political shades and may interfere or overlap with other forms of segmentation.

From 'little kingdoms' to 'little political systems'

Peasants and migration

While relations between the Rajas and the major tribal communities in their realms were of the utmost importance in the pre-colonial and even colonial periods (Kulke 2001 [1976];

Schnepel 2002; Nanda 2010; Mallebrein forthcoming), another influential group of subjects or Prajas and their links to the rulers received far less attention, namely peasants, who, for example, in the nineteenth century migrated to several Odishan feudatory states or estates. They were actively encouraged to do so by the colonial administration as well as the Rajas. Military roads, for example, from Calcutta to Sambalpur, accelerated this process by making the area more accessible. Ahuja (2009) has recently highlighted the crucial importance of 'infrastructure' and 'public work' in the colonial project that transformed Odisha.

Peasant communities such as the Kurmi or Kulta, but also communities such as the Mali (gardeners), Gouda (herdsmen), Sundi (distillers) or Rona (Otten 2007, 2008), often classified as Other Backward Classes, made use of these new opportunities and settled in high concentrations, particularly in western Odisha. As Skoda (2005) shows for the Aghria community and Otten mentioned for the Rona (Otten 2006: 11f.), the newly arriving peasants did not just occupy land, but took up the headmanship of villages and became revenue collectors for the petty Rajas as 'village kings', often structurally replicating the functions of kings on the village level. They were instrumental in transforming not only the landscape (notably by clearing the forests and promoting intensive wet-rice cultivation using ploughs), but also society, that is, by supporting the state through revenue generation. The latter is considered typical for peasantry in the model of Wolf, that is, in contrast to tribes, peasants are expected and obliged to transfer their surpluses to a dominant group of rulers, which utilizes it for its own standard of living and distributes the remainder to groups in society that do not cultivate (Wolf 1966: 3f.).

Such transformations were augmented by 'permanent settlements' initiated by the colonial administration to survey and tax the land and by a general bureaucratization of the states, that is, the establishment of separate departments for forest, revenue, police and the like. While previously local Brahmins or relatives of the Rajas were often engaged in the much less specialized administration, subsequently these departments were very often staffed prominently with specialists from outside, that is, from Bengal, the coastal belt of Odisha or even with British officers, the latter acting particularly as Diwans or heads of administration. Thus, another group of newcomers and sometimes temporary migrants arrived in the feudatory states in the late nineteenth and early twentieth centuries, being instrumental in establishing the structures of modern princely states.

This migration process, resulting in a constant influx of settlers, also included communities such as the Munda, Kharia and Oraon coming from Chota Nagpur (Jharkhand), nowadays considered Adivasi or Scheduled Tribes. It increased considerably the density of the population in the feudatory states of Western Odisha, which almost doubled between 1881 and 1931 (Schwerin 1977: 48). Schwerin further argues that the indigenous population did not decrease in absolute, but only in relative numbers, while Rothermund (1978: 4) did not find evidence of a large-scale transfer of peasants from overpopulated areas to cultivable wasteland, but rather saw a spillover from neighbouring areas. Vis-à-vis the Rajas the role of these migrants often resembled that of peasant communities such as the Aghria, while in many cases they were also employed by other peasants as agricultural labourers, indicating another (ongoing) transformation. This means that the latter are paid wages just like an industrial worker in a market-oriented economy, or in Wolf's (1966: 12) typology they are agricultural workers or farmers rather than peasants. As wage labourers, Adivasis are also employed in new industrial sites, which, however, as Strümpell (2008) has shown, are often dominated by a 'public sector "labour aristocracy"' (2008: 355) of still more recent migrants. Remaining by and large on the margins of industrial projects, Adivasi–state relations in Odisha are increasingly discussed in a discourse of citizenship, particularly 'dual citizenship', which would favour Adivasis settled in the province vis-à-vis outsiders.

'Little kingdoms' and 'princely states'

As Peabody (2006) has stressed in relation to the Rajasthani kingdom of Kota:

> colonial power did not impose itself monolithically from outside, but arose much more
> dialogically from within the conditions that were manifest locally, with local agents
> often able to redirect the potentialities of colonial power to serve agendas at a tangent
> from, if not diametrically opposite to, the agendas of colonial power.
>
> (Peabody 2006: 3)

Such a 'dialogical process' not only took migrants into account, but more importantly existing power configurations. Ahuja observed that the British opted for a policy of very limited interference and in 'administrative practice, the British government often rather preferred to leave the country "closed"'. Furthermore, 'despite all rhetoric, the early colonizers' interest in Odisha consisted not so much in "opening it up" towards "civilisation", the "rule of law" and "commerce", but in getting past it and securing control over this strategic region as cheaply as possible' (2007: 315). Thus, as Berkemer (1993: 321) argued, internally intact to a large extent in the nineteenth and even early twentieth centuries in many cases, political or ritual relations were largely preserved and expressed, while the British maintained their paramountcy and concentrated on upholding the Pax Britannica.

Yet, how fragile and tenuous this Pax Britannica used to be is indicated by the number of uprisings that occurred in the nineteenth and twentieth centuries (see for example Mojumdar 1998). For example, the so-called 'Gond disturbances' in the former princely state of Bonai at the end of the nineteenth century (Skoda 2011a) were linked to land settlements made there after 1880. However, to read these 'disturbances' simply as a straightforward reaction by Gond to a specific settlement and increased rents would miss the complex interaction between Gond 'tribal' chiefs, the Bonai Raja and the British. These events were embedded into a larger 'civilising mission' on the part of the colonial power, which – apart from the 'taming of the savages' – tried to implement newly codified property rights, as well as what it perceived to be the rule of law and good government (Mann 2004: 8). Yet, the supposed looting by the Gond can also be seen as a continuation of a pre-colonial regime revolving around conflicts, withdrawal and compromise, rather than 'honouring' the contractual relations or 'permanent' settlements that British administrators tried to introduce. The Gond chiefs continued to operate within a framework of a 'little kingdom' rather than a 'princely state', preferring withdrawal and ignorance of warrants to appearances in courts. Yet, disputes that were relatively common in the pre-colonial era and at times violent were now framed as 'disturbances' that threatened the more highly valued public tranquillity and smooth functioning of the courts to which the British persistently referred in order to solve conflicts. Leaving aside the problem of revenue collection, even greater resistance arose from the demand of a cess to set up and maintain a police force ('police cess') linked to the idea of 'pacification'. The establishment of such a centralized police force threatened the Gond' identity as 'Paiks' or 'peasant-warriors' who had guaranteed the pre-colonial and early colonial state its security. The abolition of the police cess soon after the 'disturbances', as well as the continuation of the newly established but contested police stations, is apparently a result of the conflict and hints at a certain compromise between the Gond chiefs, the Raja and the British, as well as the fact that, 'the colonial regime changed things far less than its discursive self-representations would lead one to believe' (Dirks 1992: 176).

Re-evaluating the concepts of 'little kingdom' and 'princely state', Berkemer and Frenz (2005) argue that a comparison is necessarily oblique, given the very different conceptual background: the 'princely state' as an administrative and legal category of historically existing states on the one hand, and the 'little kingdom' as a purely analytical category emerging two centuries later on the other, that is, after the abolition of the states, and referring only loosely to 'traditional' or 'early modern' kingdoms. However, instead of a linear transition from little kingdom to princely state, they propose rather the co-existence of divergent notions of the state in the colonial era, in which the kings played a dual role: as 'Raja', for example, in rituals whose performance was informed by notions of a 'little kingdom', and as 'Prince' under colonial conditions, depending on the context.[2]

Post-colonial, post-abolition kingship

With independence and the subsequent merger of the feudatory states with the province of Odisha in 1948–49, a century-old history of kingship was formally abolished, and despite other visions, present-day 'modern' Odisha came into being. However, as Galey (1990) found elsewhere in India, the idea of kingship is very much alive, and the memory of the kingdoms and former princely states continues to inform the imagination of former subjects, as well as younger generations, and may be used in future to articulate separate identities and political goals such as the state of Koshal.

While Mubayi (2005) shows that ritual kingship had already undergone processes of disintegration after the colonial conquest, Banerjee-Dube (2001) emphasizes that 'mutations' for Raja and temple in Puri were not limited to the colonial period. Being briefly dethroned, the Gajapati kings were afterwards appointed by the colonial regime to a new position of 'superintendent' of the Jagannath temple and were henceforth also referred to as 'Rajas of Puri'. Despite their diminished sphere of influence (territorially as well as financially), they were able to use their new post to influence existing power configurations by manipulating ritual relationships to their advantage and inventing novel forms of ritualization (see also Kulke (2001 [1976]: 82ff.). Banerjee-Dube argues that the end of the Gajapati's superintendency in 1955 and the appointment of a committee with the Raja as chairman, though with an administrator as secretary in charge of the everyday affairs of the temple, indicate that a division between state power and royal authority that was established under colonial rule continues in post-colonial India. Moreover, the authority of the colonial state was used by courts in independent India to validate the power of the state over temple affairs. The state continues its surveillance of the temple's affairs after independence, yet it hardly depends on the temple anymore, as the Gajapatis did. With the Supreme Court decision in 1960, the 'King of Puri', like every other king, lost all his political authority over the land and its subjects. Yet in spite of this progressive 'fragmentation of monarchical cosmology' (Price 1996: 106), he still takes part in activities in which the idea of kingship is represented. The rituals are now carried out on a smaller scale, due to economic constraints and the declining interest of the king's former 'subjects', his 'Prajas', but at the beginning of the third millennium they still mirror the relationships which constituted Hindu kingdoms in the last millennium (Hardenberg 2000).

At the same time, former rulers have often pursued political careers. While some former princes joined the Congress, in Odisha a greater number supported the Ganatantra Parishad (later merged with the Swatantra Party) founded with the help of former rulers, for example, of Kalahandi. Yet, these political transformations remained relatively marginal in anthropological discourses, in which the 'political', especially with reference to the post-colonial state, was often treated as a somehow familiar and 'transparent' category (Spencer 1997). An early exception is the work of Bailey (1959, 1963), who accompanied the Maharaja of Kalahandi during his election campaign and examined more generally the relationship between the new parliamentary democracy and older forms of social and political organization. Bailey's early insights were also supplemented from a political science angle in the 1970s through the studies of Richter (1971, 1978), who carefully analysed election results and found that more than half of the royal families of Odisha were politically active in the assembly as well as the Lok Sabha. In fact, Richter's statistics show that the number of democratic representatives with a royal background increased after independence. More recent analyses are now required, but it is certainly not just a coincidence that the first royal to become a chief minister in post-independence India in 1967 came from Odisha.

Looking at voting behaviour in a village in the former princely state of Dhenkanal, Mitra (1979) stresses that 'benefit-maximisation' and 'obligation' decisively influenced political choice, that is, material or immaterial spoils on the one hand, and social relationships on the other. One might add that loyalties to a Raja – including the Raja of Dhenkanal, who had a distinguished political career – also constitute an important form of capital, which Rajas try to mobilize, as the introduction illustrated. Mitra (2001) later reanalysed his data, emphasizing not only the interpenetration of politics and rituals, but also the interweaving of caste, faction, ritual and election as exemplified in a separate Durga Puja for the Scheduled Castes coinciding with political upward mobility. The entanglement between electoral politics and local or regional struggles led, according to Mitra, to the creation of innumerable 'little political systems' within the political entity of India, overlapping with or transforming earlier domains such as 'little kingdoms'.

The recent work of Tanabe (2007) points in a similar direction as Mitra as far as the role of subalterns (Scheduled Tribes, Scheduled Castes, women etc.) is concerned. He argued that the introduction of the Panchayati Raj system in the early 1990s and increased participation in the democratic process mark a 'post-post-colonial' transformation transcending the post-colonial predicament of separating a socio-ritual 'inner tradition' from a politico-economic 'outer modernity':

> Subalterns have been given the opportunity to exert their capacity as agents, under the institutional change, to challenge the imposed hegemony and to create a new framework of discourse and practice from hybrid resources—the sacrificial ethics of caste and the institution and value of egalitarian representation.
>
> (Tanabe 2007: 558)

Approaching the democratic process and the ways in which it is culturally inflected from an opposite angle, Skoda (2008, 2011b) studied royal campaigners and their rhetoric. With reference to Weber and Morris-Jones, he highlighted 'royal' attempts to occupy positions above politics while speaking a 'traditional' language, yet at the same time emphasizing a living for politics or saintly language and demonizing opponents accused of living off politics. At the same time, one has to acknowledge that detailed empirical studies on perceptions as well as the agency of Adivasi vis-à-vis the democratic system and the state in Odisha are by and large missing. Studies such as Shah's (2007) on the Munda in neighbouring Jharkhand offer clues that might be echoed in Odisha as well. Here, paradoxically, Munda participate in elections to 'keep the state away' because it is considered alien and is contrasted with a sacral, but vulnerable polity headed by a Raja.

Conclusion

Reconsidering power and influence in India, Price and Ruud (2010) have argued recently that:

> Long periods of relatively slow state-formation in early South Asian history produced social and political communities with high degrees of self-rule and regulation. [...] Castes, villages, chieftaincies and little kingdoms produced and reproduced ideologies which aimed to legitimize personal rule and authority in small-scale polities.
>
> (Price and Ruud 2010: xxii)

The present Union State of Odisha and its history offer ample evidence for such segmented political and social structures, or 'little political systems' in Mitra's terms, that have historically evolved and continue to inform the worldviews of rulers and ruled. Overlords and 'imperial kingdoms' such as the Ganga kingdom centred in coastal Odisha and tied to the temple of Lord Jagannath have influenced, but perhaps more importantly, co-existed with smaller kingdoms in a dynamic and multi-level political system, in which Rajas were either little kings vis-à-vis their overlords or (over)lords themselves vis-à-vis their subjects. A segmented political structure overlapped with, and was perhaps particularly apt to co-exist with, an equally segmented tribal society, which has, as Bailey showed, interacted with state structures without being fully integrated into them.

Relationships with a king, though they might be contested, imply power and influence. Both are nurtured, even if nowadays through various recourses to a 'glorious' past. Though no longer existing in a legal sense, kingship continues to inform the imagination of Praja and identity politics in the state like, for example, the Koshal movement for a separate province, which refers to and tries to revive the legacy of the Garhjat states. Yet, the segmentation is manifold and goes beyond the realms of kingship, or rather coincides with it. Divisions and fissures between senior and junior segments or between patrons or first settlers and their clients decisively structure and rank tribal society. Ideas and values such as the principle of seniority permeate kingship structures and ritual and redistributive relationships, yet they are further complicated by societal transformations, for example, the migrations of peasants and Brahmins, colonial interventions and the extension of state structures and bureaucracies or, more recently, the arrival of industrialists, migrant labourers or senior party leaders.

Notes

1   Odisha was spelled 'Orissa' before 2011. The literature cited in the text refers to the version 'Orissa', while the chapter itself employs the new form.
2   Moreover, with reference to a south Indian *zamindari*, Price has analysed the 'powerful processes' that led to 'the continuing evolution of royal symbols and values under colonial rule' (1996: 6, 77). In this regard she disagrees with statements by Dirks (1987) that political structures were in 'deep freeze' under colonial rule and that pre-colonial kingdoms rather turned into theatre states. Instead, Rajas, chiefs and *zamindars* were able to influence the social and political order, for example, through royal largesse. As a 'strategy for status', the importance of largesse, i.e. the opportunity to distribute wealth, increased during colonial rule after the establishment of the Pax Britannica.

References

Ahuja, R. (2007) 'Captain Kittoe's Road: Early Colonialism and the Politics of Road Construction in Nineteenth-century Peripheral Orissa', in G. Pfeffer (ed.), *Periphery and Centre in Orissa: Studies in Orissan History, Religion and Anthropology*. New Delhi: Manohar.

*——(2009) *Pathways of Empire: Circulation, 'Public Works' and Social Space in Colonial Orissa, c. 1780–1914*. Delhi: Orient BlackSwan.

Bailey, F. G. (1957) *Caste and the Economic Frontier*. Manchester: Manchester University Press.

——(1959) 'The Ganatantra Parishad', *Economic Weekly*, 24: 1469–76.

*——(1960) *Tribe, Caste and Nation: A Study of Political Activity and Political Change in Highland Orissa*. Bombay: Oxford University Press.

——(1961) '"Tribe" and "Caste" in India', *Contributions to Indian Sociology*, 5: 6–19.

——(1963) *Politics and Social Change: Orissa in 1959*. Berkeley: University of California Press.

Banerjee-Dube, I. (2001) *Divine Affairs: Religion, Pilgrimage, and the State in Colonial and Postcolonial India*. Shimla: Indian Institute of Advanced Studies.

Bates, C. (2006) 'Human Sacrifice in Colonial Middle India: Myths, Agency and Representation', in C. Bates (ed.), *Beyond Representation: Colonial and Postcolonial Constructions of Indian Identity*. New Delhi: Oxford University Press.

Berger, P. (2002) 'The Gadaba and the "non-ST" Desia of Koraput', in G. Pfeffer and D. K. Behera (eds), *Contemporary Society: Tribal Studies, Vol. 5*. New Delhi: Concept Publishing Company.

——(2007) *Füttern, Speisen und Verschlingen: Ritual und Gesellschaft im Hochland von Orissa, Indien*. Berlin: Lit Verlag.

Berkemer, G. (1993) *Little Kingdoms in Kalinga: Ideologie, Legitimation und Politik Regionaler Eliten*. Stuttgart: Franz Steiner.

Berkemer, G. and Frenz, M. (2005) 'Little Kingdoms or Princely States? Trajectories Towards a (Theoretical) Conception', *The Indian Historical Review*, 32: 104–21.

Boal, B. M. (1982) *The Konds: Human Sacrifice and Religious Change*. Warminster: Aris & Phillips.

Campbell, J. (1986) *Human Sacrifices in India*. Delhi: Mittal Publications.

Cohn, B. S. (2001 [1959]) 'Some Notes on Law and Change in North India', in B. S. Cohn, *An Anthropologist Among the Historians and Other Essays*. Delhi: Oxford.

——(2001 [1962]) 'Political Systems in Eighteenth-Century India: The Banares Region', in B. S. Cohn, *An Anthropologist Among the Historians and Other Essays*. Delhi: Oxford.

Dalton, E. T. (1872) *Descriptive Ethnology on Bengal*. Calcutta: Govt. Printing Press.

Dirks, N. B. (1979) 'The Structure and Meaning of Political Relations in a South Indian Little Kingdom', *Contributions to Indian Sociology* (NS), 13 (2): 169–206.

——(1987) *The Hollow Crown: Ethnohistory of an Indian Kingdom*. Cambridge: Cambridge University Press.

——(1992) 'From Little King to Landlord: Colonial Discourse and Colonial Rule', in N. B. Dirks (ed.), *Colonialism and Culture*. Ann Arbor: The University of Michigan Press.

Eschmann, A. (1978) 'Hinduization of Tribal Deities in Orissa: The Sakta and Saiva Typology', in A. Eschmann, H. Kulke and G. C. Tripathi (eds), *The Cult of Jagannath and the Regional Tradition of Orissa*. New Delhi: Manohar.

——(1994 [1975]) 'Sign and Icon: Symbolism in the Indian Folk Religion', in H. Kulke and G. C. Tripathi (eds), *Religion and Society in Eastern India*. Delhi: Manohar.

Galey, J.-C. (1990) 'Reconsidering Kingship in India: An Ethnological Perspective', in J.-C. Galey, *Kingship and the Kings*. Chur: Harwood Academic Publishers.

Gell, A. (1997) 'Exalting the King and Obstructing the State: A Political Interpretation of Royal Ritual in Bastar District, Central India', *Journal of the Royal Anthropological Institute*, 3: 433–50.

Guzy, L. (2002) *Baba-s and Alekh-s: Askese und Ekstase einer Religion im Werden*. Berlin: Weissensee Verlag.

Hardenberg, R. (1999) *Die Wiedergeburt der Götter: Ritual and Gesellschaft in Orissa*. Hamburg: Kovac Verlag.

——(2000) *Die Ideologie eines Hindu-Königtums: Struktur und Bedeutung der Rituale des Königs von Puri' Orissa / Indien*. Berlin: Arabisches Buch.

——(2005) 'Children of the Earth Goddess: Society, Marriage, and Sacrifice in the Highlands of Orissa (India)', unpublished habilitation thesis, Westfälische Wilhelms-Universität Münster.

——(2010) 'A Reconsideration of Hinduization and the Caste-Tribe Continuum Model', in P. Berger, R. Hardenberg, E. Kattner and M. Prager (eds), *The Anthropology of Values: Essays in Honour of Georg Pfeffer*. Delhi: Longman Pearson.

*——(forthcoming) *The Renewal of Jagannatha's Body: Ritual and Society in Coastal Orissa*. New Delhi: Manak Publications.

Kulke, H. (1979) *Jagannātha-Kult und Gajapati-Königtum: Ein Beitrag zur Geschichte religiöser Legitimation hinduistischer Herrscher*. Wiesbaden: Franz Steiner.

——(2005 [1978]) 'Early Royal Patronage of the Jagannātha Cult', in A. Eschmann, H. Kulke and G. C. Tripathi (eds), *The Cult of Jagannath and the Regional Tradition of Orissa*. Delhi: Manohar.

*——(2001 [1976]) 'Kshatriyaization and Social Change: A Study in the Orissan Setting', in H. Kulke, *Kings and Cults: State Formation and Legitimation in India and South East Asia*. Delhi: Manohar.

McDougal, C. W. (1963) *The Social Structure of the Hill Juang*, unpublished thesis, University of New Mexiko.

Mahapatra, L. K. (1987) 'Mayurbhanj, Keonjhar, and Bonai Ex-Princely States of Orissa', in S. Sinha, *Tribal Polities and Pre-Colonial State Systems in Eastern and Northeastern India*. Calcutta: K. P. Bagchi.

Mallebrein, C. (2004) 'Creating a Kshetra: Goddess Tarini from Ghatagaon and her Development from a Forest Goddess to a Pan-Orissan Deity', *Journal of Social Sciences*, 8 (2) (special issue: Facets of Orissan Studies, eds. L. Guzy and C. Mallebrein): 155–65.

——(2006) 'When the Buffalo Becomes a Pumpkin: The Animal Sacrifice Contested', in G. Pfeffer (ed.), *Periphery and Centre: Studies in Orissan History, Religion and Anthropology*. New Delhi: Manohar, pp. 443–72.

——(forthcoming) 'Sitting on the Tribal Chief's Lap: Coronation Rituals in Ex-Princely States of Orissa', in H. Kulke and G. Berkemer (eds), *Centres Out There? Facets of Subregional Identities*. New Delhi: Manohar.

Mann, M. (2004) '"Torchbearers upon the Path of Progress": Britain's Ideology of a "Moral and Material Progress" in India. An Introductory Essay', in H. Fischer-Tiné and M. Mann (eds), *Colonialism as Civilizing Mission: Cultural Ideology in British India*. London: Anthem Press.

*Marglin, F. A. (1989 [1985]) *Wives of the God-King: The Rituals of the Devadasis of Puri*. Delhi: Oxford University Press.

Mitra, S. K. (1979) 'Ballot box and local power: electoral politics in an Indian village', *Journal of Commonwealth and Comparative Politics*, 17: 283–99.

——(2001) 'Kashipur Revisited: Social Ritual, Electoral Politics and the State in India', in H. Kulke, and B. Schnepel (eds), *Jagannath Revisited*. New Delhi: Manohar.

Mojumdar, K. (1998) *Changing Tribal Life in British Orissa*. New Delhi: Kaveri Books.

Mubayi, Y. (2005) *Altar of Power: The Temple and the State in the Land of Jagannatha*. New Delhi: Manohar.

Nanda, C. P. (2010) 'Rethinking "Politico-Ritual States"': Sitting on the Lap of a Bhuiyan: Coronation Ceremonies in Keonjhar', in M. Kitts, B. Schneidmüller, G. Schwedler, E. Tounta and U. Skoda (eds), *State, Power and Violence*. Wiesbaden: Harrassowitz Verlag.

Niggemeyer, H. (1964) *Kuttia Kond: Dschungel-Bauern in Orissa*. Munich: Renner.

Otten, T. (2006) *Heilung durch Rituale: Vom Umgang mit Krankheit bei den Rona im Hochland Orissas, Indien*. Münster: LIT Verlag.

——(2007) 'Given From God and Come In Its Own Will: The Hierarchy of Illness Causes among the Rona of Tribal Orissa', in G. Pfeffer (ed.), *Periphery and Centre: Studies in Orissan History, Religion and Anthropology*. New Delhi: Manohar.

——(2008) 'People of the Hills: How Rona Deal with Social Change', in M. Carrin (ed.), *People of the Jangal: Reformulating Identities and Adaptations in Crisis*. Copenhagen: Curzon Press.

*Padel, F. (1995) *The Sacrifice of Human Being: British Rule and the Konds of Orissa*. Delhi: Oxford University Press.

*Parkin, R. (1992) *The Munda of Central India: An Account of their Social Organization*. Delhi: Oxford University Press.

Peabody, N. (2006) *Hindu Kingship and Polity in Precolonial India*. Cambridge: Cambridge University Press.

Pfeffer, G. (1976) 'Puris Sasana-Dörfer: Basis einer regionalen Elite', unpublished habilitation thesis, University of Heidelberg.

——(1982) *Status and Affinity in Middle India*. Wiesbaden: Steiner.

——(1997) 'The Scheduled Tribes of Middle India as a Unit: Problems of Internal and External Comparison', in G. Pfeffer and D. K. Behera (eds), *Contemporary Society: Tribal Studies I: Structure and Process*. New Delhi: Concept Publishers.

——(2000) 'Tribal Ideas', *Journal of Social Sciences*, 4 (4): 331–46.

——(2002) 'The Structure of Middle Indian Tribal Society Compared', in G. Pfeffer and D. K. Behera (eds), *Contemporary Society: Tribal Studies V: Concept of Tribal Society*. New Delhi: Concept Publishers.

——(2003) *Hunters, Tribes, Peasants: Cultural Crisis and Comparison (Ambedkar Memorial Lectures)*. Bhubaneshwar: NISWASS.

——(2004a) 'Tribal Society of Highland Orissa, Highland Burma, and Elsewhere', in A. Malinar, J. Beltz and H. Freese (eds), *Text and Context in the History, Literature and Religion of Orissa*. New Delhi: Manohar.

——(2004b) 'Order in Middle Indian Kinship', *Anthropos*, 99: 381–409.

——(2007) 'Bailey's Kondh Structure on the Tribal Frontier', in Georg Pfeffer (ed.), *Periphery and Centre: Studies in Orissan History, Religion and in Anthropology*. New Delhi: Manohar.

——(2009) 'Sahlins' *Tribesmen* (1968) Reconsidered: Tribes of Highland Orissa in Perspective', *Journal of Social Anthropology*, 6 (1–2): 127–35.

Price, P. G. (1996) *Kingship and Political Practice in Colonial India*. Cambridge: Cambridge University Press.

Price, P. and Ruud, A. E. (eds) (2010) *Power and Influence in India: Bosses, Lords and Captains: Exploring the Political in South Asia*. Delhi: Routledge.

Rajaguru, S. N. (1968/72) *The History of the Gangas* (2 vols). Bhubaneswar: Orissa State Museum.

Richter, W. L. (1971) 'Princes in Indian Politics', *Economic and Political Weekly*, 6 (9): 535–42.

——(1978) 'Traditional Rulers in Post-Traditional Societies: The Princes of India and Pakistan', in R. Jeffrey (ed.), *People, Princes and Paramount Power*. New Delhi: Oxford University Press.

Rothermund, D. (1978) *Government, Landlord, and Peasant in India: Agrarian Relations under British rule 1865–1935*. Wiesbaden: Steiner.

Rousseleau, R. (2008) *Les creatures de Yama: Ethnohistoire d'une tribu de l'Inde (Orissa)*. Bologna: CLUEB.

——(2009) 'The King's Elder brother. Forest King and "Political Imagination" in Southern Orissa', *Rivista di Studi Sudasiatici*, 9: 39–62.

*Roy, S. C. (1970 [1912]) *The Mundas and their Country*. Calcutta: Kuntaline Press.

Sahlins, M. D. (1968) *Tribesmen*. New Jersey: Prentice-Hall.

Samaddar, R. (1998) *Memory, Identity, Power: Politics in the Jungle Mahals 1890–1950*. Chennai: Orient Longman.

*Schnepel, B. (2002) *The Jungle Kings: Ethnohistorical Aspects of Politics and Ritual in Orissa*. New Delhi: Manohar.

Schwerin, D. (1977) *Von Armut zu Elend: Kolonialherrschaft und Agrarverfassung in Chota Nagpur, 1858–1908*. Wiesbaden: Steiner.

Shah, A. (2007) 'Keeping the State Away: Democracy, Politics and Imaginations of the State in India's Jharkhand', *Journal of Royal Anthropological Society*, 13 (1): 129–45.

Skoda, U. (2005) *The Aghria: A Peasant Caste on a Tribal Frontier*. New Delhi: Manohar.

——(2008) '"Coming Out" of the Palace: The Bamra Royal Family and the Performance of Power During the Elections 2004', in L. Guzy and U. Skoda (eds), *Power Plays: Politics, Rituals, Performances in South Asia*. Berlin: Weissensee Verlag.

——(2011a) 'From Dispute to "Disturbance": The "Gond Disturbances" in Late 19th century Bonai / Orissa', in B. Pati (ed.), *Adivasis in Colonial India: Survival, Resistance and Negotiation*. New Delhi: Orient BlackSwan.

——(2011b) 'Princely Politician in an Indigenized Democracy: A Raja and his Electoral Situation in Rural Orissa 2004', in K. Nielsen, S. T. Madsen and U. Skoda (eds), *Trysts with Democracy: Political Practice in South Asia*. London: Anthem Press.

——(2012) 'The Family Chronicles of the Royal Family of Bonai: Texts, Centres and Authorities', in M. Carrin and L. Guzy (eds), *Voices from the Periphery*. London: Routledge.

Spencer, J. (1997) 'Post-colonialism and the Political Imagination', *Journal of the Royal Anthropological Institute*, 3 (1): 1–19.

Stein, B. (1975) 'The State and the Agrarian Order in Medieval South Asia: A Historiographical Critique', in B. Stein (ed.), *Essays on South India*. Hawaii: University Press of Hawaii.

Stewart, C. (2002) 'Great and Little Traditions', in A. Barnard and J. Spencer (eds), *Encyclopedia of Social and Cultural Anthropology*. London: Routledge.

Strümpell, C. (2008) '"We Work Together, We Eat Together": Conviviality and Modernity in a Company Settlement in South Orissa', *Contributions to Indian Sociology*, (NS) 42(3): 351–81.

Tambiah, S. J. (1985) 'The Galactic Polity in Southeast Asia', in S. J. Tambiah, *Culture, Thought, and Social Action*. Cambridge: Harvard University Press.

Tanabe, A. (2007) 'Toward Vernacular Democracy: Moral Society and Post-postcolonial Transformation in Rural Orissa, India', *American Ethnologist* 34 (3): 558–74.

*Vitebsky, P. (1993) *Dialogues with the Dead: Discussions of Mortality Among the Sora of Eastern India*. Cambridge: Cambridge University Press.

——(2008) 'Loving and Forgetting: Moments of Inarticulacy in Tribal India', *Journal of the Royal Anthropological Institute (N.S.)*, 14: 243–61.

Wolf, E. (1966) *Peasants*. New Jersey: Prentice-Hall.

14 Punjab and Haryana

Kinship and marriage

Georg Pfeffer

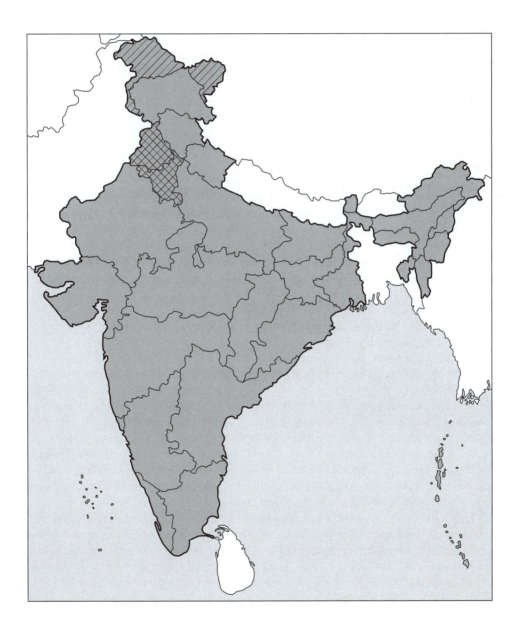

> Sonia and her husband Rampal live under security cover. The two were married for over a year and expecting their first child when a khap declared them brother and sister. They were compelled to sign divorce papers but refused to obey the khap's orders. They moved court and got police protection.
>
> (*The Tribune,* April 26, 2009)

Dramas on marriage, kinship and caste figure frequently in the media of the twin provinces Haryana and Punjab. A man is killed for marrying within his own clan (*The Tribune,* November 26, 2003); another man of the Jat caste is killed because his bride was of the—higher—Rajput caste (*The Tribune,* November 25, 2003), or the lives of both bride and bridegroom are threatened since the two belong to separate but "fraternal" clans that prohibit intermarriage (*The Tribune,* April 26, 2009). In any of such cases, the assembly of a caste or of a clan meets and, after much public deliberation, reaches a verdict. Thereafter, an angry mob goes against the reprimanded individuals, at times openly attacking a protective police force. Though the liberal public—as represented by journalists, academics, or government officers—strongly condemns such "self-styled" authorities and, even more so, any transgressions against the Indian Penal Code, the elders of such an assembly, and those implementing their verdict will not be persecuted. In case civil litigation is to decide the controversy, the view of the council members frequently prevails over that of the couples concerned.

The following chapter will discuss basic anthropological issues relating to the two north-western provinces by focusing on kinship and marriage. The themes are central, even though both governmental institutions and religious authorities openly disapprove of caste and clan discrimination, just as people known for their "advanced" views will reject "backward" marriage conventions, the details of which may even be unknown to liberal urban men. However, the overwhelming majority of the population, liberals included, will "be married"—the passive voice is important—by their families according to specific rules that determine social status. Initially, a reduced version of these rules may read as follows:

1   Every person who is regularly involved in worldly affairs *must* be married.
2   Before marriage, a person must *avoid* erotic advances towards a future spouse.
3   A person must be married within their *own* "kind," or caste, as ascribed by birth.
4   A person must *not* be married to anyone conventionally defined as a "sibling."

The obvious outcome of these restrictions amounts to a strategic importance of marriage networks and local groups like clan or caste. These unofficial loyalties will indicate a family's reputation as a potential marriage partner, while the individual decision-making process of selecting a spouse will be limited. A person's bearing in marriage matters must be generally open to public scrutiny, since any individual misconduct will reflect upon the prestige and the socio-economic opportunities of all other family members. The latter are likely to exert open or implicit pressure upon one another to ensure conformity.

In highly individualistic societies, such as those of Europe, such systemic regulations will rarely be understood and will be frequently opposed with great vigour, just as most Punjabis turn the tables by disapproving strongly of Western conventions with regard to mating and gender. Mistakenly, outsiders may also associate Punjabi kinship rules with the obsolete or marginal notions of a few, rather than the firm standards of the most reputable societal core. Few Europeans would probably connect conformity in marriage matters with general opportunities of socio-political and economic success. In north-western India, however, 'right' or 'wrong' marital policies will be of major and lasting consequence in all other spheres of social life.

To clarify the most important of these Punjabi patterns involving social conduct and social values, the chapter will rely on a rather refined type of anthropological research, as had been the accepted standard in the decades after Indian independence. Kinship studies had been the major domain of British social anthropology until the late 1980s, or in the epoch when leading Commonwealth scholars had gained highest international repute in the discipline and before the educational interventions of the Thatcher government. The subsequent account will draw extensively on such studies, though initially the modern Indian provinces of Punjab and Haryana will be introduced in a wider context.

Punjab and Haryana: a brief profile

'Punjab' is a term in Persian, the language of the Muslim imperial governments in much of the second millennium AD. The name refers to the land of 'five waters' at the foot of the mountains in the northwest of the subcontinent, the fertile plain of alluvial soil as deposited by seasonally swelling rivers that flow down from the Himalayas towards the Indus, each fluctuating through time within a bed of some ten kilometres' breadth. Manjha, the central Punjab around the cities of Lahore and Amritsar, as well as Malwa, adjoining to the southeast, are known as the historical heartlands of the province.

Water and its management has always been the crucial aspect of the Punjab economy. Since the late nineteenth century, the British colonial power organized the construction of the world's largest canal system in the western steppes between the rivers Jhelum, Chenab, Ravi, and Sutlej. As the eastern Punjab, including the land between Sutlej and Beas, was overpopulated, the administration encouraged "junior siblings" within families of peasant proprietors—as well as those of their hereditary clients—to migrate into the western wilderness as pioneer cultivators. They were to grow cotton for the world market or raise horses for the army.

Being conquered by the British only in 1849 as the latest of the Indic provinces and, accordingly, not being involved in the great uprising of 1857, the Punjab was to supply the soldiery for the new army of the Empire (see Mazumdar 2003). Census ethnographers classified the castes of these newly enlisted professionals as "martial races" to be provided with hereditary quotas. In the course of the twentieth century, many positions in the imperial forces were, as a matter of policy, assigned to members of the Sikh religion, the indigenous creed of the Punjab known for its inner-worldly commitment and its devotion to steel as a sacred material. Subsequently, in the spirit of such colonial traditions, Punjabi soldiers have been active on all of India's military fronts ever since World War I. They have also been, and are at present, the major contingent of inner-Indian and global waves of migration, just as they have excelled in the innovative management of agriculture, trade, commerce, and industry. Again and again, however, disturbances over non-economic issues have prevented the provinces from becoming the most prosperous of the subcontinent.[1]

The major and lasting 'wound' resulting from the partition of British India in 1947 was afflicted to the Punjab, with about seven million Hindus and Sikhs being driven out of newly founded Pakistan to re-organize their lives where an equal number of Muslims had been forced to leave the now independent Republic of India. Hundreds of thousands—or more—were killed in this major catastrophe of the century, before two different provinces were created under the name "Punjab," the Indian one as the smaller eastern segment. Ever since partition, next to no regular exchanges of any sort have been conducted across the new frontier, even though the two kinds of Punjabis had earlier shared the same neighbourhoods, castes, and clans. Whereas the inhabitants of West Bengal in eastern India have had fairly open borders and frequent interactions with the Bengalis of Bangladesh, the people and the governments of the two Punjabs have conspicuously ignored the respective other throughout the decades after the communal bloodshed.

In 1965, after much civil agitation for a Sikh majority province and for Punjabi as the "official language," the Indian Punjab was further subdivided, though Punjabi formally became the "second language" in the new federal state of Haryana, while Hindi attained this status in what remained as Punjab. In fact, the people of both provinces master both tongues. Later demands for complete independence led to militant conflicts. Throughout the 1980s and the 1990s, only the massive intervention of the Indian Army—ruling out civil liberties and ordinary democratic process—could suffocate multi-layered attempts to create *Khalistan*, a Sikh "land of the pure." Since then, some implicit reconciliation seems to have set in gradually, and yet communal riots, such as those involving the Sikh minority sects Nirankari or Dera Suchkhand, continue to threaten peace.[2]

Research efforts

Recurrent and often unpredictable outbursts of communal violence throughout the past century, as well as the separatist militancy, may have supplied reasons for the amazing lack of anthropological field research in the Punjab. Hershman, writing in 1974, points out:

> there has been to date no adequate exposition of the basic facts of Punjab village life. Punjab seems to have been shamefully neglected by modern anthropologists and this is true both of West Punjab, now part of the state of Pakistan, and central and eastern Punjab in the Republic of India.
>
> (Hershman 1981: 3)

The situation has not changed significantly during later decades of which two have witnessed the state of emergency and President's Rule in the province, as was proclaimed by the central government to oust the state leadership in the Indian version of rule by ordinance.

At the same time, it must be conceded that truckloads full of literature on the political and economic development of the provinces have been produced, many times being the results of meticulous research on the micro-level (for example H. Singh 2001), thereby indicating that phases or locations of reasonable tranquillity should have allowed inconspicuous anthropological fieldwork in an environment that is open to people of the rest of the world and keen to promote ambitious scholarship. The general abstention from fieldwork could, in fact, have arisen from the very obvious modernity, as witnessed everywhere in Punjab and Haryana. Western science and technology have been adopted and promoted on a wide scale and the latest technical gadgets of consumerism or agricultural production are adopted with little delay. By contrast to other Indian provinces, visitors may find adequate health services within a short distance and, as a rare support for socio-cultural research, universities offer graded language courses of Punjabi for anyone. They also have excellent facilities in the study of the specific history, literature, and religions of the land.

Anyone traveling through the two provinces may reach the villages in comfortable coaches on metalled roads. It will be hard to discover any of the remaining traditional loam houses, renowned for their excellent micro-climate during the freezing winters, the extreme heat from April to June, or the highly irregular rains in later months. The people in the provinces have nothing in common with some "primitive society" that used to be the subject of anthropology in earlier phases of the discipline. Taking the opportunities of a modern political economy, many peasants had migrated westwards at the beginning and re-migrated at the end of British rule. Within India, Punjabis can be found where steel is being processed or oil is being drilled. Accordingly, any anthropologist in search of some "traditional society" will fail to obtain the stereotyped external markers of such a scheme.

Given all of these developments, any significant difference, when compared to western European societies, must be found within spheres beyond the external indicators, or in the domains of morality and sociality, the prevalent value-ideas. In the 1930s, the applied social research of the colonial administration had, through several village monographs (R. Singh 1932; Dass 1934) of the *Board of Economic Inquiry*, offered ample evidence of the cultivators' exceptional talents and thrift while, at the same time, the experienced administrator Malcolm Darling had described the *Punjabi Peasant in Prosperity and Debt* (1925) in rather ambivalent terms. Whenever locusts or hailstorms, floods or droughts had destroyed the crops, tremendous skills and stamina, austerity and determination were applied by this prototype that was preferably named in the "ethnic singular" by the British masters of social engineering. In times of plenty, however, village folk supposedly spent whatever they had—and what their moneylenders would give them on top of it—on liquor and the prestations of grandiose weddings, or, even more frequently, on factional disputes and litigation, as facilitated by the newly introduced colonial courts of law. In fact, "the Punjabi peasant" became the favourite of the European empire builders when compared to cultivators of other provinces or the rather unimportant client castes. Even more so, he was juxtaposed to "the" Bania, i.e. members of the mercantile castes who allegedly "alienated" peasant land when mortgages failed to be paid up. Supplanting older systems that included hereditary credit relations, the colonial law had introduced state protection for individualistic banking operations and yet, when the specialists applied these new laws, colonial ethnographers, unabashedly racist in their judgements, maligned the creditors in a style[3] comparable to anti-Semitic polemics elsewhere.

The first research project of a trained modern anthropologist, a traditional "village study" in the last year of undivided Punjab, was later published by Marian Smith (1955) in a very short version. Subsequently, Murray Leaf, an adherent of the now defunct approach called "cognitive anthropology," discussed a Sikh merchant clan in a book (1972) that may be attractive for methodological but not for ethnographic reasons. The economic historian Thomas Kessinger reconstructed the past of a Punjabi village from its revenue records (1974), but the best known anthropological work is that of Joyce Pettigrew on *Robber Noblemen* (1975) recalling the factional in-fighting of the Indian National Congress, then the only major political party, that culminated in the assassination of the first Chief Minister Pratap Singh Kairon. The book described intrigues and confrontations in the political arena, as dominated by the Jat caste leadership, without involving the general standards. Pettigrew, who at that time was married to a Punjabi, continued to write on Jat and Punjabi politics and later on the Khalistan movement (Pettigrew 1995). Finally, the most ambitious anthropological work on the social order of the Punjab is the late Paul Hershman's study (1981) of a village in the vicinity of metropolitan Jullundur. As such, it explicitly does not, like traditional village monographs, imply some rural isolation or self-sufficiency but is concerned with local and regional commuters as well as intercontinental migration, though the "hard and fast" data on restricted landownership and class dependencies are forwarded as detailed and impeccable evidence. Since the book offers much insight into matters of kinship and marriage, its results, along with my own findings over four decades, will be discussed in this chapter.

Jat standards

The colonial *District Gazetteers* and *Settlement Reports* had taken fancy to a certain construct known as "the sturdy Jat" which, for want of modern research in the Punjab, has been reprinted in post-colonial decades (i.e. Rose 1883 [1970]: 366). People belonging to the largest regional caste of cereal cultivators—and about equally distributed among Hindus, Sikhs, and Muslims in undivided Punjab—were supplied with this attribute. Associated with the *sudra varna*, or the lowest of the four estates in the Hindu sacred order, the Jat—rather than the Brahmins—are seen to set the general social-religious standards of the land along with allied smaller and slightly lower cultivating castes like the Kamboh, the traditional vegetable growers. Their insignificant ritual status and the lasting influence of Islam, the rulers' creed for some 800 years before the short Sikh Kingdom (1799–1849), have had obvious effects upon Sikhism, the indigenous religion "born out of wedlock between Hinduism and Islam after they had known each other for a period of nearly nine hundred years" (K. Singh 1966: 17). The message of the Qur'an, as propagated by reckless conquerors and saintly paupers, has even had a visible impact upon the regional version of Hinduism with its most prominent sect, the decidedly anti-Muslim Arya Samaj, being openly adverse to much of the ritualism and hierarchical thinking as is found in other provinces.

Agnation and affinity, gifts and credibility

Given these socio-cultural commonalities at the face of an appalling lack of anthropological research, Eglar's work on a Jat village in Pakistan (1960) must be mentioned, since it concerns a general feature, the regular gift exchange system described as *vartan bhanji*, meaning "trading of sweets." Generally speaking, this is a man's obligation towards those to whom a "sister" has been "lost" in the past. The *bhanji*, or "sister's daughter," and her children continue the line of legitimate unilateral claims.

All Punjabis are members of specific agnatic or patrilineal descent groups and a sister, being the "sweetest" of the relatives, is bound to move out to ensure the continuation of another such group. She is the greatest of any imaginable "selfless" gifts for the sake of the intermarrying regional caste community. Muslims may, minding only the detailed Mosaic prohibitions, also "take" a bride in exchange for a sister, though a slight stain will remain in such a case. They may even marry a woman to her "father's brother's son,", i.e. an agnate, though both kinds of transactions are horrendous sins in Hindu and Sikh family law. Eglar's village data of the 1950s indicate a trend towards marriages with a "father's sister's son," or a bridegroom of a different agnatic descent group who is still "too near" to be acceptable for Hindus and Sikhs. However, such a marriage is not, as the exchange or the inner-agnatic union, a sacrilege. Beyond this, Tiemann's (1970) data show how the Hindu and Sikh Jat are able to follow the three central marriage rules strictly while simultaneously maintaining a system of mutual marital exchange between a very limited number of regionally represented agnatic descent groups through time. These three rules demand out-marriage, or exogamy, of the descent group while prohibiting any repetition of intermarriage within memory and the exchange of a sister for a bride between any two men.

Agnatic solidarity and obligations of "bride-givers" towards "bride-takers" have been the foremost structural principles of Punjabi social organization as long as memory goes. Agnates comprise the members of a male or female person's paternal clan and its "fraternally" linked clans. In practical terms, this implies that a father will leave his land jointly to all of his sons and, if no son exists, to the nearest male agnates, irrespective of any legal provisions by the state. Brothers may proceed to partition their land publically or continue with a joint holding. In the latter case, one of them may cultivate the fields while the others follow different callings, such as serving in the armed forces or being engaged in business at home or abroad while, at the same time, retaining close and regular ties to the native village. The highly ranked ideal of "brotherhood" is frequently asserted, and yet, such a multiplicity of claims to landed property, especially if inherited through several generations, is bound to lead to factional disputes, since the system of patrilineal descent implies the segmentary relativity of closer as opposed to more distant "brothers" and loyalties through time.

The inherited agnatic bond will create a deep—and formally expressed—sense of loss with regard to a female agnate. Emotional ties between father and daughter or between brother and sister are known to be stronger than any others. In fact, a major preoccupation in a man's life is to arrange the best possible marriage for his daughter in a social system prescribing marriage universally. A woman must be given away within a specified phase of her life. The active search on the bride's side—facing a hesitant and bargaining attitude of the bridegroom's relatives—as well as the deliberations over the qualities of potential husbands and the preliminary negotiations will be conducted by all of the bride's closer family members, especially the female ones, and extended to her more distant relatives. Insurmountable dissent in this matter is known as a major and lasting source of strife. While the women, including the bride herself, have many informal ways to gather detailed information when advancing their own or hampering any rival strategies, the final decision, followed by the formal proposal, is executed by the bride's father or, in case he is dead or disabled, by her brothers.

Dowry negotiations have always been a major factor of such a decision-making process and they have, especially in the most modernized urban sector, reached an ever-growing importance during the last decades. Since a flat, furniture and household goods, electronic devices and vehicles, jewellery as well as an enormous amount of money—but never cultivable land—will have to be transferred to the new husband of a daughter, the search for a bridegroom is a highly sensitive affair involving considerable commitments on the side of the bride's closer agnates who will have to be compensated reciprocally in due course of time, or when the bride-givers become bride-takers in another context. In a snowball effect much of the local caste community is thus interrelated by such credit obligations of ritual gifts carrying substantial material value.

Along with the sacred "gift of the virgin," or *kanyadan*, a family offers such prestations to rule out any open idea of some kind of a material advantage attached to, or derived from, the departure of its "sweetest" member. The gift must be "selfless." Punjabis consider a financial or any other profit on the side of the bride's family as an indicator of low caste status, even though such low-ranking units have mostly given up brideprice transactions a long time ago. At the same time, bride-givers of all castes may, in spite of their obvious surrender of a sister along with material prestations, derive an indirect advantage out of specific connections through marriage. It would be exceptionally naive not to assume an implicit awareness of such a potential. However, the law of hypergamy, openly defining the status of any bride-takers as superior, is as explicit in the Punjab as in other Indian provinces.

Dowry transactions along with the gift of the bride are the initial prestations of many more to follow in the same direction through generations. On any given ritual occasion, such as life cycle ceremonies of a daughter or a sister, and any joyful event, such as the birth of a male child in his own family, a man must, to safeguard the honor of his name for any future negotiations, make substantial gifts to his daughter or sister and to their children or grandchildren who will not be his agnates. In anthropological jargon, the link continues as an "affinal" relation. Such affinal gift obligations are inherited within the descent line by the cousins of the receivers, until, after three or more generations, this bond is gradually "forgotten" so that a new marriage will be allowed to reopen it. For three generations the givers view the affinal receivers of their gifts as loyal allies who will also be helpful in arranging further marriages in their vicinity (Hershman 1981: 150, 154). Ideally, women are "taken" from villages situated in the east and "given" towards the west. This may be one—unmentionable—reason for the fact that the surplus of males in western border districts is even higher than in others.

The affinal gifts, delivered by or addressed to a man's household, are practically handled by his wife or his daughter-in-law. The mistress of a house, or the woman she has formally installed to succeed her, has the keys to several tin boxes in which she keeps the many textile sets of clothes which she has received in the course of her career and from which she will carefully select those meant for others on some ritual occasion. Ceremonial giving is a medium of female politics. A woman will buy, or choose from her box, a certain quality of cloth for the prestations to indicate rather directly her ideas on the quality of the relationship in question.

In more recent research among high-caste Rajput, Anjum Alvi (1999, 2001) has studied these gift exchange systems in their many details and elaborated on an important differentiation: whereas *dhian*, the affinal obligation of a man towards his sister's household, her children, and her grandchildren, will always be a unilateral gift, *bhaji*, the obligation to give to agnates, neighbors, and formally defined friends, is of the reciprocal type, being returned during lifecycle ceremonies with an additional raise, lest the debt could be balanced. Much of the household economy, as conducted by the senior females, is concerned with funds derived out of a commodity economy before being channelled into the cycles of such a gift economy and, within the latter, from the non-reciprocal to the reciprocal type.

Significantly, such female-featured operations have not received general attention within gender studies.[4] When the 2006 Nobel Prize laureate Mohammad Yunus demonstrated to the world how illiterate Bangladeshi women should be supported by small-scale credits of the World Bank since they had been highly successful in their locally organized mutual aid operations, these data, taken out of their cultural context, were received as a kind of sensation. However, in Haryana and Punjab women of all status groups, even those of the lowest, have "always," while applying a formalized style of diligence and reliability, involved themselves in ceremonial gift exchange systems as related to agnatic and affinal ties. Beyond these specific lifecycle obligations, it should be emphasized that many women enhance their reputation by engaging in comparable—but 'free-floating'—rotating credit associations. Managing loans as such is a desired and honorable female pastime. The associations offer to a single receiver a larger sum, as is periodically collected in small amounts from the remaining women. Either by lot or on account of a particular situation of need, convincingly described by the woman in question and certified by other members of the circle who will be her neighbors or acquaintances, the receiving person is selected on a weekly or a monthly basis. Whereas male honor is by definition linked to virility (Pfeffer 1995), such as the power to defend or take by force, the reliability of a person in debt is at issue among women. Again, special empirical research in this field is lacking.

Today, anyone going for lunch in a middle-class restaurant of Jullundur or Amritsar is likely to observe some 30 to 40 well-dressed female guests who are not just engaged in small talk but have come to pay their regular contribution and expect a lot to assign the next receiver of the aggregate. These women are aware of moving within "the right circle," which implies the same or a "near" caste and professional status of their husbands. Accordingly, they are not just highly conscientious in paying their dues but also likely to find support in core issues like marriages and professional promotions of daughters and sons. In the same manner, the women of a sweepers' slum will organize each other's mutual support with smaller amounts of money at stake. They, too, have been socialized to be reliable through the obligations of affinal and agnatic gift exchange. The slightly older women who have been able to initiate and maintain such circles will bear the highest respect. In fact, the "gift of the virgin" along with the subsequent affinal gifts within the marriage circle of a caste group serves as the model for such other honorable exchanges among the same "kind" of people.

Order and spirit of descent

Patrilineal or agnatic descent involves multiple levels. Hershman has elaborated in practical detail the segmentation of the major clan within the Jat caste of "his" village (1981: 102–28) and due to his additional research in Southall, a town to the west of London, he has also learnt that, in matters of agnatic solidarity, overseas communities tend to be stricter than those "at home." The smallest operating unit is the household, which may include a single couple along with the children and the surviving parents of the husband or several married brothers in a joint family. Veena Das (1976) has elaborated on the emotional contradictions of such a fraternally composed household in which the brothers are supposed to be equivalent authorities for all children, though inevitably the strains of relative distance are bound to appear. Her article 'Masks and Faces' juxtaposes Punjabi concepts of innate drives, such as lust, greed, and dominance, with those of moral forces. Both are accepted as given, but morality is to enchain a person's animal instincts. Thus a man must—by domestic violence if required—uphold the authority of his mother against his wife, though his "natural" proximity as a nocturnal partner is supposed to compensate the latter. Since fraternal solidarity ought to be unlimited, the in-marrying wives are frequently made responsible for any cleavage between brothers. But Pettigrew (1975: 53) has also shown how the women of a household may aid and favor one another within a rather complex system of avoidance—towards the husband's elder siblings—and of ritualized joking with the husband's younger sisters and brothers. She has also demonstrated (ibid.) fraternal cohesion in cases of only the eldest among several brothers being married and sharing his wife with the juniors.

An *al*, or a minimal agnatic lineage, is named after the nickname of its founding ancestor some three generations above the living adult members (Hershman 1981: 110–11) whose households own adjacent fields and often share rights in a common well while worshipping in the shrine of a common ancestor. They also, if a man lacks male descendents, inherit each other's land and belong to the same faction in any of the many local political disputes. A unit comprising the paternal *and* maternal relatives of the last three generations may also operate as the effective political pressure group from one generation to the next. Thus, since 1947 almost all chief ministers in the Indian state of Punjab have been mutually related in this manner. The lasting agnatic descent group is, in every new generation, supported by a new affinally-related clan group, though descendents of former affinal partners will become re-eligible in due course of time. Consequently, the same affinal links reappear periodically, after a minimal three generations, in spite of the formal prohibition to repeat intermarriage. Only a handful of clan groups may continue such rotating marriage alliances through time and may form the backbone of a local and provincial political faction. Simultaneously, each participating *al* must, from one generation to the next, offer sufficient evidence of its power and cohesion in order to remain within such a circle of intermarrying units. To qualify for marriage, the ascribed status of an *al* will be seen against the light of the economically or educationally achieved status of its families rather than that of individuals.

Five major lineages, or *patti,* of the dominant clan were represented in Hershman's village, the members of each occupying the same residential ward with adjoining fields and employing the same members of service castes. These five lineages used to pay their land rent jointly to the government. To this day, their members will be potential inheritors of each other's fields, just as they are supposed to defend their common interests as a single unit, though the mutual relationship is, more than among other agnates, of an ambivalent quality. They are "brothers" within the same corporate action group and yet they—more openly than "real" brothers—vie for each other's land. Generally, any two sons of a man, being tied together by multiple duties, are not supposed to ever entertain jocular or casual relations with one another, but within the *patti*, an increased reserve, as opposed to friendly or informal terms between affines, is an open marker of rivalry. Members must help each other. One of each household will accompany an "own" bridegroom on a wedding excursion to take home the bride and defend the bridegroom against the ceremonial—and sometimes rather physical—resistance of her people, and yet sharing obligations does not imply mutual love, just as it does not exclude mistrust or deceit.

At the highest descent level, the localized agnatic clan group—like the general and dispersed clan category—is called *got* in Punjabi and includes lineage groups of several segmentary levels in the village. Its assembly intends to solve all internal disputes, which will be primarily those relating to kinship and marriage. Members share a common temple and mourn jointly for the deceased. With regard to land, clan members have "the first right of refusal" (Hershman 1981: 103) before it can be "alienated" by outsiders. To this day, any corporate descent group is a unit of action that combines mutually ambivalent "brothers" in their common as well as their divisive interests, their joint sacrifice, and their mutual mistrust. Sometimes, the localized clan is even bound to others of the kind by formally fraternal relations.

Caste groups and categories

For Hershman (1981: 83) the concept of a status hierarchy, as developed out of different supra-regional caste *categories*, is to be distinguished from the empirical observation of corporate regional *groups*, each bound together by endogamy or in-marriage. All over India, caste categories such as Brahmins, Herders, or Weavers stand for the theory of separate but interdependent and hierarchically ranked professional specialists making up society. At the same time, empirically operating groups, each of intermarrying members, inhabit a certain region and each is referring to one of the supra-regional categories when collective status is involved. The land between the rivers Beas and Sutlej, known as Jullundur Doab, offers an example of such a region where given caste corporations exert tremendous practical influence. Each one of them unites a number of dispersed agnatic clans, or out-marrying descent categories.

Within any village, the members of a particular caste will often be of the same "localized clan" (Hershman 1981: 83). In Hershman's village the Jat caste, as is frequent, dominated the settlement. Practically all members—grouped in some 156 households—belonged to a single clan, though nine other houses were only maternally related to add to the local caste but not to the local clan. All Jat were self-cultivating peasants while other inhabitants belonged to service castes of sorts, with the 40 Brahmin households being actually engaged in the urban businesses of the nearby city, since the landowners were Sikhs who did not require hereditary Hindu priests.

Of the other castes, Carpenters, Tailors, Goldsmiths, Water-Carriers, Barbers, and Sweepers, each numbered between 10 and 28 households. Individual members either commuted to the city for employment or were engaged in the respective hereditary services for which they used to be rewarded from the common grain heap at harvest time, but since the 1950s were paid in cash. The largest service caste in the village was that of Tanners who, in fact, were landless laborers employed on a daily basis. Within three major Tanner clans some 197 households, or more than those of the localized Jat caste, had to cope with such a precarious existence.

Like the Sweepers, the Tanners used to be so-called "untouchables," though they are known as *dalit*, or "surpressed ones," in modern parlance and the administration registers them among the Scheduled Castes for which the constitution of India guarantees special provisions in matters of education, employment, and parliamentary seats. All over India, Tanners will automatically be associated with work relating to hides and skins, though in fact they mostly serve as field laborers. The same holds true for the Sweepers who may be latrine cleaners in the cities but mostly work as farm servants in rural areas. Wherever Sweepers engage in agricultural labor, Tanners will be a rather small minority following the traditional occupation and vice versa. In short, the two major *dalit* castes locally compete with each other in a society that is divided by classes, or an unequal access to the means of production that discriminates a large section of the population. The stigmatising caste specializations, being only nominally the main occupations, are as such without any competitive aspect. In fact, the ideological reference to caste status covers up the ongoing class exploitation. In the northwest and many other Indian regions, landowners, for their class interests, let one *dalit* unit collectively compete with another for employment, though such labor relations are being camouflaged by a language of ritual purity or impurity of the castes.

Another significant aspect of such classification is the status difference between the two *dalit* categories. Though each one of them is severely discriminated in every aspect of social life, the two would never view one another as equals. The Tanners are said to carry a higher status and, accordingly, most will disallow Sweepers to enter any temple of their caste. The separation will also become obvious in political elections. While Tanners will favor and even dominate a certain political party, Sweepers will use their numerical strength to wield influence, though not dominance, in another one. Technically, the very caste name of a tanner (Chamar) or sweeper (Chura or Chuhra) is insulting as such and should always be substituted by the honorific term Jatav for the former and the sectarian title Balmiki for the latter. Balmik is the sweeper saint or ancestor. Mark Juergensmeyer (1982) has presented an impressive monograph on the socio-religious history of the Sweepers in the Jullundur region, though their recent history in the Punjab as a whole is significant for their current standing.

The socially despised followers of Balmik appear—along with Tanners and Jat—among the numerically largest castes of the Punjab. During the nineteenth century, a significant minority of them converted to Christianity in a mass movement (Heinrich 1937). They were, apart from a few individual cases, the only Punjabis who—collectively and within a short span of time—gave in to the efforts of Western missionaries. As reports of the decennial *Census of India* between 1901 and 1931 indicate, the collective crossover of the Sweepers was not restricted to Christianity, since numerous conversions to Sikhism and Islam were also counted, with the names for the converts referring to some presumed faithfulness that, if properly understood, implied an ironical meaning.

With the respective religion of Punjabis being the political issue during the partition of the province at independence, the Sweepers did not, like others when caught on the wrong side, cross the new international border but remained wherever they had been before. In rural western Punjab, all non-Muslim sweepers practically over night were known as Christians, though in the big cities many remained attached to saint Balmik and the Hindu traditions.

Similarly, Muslim sweepers of Indian Punjab joined the local churches without much ado, though any such "blurred" categories remained formally unknown ever after. Until today, the most esteemed scholars of Punjab history will recall the fate of *Divided Cities: Partition and Its Aftermath in Lahore and Amritsar 1947–57* (Talbot 2006) without considering the rather special and highly significant fate of the large Sweeper caste that is equally despised and indispensable (Pfeffer 1970).

Urban groups of the subcontinent may have generally been neglected in anthropological writing, though Hazlehurst (1966) provides an exception. His work examines caste and kinship of merchant communities—mainly those of refugees—in a small Indian town. Among these internally ranked units, partition had erased many highly refined sub-caste distinctions as well as extended marriage networks, and yet the typical clan exogamy involving affinal responsibilities had remained. The work deals with well-established groups engaging in commercial activities. The Agarwal sub-caste of Bania merchants, just as the Sud caste—the word meaning "interest"—of traditional money lenders, each have their own secret script and system of accounting. Even more prominent and numerous than these two are the Khatri, traditionally engaged as grain merchants but today—like the others—found in all literate and ambitious professions. Most Hindu and Sikh Khatri alike claim to belong to the second estate, or *kshatriya varna*, within the Hindu religious order, but in practice such classification just alludes to their general respectability. Urban centers and their intellectuals have been established in the region for millennia, even though landowners have always dominated the political leadership. Cities like Rohtak and Amritsar are, to this day, divided into modern colonial or post-colonial wards and their counterpoints, the ancient walled towns with a number of gates and specific quarters for each of the different caste groups of traders, craftsmen, and service-holders. Traditionally, merchants and bankers had writers and religiously exceptional individuals in their midst as the intellectual elite of northwest India.

Sikhism as the unique religion of the Punjab

Before the European colonialists approached India by sea, all invasions of the subcontinent crossed through the Punjab because the few passes in the north-western mountains were the only "entries" for invaders from western and central Asia. The latter left their marks in the Land of the Five Rivers. Extended phases of aggression made the victims yearn for peace. The founder of Sikhism established himself as a pacifist messenger of universal brotherhood and love. Born into a family of grain merchants, Guru Nanak (1469–1539) was, like the subsequent nine Gurus, of Khatri caste. He propagated tolerance and personal salvation irrespective of caste or creed and his message was not communicated through esoteric Sanskrit scriptures but in religious *bhajan*, or emotional songs, conveyed in the language of the common folk. Nanak's movement of the learned—or 'Sikh'—propagated monotheism without ritual exaggerations and his mysticism found followers among Hindus and Muslims alike.

In subsequent centuries this pacifist community became increasingly popular though persecuted by the state authorities, with the ninth Guru Tegh Bahadur (1621–75) being sentenced to death and executed. His son and successor Gobind (1666–1708) then transformed the community of the faithful into a militant movement. In spring 1699 he assembled his followers at Anantpur for the decisive session. Drawing his sword out of his scabbard, he is said to have demanded five men to sacrifice their lives and five—each of a different caste— followed him into his tent. Having slaughtered a goat for each of them, he declared the *panj piyare*, the five beloved ones, to form the nucleus of the new congregation called *khalsa*, or the pure. They were baptized with sugary water churned by the Guru with a double-edged dagger, the symbol of both religious and secular leadership. Subsequently, all male followers received the surname Singh, or lion, all female ones that of Kaur, or princess, in order to promote the equality of believers beyond the boundaries of caste.

Any male member of the *khalsa* would henceforth openly bear witness of his faith, since the Guru had commanded them to embrace the *panj kakke*, the five symbols of Sikh faith: *kes*, or uncut hair; *kangha*, or a comb to tie it; *kara*, a steel bangle on the right wrist; *kirpan*, a dagger or a sword; and finally *kachcha*, the short undergarment. The eminent Sikh psychologist Jit P. Singh Uberoi (1969) has interpreted these symbols as an admission of innate human inclinations, as symbolized by the hair and the sword, the latter standing for aggressiveness. The Guru's disciples, however, were to control these forces as symbolized by the comb, the steel bangle, and the undergarment. Irrespective of such an interpretation, Guru Gobind Singh had clearly instituted expressive membership rules of an organization that, more than any other religious formations, resembles that of a church. The tenth Guru was not succeeded by a human guide. In 1708, the Guru Granth Sahib, as the sacred book of the Sikhs compiling writings of several Punjabi sages of all faiths, became his permanent successor to this day.

Sikhism has retained many Hindu rules, such as the prohibition of beef. A hundred years ago, the children of a family might grow up as either Hindus or Sikhs, the distinctions being of minor importance. At the same time, Sikh monotheism and the central importance of the Sikh scripture, the expressed egalitarianism of the creed, and the disregard for icons reveals obvious commonalities with Islam. Like Indian Muslims and Christians, Sikhs practically continue to observe caste distinctions. Many of their temples are organized by either Khatri, Jat, or Tanner caste groups who will have companions in minor allied castes. A Sikh of a prominent caste would normally avoid the house of a *dalit* or a meal in the company of a former "untouchable." Today, members of the same office or labor unit, school or sports club may come from all castes and, *as members*, will interdine without hesitation. Without such a common ground, *dalit* Sikhs would frequently be excluded from private meals among members of other castes. The exceptional feature among the followers of Nanak and Gobind Singh are the regional roots. In the undivided Punjab many sacred sites and memorials are associated with Sikh glory and martyrdom. The religion is open to anybody and Sikhs are found all over the world, though the Land of the Five Rivers remains the home ground.

Conclusion

In introducing the two modern provinces on the margin of north-western India, a historical and geographic outline described the effects of specific technological innovations, such as the canal system, as well as class and gender contradictions and the given center of gravity of the Punjabi religion and the caste system. Its central considerations viewed kinship in the light of a theoretical approach known as "alliance theory" that was developed by Louis Dumont (1983) from the 1960s onwards. The latter stressed affinal—or marriage—constraints in their impact upon consanguinal—or kin—classification. Paul Hershman (1981), the major contributor to Punjab social anthropology, applied this theory rather critically by relating formal kinship considerations to the basic forces of the political economy. Later research trends in the same field, known as "New Kinship" (Carsten 2004) today, had been foreshadowed in Punjab studies by the articles of Das (1976) and Pfeffer (1995). These involved specific cultural constructs of kinship rather than formal universals. This chapter as a whole demonstrates how kinship and caste, gender and class, as well as religious controversies cannot be understood as separated domains but rather as a unified cultural complex developed on the basis of ecological and historical factors.

Notes

1 Earlier Punjabi religious and caste conflicts are described in Khushwant Singh (1966). Satya M. Rai (1965) gives details on the partition of 1947.
2 Grover (2000) edits the biography of Master Tara Singh, the leader of the "Punjabi Suba Movement" described by Lamba (1999). A Sikh view on "Operation Blue Star" is translated and edited by Anurag Singh (1999), while Mahmood (1996) presents dialogues with pro-Khalistan militants. An emotional analysis of *My Bleeding Punjab* (Khushwant Singh 2005) is most significant. Ongoing militant conflicts involving the "Dera" minority sect are covered by the newspapers (e.g. *The Tribune*, May 25, 2009).
3 Thus of a Bania "his utter want of manliness" (Rose 1883: 60) is attested.
4 Only the work of Chowdhry (1994) is concerned with women in Haryana.

References

Alvi, A. (1999) 'Bearers of Grief: Death, Women, Gifts, and Kinship in Muslim Punjab,' unpublished thesis, Freie Universität Berlin.
*——(2001) 'The Category of the Person in Muslim Punjab,' *Social Anthropology*, 13: 45–64.
Carsten, J. (2004) *After Kinship*. Cambridge: Cambridge University Press.
*Chowdhry, P. (1994) *Veiled Women: Shifting Gender Equations in Rural Haryana 1880–1990*. New Delhi: Oxford University Press.
Darling, M. (1925) *The Punjab Peasant in Prosperity and Debt*. London: Oxford University Press.
*Das, V. (1976) 'Masks and Faces: an Essay on Punjabi Kinship,' *Contributions to Indian Sociology*, 6: 1–27.
Dass, A. (1934) *An Economic Survey of Gajju Chak, a Village in the Gujranwala District of the Punjab*. Lahore: The Board of Economic Inquiry, Punjab.
Dumont, L. (1983) *Affinity as a Value: Marriage Alliance in South India, with Comparative Essays on Australia*. Chicago: University of Chicago Press.
Eglar, Z. (1960) *A Punjabi Village in Pakistan*. New York: Columbia University Press.
Grover, V. (2000) *Master Tara Singh: A Biography*. New Delhi: Deep & Deep Publications.
*Hazlehurst, L. W. (1966) *Entrepreneurship and the Merchant Castes in a Punjabi City*. Durham NC: Duke University Press.
Heinrich, J. C. (1937) *The Psychology of a Suppressed People*. London: George Allen & Unwin.
*Hershman, P. (1981) *Punjabi Kinship and Marriage*. Delhi: Hindustan Publishing Corporation.
*Juergensmeyer, M. (1982) *Religion as Social Vision: The Movement Against Untouchability in 20th Century Punjab*. Berkeley: University of California Press.
*Kessinger, T. G. (1974) *Vilayatpur 1848–1958: Social and Economic Change in a North Indian Village*. Berkeley: University of California Press.
Lamba, K. G. (1999) *Dynamics of Punjabi Suba Movement*. New Delhi: Deep & Deep Publications.
Leaf, M. (1972) *Information and Behaviour in a Sikh Village*. Berkeley: University of California Press.
*Mahmood, C. K. (1996) *Fighting for Faith and Nation: Dialogues with Sikh Militants*. Philadelphia: University of Pennsylvania Press.
Mazumdar, R. K. (2003) *The Indian Army and the Making of Punjab*. New Delhi: Permanent Black.
Pettigrew, J. (1975) *Robber Noblemen: A Study of the Political System of the Sikh Jats*. London: Routledge.
*——(1995) *The Sikhs of the Punjab: Unheard Voices of State and Guerilla Violence*. Atlantic Highlands NJ: Zed Books.
Pfeffer, G. (1970) *Pariagruppen des Pandschab*. Munich: Renner.
*——(1995) 'Manliness in the Punjab: Male Sexuality and the Khusra,' *Sociologus*, 45: 26–39.

Rai, S. M. (1965) *Partition of the Punjab.* London: Asia Publishing House.

Rose, H. A. (1883) [1970] *A Glossary of the Tribes and Castes of the Punjab and the N.W.F. Province.* Vol. II. Reprinted by Languages Department Punjab, 1970. Delhi: Punjab National Press.

Singh A. (1999) *Giani Kirpal Sigh's Eye Witness Account of Operation Blue Star. Mighty Murderous Army Attack on the Golden Temple Complex.* Amritsar: B. Chattar Singh Jiwan Singh.

Singh, H. (2001) *Green Revolutions Reconsidered: The Rural World of the Punjab.* Delhi: Oxford University Press.

Singh, K. (1966) *A History of the Punjab*, two vols. Princeton: Princeton University Press.

——(2005) *My Bleeding Punjab*, 2nd Edition. New Delhi: UBSPD.

Singh, R. (1932) *An Economic Survey of Kala Gaddi Thamman (Chak 73 G.B), a Village in the Lyllpur District of the Punjab.* Lahore: The Board of Economic Inquiry, Punjab.

Smith, M. W. (1955) 'Social Structure in the Punjab,' in M. N. Srinivas (ed.), *India's Villages*. London: Asia Publishing House.

*Talbot, I. (2006) *Divided Cities: Partition and its Aftermath in Lahore and Amritsar 1947–1957.* Oxford: Oxford University Press.

Tiemann, G. (1970) 'The four-got-rule among the *Jat of Haryana* in northern India,' *Anthropos*, 65 (1/2): 166–77.

The Tribune, Chandigarh, November 25, 2003: 'Boy hacked to death for marrying out of caste'.

The Tribune, Chandigarh, April 25, 2009: 'Curfew in Jalandhar as mob goes on rampage'.

The Tribune, Chandigarh, April 26, 2009: 'In the name of justice.' Spectrum (Sunday supplement).

Uberoi, J. P. S. (1969) 'The Five Symbols of Sikhism,' in J. P. S. Uberoi, *Religion, Civil Society and the State: A Study of Sikhism.* Delhi: Oxford University Press.

15 Rajasthan

Anthropological perspectives on tribal identity

Maxine Weisgrau

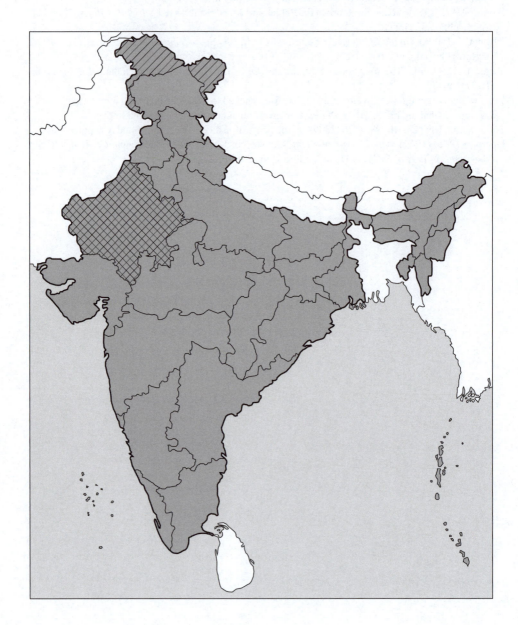

While in India on a research trip in the mid-1990s, I met a British anthropologist also doing field research in Udaipur District in Rajasthan. Because of our shared interests and the chance contiguity of our residences we spent a great deal of time together, endlessly discussing our respective research projects. By this time I had immersed myself in the theories and debates around Bhil and tribal identities, historically and in contemporary life. My colleague made an intriguing offer: if I collect hair samples from Bhils in the communities in which I was doing fieldwork, she would send them to a human genome laboratory where a researcher was analyzing the genetic histories of people identified as Bhil and Rajput (the dominant caste of Rajasthan). This DNA-based research, the genetic scientists were suggesting, would resolve the highly contentious and political debates over the time depth of Bhil residence in the district, and their genetic distinction from, or alternatively close genetic connections to, other identity groups in the district. In retrospect, this proposed undertaking resonates with the racialized narratives of Bhil identity roundly rejected by most anthropologists, but still present in the quest for genetic evidence of presumed identity markers. Years later, the hair samples I collected and carefully labeled remain in a desk drawer, unopened and unstudied.

This unopened envelope is a constant reminder to me of the complexity of identity labels; the political nature of identity claims; the multiple, conflicting, and often shifting forms of information invoked by competing groups over identity categories; and most importantly, the responsibilities of anthropologists whose research may be inserted into policy debates. I am however also keenly aware of the political uses, especially among Bhils of Rajasthan, of their claims to land and political rights that draw on historical, intergenerational, and extensive time depth of local occupation and identity. This political dimension of indigenous identity broadly conceptualized through rights conferred by states by virtue of an identity in distinction to others, conceptually links the identities of Rajasthan's Bhils in India to global discourses and rights movements around the world (Merlan 2009).

This chapter reflects on the production of anthropological knowledge about Bhils and other so-called "tribal" identity groups in Rajasthan. For three centuries travelers, ethnologists, colonial administrators, historians, and social scientists have written about these subjects, sometimes based on personal experience and observation and always shaped by Western preconceptions (Inden 1990); some of these observations resonate uncritically in the extensive corpus of twentieth-century anthropological literature on Bhils in Rajasthan. Many of the early observers speculate on the origins of Bhils in particular, as well as on broader questions of tribal identity and the characteristics of tribal communities in India more generally (see Deliège 1985). These studies reflect virtually every major school of thought and methodological approach in the history of anthropology. They document the multiple social and political uses of categories and assumptions about indigenous peoples in general, and tribal categories of identity in Rajasthan in particular.

The circulation of tribal identity categories in anthropological and political discourses illustrates the ongoing and politicized processes of group identification. Historically these group categories were created during colonial regimes, interpreted by the postcolonial state, and written about by travelers, missionaries, and other observers. Throughout the twentieth century anthropologists and other social scientists have contributed to the proliferation of ethnographic studies of individual tribal groups throughout India; anthropological literature includes efforts at "defining the tribe as a social formation and to distinguish it from other social formations" (Béteille 1998: 187). This effort at defining a tribal group in India is confounded by the wide variety of regional, social, economic, political, environmental, linguistic, and familial arrangements that groups so-designated exhibit. It is further complicated by the indiscriminate use of the term "tribe" in ethnographic descriptions both inside and outside of India.

Currently the debates about tribal identity in India are embedded in national political movements and global human rights discourses on indigenous peoples. Simultaneously specific tribal identity categories have been resisted and re-negotiated by local communities. As these local groups extend their political participation and amplify their own voices in local and national political discourse, their understanding of empowerment includes the right to self-designation and self identity; within these self designations however are the residues of multiple layers of identity claims informed by generations of discourses translated into local knowledge. In this chapter I therefore propose that Bhil identity is best understood in contemporary Rajasthan as political assertion in conversation with historical and modernization discourses by Bhils negotiating their multiple statuses as citizens, voters, laborers, land owners, and participants in development programs and agendas.

Rajasthan: a brief overview

Rajasthan ("land of kings") invokes images of northwestern India at its most complex and alluring. Its eastern hills and western deserts were the sites of famous battles led by rulers of the princely states that were consolidated in 1947 to form the state of Rajasthan at Independence. The borders of the contemporary state of Rajasthan reflect the historical association of this geographic region of India with Rajput political domination; this conception of Rajasthan with Rajput rule is due in part to the resistance of the Mewar and Marwar courts to the Delhi Sultanate during the thirteenth century. "The popular conception of the Rajput as a chivalrous warrior, defending honor and religion against the Muslim invader in the hills and deserts of Rajasthan is drawn from this period of Indian history" (Lodrick 1994: 6). This dominant Rajput identity of the northwestern region of India carried over into British administration; nineteen Rajput princely states in northwestern India were eventually consolidated and administered under the Rajputana Agency in the early nineteenth century.

British administration of the region focused on the interests of the Rajput rulers as understood by the officials of the British East India Company, and later the representatives of colonial administration. James Tod (1782–1835), political agent to the princely courts of Western Rajasthan from 1818 to 1822, enshrined the ideas of Rajput political acumen and military exploits in his extensive writings about the region (1983). To his superiors Tod was excessively sympathetic to the interests and mythologies of the Rajput rulers; he was eventually dismissed from his post and returned to England; however, it was this "romantic picture of a noble, feudal aristocracy ... that became part of the British consciousness, and subsequently came to dominate British views of Rajputs and of Rajasthan" (Lodrick 1994: 10).

This history of political boundary formation paralleled the cultural constructions of Rajasthan. George A. Grierson (1851–1941) in his discussion of Rajasthan in the *Linguistic Survey of India* classified the multiple dialects spoken in Rajputana as Rajasthani, "the language of Rajasthani or Rajwara, the country of the Rajputs" (Grierson 1908: 1). Grierson described the five major dialects of Rajasthani as comprising a language distinct from the Western Hindi spoken across northern India; subsequent scholarship challenges this linguistic classification. "More recent linguistic scholarship ... suggests that the Rajasthani language is not so easily defined. Although the dialects in the northwest and southeast of Rajasthan are clearly distinguishable for the neighboring Punjabi and Marathi tongues the boundaries of the Rajasthani language are not so clear elsewhere" (Lodrick 1994: 17). The official language of the state is Hindi, although most people born in Rajasthan also speak one of five major dialects. As in other parts of India, English medium schools now compete with the state's

Hindi medium school system; among all classes and strata of society English language fluency is seen as a major advantage for economic mobility in business, computer and software industries, and participation in the tourism industry.

The Rajput-dominated imaginings of Rajasthan's past are encoded in the state's tourist destinations of the present (Henderson and Weisgrau 2007). The palaces, fortresses, and residences of the *maharajas*, *maharanas* (erstwhile princes), and *thakurs* (local rulers and land owners) are now an integral aspect of the state's tourism infrastructure. The cities and surrounding communities of Jaipur, Udaipur, Jaiselmeer, and Jodhpur draw domestic and international tourists. Despite its robust tourism economy and urban industrial growth, Rajasthan continually ranks in the lower ranges of national indicators for literacy, health, economic development, and political empowerment, especially for rural Scheduled Caste (SC) and Scheduled Tribe (ST) communities.

Rajasthan's population of approximately 58 million people is concentrated in rural communities; despite the growth of urban centers and labor markets, three-quarters of the state's population lives in rural areas and is engaged in an aspect of agricultural production. Roughly diamond-shaped, Rajasthan is divided into two geographical areas by the Aravalli mountain range, one of the oldest mountain systems in the world. Roughly two-thirds of the state lies in the arid, sparsely populated Thar Desert region, which begins at the easternmost ridge of the Aravallis and extends westward to the Pakistan border. Areas to the south and east of the Aravallis have historically benefitted from a more temperate climate, intermittently generous and unreliable monsoons, and proximity to New Delhi, making the eastern section generally more fertile and densely populated than the west (Agarwal 1979; Rosin 1994). Environmental conditions in Rajasthan, including deforestation in the Aravallis and expansion westward of the Thar Desert region ecosystem, have been exacerbated by recurrent periods of drought. Social forestry, watershed management, and other resource protection programs addressing these environmental problems have been undertaken throughout the state by governmental and non-governmental organizations and are the focus of community-based resource management and internationally-funded interventions (Saint 1988; Henderson 1994; Mosse 2005).

Literacy and educational levels, electrification, communication technologies, access to health facilities, and income levels all display a marked urban bias. Rajasthan's extensive system of rural development programs is gradually extending educational, medical, and technological benefits to underdeveloped rural areas. State-wise an aggressive educational commitment has raised the literacy rate overall to about 60 percent; however, women's literacy state-wide is about 44 percent, and 38 percent in rural areas. Among the Scheduled Tribes of Rajasthan these rates are lower than the state-wide averages: among all Bhils literacy rates are estimated at 35.2 percent; among Bhil women 19.1 percent. Less than half of Bhil children aged 5–14 attend school (Office of the Registrar General, India 2001: 1–5).

Anthropology of Rajasthan: themes and issues

The Indian caste system imagined as a rigid and fixed system of social hierarchy has dominated the Western representation of Indian society for the past two centuries (Inden 1990: 49–90; Gupta 2005); this master narrative of caste influenced the anthropological study of caste relations in Rajasthan throughout the twentieth century. In Rajasthan Rajput social and political influence is a major theme in the social science literature of Rajasthan (Rudolph and Rudolph 1984; Lodrick 1994: 6; Balzani 2003); ethnographic studies have historically focused on inter-caste relations between Rajputs as the dominant community and their social, economic, and ritual relationships with other castes. Contemporary ethnography focuses on how Rajput political history is invoked in the deployment of political ritual and ideology in contemporary settings, including Rajasthan's tourism industry (Ramusack 1994; Jhala 2007; Bautes 2007; Snodgrass 2009).

In rural communities of Rajasthan, *jati* (local caste group) categories and hierarchies continue to influence residence patterns and marriage, as well as socioeconomic and education levels. But as contemporary empirical studies of communities throughout Rajasthan illustrate, *jati* does not automatically determine occupation or class position. The decline of Rajput landholdings and influence, and the dismantling of hereditary estates over generations, have weakened the dominant position status of Rajputs as patrons and employers in many rural communities (Sharma 1993). Participation in tourism activities has provided previously marginalized low-caste communities with possibilities for accumulating wealth and status by participating in newly-emerging industries and occupations. Snodgrass documents the transformation of Rajasthani Bhats in Udaipur District (a major tourism center in Rajasthan) from traditionally low-status leatherworkers to primarily puppeteers and performers. Income from tourism performance is providing this community with both wealth and social capital, allowing it to manipulate and subvert traditional caste hierarchies (2004, 2007).

Political party participation and electoral alliances also challenge some traditional patterns of caste hierarchy (Sharma 1996). During the 1989 elections in Rajasthan, the decades-long domination of the Congress Party came to an end; the BJP party launched a successful local effort to recruit Scheduled Tribe voters; local electioneering rhetoric claimed that Congress was the party of the Scheduled Castes. This strategy effectively dismantled traditional political alliances and voting blocs among the local low-caste communities (Weisgrau 1997: 174–185).

Gender-specific studies document the wide range of disadvantages women and girls continue to face, particularly in the rural communities of Rajasthan. Adverse female sex ratios state-wide were 910/1,000 males in 1991, rising to 922 in 2001 (Mathur 2004: 17), and are attributed in part to early marriage, child-bearing risks, and multiple forms of gender-based violence. Other factors documented throughout northern India include male-biased differentials in nutrition, access to medical services, child-care practices, and rates of infant death (Miller 1981). Social conservatism influences appropriate and acceptable behavior for all women; conventions restricting women's behavior are often drawn from Rajput ideals of household gender segregation and exclusion from public activities (Harlan 1992).

Most marriages in Rajasthan are arranged by parents or other kin, and follow the northern Indian norms of village exogamy, *jati* endogamy, and virilocal postmarital residence patterns, resulting in the dominant pattern of joint households (Kolenda 2003: 241–305). The life cycle, particularly of young rural women, turns on this significant transformation; anticipation of marriage combines with the sorrow of separation of young women from their natal households and the uncertainties of their reception by their in-laws in their husband's home. These themes dominate the mournful songs sung by young girls during the wedding season as they walk through their villages as carefree daughters for the last time, accompanied by sisters and female kin prior to their marriages and departure to their husband's household and the strangers they will reside with for the rest of their lives (Weisgrau 1997). But as Raheja and Gold (1994) demonstrate, women's songs and stories confront and satirize the conventions of behavior placed on them, while outwardly conforming to gender-based expectations.

Religious practice and spiritual spaces in India have long drawn the attention of Western observers; the over-determined view that religion uniquely dominates the actions and consciousness of people in India is widespread and often repeated in Western media. India imagined as a world center of spirituality continues to lure travelers, tourists, devotees, and journalists to its public centers of religious practice. Religious identity in Rajasthan today combines the public practices of temple visitation and *darshan*, the viewing of images and relics, with private, household-based prayer and worship (Weisgrau 1999). Religious identity is enacted within family and life stage rituals, as well as in national and local political party discourse (Joseph 2007), through transnational networks and electronic media, and within economic transactions (Carrithers and Humphrey 1991). Hinduism is the numerically dominant religion in Rajasthan; the wide range of goals and local ideologies that motivate Hindu pilgrimage are explored ethnographically by Gold (1988, 1994). Exquisitely-carved Jain temples throughout Rajasthan draw throngs of devotees and other Indian and international visitors (Cort 2007), as does the Muslim shrine of Mu'in al-Din Chisti in Ajmer (Sanyal 2007). Ethnographic explorations describe the diversity of worship forms and participants in religious centers and shrines throughout the state. The above-cited scholars explore how conflicting conceptions of self and other, of ideas about ownership, control, and appropriate behaviors are (often acrimoniously) negotiated within these densely populated religious settings.

Musical, dance, oral narrative and artistic traditions are intertwined with multiple religious themes throughout Rajasthan, and are enacted in public and within family settings (Kothari 1994; Gold 1994). The social and political relationships between artists, artisans, and their patrons are therefore significant aspects of both the histories of these art forms as well as the contemporary artistic environments (Erdman 1985; Haynes 1994). Mayaram explores how Meo Muslim ballads, myths, and other oral performance traditions of this marginal social and religious group in Alwar District are evidence of resistance to the dominance of Hindu princely rulers and the pan-Indian discourses of nationalism (1997, 2003). Her research on oral traditions and subaltern identity in Rajasthan draws on the broader traditions of subaltern studies and ethnohistory, inserting previously ignored marginal groups into narratives of Indian history and political resistance.

Scheduled Tribes of Rajasthan

The 45 Scheduled Tribes of Rajasthan listed in the 2001 Census, comprise approximately 12 percent of the state's population, but feature disproportionately in Rajasthan's touristic marketing. Websites and brochures prominently feature images of Bhil women and other tribal groups displaying their distinctive dress and ornamentation. The majority of Rajasthan's tribals self-identify as either Bhil or Mina. Over 95 percent of the tribal population in Rajasthan lives in rural areas but has economic and social connections to the markets and institutions of the towns and cities (Office of the Registrar General, India 2001: 1–5).

Contemporary Bhils are a diverse ethnic group of approximately seven million people in the northern Indian states of Gujarat, Madhya Pradesh, Maharashtra, and Rajasthan. They engage in many different occupations in both urban and rural settings. Many social and economic activities in Bhil communities are based on kinship and lineage connections; marriages are generally arranged between Bhil *jati* members, as determined through patrilineages, in other villages. Life cycle rituals and religious festivals are enacted within these local clusters of related villages and lineages. Although a major theme in the anthropological literature of the past has focused on the distinctions between Bhil and caste Hindu religion, virtually all self-identify as Hindus. Their religion, ritual cycles, and social patterns combine Hindu norms with localized practices, systems of worship, and ritual cycles (Weisgrau 1999, 2003).

The designation "Bhil" is controversial and laden with myths and stereotypes of tribal identity in India. A widely-held and often repeated assumption that contemporary people designated as Bhils are the descendants of ancient indigenous South Asians is based largely on references in the *Mahabharaata* and *Ramayana* to short, dark-skinned forest dwellers. The English language translations of Sanskrit texts influenced colonial discourse that subsequently linked these mythic forest dwellers to contemporary Bhils. In the nineteenth and early twentieth centuries tribals were generally categorized as a "race" consistent with prevailing assumptions about phenotypic (physical) and linguistic characteristics (see Risley 1969). Although all the observers of Bhil communities throughout Central Western India during this period noted physical, economic, and linguistic diversity, as well as the physical resemblance of Bhils to other local caste group members, the idea of the Bhils as a separate race of people with distinct physical, linguistic, and social characteristics persists.

Scholars documenting the social histories of Rajasthan now suggest much more recent, localized processes of class-based differentiation to account for the separation and subsequent marginalization of Bhils and other tribal communities from caste-based Hindu society. Contemporary research on Bhils in Rajasthan generally challenges the assumption of the historical existence of "tribal" society in relation to its presumed opposite, "caste" society, as well as the presumed isolation from other agricultural and entrepreneurial castes and classes (e.g. Unnithan-Kumar 1997). Evidence of economic interaction between Bhils and merchants of other caste and religious groups pre-dates the colonial period, and often shows the Bhils at a disadvantage in these commercial transactions (Hardiman 1987). Bhil agriculturalists historically practiced slash and burn, or swidden agriculture, and frequently relocated in small family groups. This may account for their subsequent social marginalization as well as their settlement patterns on less desirable hilltop farmland.

Flexibility in self-designation terminology was reported by colonial census administrators and continues among contemporary Bhils. In Rajasthan, tribal people may refer to themselves as Minas, a higher status tribal group, while outsiders believe them to be Bhils; Gameti and Gameti-Bhil are also terms of local self-designation that have been incorporated into census designations and the Government of India's Schedule of Tribes.

Bhils have politically mobilized around the identity of Adivasi, a pan-Indian term for tribals coined during the Independence movement, as well as around the identity category of Dalit, which expresses alliance with other Scheduled Tribe and Scheduled Caste groups throughout India. In many parts of western India the right of access to forestland controlled by the state and national governments is linked to tribal identity; the categories of tribal and Bhil, therefore, have profound significance in struggles for political and economic rights.

Identity discourses from the local to the global

In contemporary Rajasthan tribal groups all participate in on-going processes of identity group manipulation. The noted Rajasthani folklorist Komal Kothari observed that there are at least three categories of names for each caste group designation in Rajasthan: "one which is respectful, a second which is general or neutral, and a third which is abusive or demeaning" (Kothari 1994: 205). Among tribal communities in Rajasthan this observation of multiplicity of names can be described within the following categories: what they call themselves amongst themselves; what outsiders call them (outsiders of a wide range of identities—colonial bureaucrats, post-colonial administrators, local elites, anthropologists, and sociologists); and the names they use for themselves to talk about themselves (Weisgrau 1997: 66). A. W. T. Webb, political agent of the Bombay Presidency who supervised compilation of the Rajputana

Census of 1941, documented the self-appropriation of different group names by tribal community members during the late colonial period. He reports that when gathering data for the census few respondents in areas known to be populated with Bhils identified themselves as such. Webb describes a conversation with a Bhil woman, who explained the ambiguity of self-identification to the census takers. She stated that Bhils routinely report their identity to census takers as Mina, a higher status tribal group in Rajasthan, consciously manipulating the administrative categories to elevate their community status (Webb 1941: 191).

When the so-called tribals of India are placed in global discourse, the contested terms "indigenous peoples" or "Fourth World Peoples" are added to the layered and contentious naming process. The anthropology of indigenism, along with the languages of universal rights and intellectual property movements, suggests terminologies and typologies deriving from historical events and ethnographic settings outside of South Asia. In an effort to address this geographic bias, Richard Lee (2000) proposed that the study of indigenous peoples recognize two major categories of global interaction:

> Indigenous One describes the Americas after 1492, Australia after 1788 and probably Siberia after 1600 in the period of Russian eastward expansion; small peoples facing Eurocolonial invasion and conquest, Native Americans, from the Arctic to Tierra del Fuego are the classic cases. Indigenous Two: deals with the parts of the world where those claiming to be indigenous are encapsulated, not by European settler states, but by agrarian polities in which the dominant ethnicity situates itself in one or another of the Great Traditions from which the indigenes are excluded. Thus we have India and its scheduled tribes, Malaysia with its Orang Asii, and Indo-China and its Montagnards.
>
> (6–7)

This effort is significant in the South Asian context, as it challenges the assumption of India as a "special case" in the analysis of social and economic groupings and therefore non-comparable to the rights movements deriving from New World histories of conquest and subjugation. A growing body of literature therefore addresses the relationship of India's Scheduled Tribe communities to global rights discourses on and transnational rights movements of indigenous peoples (Xaxa 1999; Karlsson 2003). Some scholars of South Asia suggest that this global discourse, which originates in the political rights traditions of the west, is of questionable utility in illuminating the discussion on contemporary tribal issues in India. The histories of indigenous peoples in other parts of the world focus on the documentable events of European exploration, colonial rule and subjugation. India's tribal histories pre-date these historical scenarios of existing populations subjugated by foreign invasions and migrations. Histories of tribal identity in India draw in part on religious and epic mythology as well as local oral traditions; they are of a much deeper time depth than the European expansion and colonization that forms much of the basis of identification of indigenous peoples in other parts of the world. These historical narratives document long periods of interaction between tribal and nontribal populations during which "both populations have undergone many transformations through usurpation, miscegenation, and migration" (Béteille 1998: 189).

Other scholars note that the identities of, and political strategies resulting from, the adoption of "external" categories of identity is an ongoing process in the political life of tribal people in India and elsewhere (see Xaxa 1999). The globally situated discourses on indigenous identity and political rights integrated into the political consciousness of India's tribal groups is therefore part of an ongoing and continuous process of identity formation accompanied by a recognition of political rights in local, national, and international settings. Anthropologist

Sally Engle Merry, in her studies of the global circulation of international rights discourse, suggests that their origins in the European Enlightenment is not of primary importance in understanding their power among contemporary non-Western communities; what is significant is how these ideas are integrated, translated, and adopted into local discourses by local groups around the world (Merry 2006).

"Tribe" and "tribals" in anthropology

The colonial and post-colonial histories of India that inform the particulars of the creation and use of tribal categories of identity in India are clearly documentable and have a framework familiar to other places: the role of the state in generating identity categories that, on the ground and in local discourse, imagine identity categories as fixed, communal (dispersed throughout a community and applying to all within that designated community) intergenerational, inherited, and permanently ascribed. Nineteenth- and twentieth-century Western theorizing about tribal communities in India in general and in Rajasthan in particular focused around two interrelated intellectual efforts: defining the structural characteristics of tribal society and distinguishing it collectively from caste-based Hindu society. Embedded within theorizing about tribe and caste in India is the net of an evolving European discourse on race, racial categories, and racial characteristics, cast wide on the diversity of colonized peoples around the world (Robb 1997; Bayley 1997).

Broadly speaking the extensive anthropological literature on tribe and tribals in India draws on one of three major perspectives on tribal identity (see Deliège 1985; Pfeffer and Behera 2002, for a more detailed discussion of the history of anthropological perspectives on tribes in Rajasthan and in India). Social evolutionary theorists reflect the broader efforts in the history of anthropology that attempt the creation of universally applicable scenarios of the evolution of political and social typologies (see Sahlins 1960). Others focus on documenting and analyzing the unique characteristics of India's various Scheduled Tribes, their relative separation from other communities, and their systems of resource exploitation (see for example Pfeffer 1997; Pfeffer and Behera 2002; Parkin 1992). As discussed above, many scholars of tribal society in Rajasthan stress the processes of "devolution" of tribal communities from agricultural cultivators with caste status to social and economic outliers as the result of losing land and status to more powerful groups. This approach focuses on the historical relationships of groups now designed as Scheduled Tribes with local elites, colonial rulers, and the post-colonial states as primary determinants of identity and social status. Some of the evidence cited for historically constructed processes draws on the origin stories told by tribal groups themselves (Fortier 2009). Proponents of all theoretical perspectives agree that whatever the processes involved, there are critical economic, social, and political implications to the lived experiences of people in contemporary India now designated as Scheduled Tribes.

British social anthropologists drawing on ethnographic research in Africa

> have been inclined to take the boundaries of the tribe for granted, focusing their attention on its internal structure. It is as if a tribe could be understood on its own terms without taking into account other tribes or other societies of a different kind.
>
> (Béteille 1987: 78)

Attempts at a rigorous and generalizable usage of the term "tribe" as a political entity is associated with cultural evolutionary schools of anthropology, and with scholars developing universal typologies for the evolution of political systems across time and geography.

Fried (1966, 1967) challenged the evolutionary approaches to understanding the concept of tribe, and proposed that they can best be understood as a secondary reaction to external circumstances. Tribes, he states, "have been consciously synthesized to advance a scheme of external political control" (1967: 173). They arise particularly within situations of colonialism or imperialism, and are the result of interaction between complex cultures (states) and simpler organized societies. This interaction requires a minimal organizational structure by which the state can exert its external political control; the emergence of the tribe is a response to that interactive requirement (1966: 540–41).

In the mid-twentieth century anthropologists and sociologists contributed to the massive amount of literature published on the subject of tribals and tribal life based on field studies and careful observations of communities. In lieu of analytic definition anthropologists in India developed a trait list approach to identify specific tribes and tribals. For example, Fuchs suggests the following traits:

> As far as Indian tribes go, the essentials seem to be only a comparatively simple and primitive economy, combined with a certain degree of residential instability, a simple, though not always, classless social organisation, and especially that feeling of being a different and separate social unit—apart from the majority communities of India.
>
> (Fuchs 1973: 25)

F. G. Bailey states that the dichotomous distinction between "tribe" and "caste" is problematic; he challenges the diagnostic models that draw sharp distinctions between these two categories. He states that the relevant distinctions between tribe and caste society lie in political systems, and that these distinctions are more accurately described as a continuum rather than discrete categorical variation:

> The only solution to the problem [of identifying tribe from caste] is to postulate a continuum, at one end of which is a society whose political system is entirely of the segmentary egalitarian type, and which contains no dependents whatsoever; at the other of which is a society in which segmentary political relations exist only between a very small proportion of the total society, and most people act in the system in the role of dependents.
>
> (Bailey 1960: 264–65)

Tribal structural organization is not a pan-Indian system; tribal groups are not ranked hierarchically; a Santal in West Bengal, for example, has no affinity with or structural, hierarchical relationship to a Bhil of Rajasthan. Tribal group designations and hierarchical ranking may be localized as a result of religious conversion or Sanskritization, the collective emulation of upper caste practices by a Scheduled Tribe for the purposes of social elevation (Srinivas 1962; Rao 1988). The state's designation of Scheduled Tribes places unrelated groups exhibiting a tremendous amount of historical, political, linguistic, social, and economic variation under one administrative category.

Colonial narratives on Bhil identity: tribes and race

For two centuries the anthropological and historical literature on the Bhils was dominated by the assumption that they are descended from Dravidian peoples replaced by migrating Indo-Europeans whose culture evolved in South Asia into Hindu, caste-based Indian society.

Linguistic, archaeological, and anthropometric data question this hypothesis of the ancient origins of the Bhils or their assumed millennia-long separate identity, distinct from other castes and classes of Rajasthan. However, this migration-conquest scenario continues to resonate in scholarly and general discourse in India, along with the model of tribes and tribals as separate and distinct from Hindu caste-based society. Many of the political claims that India's indigenous people make to land access and related rights draw on the presumption of descent from the original peoples of South Asia. The collective designation "Adivasi" used in the decades after Independence in 1947 specifically references this collective identity category as the original people of India.

Alternative narratives of Bhil identity related to social status formation and access to property appear intermittently in the nineteenth-century British administrative record (e.g. Malcolm 1827), but are eventually discarded in favor of a unified and hegemonic hierarchicalized, racialized discourse on Bhils and other tribes (Skaria 1997). This later discourse draws almost exclusively on the vocabulary of racial categories and the biological and communal inheritance of social characteristics.

The racialized master narrative on the presumed ancient origins of the Bhils served as the context to nineteenth- and early twentieth-century explorations of Bhil identity, practices, physical characteristics, and language. Many scholars have documented the British colonial processes of classification of Indian subjects into groups with assigned, essential characteristics attributed communally across the group.

The exigencies of colonial transformation and prevalent European ideas provided British rule with the frames of reference for the classification of the "native" population of India. Through an elaborate corpus of revenue, juridical, and police records the British Raj produced for itself a colonial archive: a ready-at-hand knowledge which, in turn, provided manuals for codifying and when necessary thwarting the challenge of traditional, unchanging—and to that extent anticipated—behavior of subject population. Inherent in the production of this colonialist knowledge was the conception of the *essential types* without history [emphasis in original] (Nigam 1990: 131).

For example, the British *Imperial Gazetteer* (n.a. 1908, vol. 8, pp. 101–105) entry on "The Bhil Tribes" is representative of this racialized master narrative. Despite acknowledging great diversity in the group referred to as Bhils the text nevertheless draws conclusions confidently about the physical characteristics of the "typical" Bhil:

> The name Bhilla seems to occur for the first time about A.D. 600. It is supposed to be derived from the Dravidian word for a bow, which is the characteristic weapon of the tribe known as Bhil. The Bhils seem to be the 'Pygmies' of Ctesias (400 B.C.), and the *Poulindai* and *Phyllitae* of Ptolemy (A.D. 150); … The Bhils have been settled in this part of India from time immemorial … It is not easy to describe a tribe that includes every stage of civilisation, from the wild hunter of the hills to the orderly and hard-working peasant of the lowlands. A further difficulty arises from the fact that the name Bhil is often given to half-wild tribes … who do not seem to be true Bhils. The typical Bhil is small, dark, broad-nosed and ugly, but well built and active.
>
> (*Imperial Gazetteer* 1908: 101–02).

Sir Herbert Risley, the late nineteenth-century British administrator/ethnologist was one of the more prolific categorizers of the so-called races of South Asia. It is difficult to escape the conclusion that Risley was obsessed by race, racial characteristics, and racial separation, finding evidence of it everywhere in India—even in ancient statuary. Based on scant anthropometric data Risley established a system of physical characteristics associated with the different "races of the Indian Empire." The physical variables included stature, complexion, facial hair, eye color, head shape, and nasal shape and length. He examined data on 200 "Rajputana Bhils" and from these measurements concluded that the Bhils belong to the "Dravidian" racial type (Risley 1969: 370).

Despite the eventual discrediting of much of the evidence to support it, the racialized narrative of Bhil identity persists well into the twentieth century. This narrative jumps in time from the ancient past to the historic landscape and descriptions of poverty and social marginalization—all in a somewhat single trajectory over vast periods of time and unspecified space. This flawed identity narrative alone may provide ample justification to replace the term Bhil in scholarly discussion due in part to the often derogatory connotations these group designations have in local discourses. Many scholars have rejected the use of particular tribal designations such as Bhil, substituting Adivasi, a term now enfolded by some into the term Dalit.

Tribal as a government/administrative category

The economic and social diversity of these population groups categorized as tribes is ignored in the trait-based definitional models, as was their enormous variation in group size. But the question of what population groups officially belong to the Government of India's category of Tribes was "more or less settled definitively" by the Constitution of India (Fuchs 1973: 23). Various articles and provisions provided special safeguards and protection to the population groups categorized as "Scheduled Tribes" as well as to those categorized as "Scheduled Castes" and "Other Backward Classes." The Constitution did not state explicitly how a "tribe" is to be recognized or identified nor how it is to be distinguished from a caste (ibid.: 24). This national policy evolved into a highly complex compensatory discrimination and benefits program. Benefits are extended on a communal basis; all members of a scheduled community are eligible to receive the designated benefits and preferences despite income or property ownership levels.

The framers of the Indian Constitution originally envisioned this benefits scheme as a temporary one; it was to have expired ten years after its initial phase of operations. However, the system continues in place, continually modified through successive federal administrations, and it continues to be a recurrent divisive political issue. The proposed extension of the benefits and or revisions to the schedules or lists of eligible groups are inevitably accompanied by intense political debate that often erupts into violent demonstrations across India. Simultaneously groups that were not originally "Scheduled" for special benefits are agitating for inclusion in order to access entitlements.

Anthropology and development discourse

Rajasthani Bhils are citizens of the world's largest democracy, but illiteracy coupled with grinding poverty result in their disenfranchisement and social marginalization. State organizations and non-governmental organizations (NGOs) are attempting to elevate the standard of living of Bhils and other groups of the rural poor by, among other strategies, literacy training; political organization and activism; social and ritual reform; and the protection of natural resources (Weisgrau 1997; Mosse 2005). These organizations are increasing local awareness of social and political issues as well as encouraging participation in the local political process.

The emergence of NGOs in the second half of the twentieth century as a highly significant vehicle of local development was represented by NGOs themselves and the donors who fund them as a viable locally responsive alternative to the previous failures of large-scale, bureaucratically driven, inflexible governmental development. As the development sector in India matures in the twenty-first century the boundary between "government" and "non-governmental" development approaches are blurred (Weisgrau 1997: 102–16); current strategies integrate the priorities and resources of the state and the private sector with local organizations, all aimed at increasing the political and economic empowerment of the rural poor.

A gender perspective on all aspects of development programs is therefore currently mainstreamed into both state and non-governmental strategies; "the idea that women are more oppressed in Rajasthan than anywhere else in India inspires a huge bureaucratic apparatus and a pervasive discourse about the need for women's uplift in the state" (Moodie 2008: 454). Women's empowerment in Rajasthan has translated into a focused effort to elevate the skills, knowledge base, literacy, and political acumen of poor rural women throughout the state; in many parts of rural Rajasthan this means targeting tribal communities in general, and tribal women particularly for delivery of state and NGO development programs. Development languages, strategies, policies, and actors are now part of the daily lived experiences of men and women in Bhil communities, as are the anthropologists who study and write about them.

Anthropological engagement with the issues of tribe and gender in Rajasthan have therefore shifted away from the definitional and theoretical distinctions between tribe and caste communities and into the elucidation of the complexity of contemporary lived experiences of participating in development regimes. As many of these studies demonstrate, development discourse contains many parallels with earlier constructed imaginings of tribal communities; contemporary poverty and marginalization are seen as continuous with earlier forms of discrimination and marginalization (see for example Unnithan-Kumar 1997; Weisgrau 1997).

In many ethnographic explorations of development and poverty alleviation in tribal communities in Rajasthan, scholars note the marginalization of Bhil and other community voices to those of outside organizations in planning and instituting development strategies. They also note simultaneously the ability of community members to appropriate the resources offered, despite their origination, to serve important needs as defined by community members. For example, in her discussion of a microcredit program in rural Rajasthan Moodie (2008) documents how credit-based self-help groups provide an arena in which local women can confront caste and hierarchy relationships in rural villages in ways unanticipated by the architects of this poverty-alleviation strategy. The women participating in these programs employ strategies and gain knowledge that has little to do with the financial gain and ideas of sisterhood that microcredit organizers espouse (Moodie 2008: 463). This is an example of what anthropologists often explore as the unintended consequences of development strategy; the forms of knowledge and empowerment that derive from participating in development programs may not conform to the official rhetoric about benefits and outcomes of the development planners.

Claiming self-identification

Local resistance to the assumptions and racist stereotypes embedded in narrative of Bhil identity emerges through the reports of local administrators in the early twentieth century. As described above, census takers report that people they presume to be Bhils self-identity with a different name or modification of an existing group name, in an effort to distinguish themselves from other lower-status tribal groups. The subsequent proliferation of census category terms for tribal groups in Rajasthan therefore reflects in part an attempt of a particular group to take control of its own designation, often disassociating itself from the stigmas of non-Hindu practices of ritual and diet that further marginalize these already economically and politically disempowered people.

Ethnographic research in contemporary settings documents the fluidity over time in group categories and designations (e.g. Corbridge 1988, Unnithan-Kumar 1991). Ethnographic studies stress that these categories evolved as designations for economically marginalized population groups whose identity as tribals resulted from shifting economic and political relationships between themselves and dominant political and economic groups. This naming and re-naming process is constant and ongoing, with tribal categories continuously being negotiated and re-negotiated over time, and encoded in the apparatus of the state, particularly the census.

Skaria (2001) in his historical analysis of the relationship of Bhils and other groups in western India stresses the persistence of the trope of "wildness" in British constructions of tribal groups; this presumed wildness is understood in multiple ways but it is primarily linked to their historical connections to the forests and wilderness landscapes, in distinction to and threatening to land-owning, settled agricultural "civilized" society. It is also understood as a metaphor for the forest-dwelling and marginal social and economic existence imagined for groups so identified. Their self-identification as Adivasis links them to an identity as indigenous forest dwellers. Their acceptance of this nomenclature, Skaria suggests, can be understood as both recognition of their marginality, as well as a resistance to it (2001: 281).

The documentation of the public use of the many identity categories Bhils invoke in different settings demonstrates their agency in taking control over what they are called under what circumstances. The choice of designations in different arenas elucidates political and economic competition both within and across groups. Group designation also demonstrates agency among the Bhils and their ability to negotiate the agendas and interests of the patrons and agents with whom they continually interact, including NGOs, anthropologists, journalists, and representatives of both local and state-based political institutions. The name, its history, and its contemporary uses have meaning to people who so-designate; perhaps the ultimate violence against the Bhils would be the removal of that name and that identity from local, historic, and scholarly memory.

Conclusion

Observers of all disciplines agree minimally that there is a recurrent and often repeated term, "tribe," that continues to be used in scholarly, popular, and administrative discourses in India. Its definitions and contours depend in some part on the region of India being explored. These regional histories document the relationships between groups of people so-designated with the political and social elites around them who have the power of designation, as well as the authority of decision-making about those designations. Contemporary anthropologists who study these issues draw on a spectrum of analytic and methodological approaches to document and describe the varieties and strategies of groups increasingly claiming the right to political self-determination. These scholars generally work to separate the concept of tribe "irrespective of the pushes and pulls from the administrative domains … from the particular policy of particular states" (Pfeffer and Behera 2002: 11) as well as make explicit their assumptions and intellectual frameworks.

References

Agarwal, B. D. (1979) *Rajasthan District Gazetteers Udaipur*. Jaipur: Directorate of District Gazetteers, Government of Rajasthan.

Bailey, F. G. (1960) *Tribe, Caste and Nation: A Study of Political Activity and Political Change in Highland Orissa*. Manchester: Manchester University Press.

Balzani, M. (2003) *Modern Indian Kingship: Tradition, Legitimacy and Power in Rajasthan*. Oxford: James Curry.

Bautes, N. (2007) 'Exclusion and election in Udaipur urban space: implications of tourism' in C. Henderson and M. Weisgrau (eds), *Raj Rhapsodies: Tourism, Heritage and the Seduction of History*. Hampshire, UK: Ashgate Publishing.

Bayley, S. (1997) 'Caste and "race" in the colonial ethnography of India' in P. Robb (ed.), *The Concept of Race in South Asia*. Oxford: Oxford University Press.

Béteille, A. (1987) *Essays in Comparative Sociology*. Delhi: Oxford University Press.

——(1998) 'The idea of indigenous people,' *Current Anthropology*, 39: 187–91.

Carrithers, M. and Humphrey, C. (eds) (1991) *The Assembly of Listeners: Jains in Society*. Cambridge: Cambridge University Press.

Corbridge, S. (1988) 'The ideology of tribal economy and society: politics in the Jharkand 1950–1980,' *Modern Asian Studies*, 22: 1–42.

Cort, J. (2007) 'Devotees, families and tourists: pilgrims and shrines in Rajasthan' in C. Henderson and M. Weisgrau (eds), *Raj Rhapsodies: Tourism, Heritage and the Seduction of History*. Hampshire, UK: Ashgate Publishing.

*Deliège, R. (1985) *The Bhils of Western India: Some Empirical and Theoretical Issues in Anthropology in India*. New Delhi: National Publishing House.

Erdman, J. (1985) *Patrons and Performers in Rajasthan: The Subtle Tradition*. New Delhi: Chanakya Publications.

Fortier, J. (2009) 'The ethnography of South Asian foragers,' *Annual Review of Anthropology*, 38: 99–114.

Fried, M. (1966) 'On the concept of "tribe" and "tribal society",' *Transactions of The New York Academy of Sciences Ser. II*, 29: 527–40.

——(1967) *The Evolution of Political Society: An Essay in Political Anthropology*. New York: Random House.

Fuchs, S. (1973) *The Aboriginal Tribes of India*. New Delhi: McMillan India.

*Gold, A. (1988) *Fruitful Journeys: The Ways of Rajasthani Pilgrims*. Berkeley: University of California Press.

——(1994) '*Jatra, yatra*, and the pressing down pebbles: pilgrimage within and beyond Rajasthan' in K. Schomer, J. Erdman, D. Lodrick, and L. Rudolph (eds), *The Idea of Rajasthan: Explorations in Regional Identity, Vol. I Constructions*. New Delhi: Manohar Publishers and Distributors: American Institute of Indian Studies.

Grierson, G. A. (1908) *Linguistic Survey of India, Vol. IX Indo-Aryan Family Central Group, Part II, Specimens of Rajasthani and Gujarati*. Calcutta: Superintendent of Government Printing.

Gupta, D. (2005) 'Caste and politics: Identity over system,' *Annual Review of Anthropology*, 21: 409–27.

Hardiman, D. (1987) *The Coming of the Devi: Adivasi Assertion in Western India*. Delhi: Oxford University Press.

Harlan, L. (1992) *Religion and Rajput Women: The Ethics of Contemporary Narratives*. Berkeley: University of California Press.

Haynes, E. (1994) 'Patronage for the arts and the rise of the Alwar state' in K. Schomer, J. Erdman, D. Lodrick and L. Rudolph (eds), *The Idea of Rajasthan: Explorations in Regional Identity, Vol. I Constructions*. New Delhi: Manohar Publishers & Distributors: American Institute of Indian Studies.

Henderson, C. (1994) 'Famines and droughts in western Rajasthan: Desert cultivators and periodic resource stress' in K. Schomer, J. Erdman, D. Lodrick, and L. Rudolph (eds), *The Idea of Rajasthan: Explorations in Regional Identity, Vol.1 Constructions*. New Delhi: Manohar Publishers & Distributors: American Institute of Indian Studies.

*Henderson, C. and Weisgrau, M. (eds) (2007) *Raj Rhapsodies: Tourism, Heritage and the Seduction of History*. Hampshire, UK: Ashgate Publishing.

*Inden, R. (1990) *Imagining India*. Bloomington: University of Indiana Press.

Jhala, J. (2007) 'From privy purse to global purse: Maharaja Gaj Singh's role in the marketing of heritage and philanthropy' in C. Henderson and M. Weisgrau (eds) *Raj Rhapsodies: Tourism, Heritage and the Seduction of History*. Hampshire, UK: Ashgate Publishing.

Joseph, C. (2007) 'Hindu nationalism, community rhetoric and the impact of tourism: the "divine dilemma" of Pushkar' in C. Henderson and M. Weisgrau (eds), *Raj Rhapsodies: Tourism, Heritage and the Seduction of History*. Hampshire, UK: Ashgate Publishing.

Karlsson, B. (2003) 'Anthropology and the "indigenous slot": claims to and debates about indigenous peoples' status in India,' *Critique of Anthropology*, 23: 403–23.

Kolenda, P. (2003) *Caste, Marriage and Inequality: Essays on North and South India*. Jaipur: Rawat Publications.

Kothari, K. (1994) 'Musicians for the people: The Manganiyars of western Rajasthan' in K. Schomer, J. Erdman, D. Lodrick, and L. Rudolph (eds), *The Idea of Rajasthan: Explorations in Regional Identity, Vol. 1 Constructions*. New Delhi: Manohar Publishers and Distributors: American Institute of Indian Studies.

Lee, R. B. (2000) 'Indigenism and its discontents: Anthropology and the small peoples at the millennium,' Paper presented at American Ethnological Society Annual Meeting, Tampa, March 2000.

Lodrick, D. (1994) 'Rajasthan as a region: myth or reality?' in K. Schomer, J. Erdman, D. Lodrick, and L. Rudolph (eds), *The Idea of Rajasthan: Explorations in Regional Identity, Vol. 1 Constructions*. New Delhi: Manohar Publishers and Distributors: American Institute of Indian Studies.

Malcolm, J. (1827) 'Essay on the Bhills,' *Transactions of the Royal Asiatic Society of Great Britain and Ireland*, I: 65–92.

Mathur, K. (2004) *Countering Gender Violence: Initiatives Towards Collective Action in Rajasthan*. New Delhi: Sage Publications.

Mayaram, S. (1997) *Resisting Regimes: Myth, Memory and the Shaping of a Muslim Identity*. Delhi: Oxford University Press.

——(2003) *Against History, Against State: Counterperspectives from the Margins*. New York: Columbia University Press.

Merlan, F. (2009) 'Indigeneity global and local,' *Current Anthropology*, 50: 303–33.

Merry, S. (2006) 'Transnational human rights and local activism: mapping the middle,' *American Anthropologist*, 108: 38–51.

Miller, B. (1981) *The Endangered Sex: Neglect of Female Children in Rural North India*. Ithaca: Cornell University Press.

Moodie, M. (2008) 'Enter microcredit: a new culture of women's empowerment in Rajasthan?,' *American Ethnologist*, 35: 454–65.

Mosse, D. (2005) *Cultivating Development: An Ethnography of Aid Policy and Practice*. London: Pluto Press.

Nigam, S. (1990) 'The making of a colonial stereotype—The criminal tribes and castes of north India',' *The Indian Economic and Social History Review*, 27: 131–64.

Office of the Registrar General, India (2001) *Rajasthan Data Highlights: The Scheduled Tribes Census of India 2001*. Available at: http://www.censusindia.gov.in/Tables_Published/SCST/dh_st_rajasthan.pdf (accessed August 4, 2010).

Parkin, R. (1992) *The Munda of Central India: An Account of their Social Organization*. New Delhi: Oxford University Press.

Pfeffer, G. (1997) 'The scheduled tribes of middle India as a unit: Problems of internal and external comparison' in G. Pfeffer and D. K. Behera (eds), *Contemporary Society: Tribal Studies, Vol. I Structure and Process*. New Delhi: Concept Publishing Company.

Pfeffer, G. and Behera, D. K. (2002) 'Introduction' in G. Pfeffer and D. K. Behera (eds), *Contemporary Society: Tribal Studies, Vol. V The Concept of Tribal Society*. New Delhi: Concept Publishing.

Raheja, G. and Gold, A. (1994) *Listen to the Heron's Words: Reimagining Gender and Kinship in North India*. Berkeley: University of California Press.

Ramusack, B. (1994) 'Tourism and icons: the packaging of princely states in Rajasthan' in C. Asher and T. Medcalf (eds), *Perceptions of South Asia's Visual Past*. New Delhi: Oxford University Press.

Rao, A. (1988) *Tribal Social Stratification*. Udaipur: Himanshu Publications.

Risley, H. H. (1969 [1915]) *The People of India*. Delhi: Oriental Books Reprint Corporation.

Robb, P. (1997) 'Introduction' in P. Robb (ed.), *The Concept of Race in South Asia*. Oxford: Oxford University Press.

Rosin, R. (1994) 'Locality and frontier: Securing livelihood in the Aravalli zone of central Rajasthan' in K. Schomer, J. Erdman, D. Lodrick, and L. Rudolph (eds), *The Idea of Rajasthan: Explorations in Regional Identity Vol. II Institutions*. New Delhi: Manohar Publishers and Distributors: American Institute of Indian Studies.

*Rudolph, L. and Rudolph, S. (1984) *Essays on Rajputana: Reflections on History, Culture and Administration*. New Delhi: Concept Publishing.

Sahlins, M. (1960) 'Evolution: Specific and general' in M. Sahlins and E. Service (eds), *Evolution and Culture*. Ann Arbor: University of Michigan Press.

Saint, K. (1988) 'Drought in the Aravallis,' *Social Action*, 38: 129–37.

Sanyal, U. (2007) 'Tourists, pilgrims and saints: the shrine of Mu'in al-Din Chisti of Ajmer' in C. Henderson and M. Weisgrau (eds), *Raj Rhapsodies: Tourism, Heritage and the Seduction of History*. Hampshire, UK: Ashgate Publishing.

Sharma, C. (1993) *Ruling Elites of Rajasthan: A Changing Profile*. New Delhi: MD Publications.

Sharma, C. L. (1996) *Social Mobility Among Scheduled Castes*. New Delhi: MD Publications.

*Skaria, A. (1997) 'Shades of wildness: tribe, caste and gender in western India,' *Journal of Asian Studies*, 56: 726–45.

——(2001) *Hybrid Histories Forests, Frontiers and Wildness in Western India*. New Delhi: Oxford India Paperbacks.

Snodgrass, J. (2004) 'The future is not ours to see: Puppetry and modernity in Rajasthan,' *Ethnos*, 69: 63–88.

——(2007) 'Names, but not homes, of stone: tourism heritage and the play of memory in a bhat funeral feast' in C. E. Henderson and M. Weisgrau (eds), *Raj Rhapsodies*. Aldershot, Hampshire, UK: Ashgate Publishing, pp. 107–22.

——(2009) *Casting Kings Bards and Indian Modernity*. New York: Oxford University Press.

Srinivas, M. (1962) *Caste in Modern India and Other Essays*. Bombay: MMP Ltd.

Tod, J. (1983) *Annals and Antiquities of Rajasthan, Vols. I and II*. New Delhi: Oriental Books Reprint Corp.

Unnithan-Kumar, M. (1991) 'Caste, "tribe" and gender in south Rajasthan,' *Cambridge Anthropology*, 15: 27–45.

——(1997) *Identity, Gender and Poverty: New Perspectives on Caste and Tribe in Rajasthan*. Providence: Berghahn Books.

Webb, A. W. T. (1941) 'These ten years: a short account of the 1941 Census Operations in Rajputana and Ajmer-Merwara,' *Rajputana Census, Volume XXIV—Part 1*. Bombay: Census Department of India.

Weisgrau, M. (1997) *Interpreting Development: Local Histories, Local Strategies*. Lanham, MD: University Press of America.

——(1999) 'Vedic and Hindu traditions,' in R. Scupin (ed.), *Religion and Culture: An Anthropological Focus*. New York: Prentice Hall.

——(2003) 'Gavari' in M. Mills, P. Claus, and S. Diamond (eds), *South Asian Folklore: An Encyclopedia*. New York: Routledge Press.

Xaxa, V. (1999) 'Tribes as indigenous people of India,' *Economic and Political Weekly*, 34: 3589–95.

n.a. (1908) *Imperial Gazetteer*, viii: 101.

16 Tamil Nadu

Inequality and status

Gabriele Alex and Frank Heidemann

In June 2000, after a number of killings of people of Dalit origin, the journal *Frontline* reported about yet another caste-based act of violence with the article: 'Victims of bias: The recent murder of three Dalits in Cuddalore district shows that caste oppression is a living reality in rural Tamil Nadu'. This articulated what was being widely discussed in the public and in the private sphere of Tamil Nadu: conflicts along the lines of caste are common and often brutally exercised. Reports about caste-based murder, violence and discrimination are not only part of everyday news, but also of everyday communication with low caste people, who told me countless stories about the potency of caste up until today.

Tamil Nadu: a brief profile

Over the last 70 years, the nexus of caste, inequality and status has also been one of the main topics dealt with in the ethnographic and anthropological writings on South India. In order to understand the salience of caste and inequality, one needs to look at the geography and history that has emerged as Tamil Nadu, literally 'Land of Tamils'. Tamil Nadu lies in the south-east of India and from Chennai, the state capital formerly called Madras, its long coastline stretches up to the southern tip of the subcontinent and even beyond. The other state boundaries were created through linguistic criteria. Tamil is one of the four major Dravidian languages; the others are Telugu, spoken in the north in Andhra Pradesh; Kannada, spoken in the north-west in Karnataka; and Malayalam, spoken in Kerala. There are a number of smaller language groups, mostly without script, spoken by ethnic minorities. Tamil is – besides English – the official language in the state, and considered as a major marker of identity. Within the political rhetoric, the southern states place themselves in contrast to the north, where Hindi and other Indo-European languages are spoken. At the same time, a trans-national solidarity is expressed towards the Tamil-speaking minority in Sri Lanka. Old Tamil literature and poetry, the history of former Tamil kingdoms and Tamil culture are omnipresent in political speech.

In 2011 the total population of Tamil Nadu was 72 million people; the state, covering more than 130,000 square kilometres, hosts a variety of climatic zones. The coastal areas and the 'wet' river zones are used mainly for agriculture; paddy, peanuts, oilseed, bananas, sugarcane, mangos and tapioca are grown here. In the irrigated regions, a high population density contrasts to the 'dry' regions with only one paddy harvest and a significantly lower population density. The major rivers flow from west to east and feed into the Gulf of Mannar. The Cauvery flows from Karnataka to Tamil Nadu, making control over its water an almost permanent source of conflict. Huge dams are located in Karnataka and the water is essential for agriculture in the Cauvery delta, the major rice-producing area. In the western and northern areas of Tamil Nadu are the Ghats, hill ranges of up to 3,000 feet, where coffee, tea, spices and fruits are grown. The most western part of Tamil Nadu, the Nilgiris district, is part of this mountain area, and will be discussed later in this chapter.

Tamil Nadu looks back on a documented history of more than 6,000 years and four great dynasties that ruled the Tamil land: the Cholas, Cheras, Pandyas and Pallavas. The oldest dynasty, the Cholas, established their supremacy between AD 100 and AD 200. They are markably known for building a wide-ranging irrigation system, which enabled year-round agricultural cultivation. This, in turn, led to a perpetual settlement of groups of landless, low caste agricultural workers, from which many belonged to the castes classified as 'untouchables'. The Cholas also established an extensive trade network, a well-developed and effective administration, and taxation system. This allowed villages to operate as autonomous entities. They created geographical districts referred to as nadus, conglomerations of mostly 18 villages. Nadus organized the religious, political, jural and affinal relations between villages and villagers. The Chola rulers lost their supremacy in the thirteenth century to the Vijayanagar dynasty. After the breakdown of the Vijayanagar Empire power was distributed to small kingdoms, who declared independence and fought against each other. With the arrival of the East India Company in 1639 and the subsequent process of colonization, the little kingdoms gained influence, mainly as a result of the concept of indirect rule. This meant that the British left the 'little kings' in their positions to exercise power and collect taxes through them. The British created what was known as the Madras Presidency, comprising present-day Tamil Nadu as well as parts of Kerala, Andhra Pradesh and Karnataka. After Independence in 1947, the Madras Presidency was divided into the contemporary federal states, and Madras (named Chennai in 1996) became the capital of Tamil Nadu.

Tamil Nadu is also referred to as the 'ricebowl of India', since the area has water in abundance and has developed excellent agricultural practices and crop yields. The majority of the population belongs to the lower status strata of society that until Independence was in a feudal relationship with the ruling landowning caste groups (Srinivas 1962). After Independence, the position of these agricultural castes changed in many respects: they were given land through land reforms and settlement programmes, giving them a level of independence from the former feudal lords. They were further given full citizen status, opening the doors to education and participation in politics. Special housing programmes as well as education and loan schemes meant to compensate for discrimination through subordination, were installed. Over the last decades, these programmes have helped to transform parts of the agricultural lower castes into a strong middle class, which entered new work sectors (Kapadia 1999). Nonetheless, 65 per cent of the population are still working in the field of agriculture and depend on it for their livelihoods, while 22 per cent of Tamil Nadu's population lives below the poverty line.[1]

The special composition of high numbers of low-status groups suppressed by a small number of high-status dominant castes found its political catharsis in the Dravidian Movement, most notably the Justice Party (also known as the South Indian Liberal Federation, initiated by T. M. Nair and Theagaraya Chetty in 1917) and the Self-Respect Movement (established by Periyar E. V. Ramasamy in 1925), which rejected Brahmin dominance and fought for a casteless society. What started as a social movement soon became a political party; after Independence the Dravida Munnetra Kazhagam or DMK (literally the Dravidian Progress Federation), and later in the 1970s the All Indian Anna Dravida Munnetra Kazhagam or AIADMK (literally the All India Anna Dravidian Progress Federation), entered the political stage and have dominated Tamil politics ever since. But one has to keep in mind that there are different lines of conflict dominating the social fabric of Tamil Nadu. The Dravidian movement stressed the Dravidian, i.e. anti-Brahmin, identity and mobilized the masses against Brahmin hegemony.[2] There is also the Dalit movement, the former 'untouchables', who united against the dominance of the caste Hindus, and even though the Dravidian movement advertized itself as a Dalit movement, there have been ongoing divisions between the Dravidian and the Dalit movements. For both parties the antagonistic lines of conflict are linked to ideological concepts surrounding purity and pollution, and with the unequal distribution of civil and political rights, which partly derive from these concepts and partly are based on historical social formations.

Anthropological approaches towards Tamil Nadu Plains

Nearly all of the anthropological writings on Tamil Nadu reflect the pre-eminence of caste and status, however from the 1950s until today we see different key issues approached. One of the core questions throughout the literature tackled the relationship between caste and class in the context of class struggle, land reforms and new modes of political participation. This was mainly indebted to a Marxist approach, though not completely.

The question whether high and low castes, Brahmins and 'untouchables' share the same principles of social organization was hotly debated and was formulated in two models: 1) rules of hierarchy are accepted throughout all strata of society (models of unity); or 2) the claim of ritual supremacy of the higher castes is rejected by the lower castes (models of diversity). This led to a further question: is hierarchy the central value, or do we find principles of an egalitarian ideology? Finally, we have ethnographies dealing with the impact of class, caste and hierarchy on gender and vice versa.

In the following we will discuss different anthropological writings, however this discussion is not encompassing but rather a selection of those studies that articulate most eloquently the different approaches outlined above.

Dumont, Dirks, Béteille and Gough on social structure

One of the earliest studies is Louis Dumont's ethnography *A South Indian Subcaste. Social Organisation and Religion of the Pramalai Kallar*, (published in French in 1957 and translated into English in 1986). This study meticulously describes the local political system, agriculture, kinship system and economic and religious organization of the Kallar, a low status but landowning and dominant caste group that constitutes the political and economical elite for wide regions in the south of Tamil Nadu. Dumont demonstrates how their dominance rests on different factors: they are the landowners and until Independence, the Dalit communities were in a relationship of bonded labour. They are also the political leaders, they decide on village matters, in the Panchayat or through violence, and finally their superior position is also exercised in the rituals surrounding the village temples, where they have the first rights to perform the rites. Dumont's work describes the mechanisms of status, hierarchy and power on different levels – between castes and subcastes, but also within castes and their segments by analysing the lineage structure and alliance patterns and strategies. Whereas *A South Indian Subcaste* is primarily an ethnographic work, *Homo Hierarchicus* (1970) builds a 'grand theory', trying to explain the relationship between status and power for India as a whole. It brings forth a structural argument that proclaims on the one hand that the purity/impurity opposition constitutes the core value in India, creating hierarchy on all levels of society, and on the other hand that status and power are separated from each other in the distinction between the Brahmin and the king or the landholding castes. It is mostly for this latter piece of work that Dumont is known and criticized. The ethno-historical study of Nicholas Dirks, titled *The Hollow Crown. Ethnohistory of a Little Kingdom* (1987) also argues against Dumont when examining the nexus of power and status of the kingly family in the former kingdom of Pudukottai. This 'Shudra-king' (who belonged to the Kallar caste – a relatively low caste which was listed as a 'criminal caste' by the British), established his power based on his political qualities and his skills in ceremonial gift-exchange, establishing thereby his autonomy and creating bonds of dependence with his subjects. Caste-hierarchy was shaped by politics, the stratification was not an outcome of rules of pollution but 'embedded in a political context of kingship' and hierarchy being created by 'royal authority and honor, and associated notions of power, dominance and order' (Dirks 1987: 7). Dirks stresses the predominance of politics over religion and not the other way round, as Dumont had it.

In *A South Indian Subcaste* the notions of purity and impurity are already raised, but not intellectually originated. It is however clear that Dumont developed his understanding of the relationship between purity and hierarchy from his knowledge of Tamil rural society (Dumont *et al.* 1986: 37). One of the most intriguing arguments in *A South Indian Subcaste* centres around the importance of affinal relations that shape ritual practices. Although *A South Indian Subcaste* is an outstanding ethnography on an endogamous caste in South India, it lacks a problem-oriented approach. This differs from the next generation of scholars studying Tamil Nadu. In the wake of the Marxist anthropology, studies came into existence looking at the relationship between caste, class and the modes of production tracing the transformation from a traditional economy of land and grain supported by a caste-based closed society to a class-based open society. Most notable is André Béteille's ethnography *Caste, Class and Power: Changing Patterns of Stratification in a Tanjore Village* (1965) on Sripuram (located in the Thanjavur district in the Cauvery Delta), which discusses the effects of the post-Independence political and agricultural reforms and analyses the different segments of the village (the 'untouchable' *ceri*, the Brahmin *agraharam* and the non-Brahmin hamlets) with a Popperian approach in "terms of conflicting tendencies and aims" (Béteille 1965: 10). He concludes that the traditional Tamil rural village society has become part of a wider economy and has thereby undergone profound changes summarized as follows: the categorical unification of low castes into Dalits and Most Backward Castes led to new reformist political associations. This increased the possibilities for political participation by the formerly subjugated strata, despite the fact that landownership (i.e. resources) had not shifted in the same manner. However, land reforms re-organized agrarian relations by securing the position of tenants and increasing their share in the harvest. New credit schemes further enabled the economically weak strata of this society to take out loans from banks, thus reversing direct dependencies from landowners, and economic relationships formerly based on status were replaced by contractual relationships where cash plays an important role (Béteille 1965: 140). For Béteille, status and caste are diminishing as class-based relations and power is no longer in the hands of the dominant castes, but rather dispersed by different political bodies and distributed to different castes.

A similar approach is taken up by Kathleen Gough, whose field of study was also the Thanjavur district. She argues that through industrialization and a new economy, the character of castes change:

> they cease to be exclusive occupational, commensal or administrative units, lose their hereditary differential rights in the produce of village lands and their economic and ritual interdependence, and (in the case of lower castes) tend either to challenge or to disregard the rules of ritual rank.

> (Gough 1960: 13)

The last point is most revealing to understand Gough's argument: the changing relations in the working relations dissolve the straightjacket of caste and create new social units, which are defined by their relationship to the modes of production and most importantly enable the peasant to increase resistance against the dominant castes. But Gough combines a historical with an ethnographic approach by dealing with social and economical changes spanning from AD 850 until the late twentieth century. She puts a special emphasis on the time of colonial rule, which was as she shows, interrupted by violent and non-violent peasant revolts against the dominant groups. Gough states that resistance against landlords and dominant castes preceded Independence for a long time (Gough 1981). She further argues that caste becomes an important factor in class-based struggles, showing how the communist movement – which drew mostly on the Adi-Dravida movement and was associated with the Dalit communities (namely the Pallar and Paraiyar) – became as a result unattractive to caste Hindus, for it was thought to represent the lower castes and thereby lost its original ideal to form a united class-based movement (Gough 1989).

Moffatt, Deliège and Mosse on 'untouchability'

Through questioning whether high and low castes share the ideology of hierarchy or not, Gough's study touches already on the debate between Michael Moffatt and Robert Deliège. Moffatt's study, *An Untouchable Community in South India: Structure and Consensus* (1979) is based on fieldwork in a village in the Chingleput district, referred to in the study as Endavur. This village comprises 32 per cent 'untouchables' where 92 per cent are Paraiyar. From his ethnography we learn that the 'untouchables' are captured in a kind of feudal relation with the dominant Reddiyar caste, which owns the land and controls the labour. Moffatt does not focus however on the Paraiyars' relationship to the dominant castes, but instead on the internal social fabric of the low castes and the relationship of the different segments and sub-castes. One of his main findings is the complexity of the untouchable community: Endavur shows a huge variety of untouchable sub-castes, organized according to status and purity, which practice an interrelationship of services and transactions very similar to the *jajmani* order of the caste-Hindu villages. The Paraiyar, viewed by caste Hindus as the most bottom-down caste segment in the society as a whole, have their own 'untouchables' who perform rituals and services, such as digging graves or removing menstrual blood – which the Paraiyar have to do traditionally in turn for the higher castes. Here is anchored the first of Moffatt's arguments: the 'untouchables' replicate the social order of the 'global village culture' (1979: 3). They share the values of those high caste Hindus from whom they experience oppression and seclusion. This leads to his second important point: there is a general consensus among these low status groups about the general principles of purity and pollution, status and hierarchy. Moffatt (1979: 98) confirms Dumont's argument of a pan-Indian shared value system. His study offers overall a brilliant ethnographic approach by giving thorough descriptions of village life and the transactions between low status individuals and groups.

Deliège's study *The Untouchables of India* (1990) portrays an 'untouchable' settlement in the Ramnad district and argues directly against Moffatt's thesis of replication. Deliège's study is located in a *ceri* populated mainly by Pallar, Christian Paraiyar and Hindu Paraiyar, and like Moffatt, he places emphasis on the relations among and within the low-status groups and their segments. He comes to a different conclusion from Moffatt: his data show that the different castes do not have a lot of interdependence. Their relationships cannot be described as hierarchical, for they rather seem to live parallel to each other, which allows for relationships based on equality. Moreover, his findings show that within these low caste groups there is a general sense of egalitarianism, contrary to Moffatt's claimed replication of the hierarchical Hindu social structure. Far from sharing the ideology of suppression, the low castes have a separate subculture, and in their own ways resent, resist and revolt against the higher castes' claims of superiority (Deliège 1990). This debate was later joined by David Mosse, who, based on his fieldwork in Alapuram in the Ramnad district, argued with Moffatt for a replicatory order among 'untouchables', which is based on 'unequal reciprocal relationships of dominance', on the necessary provision of ritual services, on the caste honours structure of the religious institutions and on the expression of social proximity and distance (Mosse and Deliège 1994: 458). In his reply Deliège acknowledged the existence of divisions among Harijans, but did not accept this as a proof of the general 'operation of an ideology of purity and impurity' or a 'timeless "global Indian village culture"' (Mosse and Deliège 1994: 460) and argued that hierarchical inter-caste relations among 'untouchables' might well be a very recent phenomena, originating from new access to resources and migration (Mosse and Deliège 1994: 460).

Mines, Kapadia and Gorringe on individuality

Mattison Mines' *Public Faces, Private Voices: Community and Individuality in South India* (1994) takes a position against Dumont's hierarchical imperative and rejects the construction of 'the Indian' as the antithesis to the Western person and offers instead a 'theory of Tamil individuality' which mainly states that:

> Tamils do recognize individuality as an essential feature of ordinary life; that individuality lies at the crux of a Tamil's sense of self, as well as his or her sense of others; and that individuality plays a vital role in civic life. Nonetheless, Tamil individuality is distinct in several respects from Western notions of the individual.
>
> (Mines 1994: 2)

His findings are based on an investigation of expressions of individuality in public life, such as the role of public leaders and their clients. He shows how the highly personalized structure of leadership provides a platform where individuals can negotiate status and image. Mines' distinction into exterior or public lives on the one hand, which reflect a person's public performance, and interior or private lives on the other hand, which deal with an individual's aspirations and senses of self, allows for an analysis of individuality which includes structure and agency. He further stresses the Tamil notion of individual responsibility that demands that a person sticks to the social norms and works as one of the key qualities to provide a distinction between individuals and thereby allows for status change. Though not really deconstructing Dumont's thesis of hierarchy and status, Mines broadens the discussion by adding a different angle and perspective: a person's concept of self and the search for expressions of individuality.

Karin Kapadia also adds a different angle through her comparative study, *Siva and her Sisters* (1998), on five castes in a village complex in the Thanjavur district. This study looks at the interplay of factors relating to caste, class, kinship and gender in a village setting characterized by new educational and economical opportunities as well as by migration to urban areas. The study focuses on women mainly of low caste groups and investigates their strategies of resistance against the multiple forms of dominance they are subjected to as well as their own representations of themselves. Kapadia argues in a similar manner to Deliège, saying that the low caste women and men "create for themselves a normative world in which they have dignity, self respect and power" (1998: 5) and further that there is a sharp dichotomy between Brahmin (upper caste) values and Tamil (non-Brahmin/lower caste values) (1998: 5), thus resenting the model of consensus as advertised by Dumont and Moffatt. Kapadia argues along the lines of critical feminist theory; she sees caste and class as constructed through gender and in this manner adds a new dimension to the former, rather androcentric ethnographic studies of the area. Kapadia's analysis of the kinship system from the woman's point of view is revealing in how it moves away from a structuralist perspective of alliance and consanguinity and stresses the actor-centred relations as well as the actual position of a woman that emerges through marriage and reproduction. Status, for Kapadia, is much more than a result or absence of purity; rather it is a conglomeration of different factors. She doesn't see status grounded in purity and caste as being replaced by class-based values, but rather shows how different factors interact and lead to new, unexpected social formations and hierarchies. She argues that non-Brahmin groups moving away from the traditional close-kin marriage to marriage with strangers, in combination with a high dowry, led to a devaluation of the status of women. Processes of sanscritization, geared at increasing caste status, have had a direct impact on women in that they were more closely guarded and kept from working outside of the house. This fact, in combination with migration into the cities and towns where women cannot work in the agricultural sector as untrained labourers anymore, has further weakened the autonomy of women and strengthened the power of men as providers.

Interestingly, from her data it evolves that the status and autonomy of women is at its highest in the lower castes, where female fertility is also highly valued and moreover ritually marked. Kapadia dissolves the concept of status from a purely caste- and class-determined perspective by bringing gender and kinship relations into the equation, thereby showing that certain groups, i.e. women, within the lower castes might have a relatively higher status within their own strata than women of the higher castes.

Finally, we would like to look at a more recent study by Hugo Gorringe, *Untouchable Citizens: The Dalit Panthers and Democratisation in Tamilnadu* (2005), which investigates caste and status in the light of the political movements of low status groups. His research on processes of democratization and social movements, especially the Liberation Panthers (a movement that started from Madurai but soon became installed in wider Tamil Nadu), investigates the implications of the socio-political category Dalit, which is used for the formerly 'untouchable' castes. Dalit movements bank on the uniting power of the term by mobilizing the masses for a common political goal. Caste-based identities, however, are still strong: the symbolical, practical and material substance of caste is still very much prevalent in the interaction of members of different status groups. Marginalized 'untouchable' communities such as the Paraiyar or Chakkiliar had to fight their way into politics against the prejudices of the higher castes represented in the Tamil movements relying on a Dravidian identity.

Paradoxically, the Liberation Panther movement propagates a caste-free democratic society and at the same time mobilizes and organizes itself on the basis of caste, kinship and patronage, working rather as a network than a bounded group. The Liberation panthers "thus face a Hobson's choice between a protectionist Tamil identity in alliance with the PMK [Paatali Makkan Katchi, a working class party – author's note] whose adherents are opposed to Dalit uplift, and a "Dalit" identity that continues to be a proxy for "untouchable"" (Gorringe 2009: 170). Another important aspect Gorringe's study touches is the question of whether Dalits share the hegemonic ideology of the higher castes. Unlike Moffatt's and Deliège's rather generalizing positions, Gorringe's analysis is much more complex, showing that Dalits are aware that voicing resistance might lead to very unpleasant consequences, which makes it difficult to evaluate the actual degree of acceptance or resistance. Conversely, he argues that there are huge differences in the ways Dalits perceive of their position, depending on factors such as age, the rural/urban divide or education.

Other themes and approaches

There are, of course, a number of commendable ethnographies which are omitted here, mainly because they do not deal primarily with status and hierarchy, such as Isabelle Nabokov's *Religion against the Self: An Ethnography on Tamil Rituals* (2000) on those Tamil rituals that mediate the transgression between humans and supernatural beings, often the deceased relatives. Nabokov investigates possession, exorcism and counter-sorcery showing how demons and ghosts inflict themselves in different ways on men and women, and how the rituals around these inflictions facilitate the social integration of individuals, help them to deal with feelings of grief and further transform their identities. Another important study is Margaret Trawick's ethnography *Notes on Love in a Tamil Family* (1990), a detailed in-depth study on the ambiguities of those emotions and social bonds that cement kinship ties and the family structure. The strength and the weakness of Trawick's work is the narrow focus: the monograph focuses exclusively on one single Tamil extended family where she lived for more than a year, and there is no comparative material to enable the reader to get a broader picture. Valentine Daniel's study, *Fluid Signs. Becoming a Person the Tamil Way* (1984), is a thorough study of Tamil emic categories and concepts and personhood. He explains personhood with the notions of 'substance' and 'transaction' and by processes of transactions between humans and humans, humans and land, and humans and substances. He unpacks Tamil central categories, such as the *uur*, the land a person originates from and lives on, or the notion of the *kunam*, the qualities of people and things that are inherent in everything, and shows how relations and qualities are always in flow and never fixed. It depends largely on the degree of compatibility as to what these transactions effectuate. The eminent role of the *maman* (the mother's brother) and the affinal relatives is analysed by Antony Good in his monograph *The Female Bridegroom* (1991). He shows with very well presented ethnographic material on mainly puberty rituals and wedding ceremonies how the relations between brother and sister and the maternal uncle and his nieces and nephews are characterized by mutual obligations and exchanges, which lead to special emotional and economic ties. The Tamil prefer cross-cousin marriage and so the *maman* and his wife are always potential parents-in-law. They further play an important part in the puberty ritual, which symbolizes female fertility. Christopher Fuller's book *The Renewal of the Priesthood: Modernity and Traditionalism in a South Indian Temple* (2003) is a study on the changing lives of the priests of one of the largest temples in India, the Meenaksi-Sundaresvara Tirrukoyil, in Madurai. Fuller describes how what can be broadly termed processes of modernity (which included the involvement of the state and the political parties into the organization of the temple) have impacted on the organization and running of the temple since the 1970s. A growing traditionalism of the temple's priesthood was accompanied by practices that are seen as characteristic of modernity, for example priestly education was moved to the universities, and the priests' power and autonomy was strengthened by state law and bureaucracy. This study shows how this "apparently paradoxical amalgam" (Fuller 2003: 152) of tradition and modernity shapes religion as well as the institution of the temple in today's Tamil Nadu.

Finally, we would like to mention Lukas Werth's study, titled *Von Göttinnen und ihren Menschen. Die Vagri, Vaganten Südindiens* (1996), about the Vagri, a formerly peripatetic community that migrated to Tamil Nadu from Gujarath a few hundred years ago. The Vagri earn their living by hunting, trade of petty wares and folk healing. The community is divided into moieties, and affinal relations are expressed and mirrored in the animal sacrifices, which men have to perform in order to pacify and satisfy their respective house goddesses. Werth argues that although the Vagri belong to Tamil society, they are not integrated in the caste hierarchy on the basis of purity and pollution and exchange of services like other low castes. Even though they are considered as extremely impure, due to their lifestyle and their buffalo sacrifices, they are not on a par with the 'untouchables'.

The Nilgiri region

The debates on caste, class and gender, on reduplication, resistance and individuality and on status, purity and hierarchy are only partly reflected in the anthropological writings on the Nilgiris. The landscape, the social formation and the focus of anthropological writing clearly differs from what has been discussed above. The Nilgiris are obviously different, but at the same time clearly linked to the societies in the plains.

Also known as the 'Blue Mountains' (nil = blue; giri = hill), they rise up steeply from the surrounding plains, up to a plateau about 1,800 to 2,000 metres above sea level. In terms of administration, these hills today make up the Nilgiris District, a rather small area of 2,549 square kilometres, located in the most western part of Tamil Nadu at the borders with Kerala and Karnataka. In spite of its small size the region is rather famous. Among middle-class Indians the short form of the district capital 'Ooty' – from Ootacamund – stands for a Hill Station with a pleasant cool climate, lush green forests and colonial houses, giving it a reputation as a preferred holiday destination. The landscape features in countless Indian movies, often as a backdrop for dance scenes. Documentaries distributed worldwide tell about the unique flora, fauna and local people, or about the toy train leading up to Ooty, once the summer residence of the Madras Presidency administration.

In the nineteenth century, a great number of ethnographic descriptions were published, often by Europeans who lived a professional or retired life in Ooty. One of the best monographs was authored by a priest from the Basel Mission, J. F. Metz (1864), and one of the more famous visitors to the Hills was Sir Richard Burton (1851). The descriptions are coloured by their times. Dane Kennedy (1996: 86) observed that 'hill tribes' living close to British Hill stations in various parts of India were described in a similar manner, usually as noble savages – a role ascribed to the Todas in the Nilgiri. Most sources, including the first District Manual of the region, mention several 'tribes' (Grigg 1880: 180) or 'communities' (Francis 1908): 'the Badagas (cultivators), Kotas (artisans and musicians) and Todas (graziers)' as inhabitants of the plateau. These formerly three small groups differ clearly in size. Today, there are less than 2,000 Kota, more than 1,000 Toda, and an estimated 200,000 Badaga (or even more), forming a rather substantial community. The size of a population is always a political statement because claims are linked to potential voters. Other sections of the local society immigrated in the late nineteenth century as plantation labourers, or settled as service groups in local bazaars or taluk headquarters. A rather large group is known as 'Ceylon repatriates', who had to leave Sri Lanka as a result of Indo-Ceylon agreements after Independence (Heidemann 1997). The total population living in the district was – according to the Census 2001 – 762,141 people. Among the communities living on the slopes of the hills and in the Moyar basin north of the Nilgiri are the Kasuva, Sholega, Irula and Kurumba, the latter two described as 'forest tribes' (Francis 1908: 128; see also Zvelebil 1988, 2001). Kapp and Hockings (1989) distinguish seven different Kurumba groups. Contemporary ethnographers working on the Kurumbas are Ulrich Demmer (2007), who has worked on the social system and on ritual healing, and Nurit Bird-David (1999) with a focus on the hunter-gatherer discourse. Due to lack of space, we will not go into further detail.

Ethnographic research in the Nilgiri influenced the theoretical debates in anthropology and also had an impact on its methods. The complex social system of the Todas gained wide attention. They were vegetarian herders, lived partly mobile lives in rather small units and were divided into two moieties (or endogamous groups). Polyandry was the common rule, but paternity was a different matter, since institutionalized relationships with a partner of the opposite sex from the other moiety (and only from the other moiety) were permitted. The social father was chosen among the husbands, i.e. one of the biological brothers, and confirmed with a bow-and-arrow ceremony (Walker 1986: 190–92). In short, Todas had much to offer to anthropological theory-building. W. H. R. Rivers (1906) developed the genealogical method with his Toda material and contributed to their lasting fame. In the 1930s, the famous linguist M. B. Emeneau (1971) conducted fieldwork in the hills and proved the close link of the Toda language with other Dravidian languages. Speculations about Toda, as huge, bearded men with Roman togas, as descendants of Europeans, maybe soldiers of Alexander the Great, has lost ground. David Mandelbaum, an anthropologist and colleague of Emeneau at Berkeley, followed the same line of argument: the people of the Nilgiri "are clearly part of the culture of South India and of the civilization of India" (1989: 19).

In spite of the vast amount of literature, there are only a few anthropologists who conducted long-term fieldwork on the plateau.[3] Paul Hockings, the dean of Niligiri anthropologists, has published several monographs, including a bibliography (1978), two important Nilgiri readers (1989, 1997), and his Nilgiri Encyclopaedia, which is currently in print. His approach is descriptive and encyclopaedic; he combines history, linguistic and social anthropology and has contributed valuable materials on ethnography and social change. His main ethnography is based on fieldwork and contains a history of the Badaga, a short account of all Badaga sub-groups and extensive chapters on modern changes (Hockings 1980). Anthony Walker began – like Hockings – his life-long engagement with the Blue Mountains in the early 1960s, compiling his enormous amount of data into his opus magnum, *The Toda of South India – A New Look* (1986). His detailed description of the dairy cult, life-cycle rituals, social organization and 'Changing Toda World 1819–1981' (1986: chapter 8) emphasizes unique institutions, while at the same time stressing the structural parallels with the South Indian ethnographic context. In the 1980s, Frank Heidemann (2006, 2010) took up his work on the religion and politics of the Badaga society and a few years later Richard Kent Wolf commenced his fieldwork on the Kota community. Wolf's thick description focuses on Kota ceremonies and music, especially on drumming, and develops a theory of 'space times' and 'anchorpoints', spacio-temporal forms of thought and identity. In great detail, Wolf discusses the multiple views and experiences of time and space, which are not experienced as contradictions, but form the basis for Kota timespace (Wolf 2005).

Debates on status and purity

If we consider ritual purity as the prime marker of status, as Louis Dumont suggests, we find obvious parallels in the Nilgiris. Todas are vegetarians and rank high in status. Internally their priestly moiety obtains a higher status than the other. Among the Badagas the internal hierarchy places Lingayats – vegetarians and priests – above the other Badaga groups. Like Toda priests, Lingayats marry among themselves. Kotas do not have endogamous units but are organized into three exogamous groups, usually living in separate rows of houses in each village. The kinship system of the Kurumba groups is less explicit, boundaries are blurred, and lineages are hardly considered. However, major rules of South Indian kinship are shared by all communities: parallel cousins are classified as siblings; cross-cousins form potential marriage partners. Kinship connects and divides sections of each local society. Divisions are underlined by territorial cluster, and a hierarchy is formed on the basis of diet and professional occupation. This, we must keep in mind, is the classificatory system, an ideal form based on norms and ideas – like anywhere in India. In the past and in the present, these systems of classification did not constitute strong restrictions on the economic field. Once we found hunters among the Badagas while Kotas kept cows and were engaged in farming. Today some Kurumbas have government jobs and Todas cultivate. The question is now whether these empirical findings contradict the normative order.

The previously mentioned first core question by Moffatt and Deliège is about the consensus of the ritual order. Does the lower section of society reject the local hierarchy and ritual principles? A look at drumming – classified as a performance of low status groups – can offer a partial answer. Kotas used to play music for Badagas and Todas; drums and flutes were the main instruments. The musicians were paid for the task; they were the clients. Richard Wolf is explicit that it 'would be a mistake to assume that the Kotas accepted inferior ranking' (Wolf 2005: 26). However, they stopped playing music in the 1930s in most Badaga villages for exactly this reason. It might be speculated to what extent the system of purity entered the hills along with other migrants, or whether other factors contributed to the boycott. In my view, the fact that they stopped playing drums underlines the idea of low status ascribed to drumming. Today, Kurumbas (partly in team with Irulas) play music at Badaga festivals on the eastern plateau. They come to the Badaga villages, perform rituals, play music, bargain for their honorarium and receive the negotiated amount of cash. But at times, Badagas take the instruments and play the drums without having the slightest sense of polluting themselves. Touching the drums with their hands does not inflict any pollution at all. The lower status results from a configuration of a number of facts like playing for others, being clients and touching leather.

In various ways Kurumbas claim higher status, but – unlike Kotas – they continue to drum. They demand higher remuneration for their services and insist on equal treatment at festival time. They refuse to eat in separate places after the main meal is taken by the hosts. Today they eat the same food at the same place at the same time as Badagas. Another way of status negotiation refers to the roles and privileges in the ritual. In a few villages, Kurumbas demanded to participate in fire walking, from which they were previously banned. Today they walk on the fire, but Badagas make it clear that Kurumbas are the last to walk. Kurumba leaders say that they avoid going *to* Badaga villages to ask for an assignment, but wait for the villagers to come to their hamlet. Movement in time and space indicates status; lower status positions have to go to higher positions. In other words, the system of purity is a matter of negotiation, local norms and rules are subject to disagreement and to change. What Moffatt (1979: 304) said about the 'untouchables' and underprivileged in general holds true in the Nilgiris: among the most suppressed are the strongest believers in the system. Kurumba reject their status and use the symbolic system for status elevation, not unlike the process of sanscritization.

Verbal rejection of the ritual order and of a purity-based hierarchy is found in all sections of society. Commenting on the priestly and vegetarian section of society, be it in the local or in the national context, successful entrepreneurs, professionals or politicians make fun of the system in asking whether observing a vegetarian diet is considered an achievement in Europe? The ritual system does not allow an easy escape. Let us take up a hypothetical case. If a low status group rejects the idea of hierarchically ordered endogamous groups, actors are caught in contradictions. In the case of taking a bride from a higher status, they will cause direct – most likely violent – action from the bride-givers. In the case of marrying from a lower status, they will lose status. The third possibility, offering a bride to a lower status group, will cause problems to the bridegroom or he will be rejected right away. We find ethnographic evidence for all these possibilities, even though these are rare exceptions. Almost all actors from all sections of society like to marry their daughters or sisters to persons of equal status. The principles of Hindu society around the idea of ritual purity are shared knowledge. The norms deriving from these principles constitute a battlefield for status bargaining. The impact of the ritual system overshadows the question whether the actors believe in the system or not.

Egalitarian ideologies

In the time of pre-colonial Nilgiris, there were no palaces, no towns, no markets, no Brahmins and no script. Compared to the social setting in Tamil villages, the Nilgiri society appeared much more egalitarian. There were no separate wells for different status groups and all could touch each other. Today, local leaders of all communities claim to represent a rather egalitarian group with equal status for all members, liberties for women including mobility and a chance for re-marriage, education for both sexes and freedom of speech for everyone. There is also no professional group of priests and everyone can become a headman. This rhetoric joins hands with the Indian constitution and ideas of modernity. As a matter of fact, Nilgiri society – like caste society in the plains – cannot be explained by the Dumontian notion of purity alone. The hierarchy among two brothers is obscured if the younger is more successful in his professional life. At home and at village rituals, the elder might receive respect from his younger brother, but in the spheres of modernity, in government offices and on public stages – or even in private – there is a certain ambivalence, often resulting in mutual respect. In such cases, there is no fixed norm or rule. Actors have to choose their system of reference, which is locally distinguished as 'modern' or 'traditional' (Heidemann 2006: 39–48). There is thus much room for individual choice.

Public debates, however, aim at restricting choices and including the individual in a common framework of action. A few years ago, Badagas – in the past supporters of the Congress (I) Party – did not achieve getting the 'ticket' (a permission to canvass as a candidate for a political party) and a Tamil person became the party's candidate. Local leaders tried for a 'ticket' from other parties and expected all Badaga to vote for a Badaga candidate, regardless of the political party. They claimed 'community first' and expected all to join this slogan. Others insisted on their party loyalty and wanted to vote as usual, while a minority claimed – in the name of democracy – their free choice. Another area that demonstrates the tension between structure and agency, or between normative rules and individual choice, becomes evident in the context of marriage arrangements. In many cases the solution turns out to be a kind of marriage arrangement *ex post*, i.e. two partners join on the basis of their affection and in line with marriage rules, and parents fulfil their role in fixing the alliance according to community rules.

Conclusion

Caste and status are the prevalent themes in the anthropology on Tamil Nadu, moreover they linger largely in the political discourse and in the public media. The issues of caste, status, Dravidian versus non-Dravidian identity, gender and class have been echoed in the anthropological writings. The different studies discussed here mirror the theoretical and thematic foci of the respective time periods they come from. However, there is no doubt that status and 'untouchability' are the core themes in Tamil Nadu. According to Mattison Mines, individualism and egalitarian values shape identity and interaction in South India. In our view, complex interactions cannot be understood by excluding the Dumontian model of hierarchy or the egalitarian claim of the Indian constitution. For more than six decades, Indian citizens have experienced elections at local, regional and national levels; they have learnt that 'untouchability' is a crime and that women and men enjoy the same rights. Any debate within the family, the village or the community includes arguments of both models – as the case studies of voting for a party or choosing a bride have illustrated. The same applies for temple entries or labour contracts. In many contexts, an equal status of two people towards an institution, law or God may be agreed on. At the same time, mutual status positions, i.e. face to face, remain contested. Heidemann (2010) has argued that an unclear hierarchy may lead to the avoidance of status evaluations. This, however, brings about an absence of hierarchy, but is not to be confused with the European notion of equality.

The concept of dual sovereignty (Needham 1980) offers a partial answer to unclear status positions. The central claim of this concept is that the fundamental distinction of status and power leads to a twin hierarchy and to two peak positions in the hierarchical system. At the top of the hierarchy, we find therefore two positions: in the *varna* model Brahmins stand for status, Kshatriyas for power; in the Nilgiris respectively Todas and Badagas, and in the villages priests and headmen. This system of dual sovereignty is translated into social action: in village festivals, priest and headman avoid status evaluation and act in a parallel mode. They lead the processions – shoulder to shoulder – and, if necessary, they find a way to divide responsibilities. The headman may open the temple with his key, and the priest is the first to enter. Heidemann (2006) argues that the concept of dual sovereignty offers a suitable interpretation for local hierarchies and for the relationship of 'tradition' (in Badaga *akala* for status) and 'modernity' (*ikala* for power). Agency, i.e. debates on the appropriate system of reference (for elections, for marriages, for ritual procedures, etc.), unfolds against the backdrop of larger concepts. In this sense, the anthropology of Tamil Nadu is a discipline of small places and larger issues.

Notes

1 Tamil Nadu Government, Department of Evaluation and Applied Research, *Economic Appraisal 2005–2006*.
2 The difference between Dravidian and Aryan refers originally to the two different language families, but was then used to refer to supposedly different ethnic groups and different cultures.
3 Other important contributions to our understanding of Nilgiri society come from Gunnel Cederlöf (History), Dieter B. Kapp (Indology), Bill Noble (Geography), Christiane Pilot-Raichoor (Linguistics), Deborah Sutton (History) and Allan Zagarell (Archeology).

References

Béteille, A. (1965) *Caste, Class and Power: Changing Patterns of Stratification in a Tanjore Village.* Berkeley: University of California Press.
Bird-David, N. (1999) Personhood, Environment, and Relational Epistemology, *Current Anthropology*, 40(1): 67–91.
Burton, R. F. (1851) *Goa, and the Blue Mountains, or Six Months of Sick Leave.* London: Richard Bentley.
Daniel, V. (1984) *Fluid Signs: Being a Person the Tamil Way.* Berkeley: University of California Press.
Deliège, R. (1990) *The Untouchables of India.* Oxford: Oxford University Press.
——(1997 [1988]) *The World of the Untouchables: Paraiyars of Tamil Nadu.* Delhi: Oxford University Press.

Demmer, U. (2007) 'The Power of Rhetoric. Dialogue and Dynamic Persuasion in Healing Rituals of a South Indian Community' in U. Demmer and M. Gaenzle (eds), *The Power of Discourse in Ritual Performances*. Berlin: Lit Verlag.

*Dirks, N. B. (1987) *The Hollow Crown: Ethnohistory of an Indian Kingdom*. Cambridge: Cambridge University Press.

*Dumont, L. (1957) *Une sous-caste de l'Inde du Sud: Organisation sociale et religion des Pramalai Kallar*. Paris-La Haye: Mouton.

——(1970) *Homo Hierarchicus: An Essay on the Caste System*. Chicago: University of Chicago Press.

Dumont, L., Moffatt, M. and Stern, A. (1986) *A South Indian Subcaste: Social Organization and Religion of the Pramalai Kallar*. Delhi, Oxford: Oxford University Press.

Emeneau, M. B. (1971) *Toda Songs*. Oxford: Clarendon Press.

Francis, W. (1908) *The Nilgiris: Madras District Ga: Modernity and Traditionalism in a South Indian Temple*. Princeton: Princeton University Press.

Good, A. (1991) *The Female Bridegroom: A Comparative Study of Life-Crisis Rituals in South India and Sri Lanka*. Oxford: Clarendon Press.

*Gorringe, H. (2005) *Untouchable Citizens, The Dalit Panthers and Democratisation in Tamilnadu*. New Delhi: Sage.

——(2009) 'Becoming a Dalit Panther' in D. Gellner (ed.), *Ethnic Activism and Civil Society in South Asia*. New Delhi: Sage, pp. 145–74.

Gough, K. (1960) 'Caste in a Tanjore village' in E. Leach (ed.), *Aspects of Caste in South India, Ceylon and North-West Pakistan*. Cambridge: Cambridge University Press.

——(1981) *Rural Society in Southeast India*. Cambridge: Cambridge University Press.

——(1989) *Rural Change in Southeast India, 1950s–1980s*. Delhi: Oxford University Press

Grigg, H. B. (ed.) (1880) *A Manual of the Nilagiri District in the Madras Presidency*: Madras: Government Press.

Heidemann, F. (1997) 'Immigrant Labour and Local Networks in the Nilgiris' in P. Hockings (ed.), *Blue Mountains Revisited: Cultural Studies on the Nilgiri Hills*. New Delhi: Oxford University Press, pp. 148–63.

——(2006) *Akka Bakka. Religion, Politik und duale Souveränität der Badaga in den Nilgiri Südindiens*. Berlin: Lit Verlag.

——(2010) 'The Priest and the Village Headman. Dual Sovereignty in the Nilgiri Hills' in P. Berger; R. Hardenberg, E. Kattner and M. Prager (eds), *The Anthropology of Values. Essays in Honor of Georg Pfeffer*. Delhi: Pearson, pp. 104–19.

Hockings, P. (1978) *A Bibliography for the Nilgiri Hills of Southern India*, Revised Edition. New Haven, CT: Human Relation Area Files.

——(1980) *Ancient Hindu Refugees: Badaga Social History 1550–1975*. New Delhi: Vikas.

*——(ed.) (1989) *Blue Mountains: The Ethnography and Biogeography of a South Indian Region*. Delhi, Oxford University Press.

*——(ed.) (1997) *Blue Mountains Revisited: Cultural Studies on the Nilgiri Hills*. Delhi: Oxford University Press.

*Kapadia, K. (1998) *Siva and her Sisters: Gender, Caste and Class in South India*. San Francisco: Westview Press.

——(1999) 'Gender ideologies and the formation of rural industrial classes in South India today', *Contributions to Indian Sociology* (NS) 33, pp. 329–52.

Kapp, D. and Hockings P. (1989) 'The Kurumba Tribes' in P. Hockings (ed.), *Blue Mountains: The Ethnography and Biogeography of a South Indian Region*. Delhi: Oxford University Press.

Kennedy, D. (1996) *The Magic Mountains: Hill Stations and the British Raj*. Berkeley: University of California Press.

Mandelbaum, D. G. (1989) 'The Nilgiris as a Region' in P. Hockings (ed.), *Blue Mountains: The Ethnography and Biogeography of a South Indian Region*. Delhi: Oxford University Press.

Metz, J. F. (1864) *The Tribes Inhabiting the Neilgherry Hills: Their Social Customs and Religious Rites*. Mangalore: Basel Mission Press.

*Mines, M. (1994) *Public Faces, Private Voices: Community and Individuality in South India.* Berkeley, London: University of California Press.

*Moffatt, M. (1979) *An Untouchable Community in South India: Structure and Consensus.* Princeton: Princeton University Press.

Mosse, D. and Deliège, R. (1994) 'Replication and Consensus Among Indian Untouchable (Harijan) Castes', *Man*, New Series, 29(2): 457–61.

Nabokov, I. (2000) *Religion Against the Self: An Ethnography on Tamil Rituals.* Oxford: Oxford University Press.

Needham, R. (1980) *Reconnaissances.* Toronto: University of Toronto Press.

Rivers, W. H. R. (1906) *The Todas.* London: Macmillan.

Srinivas, M. N. (1962) *Caste in Modern India and Other Essays*: Bombay: Asia Publishing House.

Tamil Nadu Government Department of Evaluation and Applied Research (2007) *Economic Appraisal 2005–2006.* Chennai.

*Trawick, M. (1990) *Notes on Love in a Tamil Family.* Berkeley: University of California Press.

*Walker, A. (1986) *The Todas of South India – A New Look.* Delhi: Hindustan.

Werth, L. (1996) *Von Göttinnen und ihren Menschen: Die Vagri, Vaganten Südindiens.* Berlin: Das Arabische Buch.

Wolf, R. K. (2005) *The Black Cow's Footprint: Time, Space and Music in the Lives of the Kotas of South India.* Delhi: Permanent Black.

Zvelebil, K. V. (1988) *The Irulas of the Blue Mountains.* Syracuse: Maxwell School of Citizenship and Public Affairs, Syracuse University.

——(2001) *Nilgiri Areal Studies*, J. Vacek and J. Dvorak (eds), Charles University in Prague. Prague: Karolinum Press.

17 Uttarakhand and Himachal Pradesh

Ritual healing

William S. Sax

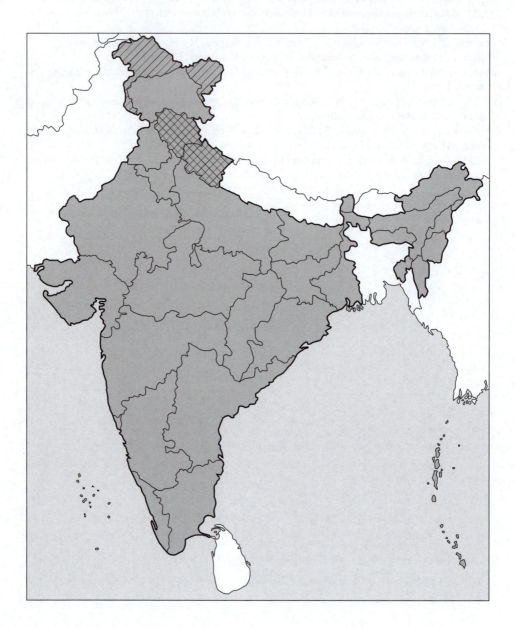

In the late 1990s, I conceived the idea of conducting research on the religion of the lowest castes of Uttarakhand, an Indian state in the Western Himalayas. I knew many Harijans[1], I had interviewed them, recorded and translated their songs, and visited them in their homes. But I had never done proper ethnographic research amongst them, never lived with them for long periods of time, never focused on their social life and customs, or asked them in detail about their lives. Now I thought that it was time to do so, and I wanted to focus on their religious practices.

Such were my general and rather vague ideas, but I did not know exactly how to pursue them. I only knew that certain low-caste men, the so-called "gurus," functioned as priests in a local religious cult that was very popular amongst the Harijans. I was trying to find out more about the cult, its rituals and other practices, but I wasn't having much success. I had taken a long bus trip to the village of one of the best-known local gurus (who had a rather dark reputation as a sorcerer), where I was told that he had gone to the fields. It was there that I found him, a hardy eighty-year-old man working alone, planting the spring crop. He was polite but reserved, first inviting me to accompany him during a ritual that he was going to perform a few days later, then rescinding the offer a few days after that, because it was a secret ritual. Perhaps a client had hired him to curse someone, and he didn't want to be seen engaging in such morally suspect activities.

Then I went to see a Harijan woman who occasionally acted as an oracle. Clients would come to her with their problems and she would go into a trance. Speaking through her, the god would diagnose the causes of the illness or misfortune, and prescribe a remedy, normally a ritual of some kind. She and her husband told me that they needed to sponsor a lengthy ritual, but they didn't have enough money to go and summon the guru, so I gave them 100 rupees for their travel costs, and they told me to return in a few days and we would make further plans. I came back several days later at the appointed time, but they had done nothing. So now I was not only irritated, but also rather worried. The invitation to see the secret ritual had been rescinded, the Harijan oracle had taken my money but done nothing, and several other leads had also failed to bring results. I was irritated, frustrated, and worried about my lack of progress. But as I left the oracle's village, I ran into a young man on the path. He called himself Satyeshvar Himalaya, but to the villagers he was just "Sacchu," and in the following months and years he became my major informant and a good friend. He charmed and delighted me with his ready smile and quick laughter, his irreverent stories about high-caste people, and his tales of adventures around India. He seemed to understand my difficulty immediately, and told me that he and his father were gurus themselves, and that they could arrange for me to see one of the rituals in which I was so interested. In the end, this led to my participation in the first of many exorcisms that I was to witness, a dramatic and exciting event that conveyed to me how very fascinating this topic was. Ritual healing became the focus of a series of research projects that I pursued for over a decade (e.g. Sax 2009), and during this time it became clear to me that in order to understand these rituals, I had to know a great deal about the history of the region, its geography, and especially its ethnography.

The Western Himalayas: a brief historical profile

There are few sources for the ancient history of this region. The so-called "Khasa Malla" kings ruled western Nepal and parts of present-day Uttarakhand (and Tibet) from the twelfth to the fifteenth century, but very little is known about them. The oldest well-attested rulers in present-day Uttarakhand were the Katyuris, who ruled from Joshimath from the seventh century but later shifted their capital to the Katyuri plain in present-day Kumaon, and subsequently were displaced by the Chand dynasty, which ruled until 1790 when it was defeated by the Gurkhas from Nepal. With its much rougher geography, Garhwal had been ruled since ancient times by a number of independent chieftains from small fortresses or *gadhi*, hence the name Garhwal, the "land of forts." These small chiefdoms—traditionally numbered at fifty-two—were first consolidated by Ajaypal Pamvar in the thirteenth century. Further north, in what is now Himachal Pradesh, there were a number of small Hindu kingdoms that came, in colonial times, to be known as the "Shimla Hill States." Some of these, like Rampur Bushahr, were very large, and derived considerable revenue from trade with Tibet. Though claims for the antiquity of this state are often made, there is no good evidence for its existence earlier than the late seventeenth century. Unlike the rulers of most hill states, the rulers of Rampur Bushahr did not claim descent from invaders from the plains, but rather that their ancestors came from the Sangla valley in Kinnaur, near the Tibetan border, a region about which very little has been written.

In 1793, the Gurkhas of Nepal defeated the last king of Kumaon and in 1804 they defeated the Pamvar dynasty of Garhwal and killed the reigning king Pradyuman Shah in a battle near Dehra Dun. In 1815 the British defeated the Gurkhas and reinstalled Pradyuman Shah's son, Sudarshan Shah, as king of the new state of Tehri Garhwal, which consisted of the western portion of the former kingdom, the British retaining control over the eastern portion. The Chand dynasty was not reinstated, but most of the kings in Himachal Pradesh were. Under colonial rule, Himachal Pradesh was part of the state of Punjab, while Uttarakhand was part of the United Provinces. In 1950, the United Provinces were re-named "Uttar Pradesh," while parts of Punjab were separately administered as the Union Territory of Himachal Pradesh. Himachal Pradesh became a state in 1971, and in 2000 the hill regions of Uttar Pradesh became a separate state called "Uttaranchal," whose name was subsequently changed to "Uttarakhand." One of the earliest and most comprehensive histories of Uttarakhand in a European language, and one upon which subsequent historians have relied rather heavily, is Edwin T. Atkinson's six-volume history, first published in 1882 and subsequently republished numerous times. Another important history was written by Ratudi (1980 [1928]), who was a minister in the court of the King of Garhwal, and whose book repeats a number of courtly traditions, not all of which are historically warranted. We are fortunate to have two sources on customary law, one by L. D. Joshi (1984 [1929]), a high-caste Brahman who had important contacts in London, and a rather more detailed one written by the low-caste barrister Panna Lal (1942 [1929]). The most comprehensive history of Uttarakhand is contained within the eight volumes published in Hindi by Shiva Prasad Dabaral between 1965 and 1978, and since then a number of shorter histories have been published, including Chetan Singh's excellent environmental history of the region (1998), Ramachandra Guha's highly influential book on a local environmental movement (1991), and histories by Handa (2002), Saklani (1987), and Kumar (2011). Radheshyam Bijlawan has written an excellent history of pastoral conflicts and local protest movements in the pre-colonial period in Hindi (2003), and more recently Aniket Alam (2007) has discussed the transition from pre-colonial to colonial rule in the region, describing a kind of pre-colonial "divine polity" that is consistent with Bijlawan's work and my own (Sax 2006a, 2006b). M. P. Joshi's edited volumes (1993–94) are a good source of information, and so is the magazine *Pahad*, published in Nainital by Shekhar Pathak, Girija Pande, and their associates.

Ethnography after Independence

The region is ethnically diverse, but the majority of its residents are Hindus who speak various local dialects of Hindi, and who have a relatively simple caste system. In addition, there are a number of scheduled tribes: the Bhoksha of the *tarai* region at the foot of the Himalayas, the Rajji in a tiny pocket of Kumaon, and along the Chinese border a number of Tibet-influenced groups who conducted trade between India and Tibet until the border was closed following the war with China in 1962. These tribes are particularly numerous in the districts of Kinnaur, and Lahul and Spiti in neighboring Himachal Pradesh, where they are mostly Buddhists, speak a number of Tibetan dialects, and constitute the majority community. There are also small numbers of Sikh and Muslim immigrants throughout the region, an even smaller number of Muslim communities scattered throughout the hills, and a group of nomadic, Gujarati-speaking Muslim buffalo-herders, the so-called "Van Gujjars."

Given its historical importance, ethnic diversity, and proximity to Delhi, it is surprising that so few good ethnographies from the region have been published; however there are some exceptions. S. D. Pant's classic (1935) study focuses on the economic practices of the "Bhotiya" tribes of Kumaon, and provides a great deal of ethnographic information as well. A more recent study of this group is by Vineeta Hoon (1996). The published outcome of Christoph Bergmann's doctoral research in the Darma valley is keenly awaited. Across the Kali River to the east lies Nepal, but despite the fact that this border is rather artificial, i.e. that cultural differences between the two regions are slight, little work has been done on the region. One of the few exceptions is Lecomte-Tilouine's edited volume (2009) dealing with religion and politics in far western Nepal. The Van Gujjars have been described in an ethnographic monograph by Gooch (1998), and the remaining tribes have occasionally been the subjects of scattered articles, primarily in Indian anthropological periodicals.

The dominant group in the region is the Hindus inhabiting the middle ranges of the Himalayas, usually called *Pahari* or "mountain people," both in Hindi and in the anthropological literature. One of the earliest ethnographic studies of this group was Rami Sanwal's brilliant (1976) historical study, which explained an important fact that has eluded many other ethnographers; namely the dual nature of the local caste system, where immigrants from the plains rank higher than indigenous groups, such that even immigrant Kshatriyas rank higher than indigenous Brahmans. Gerald Berreman's 1972 ethnography was one of the last to be written in the "comprehensive" style that attempted to cover all major aspects of social life (economics, politics, caste, religion, etc.). It advanced the thesis that members of the lower castes "see through" the caste system, and recognize that it is based upon economic exploitation (a thesis that Berreman shared with Kathleen Gough, amongst others). Recent ethnographies have been more problem-focused, with my own work for example focusing on local women's lives by means of the study of a goddess cult (Sax 1991); on notions of personhood as these are reflected in dramatizations of *Mahabharata* (Sax 2002), and on issues of social justice and ritual healing (Sax 2009). Karin Polit's monograph (2011) focuses on the concept of "honor" in the lives of Pahari women, and Capila (2002) uses folk songs as a resource for describing women's lives. In general, it can be said that the Pahari Hindus have a caste structure that is much simpler than that of the plains, along with very slight class differences, and characterized by "heteroprax" customs amongst the Brahmans, such as meat-eating and animal sacrifice. Alongside more conventional ethnographies, anthropologist Joseph Alter has written the quasi-biography of a local hunter (2000) that is of anthropological interest, and his brother, ethnomusicologist Andrew Alter, has produced a book on the sophisticated local art of folk drumming (2008).

The linguist Anoop Chandola has also written a book on folk drumming (1977), in which he advances his own linguistic theory.

There are a number of slight but noticeable differences in culture and language when one leaves the Ganges river basin and enters the Yamuna river basin. Anthropologists have been particularly interested in polyandry, which was once widespread in the Yamuna basin, and was the ostensible subject of D. N. Majumdar's 1962 classic *Himalayan Polyandry*. (In fact, the book was more about long-term civilizational change than polyandry.) This was the region that was ceded by the British to the King of Garhwal, when they re-instated him following the Gurkha wars in 1815, and Jean-Claude Galey has written a series of important articles (e.g. Galey 1986) pointing to the continuing importance of kingship, despite the absence of the king. Related systems are described by Alam (2007), and especially by the contributors to Sax (2006a). Ethnographic studies of Himachal Pradesh have been few. William Newell published a small number of papers on the Gaddis in the 1960s (e.g. Newell 1961). Parry wrote on Kangra social structure in 1979, and Sharma on women from the region in 1980. Vidal published a book on local religion in 1989, Erndl wrote a book on goddess-worship in 1993, and Conzelmann and Hesse published their contributions on marriage and gift exchange and the Khatri of Mandi respectively in 1996.

Ritual healing in Uttarakhand

None of these ethnographies concerned themselves with health and healing. In the case of the earlier books, this is partly due to the fact that they were written during a period when ethnographers sought to describe an entire culture between the covers of a single monograph. For the past few decades however, anthropologists in North America, the UK and France have increasingly written problem-focused ethnographies, and many of these have focused on topics in medical anthropology in South Asia. Indeed, at the time of publication of this article, medical anthropology remains the fastest-growing sub-field of the discipline. Still, there are few ethnographies on health-related issues in the region, with the exception of Berti (2001) and Sax (2009), both of whom have written about ritual healing. Much of this essay is drawn from the latter source.

Residents of Uttarakhand make use of a wide variety of healing techniques, including allopathic medicine (also called "biomedicine," "cosmopolitan medicine" and, in German, *Schulmedizin*) along with a number of alternative forms of medicine that are officially recognized and regulated by the Government of India: the ancient system of Ayurveda; homeopathy, which was invented in Germany but is very popular in urban India; Tibetan medicine in the predominantly Buddhist areas adjoining Ladakh and Tibet in Northeast Himachal Pradesh; the Greco-Muslim medical system known as Yunani-Tib, used mostly by Muslims in the few cities in the region; and domestic cures, temple worship, herbal remedies, bone-setting, and ritual healing of various kinds. Such "medical pluralism," where a number of healing systems exist side by side, is typical not only of India but also of most other countries, including for example the USA and Europe, where numerous forms of healing persist alongside the dominant system of allopathy.

My own research focused on one particular healing tradition, found in the upper Alakananda River basin, in which ideas of social justice, family unity, and illness are combined. Many local gods in the high-altitude districts of Garhwal are believed to be "gods of justice" who defend the weak and powerless against their oppressors by afflicting the latter with disease and misfortune. They also punish those responsible for family quarrels with illness, bad luck, and other problems. In order to end the god's affliction, the victim must apologize to whomever he has wronged, or resolve outstanding family conflicts by performing rituals jointly with his erstwhile enemies. Failure to do so traps the victim in an ever-deepening spiral of illness, suffering, and death. In what follows, I describe the healing tradition and its two major ritual specialists, the oracle and the exorcist, give an account of the "typical" ritual practices of each, and a description of some oracles and exorcists that I have known.

One noteworthy aspect of local healing traditions is that diagnosis and treatment are clearly separated. Diagnosis is typically done by an oracle, a person who is possessed by a local god or goddess and, while in a trance, answers the client's questions. In the anthropological literature on ritual healing, it is sometimes claimed that people visit ritual healers to avoid the expense of medical treatment. But in this region it is quite the opposite: ritual healing can be very expensive, requiring not only the purchase of sacrificial goats and other materials, but also the inviting and entertaining of a large number of family members and other guests, often for a number of days—to say nothing of the priest's fees. That is why people first go to medical professionals if they can, and visit an oracle only when an adequate diagnosis cannot be made, or when the treatment prescribed (usually pharmaceuticals) is not effective. Typical physical symptoms include sleeplessness, loss of appetite, diffuse pain, persistent headaches, and the like; however clients' complaints are not limited to "medical" matters. Repeated misfortune in business or farming, failure in school, family discord, and diffuse anxiety are other problems for which sufferers seek an explanation by visiting one or more oracles. Of course, there are problems for which a visit to the oracle is clearly the most rational first step: voices at night, ghostly appearances, disturbing dreams and visions, undesired "spirit possession," and so on.

The oracular consultation is not only a matter of supernatural revelation. It involves eliciting information, and it works best when it is a true conversation between oracle and client. This is why oracles frequently say such things as, "Answer properly! Say 'Yes' or 'No'!" In effect, this is an invitation, or a command, to the client to respond to the oracle's questions, to tell the oracle whether he or she is on the "right track."

Once the oracle has established that the affliction is caused by a supernatural being, then the client must find a guru. Both gurus and oracles come from all castes, but whereas oracles can be of either gender, gurus are exclusively male. The identity of the guru to be summoned is normally fixed, because whether the afflicting agent is a god or a demon or a ghost, it will have attached itself to the client in a particular place, and the responsibility for exorcizing and controlling such beings is distributed amongst a network of gurus, or exorcists, each of whom has responsibility for certain places. The afflicted person must then seek out the guru of that place, and engage his services. This is often a time-consuming and costly process, because the more successful gurus are very busy, especially during the "dark months" following the autumn harvest, which are particularly associated with such activities. Gurus perform many different kinds of rituals, and because this is an oral tradition with many different loci of power and authority, these rituals are not standardized.

The most frequently performed healing ritual is the *chal ki puja* or "worship of the *chal* demons," which is usually performed for women during their first few years of marriage, when they learn that they are afflicted by *chal* from their natal village and come back to supplicate them and return them to the soil from which they sprang. The ritual has many variations, but always involves transferring the *chal*, by means of mantras, offerings, and *jhar-phuk* ("sweeping" the body of the victim with feathers or plants while reciting mantras, a very widespread practice in North India) to a small figure made of barley flour. Later, the *chal* is again transferred into a chicken and/or a goat, which is sacrificed in return for the *chal* agreeing to stop afflicting the victim. The ritual is highly gendered: in the paradigm case, the daughter who has returned to her village is the only participating female, and when a goat is sacrificed, it is usually cooked and eaten by her "village brothers" in a festive atmosphere, who thus return the *chal* via their excrement to the soil from which it came.

Another common ritual is the *than ki puja*, a ritual (*puja*) for establishing or renewing the shrine (*than*) of a deity. Such rituals can be performed for many reasons: perhaps someone has had success in business or politics, and wishes to thank his family deity for it. Or maybe the family wishes to transfer the god from their old house to a new one, or perhaps they simply feel that it has been a long time since the shrine was renewed, and now is a good time to do so. Very often, a deity demands that a new shrine be built in return for bringing to an end the affliction s/he has caused. Whatever the reason, the *than ki puja* is fairly complex, and usually lasts a number of days.

Every *than* has a guru, with exclusive rights to conduct worship there because he or his predecessor built it. After the oracle tells the client that he or she must conduct a shrine ritual, then the client must locate the guru and find out what to do next. What must be purchased? What has to be collected? Will there be animal sacrifice? Should the shrine be inside or outside? The shrines of peaceful *devtas* are usually inside the house, while shrines of the more dangerous *devtas* are outdoors. The ritual has a number of steps, beginning with driving out negative energies and purifying the area where the shrine is to be constructed. After that, the guru leads the family in the *kas puja*, which resembles the fire sacrifice that is part of a conventional *samkalpa* ritual in this region. This is normally followed by the "dancing" of the *devtas*. "Dancing" is the term used for what one would call "possession" in English. The guru summons local gods by singing their songs, and they possess their human vehicles or "beasts," and dance. These sessions of music and dancing can be very dramatic and exciting: it is they more than anything else that draw a crowd (not only for the *kas puja*, but for all such public rituals). Not only do the *devtas* dance, they also speak, and during this part of the ritual there is much negotiation with them. Often the negotiation has to do with the shrine: the *devta* demands that a shrine be established, or says that he is happy (or unhappy) with his current one. Such negotiations are sometimes very prolonged, with tears and weeping, begging and threatening, on both sides.

Sessions of music and dancing may go on for days, with performances in the afternoon and again at night, and all of this culminates with the ritual that "establishes the shrine" (*than thapna*). The *than* itself has already been built according to measurements based on the body of the patron. A complicated ritual follows, involving mantras, a sacrificial fire, and many different kinds of offerings, the central purpose of which is to invite the main deity to come and take up residence in the shrine. Everything culminates with the sacrifice of further animals, normally decapitating them and spraying the blood into a pit in front of the shrine, which is the home of the deity's fierce and violent followers.

The ritual constitutes the sacrificial pit as a place of concentrated violence. Goats, chickens, and sometimes sheep or even pigs are sacrificed and their blood poured into the pit. Fish, crabs, spiders, worms, and other creatures are also sacrificed, especially to the dangerous *bahiyals* accompanying the god Bhairav. The idea is to attract these fierce beings with blood, to localize them in the pit, and to bind them there with spells and magic, so that their fierce and dangerous energy can later be used for the benefit of the client and his family. They can also be used for bloody revenge: people who feel that they have been the victim of injustice go there, remove the rock cover, and weep tears into the pit, calling upon the god to bring them justice and punish their oppressors. According to popular belief, this is typically done by women, especially low-caste women, who have been abused or mistreated in some way.

How does one become a guru? Some learn the tradition from their fathers, others desire the prestige of the gurus and the money they earn in fees, and aspire to become gurus themselves. But regardless of his motivation, a novice must seek out a guru who will teach him the mantras, songs, rituals, and other techniques, a process that can take years. Finally there comes a day when the novice feels he is ready to perform the *smashan ki puja*, the "ritual of the cremation ground." All the gurus I know tell me that they did this by going naked to the cremation ground (they all took one or several helpers who watched from a safe distance), where they summoned Masan, "king of the burning ground" in the middle of the night. Masan attempts all kinds of tricks to frighten the aspirant. Ghosts and wild animals appear, gale winds blow, there are noises, there is pleading from loved ones—but one must stay firmly inside the magic circle and not go anywhere. Shortly before dawn, Masan appears with his two queens, and they offer three bowls to the aspirant, who must choose from them. One of the bowls contains boiled rice, which indicates success. Another contains water, which is neutral. The third bowl contains meat, and if the aspirant chooses it, he will die. Evidently, none of my guru-collaborators had chosen the meat.

What kind of people become oracles? It is not usually a matter of choice. In fact, all the oracles I knew well had been compelled by a god or goddess to take on this burden. All of them claimed that they had resisted for a long time, but that ultimately the god had worn them down and forced them to be his or her vehicle, usually for a set number of years. One woman said she was "knocked down" by the god while working in the fields, and "punished" further by him until she acknowledged that she was his vehicle. A male oracle's daughter had run away when she was very young, and he was tortured by guilt and worry until the god helped him find her and bring her home, after which he agreed to be the god's oracle. One female oracle was of relatively high caste, well educated, politically active, and had travelled extensively throughout India. But after she was "chosen" by a goddess she began holding public consultations in which she was possessed. This embarrassed her male relatives, who tried to persuade her to stop. But she couldn't stop, because the goddess afflicted her when she did.

Whereas the oracles are defined by their patiency with respect to the gods, acting as mere containers for them, the gurus are defined by their agency. They summon the gods, praise them, negotiate with them, control, and even threaten them. Whether playing his drum, chanting a mantra, exorcizing a ghost, or sacrificing an animal, the *guru* must always be calm and self-assured; what the Germans (using a French word) would call *souverän*. Indeed, this is what the term "guru" means: not a spiritual master but rather a "master of the spirits." The guru may cause possession in others, but he himself is never possessed, and this simple fact is fundamental for what it means to be a guru. One of the uncanniest experiences I had during this research was when I saw a guru whom I knew well, possessed and writhing on the ground like a snake. But in this case he was sponsoring the worship of his own family deity. In other words, he was the client and not the guru, so there was no contradiction in his behavior.

The gurus have a difficult job. During several months of the year they constantly travel from one client to another, often going for days without sleep. Clients come from near and far with tales of suffering and need, begging the gurus to come to their aid. Everyday comforts like cooked food, a warm bed, and clean clothes are scarce. But the gurus love their work. Wandering from village to village over the steep mountain paths in the midst of winter, staying in the homes of different sorts of clients, even the desperately poor, while ministering to their spiritual needs—such things would hardly be attractive to most people, but for the gurus they represent freedom, adventure, and the thrill of the unknown.

Conclusion

The Central Himalayan states of Himachal Pradesh and Uttarakhand are ethnically diverse. Most of the residents are Hindus and speak local dialects of Hindi, and their caste system—in comparison to other regions—is less complex. There are a number of "tribes," both in the *tarai* region at the foot of the Himalayas and along the Chinese border, so-called "Bhotiyas." Those in the north are mostly Buddhist and speak Tibetan dialects. In sum, and despite the cultural complexity and the proximity to Delhi (and the spectacular Himalayan landscape), the region has been the subject of remarkably little ethnographic research. Moreover, despite the fact that medical anthropology continues to be one of the fastest growing sub-fields of anthropology, very few monographs on the topic have been written. Through my work on ritual healing, I hope to have contributed to filling both of these lacunae.

Notes

1   It is difficult to decide what to call these people. Nowadays, politically active members of the lowest castes usually call themselves Dalits (literally, "the oppressed"); however in Uttarakhand this term is little used, and such people normally refer to themselves as "Harijans." In this article I have followed their usage.

References

Alam, Aniket (2007) *Becoming India: Western Himalayas Under British Rule.* Cambridge: Cambridge University Press.

Alter, Andrew (2008) *Dancing with Devtās: Drums, Power and Possession in the Music of Garhwal, North India (SOAS Musicology Series).* Aldershot: Ashgate.

Alter, Joseph (2000) *Knowing Dil Das: Stories of a Himalayan Hunter.* Philadelphia: University of Pennsylvania Press.

Atkinson, Edwin T. (1974 [1882]) *Kumaon Hills: Its History, Geography and Anthropology with Reference to Garhwal and Nepal.* Delhi: Cosmo Publications. (First published in Allahabad under the title *The Himalayan Districts of the North Western Provinces of India.*)

*Berreman, Gerald D. (1972 [1963]) *Hindus of the Himalayas: Ethnography and Change.* Berkeley: University of California Press.

Berti, Daniela (2001) *La parole des dieux: Rituels de possession en Himalaya indien.* Paris: CNRS.

Bijlawan, Radheshyam (2003) *Madhya Himalaya Riyasat mem Gramin Janasangharsom ka Itihas (Riyasat Tehri Garhwal—Dhara and Dandak)* (1815–1949) (History of Village Warfare in a Central Himalayan Princely State [Rustling and Ceremonial Protest in the Princely State of Tehri Garhwal]) (1815–1949). Purola: Bijlawan Prakashan.

Capila, Anjali (2002) *Images of Women in the Folk Songs of Garhwal Himalayas: A Participatory Research.* New Delhi: Concept Publishing Company.

Chandola, Anoop (1977) *Folk Drumming in the Himalayas: A Linguistic Approach to Music.* New York: AMS Press.

Conzelmann, Elisabeth (1996) *Heirat, Gabe, Status: Kaste und Gesellschaft in Mandi.* Berlin: Das Arabische Buch.

Dabaral, Shiva Prasad (1965–78) (2022–2035 Vikrama). *Uttarakhand ka Itihas* (The history of Uttarakhand), eight vols. Dogada, Garhwal: Vir Gatha Prakashan.

Erndl, Kathleen M. (1993) *Victory to the Mother: The Hindu Goddess of Northwest India in Myth, Ritual, and Symbol.* New York: Oxford Univeristy Press.

Galey, Jean-Claude (1986) 'Totalite et hierarchie dans les sanctuaires royaux du Tehri-Garhwal,' *Purusartha*, 10: 55–95.

Gooch, Pernille (1998) *At the Tail of the Buffalo: Van Gujjar Pastoralists between the Forest and the World Arena.* Lund: Lund Monographs in Social Anthropology.

*Guha, Ramachandra (1991) *The Unquiet Woods: Ecological Change and Peasant Resistance in the Himalaya.* Delhi: Oxford University Press. (Oxford University Press, 1989; Oxford India Paperbacks, 1991.)

Handa, O. C. (2002) *History of Uttaranchal.* New Delhi: M. L. Gidwani, Indus Publishing Company.

Hesse, K. (1996) *Staatsdiener, Händler und Landbesitzer: Die Khatri und der Bazar von Mandi (Himachal Pradesh, Indien).* Münster: Lit.

Hoon, V. (1996) *Living on the Move: Bhotiyas of the Kumaon Himalaya.* New Delhi: Sage.

Joshi, L. D. (1984 [1929]) *The Khasa Family Law in the Himalayan Districts of the United Provinces, India.* Allabhad: Superintendant, Government Press, United Provinces.

Joshi, Maheshwar P., Fanger, Allen C. and Brown, Charles W. (eds) (1993–94) *Himalaya: Past and Present, Vols. I–III.* Columbia, MO: South Asia Books.

Kumar, Anup (2011) *The Making of a Small State: Populist Social Mobilisation and the Hindi Press in the Uttarakhand Movement.* New Delhi: Orient Blackswan.

Lal, Panna (1942 [1929]) *Hindu Customary Law in Kumaon.* Allahabad: Superintendant, Printing and Stationery.

Lecomte-Tilouine, M. (ed.) (2009) *Bards and Mediums: History, Culture, and Politics in the Central Himalayan Kingdoms.* Delhi: Almora Books.

*Majumdar, D. N. (1962) *Himalayan Polyandry: Structure, Functioning and Culture Change. A Case-Study of Jaunsar Bawar.* New York: Asia Publishing House.

Newell, W. H. (1961) *Census of India, 1961,* Vol. 20, 'Himachal Pradesh, pt. 5-B, The Gaddi and Affiliated Castes in the Western Himalayas, Report on Scheduled Castes and Scheduled Tribes.' Delhi: Manager of Publications.

*Pant, S. D. (1935) *The Social Economy of the Himalayans.* London: Allen and Unwin.

*Parry, J. (1979) *Caste and Kinship in Kangra.* London: Routledge.

Polit, K. (2011) *Women of Honour: Gender and Agency Among Dalit Women in the Central Himalayas.* Hyderabad: Orient Blackswan.

Ratudi, Pt. Harikrishna (1980 [1928]) *Gadhwal ka Itihas* (The History of Garhwal). Tehri: Bhagirathi Prakashan Griha. (First published by Garhwali Press, Dehra Dun.)

Saklani, Atul (1987) *The History of a Himalayan Princely State.* Delhi: Durga Publications.

*Sanwal, Rami (1976) *Social Stratification in Rural Kumaon.* Delhi: Oxford University Press.

*Sax, William S. (1991) *Mountain Goddess: Gender and Politics in a Himalayan Pilgrimage.* New York: Oxford University Press.

*——(2002) *Dancing the Self: Personhood and Performance in the Pandav Lila of Garhwal.* New York: Oxford University Press.

——(2006a) 'Divine Kingship in the Western Himalayas' in William S. Sax (ed.), *European Bulletin of Himalayan Research,* 29–30: 7–13.

——(2006b) 'Rituals of the Warrior *khund*' in William S. Sax (ed.), *European Bulletin of Himalayan Research,* 29–30: 120–34.

*——(2009) *God of Justice: Ritual Healing and Social Justice in the Central Himalayas.* Oxford: Oxford University Press.

Sharma, Ursula (1980) *Women, Work, and Property in North-West India.* London: Tavistock.

*Singh, Chetan (1998) *Natural Premises. Ecology and Peasant Life in the Western Himalaya,1800–1950.* New Delhi: Oxford University Press.

Vidal, Denis (1989) *Le culte des divinités locales dans une région de l'Himachal Pradesh.* Paris: ORSTOM.

18 Uttar Pradesh

Untouchability and politics

Manuela Ciotti

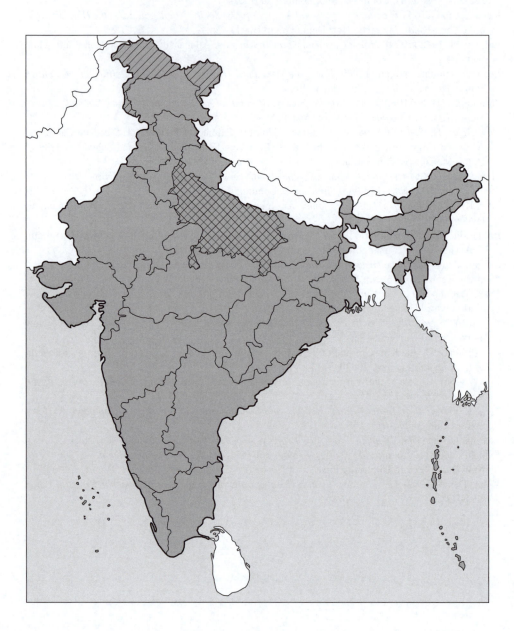

Introduction: the girl and the dog

Manupur, one of the thousand villages scattered over the Gangetic plain in the north state of Uttar Pradesh (UP): a Chamar (leatherworker, 'untouchable' caste) girl tries to fetch water from a water pump but she is told off by members of a local agricultural caste – explicitly reacting against her 'polluting' presence. Prior to the girl being chased away, her father had watched a dog licking off water from the same pump. The dog had encountered no resistance. The girl's father, who narrates the episode to me many years after its occurrence, remarks 'Is my daughter less than a dog?'[1]

Preference of dogs – considered rather impure creatures – over humans testifies to caste as '*a state of mind*' that can be only comprehended within a relational framework (Dumont 1970: 34, emphasis in the original). One of the most influential books of all times on caste society, Louis Dumont's *Homo Hierarchicus: The caste system and its implications*, distilled what, according to the author, was the main organizing ideological principle governing the caste system: the opposition between purity and impurity. The 'untouchables' were conceived as an organic element in this opposition: in Dumont's view, the attributes of purity of the higher castes – especially Brahmans – were to be upheld by the 'untouchables'' professional services, aimed to keep cleanliness – material and symbolic – around them. These services however, represented only a small fraction of these castes' occupations as the overwhelming majority of their members were part of the agrarian economy. According to Dumont, purity and impurity were to exist in a separate realm from that of power, and would encompass both the economic and the political spheres (see Basu, this volume).

A wave of criticism has accompanied Dumont's work over the past decades and rehearsing it here is beyond the scope of this chapter. However, the pervasiveness of untouchability practices in contemporary Indian society testifies to the enduring salience of purity and pollution in everyday life – against existing legislation aiming to curb such practices – in the modern forms such practices have come to be embodied and the spaces of this embodiment. As will be discussed in the course of this chapter, the anthropological imagination of UP has showcased forms of political participation enacted by Dalits – as those historically deemed as 'untouchables' are now addressed – in order to overcome their multiple marginalities. That of politics and culture within an overall frame of a political economy-oriented analysis for UP 'untouchables' is an analytical matrix, which has made its appearance in anthropological works since early post-Independence India. This has meant an attention to conflict – one which has not always translated in the Dalit strident opposition to Hindu culture. What is more, this matrix has continued to exercise its influence also on anthropological work carried out post-*Homo Hierarchicus*, and prevented the latter from becoming paradigmatic in the study of these communities in UP.

To examine the relation between Dalits' symbolic and power struggles, and the forms of political mobilization ensuing from them, this chapter chronologically analyses ethnographies centred on members of the above communities – or where they feature in a significant way. In mapping the journey of the relation between Dalit identity and the political manifestations it has spurred – and the gradual acquisition of the use of political means to fight discrimination – this chapter aims to provide a narrative that helps explain the emergence of mobilization modes which can be observed in contemporary UP polity and society. To this end, and to that of situating the 'field of politics' within the social and cultural landscapes of the state, the chapter will include an analysis of the cultural economies upholding the interplay between Dalit identity and politics. As untouchability pervasively manifests itself in the economic, the social, the cultural and political spheres, these economies form an organic component to the history of social and political change in north India.

Untouchability, caste public-ness and assertion

The refusal of water to 'untouchables' out of fear of contamination of the village wells has been recorded in the colonial administrators' writings. After Independence, both pre- and post-Dumont studies have shown the intricate ways in which the local political economy, power regimes and religious practices have come together in determining how caste hierarchies are actualized in everyday life. Denying water to 'untouchables' – with the content of symbolic violence carried by the gesture – is one of the many crude realities ensuing from such actualization. Preventing the 'defilement' of water sources is part of a repertoire of discriminatory practices ranging from social avoidance to open violence, which aims to keep at bay contamination and disruption of social norms. Pace Dumont, the anthropological imagination in UP – possibly more vigorously than that arising from other regions of India – has shown how the battle between purity and impurity pervading caste society acquires full salience only when framed against the local agrarian economy and related property ownership, old and new regimes of power and authority, local and supralocal political organizations and electoral democracy amongst others. What is more, class considerations are of paramount importance: suffice to say, as Brass has argued, the 'bottom of the economic hierarchy in rural U.P. corresponds strongly with the status hierarchy in the sense that most of the landless come from the lowest caste groups' (1997: 205). As will be shown later, Dalit class upward mobility is intimately linked to autonomous political participation.

Untouchability was abolished in 1950 with the Indian constitution: additional legislation that aimed to further protect individuals from this practice and related violence followed.[2] Despite the introduction of legal measures against it, untouchability practices see their daily re-enactment in contemporary India. The enactment of these practices should also be thought of as intersecting with the high heterogeneity of the large body of Dalit castes in UP (and elsewhere in India), as inflected by their urban and rural location and their profession (be they 'traditional' ones from which the association to their untouchability label stemmed out or 'modern' ones), and their diverse socio-economic positioning amongst others. Against this backdrop, the historicity of this spectrum is important: that is, the forms it has taken over time, and how 'untouchable' identities have been made salient in time and place by others and by Dalits themselves to fight discrimination. For example, the reasons behind similar discriminatory acts in the 1950s and in twenty-first century UP might well be different as identities are framed by the socio-economic and political climate of the time.

Concerning the wider contexts of the social practices that come under the label of untouchability, the opening episode marking the childhood of a woman in her mid-thirties at the time of writing, took place at a time (sometime in the 1980s) when caste discrimination did not have the public resonance it has today. This is largely an achievement of social and political movements and a plurality of voices within civil society, in particular Dalit intellectuals, activists and scholars who have contributed towards a vibrant counter-public sphere. Moreover, the new media have fostered the spreading of awareness around discrimination and aided the global campaign to put an end to it. The past two decades have seen a surge of 'caste' in the public arena – with the Mandal affair in the early 1990s as a landmark event.[3] Caste has become the idiom through which claims against backwardness and untouchability have been expressed more vehemently since then. In 1997, Chris Fuller wrote that 'contemporary understandings of caste – what it is and what it means – are above all a denial, most explicitly in the public domain, of the existence or continuing significance of caste in its "traditional" form' (1997: 21). The standpoints from which such understandings are to be evaluated, argued Fuller, are the Brahmanical ideology and purity and pollution, both of which were first written up by colonial ethnographers and subsequently consolidated through village ethnographies (ibid.: 21); caste is talked about in terms of cultural distinctiveness while inequalities that sustain this distinctiveness can no longer be supported in public (ibid.: 21). For Dalit communities, especially after Mandal, this argument holds only a partial explanatory salience: while for some of them the ways in which their cultures and pasts have come to be rewritten form a body of cultural distinctiveness, at the same time, caste has become a public rallying banner. In other words, the invisibility of (high) caste and related privileges, together with the impossibility of openly supporting caste in the public sphere, contrast with the high visibility of low-caste identity as a call for politics, and of 'caste' as the material and symbolic burden that hinders these communities' development. The emergence of Dalit politics can be traced back to the historical political forces' combined failure in tackling this legacy and satisfying the representational demands of upwardly mobile Dalits (see Chandra 2004).

Where the invisibility/visibility of caste is an important theme in Indian public life and certainly in UP, the growth of the public-ness of caste consciousness amongst the lower strata of the society is intertwined with its political manifestations – and they have both increased spectacularly over the past decades. In absolute terms, UP hosts the highest Scheduled Caste (SC) population all over India: they constituted 21.1 per cent of the state population (35 million) out of 166 million according to the census of 2001. The SC population is divided into 66 different legally recognized castes,[4] suggesting a degree of heterogeneity amongst them. This social subdivision needs to be situated against the overall population's religious composition: this is overwhelmingly Hindu (80 per cent); Muslims constitute 18 per cent and religious minorities such as Buddhists, Christians, Jains and Sikhs make up the rest. UP has been a site where untouchability and the world of politics have conjugated one another in interesting ways. Over half a century, Dalits have grown from participating in sporadic and poorly organized village-based political activities to full-scale autonomous institutionalized politics. Since the 1920s, UP has been the site of important reform movements and the formulation of alternative worldviews (Jaffrelot 2003). However, it was only over the past three decades that the socio-cultural and political legacy of such movements was catalysed by a political formation that turned them into a platform for institutionalized Dalit politics and rights claims. Given the many castes and many histories, this political formation is only but one manifestation – albeit spectacularly large – of Dalit assertion in UP.[5] This consists of the Bahujan Samaj Party (the majority of the people's party or BSP), which has its stronghold in the state, and is supported by the Chamar community, the largest SC in UP. Preceded by a number of Dalit organizations, the BSP was founded in 1984 by Dalits themselves and gradually attained a pivotal position within the UP polity. Prior to its creation, Dalits had overwhelmingly been affiliated to the historical Congress Party, together with upper castes and Muslims. After brief stints in power thanks to heterogeneous political coalitions, the BSP headed a majority government from 2007 to 2012, and a Dalit woman, Mayawati, was the state's Chief Minister. The 2007 election was won by a gradual process of attracting members of other caste communities – including the upper caste ones – within its fold, and diluting the party's original staunch anti-upper-caste rhetoric.[6]

Sixty years after India's Independence, this result is truly unprecedented – while the BSP's impact on the lives of ordinary Dalits calls for evaluation. The BSP's ascendance to power is the expression of a degree of social mobility amongst sections of the SCs (see Chandra 2004; Ciotti 2012; Mendelsohn and Vicziany 1998). If the BSP's political successes culminating in the conquest of state power in 2007 and the bringing together of different caste communities under the same political organization would suggest Dalits' social acceptance, violence against them in contemporary UP strongly challenges such an assumption. On this matter, Venkitesh Ramakrishnan and Ajoy Ashirwad Mahaprashasta (2009) have rightly argued that at a time of unprecedented visibility of the 'Dalit question', UP has been reported as the state with the highest number of atrocities committed against the SC/Scheduled Tribe (ST) population in India: in 2007, UP registered 20.5 per cent of all such cases in the country. This datum points to a major contradiction in the state:

> Dalits were at the receiving end in large parts of Uttar Pradesh, where the politics of empowerment of the S.Cs and the S.Ts, the protection of their interests, their physical safety and the assertion of their constitutional rights had acquired, in comparative terms, the highest political and electoral acceptability.
>
> (Ramakrishnan and Mahaprashasta 2009)

As a result, UP society features a discrepancy between Dalit political emancipation, representation and power *and* the resilience of their poor social acceptance within society – together with a rising hostility against them (Chowdhry 2009). Actually, analysts agree that atrocities are a direct response to Dalit assertiveness. If contemporary politics and society appear to be 'colliding' on the untouchability question at this particular historical juncture, this datum is telling of social transformation trends concerning these communities in the state and within society at large. It is also suggestive of the ways in which mere considerations of purity and pollution are insufficient to explain power struggles within north Indian society and the policing of caste boundaries and local ranking in the face of shifting circumstances. The discrepancy outlined above could also be read as the modern embodiment of caste as *a state of mind* and materialized in the strong reaction to the threat Dalits pose to established caste regimes in their efforts towards erasing untouchability and achieving socio-economic equality. As will be shown in the course of this chapter, higher castes' reaction to curb Dalit assertion is not a new feature in UP. What matters, however, is the magnitude of the threat often posed to caste society in north India: the action of landless and often politically unorganized 'untouchables' in the first decades of post-Independence India is not remotely comparable to that posed by a fully-fledged political party, the agenda it pursues, and the bureaucratic power attained by members of Dalit communities.

Uttar Pradesh: a brief profile

Since the late nineteenth century, UP was envisioned as a 'heartland' in multiple (and conflicting) ways: as a model province by the British, as a site of the freedom struggle, as a centre of Muslim politics, and as Hindu heartland by Hindutva forces (Kudaisya 2007: 282–83). It was in the decade after India's Independence, Gyanesh Kudaisya argues, that UP came to be constructed not only as a 'Hindi heartland' but it also came to be institutionalized as a 'political heartland' where the electoral battles for the control of India had to be fought (2007: 283). UP's historical importance together with the political weight of the number of representatives it has contributed to the national parliament or Lok Sabha, is accompanied by a record of poor governance and economic status, with appalling indicators and very unfavourable living conditions for its low castes and women. Zoya Hasan points out that 'towards the end of British rule in India the rural economic structure of UP was marked by extreme inequality in the ownership of land and means of production' (1989: 152) – an inequality that was higher in central and eastern UP (ibid.). As a result of the Zamindari

Abolition Act of 1952, 'in some areas, particularly in the eastern districts, the great thakur, bania, Kayastha and Muslim landlords lost a good deal of land which vastly reduced their economic influence. At the same time, not all large zamindars suffered irretrievably' (ibid.: 158). In these regions, amongst the Backward Caste beneficiaries were Ahirs, Kurmis and Lodhs (ibid.). Against this backdrop, the impact of new agricultural technologies during the 1960s' Green Revolution was uneven: while the western and eastern regions of the state both lie in the vast Gangetic plain, western UP benefited most from the Revolution even if the eastern region had the more fertile and rain-fed land. Hasan attributes this to absentee landlordism, a general aversion to manual work, an apathy towards innovation in lands cultivated with rice, and a surplus of labour (ibid.: 164). The western region has fared better not only in terms of agrarian development but also of industrialization and urbanization. If the population in eastern UP mostly lives in villages that are small in size compared to those in central and western UP, it is because these regions were positively influenced by the Green Revolution.

The state has been included as part of the BIMARU group of Indian states that also includes Bihar, Madhya Pradesh and Rajasthan, all of which share with UP poor indicators of human development and economic growth. Jens Lerche and Roger Jeffery argue that UP's 'social development record is dreadful and in the 1990s it has become known as one of the main development failures in India' (2003: 18) and one characterized by 'high levels of illiteracy and infant and child mortality; poor health and education provisions; and markedly unequal gender relations' (ibid.: 18). However, they also point out that, historically, UP's economic performance – mainly based on agriculture – in the 1970s compared well with that of the rest of India, but that since the 1980s per capita income has not grown as fast as that of India as a whole, and there has been a neglect of social development in the state (ibid.). The State Development Report, included in the Eleventh Five-Year Plan 2007–12,[7] shows how UP saw a decline in economic growth during the 1990s, with a low and uneven growth in agriculture – the strongest sector of UP economy – but also a decline in the growth of its industrial and services sectors. Further, the rate of poverty reduction proceeded below the national average, with rural UP faring better than urban areas. When compared to other Indian states, the state as a whole signals a low rate of urbanization so that the majority of UP's population (80 per cent) lives in rural areas (ibid.: 110–11). Jean Drèze and Haris Gazdar have argued that 'material poverty is not the main cause of Uttar Pradesh's social failure' (1997: 49), since this state shares poverty indicators with other Indian states, which, as compared to UP, have a much higher degree of social achievements. Rather, Drèze and Gazdar argue, one of the main causes of UP's failure is 'the apathy of the state, but an equally important factor is the failure of civil society to challenge oppressive patterns of caste, class, and gender relations' (ibid.: 61). Such patterns are operated by upper-caste communities which feature in much higher numbers than in other states: these elites make up 20 per cent of the population (Lerche and Jeffery 2003: 19). In addition to this, they failed, over time, to respond to the needs of emerging groups which increasingly claimed power and representation such as the mid-ranking farmers in the 1960s and the Dalits later on (ibid.: 18–19). The absence of reforms and socio-economic inclusion of a whole range of communities led, in the 1980s, to the break-up of the political alignment the historical Congress Party had set up since Independence (ibid.: 19). By deploying the anthropological research on Dalit communities as a standpoint, this chapter maps the socio-economic and cultural landscapes that led to the above break-up and the events that followed.

Histories and categories

The ethnographies discussed in this chapter form an invaluable body of knowledge on Dalit communities: in this regard, they testify to M. N. Srinivas' argument which, reinforcing Raymond Firth's idea of 'the significance of anthropological field materials as historical record' (Firth 1975: 20 in Srinivas 1997: 20), sees ethnographies of villages and tribes in India as providing 'future historians of India with information of a depth and quality not available from any other source' (1997: 20). Like all histories, the one offered here centres around categories, and in particular that of 'untouchable'. As mentioned previously, the presence of untouchability in north India was recorded by colonial administrators and ethnographers, and hence caste 'characters' were etched in their records and went to consolidate a particular representation of the texture of Indian society. Parallel to the widely analysed process of objectification of castes through the census, historical research has also shown that untouchability was not a crystallized social practice. In particular, Susan Bayly argues that 'untouchability as we know it is thus very largely a product of colonial modernity' (1999: 226). She argues that with the entry of the low castes into emerging sectors of the economy, a new construction of untouchability took shape. At the height of colonialism in the period before World War I, the 'pollution barrier' (that is, the boundary between the superior castes and those considered unclean and inauspicious) gradually acquired a rigid character (ibid.: 224). This process did not originate from domestic traditions concerning pollution and untouchability, but rather from the employment of members of unclean castes in the modern arena, where workers were placed in a significantly different position from the one they had inhabited back in their villages (ibid.: 225–26).

In response to post-colonial scholarship, Oliver Mendelsohn and Marika Vicziany, who extensively researched Dalit communities in north India, have argued:

> it is not really true that 'the Untouchables' were 'invented' during the colonial period. Rather, their description was simplified and objectified at a particular political moment so as to fit them into a bureaucratic and welfare model understandable to the modern state.
>
> (Mendelsohn and Vicziany 1998: 260)

Moreover, 'the Untouchables were a subordinate people long before twentieth-century politics transformed them into a category of political relevance' (ibid.: 2). These arguments point to the confluence of various trends, which as a result of a number of compulsions – analytical, legal and political – concomitantly fixed the contours of a category encapsulating an otherwise highly heterogeneous historically marginalized population. What is of interest here is how the resulting category has been deployed in the anthropological discourse. A scholar working on Dalit communities in south India, Simon Charsley, has scrutinized the category's validity in this context and has argued:

> the 'Untouchable' as a twentieth century construction which became both an interpretation of the past and the basis for affirmative action in the present must give pause to any theorising which takes the existence of the category, and of a section of the population corresponding to it, as axiomatic rather than problematic. The category is on the one hand too arbitrary, and on the other too deeply implicated in the processes and values of Indian society, for it not to be seriously misleading when used as a quasi-technical term by anthropologists concerned to locate and relate the village-focused studies. The current

debate as to whether Untouchables replicate or reject the caste system which devalues them illustrates the danger here of creating an unreal problem by misreading the nature of the category.

(Charsley 1996: 18)

Charsley advocates transcending the category and replacing it with a study of how castes who come under this denomination are 'differently placed economically, socially, culturally and politically' in order to produce 'configurations of relative disadvantage' (ibid.: 19). If the 'untouchable' category needs to be replaced with the ethnographic portrayal of castes – and, it should be added, of individuals – Charsley's critique calls into question also the debates that have been premised on the category itself. One of the driving questions within the anthropological literature on 'untouchable' castes, and in particular those put forward by scholars who carried out ethnographic fieldwork in south India, consisted in whether the 'untouchables' accept, show consensus to and hence replicate the ideological foundations of the system in which they live or whether they refuse them. Research in UP was concerned with social reproduction, too, for example the adoption of upper-caste social practices; however, these issues (and in particular that of caste society ritualistic behaviour) were not treated as caste ideology disconnected from the broader world of politics, the division of labour or land ownership amongst others. Moreover, they were not simply regarded as an epiphenomenon of Sanskritization, despite the importance this strategy had held for a wide range of low castes in north India in the early twentieth century and onwards. For example, in Pauline Kolenda's and Michael Mahar's work, discussed later, caste ideology was interrogated vis-à-vis the changes that newly independent India had brought about, and in particular, the constitutional emphasis on equality. An exemplification of the breadth of the anthropological imagination which emerged from UP – and which was passed on to the next generations of scholars – can be found in Bernard Cohn's writings, the first anthropologist to produce an ethnography of 'untouchables' in UP. In an essay originally published in 1962, and outlining the relation between anthropology and history, he stated:

Spending a year studying seven hundred untouchables in one north Indian village for their own sake is a waste of time. But the attempt to place one's knowledge of these people into a wider social and cultural framework of a nation-state and civilization, and try to relate this knowledge to general questions of stratification theory and theories of social and cultural change is far from insignificant activity.

(Cohn 1990: 13)

Cohn's ecumenical call for inquiry speaks of 'untouchables' *and* nation-state, civilization, stratification, social and cultural change: these scapes far exceed the domain of the caste system, although they are certainly inflected by it as well as by purity and pollution concerns.

As it will be clear from the literature analysed in the next section, the above approach has remained key to the analysis of untouchability and caste – an approach that did not prevent Cohn from analysing culture and social reproduction amongst the Chamars. What is more, scholars of UP are part of a broader community who worked on 'untouchable' communities and have returned accounts inspired by conflict, domination and cultural critique. Differences in terms of low-caste assertion between north and south India notwithstanding (see Jaffrelot 2003: 144ff), research across disciplines focusing on important sites for Dalit social mobility and cultural and political assertion, that is the states of Maharashtra and Punjab, have shown rebellion, alternative identities, conversion and protest literature production as key features (see Juergensmeyer 1982; Contursi 1993; Zelliott 1996; Chandra 2004; Rao 2009). It follows that the approach to the study of Dalit communities has mainly focused on their acute dissonance with the power, economic and religious hierarchies in which they found themselves embedded. What is more, Dalits have not been the only communities for whom a political economy-oriented analysis has been deployed in UP: the ways in which development processes have been deeply moulded by caste, community and gender has been a long-standing framework of enquiry.[8]

Intersecting with the formation and consolidation of the 'untouchable' category and the debates that revolved around it are those debates concerning the various denominations for 'untouchable' castes encountered in the literature. These form *competing categories* as, historically, they all attempted to deploy for those with an 'untouchable' background, labels which reflected socio-political agendas. Labels range from 'Harijan' (children of God) used by Gandhi, to the legal classification 'SC', to the widely used and political 'Dalit'. In addition, there are caste names, which without proper contextualization might convey offending meanings but which are also used by caste members themselves. These labels have all been used for self-representation by these castes and for representation by others over time – while all labels are also used simultaneously by the above castes (see Ciotti 2010a: 204–06, 2010b). Their use is highly contextual, politicized and uneven. The term 'Harijan' is a case in point. Being dropped as a result of political rallies against its patronizing implications, it has been publicly substituted by the term 'Dalit'. In UP, however, this term is not universally deployed by the castes it wishes to represent (see Guru 2001; Ciotti 2010b, 2010c, for different explanations of this phenomenon). Reflections over the salience of these labels started two decades ago (see Zelliott 1996) and have increasingly appeared in the literature, as issues of representation, recognition and the politics of knowledge production have become ever more relevant in the study of such communities.

The anthropological imagination at work in UP

Research originating from UP has contributed to the birth of key themes in South Asian Studies such as the relation between anthropology and history, forms of imperial knowledge and power through the working of the colonial census amongst others (see Cohn 1990). The investigation of local politics through village studies in the wake of the assessment of planned development in independent India has led an analyst of UP society and politics, Harold Gould, to state: 'the field of South Asian area studies grew out of these beginnings' (2003: 1494). Research on UP has greatly contributed towards such studies and towards a framework for the study of Indian politics in truly ethnographic fashion.[9] Moreover, when, in the 1980s, the study of caste increasingly acquired historical depth and started to explicitly attend to questions of power, the anthropological imagination from UP can be considered at the vanguard on these issues as both 'the past' and 'power' had been avenues of investigation well before these emerged as research interests within anthropology. When low-caste politics, communalism and political violence – especially following the destruction of the Babri Mosque in Ayodhya in 1992 – increased in importance in the UP polity during the 1990s, the understanding of these phenomena found many analytical tools in the interdisciplinary body of literature produced on this state.

UP villages were studied by several researchers as part of the US Cornell Project headed by Morris Opler. These early anthropological studies mapped the nature of social structures – in particular the ways in which caste organization translated into a division of labour – and social change. An article titled 'Two villages in eastern UP' by Opler and Rudra Datt Singh published in 1952 acts in lieu of introduction to the kind of studies being carried out at the time. Although not focusing on Dalit communities, both analysed villages, Madhopur and Ramapur, featured a considerable population from the Chamar and the Pasi (traditionally pig-raisers) caste respectively. Situated in the Jaunpur district, eastern UP, Madhopur was a Thakur- (Rajput-) dominated multi-caste village where they owned most of the land. While the above scholars recorded villagers working in other cities of UP, as well as India and abroad, agriculture formed the key source of livelihood in the village. Chamars were the largest caste community: about them, the authors observed that they were field workers and that:

> Being untouchables, they have a low place in Hindu society. For the most part they live in a social world of their own. We have no evidence of their interest in the power politics of the village before 1947 [...] We have cases illustrating active assertion of their will by the Chamars during the pre-independence period, but these were all connected with their desire to obtain higher wages or better treatment from their employers.
>
> (Opler and Singh 1952: 181)

What is fascinating is the importance of the politics of caste numbers in local governance, and its critical role in Indian politics noticed by the above scholars in 1949. Then, a village governing body had to be elected for Madhopur, and the low-caste Ahirs and Noniyas, traditionally cowherders and salt-makers, opposed the Thakur leadership and gained a majority in this body. These caste communities had thus managed to improve their status but, given their lack of experience and the non-cooperation of the Thakurs, not much progress could be made in the conduct of village affairs. Opler and Singh argued how Thakurs could not ignore these low castes and their expectations – because of their numerical presence – while the low castes needed the Thakurs' experience in addition to being dependent on them as landowners (ibid.: 182). Over the following 60 years, these dynamics, tensions and challenges to traditional leadership have been rehearsed countless times in UP.

The second village analysed by Opler and Singh is Ramapur. Situated near the city of Allahabad, the village enjoyed the proximity of one of the most important Hindu pilgrimage sites at the confluence of the Ganges and the Yamuna rivers. Ramapur was a multi-caste village whose economy was shaped by the proximity to the rivers and the sacred economies built around them – and where the Mallah Boatmen and the Brahman ritual specialists played a major role. Ramapur featured a 400-member Pasi community. Their untouchability was attributed to their traditional occupation of pig-raising, which Pasis attempted to shed in the effort to raise their status (1952: 186). Shedding activities considered to be 'impure' and 'polluting' is a practice often found amongst Dalits who aim to improve their status within society. As a result, they had to rely on casual agricultural labour and on cultivating small plots of land. Despite Opler and Singh finding 'murmurs' and 'complaints' about those who wanted to keep the status quo, and on the differential treatment of Pasi children at school, they argued that the Pasis 'do not yet have enough self-confidence and political consciousness to use their votes and their numbers effectively to gain additional rights' (ibid.: 186). In Ramapur, there was also a small group of Chamars who worked as agricultural day labourers, cobblers, midwives, and disposers of dead cattle. The above scholars contended that they seemed 'resigned to their lot. They are poor, dependent, illiterate, and too few in numbers to press demands as a separate group' (ibid.). Madhopur featured landowning by Thakurs and intensive cultivation while in Ramapur land was owned by Ahirs, and factors such as wealth, numbers and traditional status next to the river economy made for more diversified hierarchies and social distinctions. Despite the different sources of livelihood and the identity of property ownership in the two villages, the Chamar and Pasi communities in them resembled one another and they both showed poor bargaining power, a similar class status and the absence of political mobilization.

Building on the material collected by Opler and Singh in Madhopur, Cohn provided an all-round account of the Chamar community.[10] He set the analytical directions through which to explore the lowly conditions of the Chamars in 'wealth, power and caste position' (1990: 255). Concerning this intertwined set of features, Cohn observed that the Chamars from Madhopur village were not tanners in the early 1950s as they had been before – but they still had to remove dead cattle for a number of castes. Both activities were strictly tied to 'untouchable' identity: regarding this, Cohn wrote, 'in North India this is a not a literal untouchability, but rather a situation where high-caste men will not take water or cooked food from the Chamars' (1990: 284). As a result of the prohibition to reside in the high-caste settlements, Chamars lived in hamlets on the margins of other castes' settlements.[11] They were dependent on the Thakurs as landowners and worked as ploughmen and casual day labourers in the fields. Cohn observed how the Zamindari abolition (Land Ceiling Act) of 1952 did not much affect the economic and political dominance of the landlords (ibid.: 257). Prior to this abolition, 'no Chamars owned land in the strict sense of the word' (ibid.: 301), while following the abolition, 'very few of the Chamars got any rights in the land at all' (ibid.). This resulted in labour-related migration as many Chamars sought employment in nearby centres of commerce.

Madhopur and its surroundings were all but static and bounded places however. 'Seeds of change', Cohn wrote, had reached the village already in the early twentieth century through the construction of a railroad, the spread of higher education, the increasing role of courts in settling disputes, the Arya Samaj reform movement, elections and the nationalist struggle for Independence. As a result, changes were notable in all spheres of social life. Moreover demographic growth had pushed villagers from all castes in search of work into cities. In addition to changes in the family structure, gender roles and religious beliefs on which Cohn wrote, it is the political change that interests us more here: since 1900 Thakurs had taken up employment in government and business outside the village and they had witnessed the break-up of their caste panchayats, which had dominated the village and the whole area. If this authority weakened together with the patron–client structure, that of Chamar caste organizations grew stronger, while they also had to settle their disputes by themselves. Cohn's portrayal of Madhopur Chamars showed a much higher degree of assertion than that offered by Opler and Singh. Cohn reported how the Chamar caste tried to punish offenders in sexual relations between Thakur men and Chamar women – relations that Cohn says were commonplace a generation previously. Moreover, Chamars had tightened their caste boundaries by enforcing eating and drinking boundaries with other 'untouchable' castes – boundaries that did not exist previously. The punishment used was ostracism or outcasting. There were also records of nascent political mobilization: after the provincial elections in 1937 – when a few low-castes were entitled to vote – for the first time the Chamars challenged Thakur authority and experimented with an alliance and solidarity with low-caste Nonyas by supporting them in a land dispute against the landlords. In retaliation, the Thakurs beat the Chamars and destroyed the thatched roofs of their houses. Under the suggestion of a member of the Nonya community, they complained to the District Magistrate and took their belongings to Jaunpur, where they were hosted by the District Congress Committee. They hired a lawyer but they eventually had to come to a compromise with the Thakurs over the disputed land. The Thakurs, in the meantime, had mobilized all of their social capital to move the case across courts and delay the case, and they had also resorted to bribing the police. The next episode of Chamar rebellion took place in the wake of the UP Panchayat Raj Act of 1947: the subsequent year a party bringing together all of the lower castes in Madhopur – against the Thakurs – was formed: the Tenant (Praja) Party. The Chamars joined in. In view of their imminent defeat, the Thakurs refused to vote against the Tenant Party. So the party elected a village council and a rural court, as the above Act ruled. However, all council ordinances passed could not be implemented because of the opposition of the Thakur and other high-caste traditional leaders. Eventually, the party faced bribing of its members, lawsuits by Thakurs and the murder of one of the party leaders by a Thakur. Chamars did not have the means to fight against them, and even if they had experienced the benefits of a low-caste electoral alliance, 'they found also that they could not sustain themselves in a position of effective dominance' (ibid.: 278). Political solidarity vanished after that. In the late 1950s Cohn returned to the village he had studied in 1952–53. He found that Chamar conditions had deteriorated – more of them had migrated to cities as they realized they could not get hold of cultivating rights, while they complained bitterly about Thakurs.

In addition to embryonic political mobilization and the alternating fortunes of caste alliances, most prophetically Cohn had focused on what would become a very important issue in low-caste and middle-ranking caste politics: the past and the politics around it. Cohn distinguished between the 'historic past', which 'explains, supports, or provides a basis for action in the local social system' (ibid.: 89), and the 'traditional past', which serves to validate and maintain a social position (ibid.). Concerning the first, Cohn pointed out the absence of genealogical knowledge amongst the Chamars, compared to the vast knowledge of their own ancestors amongst their upper-caste landlords.[12] In his explanation of the 'traditional past', Cohn explained that for the upper-caste landlords, this past traces back to the epics of the *Ramayana* and the *Mahabharata*, whose heroes are considered as caste ancestors (ibid.: 90). Amongst the Chamars, Cohn argued, the traditional past consisted of origin myths and Chamar holy men such as Ravidas. Cohn also remarked on the birth of a 'corporate historic past', which stemmed from a movement of Chamar and low-caste groups towards political power (ibid.: 93). Almost half a century later, the politics of the past has gained increased salience in north India. Low-caste political mobilization has called for the need for a dignified and unifying past for the constituencies they address, which demanded the incorporation of religious and historical figures of prominence (see Narayan 2006).

In addition to Cohn's all-round portrait of 'untouchables' in the 1950s, an additional one emerged from research in Khalapur village in Saharanpur District, western UP. Out of the team of scholars from the Cornell Project who carried out fieldwork in this village, Pauline Kolenda had focused on the 'untouchable' village sweepers (Chuhras). She carried out fieldwork in the mid-1950s and 30 years later, undertook a village restudy. Kolenda had a wide range of research interests ranging from caste ideology, women and marriage, to women's role as midwives. Moreover, in line with the wider anthropological research agenda of her time, she looked at the 'great tradition of Hinduism' and the ways in which its religious tenets were reformulated in everyday practices by 'untouchables'. She conducted research on the theory of Hindu fate and offered arguments that were linked to tales of caste origins and their re-making – a theme that increasingly acquired salience and political currency. Drawing on fieldwork between 1954 and 1956, she showed how sweepers circumvented the link between their low-caste status and the law of karma (according to which this status would be explained on the basis of the sins committed in the previous life) – which would create anxiety amongst them. Instead, she put forward an alternative explanation focused on 'caste history' (1964: 75). She argued that '[t]hey console themselves that their low-caste rank may all be just a terrible historical accident, and they told at least three different status-legends to justify this position' (ibid.: 75). Taking cue from the sweepers' religious beliefs, Kolenda pointed out the gap between the high ideals of philosophical Hinduism and its popular understandings. More generally, that Hindus do not live by the Scriptures is the general point harnessed by Kolenda, which places the attention on vernacular understandings and appropriation of religious traditions. What needs to be emphasized here are 'untouchables'' attempts to make sense of their origins, again a theme that has grown in prominence with political mobilization and with the assertion of alternative explanations such as the Adi Hindu theme.[13]

Part of the above work framed Kolenda's investigation on perceptions of the caste system in Khalapur which, as mentioned earlier, she recorded twice: first in the 1950s and then in 1984. In the 1950s, she interviewed four leaders of different castes (Rajput, a Baniya, sweeper and Chamar) and then repeated the experiment, asking the same questions, in her restudy. Her primary question concerned the introduction of the new constitution after India's Independence, and its impact on citizens differently positioned in the caste system: she was interested in the long-standing question of the relation between legal infrastructure and social practices – a question which is key to the lives of those deemed as 'untouchables' as well as others. In particular, Kolenda asked 'How do Hindu villagers reconcile the new legal rights for ex-untouchables with a traditional caste ideology which justifies the restriction of untouchables to subordinate socio-economic position in Indian society?' (1958: 51). It emerged that while the abolition of untouchability and 'untouchables'' advancement were the goal of independent India, in the Chamar view, she recorded a decline in the hope for equality (ibid.: 63). From opposite sides of the caste spectrum, Kolenda found the Rajput felt subordinated to the Muslims, the British and subsequently the central government. In turn, 'untouchable' interviewees expressed the same subordinate feeling vis-à-vis the Rajputs. Whereas the sweeper and the Baniya agreed on the need for inter-caste equality, the Chamar and the Rajput dreaded the possibility of inter-caste marriage (ibid.). None of the respondents envisioned a world free of caste rules (ibid.: 64). If the complexities of caste society seen through the lens of male caste leaders showed multiple concerns, this data provide the image of the village as an 'early social laboratory' in which ideas of the old and new social orders were being reflexively tested. When Kolenda returned to Khalapur in 1984, she used the same interview guide to ask questions of two of the four original respondents (two had died) and new ones (seven in total). She recorded a shift in the ways caste was being talked about: 'No longer are the issues of access for facilities, inter-caste etiquette and untouchables' rights to jobs and education. These changes have been absorbed' (ibid.: 1836), while 'inter-caste marriage, the questioning of caste as a social system, and the expectation of social change' (ibid.: 1836) had emerged as new topics. In addition to such shift, she was also surprised by the unanimous opinion of the seven young men against caste as a system (ibid.: 1837), providing a rare account of ideological change among the young generation.

Kolenda's husband, Michael Mahar, also carried out research in Khalapur and was equally interested in the encounter between what he called the 'old' dharma (the Hindu caste system ideology) and the 'new' one inaugurated by the Indian constitution. Epitomising this transition, Mahar wrote about meetings held by well-known Congress leaders together with the UP Chief Minister announcing the new citizenship rights and the end of untouchability to the villagers. In a public demonstration of such an end, the governor drank a glass of water provided by a village sweeper before the inhabitants (1972: 26). After the initial enthusiasm, Mahar wrote, many of the old restrictions kept on being observed and untouchability practices continued unabated (ibid.). At the political level, it was the village Rajputs who 'introduced' the 'untouchables' to electoral politics: already in 1949, the latter had understood the power of electoral democracy and that of its numbers, as already noticed earlier, when the Rajputs sought their votes for their candidates for the post of *pradhan* (village chairman) – even when intimidation was used to secure their vote (ibid.: 28–29). In the late 1960s, Mahar returned to the village to observe that the 'old' dharma still ruled social life, though in a 'muted form' (ibid.: 31). The prosperity deriving from improvements in agriculture in the village did not show in the lives of the 'untouchables' although a little material progress was visible, for example in higher school enrolment, while some had obtained government jobs. However, restrictions to 'untouchables'' use of the village temple and upper caste wells were still in place (ibid.: 32).[14] Mahar also observed that although the village panchayat had lost importance over the previous decade, their presence in the village council 'was still a physical affirmation of the Untouchables' right to hold public office' (ibid.: 34).[15] One notable change took place in the 1964 national election. This saw a candidate of 'untouchable' origin contesting for the Republican Party of India (RPI), which enjoyed almost no support amongst Khalapur 'untouchables'. However, they had attended a rally where the son of Dr. Ambedkar had given a speech (ibid.: 35).[16] At the time of voting, the 'untouchables' turned en masse to the Congress party – also out of the reasoning that the RPI did not have much chance to win – while the Congress was a political force which pursued their interest (ibid.: 35). An additional argument explaining their electoral choice then, and on the subsequent election held in 1969, was that voting for Congress would prevent the Hindu party Jana Sangh from winning – an option the 'untouchables' looked at unfavourably (ibid.: 35). The more general landscape of political participation amongst them was also connoted by the lack of leadership and resources in the Republican Party, and this reinforced the reluctance of the 'untouchables' to enter political activism – which should be seen in conjunction with their concerns about Rajputs' backlash in case of such an event. Mahar also pointed out how the Buddhist movement which had been joined in by 'untouchables' in Agra and Maharasthra in the 1950s and 1960s had found no supporters in Khalapur, as they were sceptical that a substantial change would follow from conversion.

Madhopur and Khalapur villages provide some evidence of organized politics in the 1950s, of the social ferment amongst these castes – especially since citizenship rights were made available to them – and on the dynamics of contemporary political mobilization. It is with American anthropologist Owen Lynch that fullyfledged institutionalized political participation amongst 'untouchables' became a central research focus. In the book titled *The Politics of Untouchability*, published in 1969, Lynch provided an in-depth account of Jatavs' mobilization in the city of Agra, western UP.[17] This mobilization rests on a history of social mobility based on Sankritization in the early decades of the twentieth century, and on a claim to Kshatriya status in order to raise their position within the caste system (1969: 69ff). Interestingly, this and their exposure to the Arya Samaj, led them to reject the anti-caste teachings of Swami Achhutanand who in the 1930s led the Adi Hindu movement in UP, introducing the idea of the 'untouchables' as the original inhabitants of India (ibid.: 76). The Jatav elite benefited from such reform movements, from education and lobbying with the British for their inclusion into the legislative council and the district and municipal administration. This Jatav elite also engaged with events on the international scene in the 1930s, which saw Dr. Ambedkar and Gandhi pitted against one another, as well as in local protest activities against untouchability. While the earlier period saw the Jatavs pressing for their Kshatriya status to be legally recognized, with the Independence movement new issues emerged on the horizon. In 1944–45 the Jatavs formed the Scheduled Caste Federation of Agra, which had ties with the Dr. Ambedkar-led All-India Scheduled Caste Federation (ibid.: 86). Not only had they started to recognize themselves as SCs, and hence 'untouchable' to others, but they had increasingly come under the influence of Dr. Ambedkar's ideas and therefore against the caste system. Lynch observed how it was clear why the Jatavs had abandoned Sanskritization and their efforts in gaining a higher caste status:

> The change is due to the fact that Sanskritization is no longer as effective a means as is political participation for achieving a change in style of life and a rise in the Indian social system, now composed of both caste and class elements.
>
> (Lynch 1969: 97)

His analysis of the changes that electoral democracy engendered amongst the Jatavs is most detailed: it showed the strenuous political commitment, the rise of a new leadership, as well as the internal divisions within the Republican Party and the Jatav community as a whole. In addition to factionalism within the party, Lynch also signalled its lack of financial resources and its one-caste-only (Jatav) membership as a major drawback (ibid.: 125–26).

When compared to the BSP phenomenon starting in the 1980s, a number of elements should be pointed out: the first concerns the ways in which in the 1960s it was artisanal work and business in the leather industry,[18] rather than government employment, that fostered social mobility and politicization. In both cases, untouchability did not directly engender politics: rather, it was forms of social mobility amongst 'untouchables' that demanded their entry into politics. Second, both phenomena of political mobilization within party politics occurred within autonomous 'untouchable' political parties rather than within the upper-caste-led Congress. Third, autonomous political organizations such as the Republican Party and the BSP were both under the deep influence of Dr. Ambedkar. Finally, both phenomena saw urban areas as their epicentres.

Lynch's portrait of the Jatavs in western UP was complemented by the research in this region by political scientist Jagpal Singh (1998). Building on the Jatavs' mobilization and support for the RPI in the 1960s, Singh analysed the Jatavs' participation in the grassroots process termed as 'Ambedkarization'. This translated as the spread of knowledge about Dr. Ambedkar's life and ideas, the erection of statues of the leader, the construction of libraries and schools, the celebration of the leader's birthday, and other cultural activities. After the RPI, Singh argued, mobilization had continued in the 1970s with a second generation of Dalits who attended colleges and universities and mainly sought employment outside their villages. This was followed by a third generation, involving a wide socio-economic range amongst the Jatavs who began to support the BSP created in 1984.[19] The period preceding the founding of the BSP was a fertile one also for the study of intellectual life amongst UP 'untouchables'. The year 1984 in fact saw the publication of a monograph on Lucknow Chamars entitled *The Untouchable as Himself: Ideology, Identity, and Pragmatism among the Lucknow Chamars* by Ravindra Khare. Instead of 'Hindu categories', which had interested the anthropologist McKim Marriott working in villages in Aligarh district in UP since the 1950s, Khare produced a work on alternative ones enlivening 'untouchable' cultural ideology. Drawing on both fieldwork and textual analysis of the reform literature Khare found in the city, one of the merits of this book lays in focusing on the 'untouchable as a thinker' and in highlighting the multifaceted and nuanced positioning of 'untouchables' vis-à-vis Hindu culture, and the impossibility, and possibly the futility of the effort, to 'place' them inside or outside it. Khare argued:

> The Untouchable thinker often presents his case this way: He considers his group to be simply neither Hindu nor outside Indian civilization; neither merely consensual nor entirely alienated. He claims a positive and different civilizational place for his kind

essentially on the same lines as did the Buddhists and the Jains. Recently he has illustrated the two positions available to him; first as neo-Buddhists (an Ambedkar-led option), and second as a distinct community of the ādi-Hindus (i.e. the original Hindus of the subcontinent). Such points about self and society are critical for the Untouchable's ideological position.

(Khare 1984: 6)

The fluidity of the 'untouchable's' self-positioning within society conveyed by Khare's analysis found confirmation amongst other scholars some years later. While 'untouchable' thinking flourished in Lucknow, the UP polity in the 1980s and early 1990s featured two major trends: the acute polarization of upper castes *and* backward and lower castes in the political struggle for power, and the intensification of Muslim–Hindu conflict (Hasan 1996). Referring to Mandal and the rise of the Hindu Right, in 1998 Mendelsohn and Vicziany claimed that '[p]olitical developments over the last decade or so have by now overtaken the earlier (somewhat bloodless) debate over the relation of Untouchables to wider Indian society' (1998: 21). This was an acute point, not only because of what scholars like Khare (and later f Mosse (1994) for south India) were observing on the ground, but because the relation between 'untouchables' and their sense of belonging to Indian and Hindu society were much more conflicting and nuanced than structuralist accounts had ever claimed them to be.

In addition to the above analytical reflections, the broader political and religious trends, as highlighted by Hasan, had begun to have an impact on the lives of 'untouchable' communities in UP. Two studies carried out at different temporal junctures documented them: the first consists of Mary Searle-Chatterjee's ethnographical study of Benares (Varanasi) 'untouchable' sweepers in the 1980s and 1990s. Her earlier work focused on gender and the division of labour while later she researched caste and religious identities (1981, 1994a, 1994b). Searle-Chatterjee pointed out that the sweepers did not subscribe to their Hindu identity and 'use the term "Hindu" very differently from the way the high castes did, and in terms of a different set of conceptual oppositions' (1994a: 160). She included Chamar leatherworkers in her discussion, arguing that their use of the Adi Hindu theme further strengthened the division between Hindu upper castes and 'untouchable' original inhabitants (ibid.: 161). 'We are neither Hindus nor Muslims. We are the original inhabitants of India', claimed the Ravidasi priest of a large Benares temple dedicated to Ravidas (Searle-Chatterjee 1994b: 18).[20] Against this backdrop, Searle-Chatterjee also observed that the difference between the 'untouchables' and Hindu upper castes had come under scrutiny following the greater prevalence of Hindu nationalism, which forced the former to choose to be either Hindu or Muslim. This, in her view, contrasted with the absence of similar differentiation amongst the low castes (ibid.: 19ff.). In addition to the fact that the members of 'untouchable' communities with whom Searle-Chatterjee carried out her research could not place themselves in either Hindu or Muslim categories, she observed that they ate pork, buried or immersed their dead and visited minor Hindu shrines and Muslim tombs. Thus Searle-Chatterjee concluded, 'it is inappropriate to use the term "Hindu" in relation to the "lowest castes"' (ibid.: 162). About a decade later, Kathinka Frøystad's research in the city of Kanpur (2005) analysed the shift from the processes that saw Hindu upper castes 'othering' Muslims in the wake of the events around Ayodhya, to those 'othering' Dalits in response to the growing importance of their political assertion and that of the Backward Castes. The pivotal moment for the negative essentialization of the Dalits came in 1997 when Mayawati became Chief Minister for the second time (ibid.: 228). This essentialization was predicated on a theory of caste qualities by which upper castes associated Dalits with corruption, laziness and stupidity (ibid.: 31). Frøystad monitored the effects of this essentialization in master–servant relationships: despite upper-caste employers passing remarks on Dalits and on reservations and speculating that their servants' prolonged absence was explainable in terms of Dalits' empowerment, she concluded that such relationships 'were entirely unaffected by the politicization of caste' (ibid.: 251). Actually, her upper-caste informants had increased their contacts with Dalit bureaucrats to gain advantages for themselves (ibid.: 255). The overall political climate had led to a polarization of the different orders of society: as different upper-caste communities felt themselves 'victims' and coalesced together, Frøystad observed 'horizontal loyalties (between forwards of different castes) grew while vertical loyalties (between forwards and backwards) were eroded' (ibid.: 255). While Frøystad's analysis helps explain the rising hostility against Dalits following their growing empowerment, it also shows the contextual failure to reform the modalities of the vertical loyalties between upper castes and Dalits, often of a patronage nature. This patronage was marked by untouchability practices, which in the case of Frøystad's work had turned from being imputed to caste to hygiene issues – whereby 'untouchable' servants were not allowed to enter the kitchen and were physically avoided and given separate utensils (ibid.: 27).

During the 1990s and early 2000s, the BSP was part of coalition governments in UP, which led the leader Mayawati to become Chief Minister. During this period, three books appeared that testified to the increasing importance of 'untouchables'/Dalits as a political force. The books dealt with separate but intertwined aspects in the constitution of such force and mapped their genealogies. Mendelsohn and Vicziany (1998) produced the first comprehensive study of the rise of the new Dalit politicians in north India starting from the second decade after Independence, and of the policies that have targeted their communities. Their book *The Untouchables: Subordination, Poverty and the State in Modern India* traces the birth of the BSP in leaders' biographies and the forms of social mobility which led to Dalits' entry into parliaments. In 2003, Christophe Jaffrelot published a book titled *The Silent Revolution: The Rise of the Low Castes in North Indian Politics* and systematized the socio-cultural trends which had led to Dalit and low-caste political mobilization and power. In *Women Heroes and Dalit Assertion in North India: Culture, Identity and Politics*, Badri Narayan (2006) attended to the cultural economies that had brewed over the past decades and which had prepared the terrain for political assertion, turning them into an object of study. In particular, this book was concerned with Dalit rewriting of the past, namely the inclusion of low-caste women viranganas (women warriors) into national historical events (such as the 1857 mutiny), and the use of the former in the construction of contemporary Dalit political figures. As a result, Cohn's early work on the different 'pasts' of an Indian village and its uses discussed earlier saw a new 'chapter' in Narayan's book: from traces of a Chamar corporate past recorded then, to the flourishing of Dalit historiography – textual and visual – under the form of printed literature first and then through new media.

The 2000s were also the time for the appearance of narratives expanding the empirical and analytical horizon in the study of Dalits. This was also accompanied by the appearance of other communities on the 'anthropological' and 'historical' scene besides Chamars and Pasis, which numerically make up for over half of the SC population in UP. New work showed a number of communities entering Hindu Right politics, testifying to the fact that the relation between Dalits and politics was not only a synonym of Dalits in the BSP. This is the case of the Khatik 'untouchable' caste in Kanpur, broadly associated with masonry and working as butchers, analysed by Maren Bellwinkel-Schempp (2005).[21] This scholar argued that '[t]he infatuation of the Khatik with the BJP is even more surprising, as they were once at the forefront of the Dalit movement in Kanpur' (Bellwinkel-Schempp 2005).[22] Khatiks were a relatively small SC caste in the city and caste sections inhabiting different areas of town had different labour and social histories since the colonial era, and were differently associated with the business of piggery and bristle.[23] It was the British who initiated the relationship between Khatiks and pigs in order to procure bristles and foster the British brush industry. After the 1930s, Bellwinkel-Schempp contended, the Khatiks from a city neighbourhood set up firms, profited from the bristle industry and invested in real estate up to the 1940s. In a similar way to Agra Jatavs, the Khatiks are another case of 'untouchable' entrepreneurship – capitalizing on commodities such as leather and bristle derived from 'untouchable' and despised professions. However, the bristle lost its 'untouchable' occupation connotation to become a respectable commodity sold in London markets. Bellwinkel-Schempp argued, however, that Khatiks' fortunes translated into higher rank only amongst Kanpur Dalits and not in the wider society. The additional business of piggery had been initiated amongst the Khatiks by the British over the previous decades. This business was closely supervised by the British because of hygiene issues. While slaughtering pigs, the Khatiks considered themselves as Hindu and embraced the cow protection movement, while this allegiance was used against Muslims and Chamars. In the 1970s, both the textile and leather industries went into decline in Kanpur and the bristle industry encountered a similar destiny. The Khatiks took up vegetable selling while one family started to rear pigs in the public space, feeding the animals on garbage. This family expanded its business across the whole city, joined BJP politics, and contested elections at different levels of the polity. While they were unsuccessful, other political forces took over the problem of the pigs and the related degradation pervading the city.

If this research on Kanpur draws on the re-signification of 'untouchable' professions such as bristle manufacture and piggery fostered by the British – with the Khatiks rebranding their identity in the process – Narayan's book *Fascinating Hindutva: Saffron Politics and Dalit Mobilisation* (2009) sheds light on the BJP use of the past amongst 'untouchables' in north India. In order to attract into its folds Pasi, Nishad, Musahar and Dusadh communities in Bihar and Uttar Pradesh, the BJP created for them low-caste male heroes belonging to a faraway Vedic or pre-medieval past.

If these new trends showed the multiplicity of the nexus between politics and Dalits in UP, there have been a number of new directions in the study of Dalits which were often inaugurated by BSP's institutionalized politics. First, tied to the rewriting of the past, the politics of symbols and the transformation of the built environment has emerged: Nicolas Jaoul's analysis of Dr. Ambedkar statues (2006) focused on the political meanings of symbols, and their role in Dalits' reconciliation with a nation whose actualization had systematically excluded them. Scholars also began to trace the local and global dynamics of the Dalit movement in the diaspora (Hardtmann 2008). In addition, studies appeared that showed the need of a generational inflection in the study of Dalit communities. In the book *Degrees Without Freedom? Education, Masculinities, and Unemployment in North India'*, which focuses on education and its effects on social reproduction across landed Jat, Muslim and Dalit communities in western UP, Craig Jeffrey, Patricia Jeffery and Roger Jeffery (2008) mapped the dilemma between increasing schooling and the reduction of employment opportunities for educated youth. By focusing on education as a contradictory resource, the authors portray young Dalits' political entrepreneurship and the surrounding masculine cultures as forms of modernity. The theme of modernity is central to the book *Retro-modern India. Forging the Low-caste Self* (Ciotti 2010a). Manuela Ciotti argues that modernity amongst a Chamar community in the village of Manupur, eastern UP, is the outcome of two intertwined trajectories: the first trajectory is one of the reproduction of practices and ideologies that emerged in the nineteenth century amongst Indian middle classes in their encounter with colonial modernity. The second process observed amongst the Chamars is one of the subversion of established powers, hierarchies and worldviews through movements for self-respect and political empowerment (in particular through mobilization with the BSP) and the cultural production that has accompanied these movements.

The history of UP has often been recorded as a history of male 'untouchable' actors – so that the female gender amongst Dalit communities is still largely unexplored. The analysis of Dalits, gender and politics has recently emerged on the anthropological horizon in UP. *Political Agency and Gender in India* (Ciotti forthcoming) is the first ethnography of Dalit and low-caste women within institutionalized politics. Drawing on the process of upward class mobility leading to the creation of the BSP, the book explores the articulation of class, caste and gender emerging from the ethnography of BSP women activists in Lucknow (see Ciotti 2006, 2009, 2010b, 2012). As shown in the course of this chapter, Dalit women never featured in the realm of politics both in rural and urban areas. From the standpoint of individual agency, rather than that of caste collectives, this book shows low-caste women activists – underrepresented in Indian political history – appropriating and re-enacting gender idioms and models coined in colonial India, and refashioning them for the exigencies of contemporary politics. These idioms and models are particularly visible in women's mobilization activities and in their liaison roles between the developmental state and its citizens. The book testifies to the presence of underlying deeper structures of gendered political agency cutting across time, class and caste amongst Dalit/low-caste communities usually considered as 'others'. Further, the ethnographic focus on agency challenges the usual images of Dalit/low-caste women as 'victims', thus interrogating the burgeoning field of Dalit studies.

Conclusions

By exploring the dynamics between untouchability and politics, this chapter has provided an anatomy of UP society, politics and culture since India's Independence. What is more, the journey into the anthropological imagination on UP has returned an account of social change addressing wide religious, societal, regional and national scapes. The analysis of trends in the study of Dalit castes in UP has shown an emphasis on political economy, conflict and worldview alternatives. If, on the one hand, UP offers histories of domination, of the production and resilience of inequality, on the other hand it also shows trends towards equality: this chapter offered portraits of 'untouchables' as ploughmen at the beck and call of upper-caste landlords as well as of business leaders, government employees and politicians. In the process, *caste as culture* has emerged over time – a consequence of the growing involvement of Dalit caste members in politics.

Against this backdrop, the proliferation of works on Dalits from UP over the past two decades calls for reflection. The histories produced so far are incomplete: the anthropological imagination from UP, historically and in the present, can only provide an impressionistic picture given the geographical extension of the state and the size of the Dalit population and many castes within it. The existing literature shows a focus on the most numerous communities so that others have remained largely unknown and their path of mobility and politics is still left to explore. Knowledge of these castes will provide a more nuanced picture of how the production of (in)equality has shifted historically, but also of the particular trajectories that it has taken. In addition to expanding the range of communities analysed, there are themes that need to be addressed. As shown by a recent article on Dalit social history by Narayan (2010), an important theme is violence. Narayan wrote about UP Dalits' struggle at the time of abandoning the polluting activities of removing dead cattle from the fields and cutting the umbilical cord of newly born babies. This decision led to brutal violence against the Dalits.[24] Narayan argues that '[t]he absence and long silence on the history of this violence in sociological literature, governmental documents and contemporary literary texts raises serious questions about the nature and politics of knowledge production about Dalits in brahminical society like India' (2010: 112). While there is a history of hidden violence to unearth, given the number of atrocities in UP the investigation of contemporary violence remains an urgent task. Contextually, more research is needed to make sense of violence vis-à-vis positive data emerging from UP. A survey carried out on a large sample of Dalit households in eastern and western UP (Kapur, Prasad, Pritchett, Babu 2010) shows how the past two decades (1990s to 2000s) have brought about socio-economic advancement. The survey reveals massive changes in Dalit self-perception in the social, economic and cultural spheres while social gains appear to have reached them in a stronger sense than economic ones (although these are also present). A picture of the ongoing urbanization and liberalization processes also emerges. The survey also returns a picture of the progressive disappearance of those forms of untouchability that have historically disallowed sociality, have confined workers in specific domains of the economy, and excluded them from public spaces such as schools and temples.

While the simultaneous presence of violence and of socio-economic inclusion processes calls for nuanced analysis, additional research is missing on those who tragically re-enact discriminatory acts such as the one described at the beginning of this chapter. Both analysis and research are important as the compulsions of neoliberal India do not eliminate caste wars – but possibly exacerbate them – and engender many other conflicts, for example around land, employment and natural resources. Research is needed to understand the causes of the persistent incommensurability between the principle of equality and what I have defined as the most arduous principle to meet wide acceptance, that is that all individuals share the same substance (Ciotti 2010a: 144). In other words, there is an urgent need to understand better and overcome 'caste as a state of mind' in its contemporary private, public and neoliberal manifestations, which ultimately sustains that incommensurability.

Notes

1 See Ciotti 2010a: 1ff for an example of political mobilization spurred by water-related discrimination practices.
2 See the Untouchability (Offences) Act (1955) and the Scheduled Castes and Scheduled Tribes (Prevention of Atrocities) Act (1989).
3 In 1991 the Indian government decided to reserve 27 per cent of the posts in the central government for members of the OBCs, following the recommendation of the Backward Classes Commission, alias the Mandal Commission. This decision sparked widespread protests amongst upper castes who saw their employment chances further reduced.
4 A complete list is found at http://www.socialjustice.nic.in/pdf/scorderuttarpradesh.pdf
5 As discussed in the course of the chapter, it should be noted that BSP party politics does not exhaust the multiplicity of Dalit politics and accounts of social mobility in UP, which still await to be written.
6 Many accounts exist of the emergence of the BSP, its ideology and its performance (see Chandra 2004; Ciotti 2009, 2010a, 2012; Hasan 2000; Kumar 1999; Mendelsohn and Viciany 1998; Pai 2002, 2009; Jaffrelot 2003).
7 State Development Report at: http://www.planningcommission.nic.in/plans/stateplan/upsdr/sdr_ up.htm (accessed 12 November 2008).
8 A notable example being the research by Patricia Jeffery and Roger Jeffery in western UP spanning several decades.
9 The work by Paul Brass over the decades has laid the foundations for the writing of UP political history.

10 In Cohn's writings, Madhopur village is at times named as Senapur.
11 This is a standard residential pattern for such communities.
12 This is also noticed by Mahar 1972 and Ciotti 2010a.
13 Myths of origin amongst Dalits – such as those recorded by Kolenda – have undergone significant transformations. Deliège (1999) argues that there is a common underlying structure in all myths recounted by Dalits in different parts of India. The 'sibling' myth, as it is called, narrates the story of four brothers, one of whom made the mistake of handling the body of a dead animal. He was labelled 'untouchable', and considered as the ancestor of the 'untouchable' castes. Deliège's analysis supports the idea that while, on the one hand, Dalits criticize their position within society through these myths, on the other, 'they do not question the ideological foundations of the system, nor the system itself, which they present almost as natural' (1999: 73). By contrast, to critique the unequal caste social order, Dalit politics has revitalized the Adi Hindu theme. The Adi Hindu movement was initiated by Swami Achutanand in the 1920s in UP, and together with other similar movements in other parts of India, centred around the idea of the low castes as the original inhabitants of India, who were deprived of their lands and subjugated by Aryan invaders.
14 By contrast, inter-caste relations appeared to be loosening up in the spaces outside the village.
15 The introduction of reservations for SCs in the Panchayati Raj allowed members of these communities to enter otherwise inaccessible local governance bodies. See Ciotti 2011 for an analysis of rural elections and reserved quotas.
16 Dr. Ambedkar is the historical Dalit leader, also chairman of the constitution drafting committee, who enjoys universal recognition amongst Dalits in India and beyond.
17 Jatav is the Sankritized name for 'Chamar'.
18 Processes of capitalization on leatherwork which took place within the Ad Dharma movement amongst the Chamars in Punjab (Juergensmeyer 1982) and the Jatavs (Chamars) in Agra in western UP (Lynch 1969) were accompanied by self-respect movements and political assertion.
19 For an in-depth analysis of the transition from the Congress Party to the BSP amongst a Chamar community in eastern UP see Ciotti 2010a: 191ff.
20 Concerning the multifaceted religious identities and practices amongst 'untouchables' in UP – ranging from Bhakti, to Catholicism, to Hinduism – see Bellwinkel-Schempp 2007; Ciotti 2010a; Schaller 1996; Schmalz 2005.
21 Chapter accessed at http://www.maren-bellwinkel.de/artikel/pigsandpower.pdf on 1 March 2011.
22 The BJP is the Hindu right Bharatya Janata Party.
23 The pig is an impure animal associated with 'untouchables'.
24 This struggle is known as the Nara-Maveshi movement and took place in UP between the 1950s and 1980s.

References

Bayly, S. (1999) *Caste, Society and Politics in India from the Eighteenth Century to the Modern Age.* Cambridge: Cambridge University Press.

Bellwinkel-Schempp, M. (2005) 'Pigs and power: Urban space and urban decay', in E. Hust and M. Mann (eds), *Urbanization and Governance in India.* New Delhi: Manohar, pp. 201–26. Available at: http://www.maren-bellwinkel.de/artikel/pigsandpower.pdf (accessed 1 March 2011).

——(2007) 'From Bhakti to Buddhism: Ravidas and Ambedkar', *Economic and Political Weekly*, 42(23): 2177–83.

Brass, P. R. (1997) 'The politicisation of the peasantry in a north Indian state', in S. Kaviraj (ed.), *Politics in India.* Delhi: Oxford University Press.

Chandra, K. (2004) *Why Ethnic parties Succeed: Patronage and Ethnic Head Counts in India.* Cambridge: Cambridge University Press.

Charsley, S. R. (1996) 'Untouchable': What is in a name?', *Journal of the Royal Anthropological Institute* (n.s.), 2(1): 1–23.

Chowdhry, P. (2009) '"First our jobs then our girls": The dominant caste perceptions on the "rising" Dalits', *Modern Asian Studies*, 43(2): 437–79.

Ciotti, M. (2006) 'At the margins of feminist politics? Everyday lives of women activists in northern India', *Contemporary South Asia*, 15(4) 437–52.

——(2009) 'The conditions of politics: Low-caste women and political agency in a northern Indian city', *Feminist Review*, 91:113–34.

*——(2010a) *Retro-modern India. Forging the Low-caste Self*. New Delhi, London: Routledge.

——(2010b) 'Futurity in words: Low-caste women politicians' self-representation and post-Dalit scenarios in north India', *Contemporary South Asia*, 18(1): 43–56.

——(2010c) 'The private and public life of social categories in India: Interrogating the "Dalit"', Paper presented at the conference, Mobility or Marginalisation? Dalits in Neoliberal India, University of Oxford, September 2010.

——(2012) 'Resurrecting *seva* (social service): Dalit and low-caste women party activists as producers and consumers of political culture and practice in urban north India', *The Journal of Asian Studies*, 71(1): 149–70.

——(forthcoming) *Political Agency and Gender in India*. London, New York: Routledge.

*Cohn, B. S. (1990 [1962]) *An Anthropologist among Historians and Other Essays*. Delhi: Oxford University Press.

Contursi, J. (1993) 'Political theology: Text and practice in a Dalit panther', *Journal of Asian Studies*, 52(2): 320–39.

Deliège, R. (1999) *The Untouchables of India*. Oxford: Berg Publishers.

Drèze, J. and Gazdar, H. (1997) 'Uttar Pradesh: The burden of inertia', in J. Drèze and A. Sen (eds), *Indian Development: Selected Regional Perspectives*. Delhi: Oxford University Press.

Dumont, L. (1970) *Homo Hierarchicus: The Caste System and its Implications*. Chicago: Chicago University Press.

Frøystad, K. (2005) *Blended Boundaries: Caste, Class and Shifting Faces of 'Hinduness' in a North Indian City*. Delhi: Oxford University Press.

Fuller, C. (1997) 'Introduction: Caste today', in C. Fuller (ed.), *Caste Today*. Delhi: Oxford University Press.

Gould, H. (2003) 'Local-level/Grassroots political studies' in V. Das (ed.), *The Oxford India Companion to Sociology and Social Anthropology*. Delhi: Oxford University Press.

Guru, G. (2001) 'The language of Dalit-Bahujan political discourse', in G. Shah (ed.), *Dalit Identity and Politics: Cultural Subordination and the Dalit Challenge*. Vol. 2. New Delhi: Sage.

Hardtmann, E. (2008) *The Dalit Movement in India: Local Practices, Global Connections*. New Delhi: Oxford University Press.

Hasan, Z. (1989) 'Power and mobilization: Patterns of resilience and change in Uttar Pradesh Politics', in F. R. Frankel and M. S. A. Rao (eds), *Dominance and State Power in Modern India: Decline of a Social Order*, vol. I. Delhi: Oxford University Press.

——(1996) 'Communal mobilization and changing majority in Uttar Pradesh', in D. Ludden (ed.), *Contesting the Nation: Religion, Community, and the Politics of Democracy in India*. Philadelphia: University of Pennsylvania Press.

——(2000) 'Representation and redistribution: The new lower caste politics in northern India', in F. Frankel, Z. Hasan, R. Bhargava and B. Arora (eds), *Transforming India: Social and Political Dynamics of Democracy*. Delhi: Oxford University Press.

Jaffrelot, C. (2003) *India's Silent Revolution: The Rise of the Low Castes in North Indian Politics*. Delhi: Manohar.

Jaoul, N. (2006) 'Learning the use of symbolic means: Dalits, Ambedkar statues and the state in Uttar Pradesh', *Contributions to Indian Sociology*, 40(2): 175–207.

Jeffrey, C., Jeffery, P. and Jeffery, R. (2008) *Degrees Without Freedom? Education, Masculinities, and Unemployment in North India*. Stanford: Stanford University Press.

Juergensmeyer, M. (1982) *Religion as Social Vision: The Movement Against Untouchability in 20th Century Punjab*. Berkeley: University of California Press.

Kapur, D., Bhan Prasad, C., Pritchett, L. and Shyam Babu, D. (2010) 'Rethinking inequality: Dalits in Uttar Pradesh in the market reform era', *Economic and Political Weekly*, 35: 39–49.

*Khare, R. S. (1984) *The Untouchable as Himself: Ideology, Identity, and Pragmatism among the Lucknow Chamars*. Cambridge: Cambridge University Press.

Kolenda, P. (1958) 'Changing caste ideology in a north Indian village', *Journal of Social Issues*, 14(4): 51–65.

——(1964) 'Religious anxiety and Hindu fate', *Journal of Asian Studies*, 23: 71–81.

——(1989) 'Micro-ideology and micro-utopia in Khalapur. Changes in the discourse on caste over thirty years', *Economic and Political Weekly*, 24(32): 1831–38.

Kudaisya, G. (2007) 'Aryavarta, "Hind", or "Uttar Pradesh". The postcolonial naming and framing of a "region"', in D. Chakrabarty, R. Majumdar and A. Sartori (eds), *From the Colonial to the Postcolonial. India and Pakistan in Transition*. Oxford: Oxford University Press.

Lerche, J. and Jeffery, R. (2003) 'Uttar Pradesh: Into the Twenty-first Century', in R. Jeffery and J. Lerche (eds), *Social and Political Change in Uttar Pradesh: European Perspectives*. New Delhi: Manohar.

*Lynch, O. M. (1969) *The Politics of Untouchability: Social Mobility and Social Change in a City of India*. New York: Columbia University Press.

Mahar, J. M. (1972) 'Agents of dharma in a north Indian village', in J. M. Mahar (ed.), *The Untouchables in Contemporary India*. Tucson: University of Arizona Press.

Mendelsohn, O. and Vicziany, M. (1998) *The Untouchables: Subordination, Poverty and the State in Modern India*. New Delhi: Cambridge University Press.

Mosse, D. (1994) 'Idioms of subordination and styles of protest among Christian and Hindu Harijan castes in Tamil Nadu', *Contributions to Indian Sociology*, 28(1): 67–106.

*Narayan, B. (2006) *Women Heroes and Dalit Assertion in North India: Culture, Identity and Politics*. New Delhi: Sage Publications.

——(2009) *Fascinating Hindutva: Saffron Politics and Dalit Mobilisation*. New Delhi: Sage.

——(2010) 'History produces politics: The *Nara-Maveshi* movement in Uttar Pradesh', *Economic and Political Weekly*, 45: 111–19.

Opler, E. M. and Singh, R. D. (1952) 'Two villages of eastern Uttar Pradesh (U. P.), India: An analysis of similarities and differences', *American Anthropologist*, n.s., 54(2), Part 1: 179–90.

Pai, S. (2002) *Dalit Assertion and the Unfinished Democratic Revolution*. New Delhi: Sage.

——(2009) 'New social engineering agenda of the Bahujan Samaj Party: Implications for state and national politics', *South Asia: Journal of South Asian Studies*, n.s., 23(3): 338–53.

Ramakrishnan, V. and Mahaprashasta, A. A. (2009) 'Victims always', *Frontline* 26(24): November 21–December 4. Available at: http://www.frontlineonnet.com/stories/20091204262400400.htm (accessed 19 November 2009).

Rao, A. (2009) *The Caste Question: Dalits and the Politics of Modern India*. Berkeley: California University Press.

Schaller, J. (1996) 'Sankritization, caste uplift and social dissidence in the Sant Ravidas Panth', in N. D. Lorenzen (ed.), *Bhakti Religion in North India: Community, Identity and Political Action*. New Delhi: Manohar.

Schmalz, M. (2005) 'Dalit catholic tactics of marginality at a north Indian mission', *History of Religions*, 44(3): 216–51.

Searle-Chatterjee, M. (1981) *Reversible Sex Roles: The Special Case of Benares Sweepers*. Oxford: Pergamon Press.

——(1994a) 'Caste, religion and other identities', in M. Searle-Chatterjee and V. Sharma (eds), *Contextualizing Caste*. Oxford: Blackwell Publishers.

——(1994b) 'Urban untouchables and Hindu nationalism', *Immigrants and Minorities*, 13:12–25.

Singh, J. (1998) 'Ambedkarisation and assertion of Dalit identity: Socio-cultural protest in Meerut district of western Uttar Pradesh', *Economic and Political Weekly*, 33(40): 2611–18.

Srinivas, M. N. (1997) 'Practicing social anthropology in India', *Annual Review of Anthropology*, 26: 1–24.

Uttar Pradesh: State Development Report (Vols I and II), http://planningcommission.nic.in/plans/stateplan/index.php?state=sdr_up.htm (accessed 12 November 2008).

Zelliott, E. (1996) *From Untouchable to Dalit: Essays on the Ambedkar Movement*. New Delhi: Manohar.

19 West Bengal

Colonial legacy, class formation and politics

Henrike Donner

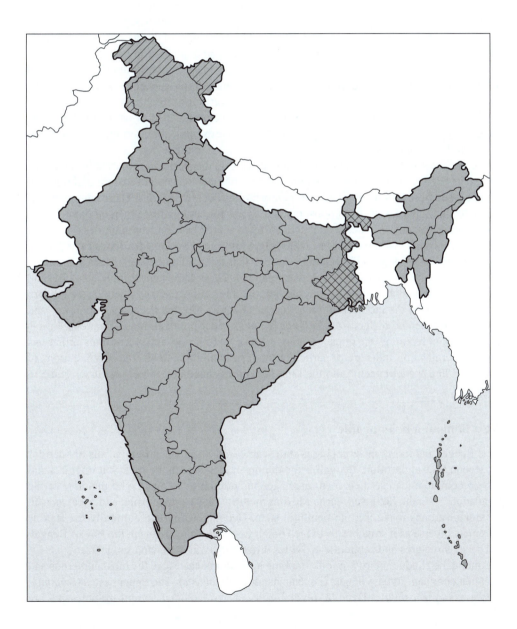

In what gave the ceremony a touch of uniqueness, members of the families of those killed in police firing in Nandigram on March 7, 2007, victims' families of Singur and a section of sex workers of the city were all witness of this historic swearing-in. Nandigram was the starting point of Ms Banerjee and her party to build up a strong anti-Government movement on the issue of land acquisition, which ultimately raked up several other issues and touched the chord of anti-incumbency sentiment.

(*United News of India* on the swearing in of
Chief Minister Mamata Banerjee, 20 May 2011)

The history of Bengal has been marked by discourses on politics since the colonial encounter, during which this former presidency became the capital of the British 'raj'. An ethnographic overview on West Bengal can only be understood in the context of this history, with the main theme running through all sections related to the reality of modernity in India.

Firstly, this chapter focuses on the way Western ideas and institutions forced local communities to rethink and reorganize with the impact of education and agricultural transformations highlighted in the context of politics resulting from these processes. Given the extensive literature on how earlier formations contributed to what might be called 'modernity', the ethnography of Bengal provides a prime example for the multiple institutions, idioms and symbolic systems that shaped distinct politics in the region.

Secondly, a set of ethnographies draw our attention to the particularities established in this context as 'Bengali culture' from the point of view of kinship, gender relations and religion, but also take a fresh look at caste and community through local categories. These ethnographies testify to the importance of relationships and social formations that emerged from highly idiosyncratic systems of beliefs and practices, often shared between communities.

Yet it is through historical studies, which allow us to see how larger processes challenged and reshaped such ideas in the 'modern' world, that these ethnographies help us to situate culturally specific practices within power relations. These may stem from sources beyond the local and immediate, for instance colonial rule, the nationalist movement or the modern nation state. Thus, the last section redirects our attention towards the 'play of politics' and the way West Bengal differs from and conforms to wider political transformations. In this respect, labour relations, the impact of long-term Left Front rule, and recent transformations in post-liberalization India are of particular interest. In all three fields, the contradictions of 'progress' and 'development' and the kind of politics shaped by these discourses come to the fore.

West Bengal: a brief profile

West Bengal, the fourth most populous state, came into being when Bengal was divided for the second time at partition. Bengali is the dominant language in the state, but migrants and *adivasi* communities use their own languages in addition to Bengali. The majority of the population is Hindu, but a very large Muslim minority plays a major role, and tribal as well as migrant groups make it a multicultural state. Geographically and culturally the state is extremely diverse as it stretches from the Himalayas to the Sunderbans in the Bay of Bengal, and social structures and economic activities differ greatly in these environments.

Among the Hindu majority, middle-ranking agricultural castes are the most numerous and are often dominant in the villages (i.e. Namasudras, Rajbansis). The upper castes (*Brahmin*, *Vaidhya* and *Kasthya*) played a pivotal role in the colonial administration and are overrepresented in urban, educated sections of the population. The main festivals are related to female goddesses, especially Durga, Lakshmi and Kali. Local cults and festivals abound, which often draw on Hindu sects (Vaishnavism in particular). When the East India Company was formed, Muslim *nawabs* ruled Bengal but with partition most affluent Muslim families have left. The remaining Muslim population is constituted mostly of poor peasants and migrant labour. Whilst the state as a whole ranks among those in the middle where indicators of development are concerned Muslims lag behind in literacy, male to female ratio and maternal mortality rates. Tribal groups make up a significant percentage of the rural population, whilst a large number of northern working-class migrants and business communities account for the multicultural character of the cities.

The capital Kolkata (Calcutta), with five million residents, is by far the largest city, followed by Howrah (one million) and regional centres including Durgapur, Bardhaman, Kharagpur, Siliguri, Asansol and Barasat, with between 200,000 to 500,000 residents. However, the majority of West Bengal's population lives in more than 50,000 villages and agriculture plays a vital role in the state's economy, with the main crops being paddy, wheat, jute, vegetables, sugarcane, pulses and oilseeds, most of which are cultivated by hand. In addition, tea is produced on large-scale plantations in the north and fish and prawns are farmed commercially on the coast. Though West Bengal is the most important producer of rice in India, output remains a concern and has been a major site for investment by the state government, as have vegetable growing, fisheries and the like. The service sector makes for the highest percentage of the state domestic product, followed by manufacture, which only constitutes 22 per cent of the state's income. Major steel industries exist along the Durgapur-Asansol corridor and the port of Haldia is a petrochemical hub, whilst smaller industries are located in and around Calcutta, for instance metal, leather, engineering, jute and textiles.

After Independence the Congress Party ruled the state until the 1960s when a Left Front led by the Communist Party of India (Marxist) [CPI(M)] joined the government. They came to power after a period of unrest in 1977 and governed until ousted after 34 years by the Trinamool Congress Party in 2011. West Bengal's political and economic fate was shaped by partition, when over five million refugees settled in the state. More recently, rural reform, resettlement and strong trade unions marked politics until the 1990s when the Left Front introduced neoliberal policies to attract investment and the political opposition gained momentum, resulting in a change of government.

From company to colonial rule: the making of politics

Bengal was the first of the three 'presidencies' established by the East India Company and provided the blueprint for British expansion into other regions (Bose and Jalal 1997). Locals got involved with the British as brokers, contractors and speculators (see Mukherjee 1987: 42) and initially, such contact was as much about networks, trade, taxes and credit, as about conflict and domination. But soon governing the province became a necessity, and knowledge had to be acquired in a systematic way (Rocher 1993) in order to establish a suitable legal framework to regulate trade relations (Sarkar 1997: 25). Pre-colonial Bengal was characterized by its many cultural and sectarian groups, distinctive urban centres, court and upper-caste cultures' opposition to vernacular practices, but also a common language, literature and popular religion.

Whilst all these factors merged into a narrative of a unified region, culminating in the nationalist imagery of 'Golden Bengal' (Bayly 1998: 29–30), Hastings, the first governor, stipulated that colonial rule should allow firstly that Indians would come under separate laws and administer these; secondly that Hindus and Muslims would be dealt with separately; thirdly that 'customs' would be extracted from written sources; and fourthly that 'religious institutions' (including relations between kin, persons and property) would be subject to a separate legal domain.

Whilst Muslims apparently had scriptures to fall back on, what constituted Hindu culture was much more contested.

Debates about 'custom' and 'community' emerged, which brought the Hindu upper castes into colonial politics. They saw themselves as guardians of 'true' Hindu culture and soon set out to reform Hinduism for a modern world. Throughout the colonial period Hindu and Muslim elites expanded their hegemonic hold over lower classes through their participation in the emerging public sphere, and this engagement led to nationalist claims for sovereignty, which were formulated on the basis of distinctive communal and regional cultures in the late colonial period.

But Bengal's history demonstrates the complexity of colonialism, which was not a one-way process. Locals were as eager to learn about the 'other' as the colonial rulers were to define different communities. From the late eighteenth century onwards institutions dedicated to the 'enlightenment' of 'natives', including the Calcutta Madrassa (1780), the Asiatic Society (1784) and Hindu College (1817), were founded. These institutions provided formal English education as well as tuition in other languages to the sons of wealthy families, and they established English-medium education as a privilege of the ruling classes, which it remained up until the 1980s (see Scrase 1993). These sites became centres of debates about reforms in a movement known as the 'Bengali Renaissance'.

The focus on recognition of local customs and communities and the reform of the same later on fed into the nationalist movement. In the process urbanized Bengalis were highlighted as 'modern' and progressive, refined 'custom' turned into a revered, homogenized 'tradition', and upper-caste practices became codified law. Debates that highlighted these tensions and demonstrated the structural and institutional changes taking place in Bengali society emerged around questions of family and gender, most prominently the 'Prevention of Sati Act' (1829) banning 'widow burning', and the 'Age of Consent Act' (1891) prohibiting 'child marriage'(Ray 1996; Raychaudhuri 1999). Both debates also show how crucial the link between class and community practice became in the colonial situation, a link that hinges on the overdetermined symbolism of Bengali women, which later fed into the notion of Mother India.

Colonial power framed the transformation of the region, notably through the 'Permanent Settlement Act' (1793), which made *zamindars* (landowners) liable for tax collection amongst villagers and gave rise to Calcutta as centre of trade and industries. The commodification of land and rights in land created an upper-caste class of absentee landlords and great economic insecurity amongst those working the land. Estate managers and debt collectors became the most powerful figures in the countryside, and coerced and evicted peasants in their search for revenue.

In the wake of the politico-economic transformations two projects were initiated: firstly, the production of knowledge that served the purpose of governance; secondly the creation of a class, as Governor Macaulay stipulated in 1835, 'Indian in blood and colour, but English in taste, in opinions, in morals, and in intellect' (cited in Burton 2001: 18). More so than in other provinces, this engagement created a distinct, though not uniform, urban section of the population, which became the Bengali middle class. The term associated with this elite is *bhadralok* (literally gentlefolk), and is often mistakenly used to describe a 'community'. However, it refers to a subculture, a new way of life that emerged in the city. As a term indicating social status it replaced references to caste, ritual status and its cultural underpinnings amongst the upper castes (Broomfield 1968). Within this colonial context ethnography developed as a way to create knowledge for governance, but soon contributed to debates around reforms that were posed in Bengali society itself. If knowledge about India became a valuable resource for those ruling, it also figured in contestations of the status quo, and it is equally true that knowledge from and about the West was highly valued amongst a class whose world had become distinctly different from that of their forefathers and that of peasant populations.

Rural Bengal: community and caste

Whilst caste relations were subject to change before, the rapid and fundamental economic transformations of the nineteenth century had a powerful effect on rural populations. The colonial administration introduced the notion of a 'community' as a defining factor in dealings with locals, and the Permanent Settlement Act benefitted aristocratic Muslims and the three upper Hindu castes (Brahmin, Baidya and Kayastha), who came to control large landholdings from afar. Both, the detachment of the indigenous elite from the land and the segregation between the two communities have had lasting effects on the politics of West Bengal, palpable even today. From early on, the idea that Muslims and Hindus ought to be governed by separate laws, for instance where inheritance was concerned, created a strong emphasis on the legal domain. Throughout the colonial period the number of court cases soared, and as public laws emphasized 'Western' values of property and individual rights, they often clashed with 'custom' and local interest groups. However, as Washbrook (1981) points out, 'private law' often worked against individual interests, as it presupposed shared 'traditions' and a 'community'. Such law supported a politics of differentiation and in Bengal differences between Hindus and Muslims became more pronounced as shared identities emerged as political entities (Cohn 1987). Another effect of these processes was the struggle of upwardly mobile 'communities', no longer tied into rigid rural caste structures, for recognition and higher status. As untouchable communities are rare in the region (Bandyopadhyay 1994: 94) these movements became prominent among agricultural lower castes.

   Anthropologists have always had a strong interest in the politics of 'caste' in all its forms as well as the transformations that occurred (for an account of the inner workings of the upper castes see Inden 1976, for intra-caste relations Davis 1983). Apart from the obvious economic relationships, villages were divided into strictly segregated *paras* (neighbourhoods), a form of organization still found in rural Bengal today (see for example Davis 1983 and Lamb 2000). The upper castes in Bengal were organized and worked similarly to upper castes in other regions, but the agricultural castes and middle-section Muslims, who owned smallholdings but were never huge landowners, were often of very malleable status and economic standing. In the western districts, the middle-ranking castes, for instance the Mahishas, mostly worked their own land, whilst the lower castes and untouchables, for instance the Rajbansis, could own land or work as sharecroppers. In the villages of the northern and eastern districts, middle-sized landholdings often belonged to communities of converted Muslims, who dominated their landless brethren in the same way as middle-caste Hindus would have done. As artisan castes found themselves competing with others for jobs and opportunities (Sarkar 1994), in the late colonial period certain middle-ranking castes such as the Namasudras and even lower castes, like the Rajbansis, and at the end opted for social reform and political mobilization, claimed higher status by adopting upper caste practices including vegetarianism and hypergamous marriages. This challenged older ideas about caste as an integrated system.

Instead, caste came to be understood as a social identity (Bandyopadhyay 1994). Caste movements were most successful among those with small landholdings and artisan communities and were not usually directed against upper castes per se. They drew heavily on the more egalitarian ethos of Hindu Vaishnavite sects prominent in the region. Furthermore, especially in the eastern and northern parts of the province, the distinction between Hindu landlords and Muslim labourers became a powerful force in politics.

In response to these complexities colonial administrators began to develop a distinct 'ethnographic' interest in groups, their workings and boundaries. In 1874 a committee of the Anthropological Institute undertook a survey, 'framed so as to adapt to Indian conditions the methods of research sanctioned by European men of science' (Risley 1891: 290). These surveys defined 'community' in accordance with ideas about caste and religious affiliation, and served as a basis for debates about political participation in the future, as 'the colonial concept of an Indian society divided along religious and caste lines had an important impact on the way communities were formed and dissolved in nineteenth and twentieth century Bengal' (Bandyopadhyay 1994: 6). They also highlighted how the idiom of caste was reshaped, as occupation, ritual status and economic opportunities came to be disconnected.

Metropolis: class and reform

The possibilities the idiom and practices related to caste flexibly came to bear on class formation throughout the colonial period. Upper castes migrated to Calcutta, harnessed new opportunities and engaged with *bhadralok* culture. Members of business families, absentee landlords, service holders and artisans, both, Hindus as well as high-status *ashraf* Muslims became entirely urbanized (Chatterjee 1993; Amin 1996; Murshid 1983), and the reform of personal and religious lives emerged as a marker of 'modern' political identities. Discourses on appropriate 'customs' could be found amongst traditionalists and radicals alike (Chatterjee 2007), and the orientation towards reform constitutes a common denominator of Bengali, middle-class and urban politics, even where local interest groups focused on apparently conservative values like 'caste' and gender relations (see Sarkar 2001). Bengali women emerged as imagined and embodied 'repositories' of essentialized pan-Bengali identities. Such debates were conducted in the public sphere of meetings, journals and letters and gradually differences between upper castes faded into the background (see Broomfield 1968; Murshid 1983; Borthwick 1984; Mukherjee 1987; Sarkar 2001).

What marked out the middle classes was the zest with which reforms were debated and embraced, and the importance afforded to this progressive orientation in the course of nationalist agitations. But as careful social history has shown, the ethnography of the *bhadralok* sections of society cannot be read off ostentatiously 'modern' sects like the Brahmo Samaj, liberal musings of figureheads like Ramohan Roy, or the outward-looking spirituality of religious reformers like Vidhyasagar. All these did play an important role in how middle-class urbanites conducted their lives (Kopf 1979), but reforms were subject to a range of ideological structural foundations, and thus resulted in disparate and sometimes contradictory practices. Sarkar charts these structural changes in relation to new regimes of time, which ruled the middle-class home in the form of a salaried job (*chakri*) and *bhadralok* pre-occupations, including 'education, religious reform or revival, philanthropy, nationalist politics' (Sarkar 1997: 190–91).

In the case of *bhadralok* culture hegemony did not imply dominance, as subaltern orders prevailed as well, which drew on very different kinds of knowledge and politics (Sarkar 1989). Much of this vernacular stemmed from devotional *bhakti* cults and women's sub-cultures (Banerjee 1989), others emerged at the convergence of English and Bengali popular forms with new technologies, in particular print media. Thus, no single approach to becoming 'suitably modern' is in evidence; secondly, the change that was envisaged by intellectuals was not necessarily circumscribed by Western models (Raychaudhuri 1988). The history of nationalism in the region links anti-colonial struggles with the spread of progressive ideas formed part and parcel of a Bengali society engaged in very distinct ways with nationalism. Whilst the majority of nationalists adopted conservative discourses based on essentialized cultural differences emergent progressive parties fed more secular impulses into the movement (Chatterjee 1993).

Defining 'tradition', 'community' and 'culture'

In common with other parts of India, much of the early ethnography produced on Bengal focused on the caste system not least due to its importance for legal procedures, for instance Jogendra Nath Bhattacharya's 'Hindu Castes and Sects' published in English in 1896 (Bhattacharya 1995). Here, separate *jatis* were described in fixed terms through 'custom', for instance the infamous *kulin* Brahmins in terms of hypergamous polygamy (marriage into a higher status group with the possibility of more than one wife). However, the disintegration of caste as a system in the course of urbanization already materialized in the form of caste organizations, as debates around the changing status of a Kayastha sub-caste shows:

> Among the Babus of Calcutta, the number of Dākshina Rarhi Kāyasthas is far larger than that of any other caste. The majority of the Dākshina Rarhis are Sakti worshippers of the moderate type. The deities they worship most generally are Durgā and Kali. But their orthodox members follow the discipline imposed upon them by their Brahman Gurus, and they neither drink any kind of spirituous liquor, nor eat any kind of flesh excepting that of goats offered in sacrifice to some god or goddess. Of all the classes of Kāyasthas in Bengal, the Dākshina Rarhis have, under British rule, made the greatest progress in education, and in securing official positions.
>
> (Bhattacharya 1995: 143)

As a politics of cultural difference emerged 'local' customs became prominent, features of accounts focused on 'Bengali' culture (Dey 1969), which was increasingly attributed to a rural idyll. Thus, Rabindranath Tagore founded a university in the countryside with a view to capturing the authentic spirit of Bengal. New assertions of 'culture' fed into nationalist discourses and created a whole cottage industry of 'folk-lore'. The collection and documentation of 'folk' art and craft shows demonstrated to the colonial rulers the value of local distinctiveness whilst providing a focus for the urbanized middle classes when showcased in societies and festivals. Bengali crafts and performative arts began to feature as a 'heritage' to be preserved and consumed by urbanites (Bandyopadhyay 1990: xix; Hauser 2002).

But there emerged an interest in social structures as well, as the work of anthropologist Nirmal Kumar Bose (1901–72) shows, carried on into the period after independence. Educated within the narrowly defined ethnographic tradition that saw anthropology as concerned with 'tribal' populations, he began to work for the Anthropological Survey of India after Independence and saw anthropological research as an (often inconvenient) part of nation-building. His commitment to the Commission for Scheduled Tribes and Castes, of which he became a prominent advocate, followed in the footsteps of British administrators, but he later on initiated much broader studies of social processes, as his work on Calcutta

(Bose 1968), which directed the attention of colleagues towards urban issues (Sinha 1972; Siddiqui 1982).

A very different and not practice-orientated anthropological approach was employed in a later series of monographs dealing with 'Bengali culture' largely produced by American anthropologists. Inspired by Marriott's critique of functionalist and structuralist approaches, these ethnosociological studies aimed at an exploration of meaning rather than social structures (see Marriott and Inden 1977). They emphasized the need to study 'Hindu society' through 'Hindu categories', foregrounding South Asian ideas about persons, bodies, caste, present in the terminologies employed. Rather than studying ritual status based on the structural distinction between pure and impure (or purity and pollution, as argued by Dumont) and boundaries between groups, species and the like, these anthropologists focused on social worlds. They suggested that transubstantiality, shared substances that are seen as moral agents in exchanges (for example between two persons having sexual intercourse, but also those sharing food, those sharing the same *guru*, those belonging to the same *jati*), played a key role in defining belonging and social groups.

Their efforts that were particularly fruitful were studies of kinship, caste and ritual were concerned, and demonstrated how social relationships can be understood if basic processes of reproduction and everyday actions like food-sharing are taken into account. They highlighted embodied ideas evoked in mundane practices, a view that challenged rule-based models based on an overarching ideology. Thus, for instance, these accounts show how kin who share food and intercourse are related in the same way to members of their caste, and the idiom of *jati* can be expanded to include those of a *desh* (country), who also share substances (Inden and Nicholas 1977).

Today a wealth of ethnography on 'Bengali' personhood, lifecycle rituals and popular religion exists (see for example Roy 1972; Barnett *et al.* 1976; Inden and Nicholas 1977; Östör 1980; Fruzzetti 1982; Östör and Barnett 1982; Davis 1983; Fruzzetti, Lamb 2000; Nicholas 1981, 2003), which attends to micro-politics that shape intimate and associational life. But whilst such studies allow us to see how folk understandings are shared between Hindus, Muslims and Christians in the region, who mostly use the same language constituting 'Bengali culture,' this universe is governed as much by ritual, devotional cults, kinship and village or neighbourhood relationships as by 'modern politics' (see Rozario 1992; Kotalova 1996, Hauser 2012). Whilst ethnosociology highlights how the sharing of substances makes persons and relates people within a group, it fails to link these cognitive categories to modern institutions and their registers, for example discourses on the body to ideas about hygiene and medicine, which challenge this framework. Thus, focusing on language and ritual practices alone these studies often fail to address historical change.

The literature on the reforms of the nineteenth century is illuminating here, as it charts the continuous tension between 'indigenous' categories and new ontologies and 'modern' lifestyles. But recent ethnography of urban middle-class culture also testifies to the resilience of such meaningful cultural categories and interpretations, for example where emic perspectives extend into the political arena, as in discourses on the environment, schooling and healthcare (Kaviraj 1997; Ecks 2004; Donner 2004, 2006, 2008).

Migration: labour and refugees

The processual character of social relations and institutions is highlighted in a very different set of studies, which are also relevant to understand West Bengal politics today and focus on labour relations. The arguments made in these studies are related to two broad fields: firstly, questions around the emergence of a working class, and secondly the interplay between labour relations, legislation and the state.

By the beginning of the twentieth century Calcutta's industries had begun to thrive. Most enterprises belonged to North Indian business communities and processed jute, a cash crop grown in the hinterland. These industries drew masses of migrants to Bengal and their founders, the Marwaris, as these communities are commonly known, played a major role in the development of trade and commerce in the region (Timberg 1977; Hardgrove 2004). Crucially, it was their business culture, networks and capital that allowed for the vast increase in industrial output in the first decades of the twentieth century, when thousands of working-class migrants, whose lives and politics have been studied in much detail (see Chakrabarty 1989; de Haan 1994; Fernandes 1997; Sen 1999) came to Bengal. The questions that have been debated relate to the formal as well as the informal sector, discuss how and whether a working class emerged in this non-European context, and showcase the multiple ways in which labour relations were shaped by state action and legislation. Labour relations and labour organizations played a major role in the history of Bengal, and shaped politics in the city of Calcutta as well as the whole state's life.

A second wave of migrants emerged in the aftermath of partition, and the massive influx of refugees after partition and the integration of these Hindu refugees in West Bengal dominated state-wide politics well into the 1980s (Chatterjee 2007). Refugee colonies in Calcutta developed a vibrant cultural and political life, and the neighbourhood emerged as a site of distinct sociality and subject formation for this mostly middle-class Hindu population (Ray 2002). Slowly but steadily these localities became emblems of successful 'modern' political integration, as fully contemporary middle-class lifestyles with scope for social mobility emerged. Here, as in the case of labour, a distinct 'politics of recognition' was established, which made party affiliation a matter of access to specific resources, a means for social mobility, and a way of life.

Left Front rule: reform, debate, transformation

Few ethnographies relate the transformations the countryside was undergoing in the period before Independence and before the rule of the Left Front. However, Greenough's detailed study of the man-made 'Great Famine' in 1943 details rural networks, differences of class and caste, as well as gender relations and kinship in the early 1940s (Greenough 1982). As the time such interdependencies and 'traditional' ontologies are challenged in the course of modernization, and Marxist mobilizations like the Tebhaga movement in the mid-1940s and the Maoist insurgence in the late 1960s, which provided new understandings of the world and made the success of the Left Front in the aftermath of political turmoil possible.

The Communists joined the state government in the 1960s, but only came to power in 1977. The history of Left Front – ousted from government in early 2011 – is unique to West Bengal, and the policies employed have been examined in much detail.

The enthusiasm for elections and the general support for electoral democracy in India is well documented, but during the years of Left Front rule in Bengal voter turn-out, especially among the rural populace, has been remarkable (see Chatterjee 1997; Ruud 2003). Among other factors, this success is commonly attributed to the land reforms, which have been debated ever since.

Whilst the CPI(M) has always taken credit for the increased stability of livelihoods in the countryside, scholarship suggests that the relationship between agrarian structure and growth is difficult to disentangle (Rogaly *et al.* 1999). Even Greenough observes that older villagers often claimed that the food situation had improved with Independence (Greenough 1982). Land reforms had been attempted by previous governments but the Left Front's 'Operation Barga', which gave sharecroppers titles in land, was also supported by far-reaching policies aimed at the empowerment of the rural poor. However, critics have highlighted that land has not been distributed amongst the poorest of the poor. Instead the Left Front policies benefitted middle-caste peasants and the rural middle class. Secondly, it has been argued that the land reforms were implemented during a period of relative growth, brought about by other factors (see Mallick 1993).

It is, of course, impossible to show through ethnographic evidence whether or not a land reform is successful, but the second objective – political empowerment – can be discussed in this context. In a study Ruud shows how by the 1990s villagers had embraced electoral politics and drew on the 'modern' discourse of rights and entitlements, parties and state institutions with ease (Ruud 2003). Thus, scholars observing the implementation of various policies and the performance of the state in West Bengal up until the late 1980s agreed that the Left Front created a reform-orientated state apparatus that functioned well (see Kohli 1987; Nossiter 1988). The uniquely effective line of command employed by the CPI(M) linked the rural areas directly with Calcutta, and as local cadres were recruited en masse, vote-banks could be created across caste, ethnic or religious communities. In fact its anti-communalist stance has been hailed as the main virtue of the Left Front.

To this effect, the Left Front strengthened the role of the village councils (*gram panchajat*), where empowerment was achieved, although affirmative action for marginalized communities and women was only introduced in 1998. This empowerment on the local level has been embraced by the electorate and in the process the party and the state merged into one. Among rural and urban poor communities they combine to constitute '*sarkar*' (government) (Davis 1983; Basu 1992; Williams 1999; Roy 2003; Ruud 2003). But critical ethnography also shows how the discourses on 'development' and 'progress' spurned by such a regime are transformed and employed selectively (Agnihotri 2001). Thus, Davis found in the 1970s that villagers distinguished between two distinct modes of political activities, one 'traditional' referred to as 'work of the village' (*gramer kaj*), based on patron–client relationships, caste hierarchies and paternalism; the other 'modern', referencing links beyond the village with unmediated access and entitlements described as 'work of government' (*sarkari kaj*). According to Ruud, whilst both notions were in evidence in the 1980s and 1990s, the CPI(M) had successfully merged them through the institution of the party (Ruud 2003). But mobilization remained uneven, and critics pointed at prevailing exclusions at the margins, where for instance tribals, or refugees, live precariously in geographical and political borderlands (van Schendel 2005; Jalais 2009; Rogaly et al. 2009).

However, it was the success of reform rather than the blind spots that came to haunt the Left Front. Roy's monograph on contemporary politics in West Bengal (Roy 2003) shows how land reforms actually enhanced 'accumulation by dispossession' (Harvey 2003), as land rapidly changed its status from being the means of production for the masses towards becoming an investment for the middle classes (Roy 2003). Those who lost their livelihood turned into urban squatters protected by politicians in exchange for votes. Their communities are pawns as the urban middle class is vowed by the Left Front in post-liberalization contestations over the distribution of state resources and real estate development that took off from the mid-1990s onwards.

Politics in a New World: land, state, conflict

Conflicts over resources shape politics in the rural areas as well as the cities (Chatterji 2001; van Schendel 2005) and have resurfaced recently in the form of violent confrontations over land acquisition for Special Economic Zones in Singur and Nandigram.

The redistribution of land to those who tilled it, and the settlement of refugees in Calcutta, had been important themes for the Communists before 1977, and much effort went into land reforms and the legalization of refugee colonies after the Left Front came to power. However, instances like the so-called 'Morichjhanpi massacre', when low-caste refugees from Bangladesh were shot at by the police five years after they had been invited to settle in West Bengal, demonstrate that communities without political clout were excluded from redistribution, even where they had access to the powers to be (Mallick 1999; Jalais 2005). The ethnography of such contestations suggests that the structural 'violence of development' (Kothari and Hartcourt 2004) increased with the expansion of the state.

Scholars and critics were quick to cast the ousting of the Left Front from power in the mould of grand debates on industrialization, globalization and development, the role of land in Marxist theorizing and mobilization and the workings of democracy, but a detailed analysis of the workings of politics can complicate the picture considerably (see for the most obvious points Majumdar 2010).

Politics, understood not as a mechanism of state power and governmentality, but as constituting and being constituted through a multitude of social relationships, has been the subject of detailed ethnography in West Bengal. Whilst the rule of the Comrades was supported by substantial violence, when voters are cynical about politicians they often also assert that democracy works for them, a view that is evident in the great symbolic significance attributed to elections themselves (see Chatterjee 1997; Williams 1999; Banerjee 2007). Earlier, Left Front paradigms of redistribution and empowerment had been embraced, if grudgingly, by the majority of voters, including a middle class that gained disproportionately through the expansion of the state. Under the Left Front, resources and privileges were distributed through political parties in both the countryside and in urban areas, but rural areas with their massive vote-banks were clearly favoured.

By the beginning of the 1990s, urbanites, who had felt left out from 1977 onwards, needed to be appeased, whilst rural communities began to rebel against the combination of political patronage and corruption even where substantial improvements had been made. Ethnography shows that decades of disinvestment in state services and jobs led to the disenchantment of middle-class voters, who increasingly withdrew their support of the Left Front. This has led some scholars to assert that only the poor are increasingly left with politics (Harriss 2007) as the middle class are no longer dependent on parties to control and access resources (Chatterjee 2007). But with reference to West Bengal there can be no doubt that the party (earlier the CPI(M), but from the mid-2000s the Trinamool Congress in certain areas) is still of outmost importance in the lives of rural as well as urban communities, and ethnography shows that during its reign the Left Front was measured most promptly and directly against outcomes in the city, as city dwellers, including the middle class, were quick to officially complain or even litigate, whether the issue was health services or a conflict over environmental rights (Dembowski 2001; Chakrabarti 2006). In the rural areas, the party represents the only way to access services, but the threat of violence and entanglement in patron–client relationships made it much harder for rural communities to enforce election promises and the even distribution of allocated resources. However, as land reforms and party politics led to vicious competition for land in the central districts (see Roy 2003) and lawlessness and militant contestations at the margins, the potential for opposition grew.

The post-liberalization period forced the state to groom investors and brought the need to acquire loans, which came with structural adjustment programmes attached, and triggered a sea change in Left Front policies. It is during this period that urban restructuring and the interests of the middle class were grudgingly initiated by the Left Front, and neoliberal reforms, state disinvestment, the privatization of education, healthcare and services reshaped the 'state.' Where the first two decades of Left Front rule were marked by the focus on redistribution and empowerment in the countryside, the new regime focused on investment, clean industries and urban development.

Whilst studies of the way local democracy works in West Bengal's cities where citizens are exposed to immense bureaucracies and complex municipal politics are surprisingly scarce (for exceptions see Banerjee 1999; Tawa-Rewal 2005; Chatterjee 2007), it is clear that urban areas had been largely neglected up until the 1990s. From the 1950s onwards urban infrastructure and manufacturing had been in crisis, strikes, lock-outs and political violence had been a hallmark of Marxist agitation, and later on dominated urban politcs. To contain the growing support for the oppositional Trinamool Congress Party led by the charismatic Mamata Banerjee and in view of diminished funds, the Left Front had now turned on urban restructuring to win back the middle class in whose image neoliberal policies were developed in order to attract investment to West Bengal.

The policies employed were not different from those implemented across India, but gained a distinct flair through their interaction with local political formations, the discrepancy between socialist rhetoric and capitalist dynamics, and last but not least lack of sustainability.

State-led initiatives focussed on improvements in infrastructure, the removal of the urban poor, and the forced acquisition of land for development. A first indicator of how the interests of the middle class dominate urban restructuring, and this implies more often than not the nexus of urban planners, developers and affluent urbanites, was the dispute over the removal of 'polluting' industries from the city centre, evidenced in the long and drawn out process within which leather manufacturers and their workers were evicted from the eastern fringes of Calcutta, and resettled as compensation (Dembowski 2001).

Here, as elsewhere, the state-led evictions to follow were legitimized by a discourse that posed the poor against the rights of citizen-consumers, a discourse resonating with the urban middle classes. Along the same lines 'Operation Sunshine', the removal of hawkers from the city centre, pitched rightful 'citizens' against the illegitimate practices associated with the urban poor. In a pattern found across India, informal workers were criminalized, the difference being that hawkers in Calcutta were heavily unionized and negotiated compensation (see Bandyopadhyay 2009 for a critical assessment of this history). In a city where the consensus had for so long been that the middle class endured the dominant politics of the vote-bank, which gave the poor a certain clout, the protests accompanying this contestation over public space remained surprisingly marginal. Like other poor residents, the hawkers, most of whom were back at their old sites within weeks, are now considered illegal and left vulnerable to police harassment and eviction.

Significantly, the struggle of the hawkers marked the end of an era, in which larger discourses on what the 'modern' city should look like changed. Earlier such visions had focused on the alleviation of poverty, a concern even the hegemonic middle class had, often grudgingly, shared. The often enforced interdependence between middle class residents and slum dwellers had, by and large, protected the livelihoods and residential arrangements of the urban poor and defined a politics of representation within which local interests played an integrating role (Chatterjee 2007). With suburbanizaton, and the vision of a clean, globalized, consumer-orientated future, working-class residences and livelihoods were criminalized, and a discourse that highlighted the urban space as the domain of middle-class citizens reshaped earlier coalitions and alliances (see Dembowski 2001; Chatterjee 2007).

Initially, the state government invested heavily in infrastructure that was geared towards attracting investment, especially in Calcutta itself, where large tracts of land were acquired in order to accommodate national and international IT companies and the like, which were provided with subsidized land, services and the guarantee that in such 'zones of exception' (Ong 2006) workers' rights could not be enforced. Later, these processes were extended to include the countryside, where fertile land was bought up or taken by force in order to establish Special Economic Zones. These processes produced spatial segregation and economic stratification and institutionalized the physical and political exclusion of whole communities from full citizenship, whilst it on the other hand encouraged corruption and political violence at the nexus of state/party and private developers.

The globalized lifestyle of the affluent and the imagination and aspiration of the middle class shaped policies that materialized in the form of built environment (flyovers, suburbs, malls) and the reordering of socio-spatial relations. For the middle class, the initial years of urban reform hailed the hope of 'arrival' for the 'belated metropolis' that had never been quite modern (Bose 1968; Bose 2007; Donner 2012). But it soon became clear that even among the segment of the population usually portrayed as beneficiaries of neoliberal restructuring, next to criticism of the Left Front, ambivalent feelings towards reforms prevailed (Ganguly-Scrase and Scrase 2008; Donner 2008). Whilst large sections of the urban population have gained from new opportunities, most prominently booming real estate markets, formerly secure privileges, for example of employment in the state sector have been lost whilst the privatization of earlier subsidized services has made their lives less predictable.

The political processes producing the new urban landscapes index a new phase in Indian politics (Chatterjee 2007), in which the interests of the upwardly mobile middle class are actively promoted by the state through incentives for private investment, i.e. in education, healthcare and housing. Whilst ethnography of the way this impacts local lives is still scarce, the way political activism becomes a new field in which citizenship is negotiated through interaction between the agencies of the state and private interests is evident in the court cases that accompany every eviction that has taken place so far. Furthermore, the effects of these neoliberal policies encompass rural sites as well. Thus, the Special Economic Zones planned in Singur and Nandigram and the ensuing protest movements affect politics in the state as a whole and contributed to the Left Front's downfall. This raises questions regarding the future of politics, and in particular the role of political parties (see Harriss 2007) in West Bengal, as rural and urban sites are becoming linked through the imagination and the demands of consumerist middle-class lifestyles, which determine the direction of urban planning but increasingly also investment in the districts (Bose 2007). After all, the irony that the most symbolic land-grab attempted by any state in post-liberalization India to date was undertaken by a Communist government in the name of 'the people' and centred around the epitomy of middle-class aspirations, the family car, was not lost on anyone.

Conclusion

I started this chapter at the foundational moment of 'first' contact between the British and the 'native' populations of what was to become colonial Bengal, imagined first as a site of negotiation, new identities, governance and, above all, economic interests. The initial ethnographic evidence provides a differentiated picture of the various groups involved in this encounter, and shows how the transformations occurring in this very heterogeneous and prosperous region integrated the province.

The ethnography also charts the multiple ways in which knowledge about Bengal served governance and contributed to the formation of communities from multilayered discourses, which later on fed into the distinctive identity and regional nationalist politics. In the course of these transformations a disjuncture between an urbanized middle class and rural communities occurred, spurred by colonial rule, which transformed the economy and the social relationships in the countryside, established politics as a multifaceted but distinct arena of contestation, and allowed for subaltern (for example low-caste) and mainstream discourses to develop side by side.

These developments built upon the distinction between 'tradition' and 'modernity' and facilitated a self-conscious Bengali and Indian identity discourse to emerge, which promoted reform among the middle class, but excluded those who belonged to low-caste and class communities. Thus, claims to Bengali culture were mostly heard in the context of elite contestations, as Bengal became a unit of representation, governance and political mobilization.

The ethnography speaks vividly of how amidst massive upheaval communities were constituted, as notions of identity became tied to political representation. However, equally significantly, the example of Bengal shows how caste-based organization gave way to communal and class-based politics, for example as *bhadralok* culture fed into the nationalist movement, and later on Left-wing politics, for instance the Tebhaga struggle.

Whilst this emerging modern politics has been well documented, anthropological research focusing on personhood, ritual and the body has highlighted that folk idioms linking persons, groups and moralities through distinctive worldviews and practices remained important, as they shaped perceptions of these larger processes, mediating between the individual and society. It is through these shared concepts and practices that subjects make sense of their experiences and relate to others.

These micropolitics of community are still often evoked where village monographs are concerned, however, even if one focused exclusively on rural sites, macro-politics figure as an important framework within which local ideas are reformulated. Thus, ethnographies of vernacular politics show that ideas about justice and government link local idioms with wider histories and discourses, amongst them 'politics', which in turn challenge simplistic assumptions about shared worldviews across the state.

Given the upheaval of partition, the political ethnography from Bengal deals, not surprisingly, with the local state and its appropriation as the emerging 'culture of representative democracy' became reality (Kaviraj 1998). This is not to say that political institutions don't exist elsewhere, but that West Bengal provides ample proof for the unevenness of processes of development. Of particular interest to scholars are the more than three decades of Left Front rule, during which important questions regarding the efficacy of progressive policies, for instance of land reforms, and modes of empowerment within the parameters of electoral democracy take central-stage.

The most recent critical ethnography produced on West Bengal takes on the post-liberalization phase when the Left Front adopted neoliberal policies, with a special emphasis on the way the search for investment enabled urban restructuring. These processes directed attention away from the concerns of rural constituencies, which have developed into fiefdoms often marked by extreme political violence on the one hand, and struggles over high profile projects in the districts on the other hand. The highly symbolic protest movements in Singur and Nandigram, which contributed to the ousting of the Left Front and the victory of Mamata Banerjee's Trinamool Congress, underline the importance of an analysis that links the urban politics often made for the middle class with supposedly rural sites. In West Bengal these structural transformations are promoted by the state, which has been shown to facilitate the dispossession of large sections of the population, whose settlements and livelihoods are defined as illegitimate and who are criminalized.

These processes occur at the intersection of local political histories, linking party politics, middle-class consumerism and urbanization. In order to understand these new politics, social scientists need to study what made the victory of Mamata Banerjee's Trinamool Congress Party possible. Secondly, the future ethnography of West Bengal will have to take seriously the way this new phase of capitalist penetration, which affects citizens across caste, class and community differently, is mediated, understood and experienced. At its best, such ethnography allows us to relate the broader processes in evidence with the emergence of specific locations, individual experiences and political spaces.

References

Agnihotri, A. (2001) *Forest Interludes: A Collection of Journals and Fiction*. Delhi: Kali for Women.

Amin, S. (1996) *The World of Muslim Women in Colonial Bengal, 1876–1939*. Leiden: Brill.

Bandyopadhyay, R. (2009) 'Hawker's movement in Kolkata, 1975–2007', *Economic and Political Weekly*, 44 (17): 116–19.

Bandyopadhyay, S. (1990) 'Introduction', in G. Dutt, *Folk Arts of Bengal: The Collected Papers*. Calcutta: Seagull.

*——(1994) 'Development, differentiation and caste: the Namasudra movement in Bengal, 1872–1947', in S. Bandyopadhyay, A. Dasgupta and W. van Schendel (eds), *Bengal: Communities, Development and States*. New Delhi: Manohar Publications.

Banerjee, M. (1999) 'Mamata's Khomata', *Seminar* 480.

——(2007) 'Sacred elections', *Economic and Political Weekly*, 42 (17): 1556–62.

Banerjee, S. (1989) *The Parlour and the Street: Elite and Popular Culture in Nineteenth Century Calcutta*. Calcutta: Seagull Publishers.

Barnett, S., Fruzzetti, L. and Östör, A. (1976) *Kinship and Ritual in Bengal: Anthropological Essays*. Delhi: South Asian Publishers.

Basu, A. (1992) *Two Faces of Protest: Contrasting Modes of Women's Activism in India*. Berkeley: University of California Press.

Bayly, C. A. (1998) *Origins of Nationalism in South Asia: Patriotism and Ethical Government in the Making of Modern India*. Delhi: Oxford University Press.

Bhattacharya, J. N. (1995) *Hindu Castes and Sects: An Exposition of the Origin of the Hindu Caste System and the Bearing of the Sects Towards Each Other and Towards Other Religious Systems*. Benares: Munshiram Manoharlal.

Borthwick, M. (1984) *The Changing Role of Women in Bengal (1849–1905)*. Princeton: Princeton University Press.

Bose, N. K. (1968) *Calcutta 1964: A Social Survey*. Bombay: Lalvani Publishing House.

Bose, P. S. (2007) 'Dreaming of diasporas: urban developments and transnational identities in contemporary Kolkata', *Topia*, 17: 111–30.

Bose, S. and Jalal, A. (1997) *Modern South Asia: History, Culture, Political Economy*. Oxford: Oxford University Press.

Broomfield, J. (1968) *Elite Conflict in a Plural Society: Twentieth-Century Bengal*. Berkeley: University of California Press.

Burton, A. (2001) *Politics and Empire in Victorian Britain*. New York: Palgrave.

Chakrabarti, I. (2006) 'Local governance: politics and neighbourhood activism in Calcutta', in G. De Neve and H. Donner (eds), *The Meaning of the Local: Politics of Place in Urban India*. London: Routledge.

*Chakrabarty, D. (1989) *Rethinking Working Class History: Bengal 1890 to 1940*. Princeton: Princeton University Press.

*Chatterjee, P. (1993) *The Nation and Its Fragments: Colonial and Postcolonial Histories*. Princeton: Princeton University Press.

——(1997) *The Present History of West Bengal: Essays in Political Criticism*. Delhi: Oxford University Press.

*——(2007) *The Politics of the Governed: Reflections on Politics in Most of the World*. New York: Columbia University Press.

Chatterji, J. (2001) *The Spoils of Partition: 1947–1967*. Cambridge: Cambridge University Press.

Cohn, B. S. (1987) *An Anthropologist Among the Historians and Other Essays*. Delhi: Oxford University Press.

Davis, M. (1983) *Rank and Rivalry: The Politics of Inequality in Rural West Bengal*. Cambridge: Cambridge University Press.

de Haan, A. (1994) *Unsettled Settlers: Migrant Workers and Industrial Capitalism in Calcutta*. Rotterdam: Verloren Publishers.

Dembowski, H. (2001) *Taking the State to Court: Public Interest Litigation and the Public Sphere in Metropolitan India*. Delhi: Oxford University Press.

Dey, L. B. (1969 [1883]) *Bengal Peasant Life*. Calcutta: K. L. Mukhopadhyay.

Donner, H. (2004) 'Labour, privatisation, and class: middle-class women's experience of changing hospital births in Calcutta', in M. Unnithan-Kumar (ed.), *Reproductive Agency and the State: Cultural Transformations in Childbearing*, Oxford: Berghahn.

——(2006) 'The parlour and the *para*: class and gender in a neighbourhood of central Calcutta', in G. De Neve and H. Donner (eds), *The Meaning of the Local: Politics of Place in Urban India*. London: Routledge.

——(2008) *Domestic Goddesses: Maternity, Globalisation and Middle-class Identity in Contemporary India*. Aldershot: Ashgate.

——(2012) 'Middle-class imagination and urban restructuring in 21st century Kolkata'. *New Perspectives on Turkey*, Special Issue: Urban Classes in Comparison, 46 (Spring 2012), 129–55.

Ecks, S. (2004) 'Bodily sovereignty as political sovereignty: "self-care" in Kolkata (India)', *Anthropology and Medicine*, 11 (1): 75–89.

Fernandes, L. (1997) *Producing Workers: The Politics of Gender, Class, and Culture in the Calcutta Jute Mills*. Philadelphia: University of Pennsylvania Press.

*Fruzzetti, L. (1982) *The Gift of a Virgin: Women, Marriage Ritual and Kinship in Bengali Society*. Delhi: Oxford University Press.

Fruzzetti, L., Östör, A. and Barnett, S. (1982) *Concepts of Person: Kinship, Caste and Marriage in India*. Cambridge, MA: Harvard University Press.

Ganguly-Scrase, R. and Scrase, T. J. (2008) *Globalization and the Middle Classes in India: The Social and Cultural Impact of Neoliberal Reforms*. London: Routledge.

Greenough, P. R. (1982) *Prosperity and Misery in Modern Bengal: The Famine of 1943–44*. Oxford: Oxford University Press.

Hardgrove, A. (2004) *Community and Public Culture: The Marwaris of Calcutta, c. 1897–1997*. Oxford: Oxford University Press.

Harriss, J. (2007) 'Antinomies of empowerment: observations on civil society, politics and urban governance in India', *Economic and Political Weekly*, 42: 26, 2716–24.

Harvey, D. (2003) *The New Imperialism*. Oxford: Oxford University Press.

Hauser, B. (2002) 'From oral tradition to "folk art": re-evaluating Bengali scroll paintings', *Asian Folklore Studies*, 1 (61): 105–22.

——(2012) *Promising Rituals: Gender and Performativity in Eastern India*. London: Routledge.

Inden, R. B. (1976) *Marriage and Rank in Bengali Culture: A History of Caste and Clan in Middle-period Bengal*. Berkeley: University of California Press.

*Inden, R. B. and Nicholas, R. W. (1977) *Kinship in Bengali Culture*. Chicago: University of Chicago Press.

Jalais, A. (2005) 'Dwelling on Morichjhanpi: when tigers became "citizens", refugees "tiger-food"', *Economic and Political Weekly*, 40 (17): 1757–62.

——(2009) *Migrant Tigers and Eco-Warriors: Politics and Environment in the Sunderbans*. Delhi: Routledge.

Kaviraj, S. (1997) 'Filth and the public sphere: concepts and practices about space in Calcutta', *Public Culture*, 10 (1): 83–113.

——(1998) 'The culture of representative democracy', in P. Chatterjee (ed.), *Wages of Freedom: Fifty Years of the Indian Nation-State*. Dehli: Oxford University Press.

Kohli, A. (1987) *The State and Poverty in India: The Politics of Reform*. Cambridge: Cambridge University Press.

Kopf, D. (1979) *The Brahmo Samaj and the Shaping of the Modern Indian Mind*. Princeton: Princeton University Press.

Kotalova, J. (1996) *Belonging to Others: Cultural Construction of Womanhood among Muslims in a Village in Bangladesh*. Uppsala: Uppsala Studies in Cultural Anthropology.

Kothari, S. and Harcourt, W. (2004) 'The Violence of Development', *Development*, 47 (1): 3–7.

*Lamb, S. (2000) *White Saris, Sweet Mangos: Aging, Gender, and Body in North India*. Berkeley: University of California Press.

Majumdar, S. (2010) 'The Nano controversy: peasant identities, the land question and neoliberal industrialization in Marxist West Bengal', *Journal of Knowledge of Emerging Markets*, 2 (1): 41–66.

*Mallick R. (1993) *Development Policy of a Communist Government: West Bengal since 1977*. Cambridge: Cambridge University Press.

——(1999) 'Refugee resettlement in forest reserves: West Bengal policy reversal and the Marichjhapi massacre', *Journal of Asian Studies*, 58 (1): 102–25.

Marriott, M. and Inden, R. B. (1977) 'Towards an ethnosociology of South Asian caste systems', in K. David (ed.), *The New Wind: Changing Identities in South Asia*. The Hague: Mouton.

Mukherjee, S. N. (1987) 'Bhadralok and their dals: politics of social factions in Calcutta, c. 1820–1856', in P. Sinha (ed.), *The Urban Experience: Calcutta – Essays in Honour of Professor Nisith R. Ray*. Calcutta: Riddhi Publishers.

Murshid, G. (1983) *The Reluctant Debutante: The Response of Bengali Women to Modernization (1849–1905)*. Rajshahi: Satiya Samsad.

Nicholas, R. W. (1981) 'The goddess Sitala and epidemic smallpox in Bengal', *Journal of Asian Studies*, 41 (1): 21–45.

——(2003) *Fruits of Worship: Practical Religion in Bengal*. Bangalore: Orient Black Swan.

Nossiter, T. (1988) *Marxist State Governments in India: Politics, Economics and Society*. London: Pinter.

Ong, A. (2006) *Neoliberalism as Exception: Mutations in Citizenship and Sovereignty*. Chapel Hill: Duke University Press.

Östör, Á. (1980) *The Play of the Gods: Locality, Ideology, Structure, and Time in the Festivals of a Bengali Town*. Chicago: University of Chicago Press.

Ray, M. (2002) 'Growing up refugee', *History Workshop Journal*, 5 (1): 149–79.

*Ray, R. K. (1996) *Mind, Body, and Society: Life and Mentality in Colonial Bengal*. Delhi: Oxford University Press.

*Raychaudhuri, T. (1988) *Europe Reconsidered: Perceptions of the West in Nineteenth-century Bengal*. Delhi: Oxford University Press.

——(1999) *Perceptions, Emotions, Sensibilities: Essays on India's Colonial and Post-colonial Sensibilities*. Delhi: Oxford University Press.

Risley, H. H. (1891) 'Ethnographic researches in India', *Journal of the Anthropological Institute of Great Britain and Ireland*, 20: 290–92.

Rocher, R. (1993) 'British orientalism in eighteenth century: the dialectics of knowledge and government', in C. A. Breckenridge and P. van der Veer, (eds), *Orientalism and the Postcolonial Predicament: Perspectives on South Asia*. Philadelphia: University of Pennsylvania Press.

*Rogaly, B., Harriss-White, B. and Bose, S. (1999) 'Introduction: agricultural growth and agrarian change in West Bengal and Bangladesh', in B. Rogally, B. Harriss-White and S. Bose (eds), *Sonar Bangla? Agricultural Growth and Agrarian Change in West Bengal and Bangladesh*. Delhi: Sage Publications.

Rogaly, B., Rafique, A. and Massey, D. (2009) 'Straw in the elephant's mouth? Social protection for temporary working migrants in West Bengal' in C. R. Abrar and J. Seeley (eds), *Social Protection and Livelihoods: Marginalised Migrant Workers of India and Bangladesh*. Dhaka: University Press.

*Roy, A. (2003) *City Requiem, Calcutta: Gender and the Politics of Poverty*. Minneapolis: University of Minnesota Press.

Roy, M. (1972) *Bengali Women*. Chicago: University of Chicago Press.

Rozario, S. (1992) *Purity and Social Boundaries: Women and Social Change in a Bangladeshi Village*. London: ZED Press.

*Ruud, A. (2003) *The Poetics of Village Politics: The Making of West Bengal's Rural Communism*. Oxford: Oxford University Press.

Sarkar, S. (1989) 'The Kalki-Avatar of Bikrampur: a village scandal in early twentieth century Bengal' in Ranajit Guha (ed.), *Subaltern Studies VI: Writings on South Asian History and Society*. Delhi: Oxford University Press.

——(1994) 'Caste, occupation and social mobility: a study of the *kansaris* in colonial Bengal', in S. Bandyopadhyay, A. Dasgupta and W. van Schendel (eds), *Bengal: Communities, Development and States*. Delhi: Manohar Publications.

——(1997) *Writing Social History*. Delhi: Oxford University Press.

Sarkar, T. (2001) *Hindu Wife, Hindu Nation: Community, Religion, and Cultural Nationalism*. Bloomington: Indiana University Press.

Scrase, T. J. (1993) *Image, Ideology and Inequality: Cultural Domination, Hegemony and Schooling in India*. New Delhi, London and Newbury Park: Sage.

*Sen, S. (1999) *Women and Labour in Late Colonial India: The Bengal Jute Industry*. Cambridge: Cambridge University Press.

Siddiqui, M. K. A. (1982) *Aspects of Society and Culture in Calcutta*. Calcutta: Anthropological Survey of India.

Sinha, S. C. (1972) *Cultural Profile of Calcutta*. Calcutta: Anthropological Survey of India.

Tawa-Rewal, S. (2005) *Electorial Reservations, Political Representation and Social Change in India: A Comparative Perspective*. Delhi: Manohar.

Timberg, T. (1977) *The Marwaris: From Traders to Industrialists*. Delhi: Vikas.

van Schendel, W. (2005) *The Bengal Borderland: Beyond State and Nation in South Asia*. London: Anthem Press.

Washbrook, D. (1981) 'Law, state and agrarian society in colonial India', *Modem Asian Studies*, 15 (3): 649–721.

Williams, G. (1999) 'Panchayati raj and the changing micro-politics of West Bengal' in B. Rogaly, B. Harriss-White and S. Bose (eds), *Sonar Bangla? Agricultural Growth and Agrarian Change in West Bengal and Bangladesh*. Delhi: Sage.

Index